HANDBOOK TO LIFE
IN MEDIEVAL AND
EARLY MODERN JAPAN

HANDBOOK TO LIFE IN MEDIEVAL AND EARLY MODERN JAPAN

WILLIAM E. DEAL

Case Western Reserve University

OXFORD
UNIVERSITY PRESS

OXFORD
UNIVERSITY PRESS

Oxford University Press, Inc., publishes works that further
Oxford University's objective of excellence
in research, scholarship, and education.

Oxford New York
Auckland Cape Town Dar es Salaam Hong Kong Karachi
Kuala Lumpur Madrid Melbourne Mexico City Nairobi
New Delhi Shanghai Taipei Toronto

With offices in
Argentina Austria Brazil Chile Czech Republic France Greece
Guatemala Hungary Italy Japan Poland Portugal Singapore
South Korea Switzerland Thailand Turkey Ukraine Vietnam

First published by Facts On File, Inc., 2005

First issued as an Oxford University Press paperback, 2007
198 Madison Avenue, New York, NY 10016
www.oup.com

Oxford is a registered trademark of Oxford University Press

Library of Congress Cataloging-in-Publication Data
Deal, William E.
Handbook to life in medieval and early modern Japan / William E. Deal.
p. cm.
Originally published: New York : Facts On File, 2006.
Includes bibliographical references and index.
ISBN 978-0-19-533126-4 (pbk.)
1. Japan—Civilization—To 1868. 2. Japan—History—1185–1600. I. Title.
DS822.2.D33 2007
952'.02—dc22
2007004318

Printed in the United States of America
on acid-free paper

For Moriyama Tae

CONTENTS

LIST OF ILLUSTRATIONS

LIST OF MAPS

LIST OF TABLES AND CHARTS

ACKNOWLEDGMENTS

Writing this book has been a humbling experience. I am mindful that a book is the product of the support and guidance of many people. Both current and former students of Case Western Reserve University and Boston University assisted with research for this book: Eric Bugyis, Miriam Chusid, Christine Fergus, Elizabeth Grammatikov, and Matt Snyder. Special thanks to Julie Digianantonio for her editorial assistance. I would like to thank Cleveland artist Grace Vibbert, who rendered several expert illustrations for this volume, and Ken Clickenger, at Dodd Camera in Cleveland, who provided expert advice about photographic matters. Further, I am indebted to Joanne Eustis, Gail Reese, Bonnie Godden, and the staff at Kelvin Smith Library at Case Western Reserve University for all of their assistance with my bibliographic needs. I also enjoyed strong encouragement from my Case colleagues Tim Beal and Peter Haas. I am grateful to publishing consultant Henry Rasof for bringing this project to my attention, and to Claudia Schaab and Melissa Cullen-DuPont at Facts On File for their steadfast editorial expertise.

In Japan, I received generous assistance from Nishimura Shoji of Waseda University, who has selflessly offered support for the past 15 years. Audrey Morrell, den mother extraordinaire, transformed the drudgery of travel into an enjoyable experience. Moriyama Tae, my former Japanese teacher and travel companion, instilled a love of traditional Japanese culture that is a guiding light for this book.

Many thanks go to wonderful friends who provided support and encouragement: Jeff and Naoko Gumpf, Jeff Catts, Sid Fowler, Barbara Green, Elizabeth Kirk, Fred Land, Alyson and John Kallmeyer, and Sam Oriti (especially for reminders of Maine in Cleveland). Daniel Meckel and Betul Basaran offered steadfast friendship, scholarship, and much-needed humor.

More personally, Yuki and Sumi kept an eye on the research team every day without fail. My brothers, Bruce Deal and Robert Deal, took care of family matters at a difficult time so that I could remain focused on writing. Most of all, I thank Lisa Robertson for her creativity, ideas, expertise, writing, editing, and support.

1

HISTORICAL CONTEXT

HISTORICAL SURVEY

Introduction

Japan's medieval and early modern periods encompass nearly 700 years. Life in Japan changed significantly between the inception of medieval warrior rule in 1185, and the imperial restoration in 1868. Nonetheless, there are continuities that unify this long span of Japanese history. As the medieval period began, military clans dominated politics and society, wealth and status were hereditary, and landowners controlled the feudal economy. By the end of the early modern era, warrior families had lost the right to bear arms. They served as administrators of impoverished regional domains, though they ranked in the upper echelons of a centralized government that instituted peace after attaining power through military might. While the superior rank of the warrior classes remained an important constant from the 12th to the 19th centuries, interdependent changes in politics, religion, economic climate, culture, and daily life—to name a few—characterized medieval and early modern times in Japan.

The transition from an embattled feudal culture to a unified, peaceable Japan poised to emerge in industry and world affairs was especially rapid during the 300 years prior to 1868—the early modern period. Faced with the inevitability of new technologies and international commerce, Japan's feudal system, by now comprising hostile provincial domains that relied upon disenfranchised laborers and legions of military retainers, became ineffective. A bustling urban culture emerged, nurtured by the newfound wealth and sophisticated tastes of merchant city dwellers. The brief historical survey presented below charts continuities and changes in cultural, economic, political, and social contexts that shaped life during Japan's medieval and early modern periods.

A NOTE ON TERMINOLOGY AND DATING

Before summarizing this history, clarification is needed regarding terms, dates, and other conventions used by historians of Japan. For example, the names given to historical eras in Japanese and in English may differ. The words "medieval" and "early modern" were first used to describe eras in European history and may mislead readers who connect these terms with circumstances and dates in medieval Europe that are not necessarily applicable to Japanese history. In Japanese scholarship, the era designated medieval in this volume is commonly termed *chusei* (literally "middle period"), and *kinsei* (literally "recent period") is frequently used to describe the era identified here as "early modern." Yet medieval and early modern are convenient terms, since they are more familiar than *chusei* and *kinsei*. Thus, these terms are used here under advisement, and distinctions between medieval and/or early modern phenomena in Japan as compared with Europe will be noted as necessary.

"Feudalism" is another term that merits consideration. In histories concerning the Middle Ages in Europe, feudalism denotes a system of land ownership whereby tenants would work land owned by proprietors called vassals in exchange for protection. Aristocratic landowners assigned land parcels to vassals with the understanding that loyal vassals would be honored with land transfers from the lord they served. Similarities do exist between the Japanese feudal structure and European feudalism, since both relied upon a warrior class versed in military technologies for protection and administration, and both forms of feudalism center on the service and pledge of honor vassals provided to their lords, the landowners. While similar in principle, in practice Japan's feudal society varied somewhat from the European feudal condition. Vassals in Japan were appointed, not as proprietors of owned land parcels, but rather as stewards acting on behalf of aristocrats, temple officials, or figures of high rank in the military government, who remained the landowners although residing far from the land itself. With no tangible reward for administrating land on behalf of aristocrats, priests, or others of high position, provincial vassals in Japan could benefit from their role only if they exercised military muscle in order to acquire or defend land. In turn, these militaristic means led to unrest in the provinces, and eventually to challenges to regional landowners as well as Japan's supreme military leader, the *shogun*. Though necessarily brief, this glimpse of theory and practice in Japanese and European feudalism highlights some aspects of feudal conditions in these two cultures. Since the tenor of feudal society informed subsequent socioeconomic developments, readers may find further comparisons of European and Japanese feudalism useful.

Having considered historical terminology, guidelines for designating Japanese historical periods also require explanation. While most scholars of Japanese history agree upon names used to identify various periods, the dates specified for each era can vary a great deal. Generally, the years 1185–1615 are designated as Japan's medieval era, identified as such due to the advent of rule by the warrior class, feudal system of land allocation and administration, and characteristic political unrest. Historians identify the period 1615–1868 as the early modern age, citing socioeconomic developments, a longstanding peace, and emergence of a prosperous urban culture. Broad categorization of the medieval period encompasses the Kamakura (typically 1185–1333) and the Muromachi periods (often, but not always, 1333–1600). As with any system defined by landmark historical events, dating for Japanese eras reveals particular perspectives. For instance, some scholars label the period from 1338 to 1573 the Ashikaga period instead of the Muromachi period. Ashikaga refers to the Ashikaga family, who served as shoguns during this time, while Muromachi is the district of Kyoto, from where the Ashikaga family ruled. In some schemes for denoting periods, the Muromachi/Ashikaga era also includes subperiods: the Northern and Southern Courts and the Warring States. Other schemes treat these subperiods as historical eras of their own. The system employed here has been selected because it allows clearer focus on nuances of Japanese history obscured by the more limited—and static—era specifications Kamakura, Muromachi, and Edo. Further, the dating schema below generally corresponds to nomenclature and organization of eras used in major reference materials about Japan.

Japanese histories often provide a chronology demarcated not by broad historical periods, but rather by imperial reign names. Dates for eras may also differ because of emphasis in certain academic disciplines on particular epochs noted for cultural importance over political or military import. While the table below is intended as a guideline to significant events that altered life in Japan, overall this volume primarily distinguishes between the medieval and early modern periods as characterized by a majority of authorities in Japan and abroad.

Medieval Japan	**1185–1615**
Kamakura period	1185–1333
Muromachi period	1333–1573
Northern and Southern Courts (Nambokucho)	1336–1392
Warring States (Sengoku) period	1467–1568
Azuchi-Momoyama period	1573–1615
Early Modern Japan	**1615–1868**
Edo period	1615–1868

Medieval Japan (1185–1615)

KAMAKURA PERIOD (1185–1333)

Most historians consider the Kamakura period the dawn of medieval Japan. In the late 12th century, following a slow erosion of power begun at least 100 years earlier, the authority of the Kyoto-based imperial family and the court aristocrats (*kuge*), who ruled as regents of the throne, were eclipsed as a military government, the *bakufu*, (literally, "tent government"; commonly referred to in English by the term "shogunate") was established in Kamakura, near present-day Tokyo. As in other Japanese periods, the designated center of political power has been adopted as the name for this historical era.

While the emperor and imperial family retained their ceremonial roles as figureheads, real power was exercised by the military rulers based in Kamakura. Both civil and military affairs were managed by the warrior (*bushi*) class. Although in theory the warrior class shared political control of Japan with the Kyoto aristocracy, the warriors were the de facto rulers of Japan, and their military regime was sanctioned by the imperial court. The first military ruler, the shogun, was appointed by the court in 1192. The

shogunate established a precedent where-
... were accorded formal respect tempered
... enforcing compliance with the sho-
... :ies as well as constant surveillance.
..., the Kamakura shogunate did not pre-
... :hallenged by Emperor Go-Daigo, who
... :he *bakufu* and briefly restored imperial
rule in 1333.

Establishment of Warrior Rule

A decentralized, ineffective system of land allocation and management by vassals, established in the final century of the Heian period (794–1185) by aristocrats who preferred life at court to administrative positions in the remote provinces, contributed to the decline of court authority. In Japan's agricultural economy, political power and economic status depended in part on landholdings. Beginning in the Nara period (eighth century), a complex network of public and private land parcels, including tax-exempt plots held by imperial families, court nobles, monasteries and shrines, existed throughout the provinces. Privately held estates called *shoen* were an enviable source of wealth and power as land availability decreased and aristocrats neglected administration of their provincial lands.

In the Heian period, aristocratic reluctance to oversee estates led indirectly to uprisings challenging the authority of the imperial court. These disturbances originated in local warrior alliances formed in provincial domains. A decisive challenge to such provincial alliances came when Minamoto no Yoritomo (1147–99) was granted court authority in 1185 to appoint military agents (*shugo*) in the provinces and military stewards (*jito*) on estates, thus ensuring cooperation with, and order among, his vassals (*gokenin*). *Shugo* were given limited authority to oversee vassals. Among *shugo* responsibilities were the registration of meritorious warriors as *gokenin* and punishment of certain crimes. At first, *jito* were chiefly responsible for maintaining smooth management of *shoen* lands. Over time, the growing power of the *jito* resulted in a loss of rights among *shoen* proprietors and a corresponding increase in warrior jurisdiction over land, agricultural and artisan production, and farm laborers. Eventually, the shogunate began to recognize that bonds with wealthy provincial landholding families had to be forged to

ensure that even shogun-appointed agents were safe from the constant threat of challenges by neighboring domains.

Over time, the warriors who had first been employed by the imperial court to quell provincial uprisings became the new political and social elite, restoring centralized power and enforcing peace until invaders from China intervened. After five years of brutal battles, the Minamoto family defeated the Taira family in the Gempei War (1180–85). Shortly thereafter, the Kamakura shogunate was established by Yoritomo who gradually managed to consolidate power over various areas of Japan. He became Japan's official ruler when Emperor Go-Shirakawa (1127–92) died and Yoritomo was appointed *seii taishogun* ("barbarian-subduing great general," usually abbreviated as "shogun"). Shogun was the highest imperially designated rank for a warrior, and consequently Yoritomo became Japan's supreme military figure, and head of the warrior government in Kamakura. The shogunate ruled Japan officially with only two brief exceptions until governance by members of the warrior classes ceased in 1868. Thus warrior rule represents a vital link between medieval and early modern Japan.

Hojo Regency

The power and authority of the Minamoto family derived in part from allegiances forged with other dominant warrior families. Among these, the Hojo family was especially important. Yoritomo had relied on his connections with the Hojo to successfully accomplish his quest to defeat the Taira in the Gempei War. Yoritomo had close ties with Hojo Tokimasa (1138–1215) and married his daughter, Hojo Masako (1157–1225). Yoritomo was assisted by the Hojo family—especially Tokimasa—in setting up his rule at Kamakura.

At Yoritomo's death in 1199, real *bakufu* power fell to the Hojo family serving as hereditary regents (*shikken*) to the shoguns. The Hojo family held a low social rank and therefore they could not become shoguns themselves. However, as regents, they were able to exert control over the government by choosing shoguns from among the aristocratic Fujiwara family or from the imperial family. While appointed shoguns may have been superior in social rank, the office of regent, held by members of the Hojo family until 1333, became the true ruling position from this point on, since the emperor followed the regent's directives. It was Hojo regents who oversaw the significant events of the Kamakura period, including the Jokyu Disturbance and the Mongol invasions.

The Hojo family came to power as a result of their victories over their rivals following the power struggle that occurred after Yoritomo's death. Further, as noted above, Yoritomo was married to Masako, a Hojo woman. Masako's father, Hojo Tokimasa, became regent to the shogun in 1203.

There were challenges to Hojo power. In 1221, the retired emperor Go-Toba (1180–1239), supported by other court aristocrats, made an unsuccessful attempt to overthrow the Hojo in an incident known as the Jokyu Disturbance (*Jokyu no hen*). Yoritomo's death in 1199 and the assassination of the third shogun, Minamoto Sanetomo, in 1219, destabilized shogunal authority and created a window of opportunity for imperial family members and court nobles to attempt to seize back actual ruling power. Go-Toba issued a decree in 1221 calling for the overthrow of the Hojo regent Yoshitoki. To quell this attempt, Hojo forces led by Yasutoki—Yoshitoki's son—occupied Kyoto and suppressed imperial resistance. The current emperor, Chukyo, was deposed, and retired emperors Go-Toba and Juntoku were exiled. In Chukyo's place, the shogunate installed Go-Horikawa as emperor (r. 1221–32). As a result of this disturbance, the shogunate established a presence in Kyoto to supervise court activities—especially any activity that might lead to another plot against the shogunate—and to administrate lands in western Japan. This new institution, the Rokuhara *tandai*, acted as special administrators to the shogun. Moreover, lands owned by the defeated aristocrats were confiscated and loyal vassals were appointed *jito* for these estates as a reward for serving the shogunate. These activities assured an enhanced political status for the shogun who was now recognized as ruler of most of the country.

Other political changes were instituted by the Hojo. In 1225, Yasutoki created a Council of State (*Hyojoshu*) that consisted of his main retainers and advisers. In 1232, the Council of State promulgated the Joei Code (*Joei shikimoku*), a 51-article legal code that articulated Hojo judicial and legislative practices and the conduct of the military government in administering the country. In 1249, a judicial court (*hikitsuke*) was established to further refine the legal process.

Mongol Invasions   During the Kamakura period, in addition to the constant domestic intrigues involving Kyoto aristocrats and rival warrior families vying for power, Japan sustained a significant threat from beyond its shores. The Mongols, who had taken control of China, made two attempts to invade and conquer Japan. Kublai Khan (1215–94), grandson of Genghis Khan, founded the Yuan dynasty in 1271 and became the first Mongol emperor of China. Making the northern city Dadu (modern Beijing) his capital, he turned his attention to Japan, demanding in a letter sent to the "King of Japan" in 1268 that the Japanese pay tribute to the Yuan dynasty. This and subsequent missives were ignored by the Japanese government. As a result, Kublai Khan made his first attempt to invade Japan in 1274. He dispatched an army reportedly numbering 40,000 warriors to Kyushu. Soon after a successful landing, much of the Mongol army and its fleet of ships were destroyed by a typhoon. Those troops that survived retreated back to southern Korea, where the invasion had originated.

Undeterred, in 1275 Kublai Khan renewed his demands that the Japanese pay tribute to his empire. Despite reiterating his message on several occasions, his demands were again ignored. This time, the shogunate anticipated a second invasion. They fortified coastal defenses and built a wall around Hakata Bay in Kyushu at considerable cost to the Kyushu vassals. In 1281, the second invasion occurred. This time, two large armies were dispatched. After a brief occupation, a typhoon once again destroyed much of the invading army and navy. And once again, the Mongols were forced to retreat to the continent. The typhoons that destroyed the Mongols on these two occasions came to be known as "divine winds" (kamikaze). The Japanese believed that the Shinto gods (*kami*) had furnished divine protection for the archipelago.

Victory over the Mongols was attained at the cost of economic hardship and political ramifications. Despite the confirmation of divine favor, Japanese coastal defenses remained on guard for many years thereafter but no subsequent invasions occurred. In a response similar to the aftermath of the Jokyu Disturbance, the shogunate appointed deputies (*tandai*) in Kyushu and in the western provinces of Honshu to oversee defense efforts. Although the Japanese prevailed in battling the Mongols, the shogunate assumed considerable liabilities. Both financial and human losses were sustained in efforts to reinforce and defend the country. As reserves were depleted, the economic and political might of the Kamakura *bakufu* was thereby weakened. Many *jito* became insolvent. Such economic strains also damaged the relationship between Hojo family rulers and their vassals. Embroiled in renewed domestic instability, Japanese relations with China were not reinstated until the 14th century.

Decline of the Kamakura Shogunate Preexisting political and economic strains were exacerbated by the Mongol invasions and hastened the decline of Kamakura shogunal authority. Central events and circumstances included the continued disintegration of the land administration and estate (*shoen*) system, weakened ties between Kamakura *bakufu* and regional officials, economic costs to the *bakufu* for maintaining defense in anticipation of further Mongol invasions, the inability to sufficiently reward those who assisted the *bakufu* in defending Japan during the two invasion attempts, the ineffectual leadership of Hojo regents, and disputes within the imperial family over lines of imperial succession.

The *gokenin* suffered great hardship in the aftermath of the Mongol invasions. They were economically strapped after expending their resources to defend Japan against the Mongol invaders. Further, the mechanisms for enjoying the spoils of war were absent in the case of the Mongol invasions. Internal warfare in Japan usually resulted in the victors taking the lands of the defeated. Loyal vassals were rewarded with these lands as a way to repay military service. In the case of the Mongol invasions, neither land nor other wealth was available to the *gokenin*. The net result was often debt for vassals loyal to the Kamakura shogunate.

Economic conditions were also a cause of decline. Landowners who borrowed money to help meet mounting expenses had to forfeit their land in lieu of repayment if they could not meet the loan terms, including high interest rates. As nobles, shrines, and temples lost control of land assets, including the revenues farmers and artisans paid annually as taxes to landholders, labor and goods produced by these lowest classes were more likely to enter the marketplace. Since many farmers and artisans could barely subsist on yields left over after meeting tax obligations, diversion of their products to markets fostered economic growth. However, the lack of protection for farmers and artisans working on publicly held land or plots they had obtained through loan foreclosure led to political uncertainty and economic instability as the military, clerics, and nobles—the most educated, highest-ranking members of society—became insolvent.

Another concern with great impact on warrior society was the dearth of land. Increasing numbers of warriors required land in return for their service to and support of the shogunate, but a limited quantity of available land had to be distributed among the burgeoning warrior houses. To alleviate the problem, land inheritance was restricted, usually to the eldest son. The result was that inherited land slated to be divided among many heirs became the property of a lone descendant, and family members who would have acquired land dispensations in the past were forced to defer instead to a single family head.

Even in instances where land could be provided in return for service or loyalty to the shogun, other problems arose. Allegiance to the Kamakura *bakufu* eroded when warriors faithful to the shogunate were sent to distant areas of Japan to oversee land parcels. Further, families with powerful provincial domains—such as the Ashikaga—began to challenge the Hojo family for control. As loyalty toward the Hojo regents declined, rebellions occurred, and the regents had an increasingly difficult time suppressing insurgents. Rather than renewing their allegiance to the Hojo, provincial warrior families entered into partnerships with other local landholders. These regional powers often ignored Hojo laws and instead created their own rules and procedures, sometimes revolting against the *shoen jito*. Such unstable politics and financial insolvency eventually led to the collapse of the *bakufu*, although there were other contributing factors, as enumerated above.

A final dispute—this time over imperial succession—implicated the Hojo and became the opportunity for members of the imperial family to wrest power away from the *bakufu* and reinstate actual imperial rule, if only for a brief time. In 1275, a dispute arose over which of two of Emperor Go-Saga's sons would succeed him on the throne. Go-Saga died without choosing between the two rivals, with the result that two lines of imperial succession (senior and junior) were formed. The Hojo arbitrated this dispute by enacting a compromise calling for alternate succession between the two lines. In 1318, Prince Takaharu of the junior line became the emperor Go-Daigo (r. 1318–39). In 1326, Go-Daigo ignored the Hojo compromise by naming his son as the next in line of succession instead of agreeing to passing rule off to the senior line. The Hojo proved ineffectual in dealing with the protests that Go-Daigo's actions provoked, becoming stalemated in a standoff with Go-Daigo that lasted for five years. Finally, the *bakufu* threatened Go-Daigo militarily and the emperor fled Kyoto. The shogunate banished him to Oki Island in 1332 but he escaped exile.

Go-Daigo's cause was championed by powerful military houses displeased with Hojo rule. He joined forces with former Hojo vassals Ashikaga Takauji (1305–58) and Nitta Yoshisada (1301–38) to overthrow the Hojo regents in 1333. In Kyoto, forces led by Ashikaga Takauji attacked the Kyoto headquarters of the Hojo while Nitta Yoshisada commanded an army that assaulted the *bakufu* in Kamakura. This decisive action effectively ended the Kamakura shogunate.

MUROMACHI PERIOD (1333–1573)

The Kemmu Restoration and the Northern and Southern Courts Victorious over the Kamakura *bakufu*, Emperor Go-Daigo returned to Kyoto to recover the throne, thereby inaugurating the Kemmu Restoration (1333–36). Go-Daigo took a number of reform actions to maintain the court as the central authority, trying to assure that imperial rule would go unchallenged. To ensure control of Kyoto warriors (samurai), Go-Daigo set up a guard station (*musha-dokoro*) for overseeing samurai affairs. He also placed members of the imperial family in provincial leadership roles. As in the Kamakura era, a singular form of government did not prevail, and military chiefs posed challenges to Go-Daigo's vision of direct imperial rule.

Warriors who had aided Go-Daigo in overthrowing the Kamakura *bakufu* did not relish the restored emperor's reforms, convinced that he had deprived them of the power and authority they had earned in exchange for their military support. Further, like the Hojo in the wake of the Mongol invasions, Emperor Go-Daigo had insufficient resources to distribute as rewards to his retainers. Additional dissatisfaction arose as samurai were taxed so that renovations could be made to the imperial palace. Sensing weaknesses in the emperor's authority, Ashikaga Takauji revolted against Go-Daigo, occupying Kyoto decisively in 1336 after an initial failure. Takauji forced the emperor to retreat, though Go-Daigo rallied, thanks to pro-imperial forces, and set up a rival court at a safe distance from the capital. After this retreat, Takauji enthroned Go-Daigo's rival, Emperor Komyo, who was from the senior imperial line. Emperor Komyo immediately appointed Takauji as shogun. In the meantime, Go-Daigo, representing the junior line of succession, claimed the legitimate right to the throne from his court at Yoshino, in the mountainous Kii peninsula south of Kyoto.

The period of the Northern and Southern Courts (1336–92) lasted for nearly 60 years. The Northern Court, or senior line, was supported by the Ashikaga family and situated at Kyoto. The Southern Court, or junior line, was located at Yoshino and supported by followers of Go-Daigo. Both claimed to be the legitimate imperial line. It was not until 1392 that Ashikaga Yoshimitsu (1358–1408), Takauji's grandson and third Ashikaga shogun, was able to reconcile the two courts and reinstate imperial succession through the Northern Court line.

Establishment of the Muromachi *Bakufu* Ashikaga Takauji assumed the title shogun in 1338 and established the Muromachi *bakufu* in Kyoto, retaining the major governmental and administrative offices of the Kamakura *bakufu*. In 1378, his grandson, Ashikaga Yoshimitsu (1358–1408; r. 1368–94), moved the *bakufu* headquarters to Kyoto's Muromachi district, an area then on the northwest outskirts of the city, for which the Ashikaga shogunate is named.

As in the Kamakura era, land ownership, military reserves, and the tenor of regional politics largely determined the power and fortunes of the shogunate. Loyalty and alliances with provincial military governors (*shugo*), powerful vassals, and family factions were critical, because the Ashikaga shogunate lacked significant landholdings and military might. Takauji was careful to install his most trusted vassals, now considered lords (later called daimyo) in their own right, in the highest posts. These high-ranking lords also served as military governors in regions bordering Kyoto. Their proximity to the capital enabled close monitoring of their movements and their superior rank heightened their loyalty to the shogunate. Vassals were also situated in Kyushu, the far north, and in eastern Japan. The government of such outlying areas could vary greatly. Some regional lords did not even live on their domains, and some held territories as large as several provinces, or in many far-flung areas that they could not manage simultaneously.

As succession continued in the Ashikaga line, personal ties obligating daimyo to the shogunate weakened, and some regional lords became essentially independent of the central government. Eventually the *bakufu* took steps to stabilize the precarious lack of control over provincial affairs. In 1367 the post of deputy shogun (*kanrei*) was created, and the third Ashikaga shogun, Yoshimitsu, made judicious use of representatives of the three main military families, Hosokawa, Shiba, and Hatakeyama, alternating their appointments in that capacity. These *kanrei* and other agents of the shogun worked to suppress and even eliminate powerful *shugo* and lords who impeded *bakufu* authority—for example, assisting Yoshimitsu in crushing the Yamana family in 1391 and ousting Ouchi Yoshihiro in 1399.

Yoshimitsu also fostered positive strides in Japanese politics, society, and culture, brokering the unification of the Northern and Southern Courts, reducing the fearsome raids of Japanese pirates (*wako*), and reestablishing trade with China's Ming dynasty. Further, Yoshimitsu indulged in lavish patronage of the arts, including his monastic retreat, the Temple of the Golden Pavilion (Kinkakuji, also called Rokuonji) situated in Kyoto's Kitayama dis-

trict. Covered inside and out with gold leaf, the structure evoked a glittering tribute to the glory and splendor of the shogun. Considering these accomplishments, it is not surprising that Yoshimitsu's reign is deemed the pinnacle of Muromachi *bakufu* authority and prestige. After his death in 1408, there was a noticeable decline in Ashikaga leadership, and provincial chiefs such as lords and governors quickly filled the power void created as the *bakufu* attended to their military campaigns.

Onin War Civil war erupted in the area around Kyoto during the tenure of the eighth shogun, Ashikaga Yoshimasa (1436–90; r. 1449–76). The Onin War (1467–77), bearing the name of the reign era when the conflict began, was brought about by economic decline, famine, and disputes over succession practices for both regional military governor (*shugo*) positions and the shogunate. General economic deterioration was pushed further than before by the final unraveling of the *shoen* system. Power no longer resided with agents of the shogunate, or obligations owed to the shogun; rather, authority depended upon steadfast vassals, securely held lands, fortifications such as castles, tactical acumen, and military skills.

Concerns over shogunal succession resulted from the fact that Yoshimasa had produced no heir to follow him as shogun. Yoshimasa decided that his younger brother should become the next shogun, but when that brother fathered a son, a power struggle ensued within the Ashikaga family. Ashikaga administrators and *shugo* also entered the dispute. The Onin War started in 1467 when the forces of Hosokawa Katsumoto fought with those of Yamana Sozen (or Mochitoyo). Hosokawa's army was supported by both the emperor and the shogun. The Yamana army was assisted by the powerful Ouchi daimyo family. Fighting was concentrated in the Kyoto area and the capital was largely destroyed during the 10 years of the war. By the time hostilities ended in the capital in 1477, warfare had spread to the provinces, where it continued.

Opposition to the shogunate grew in the region around Kyoto, compounded by uprisings in the Kanto region and elsewhere. Revolts of significant scope began to occur on a nearly annual basis as the shogunate became less concerned with suppressing such disturbances. Regional lords long dependent upon *bakufu* clout to dissuade their most assertive vassals from rebelling could no longer assume that their domains were protected by loyalty. Irrefutable vassal command over provincial concerns amid Ashikaga weakness became more apparent after the sixth shogun, Ashikaga Yoshinori (1394–1441; r. 1429–41) was assassinated in 1441 by an affronted *shugo*. In circumstances even more threatening to the Ashikaga regime, certain daimyo and *shugo* had consolidated their power in domains that functioned effectively without need for a centralized government. In uncertain economic times, dramatic changes in land administration and ownership thus contributed to numerous circumstances that effected the breakdown of the Ashikaga shogunate.

The decisive collapse of Ashikaga authority in 1467 unleashed internecine struggles for land control previously deterred by vassal and daimyo obligations to the shogun. Regional lords, who became accustomed to *shugo* collecting rents, taxes, and even claims to land in domains they administrated, realized that the estates and revenues had passed out of owner control. The results could be financially and politically devastating for daimyo. In the 15th century, one court family reported that it was divested of 14 out of its 23 estates by local *shugo* and *gokenin*. *Shugo* succession, which had shifted from the shogunate to hereditary and local control, was a major factor in the formation of such powerful domains with complete disregard for official *bakufu* protocols.

Significant economic hardship persisted in Japan from the middle of the 15th century until the official end of the Muromachi shogunate in 1573. Scant Ashikaga assets had long been insufficient to cover expenditures, and the shogunate continued to neglect provincial and economic matters, ensuring its own demise. The burden of regular taxes imposed on farmers and merchants worsened as emergency measures taxed houses and rice fields. A famine in the mid-15th century and a series of weather-related catastrophes increased the spread of poverty.

Yoshimasa tried to ease economic strains by issuing debt cancellation edicts (*tokuseirei*) but this failed to alleviate the problem. Inadequate as a ruler, he compounded the problem by filling his time with cultural rather than political pursuits. Instead of addressing the significant problems of his day, he effectively retired from the world, cloistered in an elegant detached palace, the Temple of the Silver Pavilion (Ginkakuji) in Kyoto's Higashiyama district. As a result of such inattention to affairs of state, Ashikaga power was eclipsed by Ashikaga administrators, most notably those from the Hosokawa family. Their retainers, the Miyoshi family, usurped the Hosokawa in the 16th century, and, finally, the Miyoshi were superseded by the Matsunaga family.

The countryside was in disarray and farming villages banded together to defend themselves. The leaders of these affiliated villages were local samurai who sometimes took advantage of the civil unrest to proclaim themselves the heads of domains. The most powerful of these domain lords even challenged the power and authority of the established *shugo*. Besides producing extensive civil unrest, the prolonged warfare resulted in a significant loss of income for both Kyoto aristocrats and Buddhist temples, whose income generated by outlying estates was interrupted. As a result many aristocrats fled Kyoto for the provinces, sometimes seeking security in the castle towns protected by local daimyo.

There was one benefit to the internecine struggles instituted by the Onin War. Tightly controlled daimyo and *shugo* domains actually fostered increases in economic production as these landholders were more likely to institute capital improvements that would increase production, such as irrigation, or advocating commerce to enhance laborer incomes.

Technically, the shogunate survived the war and its own weak political leadership, although vassals with great military skill and resources exerted real power. These vassals usually possessed land, and in the mid-15th century, began to construct fortress-like castles to defend their territories. Ultimately, these experienced, resourceful vassals challenged the *shugo*, often overthrowing the military governors and even annexing their domains. These powerful vassals came to be known as *sengoku daimyo* during the Muromachi era. Approximately 250 daimyo domains are estimated to have existed by the early 16th century.

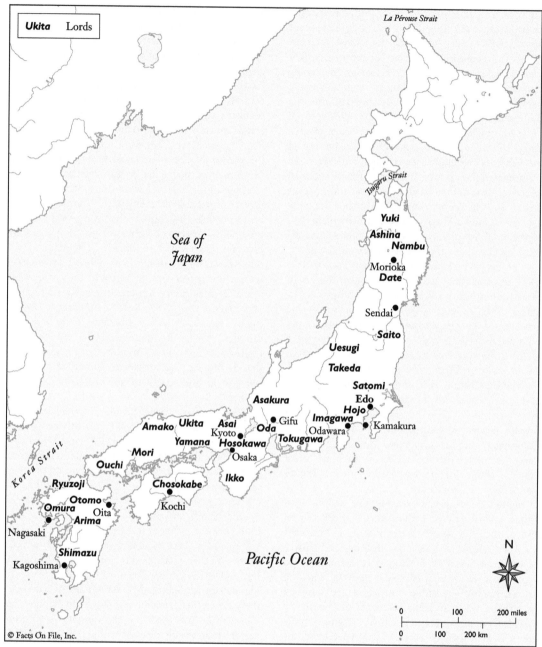

Map 1. *Important Lords in the 16th Century*

Warring States (Sengoku) Period (1467–1568)
The Warring States period refers to the 100-year era that began with the Onin War, a time marked by ongoing warfare between domain lords. Many of the circumstances of the period have been chronicled above in the events leading up to and following the Onin War. Continued political instability and the spread of warfare into the provinces were reinforced by continuities with the events surrounding the Onin War. The failure of the shogunate to maintain central control resulted in the growing power and independence of local warrior families. Those in control of the *shoen* often assumed power from their lords. The old *shugo* system, especially in the Kyoto region, was replaced by the daimyo, domain lords. The phenomenon known as *gekokujo*—"those below overthrowing those above"—also occurred when main families were overthrown by branch families, and on occasion, peasant uprisings.

For much of the Warring States period, provincial daimyo wielded considerable power with little interference by the *bakufu*. Powerful daimyo such as the Date, Imagawa, and Ouchi families controlled farming villages and gained retainers from influential local families. To assist in domain administration, legal matters, and dispute settlement, provincial daimyo issued local laws (*bunko-kuho*).

European Contacts As daimyo waged war against each other and attempted to increase their territory and authority, the governing power of the emperor and shogun remained ineffectual. Soon a new challenge confronted the Japanese—encounters with Europeans. The Portuguese arrived first: in 1543 Portuguese sailors were shipwrecked on Tanegashima off the coast of southern Kyushu. The Portuguese taught the Japanese how to make muskets, a technology new to Japan, which changed how daimyo fought battles and constructed fortifications. The Portuguese were followed by Spanish, English, and Dutch traders and missionaries. Europeans referred to Japan as *Xipangu*, a term derived from tales of Marco Polo's travels.

Among the missionaries active in Japan, the most notable was the Spanish Jesuit Francis Xavier who arrived in Kagoshima in 1549, thereby inaugurating what has come to be called Japan's "Christian Cen-

tury." Although Francis Xavier resided in Japan for less than three years, Jesuit and other missionaries worked in Japan until they were expelled by the Tokugawa shogunate in the first half of the 17th century. Some Kyushu daimyo converted to Christianity and forced their vassals to do the same to try to gain trade with Europe. These daimyo promoted Christianity in hopes of acquiring, among other things, military equipment and technology.

AZUCHI-MOMOYAMA PERIOD
(1573–1615)

The Azuchi-Momoyama period takes its name from two castles built by warrior-rulers in the second half of the 16th century. Azuchi Castle was built by Oda Nobunaga on the shores of Lake Biwa near Kyoto. Toyotomi Hideyoshi built his castle, Momoyama (Peach Mountain), at Fushimi on what was then the outskirts of Kyoto. This era is also sometimes referred to as the Shokuho period.

Unification of Japan By the 1560s, the extended period of political disorder and civil war was ending. A process of national unification began to occur as the result of the military and political shrewdness of three central figures: the warriors Oda Nobunaga (1534–82), Toyotomi Hideyoshi (1536–98), and Tokugawa Ieyasu (1542–1616). Beginning with Nobunaga, these three gradually defeated and annexed smaller daimyo, leading eventually to complete control over Japan by the Tokugawa shogunate.

Nobunaga was aware that any possibility of unifying Japan under his control meant not only defeating rival daimyo, but also controlling the imperial court at Kyoto. To this end, Nobunaga marched on Kyoto, occupying the city in 1568. He also waged war on rival warriors and powerful Buddhist temples such as the Tendai Buddhist monastery complex on Mt. Hiei, northeast of the capital, which he destroyed in 1571. As Nobunaga seized land, he gave out domains to his loyal commanders, thereby securing control over these lands.

In 1582, Nobunaga was assassinated by his vassal, Akechi Mitsuhide. Toyotomi Hideyoshi, one of Nobunaga's generals, became Nobunaga's successor. Of peasant background, Hideyoshi had become a trusted commander to Nobunaga. Hideyoshi continued the process of national unification. By 1590, most of Japan was under his control. On two different occasions—in 1592 and in 1597—he sent his armies to subjugate Korea in the first stage of what turned out to be a failed plan to conquer China. Hideyoshi also established a fixed social hierarchy consisting of warriors, farmers, artisans, and merchants that was to become institutionalized in the subsequent Edo period.

For all of Hideyoshi's military and political savvy, he failed to adequately provide for the succession of power to his son, Hideyori, who was still a young child when Hideyoshi died in 1598. Prior to his death, Hideyoshi arranged for five of his senior ministers (*tairo*)—all powerful daimyo—to protect Hideyori's interests until he came of age. Soon after Hideyoshi's death, however, rivalries between the five emerged. Tokugawa Ieyasu, a Nobunaga ally from an earlier battle in 1560 led the faction against those who supported Hideyori's right to succeed his father. The matter was settled in 1600 at the Battle of Sekigahara. Ieyasu's decisive victory cemented his control over national affairs. In order to secure his position, Ieyasu had himself appointed shogun in 1603 and established the Tokugawa shogunate (also referred to as the Tokugawa *bakufu*).

After the Battle of Sekigahara, Ieyasu made sure to secure his control over the daimyo, both those whom he was allied with and those he viewed as his rivals. In effect, Ieyasu manipulated the daimyo system to his own benefit. Depending on the daimyo, he reduced their landholdings or removed them altogether. He sometimes kept the land he confiscated for his own domains; still other land he gifted to relatives and Tokugawa family retainers. Hideyori was reduced by Ieyasu to a minor daimyo residing at his father Hideyoshi's Osaka Castle.

Eschewing day-to-day governance, Ieyasu stepped down as shogun in 1605 after only two years and gave the position to his son Hidetada. Ieyasu worked behind the scenes to strengthen the shogunate and to solidify its power and authority. Ieyasu destroyed the final threats to his regime in 1615 when he marched on Osaka Castle and there defeated rivals Hideyori and his Toyotomi family supporters. With any military threat effectively suppressed, Ieyasu issued laws that codified Tokugawa

control over the daimyo and the imperial court. These laws were the Laws for the Military Houses (*Buke Shohatto*) and the Laws for the Imperial and Court Officials (*Kinchu Narabi ni Kuge Shohatto*). Ieyasu died in 1616 having established control over the entire country and having set up rules for orderly succession of Tokugawa political power.

Early Modern Japan (1615–1868)

EDO PERIOD (1615–1868)

Early modern Japan marks the unification of the country under the Tokugawa military government and some 250 years of peace, the longest such period in Japan's history. This was possible because of the strict control and political administration of the Tokugawa shogunate. The Edo period was distinguished by strong central rule under the shoguns and strong local rule under the daimyo who reported to the shogun. Warriors were in control of all aspects of government. This, coupled with Japan's seclusion policy against influence from foreign nations, helped create a distinctive Japanese culture. It was also a time of important social and economic transformations, including the rise of cities, the development of a strong merchant class, and the expression of urban popular culture.

Early modern Japan is synonymous with the Edo period. The Edo period derives its name from the city Edo (present-day Tokyo) where the Tokugawa shogunate established its headquarters. This period is sometimes dated from 1600 to reflect the significance of the decisive victory of the Tokugawa at the Battle of Sekigahara. Alternately, the Edo period is sometimes dated from 1603, the year that Tokugawa Ieyasu became shogun. Finally, some date the Edo period from 1616, the year of Ieyasu's death. The Edo period ended in 1867 with the resignation of the last Tokugawa shogun, or according to others, in 1868 when the imperial restoration (Meiji Restoration) was proclaimed and the city of Edo was renamed Tokyo ("Eastern Capital"), replacing Kyoto as the official capital of Japan.

***Bakuhan* System of Government** Ieyasu set in motion a political structure referred to as the *bakuhan* system by modern historians. The term *bakuhan* combines the terms *bakufu* and *han* (meaning "daimyo domain") and refers to the modes of government, economy, and society central to life in the Edo period. Ieyasu's immediate successors, Hidetada (second Tokugawa shogun) and Iemitsu (third Tokugawa shogun) further refined the *bakuhan* system that was meant to maintain Tokugawa power and control over Japan.

The Tokugawa shogunate utilized several methods for consolidating their political power and authority and for suppressing the possibility of challenges to their rule from such sectors as the daimyo and the imperial court. In order to control the daimyo, Ieyasu transferred potentially hostile daimyo to strategically unimportant geographic locations. He confiscated or otherwise reduced the domain holdings of others. To further assure that these daimyo would not pose a threat, he kept them occupied with road building and other public works projects that kept them financially drained, since the daimyo were expected to provide the funds and other resources for the *bakufu*'s projects. These policies continued into the 17th century. Particularly effective was the *bakufu* practice of placing relatives and retainers as daimyo heads of domains in politically and militarily strategic districts such as Kanto and Kinki. In so doing, the Tokugawa were able to buffer themselves from the influence and potential military threats from so-called "outside lords" (*tozama*). In similar fashion, the *bakufu* secured strategic land under their own control as well as the economically and politically important cities of Kyoto, Osaka, and Nagasaki. While the *bakufu* controlled the political administration of the country, there was also a system of domain administration (*hansei*) controlled by the daimyo, whose regional authority could be quite strong.

The Tokugawa shogunate found still other ways to induce adherence to their rule. Conspicuous was the system of alternate attendance (*sankin kotai*) by the daimyo at Edo. Established in the 1630s, this system required daimyo to set up residences at Edo and to appear before the shogun every other year. Though largely ceremonial, this system had a strategic feature: daimyo families were forced to live permanently in Edo as hostages, a clear incentive for the daimyo to obey the shogunate. This system also held in check rival daimyo because of the great expense they had to bear as a result of having to maintain two separate administrative locations and the cost of traveling to Edo every other year.

Besides the daimyo, the *bakufu* was concerned about the imperial family and the aristocrats in Kyoto. The Tokugawa promulgated a legal code expressly directed at the activities of the imperial family and aristocrats that placed them in a role subservient to the interests of the shogunate. The shogunate also enforced a four-class hierarchical social system, originated by Toyotomi Hideyoshi, consisting of warriors, farmers, artisans, and merchants in this order of importance. Marriage was restricted to members of the same social class. This system of hierarchical relationships was influenced by Confucian notions of master-disciple relations.

The rigid control exerted by the Tokugawa shogunate over the country, and the peace it provided, was the foundation for the development of cities as thriving commercial centers. The increasing wealth of the merchant class produced new literary, artistic, and other cultural expressions that fit with their sensibilities and values. At the same time, this also produced tensions between warriors and merchants as the merchant class was ascending despite their lower placement in the formal social hierarchy.

National Seclusion The Tokugawa shogunate embarked on a policy of national seclusion (*sakoku*) as a means to control trade and to suppress Christianity. Ieyasu, for one, had been interested in the possibility of trade with the Dutch and the English, but trade and Christian missionary activity were closely connected and Ieyasu came to distrust the political intentions of the missionaries. The shogunate issued a series of anti-Christian directives and by 1639 Christianity was completely banned and trade radically curtailed and controlled. The only trade allowed with Europe was with the Dutch, whose activities were confined to Dejima, an island in Nagasaki harbor. National seclusion remained the national policy until the middle of the 19th century.

One of the effects of the national seclusion policy on life in the Edo period was the regulation established in the 1630s that required all families to register at a local Buddhist temple. Each year temples had to certify that none of their registered parishioners were Christians. The temple registry system was thus another means of social control.

Bakumatsu*: The End of the *Bakufu Although the basic governance structure of the Edo period was set by the middle of the 16th century and lasted until the mid-19th century, there were significant political, social, economic, and other changes that strained the *bakuhan* system and led to an increasingly ineffective government and the collapse of the Tokugawa *bakufu*.

By the middle of the 18th century, financial difficulties beset both the shogunate and the daimyo. Wealth was now concentrated in the urban merchant class. Both peasant uprisings and samurai discontent became more and more prevalent. Attempts at fiscal and social reforms were made, but they were never effective. The plight of farmers, already heavily taxed by the shogunate and the daimyo, was worsened by a series of famines. The prosperity of the merchants came to stand in stark contrast to the economic hardships of farmers and samurai.

In addition to these internal threats to Tokugawa rule, increasing contacts with uninvited American, European, and Russian ships impinged on the security of the Tokugawa. Although there had been sporadic encounters and confrontations with foreign ships prior to the middle of the 19th century, it was the arrival of Commodore Matthew Perry in 1853 in command of several U.S. warships and the demand that Japan open her ports to trade that set in motion the events that would end the Tokugawa shogunate. The *bakufu* was initially indecisive on whether to allow or ban foreigners but eventually bowed to the demands, pressures, and threats of the United States and other foreign powers and opened some ports to foreigners. Japan's long seclusion was ended. The shogunate also signed treaties with the United States and other countries against the wishes of the imperial authorities. The shogunate's assertion that it was loyal to the emperor was rendered suspect, and this unilateral action fueled significant anti-Tokugawa sentiment.

Many daimyo were against the opening of Japan to foreign influence and advocated the expulsion of the Americans and Europeans. Support grew for loyalty to the emperor even among some of the shogunate's closest allies. Those opposed to the Tokugawa shogunate and their policy of embracing foreign trade rallied behind the slogan of "Revere the emperor! Expel the barbarians!" (*sonno joi*). By 1860, activist samurai turned their wrath against the foreign "barbarians" into attacks against Japanese officials who publicly supported the Tokugawa government's foreign policy. The assassination in 1860 of Ii Naosuke, a great elder (*tairo*) of the Tokugawa shogunate and supporter of foreign trade and diplomacy, is just one example of the intense acrimony this issue engendered. The shogunate was effectively caught between the internal antiforeign movement and the external demands of foreigners.

The 1860s witnessed increasing anti-*bakufu* activities among daimyo and imperial loyalists. Despite some attempts by daimyo to forcefully prevent the entrance of foreign ships into Japanese ports, it was soon apparent that foreign military technology was superior to that of the Japanese when foreign ships engaged in naval bombardments against Japanese positions.

Discontent over the shogunate's handling of national and foreign affairs came to a flashpoint when the Choshu domain (in present-day Yamaguchi prefecture) allied with the nearby Satsuma domain in 1866 to lead a movement to oust the shogun and restore the emperor at the head of a new government. Although the Tokugawa mobilized the shogunal army to resist the daimyo, these forces were defeated by the daimyo troops. In 1867, the shogun Yoshinobu resigned under threat of further military confrontations with Choshu and Satsuma. Yoshinobu thought that he would be given an important role in any new government, but when this did not happen he dispatched his army against Kyoto only to be defeated by Choshu-Satsuma forces who declared themselves an imperial army fighting for the emperor. Choshu, Satsuma, and other daimyo sent troops against Edo, but the shogunal troops surrendered without a fight. The Tokugawa shogunate was abolished, and early in 1868, the Choshu-Satsuma faction declared a restoration of imperial rule (*osei fukko*). Emperor Mutsuhito—still a boy—replaced the shogun as leader of Japan. With this, the era of the Meiji Restoration was inaugurated, titled after Mutsuhito's reign name of Meiji ("Enlightened Rule"). The emperor moved to Edo to take up residence at Tokugawa castle and Edo was renamed Tokyo ("Eastern Capital"). The work of transforming Japan from a society ruled by warriors into a modern state was thus begun, directed by leaders of Choshu, Satsuma, and court officials who had given their allegiance to the emperor over the shogun.

TABLE OF EVENTS

Kamakura Period (1185–1333)

1185	Minamoto defeat Taira at Battle of Dannoura; end of the Gempei War; death of child emperor Antoku
	Minamoto Yoritomo establishes constable and steward system
1180s	Buddhist monk Saigyo compiles his poetry into a three-part collection known as the *Sankashu* ("Mountain Hut")
1189	Warrior Minamoto Yoshitsune forced to commit suicide
1191	Buddhist monk Eisai introduces Rinzai school of Zen Buddhism from China
1192	Minamoto Yoritomo appointed shogun by Emperor Go-Toba; establishes the Kamakura shogunate
1199	Death of Yoritomo; Hojo family assumes control of the warrior government (*bakufu*)
	Minamoto Yoriie appointed shogun
1203	Hojo Tokimasa becomes regent (*shikken*) to the shogun; exercises actual governmental power
1205	Minamoto Sanetomo appointed shogun
	Hojo Yoshitoki becomes regent to the shogun
	Fujiwara no Teika compiles *Shin Kokinshu*
1210	Genshin's *Ojoyoshu* printed

1212	Death of Buddhist priest Honen (1133–1212), founder of Pure Land school (Jodo-shu) of Buddhism
	Kamo no Chomei completes the essay *Hojoki* ("Ten-Foot-Square Hut")
1215	Death of Buddhist priest Eisai (1141–1215), founder of Rinzai school of Zen Buddhism
ca. 1218	Earliest versions of the *Tale of the Heike* (*Heike monogatari*)
1219	Sanetomo assassinated
	End of line of Minamoto shoguns; Hojo assume control over the *bakufu*
1221	Jokyu (Shokyu) Disturbance: retired emperor Go-Toba attempts to exercise real power
	Ascendancy of Hojo family regents
1224	Hojo Yasutoki becomes regent to the shogun
	Shinran founds True Pure Land (Jodo-shinshu) school of Buddhism
1226	Fujiwara no Yoritsune appointed shogun; first regent-shogun
1227	Dogen introduces Soto school of Zen Buddhism from China
1232	Hojo Yasutoki issues Joei Law Code (*Joei shikimoku*; "Formulary for Shogun's Decision of Suits")
1244	Minamoto Yoritsugu appointed shogun
	Dogen establishes Eiheiji in Echizen
1246	Hojo Tokiyori becomes regent to the shogun
1253	Nichiren school of Japanese Buddhism established
	Death of Buddhist priest Dogen (1200–53), founder of Soto school of Zen Buddhism
1262	Death of Buddhist priest Shinran (1173–1262), founder of True Pure Land school (Jodo-shinshu) of Buddhism
1272	Beginning of imperial succession disputes
1274	First Mongol invasion
1281	Second Mongol invasion

1282	Death of Buddhist priest Nichiren (1222–82), founder of Nichiren (or Lotus) school of Buddhism
1289	Death of Buddhist priest Ippen (1239–89), founder of Ji-shu ("Time") school of Buddhism
1297	*Bakufu* issues first "Virtuous Administration" (*tokusei*) edict, canceling debts of vassals
ca. 1307	Lady Nijo completes her diary called *Towazugatari* ("Unrequested Tale"; also known in English as the "Confessions of Lady Nijo")
1308	Imperial Prince Morikuni appointed shogun
1311	Hojo Munenobu becomes regent to the shogun
1318	Go-Daigo becomes emperor
1324	Shochu Disturbance: first plot by Emperor Go-Daigo to overthrow *bakufu* revealed
1325	Official embassy sent to China
ca. 1330	Yoshida Kenko completes *Tsurezuregusa*
1330s	Shoin architectural style starts to gain prominence
1331–1336	Genko Disturbance: second plot by Emperor Go-Daigo to overthrow *bakufu* revealed
1333	Ashikaga Takauji seizes Kyoto in Go-Daigo's name
	End of Hojo regency and the Kamakura *bakufu*

Muromachi Period (1333–1573)

1333–1336	Kemmu Restoration: imperial rule restored by Emperor Go-Daigo
1335	Ashikaga Takauji leads rebellion against Emperor Go-Daigo
	Nitta Yoshisada destroys Kamakura

Northern and Southern Courts (Nanbokucho) (1336–1392)

1336	Ashikaga Takauji seizes Kyoto
	Emperor Go-Daigo flees Kyoto; establishes Southern Court at Yoshino

1338	Ashikaga Takauji appointed shogun
	Takauji enthrones Northern Court emperor in Kyoto; establishes the Muromachi *bakufu*
1339	Death of Emperor Go-Daigo
1354	Death of historian Kitabatake Chikafusa (1293–1354)
1358	Nijo Yoshimoto compiles *Tsukubashu*, first linked verse (*renga*) anthology
1359	Ashikaga Yoshiakira appointed shogun
1365–1372	Prince Kanenaga and Imagawa Sadayo fight in Kyushu
1368	Ashikaga Yoshimitsu appointed shogun
1378	Ashikaga Yoshimitsu constructs the *Hana no Gosho* (Palace of Flowers) at Muromachi in Kyoto
1384	Death of Noh dramatist Kanami
1392	Unification of Southern and Northern courts; Go-Kameyama (Southern Court emperor) returns to Kyoto and surrenders imperial regalia to Go-Komatsu (Northern Court emperor)
1394	Ashikaga Yoshimochi appointed shogun
1397	Yoshimitsu constructs the Golden Pavilion (Kinkakuji) at Kitayama in Kyoto
1401	Ashikaga Yoshimitsu establishes diplomatic and trade relations with Ming China
1402	Yoshimitsu given title "King of Japan" by the Ming emperor
1404	Beginning of trade with Ming China
1429	Ashikaga Yoshinori appointed shogun
1428	Shocho peasant uprisings (*tsuchi ikki*): peasants in capital area demand that the *bakufu* cancel debts
1441	Kakitsu Uprising: Akamatsu Mitsusuke assassinates Yoshinori
	Ashikaga Yoshikatsu appointed shogun
1443	Death of Noh playwright Zeami
1450	Zen temple Ryoanji established in Kyoto

| 1454 | Ashikaga Yoshimasa appointed shogun |
| ca. 1460 | Death of Zen monk and landscape painter Tensho Shubun |

Warring States (Sengoku) (1467–1568)

1467	Start of Onin War; marks the beginning of the Warring States (Sengoku) period
1477	Ashikaga Yoshihisa appointed shogun
	End of Onin War; much of Kyoto destroyed during the 10-year disturbance
1481	Death of Buddhist priest Ikkyu
1483	Ashikaga Yoshimasa constructs Ginkakuji (Temple of the Silver Pavilion) at Higashiyama in Kyoto
1485–1493	Peasant uprisings in Yamashiro province
1488	Ikko Uprising (*ikko ikki*) in Kaga province
1506	Death of painter-monk Sesshu Toyo (1420–1506)
1525	Painting of the oldest extant scenes of daily life in Kyoto, known as *rakuchu rakugai zu* ("scenes inside and outside the capital"), by an unknown artist
1541	Ashikaga Yoshiharu appointed shogun
1543	Portuguese vessel shipwrecked at Tanegashima; introduction of European-style firearms to Japan
1547	Ashikaga Yoshiteru appointed shogun
	Last licensed trading ship sent to Ming China
1549	Introduction of Christianity to Japan: Portuguese Jesuit missionary Francis Xavier arrives in Kyushu at Kagoshima and begins missionary activities
1559	Death of Kano-school painter Kano Motonobu (1476–1559)
1560	Battle of Okehazama
1568	Ashikaga Yoshihide appointed shogun

	Oda Nobunaga seizes Kyoto; begins process of national unification
1569	Nobunaga grants permission for Christian missionaries to carry out their work
1570	Ashikaga Yoshiaki appointed shogun
	Battle of Anegawa: Oda Nobunaga defeats Asai Nagamasa and Asakura Yoshikage
	Nagasaki port opened to foreign trade
1571	Oda Nobunaga destroys the Tendai Buddhist temple complex on Mt. Hiei
	Portuguese merchant ship arrives at Nagasaki

Azuchi-Momoyama Period (1573–1615)

1573	Ashikaga *bakufu* ends: Oda Nobunaga defeats the shogun, Ashikaga Yoshiaki; Nobunaga in control of the government
	Nobunaga destroys opposition daimyo families of Asai Nagamasa and Asakura Yoshikage
1575	Battle of Nagashino; use of firearms by armies of Oda Nobunaga and Tokugawa Ieyasu; Takeda clan defeated
1576–1579	Oda Nobunaga constructs Azuchi Castle at Azuchi near Lake Biwa
1579	Supervisor of Jesuit missions in Asia, Alessandro Valignano, arrives in Japan
1580	Oda Nobunaga defeats Jodo-shinshu "League of the Single Idea" (Ikko ikki) at Ishiyama Honganji in Osaka
1582	Kyushu Christian daimyo send envoys to Rome (envoys return in 1590)
	Nobunaga orders land survey (*kenchi*) for Yamashiro province; this is later expanded to include the entire nation
	Oda Nobunaga (b. 1534) assassinated by Akechi Mitsuhide at Honnoji in Kyoto; succeeded by Toyotomi Hideyoshi

	Hideyoshi avenges Nobunaga's death; kills Akechi Mitsuhide at Battle of Yamazaki
1583	Construction of Osaka Castle begins
1585	Hideyoshi appointed imperial regent (*kampaku*) to Emperor Ogimachi
1586	Hideyoshi appointed prime minister (Dajodaijin) to Emperor Go-Yozei
	Hideyoshi given surname Toyotomi by Emperor Go-Yozei
1587	Hideyoshi takes control of Kyushu; tries to suppress pirates
	Hideyoshi issues edict restricting practice of Christianity and orders expulsion of missionaries
1588	Toyotomi Hideyoshi issues "sword hunt" order; confiscates swords held by peasants, farmers, and religious institutions
1590	Hideyoshi defeats Hojo forces at Odawara Castle; unifies control over Japan
	Hideyoshi assigns control of Kanto region to Tokugawa Ieyasu
	Death of painter Kano Eitoku (1543–90)
1591	Death of tea master Sen no Rikyu (1522–91)
1592–1593	Bunroku Campaign: Hideyoshi invades Korea
1597–1598	Keicho Campaign: Hideyoshi's second invasion of Korea; defeated by Chinese and Korean forces in 1598
1597	Twenty-Six Martyrs, first Christian persecution: crucifixion of 26 Christian missionaries and Japanese Christians at Nagasaki
	Hideyoshi issues ban on Christianity
1598	Death of Toyotomi Hideyoshi (1536–98)
	Japanese troops withdrawn from Korea
1600	Tokugawa Ieyasu victorious at the Battle of Sekigahara; gains control over entire country
	Dutch ship *Liefde* arrives in Bungo; William Adams and other crew members taken to Edo

1603	Tokugawa Ieyasu appointed shogun; establishes Tokugawa *bakufu* at Edo
ca. 1603	Izumo no Okuni begins Kabuki dance performances performed by women in Kyoto
1606	Tokugawa Hidetada appointed shogun
1609	Dutch granted permission to establish trading office and factory at Hirado
	Construction of Himeji Castle completed
1610	Construction of Nagoya Castle completed
1614	Battle of Osaka Castle (Osaka Winter Siege): Ieyasu attacks Toyotomi Hideyori at Osaka Castle
	Christianity banned throughout Japan

Edo Period (1615–1868)

1615	Battle of Osaka Castle (Osaka Summer Siege): Ieyasu captures Osaka Castle; Toyotomi clan destroyed; death of Toyotomi Hideyori (1593–1615)
	Promulgation of Ordinances for Military Houses (*Buke shohatto*) and Ordinances for Court and Courtier Families (*Kinchu narabini kuge shohatto*)
1616	Death of Tokugawa Ieyasu (1543–1616)
1617	Yoshiwara pleasure district established in Edo under government control
1620	Construction begins on the Katsura Detached Palace (Katsura Rikyu)
1623	Tokugawa Iemitsu appointed shogun
	Persecution of Christian missionaries and believers begins
1635	*Bakufu* establishes system of alternate attendance of daimyo at Edo (*sankin-kotai*)
	Foreign ships forbidden to enter all ports except for Nagasaki; overseas

	Japanese forbidden from returning to Japan	1707	Mt. Fuji erupts
1636	Japanese banned from traveling abroad	1709	Arai Hakuseki becomes adviser to the shogun, Ienobu
1636	Portuguese residents relocated to Dejima in Nagasaki	1715	Order restricting Nagasaki trade: 30 ships per year for China and two ships per year for the Dutch
	Construction of Nikko Toshogu completed	1716	Tokugawa Yoshimune appointed shogun
1637–1638	Shimabara Rebellion in Kyushu		Yoshimune inaugurates Kyoho Reforms
1638	Christianity strictly prohibited	1720s	Kyoho Reform implemented
	Decree issued forcing Portuguese to leave Japan	1720	Permission given for import of Chinese translations of Western books except for those concerning Christianity
1639	Expulsion of Portuguese traders (last of Exclusion Decrees)		
	Closing of Japan to outside world (*sakoku*)	1723	Introduction of *tashidaka* system that changes payment system for *bakufu* officials
1641	Dutch factory relocated from Hirado to Dejima at Nagasaki; Dejima only port where foreign trade is allowed		Plays dealing with love suicides forbidden
1643	Prohibition on buying and selling land	1724	Death of playwright Chikamatsu Monzaemon (1653–1724)
1655	Tokugawa Ietsuna appointed shogun	1732	Kyoho Famine in southwestern Japan
1657	Great Edo Fire		
	Tokugawa Mitsukuni begins compilation of Great History of Japan (*Dai Nihon Shi*)	1758	Aoki Konyo publishes first Dutch-Japanese dictionary and introduces the sweet potato
	Death of Neo-Confucian scholar and shogunal adviser Hayashi Razan (1583–1657)	1770	Death of woodblock artist Suzuki Harunobu (1725–70)
1688	Number of Chinese trading ships calling at Nagasaki limited to 70 per year	1772	Tanuma Okitsugu becomes a senior councilor (*roju*)
		1774	*Kaitai Shinsho*, first Japanese translation of a Dutch book: Sugita Gempaku and Maeno Ryotaku translate *Tabulae Anatomicae*, a Dutch work on dissection
1688–1704	Genroku Period: flourishing of Edo popular culture		
1693	Death of writer Ihara Saikaku (1642–93)		
1694	Death of poet Matsuo Basho (1644–94)	1779	Death of scholar Hiraga Gennai (1728–79)
1697	Dojima rice exchange (Dojima *kome ichiba*) established in Osaka	1782–1787	Temmei famines
1702	Revenge of 47 *ronin* (masterless samurai): Ako daimyo *ronin* kill Kira Yoshinaka to revenge the death of their lord	1783	Mt. Asama erupts; massive destruction to Kanto agricultural land
		1786	Death of shogun Ieharu; Tanuma Okitsugu dismissed as senior councilor
1703	Playwright Chikamatsu Monzaemon writes *The Love Suicides of Sonezaki* (*Sonezaki shinju*)	1787	Tokugawa Ienari appointed shogun Matsudaira Sadanobu becomes a senior councilor (*roju*); initiates Kansei Reforms

1790	Prohibition on unorthodox teachings	1823	German doctor Franz von Siebold arrives in Japan; serves as physician at the Dutch factory
1792	Russian envoy Adam Laxman arrives in Hokkaido; requests opening of trade relations but is denied	1824	Von Siebold opens clinic and medical school at Narutaki in Nagasaki
1793	Matsudaira Sadanobu dismissed as senior councilor	1825	Bakufu issues edict to repel any foreign ships attempting to enter Japanese ports
1798	National Learning (Kokugaku) scholar Motoori Norinaga completes commentary on the Kojiki (*Kojikiden*)	1833–1837	Tempo famines
1801	Death of National Learning (Kokugaku) scholar Motoori Norinaga (1730–1801)	1837	Osaka rice riots; Oshio Heihachiro leads insurrection in Osaka over government famine policies
1804	Russian envoy Rezanov arrives at Nagasaki; request for trade relations denied		American ship, *Morrison*, enters Edo Bay
1806	Death of woodblock artist Utamaro	1841	Mizuno Tadakuni, a senior councilor (*roju*), initiates Tempo Reforms
1808	Incident involving British ship HMS *Phaeton* at Nagasaki harbor	1843	Mizuno Tadakuni dismissed from office; Tempo Reforms are suspended
1809	Mamiya Rinzo conducts explorations of Karafuto (Sakhalin)	1849	Death of woodblock artist Katsushika Hokusai
1811	Bureau for Translation of Barbarian Writings (Bansho wage goyo) established	1852	Russian ships at Shimoda

1.1 Warriors march to defend Uraga Bay upon the arrival of Admiral Perry and his fleet from the United States in 1853. (Painting by Kano Eishu, 1854)

1853	Tokugawa Iesada appointed shogun Commodore Matthew Perry arrives in Japan at Uraga; presents official letter from U.S. president Millard Fillmore requesting establishment of diplomatic and economic relations with Japan
1854	Commodore Perry returns to Japan Treaty of Kanagawa: friendship treaty with the United States
1854–1858	Unequal treaties imposed on Japan
1856	Consul General Townsend Harris, first U.S. consul to Japan, arrives at Shimoda Office for studying barbarian books established
1858	Ansei Purge: Ii Naosuke has Yoshida Shoin assassinated Ii Naosuke appointed great councilor (*tairo*) Treaty of Amity and Commerce between Japan and the United States; first of the Ansei treaties; similar treaties later concluded between Japan and England, France, the Netherlands, and Russia Fukuzawa Yukichi founds the Dutch School (Rangaku Juku) in Edo Death of woodblock artist Ando Hiroshige
1859	Ports at Yokohama, Nagasaki, and Hakodate opened to foreign trade
1860	First Japanese embassy to the United States sent to ratify trade treaty Assassination of Ii Naosuke for signing Japan-U.S. treaty without imperial approval Tokugawa Iemochi appointed shogun
1860s	Unity of Imperial Court and Tokugawa *bakufu* (*kobu gattai*) movement
1862	Japanese students sent to Europe Namamugi Incident: Satsuma samurai murder Englishman for blocking procession near Yokohama; results in the Satsuma-England War
1863	Shimonoseki Incident: Choshu domain fires on foreign ships

	British warships bomb Kagoshima (Satsuma capital) in retaliation for Namamugi Incident Choshu forces expelled from Kyoto
1864	U.S., British, French, and Dutch ships bombard Choshu positions at Shimonoseki in retaliation for 1863 attack; Straits of Shimonoseki opened
1865	Foreign treaties ratified
1866	Satsuma and Choshu form alliance against the Tokugawa shogunate and in support of restoration of imperial rule
1867	Tokugawa Yoshinobu appointed shogun Mutsuhito enthroned as Emperor Meiji Assassination of Sakamoto Ryoma and Nakaoka Shintaro in Kyoto Tokugawa Yoshinobu resigns as shogun; end of Tokugawa shogunate; governance restored to imperial court; start of Meiji Restoration Edo renamed Tokyo ("Eastern Capital"); Edo Castle becomes the new imperial residence
1868	Proclamation of imperial restoration Shogun's forces surrender at Fushima and Toba

BIOGRAPHIES OF HISTORICAL FIGURES

Abe Masahiro (1819–1857) Daimyo and statesman. From 1843 to 1857 he served the Tokugawa shogunate as a senior councilor (*roju*). In the wake of Commodore Perry's visits to Japan, Abe orchestrated the opening of Japan to foreign trade with the United States and other Western nations. In 1854 he signed the Kanagawa Treaty with the United States, followed by peace agreements with other countries. These actions represented a significant policy shift from the shogunate's former isolationist stances.

Abe Shoo (ca. 1653–1753) Physician and botanist. Abe specialized in medicinal herbs (*honzogaku*) and studied the cultivation of sugarcane, cotton, carrots, sweet potatoes, and medicinal plants in the Edo region. His written works that detail his research include *Saiyaku shiki* and *Sambyaku shuroku*.

Abutsu-ni (unknown–1283) The nun Abutsu. Court lady, poet, and, eventually, a Buddhist nun whose travels from Kyoto to Kamakura are recounted in her poetic diary called the *Izayoi nikki* (Diary of the waning moon, 1277). She was married to Fujiwara no Tameie of the Fujiwara literary family. After her husband's death in 1275, she became a nun.

Adams, William (1564–1620) English navigator. After Adams's crippled ship landed in Kyushu, he was ordered to go to Osaka where Tokugawa Ieyasu was so impressed by Adams's immense knowledge of ships that he welcomed him to live in Japan. Adams was responsible for instituting an English trading factory for the East India Company and resided in Japan for the remainder of his life.

Aida Yasuaki (1747–1817) Mathematician. Aida was the founder of the mathematical school known as Saijo-ryu which focused on the study of systematic algebra. Among his accomplishments, Aida created the first symbolic demarcation of "equal" in Japanese mathematics.

Ajima Naonobu (ca. 1732–1796) Mathematician and fourth head of the Seki-ryu mathematical school. Ajima's accomplishments included work on logarithms and his advancement of *tetsu-jutsu* inductive methods.

Akamatsu Mitsusuke (1373–1441) Warrior and military governor (*shugo*). Akamatsu was the focal point of the Kakitsu Incident in which he assassinated the Ashikaga shogun, Yoshinori, when Yoshinori tried to reallocate Mitsusuke's land. For his precipitous actions, Mitsusuke was forced to commit suicide.

Akechi Mitsuhide (1526–1582) Warrior. He was Nobunaga's military official and the liaison between Nobunaga and Ashikaga Yoshiaki. Mitsuhide is known for the Honnoji Incident, where he betrayed Nobunaga and murdered him for reasons that are still unknown. Mitsuhide was killed in the Battle of Yamazaki.

Alcock, Rutherford (1809–1907) British consul. The first British minister of Japan, Alcock was responsible for promoting and establishing trade between Britain and Japan in 1859. After the Choshu domain assaulted Western ships that were passing through the Shimonoseki Strait, Alcock urged the British, French, Dutch, and American ships to attack the Choshu coast.

Amakusa Shiro (1621–1638) Peasant and political activist. Shiro died defending Hara Castle during the Shimabara Rebellion, a peasant uprising against oppressive taxes.

Ando Hiroshige (1797–1858) Ukiyo-e printmaker. Among the most famous of his many woodblock prints is the series of 53 prints known as the *Fifty-three Stations of the Tokaido Road* (*Tokaido goju-santsugi*) that record his impressions of everyday life and customs along the road between Edo and Kyoto.

Aoki Mokubei (1767–1833) Ceramicist. Mokubei studied pottery under Okuda Eisen (1753–1811). He was noted for his reproductions of Chinese-style ceramics, including Ming three-color ware and celadon. Along with Nonomura Seiemon and Ogata Kezan, he is known as one of the "three great potters of Kyoto." Mokubei introduced porcelain techniques to Japan.

Arai Hakuseki (1657–1725) Historian and Confucian philosopher. Hakuseki began his career in 1682 as a samurai tutor employed by the family of Hotta Masatoshi. Starting in 1694, Hakuseki acted as Confucian tutor and adviser to the sixth Tokugawa shogun, Ienobu, and later to Ienobu's son. In an effort to align the shogunate with Confucian principles he urged that the title "king" be used in place of "shogun" in interactions with Korea. In addition, he sought treasury and judicial reforms. Hakuseki wrote a number of historical works as well as his autobiography.

Arakida Reijo (1732–1806) Also known as Arakida Rei. Poet and writer. First a writer of *renga* (linked verse) poetry, and later a master of *waka*, haiku, and verse written in Chinese, she is best known for two historical novels. She also wrote short stories, travel diaries, and scholarly works.

Arima Harunobu (1567–1612) Daimyo. One of the first Christian daimyo of the latter 16th and early 17th centuries, Harunobu governed the Takaku region of Hizen province, which due to his influence became primarily Christian. He was active in the invasion of Korea and in the vermilion seal ship trade in the South China Sea. Due to a scandal involving bribery, he committed suicide and sparked anti-Christian sentiments in Japan.

Asada Goryu (1734–1799) Astronomer. Asada studied astronomy and mathematics through Chinese translations of Western scientific works. He attempted to synthesize Western and Chinese astronomical systems. In his studies Asada developed several principles fundamental to the field of astronomy. He is particularly noted for his independent discovery of Kepler's third law of planetary motion.

Asai Nagamasa (1545–1573) Warrior. Nagamasa served Oda Nobunaga during the successful 1564 campaign to take possession of Omi province. In return, Nagamasa was granted a domain in the northern part of Omi. Soon thereafter he married Nobunaga's sister, Oichi, in 1568. Two years later, in 1570, Nagamaasa joined with others in opposing Nobunaga, who had aligned himself with the shogun. Eventually defeated by Nobunaga's forces, Nagamasa was forced to commit suicide thus bringing an end to the Asai family line.

Ashikaga Takauji (1305–1358) Ruled 1338–58 as first Ashikaga shogun. In 1333, Takauji formed an alliance with Emperor Go-Daigo to oust the ruling Hojo family. Later, Takauji turned against Go-Daigo, drove him from Kyoto, and appointed Komyo emperor of what became known as the Northern Court. Komyo promptly named Takauji shogun. In exile, Go-Daigo claimed to be the legitimate emperor of what came to be called the Southern Court. The years of two claims to imperial authority have come to be called the period of the Northern and Southern Courts. Takauji spent much of his reign trying to reconcile the split between the Northern and Southern Courts but without success. A devout Buddhist, Takauji commissioned the construction of temples throughout Japan.

Ashikaga Yoshiaki (1537–1597) Ruled 1568–73 as 15th and last Ashikaga shogun. A former priest, Yoshiaki became a military dictator when he overthrew his cousin Yoshihide and became shogun. Due to contention between Yoshiaki and Oda Nobunaga, Oda removed Yoshiaki from power in 1573 and expelled him from Kyoto.

Ashikaga Yoshimasa (1436–1490) Ruled 1449–74 as eighth Ashikaga shogun. Yoshimasa is known both for his promotion of the arts and other cultural pursuits, and for his lack of political acumen that resulted in the deterioration of Muromachi power. Many of the political matters of his shogunate were taken care of by his wife, Hino Tomiko. Without an heir, Yoshimasa decided to appoint his younger brother, Yoshimi, to be his successor. Before this transfer of power occurred, however, Tomiko gave birth to a son named Yoshihisa, whom she desired to become Yoshimasa's heir. With the help of powerful Yamana family leader Sozen, Tomiko's efforts precipitated a fight for control over the shogunate that resulted in the Onin War which raged from 1467–1477. In 1474, in the midst of this struggle, Yoshimasa decided to turn power over to Yoshihisa. He then retired to the Higashiyama area of Kyoto where he built his Silver Pavilion (Ginkakuji) and immersed himself in the arts. He made significant contributions to medieval culture through his patronage of the tea ceremony and Noh drama.

Ashikaga Yoshimitsu (1358–1408) Ruled 1367–95 as third Ashikaga shogun. The Muromachi shogunate reached the height of its power under the rule of

Yoshimitsu. He brought the Yamana family and its land holdings under his control in 1391, and, the next year, he ended the stalemate between the Northern and Southern courts by convincing the Southern court to accept the sovereignty of the northern emperor. In 1395, Yoshimitsu abdicated his title as shogun and became a Buddhist monk residing in Kinkakaji (Temple of the Golden Pavilion) in Kyoto's Kitayama area. His son, Yoshimochi, became the next shogun but Yoshimitsu continued to rule in the background. In 1401, Yoshimitsu established trade with Ming China by sending a delegation on his behalf as the "King of Japan." It was only upon Yoshimitsu's death in 1408 that his son took full control of the shogunate.

Awataguchi Yoshimitsu (1227–1291) Noted Kamakura-period sword maker, Yoshimitsu was associated with the Awataguchi school of swordsmiths in Kyoto and was famous for the quality of the short swords he manufactured.

Bankei Yotaku (Bankei Eitaku) (1622–1693) Rinzai Zen Buddhist monk. Bankei was a popular monk with many disciples who taught about Zen thought and practice in ordinary language. He also traveled extensively and founded a number of temples.

Basho (Matsuo Basho) (1644–1694) Zen Buddhist monk and poet. Basho was instrumental in the development of the poetry genres known as haikai and haibun, and was a critic of classical Japanese poetry. He published his first poems in 1662 and produced a haikai volume, *Kai oi* (Covering shells), in 1672. That same year, he took up residence in Edo, making a living as a haikai instructor. His growing fame as a poet and teacher attracted many students. After 1680, he embraced Zen Buddhist practice and began a series of travels in northern and other parts of Japan that had strong spiritual overtones. Basho described his travels in poetic travel diaries, the most famous of which is *Oku no hosomichi* (Narrow road to the deep north).

Benkei (Musashibo Benkei) (unknown–1189) Buddhist priest and warrior monk. Most of what is known about Benkei has been gleaned from hagiographical depictions of him in works such as the

Heike monogatari (Tale of the Heike) and the *Gikeiki* (Yoshitsune chronicle). Benkei is revered for his loyalty to Minamoto no Yoshitsune and for his marital abilities. Benkei's legend is also told in Edo-period theater works.

Buson (Yosa Buson) (1716–1784) *Nanga* painter and *haikai* poet. At 22, Buson went to Edo to study haikai with Hayano Hajin, but after the master's death in 1742, Buson became an itinerant until settling in Yosa in 1754. As a poet, he is considered second only to Basho. Later, Buson was equated with Okyo as a superior Kyoto *nanga* painter. Along with Ike Taiga, Buson brought the *nanga* school to its apex, distinguishing himself in the Chinese scholarly tradition as both poet and painter. His spontaneous, lyrical paintings often incorporate literary themes and humor.

Cabral, Francisco (ca. 1528–1609) Portuguese Jesuit priest. Cabral, a Jesuit missionary, arrived in Japan in 1570. He demanded that the Japanese learn Western languages and culture in order to embrace Christianity, rather than have the missionaries adapt to Japanese culture. This view conflicted with the perspective of another Jesuit, Alessandro Valignano. Cabral also made it difficult for Japanese to become Jesuits. He departed Japan in 1583.

Chikamatsu Monzaemon (1653–1724) Playwright. Chikamatsu wrote some of the most important plays of the Bunraku and Kabuki theaters. See chapter 9, Performing Arts.

Chokei (1343–1394) Reigned 1368–83 as the 98th emperor. Chokei was the second emperor to the Southern Court, which operated under continuous attacks from the Northern Court. Thus Chokei was often forced to take refuge and set up temporary residence in temples throughout the course of his reign.

Date Masamune (1567–1635) Daimyo. A warrior and ruler in the provinces of Mutsu and Dewa. Masamune was responsible for quelling peasant uprisings and offering his allegiance to Tokugawa Ieyasu in the Battle of Sekigahara. Controlling the Sendai domain, he began a salt industry and endorsed repossession of land. Masamune was also adamant in his opposition to foreign relations with the West.

Dogen (1200–1253) Zen Buddhist monk. Dogen studied Tendai Buddhism on Mt. Hiei but was dissatisfied with what he learned. After studying with the Zen monk Eisai, Dogen traveled to China and there reached enlightenment after studying Soto (in Chinese, Caodong) Zen. Returning from China, he established the Soto Zen school in Japan. Dogen's assertions about the correctness of Soto teachings and practices angered the traditional Tendai school, and Dogen was forced to flee to Echizen, where he established the Eiheiji, a Soto temple, in 1246. Dogen's magnum opus, *Shobo genzo* (Eye treasures of the right Dharma), includes instructions for his disciples as well as sermons explaining his Soto perspective.

Eifuku Mon'in (1271–1342) Empress and *waka* poet. As empress to Emperor Fushimi (r. 1287–98), Eifuku was the most notable woman writer of *waka* poetry and patron of the Kyogoku poetic style. Much of her work focuses on the seasons and the ephemerality of nature, as well as on love and other complex human emotions. The bulk of her work (around 150 poems) is represented in the *Gyokuyo wakashu* (Collection of jeweled leaves) and the *Fuga wakashu* (Collection of elegance), as well as other imperial anthologies.

Eisai (1141–1215) Zen Buddhist monk. Restless with the lack of discipline emerging in the Tendai Buddhist school, Eisai embraced the principles of the Rinzai school of Zen Buddhism and brought them to Japan in 1191 after a period of study in China. Preaching this new form of Buddhist practice in Kyoto and Kyushsu, Eisai drew much criticism from Tendai leaders, facing charges of heresy. In 1199 he traveled to Kamakura where Hojo Masako embraced him, making him abbot of Kenninji monastery in 1202. There he taught his unique mixture of Zen, Tendai, and esoteric Buddhism until his death in 1215.

Eison (Eizon) (1201–1290) Ritsu school Buddhist monk. Eison studied Buddhism at the Daigoji in Kyoto. Seeking a more accessible form of Buddhism, Eison eventually embraced the ideals of the Ritsu (Vinaya or Precepts) school. Eison also labored to improve the situation of marginalized social groups such as lepers, and engaged in work to improve the community by repairing roads and bridges. At the invitation of Hojo Tokiyori in 1262, Eison spent a brief time establishing a number of temples in and around Kamakura. Eison was the author of numerous religious texts.

Ema Saiko (1787–1861) Painter and poet. Ema Saiko was one of the first female scholars of Chinese arts and letters to receive recognition for her talents. Her father, a doctor and scholar of both Confucianism and Western studies, lost both his wife and son when Saiko was three years old. Thereafter he doted on his daughter, encouraging her to develop her artistic talents by teaching her himself and later arranging for her to study painting under the Kyoto monk Gyokurin (1751–1814). During her lifetime, Saiko occupied an important place in the Japanese art world, thanks to her celebrated Chinese-style artwork, including verse, calligraphy, and ink paintings.

En'i (fl. late 13th century) *Yamato-e* painter. The details of En'i's life are unknown. Possibly a priest-painter or a professional artist, he may have belonged to a group of painters who specialized in images related to the Jodo school of Pure Land Buddhism. His name appears on an inscription at the end of one of the *Ippen shonin eden* scrolls, a famous work that illustrates the life of the priest Ippen.

Enku (ca. 1632–1695) Tendai Buddhist priest and sculptor. Enku traveled throughout Japan as an itinerant priest and beggar, preaching to the people he met along the road. He is particularly noted for his carvings of Buddhist images. His style is known as "hatchet carving" because the carvings are rough with the appearance of being unfinished.

Eshin (1182–1270s) Pure Land Buddhist nun. Also known as Eshin-ni (the nun Eshin). Eshin was the wife of Shinran Shonin, founder of the Jodo-shinshu school of Pure Land Buddhism and the first Buddhist priest to marry. Eshin is famous for her active support of her husband's Buddhist teachings. Many of her letters survive, indicating both her learning and her literary ability.

Fabian (ca. 1565–after 1620) Japanese author and Christian apostate. After studying Zen in Kyoto, Fabian converted to Christianity in 1583 and entered the Jesuit order as a brother three years later. While teaching at the Jesuit school in Amakusa, he authored a Christian-influenced version of the famous warrior narrative, *Heike monogatari* (Tale of the Heike). He spent a number of years at the Jesuit mission in Kyoto, where he gained a reputation for being an impassioned preacher. After he was denied promotion to the priesthood, Fabian suddenly left the Jesuits in 1608. He spent much of the rest of his life speaking out against his former Jesuit brothers, writing the famous work *Ha Daiusu* (*Deus Destroyed*) in 1620. This text became foundational for the anti-Christian movement of the Edo period.

Frois, Luis (1532–1597) Jesuit missionary. Frois, born in Portugal, was sent to Japan in 1563. He is important for his careful record keeping of life in 16th century Japan. His writings included missionary reports and a history of Japanese Christianity (*Historia de Japam*) that covers the years 1549 to 1593. He died in Nagasaki.

Fujiwara no Kanezane (Kujo Kanezane) (1149–1207) Statesman. Kanezane was a Kamakura-period aristocrat who started the Kujo family line. He served as an imperial regent and struggled to control retired emperors from continuing to try to direct the affairs of state from behind the scenes. This activity was the cause of his downfall in 1196, after which he became a Buddhist priest. Besides some poetry, Kanezana is known for his court diary, the *Gyokuyo*.

Fujiwara no Takanobu (1142–1205) *Yamato-e* painter and poet. Takanobu lived in Kyoto as a court noble and painted several portraits including Minamoto no Yoritomo, Fujiwara no Mitsuyoshi, and Taira no Shigemore. He first developed the style of portraiture called *nise-e*, which incorporated a detailed, realistic approach to depicting facial features. He was also one of the first to produce portraits in the secular *Yamato-e* style.

Fujiwara no Toshinari no Musume (Shunzei no Musume) (ca. 1171–1254) Poet. Fujiwara no Toshinari no Musume, literally, "Fujiwara no Toshinari's daughter" was also known as Shunzei no Musume ("Shunzei's daughter"). Despite these names, she was in fact the granddaughter of the renowned poet Fujiwara no Shunzei (Fujiwara no Toshinari). She was one of the foremost women *waka* poets. Her poetry includes themes of romance infused with symbolic language that utilizes images of the changing seasons. Her work is preserved in imperial poetry anthologies and other poetry collections.

Furuta Oribe (1544–1615) Warrior and tea master. Oribe was a tea master who distinguished himself through patronage of a ceramic type known as Oribe ware. A student of tea master Sen no Rikyu, Oribe became Japan's foremost figure in tea circles after Rikyu's death. Oribe was originally a retainer of Oda Nobunaga and Toyotomi Hideyoshi.

Geiami (1431–1485) Ink painter. Geiami, son and student of Noami and father of Soami, was an ink painter who worked in the *suiboku* style. He inherited the role of *doboshu* from Noami and passed the position to Soami. *Doboshu* retained responsibility for the connoisseurship and display of art works and other valuables owned by the Ashikaga shoguns. As *doboshu*, Geiami contributed to a catalog of Chinese works in the Ashikaga collection. He also helped compose the *Kundaikan sayu choki*, Japan's first volume of art criticism. Geiami was an established painter whose style demonstrates the influence of Chinese Southern Song masters Ma Yuan and Xia Gui, as well as the *suiboku* artist Shubun.

Gido Shushin (1325–1388) Zen Buddhist monk. Gido Shushin studied Tendai Buddhism on Mt. Hiei before embracing the teachings of the Rinzai school of Zen Buddhism in 1342, becoming a disciple of Rinzai's Japanese founder, Muso Soseki. Gido became a leading proponent of Gozan (Five Mountains) Zen literature and is considered one of the Gozan tradition's most accomplished poets.

Go-Daigo (1287–1339) Reigned 1319–39 as the 96th emperor. Go-Daigo was relentless in his opposition to Kamakura rule. After his foiled 1324

Shoshu Conspiracy to overtake the shogunate, he launched a second unsuccessful attempt in 1331, known as the Genko Incident, when he marched his imperial army on Kamakura and was soundly defeated by Hojo Takaoki. He was subsequently exiled to the Oki Islands, leaving his throne in Kyoto to be filled by the first Northern Court emperor, Kogon. He regrouped two years later, and with the support of the famed warrior Kusunoki Masashige and the recently defected Hojo general Ashikaga Takauji, he was finally successful in bringing an end to Kamakura rule by ousting Kogon and ushering in the Kemmu Restoration of 1333. Go-Daigo returned to Kyoto to restore imperial power but was forced out by an unsatisfied Takauji in 1335. Retreating to Yoshino, he established a Southern Court in opposition to the Northern Court, revived when Takauji installed Kogon's brother, Komyo, as emperor in Kyoto. This began a long and intense period of civil war known as Nambokucho (Northern and Southern Courts) lasting until 1392. The conflict finally ended when the Muromachi shogunate convinced the Southern Court to recognize Northern emperor Go-Komatsu as a legitimate ruler. The day before his death in 1339, Go-Daigo handed control of the Southern Court over to his son, Go-Murakami.

Go-Kameyama (1347–1424) Reigned 1383–92 as the 99th emperor. As the last emperor of the Southern Court, Go-Kameyama negotiated the reunification of the Northern and Southern Courts. Under this agreement the imperial rule of Northern emperor Go-Komatsu was to be accepted, with succession alternating between the Northern and Southern lines. Upon the death of Muromachi shogun Ashikaga Yoshimitsu, Go-Kameyama tried to ensure that the Northern Court would honor this arrangement. Failing to capture the attention of the Northern Court, Go-Kameyama eventually returned to Kyoto, allowing the Northern Court lineage to continue to occupy the throne.

Go-Saga (1220–1272) Reigned 1242–46 as the 88th emperor. Son of Tsuchimikado, Go-Saga left his life as a Buddhist monk and was aided by the Kamakura shogunate in taking the throne from the court-supported heir, Prince Tadanari. While Go-Saga allowed his son Go-Fukakusa to assume the throne after the father had ruled only four years, Go-Saga continued to be a strong presence in the court for 26 years, forcing Go-Fukakusa to relinquish control to his younger brother Kameyama in 1260. This created intense rivalry between the two brothers, which was not resolved until after Go-Fukakusa sought the Kamakura shogunate's help in establishing his lineage's succession. The shogunate established a compromise by alternating succession between the two lines, starting in 1287 with emperor Fushimi, Go-Fukakusa's son. The two lines of succession are known as the Jimyoin (Go-Fukakusa's line) and the Daikakuji (Kameyama's line).

Go-Toba (1180–1239) Reigned 1183–98 as the 82nd emperor. Ascending the throne at three years of age, Go-Toba handed over his position to his son Tsuchimikado after just 15 years in power. Despite this, Go-Toba continued to govern, maintaining control of the emperorship during the reigns of his second son, Juntoku, and his grandson, Chukyo. An accomplished *waka* poet, Go-Toba established a number of poetry contests and wrote an essay on poetry. Despite these interests, Go-Toba was particularly concerned with trying to oust the Kamakura shogunate and reestablish direct imperial rule. Go-Toba's opposition to the shogunate culminated in his failed attempt in 1221 to overthrow the warrior regime in an event known as the Jokyu Disturbance. Afterward Go-Toba was forced to live out the rest of his life in exile on Oki Island.

Gyokuen Bompo (1348–ca. 1420) Zen monk, painter, poet, and calligrapher. As a painter, Bompo worked in the *suiboku* ink style. He served as abbot of two major monasteries in Kyoto, Kenninji and Nanzenji.

Gyonen (1240–1321) Buddhist monk. Gyonen was ordained in 1257 at Todaiji in Nara where he learned Kegon Buddhist doctrine, Pure Land principles, and Shingon Buddhism. Gyonen was a prolific writer and is especially noted for the *Hasshu koyo* (Outline of the eight Buddhist schools, 1268).

Hakuin (Hakuin Ekaku) (1686–1769) Rinzai school Zen priest. Hakuin lived as an itinerant monk before achieving enlightenment at the age of 24. In 1716, he set out to reform the Rinzai school by introducing the practice of contemplating paradoxical questions called *koan*. His reforms were so successful that many of his rituals are still used in modern Zen practice. In addition to being a prolific writer, Hakuin took up painting and calligraphy in the twilight of his life, creating works that are still praised as significant artistic contributions.

Harunobu (ca. 1725–1770) Ukiyo-e artist. Complete name was Suzuki Harunobu. Harunobu is noted for producing polychrome woodcut prints using four to 10 colors in addition to black outlines and interior details. His subjects included young courtesans, noted beauties, actors, classical and contemporary poems, scenes of domestic life, and erotic prints called *shunga*.

Hasegawa Tohaku (1539–1610) Painter. Tohaku identified himself as successor to Sesshu Toyo after studying the Kano style in Kyoto from ca. 1570. He first worked in the Kano studio but later revolted against Kano style and founded the Hasegawa school. Late in life he served Tokugawa Ieyasu in Edo. Tohaku created daring monochrome ink landscapes in *suiboku* style, but also produced gold-screen paintings more typical of Momoyama style.

Hayashi Razan (1583–1657) Neo-Confucian scholar. The first in a line of Hayashi family advisers to the Tokugawa shogunate, Razan's early intellectual development was shaped by his study of Zen Buddhism and the Confucian philosophy of Zhu Xi (Chu Hsi). Razan created his own unique view of Neo-Confucian thought. He became one of the shogunate's most prominent advisers and scholars until his death in 1657. Using his political influence, Razan promoted Neo-Confucian ideals within the government and among the populace. He did this by drafting a number of legal codes for both the military class and shogunal vassals as well as lobbying for anti-Christian legislation.

Hayashi Shihei (1738–1793) Scholar and politician. An authority in military science, Hayashi criticized and drew attention to the inadequacy of Japanese military protection. He became adamant about the stabilization of domestic affairs and began to advocate various political and economical reforms. Due to the Japanese fear of Western interest, Hayashi became more determined to improve domestic military and maritime forces. His fervor for change proved ill-advised, and he was placed under house arrest.

Hino Tomiko (1440–1496) Like Hojo Masako, Hino Tomiko exerted a strong influence on Japanese politics during the Kamakura period. The wife of a shogun, she held virtual control of the shogunate. She was known for raising taxes to support the arts and temple building. Tomiko later ruled through her son, after forcing her husband out of power.

Hiraga Gennai (1728–1780) Botanist. Hiraga first studied medicinal herbs in Osaka but moved to Edo around 1757. There he wrote the *Butsurui hinshitsu* (Classification of various materials) in 1763 and two satirical novels, *Nenashi-gusa* (Grass without roots) and *Furyu Shidoken den* (Brave story of Shidoken). These novels served, in part, as the foundation for the comic literature known as *kokkeibon*. Hiraga performed experiments such as making asbestos cloth, thermometers, Dutch-style pottery, and static electricity. Additionally, he learned weaving methods, ceramics, and painting techniques.

Hirata Atsutane (1776–1843) Shinto and Kokugaku (National Learning) scholar. Atsutane studied the work of Motoori Norinaga and other Kokugaku scholars. He embraced Kokugaku ideas about locating Japan's spiritual center in ancient texts that recounted the "way of the gods," and which sought to excise foreign thought, such as Buddhism and Confucianism, in order to return the Japanese to their true spiritual heritage. Atsutane established a movement known as Fukko (Restoration) Shinto to promote his nationalist agenda. Atsutane believed that Japan was a superior nation because it was the land of the gods with the imperial line directly descended from the *kami*. These nationalist ideas influenced the leaders of the movement to replace the shogunate with direct imperial rule. Atsutane was the author of numerous volumes that articulated his Shinto perspective.

Hishikawa Moronobu (ca. 1618–1694) Ukiyo-e painter, print artist, and illustrator. Moronobu first worked in the family textile business, then went to Edo to apprentice in painting around 1658. He studied several styles, including Tosa, Kamo, Hasegawa, and genre painting. Moronobu helped to elevate woodblock prints from illustrations to full-fledged works of art. Moronobu's works eliminated text and were designed to be appreciated for their skill and artistic merit, and he was the first to include his name on his printed images.

Hojo Masako (1157–1225) Political activist. Masako was the wife of Minamoto no Yoritomo, the founder of the Kamakura shogunate, and mother of Minamoto no Yoriie and Minamoto no Sanetomo. Although Masako took Buddhist vows after the death of her husband in 1199, she became increasingly active in shogunal politics, earning the nickname "nun-shogun" (*ama* shogun). Her influence and control began with the removal of the politically inept shogun Yoriie, whom she replaced him with Sanetomo. Further exerting her political prowess, Masako exiled her father upon the discovery of a plot to establish his son-in-law (from a second marriage) as shogun. As the virtual controller of the shogunate, she traveled to Kyoto in 1219 and appointed Kujo Yoritsune (1218–56) as heir to the childless Sanetomo. Masako's political influence continued until her death in 1225.

Hojo Takatoki (1303–1333) Ruled 1311–33 as ninth and last Hojo regent. Takatoki took office when he was just eight years old and was therefore assisted by his grandmother and minister in running shogunal affairs until he came of age. Takatoki's nominal involvement in government left the administration weak and vulnerable to attack by forces loyal to the imperial court that were clamoring for a restoration of direct imperial rule. After a thwarted attempt launched by Emperor Go-Daigo to take over the government in 1325, Takatoki fell ill and spent time as a Buddhist monk while retaining his position as regent. In 1331 Go-Daigo succeeded in taking over the government and ending the shogunate. Takatoki and his family were forced to commit suicide.

Hojo Tokimasa (1138–1215) Ruled 1199–1205 as first Hojo regent. From 1192 to Minamoto no Yorit-omo's death in 1199, Tokimasa worked hard to stabilize the newly created Kamakura shogunate. When his grandson Yoriie took on the shogunal title in 1199, Tokimasa assumed greater control of the government by creating the office of regent and appointing himself to it. In 1204, however, Tokimasa had Yoriie murdered, installing his younger grandson Sanetomo in his place. In spite of Tokimasa's ambitions, his daughter Masako and son Yoshitoki relieved their father of his duties as regent when Tokimasa's plot to replace Sanetomo as shogun was discovered in 1205. After being ousted, Tokimasa was forced to return to the Hojo family land in Izu where he spent his final years living as a Buddhist monk.

Hojo Tokimune (1251–1284) Ruled 1256–84 as sixth Hojo regent. In 1274 Tokimune faced the first Mongol invasion of Japan after refusing to submit to the rule of Mongol China. Luckily, violent storms severely hampered the Mongol attack and they were forced to retreat, giving Tokimune time to fortify the coast of Kyushu in preparation for a second attack that occurred in 1281. During this second attack Japan was saved yet again by violent weather conditions, prompting the Mongols to retreat and allowing Tokimune to issue a counterattack. This attack, however, proved very costly for the shogunate, leaving the government in a state of fiscal distress, a condition that plagued the Kamakura until its final collapse in 1333.

Hojo Tokiyori (1227–1263) Ruled 1246–56 as fifth Hojo regent. As regent of the Kamakura shogunate, Tokiyori instituted the Hikitsuke (High Court) in 1249, which dealt with shogunal vassals. Even though he abdicated his position to enter the Buddhist religious life, he still exercised power over the regency.

Hojo Yasutoki (1183–1242) Ruled 1224–42 as third Hojo regent. Commander of the forces that brought the imperial court under Kamakura rule, Yasutoki rose to the office of regent upon the death of his father, Yoshitoki, in 1224. During his rule, Yasutoki established the groundwork for a system of warrior government that was to rule Japan for the next five centuries. In particular, he took strides to construct a constitution, establish the State Council, and draw up a legal code for the warrior class, efforts that brought stability to shogunal rule. A Buddhist, Yasutoki employed the Zen monk Myoe as his adviser and constructed a number of temples.

Hojo Yoshitoki (1163–1224) Ruled 1205–24 as second Hojo regent. After fighting alongside Minamoto no Yoritomo in the Gempei War, Yoshitoki became the leader of the Kamakura shogunate. In 1213 Yoshitoki succeeded in destroying his most powerful military rival, Wada Yoshimori. After the assassination of Sanetomo in 1219, Yoshitoki became de facto shogun. He quieted the 1221 Jokyu Disturbance led by retired emperor Go-Toba and forced the imperial court to fully submit to shogunal authority. In doing so, he united the entire nation under Kamakura rule.

Hon'ami Koetsu (1558–1637) Artist. Koetsu is especially noted for his skills at painting, pottery, lacquerware, calligraphy, landscape gardening, poetry, and mastery of the tea ceremony. Koetsu, who came from a distinguished family of sword connoisseurs, was granted a large piece of land in Takagamine, northeast of Kyoto, where he established a colony that included craftsmen, artists, papermakers, lacquerers, and brushmakers. Considered the finest calligrapher of his time, Koetsu studied a variety of styles, including Heian courtly arts, the early 14th-century Shorenin style of calligraphy, and the calligraphic style of the fourth century Chinese aristocrat Wang Xizhi. Koetsu published the 10th-century *Tales of Ise* and the 12th-century *Hojoki*, both inscribed with his own calligraphy. Additionally, Koetsu published songbooks from the Noh theater. All of his works shared the common theme of linking the present to the past through style. He is known as one of the *Kan'ei no sampitsu* (Three brushes of the Kan'ei era); the other two were Konoe Nobutada and the monk Shokado Shojo.

Honda Toshiaki (1744–1821) Mathematician, astronomer, and political economist. A trained mathematician, astronomer, and ship navigator, Honda opened his own school of mathematics and astronomy in Edo and began to study Western scientific writings. Also a political economist, he maintained that Japan could not solve its economic crises unless it emulated Western models, such as England. In his 1798 work *Keisei hisaku* (A secret plan for governing the country), Honda recommended the colonization of Hokkaido. In *Saiiki monogatari* (Tales of the West), published that same year, he proposed moving the capital from Edo to Kamchatka, and strongly favored reopening Japan to foreign trade and overseas colonization.

Honen (1133–1212) Pure Land Buddhist priest. Honen studied Tendai Buddhism at Mt. Hiei but was unhappy with what he perceived to be the degenerate state of Buddhist practice in his own day. He discovered the Pure Land Buddhist teachings of the Chinese monk Shandao. As a result, Honen embarked on a religious career preaching the spiritual benefits of *nembutsu* practice. These efforts led to the establishment of Jodo-shu, or the Pure Land Buddhist school in Japan. Over the next several years, Honen gained many followers for his movement. Established Buddhist schools such as Tendai were wary of Honen's teachings and success. They lobbied the government to curtail Honen's preaching activities. In response, the government forbade the *nembutsu* practice in 1207. Found guilty of disrupting the public peace, Honen and his disciples were forced to flee to Shikoku. Eventually pardoned, Honen returned to Kyoto in 1211, one year before his death. Honen was the author of numerous works. Especially famous is his 1198 treatise, *Senchaku hongan nembutsu-shu*.

Hosokawa Katsumoto (1430–1473) Warrior and governor. From the middle of the Muromachi period, members of the Hosokawa family were favored by the Ashikaga shoguns for their loyalty and were given influential positions in the shogunate. Katsumoto was no exception. Beginning his career as *shugo* of the provinces of Settsu, Tamba, Tosa, and Sanuki, Katsumoto soon rose to the office of *kanrei*, which he occupied on and off until he was appointed guardian of heirless shogun Ashikaga Yoshimasa's adopted successor Yoshimi. However, when the shogun's wife, Hino Tomiko, suddenly gave birth to a son in 1465, just a year after the adoption of Yoshimi, Katsumoto's military prowess was tested when he was pitted against Tomiko's hired warrior Yamana Sozen in a battle over who would rightfully assume the office of shogun. This dispute, better known as the Onin War (1467–77), outlived both men as Sozen died in 1473, and Katsumoto was consumed by plague just two months later.

Hotta Masayoshi (1810–1864) Daimyo. Established trade between the United States and Japan, and was responsible for opening Japan to the rest of the world. Hotta urged the Japanese government to Westernize by establishing relations with the United States. This move proved disastrous for the continuation of the shogunate. His advocacy of a new foreign policy proved unfavorable with the emperor, who refused to sign the commercial treaty with the United States. Hotta was released from office and his actions helped the emperor rise to power, while weakening the Tokugawa shogunate.

Ihara Saikaku (1642–1693) Novelist and poet. Saikaku was one of the most important Edo period writers. See chapter 8, Language and Literature.

Ii Naosuke (1815–1860) Statesman. Ii attempted to strengthen the supremacy of the shogunate, but overlooked Western intrusion on Japan. His desire to secure the position of the shogunate grew stronger when he was appointed *tairo*. Due to American pressure to ratify the Harris Treaty (a commercial treaty with the United States), Ii signed it without imperial approval. Internal upheaval resulted. In response, Ii carried out the Ansei Purge, which silenced all who were opposed to trade relations with the West. Ii was assassinated in 1860.

Iinuma Yokusai (1782–1865) Scientist. Iinuma studied Dutch science (*rangaku*) in Edo, and is credited with introducing Western botanical studies in medicinal herb treatments (*honzogaku*). In 1856, he wrote a 20-volume plant atlas (*Somoku zusetsu*) in which he describes 1,215 species of plants as classified in Linnaeus's system and not in the traditional Japanese method.

Ike Taiga (1723–1776) Artist and calligrapher of the literati style. Taiga was born and lived in Kyoto where he first studied the Tosa style, but he quickly became interested in the *nanga* (Southern school) style. He studied with Japanese literati pioneers Yanagisawa Kien and Sakaki Hyakusen, and learned finger painting. Taiga continued to focus on the Chinese manner, including sources such as the *Mustard Seed Garden* manual of painting, while also studying Zen and calligraphy.

Ikkyu Sojun (1391–1481) Rinzai school Zen Buddhist monk. Ikkyu began his career at five years of age as an acolyte at Ankokuji before engaging in strict study under Ken'o Soi and receiving more severe discipline under Kaso Sodon. Ikkyu cast off all that discipline in favor of more pleasurable pursuits when he embraced "mad zen" upon moving to Sakai in the late 1420s. There he shocked the townspeople with his promiscuous and gluttonous ways before leaving to roam the countryside in the company of many prominent artists and writers of the day. His 1455 polemic "Jikaishu" harshly criticized the current extravagant state of his own sect, and after becoming abbot of the Daitokuji in 1474, he set about quelling the turmoil that had developed between groups within the monastery and also worked hard to secure the temple's financial situation. Ikkyu was also an accomplished poet.

Ingen (1592–1673) Founder of the Obaku school of Zen Buddhism in Japan. The Chinese monk Ingen had studied Zen Buddhism in China and thereafter went to Japan in 1654. In 1658 the shogun, Tokugawa Ietsuna, gave Ingen land at Uji, near Kyoto, on which Ingen built the Mampukuji as the headquarters for the Obaku school. Obaku Zen incorporates the *nembutsu* practice along with esoteric Buddhist rituals. Ingen's skills as a calligrapher popularized the Obaku style of calligraphy.

Ino Jakusui (1655–1715) Physician and chemist. Ino studied medicinal herbs (*honzogaku*) as well as the properties of around 2,000 plants listed in a Chinese text on medicinal herbs. He is best known for his *Shobutsu ruisan*, a 1,000-volume discourse on medicinal herbs. Started in 1697, he produced 362 volumes before his death. The remaining volumes were completed by his students who received support from the Tokugawa shogun, Yoshimune.

Ino Tadataka (1745–1818) Geographer. Ino Tadataka was an important Edo-period cartographer and geographer who accurately measured the length of the meridian using Japanese methods. Ino's most important work was a compilation of maps on Japan based on his own personal surveys of the entire country.

Ippen (1239–1289) Pure Land Buddhist monk. Ippen began his study of Buddhism at age nine when he entered the Tendai monastery of Enryakuji at Mt. Hiei. Three years later, he traveled to Kyushu to take up the study of Pure Land Buddhism. After a brief time out of the religious life, Ippen became an itinerant preacher. After a deep religious experience, he founded the Ji-shu (Time school) in 1276. Later, Ippen developed an ecstatic form of dance honoring Amida. Despite resistance from the Tendai school, Ippen taught this form of religious dance to his disciples. Before his death, Ippen is said to have destroyed all of his written works, leaving nothing behind for future generations.

Ito Gemboku (1800–1871) Physician. Gemboku was a prominent physician who studied Western medicine under Philipp Franz von Siebold. In 1826 he founded a school for Western science where he trained many scholars and physicians. In 1858 he was appointed the shogunate's physician. Gemboku created a vaccination center in Edo and was the first Japanese doctor to use the smallpox vaccine.

Ito Jakuchu (1716–1800) Painter and printmaker. The son of a wealthy grocer, Jakuchu lived and worked in Kyoto near the markets. He was a specialist in elegant images of the birds that roamed his garden. Although a Kano school student, he was influenced by Chinese academic painters of the Yuan and Ming dynasties in the collections of the Shokokuji. Residing at this temple after 1788, Jakuchu produced images of Buddhist subjects as well as life at Shokokuji. He remained relatively unknown until rediscovered in the late 19th century.

Ito Jinsai (1627–1705) Confucian philosopher. Jinsai embraced the Neo-Confucian philosophy of Zhu Xi (Chu Hsi) and added his own ideas and commentaries that he recorded in several works. Later he founded the Kogigaku school of Confucian scholarship in Kyoto, which focused on the interpretation of classical texts. This school was responsible for introducing the ethical principle of *makoto* (sincerity) characteristic of Edo-period values.

Ito Keisuke (1803–1901) Physician and botanist. Ito specialized in the study of medicinal herbs (*honzogaku*). Using Carl Peter Thunberg's *Flora Japonica*, a gift given to him from Philipp Franz von Siebold as a model, he wrote *Taisei honzo meiso* in 1829. This volume utilized the Latin name for plants placed within the Linnaean plant classification system.

Jien (1155–1225) Buddhist priest. Jien became abbot of the Hosshoji temple in 1178. In 1181 he accepted the highest title given to a Buddhist monk by the court: Hoin or Seal of the Law. After this honor, Jien became palace chaplain under Emperor Go-Toba, whose efforts to overthrow the shogunate were discouraged by remarks Jien made against such action in his famous work *Gukansho*. In addition to being a skilled politician, Jien was also an accomplished poet who viewed poetry as an essential part of the path toward enlightenment. Jien's poetry is included in the *Shinkokinshu*.

Jiun Onko (Jiun Sonja) (1718–1804) Shingon school Buddhist priest and scholar. In his youth, Jiun studied Confucian principles and was sent by his Shingon abbot to learn the Chinese classics under the direction of master Ito Togai. An accomplished calligrapher, Jiun is best known as a preeminent Sanskrit scholar who published a 1,000-volume language study, *Bongaku shinryo*.

Jokei (fl. 1184–1212) Kei school sculptor. Jokei was a student of Unkei but little else is known about the details of his life. Works attributed to him display a realist style influenced by Chinese Song sculpture.

Josetsu (active early 15th century) Painter and Zen monk. Little is known about the life of Josetsu except for the fact that he was a monk-painter living at Shokokuji in Kyoto, and that he was employed by shogun Ashikaga Yoshimochi as a stonecutter to carve an inscription on a stone stela in memory of the Zen master Muso Soseki (1275–1351). He is traditionally regarded as the originator of monochrome ink painting (*suibokuga*). The inscription on his most famous painting, *Catching a Catfish with a Gourd* (ca. 1413) states that it was painted in a "new style" (presumably meaning the *suibokuga* style) for Yoshimochi. Josetsu was also Shubun's teacher.

Kaempfer, Engelbert (1651–1716) German physician and writer. Kaempfer worked as a physician on the island of Dejima in Nagasaki Harbor. He accompanied the annual Dutch mission to the Edo court in 1691 and 1692. His account of his experiences in Japan is recorded in his two-volume *History of Japan* (1727–28) that served as the standard European work on Japan until the 19th century. He left Japan for Europe in 1692 and in 1712 published *Amoenitatum exoticum*, a book of observations on medicinal plants he studied while in Asia.

Kaiho Yusho (1533–1615) Painter who founded the Kaiho school. Born in a warrior family in Omi province, early in life Yusho entered the Tofukuji in Kyoto as a Buddhist novice. He eventually became a lay priest and served the abbot at Tofukuji. He turned to the study of painting with Kano Motonobu or Kano Etoku. He worked as a painter for Toyotomi Hideyoshi at Jurakudai and later served Emperor Go-Yozu. Some Yusho images emulate the monochrome manner and restrained washes of Chinese painter Liang Kai. Yusho later worked in rich colors and gold leaf fashionable during the Momoyama period. He is considered the equal of Kano Eitoku and Hasegawa Tohaku.

Kaikei (1183–1236) Kei school sculptor. Kaikei was likely the adopted son and pupil of Kokei. With Kokei's son Unkei, Kaikei is regarded as one of the greatest Kamakura-era sculptors. Kaikei executed many commissions for the Buddhist priest Chogen for the rebuilding of Todaiji in Nara after the 1180 fire. Today more than 20 images he sculpted survive, including the Nio guardians in the Great South Gate (Nandaimon) at Todaiji, completed in collaboration with Unkei. Kaikei distinguished himself from Unkei through a heightened elegance and grace also associated with late Heian period Fujiwara patronage.

Kamo Mabuchi (1697–1769) Scholar and essayist. After receiving instruction from Kada no Azumamaro and teaching classics in Edo, Mabuchi served as tutor to the son of the shogun, Tokugawa Yoshimune. The crowning achievement of Mabuchi's career was the work *Man'yoko*, a collection of essays on the classic Japanese poetry anthology, *Man'yoshu*. Besides poetic accomplishments, Mabuchi was a foundational figure in the Kokugaku (National Learning) movement.

Kamo no Chomei (1156–1216) Buddhist monk, poet, and literary critic. The quintessential literary hermit, Chomei became a Buddhist monk in 1204 after he was denied his rightful position as a Kamo Shrine Shinto priest. His most famous work, *Hojoki (An Account of My Hut)*, recounts his life as a recluse in which he ponders the ephemerality of human existence. Besides his poetry, Chomei is also known for his literary treatise, *Mumyosho*, in which he discusses the aesthetic ideal of *yugen* (mystery and depth).

Kano Eitoku (1543–1590) Kano school painter. Pupil and eldest son of Kano Shoei, Eitoku first studied with his grandfather, Kano Motonobu. Residing in Kyoto, contemporaneous diaries cite Eitoku as the most sought after artist of his time. His screens for Azuchi Castle and Jurakudai in Kyoto were commissioned by Oda Nobunaga and Toyotomi Hideyoshi respectively. As one of Japan's most important artistic figures, he had an important role in training pupils and influencing contemporaries. Many of his works were destroyed in battles and fires typical of his era. Eitoku worked in a grand manner appropriate to the scale and status of the structures he decorated. He blended ornamental sensibilities with dramatic scale and bold line heightened with gold ground and washes.

Kano Masanobu (1434–1530) Kano school painter. Tradition identifies Masanobu as the founder of the Kano school, although the style and lineage was actually by his son, Motonobu. Raised in Kano village in Izu province, Masanobu later traveled to Kyoto to serve as official painter to shogun Ashikaga Yoshimasa. Masanobu probably studied with Shokokuji painter Shubun. His works reflect the Shubun influence although few of Masanobu's paintings survive. A secular artist in an era of priest-painters, Masanobu is known for clarity of expression and brushstroke in works incorporating Chinese subjects, themes, and styles.

Kano Mitsunobu (1561 or 1565–1602 or 1608) Kano school painter. Mitsunobu became the sixth-generation leader of the Kano school after his father and teacher Eitoku died in 1590. Living in Kyoto, he collaborated with his father on Azuchi Castle paintings. Later, he served Toyotomi Hideyoshi as his father had, working at castles, temples, and palaces—all destroyed today. After Eitoku's death, Mitsunobu's style changed, becoming increasingly ornamental and focusing on *Yamato-e* themes that were rendered with less drama than his father's images. Mitsunobu later served Tokugawa Ieyasu in Edo.

Kano Motonobu (1476–1559) Kano school painter. Motonobu was Kano Masanobu's oldest son and is considered the actual founder of the Kano style. He followed his father as official painter (*goyo eshi*) to the shogunate, and also headed the court painting academy (*edokoro*). No signed works have been discovered to date yet Motonobu's style is readily identifiable. His works integrate *Yamato-e* influences with knowledge of Chinese bird-and-flower and monochrome ink modes in an official manner that appealed to imperial patrons, the shogunate, and contemporaries alike. Motonobu was especially noted for his work on large surfaces, such as *fusuma*, heralding the rise of mural painting in Japan.

Kano Tan'yu (1602–1674) Kano school painter. Tan'yu was the grandson of Eitoku and the eldest son of Takanobu. He studied with Kano Koi, and was called to serve Tokugawa Hidetada in Edo in 1617 as *goyo eshi* (official painter). Considered the foremost artist of his day, Tan'yu is credited with revitalizing the Kano school and establishing the Kano style at the court painting academy (*edokoro*). He also worked in the Tosa style and Muromachi *suiboku* manner. He changed his name from Morinobu to Tan'yu in 1636 when he took the tonsure in response to the shogun's order.

Kao Ninga (fl. early 14th century) Buddhist *suiboku* painter. Kao is regarded as one of the founders of the Muromachi *suiboku* style, along with Mokuan Reien. His identity remains uncertain, but he was probably affiliated with the Takuma school. Presumably a high-ranking priest, he resided in China for about a decade before returning to Kyoto. Kao was one of the first Japanese artists to use spontaneous and idiosyncratic strokes to depict Zen subjects in monochrome ink, thus capturing the ineffable spirit of the Zen tradition.

Kasuga no Tsubone (Fuku) (1579–1643) Shogunal nurse. Also known by her given name, Fuku, Tsubone served as nurse to the third Tokugawa shogun, Iemitsu. She accepted the position only after having divorced her husband. After Iemitsu officially became shogun in 1623, Tsubone achieved her greatest authority, controlling the entire women's quarters (*ooku*).

Katsushika Hokusai (1760–1849) Ukiyo-e painter and printmaker. During his long career, Hokusai adopted many pseudonyms. He first used the name by which he is best known, Hokusai, meaning "northern studio" beginning in 1796. Mostly he lived in Edo, where he trained to be an engraver and also learned to carve wood blocks for making prints. One of Japan's best-known and prolific artists, Hokusai was a skilled designer who was able to create innovative images incorporating various influences—even Western perspective in which he emulated the work of Shiba Kokan. His most celebrated works are series of prints, such as *Fugaku sanjurokkei* (*Thirty-six Views of Mt. Fuji*) and *Fugaku hyakkei* (*One Hundred Views of Mt. Fuji*), as well as numerous other landscapes, bird-and-flower subjects, and ghosts.

Katsushika Oi (fl. 1850) Ukiyo-e painter and printmaker. Hokusai's third daughter, Oi worked in a manner similar to her father but also used light and dark contrasts to depict volume.

Kawamoto Komin (1810–1871) Scientist and physician. Kawamoto studied "Dutch studies" (*rangaku*) and medicine in Edo. He was appointed instructor of physics and chemistry at the Bansho

Shirabesho—the shogunal school for Western studies—and counseled Shimazu Nariakira, the Satsuma lord, on the manufacture of such things as machinery and arms. His writings include chemistry texts and a 15-volume encyclopedia on physics, *Kikai kanran kogi* (Observing the waves of the sea, 1851–56).

Kenrei Mon'in (1155–1213) Imperial mother. Kenrei Mon'in was the daughter of Taira no Kiyomori, the wife of Emperor Takakura, and the mother of the child emperor Antoku. After the Taira clan was defeated in the Battle of Dannoura (1185), Kenrei Mon'in threw herself into the sea in an attempt to save her son who had been cast overboard. She survived but Antoku drowned. Devastated by these events, she became a nun and lived the rest of her life at the Jakkoin, a Buddhist convent outside of Kyoto.

Kitabatake Chikafusa (1293–1354) Government official and scholar. Chikafusa served as a high-ranking court official. In 1333, he became an adviser to emperor Go-Daigo. After Go-Daigo's attempt to restore direct imperial rule (known as the Kemmu Restoration) failed, Chikafusa was instrumental in establishing the so-called Southern Court at Yoshino in opposition to the Northern Court at Kyoto supported by the Muromachi shogunate. Chikafusa wrote a famous text, the *Jinno shotoki* (Record of the Legitimate Succession of the Divine Emperors; written in 1339, published in 1369), which argued for the legitimacy of the Southern Court on the grounds that it was the true imperial line descended from the gods. This text also had strong nationalist overtones because it asserted that Japan was a divine country superior to all other nations.

Kitagawa Utamaro (1753–1806) Ukiyo-e printmaker. One of the most influential artists of the ukiyo-e genre, Utamaro is best known for his elegant, graceful prints of courtesans and ordinary townspeople. In the late 18th century, he produced several series of prints focusing on half-torso and close-up views of women both in domestic scenes and in the licensed quarter. Little else is known about Utamaro except that he was put under house arrest in 1804 by the shogunate after having published a triptych that included Toyotomi Hideyoshi shown in a manner deemed disrespectful by authorities.

Kiuchi Sekitei (1724–1808) Archaeologist. Kiuchi collected and classified stones and other artifacts that he obtained through his extensive travels around the Japanese islands. He formulated a theory that flint arrowheads were prehistoric weapons and published this and other comparative theories in his 15-volume work *Unkonshi* (Treatise on rocks, 1773–1801).

Kokan Shiren (1278–1346) Rinzai school Zen Buddhist monk. An important writer of the Gozan literature school, Kokan wrote the first history of Japanese Buddhism (*Genko shakusho*) that was widely read and studied over the subsequent centuries.

Kokei (fl. late 12th century) Kei school sculptor. Father of Unkei and teacher to Kaikei, Kokei's work fostered the development of the realistic style in Kamakura period sculpture.

Komei (1831–1867) Reigned 1846–67 as the 121st emperor. The last emperor under Tokugawa rule, Komei was caught up in the turmoil surrounding the transition from the Edo period to the Meiji Restoration. A proponent of continuing the national seclusion policies set in place during the early years of the Edo period, Komei reluctantly agreed to treaties that allowed for foreign trade with Japan. Komei supported efforts to maintain the shogunate against factions seeking to abolish military rule and a return to direct imperial rule. In the end, the shogunate collapsed under the pressure to restore the rule of the emperor.

Kosho (fl. late 12th to early 13th century) Kei school sculptor. Fourth son and pupil of Unkei. Among Kosho's works is a sculpture of the famous Heain period monk Kuya Shonin housed at Rokuhara Mitsuji in Kyoto. Working in the realistic style typical of Kamakura period sculpture, Kosho's images exhibit a refined technical skill.

Koun (fl. early 13th century) Kei school sculptor. Koun was Unkei's second son. He worked with his father on projects at such Kyoto temples as Toji, Kofukuji, and Rokuhara Mitsuji.

Kusunoki Masashige (1294–1336) Warrior. Masashige was a staunch and loyal supporter of emperor Go-Daigo. He supported Go-Daigo's Kemmu Restoration that opposed the Muromachi shogunate and sought to return direct rule to the emperor. Masashige lead a force of imperial loyalists against the shogunate's army at the Battle of Minatogawa in 1336. After his troops were routed, Masashige committed suicide in order to avoid capture. Masashige's loyalty to the emperor was promoted by Japan's militarists during the years leading up to World War II.

Mamiya Rinzo (1775–1844) Geographer. Rinzo was a student of the geographer Ino Tadataka with whom he studied cartography. In 1800, the Tokugawa shogunate dispatched him to Hokkaido and the Kuril Islands in order to conduct a survey. In 1809 he discovered that Sakhalin was separated from the Asian continent by a strait. He crossed it, visited eastern Siberia, and then returned to Japan via China. His travel reports, *Kita Ezo zusetsu* (Illustrated notes on northern Ezo) and *Todatsu kiko* (Voyages in Manchuria), greatly expanded Japanese knowledge of the peoples and geography of these regions.

Maruyama Okyo (1733–1795) Painter and founder of the Maruyama school. Okyo studied Kano school painting in Kyoto with Ishida Yutei. In addition, he studied Rimpa and Tosa school styles, Chinese bird-and-flower painting, and Western painting techniques. Okyo devised his own style that derived from the accurate observation of nature. His paintings, using Muromachi *suiboku*, display realistic perspective along with more traditional decorative elements such as the use of gold leaf.

Matsudaira Sadanobu (1759–1829) Daimyo and government minister. Sadanobu, grandson of the eighth Tokugawa shogun, Yoshimune, served as a Tokugawa government official in several capacities. He was responsible for instituting the Kansei Reforms (1787–93) that sought to restore financial health and social order to late 18th-century Japan.

To these ends, he tried to limit the growth of powerful merchants and to enforce a rigidly Neo-Confucian curriculum at the shogunal school known as Shoheiko. Sadanobu was forced out of the government in 1793. He retired to his domain where he engaged in the further study of Neo-Confucian thought.

Matsumura Goshun (1752–1811) Painter and founder of the Shijo school. Like Maruyama Okyo, Goshun created his own style of painting that combined Western artistic elements, such as perspective, with traditional Japanese artistic subjects and themes. Goshun employed heightened realism but combined this with a Chinese-inspired literati style that he learned from his earlier study with Yosa Buson, a *nanga* (Southern school) painter. Goshun later joined Okyo's painting workshop, and after Okyo's death, Goshun established his own workshop at Shijo in Kyoto.

Matsuo Basho
See BASHO.

Meisho (1623–1696) Empress. Named Okiko at birth, this five-year-old girl became Empress Meisho following the decision by her father, Go-Mizunoo, to abdicate his reign as emperor. Empress Meisho (r. 1629–43) became the first reigning empress since the eighth century.

Minamoto no Sanetomo (1192–1219) Ruled 1203–19 as third Kamakura shogun. More famous for his poetic prowess than his political acumen, Sanetomo became shogun in 1203 after his brother Yoriie was banished to a Buddhist temple in Izu and then murdered the following year. However, actual governance was assumed by Sanetomo's mother and grandfather. Marrying the daughter of a Kyoto court adviser in 1204, Sanetomo had begun writing classical verse at the age of 14 and in 1209 forwarded a number of poems to court poet Fujiwara no Teika for critique. Sanetomo is famous for a poetry style that imitated the kinds of verse found in the *Man'yoshu*. Sanetomo's most famous work is the *Kinkai waka-shu* (1213) that contains 716 poems. Sanetomo was assassinated by his nephew Kugyo, son of Yoriie, who sought to avenge his father's death.

Minamoto no Yoritomo (1147–1199) Ruled 1192–99 as first Kamakura shogun. Yoritomo came to prominence as the commander of the Minamoto troops that defeated the powerful Taira family in the Gempei War (1180–85). With the victory, Yoritomo established the Kamakura shogunate, thereby inaugurating warrior rule of Japan that lasted until 1868. Yoritomo's warrior government was headquartered in the city of Kamakura, and in 1192 Yoritomo was named shogun by the emperor. Yoritomo established a number of governmental offices including the *samurai-dokoro*, the *kumonjo*, and the *monchujo* to oversee governance of Japan. He ruled as shogun for seven years before dying of injuries sustained during a horse-riding accident in 1199.

Minamoto no Yoshitsune (1159–1189) Warrior. Yoshitsune was one of the heroes of the Gempei War (1180–85) in which the Minamoto defeated the Taira. His brother, Minamoto no Yoritomo, became the first shogun as head of the Minamoto family.

1.2 Minamoto no Yoritomo (1147–99), founder of the Kamakura shogunate. (Illustration Kikuchi Yosai from *Zenken kojitsu*, mid-19th century)

After the war, however, Yoritomo turned against his brother, suspicious that Yoshitsune wanted to take power for himself. Eventually, Yoshitsune was forced to commit suicide. Yoshitsune's expertise as a warrior and his tragic demise became the source for later literature and drama that treated him as a tragic hero.

Mincho (Kichizan Mincho) (1352–1431) Painter. Mincho was a Zen monk based at temples in Kyoto who painted in the Muromachi *suiboku* style. His works include landscapes and portraits executed in ink. In addition, he painted Buddhist images.

Miyamoto Musashi (1584–1645) Warrior and artist. Musashi was a noted sword master who developed a two-sword fencing technique called *nito-ryu* (two-sword style). He is also the reputed author of the famous book on swordsmanship called *Gorin no sho (The Book of Five Rings)*. This text details such aspects of swordsmanship as proper posture and dress, fighting techniques, and spiritual demeanor. Musashi was also a well-known *sumi-e* (ink painting) artist.

Mogami Tokunai (1755–1836) Explorer and scientist. In 1785, after studying navigation and surveying, Tokunai embarked on a series of expeditions to Hokkaido, Sakhalin, and the Kuril Islands, where he conducted geographic surveys. As a result, he promoted the strategic importance of Hokkaido to Japan's national defense.

Mokkei (fl. 13th century) Painter. Mokkei is the Japanese name for the Chinese Chan (Zen) monk and painter Muqi. His paintings, executed in monochrome ink, depict a wide range of subjects including animals especially monkeys), birds, landscapes, and flowers. His extant works only survived in Japan. He is also significant for the influence he had on subsequent Japanese monochrome ink painters.

Mokuan Reien (unknown–ca. 1345) Painter. Reien is considered to be the founder of the Muromachi *suiboku* style of painting, along with Kao Ninga. Reien was ordained a Zen priest in Kamakura in 1323 and traveled to China in 1326 to further his study of Zen. In China, he studied ink painting with

Chinese masters and it is in China that he perfected his technique.

Motoori Norinaga (1730–1801) Kokugaku (National Learning) scholar. Norinaga was the author of numerous texts that expounded the uniqueness of Japanese culture and the character of the Japanese people. He derived his arguments from rigorous philological study of ancient Japanese texts such as the *Kojiki* (Record of Ancient Matters, compiled in 712). His writings became central to the Kokugaku movement, which sought to recover the true Japanese spirit from centuries of foreign influences such as Confucianism and Buddhism. Norinaga's idea that a pure Japanese past can be learned directly from ancient texts is reiterated in his magnum opus, the *Kojiki den*, a 44-volume study of the *Kojiki*, which took 34 years to complete. See also chapter 7, Philosophy, Education, and Science.

Mugai Nyodai (1223–1298) Zen master and first Zen priestess. She founded and served as abbess of the Keiaiji and its subtemples in northern Kyoto, whereupon she established them as a part of the Five Mountain Convents Association—a growing network of Zen convents in the Kamakura period. Born into a well-connected samurai family and highly educated in both Japanese and Chinese, she studied Zen under the Chinese priest Mugaku Sogen (also known as Bukko Kokushi, 1226–86). Mugai received her master's teachings shortly before his death, at which point he conferred upon her the character *mu*, meaning "nothingness," from his own name. Mugai became the first woman to successfully propagate Rinzai Zen teachings.

Musashibo Benkei
See BENKEI.

Muso Soseki (1275–1351) Buddhist priest. The most famous and powerful leader of the Rinzai sect of Zen Buddhism, Soseki served as spiritual counselor to many prominent figures in the Muromachi shogunate and studied under several well-known masters including Chinese master Yishan Yining and Rinzai master Koho Kennichi. Twenty years after reaching enlightenment, he became abbot of Nanzenji in Kyoto in 1325, and he established Zen

temples and monasteries throughout Japan, beginning with Saihoji in 1339. However, the crowning achievement of his career was the establishment of the Gozan system, which aided the proliferation of the Rinzai sect and its principles long after Soseki's death in 1351.

Myoe (1173–1232) Kegon school Buddhist monk. Myoe was an outspoken critic of Pure Land Buddhism in the early Kamakura period. He sought a revival of the older, established schools of Nara and Heian period Buddhism. He argued that the new forms of Buddhism developing in the early Kamakura period were a betrayal of orthodox Buddhism and that what was needed was a return to the proper Buddhist practice of the past.

Nagakubo Sekisui (1717–1801) Geographer and cartographer. Sekisui published the first Japanese map of the Japanese islands that utilized the Western system of longitudes and latitudes.

Nagasawa Rosetsu (1754–1799) Painter. Also known as Rosetsu or Nagasawa Masakatsu. Rosetsu studied painting under Maruyama Okyo. However, legend has it that Rosetsu's eccentric painting style led Okyo to rebuke and dismiss him on several occasions. Because of his talent, however, Okyo passed on commissions to Rosetsu that Okyo could not complete himself. A versatile artist, Rosetsu developed his own expressive style that included themes such as people, birds, and animals.

Nakayama Miki (1798–1887) Religious leader. Miki founded the religion known as Tenrikyo (Religion of Heavenly Principle) as a result of religious experiences that began at age 40. According to Tenrikyo tradition, Miki was possessed by a god referred to as Tenri O no Mikoto ("Lord of Heavenly Principle") who used her as a vehicle for divine revelation. As a result, Miki devoted the rest of her life to teaching the heavenly principles revealed through her that stressed the necessity of working for the benefit of others and faith healing.

Nichio (1565–1630) Nichiren school Buddhist priest. Nichio founded the Fuju Fuse ("neither giving nor receiving") sect of Nichiren Buddhism. He was a strong advocate of the Nichiren doctrine that explicitly denounced giving religious offerings to non-Nichiren believers as well as receiving their offerings. Nichio was eventually exiled for 12 years as a result of his uncompromising views and his unwillingness to yield to requests from the shogunate for religious cooperation. Fuju Fuse was officially banned by the shogunate in 1691. Adherents continued to practice clandestinely until the ban on Fuju Fuse was repealed in 1879.

Nichiren (1222–1282) Buddhist monk. Nichiren, the founder of the Buddhist school that bears his name, began his study at the age of 12 and was ordained at 16, but he was soon plagued with uncertainty about the tenets of Pure Land doctrine. Thus, after visiting many temples and spending time studying esoteric Buddhism, Nichiren embraced the *Lotus Sutra*, solidifying his dislike of Pure Land teachings. Forced out of his Awa province birthplace after speaking critically of the Pure Land (Jodo) and Zen sects of Buddhism, Nichiren moved to Kamakura where he continued to develop his own religious ideology rooted in the wisdom of the *Lotus Sutra*. Nichiren wrote "Treatise on pacifying the state by establishing orthodoxy," which resulted in his expulsion from the capital. Upon returning to Kamakura in 1263, Nichiren became militant in his opposition to other Buddhist schools, inciting armed conflicts and provoking legal action aimed at silencing him. Banished to the island of Sado in 1271, Nichiren wrote prolifically while his followers appealed for his freedom, which was granted in 1274. Nichiren emerged from exile and took up residence at Minobu, but the last five years of his life were consumed by chronic illness.

Nijo, Lady (1258–ca. 1306) Writer. Lady Nijo was an author and Buddhist nun who penned a well known autobiography called the *Towazugatari (Confessions of Lady Nijo)*. This work recounts her life as an aristocratic woman during the years 1271–1306. It includes details about her love life and her decision to become a Buddhist nun, a result of court intrigues. Lady Nijo's writing is significant for its view of aristocratic life at a time when it was being eclipsed by warrior culture and values.

Ninomiya Sontoku (1778–1856) Agrarian reformer and philosopher. With both his parents dead when he was just 16, Ninomiya spent his early years restoring the wealth of his family through discipline and frugality. This lifestyle was noticed by shogunal reformer Mizuno Tadakuni, who soon employed Ninomiya for a variety of tasks ranging from bookkeeping to complex civil engineering assignments. His success in increasing rice production on the farms of his domain earned him a post in the Tokugawa government as head of land development, but he died shortly after assuming it. He is also celebrated for his ethical virtue and for inspiring the *hotoku* movement, which his disciples furthered after the Meiji Restoration.

Nitta Yoshisada (1301–1338) Warrior. Yoshisada, along with his compatriot Kusunoki Masashige, fought in support of emperor Go-Daigo during the Kemmu Restoration that sought to restore direct imperial rule. After the defeat of the imperial cause by the Muromachi shogunate, Yoshisada was hunted down by shogunate forces and was eventually killed in 1338.

Noami (1397–1471) Painter. Noami was a Muromachi *suiboku* painter who studied with Shubun. He was the first painter appointed as *doboshu*, or curator responsible for the connoisseurship and display of art works and other valuables owned by the Ashikaga shoguns. In this capacity, Noami created a catalog of the shogunate art collection. As a painter, Noami was influenced by the Chinese painter Muqi (in Japanese, Mokkei) and by Chinese-style landscapes. In addition to his artistic skills, Noami was expert in incense and tea ceremony.

Nomura Motoni (1806–1867) Poet and political activist. Motoni was the wife of a samurai, but after her husband's death in 1859, she took the tonsure and became a Buddhist nun. She wrote poetry with a political emphasis, supporting the late Edo-period movement seeking to end warrior government and restore direct imperial rule. As a result of her political activism, she was arrested by the shogunal authorities and spent 10 months in exile. Her poetry is published in the anthology *Koryoshu* (1863).

Nonomura Ninsei (Nomomura Seiemon) (fl. mid-17th century) Potter. Ninsei is considered one of the three great Kyoto potters, along with Ogata Kenzan and Aoki Mokubei, and is the founder of Kyo, or Kyoto, ware (*Kyo-yaki*). He started his career crafting tea bowls and other objects in a subdued style that were for use in the tea ceremony. His subsequent work, however, utilized brightly colored enamel as well as silver and gold, evincing the contemporaneous aesthetic found in Kano and Rimpa school painting.

Noro Genjo (1693–1761) Physician and Dutch learning scholar. Noro became the official physician to the shogun Tokugawa Yoshimune in 1739. He began the study of Dutch in 1740 on Yoshimune's order. He later translated a Dutch book on medical botanicals into Japanese.

Oda Nobunaga (1534–1582) Warrior and military leader. Along with Toyotomi Hideyoshi and Tokugawa Ieyasu, Nobunaga was one of the military leaders responsible for the unification of Japan in the latter half of the 16th century. He was known as a ruthless warrior, but he also patronized the arts. Though Nobunaga came from a family of local domain officials, he became lord of Nagoya castle and from there began his military campaign to take control over all of Japan. By 1568 he had taken control of Kyoto and named Ashikaga Yoshiaki as shogun. It was Nobunaga, however, who was controlling the affairs of state. Nobunaga relentlessly destroyed his enemies. These included other powerful lords and warriors, and powerful Buddhist schools who owed allegiance to his rivals. With central Japan under his control, he built a castle at Azuchi on the east shore of Lake Biwa near Kyoto. This served as his official headquarters after 1579.

Nobunaga enacted a number of policies meant to secure his rule by weakening his rivals. He abolished road tolls that were a means of income for local lords and he engaged in "sword hunts" as a means of disarming farmers and the peasantry. Militarily, Nobunaga was among the first warlords to use Western firearms in battle.

In 1582, while engaged in further campaigns to seize additional territory in western Japan, Nobunaga was unexpectedly attacked by one of his own military leaders, Akechi Mitsuhide. Realizing that he would be captured by his former ally, Nobunaga committed suicide. At the time of his death, Nobunaga controlled nearly half of the country and had set in motion the possibility of national unification that was realized only some 20 years later.

Ogata Kenzan (1663–1743) Potter. Kenzan was the younger brother of the artist Ogata Korin. He studied pottery with Nonomura Ninsei. Along with Ninsei and Aoki Mokubei, he is considered one of the three great Kyoto potters. In 1699, Kenzan established a kiln called Inuiyama that was located northwest of Kyoto. At one point, Kenzan was joined by Korin and the two collaborated with Kenzan directing the creation of ceramic works that Korin would then decorate.

Ogata Korin (1658–1716) Painter. Korin is connected with the Rimpa painting school which derives its name from Korin: the term *Rimpa* means "Rin school." Despite this association between Rimpa and Korin, the school traces itself further back to the painting styles of Hon'ami Koetsu (1558–1637) and Tawaraya Sotatsu (d. c. 1643). Korin studied Kano school ink painting style with Yamamoto Soken. Korin's own work reflects both the decorative painting style of Koetsu and Sotatsu combined with aspects of the Kano style. He painted themes taken from Heian period literature, then in vogue among elite warriors. Korin is especially noted for his colorful screens set against a gold ground.

Ogyu Sorai (1666–1728) Confucian scholar. Son of an exiled shogunal physician, Sorai had a difficult childhood, leaving him disillusioned by medicine and attracting him to other pursuits such as Confucian philosophy, linguistics, poetry, music, and political and military science. Sorai's mastery of the Chinese language made him an expert in the classical Confucian texts and an intimidating critic of Neo-Confucian scholarship. He dedicated much of his life to restoring the prominent status of the classical Chinese texts in Japanese Confucian dialogue, and he is credited as a foundational influence on the development of modern philosophical discourse in

Japan. His major works include *Gakusoku*, *Bemmei*, and *Rongochu*.

Okuni (early 17th century) Actress. Okuni or Izumo no Okuni gained national recognition as the head of a women's theater company that synthesized elements of song, dance, music, drama, and erotic themes into their performances. People would gather to see these plays at the Kitano Shrine and on the banks of the Kamo River, both located in Kyoto. Some speculate that these legendary shows form the beginning of Kabuki theater. Known as Okuni Kabuki, her plays reflected popular themes resulting from the rise of the merchant class and newly found strength of the townspeople. Women, however, were officially banned from the stage by the Tokugawa in 1629, citing moral corruption. Little historical evidence exists concerning Okuni's life, and therefore it is impossible to know to what degree Okuni Kabuki influenced the later Kabuki tradition.

Ono Ozu (1559–1631) Poet and calligrapher. As a young woman, Ozu was sent to Kyoto to study painting, calligraphy, music, chanting, and *waka* poetry. It is believed that she married a retainer of the Toyotomi family but was later granted a divorce due to her husband's alcoholism. Following the divorce, she made a comfortable living as a tutor for wealthy noblewomen. A gifted poet and calligrapher, Ozu's talents caught the attention of more than one Tokugawa shogun. In addition to requesting her services as a tutor for their wives and children, some shoguns, including Ieyasu and Hidetada, commissioned work from her.

Ono Ranzan (1729–1810) Botanist and physician. Ono was a specialist in herbal medicine (*honzogaku*). In 1803, he published *Honzo komoku keimo*, a 48-volume compilation of plants used in medicine, which earned him the nickname, "the Linnaeus of Japan."

Otagaki Rengetsu (1791–1875) Poet. After the death of her husband in 1823, Otagaki assumed the Buddhist name Rengetsu, meaning "lotus moon." An active *waka* poet, calligrapher, potter, and painter, Rengetsu studied with writers Mutobe Yoshika (d. 1862) and Ueda Akinari. The imagery in her poems celebrates the banalities of everyday life.

Perry, Matthew C. (1794–1858) United States naval officer. Perry commanded the American forces that sailed into Edo Bay in 1853 and demanded, on behalf of President Millard Fillmore, that Japan end its policy of national seclusion, establish diplomatic relations, and open its ports to foreign trade. He returned to Japan in 1854 seeking an official Japanese government response to the American demands. Through negotiation, Perry concluded the Kanagawa Treaty on March 31, 1854. This and subsequent treaties contained provisions for trade and diplomatic relations with the United States and served as a model for subsequent treaties with other Western nations.

Rennyo (1415–1499) Buddhist monk. As the eighth head abbot of the True Pure Land temple Honganji, Rennyo's leadership helped the Jodo Shin school become the largest and most influential religious group of its time by focusing his missionary work on the central provinces of Japan. Threatened by this emergence, the Tendai sect sent their warrior-monks to attack Honganji in 1465, forcing Rennyo to flee. After a number of years evading capture, Rennyo settled in Yoshizaki in 1471. There he authored his primary literary work, *Ofumi*, in which he sought to discover the essential truth of Shinran's teaching. Rennyo dedicated himself to restoring prominence to Honganji.

Ryokan (1758–1831) Soto school Zen monk. Ryokan was an itinerant monk who was especially noted as a poet and calligrapher whose work celebrated the beauty of nature.

Ryonen Genso (1646–1711) Buddhist nun. Genso was an accomplished poet and painter, known for her portraits of distinguished Zen abbots. She became a nun following the death of her husband. After a conversation she had with the monk Hakuo of the Obaku Zen sect during a pilgrimage to Edo, Genso purposefully disfigured her beautiful face with a hot iron to escape her womanly appearance. She later served as one of the few female Zen abbesses of her time.

Saigo Takamori (1827–1877) Warrior and political activist. Saigo, born in the Satsuma domain in

Kyushu to a samurai family of low rank, was a leading figure in the overthrow of the Tokugawa shogunate during 1867–68 and the subsequent restoration of imperial rule. Prior to 1864, Saigo served the Shimazu family, lords of Satsuma, in various capacities and with varying degrees of success, and he was exiled on two different occasions. In 1864, once again in favor, he was dispatched to Kyoto by the Satsuma domain to command the Satsuma troops stationed there. During this time, Saigo was involved in negotiations between supporters of the shogunate and imperial loyalists in an attempt to defuse the growing tensions between these two factions. In November 1867, imperial rule was restored when Tokugawa Yoshinobu resigned, thus bringing the Tokugawa shogunate to an end. Saigo's fame, however, came when he led imperial loyalist troops against shogunate forces resisting the restoration of imperial rule. Saigo arranged for the surrender of shogunate supporters in Edo and finally routed the remaining resistance in November 1868. Saigo received honors for his service on behalf of the new imperial government. Saigo, however, ended up rebelling against the Meiji government over issues of the role of samurai in the new Japan. He died leading a force of samurai insurgents against the imperial army.

Sakai Hoitsu (1761–1829) Rimpa school painter. Hoitsu, born into a high-ranking warrior family in Edo, studied a number of different painting styles, including Kano, Maruyama, *nanga* (Southern school), and Rimpa. In 1797, at Kyoto, he took the tonsure as a True Pure Land monk because of ill health. In 1809, he returned to Edo and started a painting studio called Ukaan (Rain flower hermitage). He spent the rest of his life in relative seclusion, devoting himself to the study of the decorative artistic style of the Rimpa master, Ogata Korin. In 1815, on the 100th anniversary of Korin's death, Hoitsu published two books, *Korin hyakuzu* (One hundred paintings of Korin) and *Ogata-ryu ryakuin-fu* (Album of simplified seals in the Ogata style) that sparked a renewed interest in the work of Korin. Hoitsu's painting style reflects the Rimpa interest in depicting flowers, plants, and other natural objects. His most famous painting is a screen titled *Natsu akikusa-zu* (Summer and autumn grasses).

Sakaida Kakiemon (1596–1666) Potter. Kakiemon originated the Kakiemon style of decoration which involved multicolored painting over glazed porcelain. Although disputed, Kakiemon family genealogy places him in Nangawara, west of Arita in Kyushu, where he first made Karatsu wares under his father's supervision. Later he worked among Kyushu potters who developed Imari ware featuring underglaze blue decoration. The precise date for the invention of multicolored porcelain painting is disputed, although the traditional association with Kakiemon is confirmed by the fact that the technique has long borne his name. Typically, Kakiemon ware includes brilliant colors, such as blue, green, yellow, purple, black, and orange-red, painted atop a clear glaze that reveals the porcelain ceramic body beneath the pigments.

Sakamoto Ryoma (1836–1867) Political activist. Sakamoto was a samurai from the Tosa domain on Shikoku who was a noted swordsman. He was living in Edo in 1853 when Perry arrived in Edo Bay demanding that Japan open its ports to Western economic and diplomatic interests. Sakamoto became staunchly antiforeign and pro-imperialist, and involved himself in a plan to restore imperial rule by overthrowing the Tokugawa government. Sakamoto was murdered by forces loyal to the shogunate just prior to the Meiji Restoration.

Sakuma Shozan (1811–1864) Warrior and scholar. Also known as Sakuma Zozan. Shozan studied Western Learning (*yogaku*) and opened a private school that taught Western artillery principles. He became a strong proponent of studying the West as a means of advancing the cause of Japanese modernization. He was known for the slogan "Eastern ethics, Western techniques" (*toyo no dotoku, seiyo no geijutsu*). This referred to Shozan's belief that embracing Western technology within the framework of traditional Japanese values was necessary for Japan to take its proper place among modern nations. Shozan became an adviser to the shogunate but he was assassinated in 1864 by imperial loyalists who rejected the shogunate's willingness to sign treaties with Western nations and open Japan to outside influences.

Sasaki Shogen (ca. 17th–18th centuries) Calligrapher. Sasaki learned calligraphy from her father. She became a master of both Chinese and Japanese scripts. Her style tended to underscore outline rather than shading. She entered the nunhood after her husband's death and became a well-respected tutor of high-ranking noblemen and noblewomen.

Seki Kowa (Seki Takakazu) (1642–1708) Mathematician. Self-educated, Seki is regarded as one of the great masters of early modern Japanese mathematics. Seki established a school of mathematics known as the Seki-ryu and was noted for his creation of *tenzan-jutsu*, a system of algebra capable of dealing with complex mathematical problems.

Sen no Rikyu (1522–1591) Tea master. Rikyu revolutionized the way of tea (*chado*) and founded the Sen lineage that led to the three prominent schools of tea fostered by his three grandchildren. He first serve as tea officiant to Oda Nobunaga from 1570–73, then to his successor, warlord Toyotomi Hideyoshi. Rikyu officiated at several noted tea gatherings sponsored by Hideyoshi, including the event held at Kitano Shrine in Kyoto in 1587. Scholars are uncertain why Rikyu lost favor with Hideyoshi and was forced to commit ritual suicide in April 1591. Despite his untimely death, Rikyu's contributions to tea have endured. He favored an unpretentious aesthetic, emphasizing the quiet beauty of worn, everyday objects and simple surroundings for enjoying tea in an atmosphere of respect and restraint.

Sengai Gibon (1750–1837) Painter and calligrapher. Sengai became a Rinzai Zen monk at the age of 11. It was only during the latter 26 years of his life that he engaged in painting and calligraphy. The subjects of his works range from Buddhist figures to landscapes, plants, and animals. These are rendered solely in ink and often display quick, unrestrained brush strokes and a strong sense of humor. One of his most famous works is titled ○ △ □ (Circle, Triangle, and Square).

Sesshu Toyo (1420–1506) Muromachi *suiboku* painter. Sesshu became a Zen monk at age 11. He later took up residence at Shokokuji in Kyoto where he studied painting under Tensho Shubun. In 1467, Sesshu journeyed to China as part of a trade mission. He subsequently painted scenes of Chinese landscapes he observed on this trip. After returning to Japan, he opened a painting studio in Bungo province. Sesshu is renowned for his landscape paintings though he also did portraits and bird-and-flower painting. See also chapter 10, Art and Architecture.

Sesson Shukei (ca. 1504–ca. 1589) Muromachi *suiboku* painter. A Soto Zen monk and self-taught painter, Shukei studied the works of Sesshu and paintings from the Chinese Song and Yuan dynasties. He wrote a treatise on painting called *Setsumon teishi* (Fundamental advice for students; 1542) that expounded the importance of observing nature and making copies of acclaimed paintings. Sesson's paintings are characterized by his skillful use of light and dark tones. The subject matter of his works include figures, animals, plants, flowers, Daoist immortals, and dragons.

Shiba Kokan (ca. 1747–1818) Artist of ukiyo-e and Western-style images. Kokan produced the first engravings using copper plates in Japan, and significantly advanced oil painting in the Western manner. His interest in Western styles of art is expressed in an essay arguing for the superiority of Western depictions of light and shade and the importance of such styles for illustrating explanatory texts. Kokan trained in Kano school and later bird-and-flower painting, but turned to woodblock prints at age 23. By his mid-thirties, he created his first engravings on copper plates. His works are often a curious blend of European and Japanese techniques and imagery.

Shibukawa Shunkai (Shibukawa Harumi) (1639–1715) Astronomer. Shunkai was noted for his work on reforming the inaccurate Xuanming (in Japanese, Semmyoreki) calendar, the Chinese calendar adopted by Japan in 862. Shibukawa's new calendar was officially adopted by the Tokugawa shogunate in 1684 and used until 1754. He was also one of the first Japanese astronomers to evaluate, compare, and comment on Western methods of astronomy. As a result of his scientific achievements, Shibukawa became Japan's official astronomer in 1685.

Shinran (1173–1263) Buddhist monk. After spending his early years in study and practice at Mt. Hiei's Enryakuji, Shinran became a follower in 1201 of Jodo sect founder, Honen, whose *nembutsu* movement soon became quite powerful. It drew much criticism from the other Buddhist schools, leading to its dissolution at the hands of the government and the expulsion of Shinran to the province of Echigo, where he became the first priest to be publicly married. Pardoned in 1211, Shinran decided to move his large family to the Kanto region, where he quickly gained a large following and wrote his most accomplished work, *Kyogyoshinsho*, which described the path to rebirth in the Pure Land and delineated the foundational principles of Shinran's Jodo Shin sect of Buddhism. Returning to Kyoto in 1235, Shinran entered his most prolific period of writing, which lasted until just three years before his death in 1263. His cremated remains were placed in the Otani area of Kyoto at the future site of the Honganji.

Shinso
See SOAMI.

Shizuka Gozen (late 12th century) *Shirabyoshi* dancer and mistress of Minamoto no Yoshitsune. Yoshitsune, one of the heroes of the Gempei War (1180–85), met with suspicion from his brother Minamoto no Yoritomo, head of the Minamoto family, after the war ended. Pursued by Yoritomo's troops, Yoshitsune was forced to flee Kyoto accompanied voluntarily by his mistress Shizuka. She was unable to keep up the strenuous pace, so Yoshitsune abandoned her in the Yoshino region, where she was captured by monks and taken to Kamakura. She was allowed to return to Kyoto only after she danced for Yoritomo against her will. Her life is recounted in numerous medieval texts.

Siebold, Philipp Franz von (1796–1866) German physician. Considered the pioneer of Japanese studies in Europe, Siebold, an employee of the Dutch East India Company, was sent to Nagasaki in 1823, where he established a school of "Dutch science" (*rangaku*). In 1826, he traveled to Edo to meet the shogun where he became acquainted with the shogunate's astronomer, Takahashi Kageyasu. Siebold and Kageyasu illegally traded Dutch books for Japanese maps. When the shogunate learned of this exchange, Siebold was expelled from Japan in 1829 on the grounds that he was a spy and Kageyasu was sent to prison. He wrote a number of books about his Japanese experiences including the five-volume *Fauna Japonica* (Japanese fauna; 1833–50) and *Nippon, Archiv zur Beschreibung von Japan* (Nippon, an archive for the description of Japan; 1832–51).

Soami (Shinso) (ca. 1455–1525) Muromachi *suiboku* painter. Soami was the grandson of Noami and the son and pupil of Geiami. Besides his fame as a painter, he also designed landscape gardens, wrote poetry, and excelled at the tea ceremony. Like his grandfather and father, Soami served as *doboshu*, the curator responsible for the connoisseurship and display of art works and other valuables owned by the Ashikaga shoguns. His paintings, mostly landscapes, were deeply influenced by the Chinese painting style of Muqi (in Japanese, Mokkei). Soami is also credited with designing the famous dry landscape garden at Ryoanji in Kyoto.

Soga Shohaku (1730–1781) Painter. Shohaku studied Kano school painting, but developed his own style reminiscent of Muromachi *suibokuga* (ink painting). Much of his work was executed using monochrome ink applied in broad strokes. He is best known for his figural depictions from Chinese legend and folklore, and for his landscapes.

Sogi (1421–1502) Rinzai Zen monk and poet. Also referred to as Iio Sogi. Sogi was a famous *renga* (linked verse) poet and traveler. See chapter 8: Language and Literature.

Sotatsu (Tawaraya Sotatsu) (unknown–ca. 1643) Artist. Although little is known about his career, Sotatsu headed the Tawaraya workshop in Kyoto as a commercial painter of fans, painted screens, ink paintings, as well as other commercial art venues. He gradually rose through the ranks to achieve recognition by the Kyoto nobility. Sotatsu's vast repertoire of works comprises illustrated picture scrolls from classical literature, and ink paintings that largely depict the Chinese monochrome style as well as Zen Buddhist subjects, but he is especially associated with the revival of *Yamato-e* themes (painted on a much grander scale, using precious materials such as gold and silver) during the 16th and 17th centuries. He also created a new "boneless" technique, by using several layers of ink to create forms without the use of an outline. Although he worked in the Edo period, his works resemble the Momoyama-period style. He often collaborated with Hon'ami Koetsu.

Sugita Gempaku (1733–1817) Physician and scholar. A prominent intellectual specializing in Western learning, Sugita's main contribution was to translate and confirm the information reported in Western anatomy texts, while serving as the private physician to the ruler of the Obama domain, a post he inherited from his father. His most famous translation is the 1774 work *Kaitai shinsho*, which was the first work to spark sufficient Japanese interest in European scientific scholarship.

Suzuki Shosan (1579–1655) Warrior and Zen monk. Shosan was originally a warrior, fighting on the side of the Tokugawa at the Battle of Sekigahara (1600) and at the Siege of Osaka Castle (1614–15). In 1621 he became a Zen monk. However, he chose not to align himself with either the Rinzai or Soto Zen schools. Shosan advocated a moral Zen teaching that was based on the idea that one's daily work, if pursued in a selfless way, was a religious practice that promoted enlightenment. Eclectic in his approach to Buddhism, Shosan also taught the spiritual benefits of reciting the *nembutsu*, the practice of chanting the name of Amida Buddha closely associated with the schools of Pure Land Buddhism. Shosan also believed that it was the responsibility of the government to restore what he viewed as true Buddhism to Japan. Shosan wrote numerous texts expounding these views.

Takahashi Kageyasu (1785–1829) Geographer, astronomer, and interpreter. Kageyasu served as astronomer to the shogunate. He also published scientifically accurate maps of the Japanese islands based on surveys conducted by Ino Tadataka, Mamiya Rinzo, and Mogami Tokunai. Later, he illegally supplied maps to Philipp Franz von Siebold in exchange for Dutch books. When his actions were discovered, he was arrested by shogunal authorities

and sentenced to death. Kageyasu died in prison before his execution could be carried out.

Takahashi Yoshitoki (1764–1804) Astronomer. Yoshitoki became official astronomer to the Tokugawa shogunate in 1795. Working with Hazama Shigetomi (1756–1816), he developed the Kansei calendar, a more accurate calendar that was adopted by the shogunate in 1798. He also translated a Dutch version of a French astronomy text, the *Traité d'astronomie* authored by Joseph Jérôme Lelande (1732–1807).

Takasugi Shinsaku (1839–1867) Warrior. Takasugi was a Choshu domain retainer. He gained fame as an imperial loyalist who fought to overthrow the Tokugawa shogunate. He was also a military strategist who restructured the Choshu domain's military forces utilizing Western troop organization and fighting techniques. This contributed to the defeat of the shogunal army in battles waged in the last years of the Edo period and led to the restoration of imperial rule. Takasugi, however, succumbed to tuberculosis and died just prior to the change in government that marked the start of the Meiji Restoration.

Takayama Ukon (1553–1615) Daimyo. Also known as Takayama Nagafusa. Ukon was a noted Christian lord who was baptized in 1564. He turned against his anti-Christian lord in support of Oda Nobunaga, who was favorable toward Christianity for political reasons. At various times, Ukon tried to convert the people of the regions he had control over. He was banished from Japan in 1614, the result of the persecution of Christianity by the Tokugawa shogunate.

Takebe Katahiro (1664–1739) Mathematician. A student of Seki Kowa, Katahiro discovered the principle of integral calculus and coauthored *Taisei sankyo* in 1710, a 20-volume compendium detailing Japanese mathematics. He also ran the shogunal observatory established by Tokugawa Yoshimune in 1720.

Takeda Shingen (1521–1573) Daimyo. Shingen was a powerful lord during the Warring States and

Azuchi-Momoyama periods. He fought several famous battles against Uesugi Kenshin known as the Battles of Kawanakajima that occurred between 1553 and 1564. Shingen was involved in the shifting alliances between feudal lords who vied for power during this unsettled period of Japanese history. In 1573 he defeated the armies of Oda Nobunaga and Tokugawa Ieyasu at the Battle of Nikatagahara. However, Shingen died of a disease later that year.

Tani Buncho (1763–1840) *Nanga* (Southern school) painter. Buncho was an eclectic artist credited with bringing the literati style to Edo. Born to an Edo samurai family. His artistic education began with Kano school training and continued to include Tosa, ukiyo-e, Western traditions, Chinese style, and the Maruyama-Shijo school. Ultimately he was known as a *nanga* painter although his style varied. Buncho was especially noted for realistic portraits, and he had a strong influence on his contemporaries.

Tankei (1173–1256) Kei school sculptor. Oldest son and pupil of Unkei. Tankei worked with his father on restoring two Nara temples, Todaiji and Kofukuji, which had been damaged in fighting during the Gempei War (1180–85). Like other Kei school sculptors, Tankei's style is realistic.

Tensho Shubun (fl. 1414–1463) Muromachi *suiboku* painter. Tradition places Shubun as a student of Josetsu and teacher of Sesshu and Sotan. Shubun served as official painter to the shogunate, and he went to Korea in 1423 or 1424 with a shogunal embassy. A Zen monk, he created carvings and paintings for Shokokuji and was associated with its reconstruction from 1430 to 1440. Shubun is considered progenitor of the Chinese monochrome ink style as reimagined to suit Japanese tastes. He is usually paired with Sesshu as the two greatest painters of the mid- to late 15th century.

Tetsugen (1630–1682) Obaku school Zen monk. Tetsugen is primarily known for compiling the entire Buddhist canon—known as the Obaku or Tetsugen edition—an undertaking that took 10 years. This was the first time the entire Buddhist canon was printed in Japan.

Thunberg, Carl Peter (1743–1828) Swedish botanist and physician. Thunberg studied medicine and botany with Carolus Linnaeus (1707–78) at the University of Uppsala and later became a ship physician for the Dutch East India Company. In 1775, during a one-year stay in Nagasaki, Thunberg collected more than 800 specimens of plants, and published *Flora Japonica* in 1784.

Tokugawa Hidetada (1579–1632) Ruled 1605–23 as second Tokugawa shogun. Hidetada, Tokugawa Ieyasu's third son, became shogun in 1605 when his father retired. However, he effectively ruled in name only because Ieyasu continued to run the government. It was only after Ieyasu's death in 1616 that Hidetada took over actual control of the shogunate. Hidetada was also a general who led troops at the Battle of Sekigahara (1600) and the Siege of Osaka Castle (1614–15), both significant victories that secured Tokugawa control over Japan. As shogun, Hidetada continued the work of his father in consolidating Tokugawa power and in reforming government administration of the country. In particular, Hidetada created mechanisms for controlling the power of both the daimyo and the imperial court. Hidetada also continued the policy of strict regulation of Christianity and it was under his rule that the policy of national seclusion was enacted. Like his father before him, Hidetada retired as shogun in 1623, appointed his son Iemitsu to the position, but continued to rule behind the scenes until his death in 1632.

Tokugawa Iemitsu (1604–1651) Ruled 1623–51 as third Tokugawa shogun. Known as Takechiyo as a child, this third shogun of the Tokugawa regime took the name Iemitsu after his coming-of-age celebration in 1620. Left behind to defend Edo Castle as a young boy while his father and grandfather defeated the last of the Toyotomi family in the 1614–15 battles at Osaka Castle, Iemitsu was initiated early into the ways and means of governance in Tokugawa Japan and was more than ready to take the reins of power when his father had the imperial court bestow the title of shogun upon him in 1623. However, Iemitsu's succession came only at the behest of his wet nurse, as his father had favored Iemitsu's younger brother for the role—a rivalry that was settled for good when Iemitsu demanded his brother's suicide shortly after the death of their father.

Iemitsu's reign served to further strengthen the Tokugawa grasp on Japan, starting in the 1630s when he issued regulations to clarify the degree of battle-readiness expected of samurai retainers, updating the feudal laws known as *Buke shohatto* to further define the role of daimyo and samurai in Tokugawa society, and obligating daimyo to split their time between Kyoto and their domains, leaving their wives and children to reside full time in Kyoto as "hostages of good faith," thus guarding against daimyo revolts. While promoting Confucian and Buddhist thought, Iemitsu also watched the growing Christian population closely, and after putting down the 1637–38 Christian revolts in Kyushu, Iemitsu instituted extreme trade regulations that soon became the policy of national seclusion practiced throughout the Tokugawa peace until 1853 when the West demanded that Japan open its ports to trade and diplomatic relations. By his death in 1651, Iemitsu had cultivated the shogunate to its most mature state, ensuring continuance of the national stability that defined the Edo period.

Tokugawa Ienari (1773–1841) Ruled 1786–1837 as 11th Tokugawa shogun. Adopted by the childless Ieharu in 1781, Ienari ascended to the office of shogun in 1787 and quickly relinquished much of the initial responsibility for governance first to his head councilor, Matsudaira Sadanobu, and then to Sadanobu's successor Nobuaki. Under Sadanobu, Ienari endorsed policies known as the Kansei reforms, aimed at improving the plight of the common people and making the shogunate financially stable through the promotion of a frugal lifestyle. After Nobuaki retired from office, Ienari opted to assume all responsibility for the government. However, under Ienari's rule, the government returned to its profligate ways, which undermined public morality and created economic difficulties that were intensified by massive famines and the inflation of the 1830s. Despite these problems, Ienari was able to maintain relative peace through strict control of daimyo and other powerful warlords by way of forcing marriage to one of his many daughters. Ienari

turned the shogunate over to his son, Ieyoshi, in 1837, but continued to rule behind the scenes until his death in 1841.

Tokugawa Ieyasu (1543–1616) Ruled 1603–05 as first Tokugawa shogun. Ieyasu is one of the greatest warriors and political leaders in Japanese history. He finished the task of unifying Japan begun by Oda Nobunaga and Toyotomi Hideyoshi. Ieyasu established the Tokugawa shogunate that inaugurated the start of the Edo period and the more than 250 years of peace that characterized the era. See also the historical narrative in this chapter.

Tokugawa Kazuko (Tofuku Mon'in) (1607–1678) Daughter of the shogun Tokugawa Hidetada. In a political move to strengthen the legitimacy of the emperor Go-Mizunoo's rule, Kazuko became his consort as part of the shogunate's plan to link the shogun to the imperial court. Go-Mizunoo abdicated to Kazuko's eldest daughter, Okiko, however, after the Shie incident, in which purple robes, symbolizing the highest order of priesthood, were given to the temples of Daitokuji and Myoshinji in 1627 by Go-Mizunoo without the shogunate's approval. The shogunate pronounced them invalid and confiscated them. Even after the end of their daughter's reign, Kazuko exerted considerable influence over court affairs as the stepmother of the three successive emperors.

Tokugawa Mitsukuni (1628–1700) Daimyo. Mitsukuni, a grandson of Tokugawa Ieyasu, was the lord of the Mito domain. He became known as an effective ruler and Mito domain became one of the most powerful domains during the Edo period. Mitsukuni embraced Neo-Confucian values and was later revered as the ideal of the benevolent ruler. Mitsukuni is also noted for his project to compile a history of Japan following the model of Chinese dynastic histories. The *Dai Nihon shi* (History of great Japan) was started in 1657 and, though largely completed by the time of Mitsukuni's death, was not finally completed until 1906. The work traces the history of Japan from its origins to the 14th century by chronicling the reigns of Japan's emperors. The work was influential, in part, because of the loyalty it expressed toward the imperial family.

Tokugawa Yoshimune (1684–1751) Ruled 1716–45 as eighth Tokugawa shogun. Son of Tokugawa Mitsusada, a prominent daimyo and member of the Kii branch of the Tokugawa family tree, Yoshimune began his career when he took over the position of daimyo in 1705 after his father and brothers died suddenly. He became shogun upon the death of the childless Ietsugu in 1716, having gained the support of high-ranking government officials on the merits of his success as a daimyo. He soon made efforts to curtail the excess that had come to characterize the lifestyle of many government officials by enforcing laws promoting frugal living and a return to the practice of classical samurai values. Sensitive to the plight of peasants, Yoshimune sought to improve the economic situation of the populace by solving the financial crisis of the shogunate through his Kyoho reforms, which called for increased fiscal accountability on the part of daimyo, tax collectors, and other officials in the shogunate. Through these efforts, Yoshimune was able to bring stability to the price of rice. By lifting the ban on the import of Western books in 1722, the government learned about methods for cultivating new lands on which to grow new crops as staple food sources. Despite these reforms, including the 103-article penal code of 1742, Yoshimune failed to win the trust of the public and was constantly putting down riots and disturbances throughout his tenure before finally handing administrative responsibilities to his son, Ieshige, in 1745.

Tokugawa Yoshinobu (1837–1913) Ruled 1867–68 as 15th and last Tokugawa shogun. Although his reign as shogun lasted less than a year, Yoshinobu lived in a time of great social and political upheaval. Yoshinobu became shogun in 1867 as the shogunate was on the brink of collapse from pressure by powerful lords who wanted to restore imperial rule. After brief efforts to reform the shogunate in hopes of regaining control of the country, he was convinced to relinquish his position in favor of a return to imperial rule. This ended the shogunate and inaugurated the Meiji Restoration.

Tominaga Nakamoto (1715–1746) Scholar. Tominaga, son of an Osaka merchant, was a noted critic of religion. In his writings, such as *Shutsujo kogo* (Buddha's comments after his meditation; 1745) and *Okina no fumi* (Writings of an old man; 1746), he criticized Buddhism, Confucianism, and Shinto on the grounds that they were largely untrue because they defied common sense.

Tomoe Gozen (late 12th century) One of the best known female warriors of the 12th century and favored concubine of Minamoto no Yoshinaka. Tomoe Gozen fought alongside her male counterparts during the Gempei War (1180–85). Her biography is as much legend as history. Tomoe appears in the *Heike monogatari* as a warrior of superior skill, equal to and sometimes exceeding her male peers. Her military adventures inspired the 16th century Noh play, *Tomoe*.

Torii Kiyonaga (1752–1815) Ukiyo-e printmaker and painter. Kiyonaga was born in Uraga to a bookseller and publisher. He traveled to Edo in 1765, and studied printmaking under Torii Kiyomitsu. He was adopted into the Torii family upon his teacher's death. Kiyonaga became the fourth and final master of the Torii school and was renowned first for actor prints in the Torii tradition, then for depictions of graceful, slender beauties of the pleasure districts. His work generated strong interest and influenced numerous contemporaries through his design skill and acumen as a colorist.

Tosa Mitsunobu (1434–1525) Tosa school painter. Mitsunobu served as head of the court painting academy (*edokoro azukari*), producing works including *e-maki*, Buddhist paintings, and portraits. He was noted for restoring the Tosa reputation and is considered the family's most important figure. Mitsunobu created a formula for rendering paintings of Kyoto and its environs known as *rakuchu rakugai-zu*.

Toshusai Sharaku (fl. 1794–1795) Ukiyo-e artist. Little is known of the details of Sharaku's life; he resided in Edo and he may have been a Noh actor. He specialized in prints of Kabuki actors that were often represented in exaggerated poses or with caricatured facial features. Of the some 159 extant prints attributed to him, all were produced within a 10-month period in 1794–95.

Toyotomi Hideyori (1592–1615) Warrior. Hideyori was Toyotomi Hideyoshi's only son. Although

1.3 Tomoe Gozen (late 12th century), famed woman warrior (Illustration Kikuchi Yosai from *Zenken kojitsu*, mid-19th century)

cation of Japan during the late 16th century. Despite his humble beginnings as the son of peasants, Hideyoshi rose through the ranks to become one of Nobunaga's generals, fighting in many of the decisive battles that gained Nobunaga control over central Japan. After Nobunaga committed suicide in 1582 in order to avoid capture at the hands of a retainer who turned against him, Hideyoshi killed the retainer, secured support from the Oda family and other powerful lords, and embarked on his own campaign to unify the country under his control. His further victories in western Japan, and on the islands of Kyushu and Shikoku, and the alliances he forged with powerful daimyo, gave him control over a unified country by 1590. Hideyoshi instituted significant political, economic, and social reforms. For instance, he conducted land surveys, prohibited the possession of arms by those outside the warrior class, promoted transportation as a way to improve economic conditions, and incorporated a rigid class system that made distinctions between warriors, farmers, artisans, and merchants. Hideyoshi's aspirations were not only confined to the domestic sphere. He attempted to conquer Korea on two different occasions during the 1590s, but both of these incursions on the mainland failed. Hideyoshi died in 1598, leaving only a five-year-old son as a potential heir. However, on the death of Hideyoshi, Tokugawa Ieyasu quickly rose to power and founded the Tokugawa shogunate, thus completing the unification of Japan.

Hideyoshi had desired that Hideyori succeed him, intrigue among Hideyoshi's supporters and the victories of the Tokugawa at the Battle of Sekigahara and elsewhere conspired against Hideyori achieving national political power. Instead, Hideyori took his place among the many daimyo controlled by the Tokugawa. Tokugawa Ieyasu, though he had allowed Hideyori to occupy his father's former stronghold at Osaka Castle, was suspicious of Hideyori's intentions. As a result, the Tokugawa attacked Osaka Castle. Defeated, Hideyori committed suicide at the age of 22.

Toyotomi Hideyoshi (1536–1598) Warrior and military leader. Along with Oda Nobunaga and Tokugawa Ieyasu, Hideyoshi was one of the three great military leaders who contributed to the unifi-

Uesugi Kenshin (1530–1578) Daimyo. Also known as Uesugi Terutora. Kenshin was a powerful lord during the Warring States and Azuchi-Momoyama periods. He fought several famous battles against Takeda Shingen known as the Battles of Kawanakajima that occurred between 1553 and 1564. Kenshin was also opposed to Oda Nobunaga and was preparing a force against Nobunaga when he died.

Unkei (unknown–1223) Kei school sculptor. Unkei was the son and pupil of Kokei. Considered the greatest of the Kei school sculptors, Unkei epitomized the Kei school style with his realistic rendering of Buddhist figures. He collaborated with Kaikei on a pair of Nio guardian figures located in Great

South Gate (*nandaimon*) at Todaiji. Unkei received patronage from officials of the Kamakura shogunate who commissioned him to create portrait sculptures.

Uragami Gyokudo (1745–1820) *Nanga* (Southern school) painter, musician, and poet. Gyokudo was born to a samurai family. He served the Ikeda daimyo, accompanying his lord to Edo where he learned *koto* and studied painting, poetry, and the Chinese classics. As an artist, he was highly regarded among second generation *nanga* painters. His landscapes, rendered in monochrome ink, evoke a sense of melancholy. He is also noted for a brush technique that is spontaneous and eccentric.

Utagawa Kuniyoshi (1798–1861) Painter, printmaker, and book illustrator. Kuniyoshi was a student of ukiyo-e artist Utagawa Toyokuni. He became famous for his ukiyo-e depictions of Kabuki actors, landscapes, and animals. He is also known for his *musha-e*, or warrior prints often rendered as triptychs. In many of his prints, Kuniyoshi displays a predilection for the bizarre and phantasmic.

Valignano, Alessandro (1539–1606) Italian Jesuit missionary. Valignano visited the Jesuit mission in Japan on three different occasions between 1579 and 1603, staying between three and five years each time. He urged Jesuit missionaries to learn the Japanese language and to adapt aspects of Japanese culture as a means to more effectively promote Christianity in Japan. To this end, for instance, some Jesuits dressed like Zen monks. Valignano also founded Christian schools and a novitiate.

Watanabe Kazan (1793–1841) Painter. Kazan was born in Edo to a low-ranking samurai family. He advocated the incorporation of Western painting techniques into the *nanga* (Southern school) landscape style. He was adept at depicting figures in a realistic manner. Kazan publicly opposed the national seclusion policy advanced by the Tokugawa shogunate and consequently endured permanent house arrest in commutation of the death penalty. In 1841, he committed suicide.

Xavier, Francis (1506–1552) Spanish Jesuit missionary. Francis Xavier, one of the founders of the Society of Jesus (Jesuits), introduced Christianity into Japan upon his arrival there in 1549. Although he gained some support from local lords, his journey to Kyoto to meet Emperor Go-Nara and to gain permission to preach throughout Japan went without success on both counts. Xavier departed Japan in 1551.

Yagyu Munenori (1571–1646) Sword master. Son of Yagyu Muneyoshi (1527–1606) who founded the Yagyu-ryu (later called Yagyu Shinkage-ryu) school of swordsmanship. Munemori earned fame at the Battle of Sekigahara (1600) and the sieges of Osaka Castle in 1614 and 1615, fighting on the side of Tokugawa Ieyasu. He later was named sword instructor to Tokugawa shoguns, a post carried on by subsequent members of the Yagyu family.

Yamagata Daini (1725–1767) Confucian scholar and physician. Daini advocated the overthrow of the shogunate on the grounds of government corruption. He was eventually executed for plotting against the shogunate.

Yamana Sozen (1404–1473) Warrior. Sozen was a provincial military governor (*shugo*). He is most famous for his role in the shogunal succession dispute between Ashikaga Yoshihisa, who Sozen supported, and Ashikaga Yoshimi, supported by Sozen's rival Hosokawa Katsumoto. Sozen fought in the subsequent Onin War that was the result of this succession struggle.

Yamazaki Ansai (1619–1682) Neo-Confucian scholar. Ansai founded Suiga Shinto (or Suika Shinto), a movement combining Neo-Confucian ideals based on the Zhu Xi (Chu Hsi) school with Shinto nationalism. This form of Shinto combined Confucian moral cultivation with the notion that Japan is a unique and divine country. Ansai promoted such virtues as loyalty to one's lord and the importance of the divine descent of the imperial family. Although Ansai saw his ideas as applicable to the political and social goals of the Tokugawa shogunate, such nationalist notions as divine imperial descent were also relevant to those at the end of the

Edo period who sought to overthrow the shogunate and restore imperial rule.

Yodogimi (1567–1615) Daughter of Oda Nobunaga's sister Odani no Kata and the daimyo Asai Nagamasa. Yodogimi faced significant hardships as a girl and again as a young woman; her father was killed in 1573 by her uncle, Oda Nobunaga, and 10 years later her stepfather, Shibata Katsuie, defeated by Toyotomi Hideyoshi, was joined in suicide by Yodogimi's mother. She and her two sisters were thrown on the mercy of Hideyoshi, whereupon she was taken into his household and became his favorite concubine. She bore him two children, Tsurumatsu (1589–91) and Hideyori. Following Hideyoshi's death, Yodogimi took up residence at Osaka castle alongside Hideyori and his forces, determined to help her son preserve the power of the Toyotomi family. Osaka Castle, however, fell to the Tokugawa forces in 1615. Unable to bear defeat, Yodogimi and her son Hideyori committed suicide on June 4, 1615.

Yosa Buson
See BUSON.

Yoshida Kanetomo (1435–1511) Shinto priest. Descending from a line of court divinators, Kanetomo spent most of his life trying to unite all of Shinto under his family's control. To this end, he claimed that the newly constructed altar he placed at the Yoshida Shrine in 1484 was to be the hub from which all Shinto activity radiated. He also wrote a number of works that were heavily influenced by esoteric Buddhist practice attempting to better define Shinto belief. Many of Kanetomo's contributions are credited with inspiring the Edo-period Yoshida Shinto movement.

Yoshida Kenko (1283–1350) Buddhist monk and author. Descended from a line of Shinto diviners, Kenko's 1330 literary effort, *Tsurezuregusa*, is still praised as a quintessential *zuihitsu* genre work. Holding a number of positions in the imperial court before becoming a Buddhist monk in 1313, Kenko moved frequently, never fully embracing any one teacher or monastery. He is considered one of the

four masters of the conservative Nijo school of poetry. He first worked under the patronage of the Daikakuji imperial lineage before accepting the support of Ashikaga Takauji after emperor Go-Daigo was chased out of the capital.

Yoshida Mitsuyoshi (1598–1672) Mathematician and translator of the Chinese mathematics work *Suanfa tongzong* (1593). He also wrote an explanatory treatise on the abacus (*soroban*), *Jinkoki* (Large and small numbers, 1627), which played an important role in spreading the use of the abacus in Japan. It also partly replaced the old Japanese mathematics (*wasan*) and *sangi* calculation methods.

Yoshida Shoin (1830–1859) Warrior, scholar, and political activist. Shoin was a champion of the *sonno joi* ("Revere the emperor! Expel the barbarian") movement that sought to end the shogunate and restore imperial rule. Because of his active involvement in attempts to overthrow the shogunate and in an assassination plot against a high shogunal official, Shoin was executed as part of the Ansei Purge (1858–60) that tried to destroy opposition to the shogunate.

Yoshikawa Koretari (1616–1694) Shinto practitioner who founded the movement known as Yoshikawa Shinto. This form of Shinto was derived from Yoshida Shinto and held that Shinto was the source of all things, including all other religions. Koretari became director of Shinto affairs (*shintokata*) for the shogunate in 1682. This was a position held by subsequent members of the Yoshikawa family.

READING

General

Beasley 1999; Hall 1970; Hane 1991; Totman 1981; Totman 2000; Mason and Caiger 1997

Medieval Japan

Varley 1974; Yamamura (ed.) 1990; Arnesen 1979: daimyo in medieval Japan; Berry 1982: life and times of Hideyoshi; Berry 1993: Kyoto during the Onin War and the Warring States period; Boxer 1951: medieval Christianity; Elison and Smith (eds.) 1981: 16th-century history; Grossberg 1981: Muromachi shogunate; Hall and Mass (eds.) 1974: medieval institutional history; Hall and Toyoda (eds.) 1977: Muromachi history; Hall, Nagahara, and Yamamura (eds.) 1981: medieval political and economic history; Mass (ed.) 1982: Kamakura history; Mass 1979: Kamakura shogunate; Varley 1971: Kemmu Restoration; Totman 2000, 158–171: medieval political history, 199–217: late medieval and early Edo political history

Early Modern Japan

Totman 1974; Totman 1993; Hall (ed.) 1991; Cullen 2003, Jansen 2000, Totman 1993; Bolitho 1974: *fudai* daimyo; Hall and Jansen (eds.) 1968: early modern institutional history; Keene 1969: Japanese encounters with the West; Sheldon 1958: merchant class; Totman 1967: politics in the Tokugawa shogunate; Totman 1980: end of the Tokugawa shogunate; Mayo 1974: late Edo history; Totman 2000, 278–289: late Edo-period history; Jansen (ed.) 1989: 19th-century history

2

LAND, ENVIRONMENT, AND POPULATION

)SCAPE AND
RONMENT

Japan is an archipelago in the Pacific Ocean along the eastern coast of the Asian mainland. The archipelago includes four main islands—Honshu, Hokkaido, Kyushu, and Shikoku in descending order of size—and more than 1,000 other islands of varying sizes. The total area of Japan is approximately 145,885 square miles, slightly smaller than the state of California. The four main islands are some 1,200 miles in length (northeast to southwest) with a width of about 200 miles at the widest point. These four islands comprise approximately 95 percent of Japan's entire landmass.

The Japanese islands are situated at the intersection of four tectonic plates. The collision of these plates is the source of the many earthquakes, volcanoes, hot springs, and other geological phenomena that have occurred frequently throughout Japanese history. As a result of this geologic instability, mountains cover some 80 percent of the Japanese landscape. Historically, this mountainous land surface resulted in the division of Japan into regions set into plains between mountain ranges. Of particular importance during the medieval and early modern periods are the Kanto Plain—the site of the cities of Edo and Kamakura—and the Kansai Plain in which Kyoto and Osaka are situated.

Oceans, Bays, Lakes, and Rivers

Japan is completely surrounded by water. Thus, relative to other East Asian nations, Japan exists in geographical isolation, a feature that has allowed it to draw upon Chinese, Korean, and other continental influences when it chose to do so, and to isolate itself from outside influences at other times. The Sea of Japan separates Japan from China (500 miles at the closest point) and Korea (120 miles at the closest point). The Seto Inland Sea (Seto Naikai), a part of the Pacific Ocean, creates sea boundaries between Honshu, Shikoku, and Kyushu. Some 1,000 islands populate the Seto Inland Sea. This sea and its islands were significant to trade and transportation during the medieval and early modern periods. Other ocean boundaries between the four main islands include several straits (*kaikyo*), such as the Kammon Strait (also called Shimonoseki Strait; located between Honshu and Kyushu), the Tsugaru Strait (situated between Honshu and Hokkaido), the Naruto Strait (at the entry to Osaka Bay), and the Tsushima Strait (between Iki Island and Tsushima Island in the Pacific Ocean).

During the medieval and early modern periods, several bays (*wan*) served as calm waters for ports that conducted both domestic and foreign trade. Among the more significant in this time period were Osaka Bay, Edo Bay (present-day Tokyo Bay), Ise Bay, and Uraga Bay.

There are few lakes on the Japanese islands, though Lake Biwa (Biwako) in central Honshu, Japan's largest freshwater lake, is a notable exception. Lake Biwa (area: 259 square miles; circumference: 172 miles) was fished and used for transportation in the medieval and early modern periods. Lake Biwa also secured a place in the Japanese imagination for its Eight Views of Omi. This refers to eight locations around Lake Biwa in Omi Province (present-day Shiga Prefecture) that were praised for their beauty from at least the beginning of the 16th century and were a subject for Edo-period artists.

The Japanese landscape is marked by many rivers, but most of them are rather short. Only two rivers, the Shinanogawa and the Tonegawa on Honshu, exceed a length of 200 miles. Historically, rivers were used mostly for crop irrigation rather than ship navigation. Flooding also impacted medieval and early modern life. Some important rivers include:

Ara River (Arakawa; length: 105 miles) Originates in the Kanto Mountain, ends in Edo Bay (present-day Tokyo Bay)

Chikugo River (Chikugogawa; length: 89 miles) Longest river in Kyushu

Edo River (Edogawa; length: 37 miles) Flows into Edo Bay (Tokyo Bay)

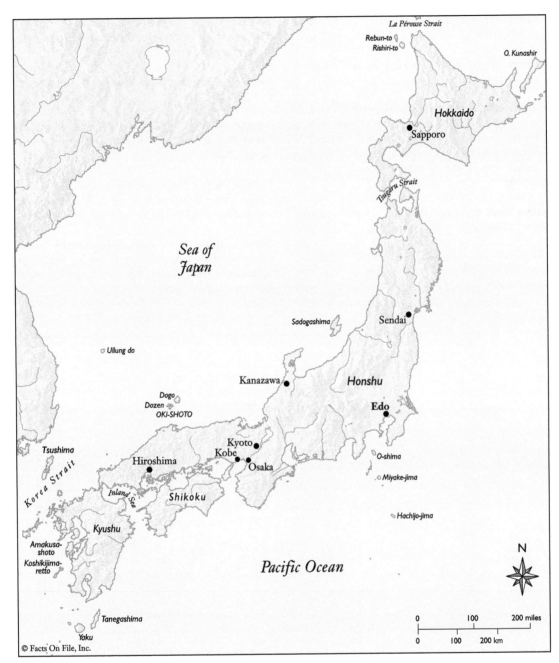

La Pérouse Strait

Rebun-to
Rishiri-to

O. Kunashir

Hokkaido

● Sapporo

Tsugaru Strait

Sea of
Japan

Sadogashima

● Sendai

○ Ullung do

Kanazawa ●

Honshu

Dogo
Dozen
OKI-SHOTO

Edo ●

Tsushima

Kyoto ●
Kobe ●
● Osaka

O-shima

Hiroshima ●

Miyake-jima

Korea Strait

Inland Sea

Shikoku

Hachijo-jima

Kyushu

Pacific Ocean

N

Amakusa-
shoto
Koshikijima-
retto

Tanegashima

0   100   200 miles

Yaku

0   100   200 km

© Facts On File, Inc.

Map 2. *Topographic Map of Japan's Main Islands*

Kamo River (Kamogawa; length: 22 miles) Flows through Kyoto

Katsura River (Katsuragawa; length: 19 miles) Flows through Kyoto

Kiso River (Kisogawa; length: 141 miles) Honshu; flows into Ise Bay at Nagoya

Kitakami River (Kitakamigawa; length: 155 miles) Longest river in the Tohoku region of northern Honshu

Kuma River (Kumagawa; length: 71 miles) Flows through Kyushu

Mogami River (Mogamigawa; length: 142 miles) Flows through the Tohoku region of northern Honshu

Nagara River (Nagaragawa; length: 87 miles) Flows through central Honshu and empties into Ise Bay; famous for cormorant fishing

Oi River (Oigawa; length: 99 miles) Flows through central Honshu and empties into Suruga Bay

Sagami River (Sagamigawa; length: 68 miles) Flows through central Honshu and empties into Sagami Bay

Shinano River (Shinanogawa; length: 228 miles) Longest river in Japan; flows through central Honshu and empties into the Sea of Japan at Niigata

Sumida River (Sumidagawa; length: 15 miles) Flows through Edo (Tokyo) as one of the lower branches of the Arakawa; important in the history of Edo culture and society

2.1 Leisure-time boating on the Sumida River in the city of Edo (Illustration Grace Vibbert)

Tama River (Tamagawa; length: 78 miles) Flows into Edo Bay (Tokyo Bay)

Tenryu River (Tenryugawa; length: 132 miles) Flows through central Honshu

Tone River (Tonegawa; length: 200 miles) Second-longest river in Japan; flows through central Honshu and empties into the Pacific Ocean at Choshi; the Tonegawa originally emptied into Edo Bay (Tokyo Bay) but in the Edo period the river's course was altered to try to prevent floods in Edo

Yodo River (Yodogawa; length: 47 miles) Flows through central Honshu; it originates in Lake Biwa and empties into Osaka Bay; at its upper reaches the river is called the Setagawa and as it flows near Kyoto it is called the Ujigawa; the Yodogawa was important in the medieval and early modern periods as a transportation route between Kyoto and Osaka.

Mountains, Volcanoes, and Earthquakes

One of the most prominent attributes of the Japanese landscape is the presence of mountains and volcanoes. Mountainous, wooded terrain comprises two-thirds of the Japanese islands, leaving only about 15 percent of arable land available. The main island of Honshu is split by mountains that run down its spine, dividing the island into a side that faces the Pacific Ocean and a side that faces the Sea of Japan.

The majority of mountains and volcanoes are a few hundred to a couple of thousand feet in altitude, but a few ranges reach 5,000–10,000 feet high. The highest mountain in Japan is Mount Fuji (Fujisan), an active volcano extending more than 10,000 feet in height. Its oft-depicted conical shape represents a common volcanic form seen throughout Japan. Traditionally, mountains, such as Mount Fuji, have been considered the abode of the gods and as such were considered sacred during the time period studied in this volume.

Mountains also created natural boundaries between different parts of Japan that had strategic implications during the medieval and early modern periods. They impeded trade and communication, and made it difficult to fight wars or to uniformly exert political influence and administer the law.

Because Japan is situated in one of the most geologically active regions of the world, volcanoes and earthquakes are frequent both historically and today. Both volcanoes and earthquakes have had a significant impact on the lives of the Japanese people throughout Japan's history. Destructive volcanic eruptions and devastating earthquakes are recorded in the medieval and early modern periods with some regularity. Earthquakes occurring under the ocean can spawn large tidal waves known as tsunami. History records the destructive power of such waves when they reach the shore. Volcanoes and earthquakes occurred with sufficient frequency and intensity that this topographic feature of the Japanese islands served as a frequent reminder to medieval and early modern Japanese of the Buddhist notion of impermanence, the idea of the fundamental instability and ephemerality of the world. Positive effects of this geologic phenomenon include hot springs, which have traditionally been used both for relaxation and for medicinal purposes, a fertile land rich in mineral deposits, and productive soil.

Some important mountains and volcanoes include:

Mount Asama (Asamayama; height: 8,425 feet) Volcano in central Honshu

Mount Aso (Asosan; height: 5,223 feet) Volcano in Kyushu

Mount Bandai (Bandaisan; height: 5,968 feet) Volcano in northern Honshu

Mount Dai (Daisen; height: 5,673 feet) Volcano in western Honshu; home of Daisenji Buddhist temple

Mount Fuji (Fujisan; height: 12,388 feet) The highest and most famous mountain in Japan; located in central Honshu; considered particularly sacred and a symbol of the Japanese nation; subject of literature and art; visible from Edo; still classified as an active volcano although it has not erupted since 1707; as a sacred mountain, Fuji was the object of pilgrimage during the Edo period—as with other sacred mountains, women were forbidden to climb it because they were considered impure

Mount Haku (Hakusan; height: 8,865 feet) Volcano in central Honshu; considered particularly sacred

Mount Hakone (Hakoneyama; height: 4,718 feet) Volcano in central Honshu

Mount Hiei (Hieizan; height: 2,782 feet) Mountain to the northeast of Kyoto; the important Tendai Buddhist temple complex of Enryakuji and the Hie Shrine are located on Hiei

Mount Koya (Koyasan; height: 3,300 feet) Mountain in central Honshu; home to the important Shingon Buddhist temple complex of Kongobuji; throughout the medieval and early modern periods women were forbidden to climb the mountain

Mount Shira (Shirayama; height: 8,865 feet) Alternate name for Hakusan (see above)

Mount Tate (Tateyama; height: 9,892 feet) Mountain in central Honshu; considered one of Japan's three most sacred mountains, along with Mount Fuji and Mount Haku

Mount Unzen (Unzendake; height: 4,459 feet) Volcano in Kyushu near Nagasaki

Mount Yari (Yarigatake; height: 10,433 feet) Mountain in central Honshu; part of the Hida Mountain range

Climate

The overall climate of Japan is marked by diversity and fluctuation, though it is generally characterized as temperate to subtropical and experiences four seasons. Because of the great length of its north/south land orientation, Japan resides in several climatic zones and experiences a variety of different weather conditions. Influencing the climate of Japan is its location in the monsoon zone of East Asia, which generates great winds and produces seasonal shifts. Local variations in climate are the result of proximity to mountains, oceans, and other geographic features. The Japanese rainy season produces an average annual rainfall of 180 inches per year. Typhoons are a yearly occurrence. Hokkaido, the northernmost of Japan's four main islands, has a climate that is both drier and cooler than the other three islands.

The winter season is characterized by monsoons dropping major snowfall on the mountainous regions of Japan. The spring season brings in warmer air currents and dry conditions, but this is soon followed by the rainy season (*baiu*) in June and July. The summer season that follows produces hot and humid weather, especially in the plains areas. Summer is brought to an end by the yearly typhoons in August and September, the end of which marks the start of the autumn season. The fall is also distinguished by continued rain, and cooler, breezier weather, finally ending with the beginning monsoons of winter.

Natural Resources

Natural resources in the Japanese islands include its abundant forests and supply of wood. More than 70 percent of Japan is wooded, and the islands are home to a variety of tree species throughout its varied regions. During the Edo period, Japan experienced a great demand for wood to build the infrastructure of its newly emerging urban centers, such as Edo and Osaka.

Mining has been prevalent throughout Japanese history. In particular, during the 16th to the 18th centuries, a number of gold and silver mines were opened, including the famous Sado Island mines. These mines produced tremendous amounts of gold and silver, which aided the income of the Tokugawa shogunate.

Flora and Fauna

Japan is home to a rich variety of plant and animal life. Flora and fauna are used for food, medicine, and other specific needs of daily life. Bamboo, for example, is used both in construction and, as young shoots (*takenoko*), for food. Plants and animals also have associations with the seasons and other symbolic meanings. Plant and animal motifs are used on traditional clothing and family crests, and certain plants are used in Japanese religious and seasonal rituals. For instance, pine is used at the New Year and symbolizes longevity.

The varied climates of Japan have produced a diverse array of plant life throughout the archipelago. Different regions are notable for different botanical characteristics. Overall, it is estimated that Japan has approximately 5,000–6,000 different plant species. During the Edo period, floriculture thrived, giving rise to the development of numerous new species of wildflowers. Similarly, Japan has a significant diversity of animal and sea life. There are more than 110 different kinds of mammals resident on the Japanese islands. Besides the fish and other sea life found in Japan's ocean waters, there are various species of seaweed, some of which are harvested for food.

2.2 Example of the use of thatch in roof construction (Photo William E. Deal)

2.3 Black pines at the Ginkakuji in Kyoto (Photo William E. Deal)

CITY, TOWN, AND COUNTRYSIDE

The rise of cities and towns in Japan during the medieval and early modern periods occurred especially with the development of castle and market towns, though temple and port towns also played a role in urban development. This urbanization process largely took place in the Edo period, although its origins date back to the medieval period. Exceptions to this general pattern during the medieval period were cities such as Kyoto and Kamakura that developed into flourishing cities due to their position as either imperial or shogunal capitals.

Castle Towns

Castle towns trace their origin to the Muromachi period and the construction of wooden defenses typically located on hills for reasons of protection and surveillance. These fortifications were the precursors to the castles and castle-building styles that grew more elaborate during the Warring States period. As the military and political significance of castles grew, they also became the focal point for economic activity within their local region. With the rise of commerce around castles, merchants, artisans, and peasants joined the warrior class in taking up residence within a castle's sphere of influence. Castles became castle towns as a result. By the Azuchi-Momoyama period (late 16th century), castle towns became the political and administrative

2.4 Dragonfly (tombo) *on a bamboo fence rail—one of many kinds of insect life native to Japan* (Photo William E. Deal)

hubs of daimyo domains, and it is estimated that in most domains one-10th of the population resided in its castle town. Some of them, at least, were to become Japan's largest cities, such as Edo and Osaka.

During the 16th century, castle towns (*joka machi*) began their transformation into town and city complexes. This occurred in part because castle towns served as government administration centers. Many daimyo and almost all samurai lived within the castle town complexes. Merchants, traders, artisans, craftspeople, and others were eventually incorporated into these towns and cities to provide the labor and market activity needed to support the work conducted there and to further build and maintain the infrastructure. As a result of this dynamic, castle and market towns came to occupy the same location.

Market Towns

Market towns (*ichiba machi*) originated in the Kamakura period as areas the government authorized to sell produce and other goods on certain days

of the month. As the population density of castle towns increased, markets assumed locations either nearby or within castle towns. Some merchants also became residents of cities while others traveled from market to market. Historically market towns represented the confluence of both rural and urban life. As city and town populations increased, market shops open on a regular basis came to largely supplant the need for the earlier periodic markets.

Temple/Shrine Towns

Temple and shrine towns (*monzen machi*) originated in the vicinity of Buddhist temples and Shinto shrines, usually along the roads leading to these religious sites. These towns served the needs of pilgrims visiting the temples and shrines. Establishments that developed along these routes provided food and lodging to pilgrims, and sold amulets and other religious items. As religious sites grew in size, so did the permanent infrastructure needed to support this activity.

Port Towns

Port towns grew up around sea ports that developed flourishing trading centers in the medieval and early modern periods. The cities of Anotsu, Bo no Tsu, Hakata, and Sakai (for details on these cities, see below) are examples of cities that developed from trade with the Asian mainland. Even after restrictions on foreign trade were enacted by the shogunate in the 16th century, ports engaged in domestic trade continued to thrive.

Post-Station Towns

Post-station towns (*shukuba machi* or *shukueki*) grew up along the medieval and early modern road systems that connected cities and towns to each other. Post stations were sometimes small towns that provided basic provisions and lodging to travelers.

Other post stations developed into substantial cities, usually as a result of their location in or near a market, or as a result of their location along the intersection of two or more roads. Post-station towns were regulated by the government. For additional details on post-station towns see chapter 11: Travel and Communication.

Countryside

The historical record concerning rural habitation in medieval Japan is often lacking in precise information. Details emerge more clearly after 1600. In general, medieval and early modern rural inhabitants lived within a village context. The village operated as a communal support for the overall well-being of the community. Everyone associated with the village was dependent on the development of the agricultural community as a whole. Typically, villages produced rice, grain, and other field crops. There were, of course, significant local variations in the way that rural communities were set up and the degree to which the terrain—for instance, flat land or hills—dispersed people or drew them together.

Village settlement began to change with the advent of large cities—like Edo and Osaka—and the increasing importance of castle towns as centers of commercial activity during the early modern period. The capriciousness of farm life with its uncertain harvests was sometimes abandoned for the draw of a town or city and its allure of steadier employment. Besides farm villages, fishing villages were a feature of medieval and early modern rural life, and mountain villages developed in the early modern period around lumber and other products that found flourishing markets in the expanding towns and cities of the Edo period.

Domains

Domains (*han*) were territories assigned by the Tokugawa shogunate and governed by provincial daimyo. The term *han* refers to both the land itself and the provincial governments that the various domains represented. Domains were provincial centers for administrative, military, and financial governance that provided both local control and connections to the shogunate in Edo. The number of domains fluctuated during the Edo period. Generally, though, there were about 260 domains in existence at any given time. The rise and fall of a particular domain was usually the result of either internal conflict or the intervention of the Tokugawa government. The shogunate would, for instance, reassign domain control when it feared possible provincial rebellion.

Daimyo domains varied in size, bureaucratic structures, and the extent of their autonomy from direct control by the Tokugawa shogunate. Generally, the greater the distance from Edo, the greater was the independence. Domains also had different rice-producing capacities. Depending on size, domains produced anywhere from 10,000 to 1 million *koku* (one *koku* = five bushels or 180 liters) of rice a year.

Having been awarded a particular domain, a daimyo was required to fulfill certain obligations to the shogunate. These responsibilities included the creation and upkeep of a local army of samurai loyal to the shogun, and compliance with the system of *sankin kotai*, whereby each daimyo was required to reside every other year in Edo in attendance on the shogun.

POPULATION STATISTICS

Total Population

Population expanded throughout Japan's early modern period. Such expansion was most notable in the 17th century where the overall population rose from 12 million to 30 million, although these numbers decreased and eventually leveled off during the 18th century. The statistics listed below for Japan's total population were gathered from population censuses conducted at the order of the shogunate. However, the accuracy of such statistics varies greatly, as the surveys often neglected different demographics like members of the samurai household, children, and others.

Year	Population
1721	26,065,425
1732	26,921,816
1744	26,153,450
1756	26,061,830
1780	26,010,600
1792	24,891,441
1804	25,517,729
1828	27,201,400
1834	27,063,907
1846	26,907,625

Source: Conrad Totman, *Early Modern Japan* (Berkeley: University of California Press, 1993): 251.

Urban Population

In 1700, around 5 to 7 percent of the populace resided in larger cities, making Japan one of the most urbanized countries in the world in this time period.

Between 1550 and 1700 Kyoto was the first city to surpass a population of 100,000 people. By 1700 the city was estimated to have approximately 350,000 individuals. Osaka had roughly 500,000 people in the mid 18th century, dropping to 375,000 in 1801 and 317,000 in 1854. While Edo began as a village, by 1678 it grew to roughly 570,361 inhabitants. This number increased to about 1.3 million in 1721 and 1.4 million by the start of the 19th century. These statistics made Edo one of the largest urban centers in the entire world at the time.

GAZETTEER OF PLACE-NAMES

Islands

CHIKUBUSHIMA

Chikubushima (area: .05 square miles) is an island located in Lake Biwa in central Honshu. It is considered a sacred island and is the site of both the Hogonji temple and the Tsukubusuma Shrine. Hogonji is also the 30th of the 33 temples that comprise the

2.5 Model of a crowded amusement area (sakariba) *in the city of Edo* (Edo-Tokyo Museum exhibit; Photo William E. Deal)

Kannon pilgrimage route. The Noh play *Chikubu-shima* is set on the island. Chikubushima is associated with such important late 16th-century warriors as Oda Nobunaga and Toyotomi Hideyoshi.

DEJIMA

An artificial island in Nagasaki harbor that was built in 1636 for foreign residents to keep them separated from the population at large. The Tokugawa shogunate used Dejima as a way to check the spread of Christian missionary activity in Japan, particularly by the Portuguese. Dejima first housed Portuguese traders, but they were expelled from Japan in 1637. At that time, the Dutch factory at Hirado Island (see below) was moved to Dejima and the Dutch occupied the island until the closing years of the Edo period. Dejima was also important as a source of Western scientific and other knowledge during the early modern period.

HIRADO ISLAND (HIRADOSHIMA)

Hiradoshima (area: 64 square miles) is an island off the northwest coast of Kyushu. In 1550, the island's port at the city of Hirado became the first port opened to foreign trade. Dutch and Portuguese merchants lived on the island until they were forced to move to Dejima in 1636. The island is also connected with the Hirado warrior family whose castle was located on the island.

HOKKAIDO

Hokkaido (area: 30,107 square miles) is the second largest and the farthest north of Japan's four main islands. The Tsugaru Strait separates Hokkaido from Honshu. To Hokkaido's west lies the Sea of Japan, to its northeast lies the Sea of Okhotsk, and to its south and east lies the Pacific Ocean. During the medieval and early modern periods, Hokkaido, then known as Ezo, was not formally a part of Japan. It was inhabited mostly by the Ainu, a people whose origins are not entirely clear. The name Ezo was changed to Hokkaido in 1869. During the early Edo period, the Matsumae domain established control over a small part of southwestern Hokkaido and gradually increased its holdings over much of Hokkaido through the 19th century.

HONSHU

Honshu (area: 87,992 square miles) is Japan's largest island and is generally viewed as Japan's mainland because it comprises roughly 60 percent of Japan's total land area. Honshu is bordered by the Pacific Ocean to its east and by the Sea of Japan to its west. Most of the key events that took place in Japan's medieval and early modern periods occurred on Honshu. The major medieval and early modern cities of Kyoto, Kamakura, Edo, and Osaka are all on Honshu. Not surprisingly, the majority of Japan's population, both historically and today, resides on this island. Japan's largest and most famous mountain and lake—Mount Fuji and Lake Biwa—are both on Honshu.

ITSUKUSHIMA

Itsukushima (or, Miyajima; area: 12 square miles) is in Hiroshima Bay in the Seto Inland Sea. The island was considered sacred throughout the medieval and early modern periods. As a result, giving birth or conducting funeral rituals—both considered ritually polluting in Shinto—were prohibited during this time period. Itsukushima Shrine, established in the sixth century, is famous for its vermilion torii (Shinto gate marking the entrance to a shrine's precincts) which appears to float in the water at high tide. The shrine is also associated with the Heike warrior family.

KYUSHU

Kyushu (area: 14,177 square miles) is the third largest and the farthest south of Japan's four main islands. Kyushu is bordered by the East China Sea to its west and by the Pacific Ocean to its east. The Shimonoseki Strait separates Kyushu from Honshu and the Tsushima Strait separates Kyushu from Korea to the northwest. One theory places the location of the early Japanese state mentioned in a late third-century Chinese history as northern Kyushu. Whether this is true or not, Kyushu, due to its proximity to the Asian mainland, was often the point of first contact by envoys and traders going between Japan and the mainland. The 13th-century Mongolian invaders attacked Kyushu, and much of the Japanese contact with Europeans in the 15th and early 16th centuries occurred on this island. When the Tokugawa shogunate severely limited contacts with the West, the little commerce and interaction that occurred was centered in Kyushu. Some leaders involved in the Meiji Restoration that overthrew the Tokugawa government in 1868 were from Kyushu.

MATSUSHIMA

Some 260 small islands constitute the Matsushima islands. They are located in Matsushima Bay in northern Honshu. There islands are known for their beauty and were often the subject of Edo-period Japanese painters. The famous haiku poet Matsuo Basho wrote a poem expressing his longing to return to Matsushima. Matsushima is also noted for the Zuiganji, patronized by, among others, the warrior Date Masamune (1567–1636) and the Date family who controlled the region that includes Matsushima.

OKI ISLANDS

The Oki Islands are an archipelago in the Sea of Japan off the coast of western Honshu. There are four main islands (combined area: 134 square miles) and nearly 200 smaller islands. The islands are famous as a place of exile during the Kamakura period. The Hojo regents dispatched rivals there, including Emperor Go-Daigo.

SADO

Sado Island (also called Sadogashima; area: 331 square miles) is the fifth-largest Japanese island. It is in the Sea of Japan off the coast of central Honshu, across from the modern city of Niigata. During the Kamakura period, Sado was a place of political and religious exile. Notable figures sent there include the Buddhist priest Nichiren, the Emperor Juntoku, and the playwright Zeami. In 1601, gold and silver mines began operation, leading to great prosperity that continued through the 1750s, after which time production slowed nearly to a halt.

SHIKOKU

Shikoku (area: 7,063 square miles) is the smallest of Japan's four main islands. It is situated between Honshu and Kyushu. The Seto Inland Sea separates Shikoku from Honshu, while the Bungo Strait sepa-rates the island from Kyushu. The Pacific Ocean lies to Shikoku's east. Although Shikoku figures some-what less prominently than Honshu and Kyushu in Japan's medieval and early modern history, it was nevertheless home to several daimyo domains and its major towns and cities were typically castle towns. Toyotomi Hideyoshi, in his quest to take control of Japan, defeated rivals on Shikoku in 1583. Shikoku is perhaps best known for the 88-temple pilgrimage associated with the famous Shingon priest Kukai who was born on the island.

TANEGASHIMA

An island (area: 172 square miles) 25 miles south of the Osumi peninsula in southern Kyushu, Tane-gashima was the site of the first encounter with the Portuguese. In 1543, a Chinese ship carrying Por-tuguese came ashore. Among the cargo were mus-kets known as harquebuses, which were copied and used by Japanese warriors.

TSUSHIMA

An archipelago of five islands located at the intersec-tion of the Tsushima and Korea Straits between northwestern Kyushu and Korea. There are two prin-cipal islands, Kami (area: 159 square miles) and Shimo (area: 115 square miles). Tsushima is historically im-portant as a waypoint between Japan and Korea, and, by extension, the rest of the Asian mainland. The islands came under attack during both Mongol inva-sions of Japan in the late 13th century. Tsushima was also subject to pirate raids. The islands were the fief of the So family throughout the medieval and early mod-ern periods. Due to its location, the So family was sometimes involved in trade and other negotiations with Korea and the Asian mainland.

Cities and Towns

AIZU WAKAMATSU

City in present-day Fukushima Prefecture. Aizu Wakamatsu was a castle town associated with the Aizu domain. The city was the site of pro-shogunate activity during the time leading up to the Meiji Restoration. One of the last battles in the struggle to defend the shogunate was fought there. Famous for its lacquerware.

AKASHI

City in present-day Hyogo Prefecture situated on the Akashi Strait in the Seto Inland Sea. The city is celebrated in literature for the scenic beauty of its coastline. Akashi was a castle town and also a post station on the San'yodo road during the Edo period.

AKITA

City in present-day Akita Prefecture situated on the Omono River (Omonogawa). Akita was a castle town controlled by the Satake family during the Edo period.

AKO

City in present-day Hyogo Prefecture situated on the Seto Inland Sea. Ako was a castle town controlled by the Ikeda family during the Edo period. The city was a center of salt and cotton production. Ako is also associated with the 47 Ronin Incident (early 18th century; see chapter 5: Warriors and Warfare, for details).

AMAGASAKI

City in present-day Hyogo Prefecture situated on Osaka Bay. Amagasaki was a castle town from the 16th century and was under the control of a successive series of lords (daimyo).

AMAKUSA

Town on Shimoshima, one of a group of islands known as the Amakusa Islands (Amakusajima) off the coast of southern Kyushu. A center of Christian activity from the 16th century, Amakusa, along with Shimabara on Kyushu's mainland, is associated with the Shimabara Rebellion (1637), an uprising of Japanese Christians.

AMANOHASHIDATE

Amanohashidate ("Bridge of Heaven") is a two-mile-long and 200-foot-wide strip of land stretching across Miyazu Bay in present-day Kyoto Prefecture. It has long been considered one of Japan's most scenic spots. Amanohashidate was sometimes the subject of medieval and early modern paintings and woodblocks.

ANOTSU

Former port town, now part of the city of Tsu in present-day Mie Prefecture. Anotsu was a major port during the Muromachi period, conducting trade with China. A late 15th-century earthquake destroyed the port infrastructure. In the Edo period, Anotsu was a pilgrim's stop on the way to Ise Shrine.

AOMORI

City in present-day Aomori Prefecture situated on Aomori Bay. Aomori's harbor was actively utilized for fishing and shipping during the Edo period.

ARITA

Town in present-day Saga Prefecture in Kyushu. It was famous for its production of fine porcelain known as Arita ware (Arita-yaki) starting in the early 17th century. Knowledge of porcelain production was first brought to Arita by Korean craftsmen.

ASHIKAGA

City in present-day Tochigi Prefecture. Ancestral home of the Ashikaga family who rose to political prominence as shoguns during the Muromachi period. The Ashikaga School (Ashikaga Gakko) was located here (see chapter 7: Philosophy, Education, and Science, for details). Ashikaga was famous for the manufacture of woven silk during the medieval and early modern periods.

AYABE

City in present-day Kyoto Prefecture. The city was originally settled by Chinese and Koreans, who were noted for their weaving skills. Ayabe was a castle town controlled first by the Bessho family and later, during the Edo period, by the Kuki family.

AZUCHI

Town in present-day Shiga Prefecture located on the northeastern shore of Lake Biwa. Azuchi is famous as the place where Oda Nobunaga built his Azuchi Castle in the 16th century.

BEPPU

City and seaport in present-day Oita Prefecture in Kyushu on Beppu Bay. As it is now, Beppu was famous for its many hot springs during the medieval and early modern periods.

BIZEN

City in present-day Okayama Prefecture situated on the Seto Inland Sea. Bizen is particularly well-known for the production of Bizen pottery (Bizen-yaki), which dates back to the Kamakura period. Ikeda Mitsumasa, the Bizen Province lord, instituted the famous Shizutani School (Shizutani Gakko) in Bizen in 1668. Mitsumasa also promoted the manufacture of Bizen pottery.

BO NO TSU

Former port town in present-day Kagoshina Prefecture. Bo no Tsu was controlled by the Shimazu family during the Muromachi period. Under their direction, the town developed into a major port engaged in trade with China.

CHIBA

City in present-day Chiba Prefecture situated on the Boso Peninsula near Edo. Chiba was a castle town during the medieval period under the control of the Chiba family. In the Edo period, Chiba was a post-station town at the intersection of several roads.

CHOFU

City in present-day Yamaguchi Prefecture that served as the capital of Nagato Province in the medieval and early modern periods. Chofu was a castle town controlled by the Mori family.

DANNOURA

Area on the coast of present-day Yamaguchi Prefecture near Shimonoseki. Dannoura is famous as the site of the Battle of Dannoura in 1185, in which the Minamoto (Genji) finally defeated the Taira (Heike), thus ending the five-year-long Gempei War and inaugurating the start of the medieval period.

DAZAIFU

City in present-day Fukuoka Prefecture. Dazaifu was especially important prior to the medieval period as the Kyushu government headquarters. By the medieval period, Dazaifu lost its importance as a government center. However, as a castle town controlled by the Shoni family, it was important to efforts to repel the two late 13th-century Mongol invasions that occurred in Kyushu.

EDO

City located on Edo Bay (present-day Tokyo Bay). Edo ("Rivergate") became the city of Tokyo ("Eastern Capital") at the beginning of the Meiji Restoration, replacing Kyoto as the nation's capital. The name "Edo," however, was used throughout the medieval and early modern periods. In the Edo period, the city became the administrative center of the Tokugawa shogunate and it was an important transportation route. Edo was also one of the centers of Edo culture.

Evidence suggests that Edo first became a warrior enclave in the mid-15th century. However, Edo began to take on prominence when the warrior Tokugawa Ieyasu established the city as his headquarters during his quest to unify Japan. After Ieyasu made Edo the location of the Tokugawa shogunate in the early 17th century, with Edo Castle at its center, the city grew quickly in both size and political importance. At the beginning of its status as a castle town, Edo was intended as the residence for government officials and samurai. By the 18th and 19th centuries, as the city's business and cultural importance grew, merchants, artisans, and laborers took up residence there as well, to take advantage of the work that large-scale construction projects offered. It is estimated that Edo's population exceeded 1 million by the early 18th century. By at least the second half of the Edo period, the city's population density likely surpassed 100,000 people per square mile. By way of comparison, the population density of Manhattan (New York City) in 2000 was estimated at around 70,000 people per square mile.

At least in part, the layout of the city reflected the Edo period's notion of four primary social classes—warrior, farmer, artisan, and merchant. The city was segregated according to class, and the size of one's home and proximity to Edo Castle also expressed one's rank. Neighborhood divisions within the city were known as wards (*cho*), of which there were nearly 1,700. These became the commoner (*chonin*) areas of the city. The city was further divided on the basis of one's occupation within a social class. Similar occupations usually clustered in the same part of the city. Edo residents also had to contend with natural disasters. A great conflagration in 1657, the Meireki Fire, reportedly killed 100,000 people and destroyed nearly two-thirds of the city.

Edo was not only the political center of Japan, but also one of its cultural centers. New forms of literature, music, theater, and other entertainments thrived in Edo. The theater form known as Kabuki,

for instance, was particularly popular among the city's residents.

Edo was rich in varied communities within the city. Some of the more important of these areas of the city are listed below:

Akasaka A section of Edo that is part of present-day Minato Ward. Akasaka was the site of daimyo residences during the Edo period.

Aoyama A section of Edo that is part of present-day Minato Ward. Temples, shrines, and warrior residences were located in Aoyama during the Edo period.

Asakusa A section of Edo that is part of present-day Taito Ward situated on the Sumida River (Sumidagawa). In the Edo period, Asakusa was both an entertainment and business area. Asakusa is famous for the Buddhist Sensoji.

Azabu A section of Edo that is part of present-day Minato Ward. Azabu was an area of samurai residences during the Edo period.

2.6 Edo shop similar to those situated in the Asakusa district (Illustration Grace Vibbert)

2.7 *Model of Edo street scene* (Edo-Tokyo Museum exhibit; Photo William E. Deal)

Ginza A section of Edo that is part of present-day Chuo Ward. The name Ginza (literally, "silver seat") reflects that area's original use as the mint district for casting silver coins. The first mint was established by the shogunate in 1612. In the late 18th century, copper and iron coins were produced in the Ginza area.

Kanda A section of Edo that is part of present-day Chiyoda Ward. During the Edo period, Kanda was both a residential and business area.

Kasumigaseki A section of Edo that is part of present-day Chiyoda Ward. During the Edo period, Kasumigaseki was home to wealthy daimyo.

Marunouchi A section of Edo that is part of present-day Chiyoda Ward. The wealthiest and most powerful daimyo resided in the Marunouchi area during the Edo period.

Nihombashi A section of Edo that is part of present-day Chuo Ward. The district is named for its centerpiece, the Nihombashi Bridge, built in 1603. Nihombashi marked the point of departure for those leaving the city along the Tokaido or one of the other road systems that crisscrossed early modern Japan. Nihombashi was the center of Edo commerce.

Ueno A section of Edo that is part of present-day Taito Ward. It was popular among Edo residents as a place to go for a day's outing. Ueno was famous for its many Buddhist temples, including the Kan'eiji, associated with the Tokugawa family. Ueno was also the location of the graves of some Tokugawa shoguns. In 1868, in the waning days of the Tokugawa shogunate, the shogunal forces lost a battle fought at Ueno to the forces in favor of an imperial restoration.

Yoshiwara A section of Edo that was located in what is now part of present-day Taito Ward. Yoshiwara was famous as the pleasure and prostitution district of Edo. The Edo government regulated the district, issuing the first business license for Yoshiwara in 1617. The district was surrounded by walls and a moat to restrict access.

FUKUI

City in present-day Fukui Prefecture. Fukui was a castle town founded in 1575 by Shibata Katsuie. Following Katsuie, Fukui was controlled by a succession of lords until it passed into the hands of Tokugawa Ieyasu's son and thereafter remained in the son's family.

FUSHIMI

Area in the Momoyama district of the present-day city of Kyoto. During the Sengoku period, Toyotomi Hideyoshi built his Fushimi Castle here, which had a great impact on the political and economic importance of the area. The Fushimi Inari Shrine is also here. Fushimi was also the site of the Battle of Toba-Fushimi in 1868. This battle pitted shogunal forces against the forces of the Satsuma, Choshu, and Tosa domains, who were fighting on the side of imperial restoration. The shogunal forces were defeated.

GIFU

City in present-day Gifu Prefecture situated on the Nagara River (Nagaragawa). In the Muromachi period, Gifu was a castle town called Inokuchi and controlled by the Toki family. In the late 16th century, Inokuchi was renamed Gifu by Oda Nobunaga who assumed control of the city. In addition to its status as a castle town, Gifu was also a post station along the Nakasendo road.

GOBO

City in present-day Wakayama Prefecture on the Hidaka River (Hidakagawa). Gobo developed as a temple town. It was the site of a branch temple of the Nishi Honganji in Kyoto, headquarters of True Pure Land Buddhism. Gobo was also home to Dojoji, a temple appearing in both the Noh and Kabuki theatrical traditions during the Edo period.

HACHINOHE

City in present-day Aomori Prefecture situated on the Pacific Ocean. Hachinohe was an Edo-period castle town controlled by a branch of the Nambu family.

HACHIOJI

City in present-day Tokyo Prefecture. Hachioji was a castle town in the medieval period and a post station along the Koshu Kaido road during the Edo period. The city was known for the production of raw silk.

HAGI

City in present-day Yamaguchi Prefecture situated on the Abu River and Sea of Japan. Hagi was an Edo-period castle town controlled by the Mori family. The city also served as the capital of the old provinces of Nagato and Suo. Hagi is perhaps best known for its ceramics called Hagi-yaki, beginning in the 17th century. Hagi is also the site of the Shoka Sonjuku, a school founded in the late Edo period by Yoshida Shoin, a staunch supporter of the imperial restoration movement.

HAKATA/FUKUOKA

City in present-day Fukuoka Prefecture. During the medieval and into the beginning of the early modern periods, Hakata's port was an important trading post between Japan, Korea, and China due to its proximity to the Asian mainland. Among the goods traded were ceramics and textiles. Hakata merchants, active in the medieval and the beginning of the early modern periods, controlled the politics of Hakata life. Hakata's merchant life was eclipsed by Hirado and Dejima after the appearance of Western traders to Japan. One unwelcome side effect of Hakata's closeness to the Asian mainland was that Hakata was attacked twice by the Mongols in their unsuccessful attempts to conquer Japan in the late 13th century. In 1600, Kuroda Nagamasa built a castle on the outskirts of Hakata that became the castle town known as Fukuoka. The Kuroda family served the Tokugawa shogunate throughout the Edo period. The modern city of Fukuoka incorporates the formerly separate port city of Hakata.

HAKODATE

City in present-day Hokkaido Prefecture situated on the Tsugaru Strait that separates Hokkaido and Honshu. Hakodate gained importance in the late Edo period when it was one of the ports made available to foreign trade under provisions of the Kanagawa Treaty (1854) that began the process of opening Japan to the West. Hakodate was also the site of the first Western-style fort, Goryokaku, constructed in the last years of the Edo period.

HAMADA

City in present-day Shimane Prefecture situated on the Sea of Japan. A castle town, during the Edo period Hamada was also an important fishing port.

HAMAMATSU

City in present-day Shizuoka Prefecture situated on the Tenryu River (Tenryugawa). The city was known as Hikuma prior to 1570. Hamamatsu was both a castle town and a post station along the Tokaido road during the Edo period. The Battle of Mikatahara was fought at Hamamatsu in 1573. In this confrontation, Takeda Shingen defeated the troops commanded by Oda Nobunaga and Tokugawa Ieyasu.

HANDA

City in present-day Aichi Prefecture situated on the Chita Peninsula. Handa was a port city during the Edo period.

HIKONE

City in present-day Shiga Prefecture situated on Lake Biwa. Hikone was a castle controlled by the Ii family during the Edo period. The city figured in events occurring at both the beginning and end of the Tokugawa shogunate. Hikone was a battleground in the struggle to unify Japan at the end of the 16th century and was the home of Ii Naosuke who was eventually assassinated for embracing policies to open Japan to Western trade at the end of the Edo period.

HIMEJI

City in present-day Hyogo Prefecture situated on the Ichi River (Ichikawa). Himeji was an area with a fortress as early as the 14th century. It became a castle town in the early 17th century with the construction of the Himeji Castle by Ikeda Terumasa.

HIRAIZUMI

City in present-day Iwate Prefecture situated on the Kitakami River (Kitakamigawa). Hiraizumi was important during the Heian period as the focus of activities of the Oshu Fujiwara family. They created a cultural and commercial center to rival that of Kyoto. Hiraizumi's significance never recovered after 1189 when Minomoto no Yoritomo destroyed much of the city in retaliation for Oshu Fujiwara's support of Yoritomo's brother and enemy, Minamoto no Yoshitsune. Despite this political misfortune, Hiraizumi retained its status as a center of religious activity for the area during the medieval period.

HIRATA

City in present-day Shimane Prefecture situated on Lake Shinji. Hirata was a market town during the Edo period.

HIROSAKI

City in present-day Aomori Prefecture situated on the Tsugaru Plain. Hirosaki was a castle town controlled by the Tsugaru family, which built Hirosaki Castle in 1611. Hirosaki was also known for its green lacquerware known as *tsugaru-nuri*.

HIROSHIMA

City in present-day Hiroshima Prefecture situated on Hiroshima Bay in the Seto Inland Sea. Hiroshima was a castle town during the Edo period and controlled by the Mori family. In the late 16th century, Mori Terumoto constructed Hiroshima Castle, but he lost power after the Tokugawa defeated him at the Battle of Sekigahara in 1600. After this time, control of Hiroshima was assumed by the Asano family, closely associated with the Tokugawa shogunate, who ruled there throughout the Edo period.

HITA

City in present-day Oita Prefecture situated on the Chikugo River (Chikugogawa) in the Hita plateau. Hita was a castle town during the Edo period. Hirose Tanso's Kangian school was located here. The city was also known for the production of Onta ceramics (Onta-yaki).

HITACHI OTA

City in present-day Ibaraki Prefecture. Hitachi Ota was a castle town during the Warring States period controlled by the Satake family. The Mito domain took control of the city after the start of the Edo period.

HITOYOSHI

City in present-day Kumamoto Prefecture situated on the Kuma River (Kumagawa). Throughout most of the medieval and early modern periods, the city was a castle town under the control of the Sagara family. The city produced a liquor distilled from rice.

IBARAKI

City in present-day Osaka Prefecture. Ibaraki was a castle town during the Edo period.

ICHINOMIYA

City in present-day Aichi Prefecture. During the medieval and early modern periods, Ichinomiya was a shrine town centered on the Masumida Shrine. During the Edo period, it also served as a market town and a station along the Gifu road.

IIYAMA

City in present-day Nagano Prefecture situated on the Chikuma River (Chikumagawa). Iiyama became a castle town in the late 16th century when a castle was constructed there by the Uesugi family. Control of the castle and city passed through a succession of lords during the Edo period.

IMABARI

City in present-day Ehime Prefecture situated on the coast of the Kurushima Strait in the Seto Inland Sea. Imabari was a castle town built by Todo Taka-tora in the early 17th century as a reward for his faithful duty to the Tokugawa during the Battle of Sekigahara. Imabari Castle was assigned to the Matsudaira family in the mid-17th century, and they controlled Imabari for the remainder of the Edo period.

IMARI

City in present-day Saga Prefecture situated on Imari Bay. During the Edo period, Imari was important both as a producer of ceramics (Imari-yaki), and as a port for the export of ceramics, including those produced in nearby Arita (Arita-yaki).

INUYAMA

City in present-day Aichi Prefecture situated on the Kiso River (Kisogawa). A castle town, Inuyama Castle was built on the Kiso River around 1440. During the Edo period, Inuyama was controlled by the Naruse family.

ISE/UJI-YAMADA

City in present-day Mie Prefecture situated on Imari Bay. Ise, formerly referred to as Uji-Yamada, was important during the medieval and early modern periods as the site of the Ise Shrine (Ise Jingu), in which the Sun Goddess, Amaterasu, is enshrined.

ISESAKI

City in present-day Gumma Prefecture. Isesaki was a castle and market town during the Edo period. It was a center for the manufacture of silk.

ITAMI

City in present-day Hyogo Prefecture. During the medieval period, Itami was a castle town controlled by the Itami family. During the Edo period, Itami was a center for brewing of the alcoholic drink known as sake.

IWAKUNI

City in present-day Yamaguchi Prefecture situated on the Nishiki River (Nishikigawa) and Hiroshima Bay. Iwakuni was a castle town whose Iwakuni Castle was completed in 1608 and controlled throughout the Edo period by the Kikkawa family, a branch of the powerful Mori family. Iwakuni is the site of Kintai Bridge (Kintaikyo) constructed in 1673 as a means of escape from floods on the Nishiki River.

IZUMI OTSU

City in present-day Osaka Prefecture situated on Osaka Bay. During the Edo period, Izumi Otsu was a port town.

IZUMO

City in present-day Shimane Prefecture situated on the Sea of Japan. Izumo was a market town, but it was best known as the site of the Izumo Shrine (Izumo Taisha).

KAGA/DAISHOJI

City in present-day Ishikawa Prefecture situated on the Daishoji River (Daishojigawa) and the Sea of Japan. Kaga, formerly known as Daishoji, was originally a temple town but became a castle town after the Maeda family constructed a castle there in the early 17th century. Kaga was a center for the production of Kutani ceramics (Kutani-yaki) and silk fabric.

KAGOSHIMA

City in present-day Kagoshima Prefecture situated on Kagoshima Bay. The former land of the Satsuma family, it was here that the first Christian missionary to Japan, the Jesuit Francis Xavier, landed in 1549. Kagoshima was a castle town and port during the Edo period. The Shimazu family built Tsurumaru Castle in 1602, leading to the growth of the city.

KAMAKURA

City in present-day Kanagawa Prefecture situated on Sagami Bay. Minamoto no Yoritomo made it the headquarters for his military government—the Kamakura shogunate—in 1192. Until the 12th century, Kamakura had been a fishing village. After the collapse of the Kamakura shogunate in 1333, political power shifted back to the capital at Kyoto. Not only was Kamakura a political center during the Kamakura period, it was also a religious one. Zen, Nichiren, and Pure Land Buddhist schools all had a presence in Kamakura, and Shinto shrines, such as the Tsurugaoka Hachiman Shrine, were also important religious institutions in the city. The Daibutsu,

a 37-foot-high bronze statue of Amida Buddha, was dedicated at Kamakura's Kotokuin Temple in 1252. After the Kamakura period when political power reverted back to Kyoto, Kamakura experienced a significant decline in its fortunes. These were never fully reversed in the medieval and early modern periods, though the city received some financial support for its cultural institutions from the Tokugawa shogunate during the Edo period.

KANAZAWA

City in present-day Ishikawa Prefecture situated on Sagami Bay. In the 15th century, the Ikko school of True Pure Land Buddhism established a temple in the area that became Kanazawa, after the school was driven from Kyoto. Ikko school supporters, however, were defeated in 1580. In 1583, Maeda Toshiie constructed Kanazawa Castle on the grounds of the Ikko temple, thereby controlling the region. From then until the end of the Edo period, the Maeda family controlled what had become the castle town of Kanazawa. Outside of the Tokugawa family, the Maeda became the most powerful and wealthy lords in Japan in the Edo period. Because of Maeda family tastes and interests, Kanazawa also became known for the quality of its arts and other cultural endeavors.

KARATSU

City in present-day Saga Prefecture situated on Karatsu Bay. Karatsu was a port and castle town during the Edo period. The city was known for the production of Karatsu ceramics (Karatsu-yaki).

KASHIMA

City in present-day Ibaraki Prefecture. Kashima was the site of the Kashima Shrine, dedicated to a deity worshipped by samurai.

KAWAGOE

City in present-day Saitama Prefecture situated on the Musashino Plateau. Kawagoe was a castle town from the 15th century, under the control of the Ota family. In the Edo period, Kawagoe was both a port and post-station town. During Edo, control of Kawagoe passed through a succession of different lords.

KIKUCHI

City in present-day Kumamoto Prefecture situated on the Kikuchi River (Kikuchigawa). During the Kamakura period, Kikuchi was controlled by the Kikuchi warrior family. During the Edo period, Kikuchi was a station on the road between Hita and Kumamoto.

KISARAZU

City in present-day Chiba Prefecture situated on Edo Bay. During the Edo period, Kisarazu was an important domestic port.

KISHIWADA

City in present-day Osaka Prefecture situated on Osaka Bay. During the Edo period, Kishiwada was a castle town controlled by the Okabe family.

KOBE/HYOGO

City in present-day Hyogo Prefecture situated on Osaka Bay and Seto Inland Sea. Kobe was an important port during the medieval and early modern periods, and was among the first Japanese ports opened to foreign trade under the provisions of the Ansei treaties signed in 1858. Kobe also was involved in the tally trade with Ming-dynasty China during the later part of the Muromachi period (for details on the tally trade, see chapter 11: Economy).

KOCHI

City in present-day Kochi Prefecture situated on Urado Bay. Under the rule of Chosokabe Motochika during the 16th century, Kochi, then called Tosa, became a castle town of the Edo period, controlled by the Yamanouchi family, lords of the Tosa domain. Kochi was also the birthplace of Sakamoto Ryoma, noted for his activities in support of an imperial restoration at the end of the Edo period.

KOFU

City in present-day Yamanashi Prefecture. Kofu was home to the Ichijo family in the Kamakura period and was ruled for three generations by the Takeda warrior family in the 16th century. During the Edo period, Kofu was a shogunal domain and post station.

KOGA

City in present-day Ibaraki Prefecture situated at the intersection of the Omoi River (Omoigawa) and the Watarase River (Watarasegawa). In the mid-15th century, Ashikaga warriors took refuge at Koga after Ashikaga Shigeuji assassinated Uesugi Noritada, his political rival. During the Edo period, Koga was a castle town under the control of a succession of lords, as well as a river port and post station along the Nikko road (Nikko Kaido).

KOMATSU

City in present-day Ishikawa Prefecture situated on the Kakehashi River (Kakehashigawa) and the Sea of Japan. Komatsu was a castle town and its castle was constructed by the leader of a religious revolt. In 1639, Maeda Toshitsune took control of the castle and under his leadership Komatsu developed into a thriving community. The city was famous for the production of Kutani ceramics (Kutani-yaki) and silk.

KOTOHIRA

City in present-day Kagawa Prefecture. Kotohira was a temple and shrine town during the Edo period, focused on Kompirasan (also known as Kotohiragu), an important temple and shrine complex that was especially popular with sailors praying for protection and safe journeys.

KUMAMOTO

City in present-day Kumamoto Prefecture. Kumamoto was an Edo-period castle town. Kumamoto Castle was built in the early 17th century by Kato Kiyomasa, but in the latter half of the century the Hosokawa family assumed control.

KURASHIKI

City in present-day Okayama Prefecture situated on the Takahashi River (Takahashigawa). Kurashiki was an important trading town for such commodities as rice, oil, and cotton during the Edo period. Kurashiki's storehouses (*kura*) were used to store harvested rice from regional farmlands. The city was controlled directly by the Edo government.

KYOTO/HEIANKYO

City in present-day Kyoto Prefecture situated on the Kamo River (Kamogawa) and the Katsura River (Katsuragawa). Kyoto, originally called Heiankyo, was Japan's capital and location of the imperial court from 794 to 1868. The term *Kyoto* came into general use by the 12th century. The city was designed in a grid pattern on a north-south axis following the model of Chang-an, the capital of Tang-dynasty China. The city measured 3.2 miles from north to south and 2.8 miles east to west. In the Heian period, the emperor, his family, and the imperial court were located in the northern section of the city. Aristocrats and bureaucrats were integral to the workings of the Japanese government at this time. Residences of influential aristocrats were situated in the center of the city, while markets were located in both the northern and southern sections of the city. By the 11th century, however, the organization of the city based on the Chinese model gave way to less gridlike settlement patterns, reflecting the real use of the urban landscape as opposed to the idealized one implied by a balanced grid.

Kyoto was the center of the Japanese universe throughout the Heian period, both as its political and cultural hub. The modern expression "classical Japanese culture" refers mainly to the Kyoto cultural sphere of the Heian period. But Kyoto's fortunes changed with the end of aristocratic rule at the end of the Heian period and the beginning of the military rule that marked the medieval and early modern periods. Although Kyoto remained home to the imperial court during the Kamakura period, real governing power shifted to the city of Kamakura, headquarters of the Kamakura shogunate.

At the end of the Kamakura period, Kyoto once again became the political center of Japan when the Ashikaga shoguns took up residence in the Muromachi section of the city and established the military government that is commonly referred to as the Muromachi period. The Ashikaga presided over both warriors and aristocrats and were great patrons of the arts and religion. Many Buddhist temples, such as Nanzenji and Ginkakuji, were built during the time of Ashikaga rule. This period of building was followed by a time of great destruction. By the middle of the 15th century, the authority of the Ashikaga shoguns was being eclipsed by powerful warrior lords. The Onin War (1467–77), precipitated by a dispute over shogunal succession, pitted powerful lords against each other. One of the significant effects of the war was that much of Kyoto was destroyed in the fighting. This war ushered in a time referred to as the Warring States period (1467–1568) during which warrior families fought against each other in a struggle for control of the country.

Kyoto never fully recovered from the devastation wrought by the Onin War, and during the Edo period, Kyoto's political and cultural centrality was once again eclipsed. This time, the Tokugawa shogunate, which had unified Japan in the early 17th

2.8 Warajiya restaurant, Kyoto, is an extant example of a storefront in Edo-period style. (Photo William E. Deal)

century, established its military rule from the city of Edo. Although Kyoto was still important as a cultural center, new cultural expressions—focused especially on the merchant rather than the aristocratic class—were taking form in castle towns such as Edo and Osaka. Kyoto was fully overshadowed when, in 1868, the capital was moved to Edo, newly named Tokyo, and the emperor took up residence there.

MAEBASHI

City in present-day Gumma Prefecture situated on the Tone River (Tonegawa). Maebashi, a castle town from the Muromachi period, was called Umayabashi in the medieval period. During the Edo period the city was controlled by the Matsudaira family and was a center for the production and distribution of silk.

MARUGAME

City in present-day Kagawa Prefecture situated on the Inland Sea. During the Edo period, Marugame was a castle town from 1597 when Marugame Castle was built. The city was controlled by a succession of lords and was also important as a point of departure for pilgrims going to the Kompira Shrine located nearby.

MATSUE

City in present-day Shimane Prefecture situated on Lake Shinji. Matsue was a castle town during the Edo period. Matsue Castle was constructed in 1611 and came under the control of the Matsudaira family in 1638.

MATSUMOTO

City in present-day Nagano Prefecture. During the Muromachi period, Matsumoto was controlled by the Ogasawara family. Matsumoto Castle was constructed in 1595. Thereafter, Matsumoto developed into a castle town. Typically, castles were situated on a mountain or hill, but Matsumoto Castle was built on a plain.

MATSUSAKA/MATSUZAKA

City in present-day Mie Prefecture overlooking Ise Bay. Matsusaka (sometimes called Matsuzaka) was

both a castle and post-station town during the Edo period. Commercially, it was known for the production of cotton.

MATSUYAMA

City in present-day Ehime Prefecture. A castle town during the Edo period, its castle was constructed in the early 17th century. The city was controlled by the Matsudaira family.

MIKI

City in present-day Hyogo Prefecture. Miki was a castle town from the 15th century when Bessho Naganori built his castle there. The castle was later captured and burned by Toyotomi Hideyoshi in 1580. During the Edo period, Miki was known for the manufacture of hardware and the production of sake.

MINO

City in present-day Gifu Prefecture situated on the Nagara River (Nagaragawa). Mino was an Edo-period castle town after the Nanamori family built a castle there in 1606. Mino was an important site for the production of paper (washi) throughout the medieval and early modern periods.

MINOBU

City in present-day Ehime Yamanashi situated on the Fuji River (Fujikawa). Minobu was a temple town associated with the Kuonji, the head temple of the Nichiren school of Buddhism, located on nearby Mount Minobu (Minobu-san). Nichiren's grave is at Kuonji.

MITO

City in present-day Ibaraki Prefecture situated on the Naka River (Nakagawa). As early as the Kamakura period, Mito was home to a fortress. At that time the area was controlled by the Daijo family. After the Edo-period unification of Japan, Mito came to be controlled by Tokugawa Yorifusa, one of Ieyasu's many sons. Yorifusa built a castle there which became the center of the Mito domain (han) during the Edo period. Yorifusa's Tokugawa family line was one of three from which a shogun could be chosen. Mito was also a center of learning known as Mitogaku, notable for its support of imperial restoration at the end of the Edo period.

MORIOKA

City in present-day Iwate Prefecture situated on the Kita River (Kitakami River). In the Edo period, Morioka was a castle town controlled by the Nambu family. It was known for the production of ironware.

NAGAHAMA

City in present-day Shiga Prefecture situated on Lake Biwa. Toyotomi constructed Nagahama Castle in 1573. Nagahama developed as a temple town around the Daitsuji, affiliated with the True Pure Land Buddhist school. Nagahama was also important as a port.

NAGANO

City in present-day Nagano Prefecture. Nagano flourished as a temple town associated with the Zenkoji throughout the medieval and early modern periods. In the Edo period, Nagano also became important as both a post-station town and a market town.

NAGAOKA

City in present-day Niigata Prefecture situated on the Shinano River (Shinanogawa). Nagaoka was an Edo-period castle town and port controlled by the Makino family.

NAGASAKI

City in present-day Nagasaki Prefecture. Nagasaki was an important port city, especially during the Edo period. Because of its proximity to the Asian continent, it has a long history of contacts with China and Korea. In 1571, Nagasaki became a center of trade with Portugal and other European countries. In 1636, in an attempt to restrict contacts with the West, the government built Dejima island in Nagasaki Bay as a way to contain the foreign presence in Japan. Japanese understanding of Western

science and other areas of learning was typically gleaned first at Nagasaki.

NAGOYA

City in present-day Aichi Prefecture situated on Ise Bay. During the Muromachi period Nagoya was associated with the Atsuta Shrine. In the Edo period, Nagoya developed into a thriving castle town after Tokugawa Ieyasu built Nagoya Castle in the early 17th century as the residence for one of his sons. This branch of the Tokugawa family was known as the Owari family and was one of three Tokugawa lineages from which a shogun could be chosen.

NAOETSU

Formerly a city in present-day Niigata Prefecture situated on the Sea of Japan. It is now part of the city of Joetsu. Naoetsu was a port in the Kamakura period and a post station from the 14th century.

NARA

City in present-day Nara Prefecture. Nara was the site of the capital during the Nara period (710–784). Although it lost some importance after the capital moved to Kyoto in the late eighth century, Nara's many shrines and temples maintained influence throughout the medieval and early modern periods.

NIIGATA

City in present-day Niigata Prefecture situated on Sea of Japan. Niigata was an important port town during the Edo period and was one of the ports opened to foreign trade under the provisions of the Ansei treaties signed in 1858.

NIKKO

City in present-day Tochigi Prefecture. Nikko is important primarily as the site of the Toshogu, built in 1634, a shrine complex that includes the mausoleum of Tokugawa Ieyasu.

ODATE

City in present-day Akita Prefecture situated on the Yoneshiro River (Yoneshirogawa). Odate was a castle and market town controlled by the Satake family during the Edo period. Odate is reportedly the site where the Akita dog breed originated.

ODAWARA

City in present-day Kanagawa Prefecture situated on Sagami Bay. The city became a castle town controlled by the Hojo family during the Muromachi period. The castle constructed by the Hojo was destroyed by Toyotomi Hideyoshi in 1590. Odawara became a flourishing post station along the Tokaido road in the Edo period. The area was controlled by the Okubo family in the Edo period.

OKAYAMA

City in present-day Okayama Prefecture situated on the Seto Inland Sea. Okayama Castle was built in the 16th century. In the Edo period, the area was under the control of the Ikeda family. A famous garden, Korakuen, was designed and built in the late 17th century.

OKAZAKI

City in present-day Aichi Prefecture situated on the Yahagi River (Yahagigawa). Okazaki Castle was constructed in 1455. The castle is famous as the site of Tokugawa Ieyasu's birth. In the Edo period, Okazaki was a thriving post station along the Tokaido road.

OMI HACHIMAN

City in present-day Shiga Prefecture situated on Lake Biwa. Omi Hachiman Castle was constructed by Toyotomi Hidetsugu, Hideyoshi's adopted son, in 1585 but abandoned a few years later. Nevertheless, Omi Hachiman developed into a thriving merchant town in the Edo period.

OSAKA

City in present-day Osaka Prefecture situated on the Yodo River (Yodogawa) and Osaka Bay. Prior to the medieval period, Osaka was a port that engaged in trade with the Asian mainland. In the Muromachi period, a militant True Pure Land Buddhist school established the Ishiyama Honganji at Osaka. The religious and secular activities that grew up around this temple complex were the genesis of the city of Osaka as an important urban center. Oda Nobunaga destroyed the temple in 1580 because he feared the influence of this group in his plans to unify Japan under his control. In 1583, Toyotomi Hideyoshi, Nobunaga's successor, built Osaka Castle on the grounds of the former temple. Hideyoshi used Osaka Castle as his headquarters in his quest to defeat his enemies and take control of Japan. Osaka Castle lost some of its significance as a power base after Hideyoshi's death in 1598, and it was largely destroyed in Tokugawa Ieyasu's campaigns in 1614 and 1615 to solidify his control of the country and to eradicate any possibility of Hideyoshi's heirs rising up against him.

Although Osaka was no longer a center of power (the Tokugawa shogunate had established its base at Edo), Edo-period Osaka developed into a major city, especially important as a market and trading area. It was one of the places where the rice tax paid to Edo was gathered for distribution. Besides being a major commercial area, Osaka also developed into a cultural center in the late 17th and early 18th centuries, producing new literary and theatrical forms that especially appealed to the interests and tastes of the new urban class so integral to the city's prosperity. Osaka was also a place to learn Dutch studies (Rangaku) and Western medicine at a time when Japan was still officially closed to most Western influence and interaction.

OTSU

City in present-day Shiga Prefecture situated on Lake Biwa. Otsu was a port and castle town during the Edo period. It was also a post station along the Tokaido road. Otsu was home to several important religious institutions, including the Miidera temple.

SAGA

City in present-day Saga Prefecture situated on the Sea of Japan and Ariake Bay. An Edo-period castle town, Saga was controlled by the Nabeshima family.

SAKAI

City in present-day Osaka Prefecture situated on Osaka Bay. Sakai was a flourishing seaport and trading center from the Muromachi period through the beginning of the Edo period. Sakai merchants, who also controlled the area's politics, conducted an active trading relationship with the Asian mainland and later with Europe. After the Tokugawa shogunate enacted the 1639 national seclusion policy severely limiting contact with the outside world, Sakai's fortunes waned quickly.

SEKIGAHARA

City in present-day Gifu Prefecture. Prior to the medieval period, Sekigahara was an important barrier station. The city is best known, however, as the site in 1600 of the Battle of Sekigahara in which Tokugawa Ieyasu finally vanquished his enemies and established both control over Japan and the supremacy of his family line. In the Edo period, Sekigahara was a post station.

SENDAI

City in present-day Miyagi Prefecture situated on the Nanakita River (Nanakitagawa) and the Hirose River (Hirosegawa). Aoba Castle (also called Sendai Castle) was built in 1601 by Date Masamune. The area was controlled in the Edo period by the Date family.

SETO

City in present-day Aichi Prefecture. Seto was important during the medieval and early modern periods as the site for the production of Seto ceramics (seto-yaki). The term *setomono*, taken from the city's name, is a generic name for ceramics.

SHIMABARA

City in present-day Nagasaki Prefecture in Kyushu situated on the Shimabara Peninsula. Shimabara was a castle town controlled by the Matsudaira family during the Edo period. It is also close to Mount Unzen, an active volcano whose 1792 eruption reportedly killed 15,000 people. Shimabara was the location of the Shimabara Rebellion (1637), an uprising of Japanese Christians.

SHIMODA

City in present-day Shizuoka Prefecture situated on the Izu Peninsula. Shimoda was a port during the Edo period, involved in the trade of goods between nearby Edo and Osaka. Shimoda is most famously associated with the arrival of Commodore Perry in Japan, first in 1853, and with the subsequent opening of Japan to the outside world after more than 200 years of isolation. The 1854 Kanagawa Treaty signed between Japan and the United States opened Shimoda's port to foreign trade. Shimoda was the residence of the first American diplomat in Japan, Townsend Harris, who set up a consular office there in 1856.

SHIMONOSEKI

City in present-day Yamaguchi Prefecture. Chofu (see above), a section of the modern city of Shimonoseki, was the capital of Nagato Province in the medieval and early modern periods. Besides it proximity to Dannoura (see above), Shimonoseki was the site of domain resistance to the opening of Japan to Western ships at the close of the Edo period. In 1863, the head of the Choshu domain fired on Dutch, French, and American ships as they passed through the ocean channel at Shimonoseki. In retaliation, Shimonoseki underwent a naval bombardment by Western ships.

SHIZUOKA

See SUMPU.

SUMPU

Former name of a city in present-day Shizuoka Prefecture situated on Suruga Bay in the Pacific Ocean. Sumpu became the present-day city of Shizuoka in 1869. During the Muromachi period, Sumpu was controlled by the Imagawa family. It was a castle town from the Azuchi-Momoyama period and throughout the Edo period. Tokugawa Ieyasu built Sumpu Castle in the 1580s, retiring there in 1605 and dying in 1616. Sumpu was also a post station along the Tokaido road.

TAKADA

Former name of a city in present-day Niigata Prefecture situated on the Sea of Japan. It is now part of the city of Joetsu. Takada was a castle town from the early 1600s, first under the control of the Uesugi family and later under the rule of the Matsudaira family.

TAKAMATSU

City in present-day Kagawa Prefecture situated on the Seto Inland Sea. A castle town, Takamatsu was first inhabited by the Ikoma family who built Takamatsu Castle there in 1588. Some 50 years later, the Matsudaira family took control of the castle and the city, maintaining their authority in the area through the end of the Edo period.

TAKAYAMA

City in present-day Gifu Prefecture situated in the mountains of the Hida region. From the late 16th century, Takayama was a castle town of the Kanamori family. It was highly regarded for its wood and timber, and for the quality of its carpenters and carpentry work. The Hida region came under direct rule by the Tokugawa shogunate in 1692.

TOKUSHIMA

City in present-day Tokushima Prefecture situated on the Yoshino River (Yoshinogawa). Tokushima was a castle town during the Edo period, controlled by the Hachisuka family, as well as a center of the indigo trade.

TOTTORI

City in present-day Tottori Prefecture. Tottori was a castle town during the Edo period, controlled by the Ikeda family.

TSUWANO

City in present-day Shimane Prefecture. Tsuwano was a castle town during the Edo period, under the control of the Kamei family. Tsuwano was noted for the production of paper (*washi*). Tsuwano was home to a school known as the Yorokan, established in 1786.

UENO

City in present-day Mie Prefecture. Ueno was a castle town in the Edo period, controlled by the Todo family. Ueno was a site for the production of Iga ceramics (Iga-yaki). Ueno is also famous as the birthplace of the poet Basho. The school of martial arts known as Iga Ninjutsu was started in Ueno.

UJI

City in present-day Kyoto Prefecture situated on the Uji River (Ujigawa). Although Uji had close associations with the Kyoto aristocracy during the Heian period, it was also the site of the Obaku Zen sect Mampukuji, built in the 17th century. Uji was important as a center for tea production.

URAGA

District in the present-day city of Yokosuka in Kanagawa Prefecture. In the Edo period, Uraga was a port situated on Edo Bay. It was of strategic importance to the shogunate located at Edo because it was from Uraga that a commissioner's office was established to inspect ships passing through Edo Bay. Uraga is also associated with Commodore Perry who landed at nearby Kurihama in 1853.

USA

City in present-day Oita Prefecture. During the medieval and early modern periods, Usa was associated with the Usa Hachiman Shrine.

USUKI

City in present-day Oita Prefecture situated on Usuki Bay. Usuki was a castle town during the Azuchi-Momoyama and Edo periods. Its castle was constructed by Otomo Sorin, a Christian lord. In the Edo period, the castle and city were under the control of the Inaba family.

UTSUNOMIYA

City in present-day Tochigi Prefecture situated at the base of Mount Nikko. In the Kamakura and

Muromachi periods, the city and area was controlled by the Utsunomiya family of military governors. In the Edo period, Utsunomiya was a castle town controlled by the Toda family. It was also a post station along the Nikko Kaido road.

WAKAYAMA

City in present-day Wakayama Prefecture situated on the Kino River (Kinokawa). Toyotomi Hideyoshi built a castle at Wakayama in 1585 for his son Hidetada. The area was later controlled by the Kii family, a branch of the Tokugawa and one of three family lines from which a shogun could be chosen in the Edo period. The last seven Tokugawa shoguns—ruling between 1716 and 1867—were selected from this family line.

YAMAGATA

City in present-day Yamagata Prefecture situated on the Mogami River (Mogamigawa). In the Edo period, Yamagata was a castle town controlled by a succession of lords. Yamagata was also important as a post station standing at the intersection of several roads.

YAMAGUCHI

City in present-day Yamaguchi Prefecture. Yamaguchi was a castle and port town under the control of the Ouchi family for two centuries beginning about 1350. During the Onin War (1467–77), as Kyoto was being destroyed by the battles being waged there, Yamaguchi became a refuge for lords and aristocrats from Kyoto. Yamaguchi developed cultural traditions that replicated what had existed in Kyoto. In 1555, the Ouchi family was replaced by the Mori family, but the Mori abandoned Yamaguchi for the nearby city of Hagi, and Yamaguchi quickly declined in importance as a result.

YOKOHAMA

City in present-day Kanagawa Prefecture. Although Yokohama is today Japan's second-largest city, it was a small fishing village until the end of the Edo period when it was developed as a port for foreign trade.

YONEZAWA

City in present-day Yamagata Prefecture. Yonezawa was a castle town from the Muromachi period through the end of the Edo period, controlled by the Uesugi family. It was famous for the manufacture of silk fabrics.

YOSHIDA/TOYOHASHI

A city now called Toyohashi in present-day Aichi Prefecture. The former Yoshida was a castle town situated on Atsumi Bay. In 1505 a castle was constructed that would later be called Yoshida Castle. In the late 16th century, the Ikeda family controlled the castle and city. In the Edo period, a succession of lords controlled Yoshida. The city was also a post station along the Tokaido road.

Domains

AIZU DOMAIN

Located in southern Mutsu Province, this domain changed hands a number of times before being granted to Hoshina Masayuki in 1643. Closely tied to the Tokugawa shogunate through his father, Tokugawa Hidetada, Masayuki was given the rank of *shimpan* (related domains). His family was later awarded the name Matsudaira, the original family name of the founder of the Tokugawa shogunate, Tokugawa Ieyasu. In the late Edo period, the Aizu domain fought against imperial restoration. Estimated annual rice production: 230,000 *koku*.

CHOSHU DOMAIN

Also known as the Hagi domain, Choshu was located in Suo and Nagato provinces. It was controlled by the Mori family. Choshu domain produced several important leaders of the Meiji Restoration. Estimated annual rice production: 369,000 *koku*.

HIKONE DOMAIN

Located in Omi Province, the Hikone domain was situated along the eastern side of Lake Biwa. It was granted to the Ii family in 1601 as reward for their service to Tokugawa Ieyasu. Later, Hikone daimyo, such as Ii Naosuke, served in the Tokugawa government. Estimated annual rice production: 350,000 *koku*.

HIZEN DOMAIN

Also referred to as Saga domain, this domain was located in Hizen province and was governed by the Nabeshima family from 1607. Hizen domain dominated both the coal and porcelain markets during the late Edo period and pioneered the introduction of Western military technology into Japan. Estimated annual rice production: 357,000 *koku*.

KAGA DOMAIN

Kaga domain, also referred to as the Kanazawa domain after the castle town that served as its headquarters, included large areas of Kaga, Noto, and Etchu provinces. It was administered by the powerful Maeda family. Estimated annual rice production: 1,025,000 *koku*.

KII DOMAIN

The Kii domain was located in Kii province and a section of Ise province. It was given to Tokugawa Yorinobu, one of Tokugawa Ieyasu's sons in 1619. The Kii domain, along with the Mito and Owari domains, belonged to one of three highly respected Gosanke families, branches of the Tokugawa family line. Tokugawa Yoshimune, the fifth daimyo of Kii, served as the eighth shogun. Estimated annual rice production: 555,000 *koku*.

MITO DOMAIN

The Mito domain was given to Tokugawa Yorifusa, one of Tokugawa Ieyasu's sons, in 1610. It was located in areas of Hitachi and Shimotsuke provinces. Like the Kii and Owari, the Mito daimyo belonged to the powerful Gosanke trio of Tokugawa branches descended from Tokugawa Ieyasu. Estimated annual rice production: 350,000 *koku*.

OKAYAMA DOMAIN

Okayama domain, located in Bizen province and a section of Bitchu province and headquartered at Okayama Castle, was granted to Ikeda Tadatsugu in 1602. The family of Ikeda Mitsumasa, a grandson of Tadatsugu's father, gained control of the domain in 1632. Estimated annual rice production: 315,200 *koku*.

OWARI DOMAIN

Located in Owari province and areas of Mino and Shinano provinces, the Owari domain was also called the Nagoya domain because of its headquarters at Nagoya Castle. The domain was awarded to Tokugawa Yoshinao, one of Tokugawa Ieyasu's sons. The Owari daimyo became the most powerful of the Gosanke—highly ranked daimyo directly descended from Tokugawa Ieyasu. Estimated annual rice production: 619,500 *koku*.

SATSUMA DOMAIN

Also referred to as Kagoshima domain, this fiefdom was located in Satsuma and Osumi provinces, as well as areas of Hyuga province. The Shimazu family ruled as lords of this domain for the entirety of the Tokugawa shogunate, profiting from a strategic geographical location that allowed them to amass significant wealth through foreign trade. Satsuma fought on the side of imperial restoration in the late Edo period. Estimated annual rice production: 729,000 *koku*.

SENDAI DOMAIN

Centered in Mutsu province, this domain was established by Date Masamune, an ambitious warrior whose nickname, Dokuganryu (One-eyed dragon) arose from his lack of eyesight in one eye. A former vassal of Toyotomi Hideyoshi, Masamune was awarded the immense Sendai domain in 1603 for his support of Tokugawa Ieyasu. In the late Edo period, the Sendai domain fought against imperial restoration. Estimated annual rice production: 620,000 *koku*.

TOSA DOMAIN

Also named Kochi domain after the castle town of Kochi, which served as its administrative center. Tosa domain occupied all of Tosa province. Dominated by the Yamanouchi family since 1603, this domain played an important role in the Meiji Restoration, supporting the cause of imperial restoration. Estimated annual rice production: 240,000 *koku*.

MEDIEVAL AND EARLY MODERN REGIONS, PROVINCES, AND EQUIVALENT MODERN PREFECTURES

Region (*do*)	Province (*kuni*)	Location in Modern Prefecture
Tosando (Eastern Mountain Region)	Mutsu	Aomori, Fukushima, Iwate, Miyagi, Akita
	Dewa	Akita, Yamagata
	Shimotsuke	Tochigi
	Kozuke	Gumma
	Shinano	Nagano
	Hida	Gifu
	Mino	Gifu
	Omi	Shiga
Hokurikudo (Northern Land Region)	Wakasa	Fukui
	Echizen	Fukui
	Kaga	Ishikawa
	Noto	Ishikawa
	Etchu	Toyama
	Echigo	Niigata
	Sado Island	Niigata
Tokaido (Eastern Sea Region)	Hitachi	Ibaraki
	Shimosa	Ibaraki
	Kazusa	Chiba
	Awa	Chiba
	Musashi	Saitama, Tokyo, Kanagawa
	Sagami	Kanagawa
	Izu	Shizuoka
	Kai	Yamanashi
	Suruga	Shizuoka
	Totomi	Shizuoka
	Mikawa	Aichi
	Owari	Aichi
	Iga	Mie
	Ise	Mie
	Shima	Mie
Kinai (Capital Provinces)	Yamashiro	Kyoto
	Settsu	Hyogo
	Kawachi	Osaka
	Yamato	Nara
	Izumi	Osaka
San'indo (Northern Mountain Region)	Tamba	Kyoto, Hyogo
	Tango	Kyoto
	Tajima	Hyogo
	Inaba	Tottori
	Hoki	Tottori
	Izumo	Shimane
	Iwami	Shimane
	Oki Island	Shimane
San'yodo (Southern Mountain Region)	Harima	Hyogo
	Mimasaka	Okayama
	Bizen	Okayama
	Bitchu	Okayama
	Bingo	Hiroshima
	Aki	Hiroshima
	Suo	Yamaguchi
	Nagato	Yamaguchi
Nankaido (Southern Sea Region)	Kii	Wakayama
	Awaji Island	Hyogo
	Sanuki	Kagawa
	Awa	Tokushima
	Tosa	Kochi
	Iyo	Ehime
Saikaido (Western Sea Region)	Tsushima Island	Nagasaki
	Iki Island	Saga
	Chikuzen	Fukuoka
	Chikugo	Fukuoka
	Buzen	Fukuoka
	Bungo	Oita
	Hizen	Saga, Nagasaki
	Higo	Kumamoto
	Hyuga	Miyazaki
	Osumi	Kagoshima
	Satsuma	Kagoshima

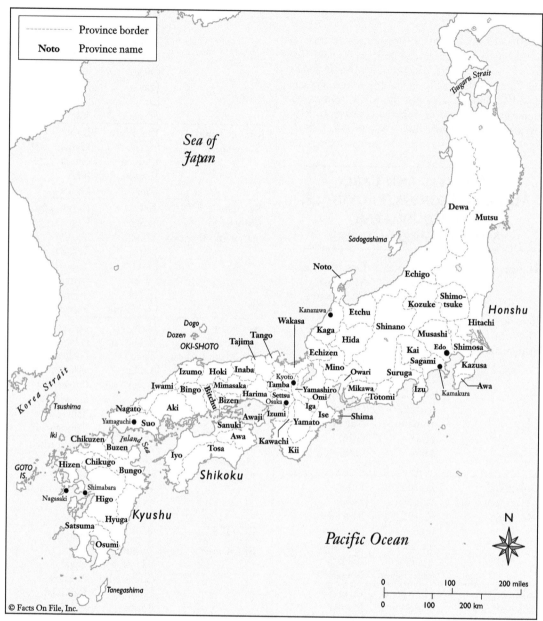

Map 3. *Provinces of Medieval and Early Modern Japan*

READING

Landscape and Environment

Trewartha 1965: geography and environment; Association of Japanese Geographers (eds.) 1980: geography and environment; Totman 1993, 3–10: geography and climate; Totman 2000, 11–19: geography, climate, and flora and fauna, 248–252: natural resources in the early modern period; Miner, Odagiri, and Morrell 1985, 415–418: geography, flora and fauna, 430–433: list of important bodies of water, mountains, and islands with their locations, 433–441: poetic place names

City, Town, and Countryside

Beasley 1999, 161–170: cities, towns, and countryside; Totman 1993, xvii: map of castle towns, 11–15: countryside, 25–28: cities and towns; Totman 1981, 189–1992: city, countryside, and social change; Frédéric 1972, 90–112: cities in the medieval period, 113–137: the countryside in the medieval period; Totman 2000, 154–158: medieval urbanization, 236–241, 260–261: Kyoto and its culture in the early modern period, 241–243: Osaka culture in the early modern period, 243–245, 261–263: Edo culture in the early modern period

Population Statistics

Hall (ed.) 1991, 519: population statistics; Totman 1993, 249–252: population statistics; Yonemoto 2003, 17: population statistics; Naito 2003, 178–179: population and population density of Edo; Hanley 1997, 129–131: early modern demographics; Totman 2000, 232–233, 247–248: early modern demographics, 261: population statistics

Regions, Provinces, and Equivalent Modern Prefectures

Miner, Odagiri, and Morrell 1985, 418–429: provinces, prefectures, and maps

3

GOVERNMENT

’ERIAL AND
⸻ITARY RULE

For the nearly 700-year span of Japan's medieval and early modern periods, warriors—with varying levels of effectiveness and hegemony—ruled the country. Although the fortunes of particular extended warrior families waxed and waned, only members of the warrior class could serve as shoguns, the military rulers. Their governments, known commonly as shogunates, were often challenged by the interests of other powerful warrior families in various parts of Japan and by the imperial family in Kyoto.

Although the warrior bureaucracy largely controlled the affairs of the state, the emperor and the imperial court were still the formal head of government. Warrior governments typically sought out—or forced—the formal imperial decrees that gave legitimacy to the shoguns. Occasionally emperors would attempt to reassert direct imperial rule. They were, however, always suppressed in favor of warrior rule. During the first part of the Kamakura period, the shogunate and the court more or less shared governmental authority. By the middle of the medieval period and into the early modern period, court power and authority became mostly a thing of the past.

Warrior governments functioned as a lord-vassal system of loyalty. This is reflected in the political structures of the different shogunates. Although they varied greatly in their organization, the notion of loyalty, whether earned or forced, always laid the foundation on which the warrior government was built.

During the earlier Nara and Heian periods, the *kuge*—members of the imperial court and powerful aristocratic families—controlled Japan. With the rise of the warrior class from the Kamakura period, however, this power was eclipsed but never replaced or abolished.

The term *tenno* (literally, "heavenly sovereign," that is, the emperor) refers to Japanese sovereigns and dates back to at least the seventh century. Imperial descent was traced through a hereditary line,

usually through males, although examples do exist of female rulers. Early in Japan's history, the emperor served both secular and religious roles. By the start of the medieval period, however, warriors largely eclipsed imperial authority. Emperors therefore took on a mostly ceremonial or symbolic role in the centuries that comprise Japan's medieval and early modern periods.

When Minamoto no Yoritomo established the Kamakura shogunate in 1185, he chose to maintain his base of operations at Kamakura, the location of the family in eastern Japan. The court stayed at Kyoto. The imperial court became an organ of the shogunate, used to appoint shoguns and for other ceremonial occasions that served mostly to legitimate warrior rule.

The shogunal regent (*shikken*) system put into effect by the Hojo family further transformed the relationship between court and shogunate. At court, the imperial government was run, in fact, not by the emperor but by an imperial regent from the aristocratic Fujiwara family. The Hojo family was now in control of the shogunate via the shogunal regency. Both forms of authority were thus controlled by regents, with the Hojo regent regulating most aspects of government. The Hojo regents also increasingly involved themselves in matters of imperial succession, thereby lending additional complications to the already divisive process of choosing emperors.

Interactions between court and shogunate also included periodic power struggles. The 1221 Jokyu Disturbance, in which the retired emperor Go-Toba unsuccessfully attempted to overthrow the shogunate, resulted in stricter control by the shogunate over the court; it came to control imperial succession. The Kemmu Restoration (1333–36), Emperor Go-Daigo's short-lived reestablishment of direct imperial rule, is the most dramatic example of court-shogunate conflict. Emperor Go-Daigo's three-year usurpation of power was overturned by Ashikaga Takauji, who thereafter established the Ashikaga shogunate inaugurating the start of the Muromachi period.

The court not only struggled against the shogunate, but it also, periodically, struggled against itself. This was especially pronounced during the period of the Northern and Southern Courts (1337–92). The 13th century witnessed two rival lines of imperial succession that led, by the 14th century, to a nearly 60-year span of dual imperial courts. These two rival lineages were the Jimyoin, descended from Go-Fukakusa (89th emperor, r. 1246–59) and the Daikakuji, descended from Kameyama (90th emperor, r. 1259–74), Go-Fukakusa's brother. Each brother vied to gain total control from the other. To quell this dispute, shogunal regent Hojo Sadatoki ruled that each line would provide the emperor in an alternating succession. This ruling, known as the Bumpo Compromise, required the emperor from each throne to rule for 10 years and then abdicate so the emperor from the other line could rule. The decision, however, only staved off the inevitable break between the Jimyoin and Daikakuji lines. In 1331, Emperor Go-Daigo, the 96th emperor, in the Daikakuji line, attempted to cut the Jimyoin line out of the imperial succession. The Jimyoin line, supported by Hojo Takatoki, resisted. In the ensuing confusion, Go-Daigo fled Kyoto with the imperial regalia (*shinki*—mirror, sword, and jewel), symbols of imperial authority and the legitimate right to rule.

The conflict led to the division into the Northern and Southern Courts, which lasted from 1337 to 1392. The Northern Court (Hokucho) was situated in Kyoto, while the Southern Court (Nancho) was located in the south at Yoshino. The first five emperors of the Northern Court—Kogon, Komyo, Suko, Go-Kogon, and Go-En'yu—were considered illegitimate *tenno* because they did not possess the imperial regalia. The separation of the Northern and Southern Courts continued for nearly 60 years before the Southern Court relinquished their claims of being the true imperial line.

At the end of the medieval period, the three great unifiers of Japan, Oda Nobunaga, Toyotomi Hideyoshi, and Tokugawa Ieyasu, each used the title-granting authority of the imperial court to accumulate titles that served to legitimate their rule. Tokugawa Ieyasu obtained the status of shogun.

Subsequent Tokugawa shoguns provided for the imperial line by restoring the imperial palace and making income available to the imperial family. On the other hand, the shogunate maintained control over the court and aristocrats by enacting legal regulations that set strict limits on their activities. As in the medieval period, the emperor was largely a figurehead whose main function was to perform public rituals.

Imperial fortunes dramatically changed toward the end of the Edo period. The Tokugawa shogunate faced increasing criticism regarding how it both handled internal affairs and permitted increasingly frequent interactions with Europeans, Americans, and other foreign powers who urged Japan to open its ports to foreign trade and, by extension, cultural influence. In this atmosphere, the slogan *sonno joi*, "revere the Emperor, expel the barbarians," became the rallying call of those who wanted to overthrow the Tokugawa shoguns and restore direct imperial rule. The result of this movement was the dismantling of the Tokugawa shogunate in 1868, and the inauguration of the Meiji Restoration.

STRUCTURE OF THE IMPERIAL COURT

The system of court ranks that organized the aristocratic hierarchy during the medieval and early modern periods was derived from the system established in the early eighth century, the Taiho Code, which had been based on Chinese models. Ranks were conferred on both aristocratic men and women. The status awarded determined the types of government positions one could hold and consequently one's relative power within the aristocratic and imperial hierarchy. Rank therefore had a large impact on one's social standing, political power, and economic wealth. Although occasionally making some allowance for ability, the Japanese rank system was mostly based on the prestige of one's family background.

The structure of the imperial court was a complex affair. The following chart depicts the basic outline, but each division and ministry contained a hierarchy of officials. Some divisions also included subdivisions. Despite the formality of this structure, the operation and functionality of any particular ministry fluctuated depending on the particular time period. There were also aristocratic families who came to dominate a particular court function through the use of heredity.

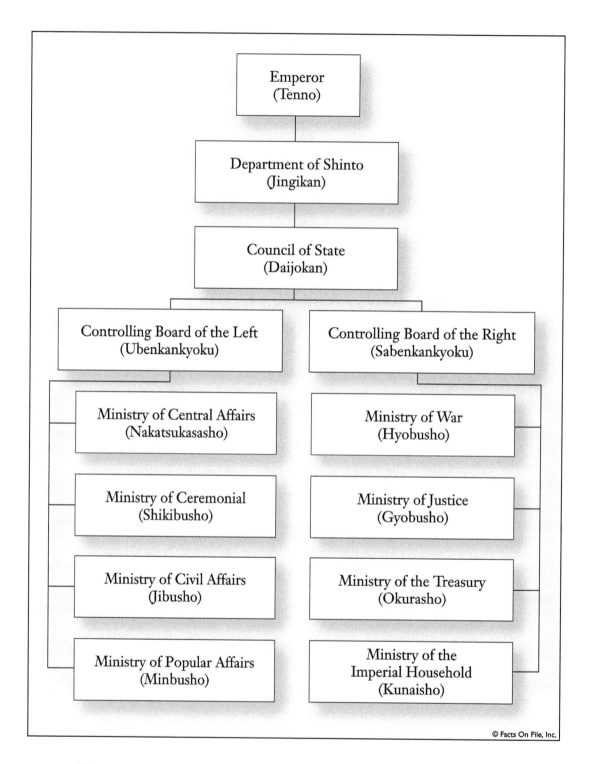

Court Ranks

Ranks for imperial princes and government officials:

IMPERIAL PRINCES

First Order (*ippon*)
Second Order (*nihon*)
Third Order (*sanbon*)
Fourth Order (*shihon*)

PRINCES AND GOVERNMENT OFFICIALS

Senior First Rank (*shoichi-i*)
Junior First Rank (*juichi-i*)
Senior Second Rank (*shoni-i*)
Junior Second Rank (*juni-i*)
Senior Third Rank (*shosan-i*)
Junior Third Rank (*jusan-i*)
Senior Fourth Rank, Upper Grade (*shoshi-ijo*)
Senior Fourth Rank, Lower Grade (*shoshi-ige*)
Junior Fourth Rank, Upper Grade (*jushi-ijo*)
Junior Fourth Rank, Lower Grade (*jushi-ige*)
Senior Fifth Rank, Upper Grade (*shogo-ijo*)
Senior Fifth Rank, Lower Grade (*shogo-ige*)
Junior Fifth Rank, Upper Grade (*jugo-ijo*)
Junior Fifth Rank, Lower Grade (*jugo-ige*)

GOVERNMENT OFFICIALS ONLY

Senior Sixth Rank, Upper Grade (*shoroku-ijo*)
Senior Sixth Rank, Lower Grade (*shoroku-ige*)
Junior Sixth Rank, Upper Grade (*juroku-ijo*)
Junior Sixth Rank, Lower Grade (*juroku-ige*)
Senior Seventh Rank, Upper Grade (*shoshichi-ijo*)
Senior Seventh Rank, Lower Grade (*shoshichi-ige*)
Junior Seventh Rank, Upper Grade (*jushichi-ijo*)
Junior Seventh Rank, Lower Grade (*jushichi-ige*)
Senior Eighth Rank, Upper Grade (*shohachi-ijo*)
Senior Eighth Rank, Lower Grade (*shohachi-ige*)
Junior Eighth Rank, Upper Grade (*juhachi-ijo*)
Junior Eighth Rank, Lower Grade (*juhachi-ige*)
Greater Initial Rank, Upper Grade (*daisho-ijo*)
Greater Initial Rank, Lower Grade (*daisho-ige*)
Lesser Initial Rank, Upper Grade (*shosho-ijo*)
Lesser Initial Rank, Lower Grade (*shosho-ige*)

LIST OF EMPERORS

	Emperor	Birth/Death	Reign Dates
82	Go-Toba	1180–1239	1183–1198
83	Tsuchimikado	1195–1231	1198–1210
84	Juntoku	1197–1242	1210–1221
85	Chukyo	1218–1234	1221
86	Go-Horikawa	1212–1234	1221–1232
87	Shijo	1231–1242	1232–1242
88	Go-Saga	1220–1272	1242–1246
89	Go-Fukakusa	1243–1304	1246–1259
90	Kameyama	1249–1305	1259–1274
91	Go-Uda	1267–1324	1274–1287
92	Fushimi	1265–1317	1287–1298
93	Go-Fushimi	1288–1336	1298–1301
94	Go-Nijo	1285–1308	1301–1308
95	Hanazono	1297–1348	1308–1318
96	Go-Daigo	1288–1339	1318–1339
97	Go-Murakami	1328–1368	1339–1368
98	Chokei	1343–1394	1368–1383
99	Go-Kameyama	1347–1424	1383–1392
100	Go-Komatsu	1377–1433	1392–1412
101	Shoko	1401–1429	1412–1428
102	Go-Hanazono	1419–1470	1428–1464
103	Go-Tsuchimikado	1442–1501	1465–1500
104	Go-Kashiwabara	1464–1527	1500–1526
105	Go-Nara	1496–1558	1526–1557
106	Ogimachi	1517–1593	1557–1586
107	Go-Yozei	1571–1617	1586–1611
108	Go-Mizunoo	1596–1680	1611–1629
109	Meisho (f)	1623–1696	1629–1643
110	Go-Komyo	1633–1655	1643–1654
111	Gosai	1637–1685	1656–1663
112	Reigen	1654–1732	1663–1687
113	Higashiyama	1675–1710	1687–1709
114	Nakamikado	1701–1737	1710–1735
115	Sakuramachi	1720–1750	1735–1747
116	Momozono	1741–1763	1747–1762
117	Go-Sakuramachi	1740–1813	1763–1770
118	Go-Momozono	1758–1780	1770–1779
119	Kokaku	1771–1840	1780–1817
120	Ninko	1800–1846	1817–1846
121	Komei	1831–1866	1846–1866

1	Kogon	1313–1364	r. 1332–1333 (Northern only)
2	Komyo	1321–1380	r. 1333–1348 (Northern only)
3	Suko	1334–1398	r. 1348–1351 (Northern only)
4	Go-Kogon	1338–1374	r. 1352–1371 (Northern only)
5	Go-En'yu	1358–1393	r. 1371–1382 (Northern only)
6	Go-Komatsu	1377–1433	r. 1382–1392 (Northern); r. 1392–1412 (reunified)

STRUCTURE OF THE SHOGUNATES

Kamakura Shogunate

shikken **(shogunal regent)** The office of shogunal regent was held by members of the Hojo family between 1203, when Hojo Tokimasa assumed the title, until the end of the Kamakura period in 1333. Lacking the necessary social rank to hold the title of shogun, it was through the office of *shikken* that the Hojo family was able to run the government behind the scene. As shogunal regents, the Hojo family not only controlled the affairs of state, they eventually came to decide who would be appointed shogun in the first place.

rensho **(cosigner)** The office of *rensho* was established by the shogunal regent Hojo Yasutoki in 1225 as a way to share power and government administration with competing branches of the Hojo family. This position created, in effect, an associate regent. Official documents required the signatures of both the regent and the cosigner.

Hyojoshu (Council of State) The Hyojoshu was established in 1225 by Hojo Yasutoki as a way to share the responsibility for governance. The council included the most important statesmen, warriors, and scholars. Matters were decided by a simple majority vote. It was the highest decision-making body in the Kamakura government.

Kumonjo (Public Documents Office) The Kumonjo was established by Minamoto no Yoritomo in 1184 as the main executive and general administrative office of his government. After the establishment of the Kamakura shogunate, this office was renamed the Mandokoro.

Mandokoro (Administrative Board) Established in 1191 by Minamoto no Yoritomo, the Mandokoro took over the functions of the Kumonjo as the main executive and general administrative office of the Kamakura shogunate. After Hojo family regents assumed real control over the shogunate, they transformed the Mandokoro into an office whose sole responsibility was to oversee the government's finances.

Monchujo (Board of Inquiry) In 1184 Minamoto no Yoritomo established the Monchujo to be responsible for legal matters, especially dealing with lawsuits and appeals. Most cases concerned disputed land rights, but over time they included such things as business matters and loans.

Samurai-dokoro (Board of Retainers) This office was established by Minamoto no Yoritomo in 1180. It functioned as a disciplinary board to regulate the activities of Yoritomo's expanding network of warrior vassals (*gokenin*). Its main responsibility was overseeing the police and the land stewards (*jito*). In the Muromachi period, added duties included security for the capital at Kyoto, and administration of shogunal and other property.

Hikitsukeshu (High Court) The Hikitsuke was established as a judicial court by shogunal regent Hojo Tokiyori in 1249. It was intended to supplement the responsibilities of the Hyojoshu (Council of State). Among the legal issues dealt with by this body were land claims and taxation.

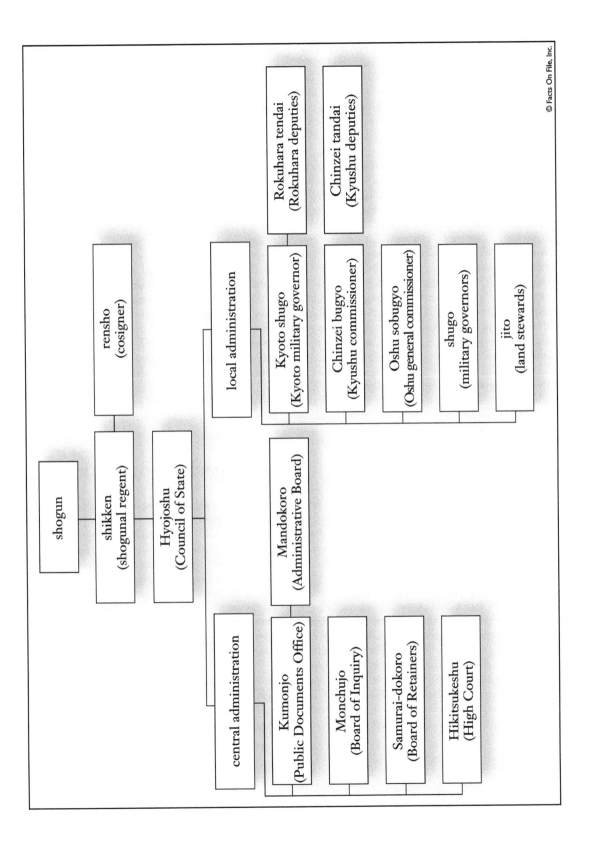

shogun

shikken
(shogunal regent)

rensho
(cosigner)

Hyojoshu
(Council of State)

central administration

Mandokoro
(Administrative Board)

Kumonjo
(Public Documents Office)

Monchujo
(Board of Inquiry)

Samurai-dokoro
(Board of Retainers)

Hikitsukeshu
(High Court)

local administration

Kyoto shugo
(Kyoto military governor)

Chinzei bugyo
(Kyushu commissioner)

Oshu sobugyo
(Oshu general commissioner)

shugo
(military governors)

jito
(land stewards)

Rokuhara tendai
(Rokuhara deputies)

Chinzei tandai
(Kyushu deputies)

© Facts On File, Inc.

Kyoto *shugo* (Kyoto military governor) The position of Kyoto military governor was established at the beginning of the Kamakura shogunate. The governor's role was to oversee the affairs of the imperial court on behalf of the shogunate. This position was replaced by the Rokuhara *tandai* in 1221.

Rokuhara *tandai* (Rokuhara deputies) The office of Rokuhara *tandai* (shogunal deputies located in the Rokuhara district of Kyoto) was established in 1221 to replace the office of Kyoto *shugo* as supervisors of political, military, and legal matters. The Rokuhara *tandai* were responsible not only for overseeing Kyoto, but also affairs in the southwestern part of Japan. This position was created as the direct effect of Emperor Go-Toba's attempt, known as the Jokyu Disturbance, to overthrow the shogunate and reestablish direct imperial rule. After Go-Toba's defeat, the Rokuhara *tandai* was set up in part to ensure that such threats to shogunal power did not occur again.

Chinzei *bugyo* (Kyushu commissioner) This position was established by the Kamakura shogunate. The shogunate appointed two commissioners to oversee local Kyushu matters, especially the activities of Minamoto vassals.

Chinzei *tandai* (Kyushu deputies) Like the Rokuhara *tandai*, the Chinzei *tandai* were overseers of political, military, and legal matters. Their sphere of responsibility was Kyushu. This office was established in 1293 in response to ongoing concerns that the Mongols would make additional attempts to invade Japan through Kyushu ports.

Oshu *sobugyo* (Oshu general commissioner) This office was established by the Kamakura shogunate at the beginning of the medieval period in an area of northeastern Japan known as Oshu (island of Honshu). This region was the domain of a warrior branch of the Fujiwara family known as the Oshu Fujiwara who ruled the area with little intervention from the imperial court during the Heian period. In 1189, Minamoto no Yoritomo, fearing the power of this domain, attacked and conquered the Oshu Fuji-

wara. The position of Oshu general commissioner was founded to manage affairs in this region for the shogunate.

shugo (military governors) The *shugo* rank was established by Minamoto no Yoritomo to maintain control over the provinces. The position became a formal part of the administrative structure of the Kamakura shogunate. Although Yoritomo hand-selected the first *shugo*, this title became hereditary over time. Duties of this office included general police and peacekeeping activities and administrative responsibilities such as investigating crimes and judging legal cases.

jito (land stewards) Land stewards, or *jito*, were officials appointed by the Kamakura shogunate from among its most trusted vassals to serve as estate (*shoen*) supervisors. *Jito* were responsible for overseeing the shogunate's tax interests on these private estates. As such, *jito* handled the collection of taxes and ensured correct distribution. The *jito* system, however, was also a means whereby the Kamakura shogunate could reward its loyal vassals (*gokenin*) for their service to the military government. Over time, *jito* became an inherited office.

Muromachi Shogunate

The Ashikaga shogunate inherited much of the administrative structure of the Kamakura government. Key offices such as the Mandokoro (Administrative Board), Samurai-dokoro (Board of Retainers), and the Monchujo (Board of Inquiry) remained. The following description of individual positions and offices only covers those not already dealt with in the section on the Kamakura administrative structure. The only exception is when a particular office or position underwent significant change in the Muromachi period.

kanrei (shogunal deputy) The office of *kanrei* was instituted by the Ashikaga shogunate. The role of the shogunal deputy was to assist the shogun in administering the warrior government. One important

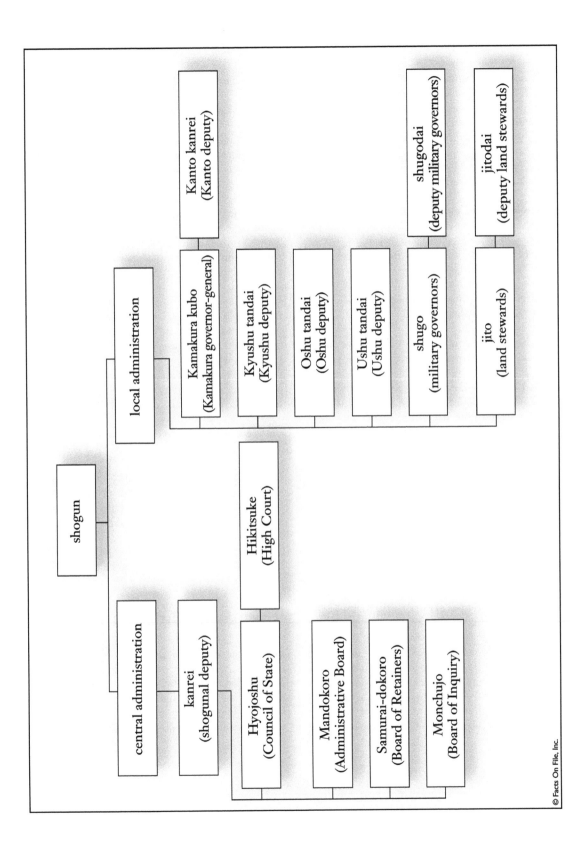

shogun

central administration

kanrei
(shogunal deputy)

Hyojoshu
(Council of State)

Mandokoro
(Administrative Board)

Samurai-dokoro
(Board of Retainers)

Monchujo
(Board of Inquiry)

Hikitsuke
(High Court)

local administration

Kamakura kubo
(Kamakura governor-general)

Kanto kanrei
(Kanto deputy)

Kyushu tandai
(Kyushu deputy)

Oshu tandai
(Oshu deputy)

Ushu tandai
(Ushu deputy)

shugo
(military governors)

shugodai
(deputy military governors)

jito
(land stewards)

jitodai
(deputy land stewards)

responsibility of the *kanrei* was to oversee relations between the shogunate and the *shugo* (military governors). Military governors had grown more powerful by this time and posed a threat to the governing authority of the shogunate. Three warrior families—the Shiba, the Hosokawa, and the Hatakeyama—shared this position on a rotating basis.

Hyojoshu (Council of State) See above under "Kamakura Shogunate."

Hikitsuke (High Court) See above under "Kamakura Shogunate."

Mandokoro (Administrative Board) See above under "Kamakura Shogunate."

Samurai-dokoro (Board of Retainers) See above under "Kamakura Shogunate."

Monchujo (Board of Inquiry) See above under "Kamakura Shogunate." In the Muromachi period, many of the responsibilities formerly carried out by the Monchujo were reassigned to the Mandokoro (Administrative Board), and the Board of Inquiry was reduced to record keeping.

Kamakura *kubo* (Kamakura governor-general) During the Muromachi period, the term *kubo* referred both to Ashikaga shoguns and to their governors-general. The post of Kamakura *kubo* was established in 1336 to monitor the interests of the shogunate in Kamakura and eastern Japan. To this end, the Kamakura *kubo* was responsible for governing affairs in this region. The Kamakura governor-general became a hereditary position within the Ashikaga family.

Kanto *kanrei* (Kanto deputy) The Kanto *kanrei* was a position initiated by the Ashikaga shogunate in 1349. Headquartered in Kyoto, the shogunate needed an overseer in the Kanto region, which included Kamakura. The Kanto deputy fulfilled this role, especially in providing assistance to Kanto area governors-general (Kamakura *kubo*). From the latter half of the 14th century, members of different branches of the Uesugi family held the position of Kanto *kanrei*.

Kyushu *tandai* (Kyushu deputy)

Oshu *tandai* (Oshu deputy)

Ushu *tandai* (Ushu deputy) As part of the Ashikaga shogunates' effort to maintain control over political and military affairs, regional deputies (*tandai*) were appointed in parts of Japan that were deemed strategically important. The Muromachi-period government placed deputies in northwestern Honshu (the Oshu and Ushu *tandai*) and in Kyushu (Kyushu *tandai*). See also "Rokuhara *tandai*" and "Chinzei *tandai*" above under "Kamakura Shogunate."

shugo **(military governors)** See above under "Kamakura Shogunate."

shugodai **(deputy military governors)** The position of *shugodai* existed during the Kamakura period. Up until the Mongol invasions in the latter half of the 13th century, *shugo* infrequently lived in the provinces they were assigned to govern. This responsibility fell to the *shugodai*. In the Muromachi period, the *shugodai* became a more formal part of the shogunate's administrative structure.

jito **(land stewards)** See above under "Kamakura Shogunate."

jitodai **(deputy land stewards)** Within the *jito* system, some shogunal vassals received appointments to oversee multiple estates. When this occurred, deputy land stewards were used to govern these additional regions. This position was significant enough to become a formal part of the Ashikaga shogunate's administrative structure.

Tokugawa Shogunate

tairo **(great elder)** Although the position of *tairo* ranked just below shogun in the Edo period's administrative structure, it was in fact an office rarely filled. When it was assigned, it was often used as a sinecure. One important exception to this pattern was Ii Naosuke (1815–60), who used this position to run the shogunate.

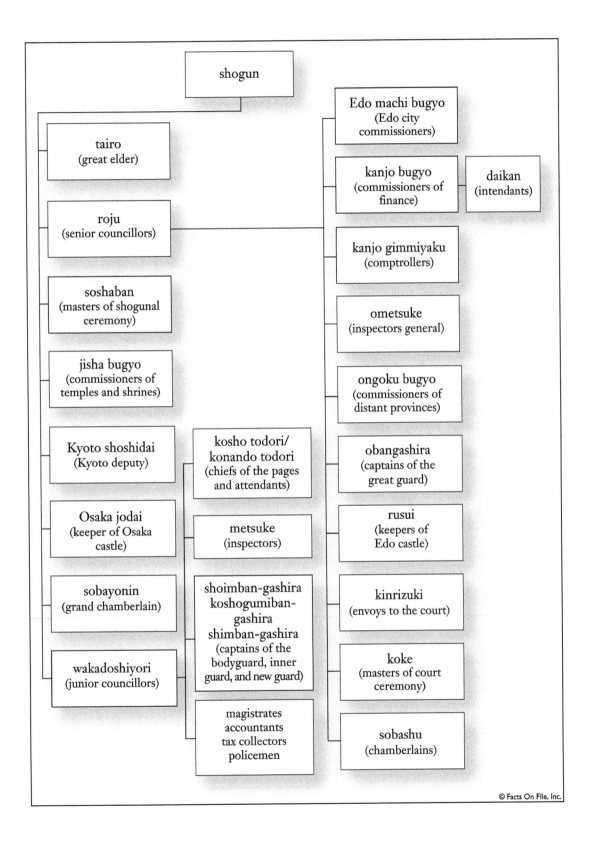

shogun

tairo
(great elder)

roju
(senior councillors)

soshaban
(masters of shogunal ceremony)

jisha bugyo
(commissioners of temples and shrines)

Kyoto shoshidai
(Kyoto deputy)

Osaka jodai
(keeper of Osaka castle)

sobayonin
(grand chamberlain)

wakadoshiyori
(junior councillors)

kosho todori/
konando todori
(chiefs of the pages and attendants)

metsuke
(inspectors)

shoimban-gashira
koshogumiban-
gashira
shimban-gashira
(captains of the bodyguard, inner guard, and new guard)

magistrates
accountants
tax collectors
policemen

Edo machi bugyo
(Edo city commissioners)

kanjo bugyo
(commissioners of finance)

daikan
(intendants)

kanjo gimmiyaku
(comptrollers)

ometsuke
(inspectors general)

ongoku bugyo
(commissioners of distant provinces)

obangashira
(captains of the great guard)

rusui
(keepers of Edo castle)

kinrizuki
(envoys to the court)

koke
(masters of court ceremony)

sobashu
(chamberlains)

roju (senior councillors) *Roju* were senior officials of the Tokugawa shogunate who watched over the entire government structure and the functioning of its many offices. In short, they administered the affairs of state, both domestic and foreign, for the shogunate. Senior councillors—usually four or five in number—were appointed from among the fudai (hereditary vassals) daimyo.

Edo *machi bugyo* (Edo city commissioners) Edo *machi bugyo* were shogunal officials charged with overseeing matters of city life concerning the *chonin* (townspeople and merchants). Edo city commissioners were selected from among those of *hatamoto* ("bannerman": direct samurai retainers of the shogunate) rank.

kanjo bugyo (commissioners of finance) Commissioners of finance served the shogunate as officials accountable for financial matters. *Kanjo bugyo* reported directly to the senior councillors (*roju*). These commissioners—usually only four in number but overseeing a large number of assistants—were appointed from those of *hatamoto* rank.

daikan (intendants) Although the office of *daikan* existed prior to the Edo period, it became a formal part of the Tokugawa shogunate's administrative structure. These local government officials supervised and managed the shogunate's personal landholdings (*tenryo*).

kanjo gimmiyaku (comptrollers) This office, created in 1682, was charged with investigating, and otherwise overseeing, the operations of the *kanjo bugyo* (commissioners of finance). Although comptrollers were structurally lower than the commissioners of finance, they functioned as a control over the higher office's activities. *Kanjo gimmiyaku* reported to the senior councillors (*roju*).

ometsuke (inspectors general) This office originated in 1632 when the third shogun, Tokugawa Iemitsu, appointed four people of *hatamoto* (bannerman) rank to oversee activities and places of potential trouble to the shogunate. Those who served as *ometsuke* were often senior officials with extensive government service. Among the areas of concern

scrutinized by the *ometsuke* were the road system, daimyo activities, and groups troublesome to the shogunate such as Christian missionaries and their Japanese followers. Inspectors general reported to the senior councillors (*roju*).

ongoku bugyo (commissioners of distant provinces) The post of *ongoku bugyo* was similar in duty to the Edo *machi bugyo* (Edo city commissioners; see above) except that these commissioners served in localities other than Edo, including Kyoto and Osaka. Like the Edo *machi bugyo*, they were selected from among families of *hatamoto* (bannerman) rank. See above under "Edo *machi bugyo*."

obangashira (captains of the great guard) Captains of the Great Guard were responsible for security at the three castles—at Edo, Kyoto, and Osaka—associated with the shogunate

rusui (keepers of Edo Castle) The *rusui* primarily supervised and when necessary, defended Edo Castle. Their post was analogous to that of *jodai* (castellan).

kinrizuki (envoys to the court) The *kinrizuki* served as imperial palace inspectors.

koke (masters of court ceremony) Literally, "elevated families," *koke* were hereditary government officials responsible for carrying out official ceremonies and rituals for the shogunate. In addition, masters of court ceremony were used as shogunal representatives at court, temple, and shrine functions.

sobashu (chamberlains) The office of *sobashu* was established in 1653 by the fourth shogun, Tokugawa Ietsuna. Chamberlains were in direct service to the shoguns and, bureaucratically, reported to the *roju*.

soshaban (masters of shogunal ceremony) Masters of shogunal ceremony were protocol officials who reported directly to the shogun. The 20-some *soshaban* were responsible for such tasks as keeping the shogun's schedule and organizing shogunal ceremonies.

3.1 Example of an Edo-period local government building (jinya) (Photo William E. Deal)

jisha bugyo (**commissioners of temples and shrines**) Temple and shrine commissioners, usually four in number, supervised temple and shrine affairs, including matters involving religious hierarchies and the landholdings of these institutions. Among other responsibilities, they also held subsidiary duties involving legal matters in regions outside of the Edo area.

Kyoto *shoshidai* (**Kyoto deputy**) The post of Kyoto deputy was first established by Oda Nobunaga and Toyotomi Hideyoshi, during the Azuchi-Momoyama period, to oversee the affairs of Kyoto, especially the activities of the imperial court and nearby territories. This office became formalized within the administrative structure of the Tokugawa shogunate.

Osaka *jodai* (**keeper of Osaka Castle**) The Osaka *jodai*, or keeper of Osaka Castle, was the senior military officer in central Japan. As the primary administrator in the region, the Osaka *jodai* maintained the military strength of Osaka Castle. During the Edo period, *jodai*, including the Osaka *jodai*, served as the proxy of the Tokugawa shogun in commanding the respective castle. This rank was reserved for middle-ranking daimyo, and holders of this rank were frequently promoted to posts of Kyoto deputy (Kyoto *shoshidai*) and senior councillor (*roju*).

sobayonin (**grand chamberlain**) The grand chamberlain was responsible for transmitting messages between the Tokugawa shogun and the *roju*, the shogun's senior councillors. This position was created in 1681.

wakadoshiyori (**junior councillors**) Junior councillors, or "young elders" assisted the *roju* and surveyed the *hatamoto* and *gokenin*. Additionally, they supervised artisans, artists, physicians, palace guards, and construction work. In case of a war, the *wakadoshiyori* led the *hatamoto* into battle. The position was created in 1633 and chosen from the fudai daimyo.

kosho todori/konando todori (**chiefs of the pages and attendants**) *Kosho todori/konando todori* served as the chiefs of shogunal pages and attendants.

metsuke (**inspectors**) *Metsuke* performed police and enforcement duties at numerous levels. Not only did they serve as high-level spies for their military rulers, but they also evaluated other shogunal officials and staff as well.

shoimban-gashira (**captains of the bodyguard**), *koshogumiban-gashira* (**captains of the inner guard**), *shimban-gashira* (**captains of the new guard**) The various bodyguards operated under the command of the junior councillors during war.

List of Shoguns and Regents

KAMAKURA SHOGUNS

Shogun	Birth/ Death	Held Office
1. Minamoto Yoritomo	1147–1199	1192–1199
2. Minamoto Yoriie	1182–1204	1202–1203
3. Minamoto Sanetomo	1192–1219	1203–1219
4. Fujiwara (Kujo) Yoritsune	1218–1256	1226–1244
5. Fujiwara (Kujo) Yoritsugu	1239–1256	1244–1252

	Birth/ Death	Held Office
6. Prince Munetaka	1242–1274	1252–1266
7. Prince Koreyasu	1264–1326	1266–1289
8. Prince Hisaakira	1276–1328	1289–1308
9. Prince Morikuni	1301–1333	1308–1333

HOJO SHOGUNAL REGENTS (*SHIKKEN*)

Regent	Birth/ Death	Held Office
1. Hojo Tokimasa	1138–1215	1203–1205
2. Hojo Yoshitoki	1163–1224	1205–1224
3. Hojo Yasutoki	1183–1242	1224–1242
4. Hojo Tsunetoki	1224–1246	1242–1246
5. Hojo Tokiyori	1227–1263	1246–1256
6. Hojo Nagatoki	1229–1264	1256–1264
7. Hojo Masamura	1205–1273	1264–1268
8. Hojo Tokimune	1251–1284	1268–1284
9. Hojo Sadatoki	1271–1311	1284–1301
10. Hojo Morotoki	1275–1311	1301–1311
11. Hojo Munenobu	d. 1312	1311–1312
12. Hojo Hirotoki	1233–1315	1312–1315
13. Hojo Mototoki	d. 1333	1315–1316
14. Hojo Takatoki	1303–1333	1316–1326
15. Hojo Sadaakira	d. 1333	1326
16. Hojo Moritoki	1295–1333	1326–1333

MUROMACHI SHOGUNS

Shogun	Birth/ Death	Held Office
1. Ashikaga Takauji	1305–1358	1338–1358
2. Ashikaga Yoshiakira	1330–1367	1358–1367
3. Ashikaga Yoshimitsu	1358–1408	1368–1394
4. Ashikaga Yoshimochi	1386–1428	1394–1423
5. Ashikaga Yoshikazu	1407–1425	1423–1425
6. Ashikaga Yoshinori	1394–1441	1429–1441
7. Ashikaga Yoshikatsu	1434–1443	1442–1443
8. Ashikaga Yoshimasa	1436–1490	1449–1473

Shogun		
9. Ashikaga Yoshihisa	1465–1489	1473–1489
10. Ashikaga Yoshitane	1466–1523	1490–1493 and 1508–1521
11. Ashikaga Yoshizumi	1480–1511	1494–1508
12. Ashikaga Yoshiharu	1511–1550	1521–1546
13. Ashikaga Yoshiteru	1536–1565	1546–1565
14. Ashikaga Yoshihide	1538–1568	1568
15. Ashikaga Yoshiaki	1537–1597	1568–1573

EDO SHOGUNS

Shogun	Birth/ Death	Held Office
1. Tokugawa Ieyasu	1542–1616	1603–1605
2. Tokugawa Hidetada	1570–1623	1605–1623
3. Tokugawa Iemitsu	1604–1651	1623–1651
4. Tokugawa Ietsuna	1641–1680	1651–1680
5. Tokugawa Tsunayoshi	1646–1709	1680–1709
6. Tokugawa Ienobu	1633–1712	1709–1712
7. Tokugawa Ietsugu	1709–1716	1713–1716
8. Tokugawa Yoshimune	1684–1751	1716–1745
9. Tokugawa Ieshige	1711–1761	1745–1760
10. Tokugawa Ieharu	1737–1786	1760–1786
11. Tokugawa Ienari	1772–1841	1787–1837
12. Tokugawa Ieyoshi	1793–1853	1837–1853
13. Tokugawa Iesada	1824–1858	1853–1858
14. Tokugawa Iemochi	1846–1866	1858–1866
15. Tokugawa Yoshinobu	1837–1913	1866–1867

LAW, CRIME, AND PUNISHMENT

Pre-Kamakura Shogunate

Prior to the establishment of the Kamakura shogunate, Japan's legal system existed mostly to define positions and behaviors within the court aristocracy (*kugeho*). As far as the common person was con-

cerned, regulations were both loosely defined and enforced by local landowners, and these laws were largely pieced together from a combination of religious codes and regulations adopted from the Chinese system. Hardly a comprehensive national legal system, the pre-Kamakura legal codes were developed locally by estate owners for those working the land, military commanders for the soldiers under them, religious leaders for lesser clergy, and high-ranking domain officials for their deputies. The penalties for violating these codes were also micromanaged and set by the whim of the superior. They included both corporal and capital forms of punishment, and were informed by Confucian ideals aimed not only to punish, but also to change the criminal's heart leading to personal betterment even if, as in the case of a death sentence, that betterment meant improvement in the next life.

Kamakura Shogunate

With the rise of the warrior class and the unification of Japan under the Kamakura shogunate, the Japanese legal system acquired the form of the traditional samurai code of ethics focused on maintenance of the hierarchy and familial honor and obligation. Thus most of the early laws set forth by the shogunate were aimed at solidifying the power of the ruling class by delineating the privileges of the samurai warlords and the obligations of their vassals. This warrior-class law, known as *bukeho*, was quickly disseminated throughout the land. By the start of the Muromachi shogunate, most of the values and obligations of the samurai had been internalized by the populace.

The first official codification of the warrior-class laws, called the Joei Shikimoku, was issued in 1232 by the Kamakura shogunate, and it would set the tone for all the edicts issued by the military government for essentially the next 700 years. This code served to clearly define the roles of samurai lords and their vassals and was based on a combination of many of the local legal codes that antedated the shogunate. Thus, it was the first centralized national legal code compiled from all of the minor regulations that had been in existence on local estates, in military regi-

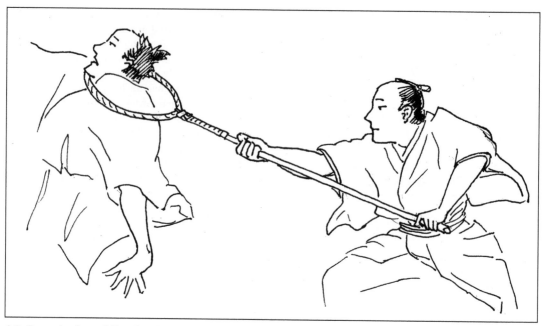

3.2 *Example of an* uchikomi, *a device used to apprehend a criminal or criminal suspect* (Illustration Grace Vibbert)

mens, in monasteries, and in regional government offices. The last, and most important, function of this new law code was to clarify the now limited authority of the imperial court at Kyoto from which the warrior class had assumed power.

Muromachi Shogunate

This first legal code remained relatively unchanged throughout the Kamakura reign with only a few amendments made in the form of supplementary edicts called *tsuika*. It was the primary national legal code of this period. After assuming power from the Kamakura government, the Ashikaga family of Muromachi shoguns continued to support legislation delineated in the Joei Shikimoku, considering their own edicts to be merely supplemental to the primacy of the original code. With the consultation

of a board of scholars and advisers, Ashikaga Takauji included the major addition made by the Muromachi in 1336. This supplemental edict, the Kemmu Shikimoku, was based on a seventh-century constitution written by Prince Shotoku and consisted of 17 articles dealing with the attitudes and behaviors expected of the warrior class. These items dealt with issues ranging from personal habits to the attention a ruler should pay the courtiers and peasants.

Another major contribution of the Muromachi period to the legal structure of Japan was the development of principles of group responsibility known as *renza* and *enza*. In accordance with these values, blame was not simply assigned to the guilty individual when a crime was committed, but it was also assigned to that individual's family and perhaps the larger community of which he was a part. Members of those groups associated with the criminal would often be subject to as severe a penalty as the one who had committed the crime. Accordingly communities

3.3 Example of shujinkago, *a bamboo basket used to transport criminals during the Edo period* (Photo William E. Deal)

were encouraged to restrain rebellious individuals before they aroused the attention of the government authorities. Legal disputes were discouraged with the promotion of the *kenka ryoseibai* policy, which stated that the factions on either side of any argument were to be held equally accountable for the disagreement. Thus, if a fight over land rights arose between two neighboring lords and they could not reach an agreement themselves, the state would confiscate both of their lands.

As the 15th century began, disputes over shogunal succession leading to the Onin War caused a destabilization within the Muromachi government resulting in a decentralization of power starting as early as the 1460s. As the governmental structure fell into disarray, the legal system again became fragmented as local daimyo rose to power, enacting individual laws for their personal domains. These domainal codes, known as *bunkokuho*, were still largely based upon the once universal laws set forth by the Kamakura and Muromachi shoguns with some additions made that were taken from the traditions of the individual daimyo family. These codes strictly defined the role of vassals, and the power of the lords to control the activities of those living and working on their lands. Regulations were also set forth that stringently prohibited the cultivation of lands by commoners without the approval of the lord, and travel into or out of the domain was also heavily restricted.

Azuchi-Momoyama Period

The regional laws set forth by the increasingly powerful daimyo continued to make up the primary form of legal structure after the Muromachi shogunate officially collapsed and the Azuchi-Momoyama period began. However, Japan as a nation was very unstable during this period, and domains changed hands often, making it hard to enforce any one legal code for very long. Thus, land rights were often abused and much criminal activity went unpunished. Still, honor was very important to even the most unruly samurai, and, at least among the warrior class, infractions of the traditional *bushi* code of ethics were dealt with swiftly within bands of samurai in the course of fighting the many skirmishes that broke out between competing daimyo.

This long period of chaos that consumed much of the 15th and 16th centuries in Japan came to a close when Tokugawa Ieyasu united the country in the early 17th century, reestablishing shogunal rule and ushering in one of the longest periods of national stability. With the newly centralized government came a new national code of laws, which quickly became more structured and sophisticated as Japanese society moved into a time of peace and prosperity. The Edo period brought many changes in class structure especially for the warrior class as they put down their swords and armor and assumed the bureaucratic duties of the peacetime ruler, and the laws set forth by the Tokugawa shoguns were aimed at clearly defining class groups and further empowering the ruling ranks.

Edo Period

The division between lord and vassal that had blurred during the period of civil war that preceded the Edo period was already becoming clearer under the leadership of Toyotomi Hideyoshi, who conducted the first sword hunt in 1588. The goal of these sword hunts was to disarm the populace living in the countryside, thus thwarting the possibility of rebellion. These actions were largely successful, and by the start of the Edo period swords were only carried by the military aristocracy and were worn as a symbol of elite status. The Tokugawa also created a new set of laws for the military houses that was reminiscent of the code put forth by the Kamakura shogunate. Known as the Buke Shohatto, these laws served to tighten the shogunate's control over conquered daimyo and were intended to structure the Edo social hierarchy in a way that conformed to the Confucian ideals for the perfect society. This initial set of laws proved very successful as it became solidly woven into the fabric of the Japanese ethos by the mid-1700s.

The shogunate continued to consolidate its power by issuing a series of laws limiting the privileges of the imperial court and the nobility as well as a legal code regulating the activity of religious institutions. The emperor and his court were ordered to concern themselves only with cultural and scholarly affairs, leaving the political responsibilities to the shogun, and religious organizations were carefully monitored to make sure that they were not breeding attitudes of dissension toward the government. One final measure that the Tokugawa shogunate took to solidify its power early in the Edo period was to require alternate-year attendance from its daimyo. This meant that each daimyo was required to move his family to the capital city and himself to alternate years in residence at Edo and at his domain governing his vassals. The daimyo was to leave his family hostage in the hands of the shogunate in Edo during the years he spent living in his domain as a sign of his loyalty to the shogun.

As the Edo period progressed, Japan felt increasing pressure from foreign powers to open its borders to allow trade of both goods and ideas. This intrusion threatened to compromise the power of the very stable Tokugawa rule, and thus was resisted by a concerted effort on the part of the government to eradicate all outside influences. This policy was known as national seclusion or *sakoku* and included laws restricting travel into or out of the country, prohibiting the actions of Christian missionaries who had been in Japan since the early 1500s, banning the importation of scientific books and other materials from Europe, and calling for the deportation of all foreign-born peoples or people born to foreign parents. Nearly all of these regulations were covered in the first 17-article *sakoku* legal code issued in 1633. Other *sakoku* edicts were aimed mostly at eradicating the presence of Christianity in Japan and included the religious inquisition *(shumon aratame)* of the mid-1600s and the anti-Christian edicts *(kinkyorei)* issued as early as the late 16th century.

The cultivation of farmlands was also an important legal matter in Edo-period Japan, and the Tokugawa shoguns issued a number of edicts regulating the use of farmland and the taxation of crop yields. Occasionally, religiously inspired laws were passed at the whim of the shogun like the edicts on compassion for living things passed by Tokugawa Tsunayoshi in 1685 in response to the guilt he felt over the death of his son. Toward the end of the 18th century, a set of legal provisions was created to aid local officials in determining the appropriate punishments for the legal infractions made by commoners. These legal codes included the establishment of labor camps called *ninsoku yoseba*, which served as early forms of prisons to house criminals as well as homeless beggars and drifters. Finally, as the shogunate began to deteriorate in the years leading up to the Meiji Restoration, a series of reforms was issued to restore the financial solvency of the government and to ameliorate class tensions that had developed after years of strict maintenance of the social structure. Thus, the Kyoho, Kansei, and Tempo reforms included laws establishing new taxes for the daimyo, providing relief for the famine-stricken peasant class, and discouraging the self-indulgent tendencies of the aristocratic ruling class.

In the end, the highly developed Tokugawa legal system was not enough to maintain order within the shogunate and hold the country together. Foreign traders and diplomats forced their way into Japan's harbors, starting with Commodore Perry in 1853, leaving the country fiercely divided over how to respond to this sudden interaction with the outside world. Still, the successes of many Tokugawa legal developments did not go unnoticed as much of Edo policy was adopted by the Meiji leaders and formed the foundation of Japan's modern legal system.

READING

Imperial and Military Rule

Jansen 2000; Totman 2000; Totman 1993; Hall and Mass (eds.) 1974; Yamamura (ed.) 1990; Hall (ed.) 1991; Jansen (ed.) 1989; Arnesen 1979; Beasley 1999; Bolitho 1974; Grossberg 1981; Hall and Jansen (eds.) 1968; Hall, Nagahara, and Yamamura (eds.) 1981; Mass 1974; Mass 1979; Mass (ed.) 1982; Totman 1967

Law, Crime, and Punishment

Frédéric 1972, 65–68: justice and punishment in the medieval period; Henderson and Anderson 1974, 576–579: Edo law

4

SOCIETY AND ECONOMY

ing Japanese society and economy through-
the medieval and early modern periods rep-
complex task. First, as in any culture over
variety of social and economic changes—
or and minor—occurred that reshaped the
ontours of social and economic development. In this survey of medieval and early modern
Japan, space prevents a detailed explication of all the
nuances of social and economic phenomena. Second, the dearth of sources from the medieval era in
particular requires that characterization of feudal
socioeconomic conditions in Japan be tenuous at
times. Even extant sources offer only a singular perspective due to the generally high social and economic status of the record keepers themselves.
Surviving sources typically represent the perspective
of elite members of medieval and early modern
Japanese society—warriors, aristocrats, and monastics. By the middle and later years of the Edo period,
however, significantly more information survives,
representing a wider range of sources and social
groups than during the medieval period.

This inquiry begins with the structures of Japanese society in the medieval and early modern periods
and then considers major economic arrangements.
In this time period, social class and occupational
group were generally interdependent. The terms for
the various social groups—such as warriors, farmers,
and merchants—are also indicators of the economic
function and social status of members of these
groups. By the Edo period, an ideal social hierarchy
had been fully articulated by the Tokugawa shogunate. This system transformed long-established
connections between economic contributions and
social rank into a formal social hierarchy that had
both behavioral and material implications. For
instance, farmers were considered socially superior
to merchants. The government-mandated social
system placed greater value on farming and agriculture than on commercial ventures. Yet this was the
ideal—the reality was that actual social influence and
economic wealth often worked in ways contrary to
this social scheme. Thus, for instance, farmers often
experienced poverty and social isolation, especially
as Edo economic conditions shifted toward an
urban, consumer-oriented culture. In this environment, merchants became increasingly wealthy
despite their officially inferior status.

SOCIETY

Prior to the start of the medieval period, aristocrats
were the center of Japanese society. As the ruling
class, as well as the landowners, the aristocracy
determined most social and cultural norms. Other
social classes—such as farmers and warriors—were
dominated by aristocratic influence to the extent
that records detailing their activities are almost
entirely nonexistent or have survived as peripheral
information in the background of aristocratic
sources. With the rise of the warrior class in the
medieval period, this situation shifts dramatically.
Along with more information about warriors, farmers and merchants with whom the military class
interacted—sometimes closely—also become more
visible in records by the end of the medieval period.

Despite the selective nature of available historical
sources, the evidence suggests that at least some
conditions remained relatively constant throughout
the medieval and early modern periods. For
instance, the warrior class maintained political control and enforced a strict system of social stratifica-
tion for this span of nearly 700 years. Yet, change is
inevitable and certain elements of Japanese society
and economic structure remained beyond the full
control of samurai rulers, particularly as the Tokugawa shogunate inadvertently fostered an inversion
of the idealized social order they formally required.
Merchants, for example, were at the bottom of the
Edo-period four-tiered social structure. However, as
samurai families patronized merchants while serving
required periods of attendance upon the shogun in
the capital, Edo, these flourishing entrepreneurs
gained respectability as their fortunes outgrew their
traditionally low social rank.

Further, besides the social hierarchies that
existed between classes, there were also significant
hierarchies that existed within particular social
classes. For example, warriors of the Edo period
were hierarchically superior to all other social
classes, but within the warrior class itself there was
also a status hierarchy. Distinctions were made
between such warriors as foot soldiers whose power
and authority differed greatly from that of warriors
who served as regional agents of the shogunate.

Aside from temporal and regional variations in both arrangement and nomenclature, feudal Japanese social structure incorporated the following basic class distinctions in ever-changing relationships: warriors, aristocrats, Shinto and Buddhist clergy, farmers and peasants, artisans, merchants, and outcastes. Notably, membership in one class did not necessarily preclude associations with another class. For instance, Buddhist monastics could have either aristocratic or peasant origins. As with other aspects of feudal experience, identifying such individuals with a particular social group—and that group's related behaviors and values—could prove problematic. In the following sections, medieval and early modern Japanese society is addressed in terms of its overall structure, the status of women, and forms of social protest.

Medieval Society

Medieval society was shaped largely by the emerging power and status of warriors who resided in the provinces. The Kamakura military government, first established by Minamoto no Yoritomo, set this social transformation in motion. While warriors did not supplant the role and social position of the emperor and aristocrats, upper-echelon warriors accumulated significant prestige and authority, with the effect that warrior interests and values became central to Japanese social structure. Medieval aristocrats, residing in Kyoto, maintained their privileged status and connections to the imperial family, but for the most part real power had passed to the warrior class. Aristocrats continued to pursue the arts, such as literature, and were purveyors of aesthetic taste. By the end of the Kamakura period, as aristocratic estates (*shoen*) were incorporated into the landholdings of regional warriors, aristocrats lost their economic base. Without a source of tax revenues and other tribute, some aristocrats were forced to earn a living by teaching aristocratic aesthetics and etiquette to warriors who were stationed in Kyoto.

One key feature of warrior-dominated society that remained figural until the end of the Edo period was the system of vassalage and vertical relationships between lords and retainers. As in other feudal cultures, the relationship and reciprocal obligations of the lord and retainer (also called vassal) had a powerful effect on Kamakura social ideals and norms. (For more information on the lord-retainer relationship especially as it affected warriors, see chapter 5: Warriors and Warfare.)

Warriors were caught up in a network of lord-retainer relationships. This hierarchy was characteristic of warrior society throughout the medieval and early modern periods. Warrior values took on increasing importance for the larger society as the centuries progressed. The periods of intense civil war that marked much of the medieval period also had a significant impact on social arrangements and the often fleeting alliances between lords, their vassals, and the farmers and peasants who worked the land.

One of the problems with trying to describe medieval society is that there was not a rigid nomenclature used to describe the different social strata. Similarly, the rights and relationships between different social classes, as for instance between landowners and peasants who worked the fields, was not fixed, so there could be a great deal of difference between domains. The nature of social interactions was as much a product of the particular relationships forged between individual landowners and peasants as it was a product of a legal recognition of social classes. Finally, there were also local variations in social organization that preclude the possibility of describing medieval society in singular terms.

WARRIORS

The most significant aspect of medieval and early modern Japanese society was its domination by the warrior class. In general, warriors were referred to by the terms *bushi* ("warrior men") or *samurai*. Although warriors began to emerge as a significant social power in the late Heian period, it was not until the Kamakura period and the establishment of military rule that samurai rapidly ascended to the top of the social hierarchy in terms of rights and political authority.

The warrior class included people from a range of both aristocratic and commoner social-class origins. For instance, while many of Minamoto no Yoritomo's followers were commoners from provincial areas of eastern Japan—far removed from the aristocratic culture of Kyoto—Yoritomo was himself descended from the imperial family. Leadership in the warrior hierarchy typically fell upon those descended from Kyoto families with at least a mid-level rank in the political or military bureaucracy, for instance those who served in the provinces as estate (*shoen*) managers and provincial governors (*shugo*). The strictly observed hierarchy of the Kamakura-period warrior class consisted of three main classes: *gokenin* (literally, "housemen"), samurai, and *zusa*.

Gokenin At the top of the warrior-class hierarchy were the *gokenin*, or shogunal vassals (also frequently termed "retainers" in English), the highest ranked and most loyal of the Kamakura shogunate's supporters. These were the direct vassals to the shogunate in both the medieval and early modern periods. There were relatively few people situated at the *gokenin* level—around 2,000 warriors—but vassals themselves also were served by subvassals loyal to their lord, and by extension, to the shogun. The *gokenin* were expected to provide military and financial support to the shogunate. Not surprisingly, *gokenin* enjoyed special privileges in return, such as land ownership and bureaucratic appointments, granted by the shogunate. For instance, the shogunate chose estate stewards (*jito*) and military governors (*shugo*) from among the *gokenin*. In the Muromachi period, besides direct vassals to the shogun, there arose vassals who also served the military governors.

Samurai Below *gokenin* was the samurai class. Although we tend now to think of the term *samurai* (literally, "one who serves") as a generic term for warrior, during the Kamakura period samurai referred to a specific social ranking. Samurai, though less powerful than *gokenin*, also commanded subvassals who were loyal to them. Like *gokenin*, samurai were cavalry soldiers.

Zusa Foot soldiers, or *zusa*, constituted the lowest of the three levels of the Kamakura warrior class. They became increasingly important during the transition from the Kamakura to the Muromachi period when warfare became more and more common in the struggle for political power between competing warrior factions.

The majority of warriors resided in villages and tended to their landholdings. They also trained and otherwise stayed prepared for the eventuality of being called into battle by their lords.

The warfare and civil strife that began during the Muromachi period also reflected the breakdown in lord-vassal relations. The loyalty that vassals displayed toward their lord was not infrequently discarded in favor of new alliances based on the shifting fortunes of local warriors. In short, loyalty was sometimes jettisoned for opportunities to enhance personal power and wealth. It was partly a result of this shift in social relations that the warrior class known as daimyo developed in the Muromachi period. Daimyo, or feudal lords, were able to establish regional centers of power on territories they came to control through warfare and strategic alliances. It was from among the ranks of the daimyo that Oda Nobunaga, Toyotomi Hideyoshi, and Tokugawa Ieyasu emerged to unify Japan in the latter half of the 16th century.

FARMERS AND PEASANTS

In the medieval period, farmers and peasants (known collectively as *hyakusho*) were free to work on either public land or on estates. In either arrangement, they paid land tax to the government or to estate authorities. As a social class, farmers and peasants were situated between warriors and aristocrats and lower-class peasants (*genin*). The living conditions and social freedoms of farmers and peasants varied depending on the particular land or estate they were associated with and the quality of the relationship they had to landowners or their proprietors.

In the medieval period, it was typically the case that peasants and farmers worked the land of their samurai lord and paid rent in the form of some percentage of their yearly harvest. In some areas of Japan—in the area of Kyoto, for instance—peasants and farmers sometimes attained at least some degree of local autonomy. This was particularly the case as the agricultural and crafts products produced by peasants and farmers became an increasingly important part of the Japanese economy. Such commerce resulted in the increased status of farmers and peasants. This increased status was further heightened on occasions when farmers and peasants created federations to protect their local villages and communities from warfare and in order to deal with communal issues such as field irrigation. Such federations usually came into being as the result of uprisings against absentee control of land. These federations were structured so that a village head was chosen to oversee federation issues, including rules for the maintenance of community harmony. Control over farmers and peasants was further weakened during the Warring States period when the resources for local control by lords were diverted to matters of civil war.

Myoshu Within the class of farmers and peasants, there also existed status differences. The most powerful farmers and peasants were known as *myoshu*. They were local landholders who usually lived on estates (*shoen*). The proprietor of the estate collected tax from the *myoshu*. These powerful independent peasants were chosen by the estate proprietor to serve in this capacity. Besides paying tax, these peasants were given the right to income from the lands they controlled.

Genin Subordinate farmers (*genin*; literally, "inferior people") worked land for the independent farmers or for other domain officials and had neither rights to independent land management nor freedom of movement. They could also be bought and sold, and were usually included in matters of estate inheritance. Despite this very lowly status, subordinate farmers were usually treated as members of the extended family that controlled or owned the land. The social status of subordinate farmers began to change in the late Muromachi period when they gained land rights as tenant farmers.

Warrior-Farmers Another distinction within the peasant-farmer class was the warrior-farmer. Socially, warrior-farmers occupied a position between independent farmers and lesser peasants. One indicator of the heightened position of warrior-farmers over other peasants was that the former were allowed to use surnames.

In the medieval period, it was possible in certain instances for farmers and peasants to ascend the social hierarchy. The opportunity to do this was usually occasioned by the chaotic social conditions produced by the century of civil war that marked the Warring States period. During this time, farmers and peasants were sometimes used by lords as foot soldiers in their armies. Those who were particularly adept at the martial arts were able to become samurai. The exemplar of this medieval social mobility was Toyotomi Hideyoshi who went from peasant to military ruler of Japan. Once the Tokugawa shogunate established and enforced the rigid social structure that characterized society in the Edo period, opportunities for social mobility were much more limited.

OUTCASTES

In the medieval period, there was a social class below that of peasant. These were the outcastes, usually known by the term *eta* (hereditary outcaste) or *hinin* (literally, "nonhuman;" outcaste by occupation or social status). These terms were used without clear distinction between them during the medieval period—it was only in the Edo period that a sharp differentiation was asserted by the shogunate (see the subheading "Outcastes" under "Early Modern Society" below). *Eta* were especially associated with tasks requiring the disposal or treatment of animals and animal hides, such as butchering or tanning. Further, the religious impurity and defilement associated with *eta* by virtue of their occupation was considered to be contagious to those who might come in contact with them. Thus, strict segregation from *eta* was often practiced. References to *eta* date back to Kamakura-period records. By contrast, *hinin* were usually outcastes as a result of some social transgression, such as committing a crime, or who were engaged in activities deemed outside of proper social roles, such as actors and performers.

Early Modern Society

Unlike medieval society, early modern social structure was, at least in the ideal, far more rigidly drawn. The ideal of a fourfold hierarchical social class—in descending order, warriors, farmers, artisans, and merchants—was a social vision borrowed from Confucian philosophy. This perspective was set in motion in Japan in 1591 when Toyotomi Hideyoshi issued a decree prohibiting movement between these four social classes. This social class division remained in effect throughout the Edo period, but the regulation of these social classes in practice was always somewhat different than the ideal would suggest.

From the perspective of the ideal society, the Tokugawa shogunate articulated a rigid fourfold social hierarchy based on notions derived from Neo-Confucian moral philosophy. This was intended, in part, to organize society in accord with the productive value of each social class to the larger society. The so-called *shi-no-ko-sho* structure—warrior (*shi*), farmer (*no*), artisan (*ko*), and merchant (*sho*)—was viewed as the ideal arrangement of society that produced order and harmony. The warrior class was the head of the hierarchy because of the warriors' role as government administrators. Farmers followed next because of the importance of their work in nourishing and sustaining the nation. Artisans comprised the next most valuable group because they were responsible for manufacturing items of utilitarian worth. Merchants followed last. They were little esteemed by the Neo-Confucian value system that animated the social hierarchy because they were viewed as producing nothing yet making a profit off the labor of others. Finally, there were groups of people who were not placed within this system, including aristocrats, monastics, and outcastes.

This system remained in place until the beginning of the Meiji period when it was abolished. According to estimates, the population at the end of the Edo period was approximately 30 million people. Of these, the samurai class made up about 6.5 percent, farmers, artisans, and merchants collectively accounted for 90.5 percent, outcastes groups numbered 1.75 percent, and some 1.25 percent consisted of such people as aristocrats and monastics. Throughout the Edo period, each social group was subject to different legal, political, criminal, and other rules and regulations.

The ideal configuration of early modern Japanese society, however, constantly, and in a variety of ways, bumped up against the actual social lives of people. For instance, from the perspective of the samurai class, one was either a samurai or a non-samurai. The term *chonin*, "townsperson," was often used to collectively describe artisans and merchants residing in cities. Moreover, the four-class-system did not account for aristocrats, monastics, and outcastes. In these and other ways, the ideal division of four social classes was breached both conceptually and in practice throughout the early modern period.

In many ways, then, Edo-period society functioned as a three-class social system: warriors, farmers, and townspeople. It was according to these three divisions that early modern government usually operated. Thus, for instance, the warrior class was governed according to relationships between lord and vassal. Townspeople were governed by a system of neighborhood officials appointed by the particular city's ruling lord. Farmers were controlled by village officials who were in turn accountable to regional officials appointed by a more powerful lord.

Whether one approaches early modern society from a three- or four-tiered class structure, it was still further complicated than just a multitiered class structure. Like the medieval period, there were hierarchies existing within each class in addition to the hierarchy between classes. There could be very wide discrepancies within a particular class. For instance, while warriors occupied the highest social class, within this class there were lords who enjoyed favor with the shogunate and lesser samurai for whom social and economic security were not guaranteed. In similar fashion, "farmers" encompassed both village heads who resided in large and well-appointed homes, and tenant farmers and those without any ownership of land who might live in quite austere, and even squalid, conditions. Artisans might produce their goods through the patronage of a wealthy client, or they might be poor, making a living by producing simple goods such as baskets or bamboo utensils. Merchants might have significant wealth, operating a large storefront, or they might be street vendors selling cheap goods or food from their carts.

WARRIORS

In several important ways, warriors were not just the highest class, but they were a class apart. They dressed differently from the rest of Edo-period society, sporting stiff-shouldered jackets and split-skirt pants. They wore their hair in a special warrior's topknot. They also were the only class allowed to carry weapons: both a long and a short sword. Warriors were subject to different laws and, if involved in a criminal case, given treatment different from non-warriors. In these and other ways, warriors were set apart as a special and privileged class.

The national peace established by the Tokugawa shogunate significantly affected the warrior class. During the previous Warring States period, warriors had been actively involved in the civil wars waged for control of Japan. With the Tokugawa peace, warriors were displaced from their usual role. While all warriors were the recipients of hereditary stipends and titles, there was a wide discrepancy between their actual situations in life. Some warriors became government administrators earning significant incomes. Many others, however, worked in bureaucratic or other routine positions—often menial—for which they were poorly compensated.

Warriors were at the ready if needed in battle, but because warfare was basically non existent in this period, they had little opportunity to hone their skills. The famous warrior code—Bushido, or the Way of the Warrior, formulated in the early modern period—provided warriors with an explicit and idealized value system and a reminder to stay prepared for war (see also chapter 5: Warriors and Warfare). The Way of the Warrior also created the image of the self-cultivated and moral warrior, dedicated to serving his lord and willing to die in the process if necessary.

Studying these idealized warrior values and trying to apply them to their lives, along with the study of other subjects intended for self-cultivation, were among the ways that warriors spent their leisure time. Warrior wives were expected to maintain the household. In their free time, these women might cultivate their interest in the arts or partake of the burgeoning popular culture of literature and theater.

FARMERS

Following warriors, farmers constituted the second-ranked social class during the early modern period. They were ranked above artisans and merchants because their labor in producing the nation's food supply was clearly indispensable to the functioning of Edo-period society. As a social class, farmers made up approximately 80 to 85 percent of the entire population situated in some 63,000 villages spread throughout the country. It has already been observed that this was a diverse group, encompassing both a wealthy and literate few and a much larger number of farmers and farm laborers. Some lived quite comfortable, if not wealthy, lives. Others, however, barely made a living working the land of others. Village heads oversaw the communal aspects of the farm community. In turn, village heads reported to domain administrators who collected the rice tax and served as regional peacekeepers. Farm women maintained the household and provided seasonal farming assistance as needed.

4.1 Stone sculpture of a "welcoming cat" (maneki neko) *used to greet customers at Edo-period shops and believed to bring prosperity to the merchant* (Photo William E. Deal)

ARTISANS AND MERCHANTS

Artisans and merchants who resided in towns and cities made up the third and fourth tiers of early modern society. They were often referred to collectively as "townspeople" (*chonin*) by the warrior class. Despite this apparent erasure of class difference, official Neo-Confucian orthodoxy made a clear distinction between artisans and merchants. The official view of artisans was positive: They contributed to society because they built the infrastructure and produced the goods and products required for society to function. Artisans, though important to the functioning of early modern society, rarely accumulated the kind of wealth associated with merchants. These skilled professionals either worked independently to produce their goods or they were employed by merchants.

By contrast, the official view of merchants was negative: they were selfish and self-interested because they accumulated wealth by dealing in goods they had not produced through their own hard work. Here again the ideal view of Edo-period society bumped up against the reality that outside of the most senior warrior authorities, merchants were the wealthiest class and enjoyed the power that wealth afforded them.

4.2 Model of the interior of an artisan's woodworking shop in Edo (Edo-Tokyo Museum exhibit; Photo William E. Deal)

OUTCASTES

Like medieval society, early modern society included groups considered to be outcastes and therefore outside the mainstream social structure articulated by the Neo-Confucian vision of the ideal society. By the end of the early modern period, it is estimated that 380,000 people were characterized as outcastes.

There were two predominant groups of outcastes: *eta* (called *burakumin*—"people of the village"—in contemporary Japan) and *hinin* (literally, "nonhuman"). In the medieval period, these two groups were not strictly demarcated. In the early modern period, however, government authorities drew a specific distinction between them: *eta* referred to those who were outcastes by birth, and *hinin* were outcastes as a result of their occupation.

The *eta* engaged in such occupations as butchering animals and tanning animal hides that were considered defiled and thus religiously polluting. As a

result, the *eta* suffered from much discrimination even when they engaged in livelihoods that were not in and of themselves considered ritually impure. The *eta* often lived in cities where they were forced to live in segregated communities. They were also restricted in where they could travel and who they could socialize with, and they were permitted to marry only other *eta*.

The *hinin* worked in occupations that were considered outside of the fourfold social class officially recognized by the shogunate. Such occupations were thought to contribute little if any value to society, and included those who were beggars, itinerant and street entertainers, prostitutes, and criminals. *Hinin* status was not hereditary as *eta* status was. It was rather a status that one fell into as a result of economic hardship or moral failing. Ironically, the warrior elites who dictated proper social values were also among those who frequented the pleasure quarters and enjoyed the various entertainments to be found there.

OTHER GROUPS

Early modern Japanese society also included groups who fell outside the fourfold social ideal. Among these other groups were lesser Buddhist and Shinto clerics who often were responsible for maintaining and administering local temples and shrines. Such clerics were usually married and also farmed and engaged in other village activities, dealing with religious matters as necessary. Household servants and shop hands were another group, usually found in urban centers like Edo and Osaka. By some estimates, this group comprised approximately 10 percent of Edo's population. Day laborers were another group who worked in cities but often came from villages. When they could not make a livelihood in the countryside, day laborers would leave home to work at menial tasks in the city, residing in the least desirable neighborhoods and housing. There were yet other groups too numerous to detail here. The significant point is that these other social classes did not fit the formal criteria of the four social classes, yet they were important to the structure and functioning of early modern society.

WOMEN

Japanese women's history is difficult to chart. On the one hand, it is easy to assume that Edo-period official pronouncements about the social status of women were the norm throughout the medieval and early modern periods. Although, in general, we might observe that women were subservient to men and had significantly less access to positions of power and authority, there were certainly exceptions to this rule through the eras covered in this book.

A study of the social status of women in Japan's medieval and early modern periods underscores the fact that social structure was not just a matter of social class but also of gender roles, both between and within specific social classes. Just as the Edo-

period ideal social structure was far from many actual class experiences, so too the official status of women does not fully convey the actual lives many women lived. In short, the social status of women was dynamic and changed over the course of the medieval and early modern periods. Over the centuries that comprise the medieval and early modern periods, the duties and rights of women changed, due both to the particular time period in which they lived and to the social class to which they belonged. The wife of a warrior, for instance, would have different duties and rights than the wife of a peasant living in the same time period. Such things as the rights to inherit property, freedom of movement—for instance, rules against women traveling alone—and divorce rights also fluctuated.

Historical sources for studying women's social lives are spotty at best. There are more sources from the early modern period than from the medieval, but the shortage of information to create a sustained narrative of women's lives extends throughout the medieval period and especially into the first half of the early modern period. Documents written by women are sparse compared to those written by men. Those written by men that include comments and observations about women invariably bear the particular bias of the author toward women. For these reasons, the following overview of women in medieval and early modern Japanese society is necessarily incomplete, providing only snapshots of the kinds of lives women might have led in the medieval and early modern periods.

Medieval Period

In the medieval period, a tradition that antedated the period continued to be exercised, reflecting the social value that women had in a predominantly patriarchal society. This tradition was for a lesser family to marry daughters into other more influential families to secure ties to these families. This practice was meant to establish strategic relationships between families. While this practice was particularly effective when it involved social and political elites, it reportedly also occurred at regional and village levels, as well.

Prior to the medieval period, the aristocratic Fujiwara family would marry daughters into the imperial family in order that the Fujiwara would gain additional power and access to ruling authority. Not only was there the direct connection to the daughter, but children born of the daughter's marriage created ongoing Fujiwara connections. Thus, for instance, if an aristocratic family married a daughter to an emperor, sons of that union would become emperors and have grandparents in the aristocratic family.

Using daughters as a commodity to buy political power and economic advantage continued in the medieval and early modern periods. In this time period, however, key alliances were created through marriage by the warrior class. This was especially the case in the latter half of the 16th century when various lords vied with one another for military control of the country. Daughters were married into other warrior families as a means to certify military agreements and arrangements between warrior groups. A further strategy was to give a daughter or other woman of one family to another family to serve as hostages for some political or military end.

This view of women in the medieval period, however, is tempered in part by the fact that there were instances of women as warriors. Warrior wives, especially, were sometimes trained in the martial arts, such as the use of different kinds of weapons, with which they would be expected to defend their homes and domains if their husbands were off fighting elsewhere.

Early Modern Period

The relative social and political stability that characterized the early modern period also produced changes in women's lives. Most notably, Neo-Confucian values and ethical pronouncements about the proper role for women in society dictated a rigid patriarchal system in which women were subservient to fathers, husbands, and in old age, to their sons. It should be stressed, though, that the Neo-Confucian ideal and the reality of women's lives could be quite different. There were always exceptions to the official status women were expected to occupy. Never-

theless, the official Neo-Confucian perspective was quite telling in its attitude toward women and women's place in Edo-period society.

One of the most important Neo-Confucian texts, and arguably the most famous, which makes specific moral pronouncements about women and how they should lead their lives, was *Higher Learning for Women* (*Onna daigaku*; early 18th century), attributed to Kaibara Ekken (1630–1714), a Neo-Confucian scholar. This text set the tone for attitudes about women for the remainder of the early modern period. According to this text, a woman should always be obedient, first to her parents, then to her husband and his family, and finally, in her old age, to her sons. Further, a woman should exhibit such qualities as working hard without complaint, frugality, and humility. This text also explains that a married woman could be justifiably divorced if her husband found her to be disobedient, unable to bear children, or in bad health.

We must keep in mind that *Higher Education for Women* was a moral guide for women and not a historical description of women's actual lives. There is ample evidence to suggest that women did not merely—or only—live a life of subservience to men and that the Neo-Confucian ideal may have been breached as often as it was met. This is certainly true for at least some classes of women in the early modern period. Older women whose children were grown had more freedom of movement than young wives. There were also occasions when a woman married a man who was adopted into the woman's family, often because that family had no male heir. The man in this case would assume the name of the wife's family. There is evidence that women living under this kind of marital arrangement had at least somewhat more control over the household than women who married outside of their own family. Lower-class women often worked in the homes of the wealthy and only later married. Although marriage was often arranged for women by the males in their families, in some instances, rural girls had more personal choice in selecting husbands than did urban girls. Finally, the literacy rate for women in the early modern period was approximately 15 percent, a figure higher than in other cultures at a similar point in economic development. Literacy afforded women opportunities for working in a family business or teaching at a private school, activities not prized in texts like the *Higher Education for Women*.

The idea of strategic marriages intended to create alliances between families has already been mentioned. This practice continued in the early modern period. Persisting also was the use of women as hostages to control the political machinations of potential rivals. This phenomenon was particularly conspicuous in the practice of alternate attendance at Edo required of lords (daimyo) by the shogunate (see chapter 1). In years when the lord returned to his domain, the lord's wife had to remain behind in Edo. Women were used, in this instance, to keep the lords loyal to shogunal authorities.

Although prostitution certainly existed in the medieval period, it became institutionalized and supervised by the shogunate in the Edo period. Licensed brothels, known as pleasure quarters, existed in major cities, but the Yoshiwara district in the city of Edo was the most famous of the period. The status of prostitutes was mixed. On the one hand, high-ranking courtesans might enjoy great fame for their beauty and musical skills. On the other hand, the life of most prostitutes was grim. They were controlled by the brothel owner and had typically been forced into prostitution as a result of poverty. It is from the pleasure quarters that women refined in the arts—the geisha—came into prominence. Geisha were not necessarily prostitutes, though they often had lovers and applied their skills to pleasing men.

SOCIAL PROTEST

A rigid and closely controlled social structure characterized medieval and early modern Japan. Nevertheless, social protest was not unknown and occurred as a result of any number of factors, including excessive taxation, crop failure resulting in famine and starvation, and religious activism and oppression. Regardless of the precipitating conditions, social protest was always a challenge to the ruling authority of a region or to the country itself.

Many medieval and early modern social protest movements are described by the term *ikki*. Ikki originally had other meanings—such as warrior leagues —but in the Muromachi period the term was used to refer especially to a local uprising led by regional warriors, peasants, and farmers who organized themselves into protest leagues. In the early modern period, *ikki* referred generally to any peasant revolt.

Social Protest in the Medieval Period

As warrior control over the country became decentralized due to the civil wars fought during the Warring States period, social protests became more frequent as the mechanisms of social control became weaker and weaker, one of the side effects of constant warfare. In the 14th century, disgruntled farmers and peasants in central Japan in the region of Kyoto banded together in "land protest leagues" (*tsuchi ikki* or *do ikki*). Their concerns over such matters as taxation and unfair treatment by estate officials were addressed to estate (*shoen*) proprietors who were the administrators of these lands. In the 15th century, some of the protests were directed to the shogunate to seek cancellation of debts (*tokusei*). Some 100 debt cancellation uprisings occurred during the 15th century. Only sometimes were these uprisings successful in getting debts excused. Of note, however, was the size of some of these protests. Although they usually began as a local matter, they sometimes spread across regions and came to include several thousand protesters. Regardless of their success, such large-scale protests became a cause of significant concern for both regional and national authorities.

Another form of regional uprising in the medieval period was carried out by leagues known as "provincial protest leagues" (*kuni ikki*). These started in the 15th century and were usually led by local landowners and provincial warriors (*kokujin*). While some of these protests were fueled in part by financial conditions, they were more typically political in nature, directed against the power and authority of provincial military governors (*shugo*), and often larger in scale than other kinds of social protest movements. The goal of provincial warriors was to oust the local military governor and take control of a region themselves. Provincial warriors created protest leagues to rally support and resources to enable them to overthrow a military governor. Peasants joined these leagues in hopes of gaining reprieve from heavy taxation. Peasants likely also hoped for favor in return for supporting provincial warriors who, if successful, would become the new regional authorities. One of the effects of these provincial uprisings was that they helped to create the system of regional lords known as the *sengoku daimyo* (see chapter 1: Historical Context, for additional information on *sengoku daimyo*).

Some social protests were based, in part, on religious activism and persecution, though these too had important political implications. Both the Jodo-shinshu and Nichiren schools formed leagues of followers that defended these sects from outside interests and influence. During the Warring States period, when these leagues were active, both Jodo-shinshu and Nichiren organized their own military forces to defend their interests. This usually meant fighting against local warlords for regional control. The success of these schools in attracting followers also provided them with a base for political activism by organizing followers into protest leagues. In some instances, these religio-political leagues wielded more power than the local lords, especially as civil war eroded the influence of warrior lords. Not only did such Buddhist schools seek to maintain or assert their interests against those of warrior authorities, but they also fought against each other as well as with the older, established Buddhist schools such as Tendai.

Jodo-shinshu Buddhists were organized into leagues known as Ikko ikki. The term *Ikko ikki* refers to leagues established by members of Jodo-shinshu, also referred to by the name *ikko*, meaning "single-minded" faith in Amida Buddha. These "League of the Single-Minded" uprisings began in the late 15th century and usually involved large numbers of militant protesters derived from the peasant class seeking self-governance. In the largest and one of the most significant Ikko ikki actions, protestors battled with the lord of Kaga province. The victorious pro-

testers forced the lord to commit suicide. These events inaugurated a nearly 100-year rule by Jodo-shinshu adherents in the Kaga region. Ikko ikki protests continued in various parts of Japan until 1580 when Oda Nobunaga destroyed the military capabilities of the League of the Single-Minded.

Hokke ikki was the name for protest leagues among followers of Nichiren Buddhism, a school that was also called the Hokke (Lotus) school because of the importance of the Lotus Sutra to its doctrines and practices. Unlike the Ikko ikki, which appealed especially to peasants, the Hokke ikki was championed particularly by members of the Kyoto merchant and artisan classes who saw these leagues as a way to protect their interests and communities. The Nichiren school had been particularly successful in attracting followers among the nonaristocratic classes in Kyoto. Conflicts arose with the Tendai school on Mt. Hiei, which had in former times been dominant in the capital. Armed conflicts erupted between these two schools in the Muromachi period and it was the Hokke ikki who rose up to defend Nichiren-school interests, both religious and commercial. In the first half of the 16th century, the Hokke protests were finally suppressed by superior forces from Mt. Hiei.

Social Protest in the Early Modern Period

Social protest in the early modern period was usually the result of heavy taxation or the high price of rice that precipitated poverty and starvation especially among farmers, peasants, and the urban poor. Such conditions led to both farmer-peasant uprisings in the countryside and urban riots. Farmer-peasant uprisings (Hyakusho ikki; "farmer protest leagues") occurred to protest the treatment of farmers and peasants by the Tokugawa shogunate and domain lords. During the Edo period, some 2,500 such farmer league uprisings occurred throughout the country to protest excessive taxation and the hardships it fostered.

During the first half of the Edo period, farmer protests varied in their level of militancy. Sometimes farmers would simply abandon the lands they worked in order to avoid taxation. Other times, farmers would submit appeals to the authorities protesting the conditions they were forced to endure. Later in the Edo period, farmer protests often involved leagues of protesters drawn from much wider areas and constituting a much larger number of participants, sometimes numbering in the thousands. Such protests were both more violent and more widespread than those that occurred earlier in the period; they took on greater national urgency because they involved farmers from more than one region. If the shogunate could ignore the more limited protests, they could not afford to ignore these larger uprisings. One other change in the development of these more militant protests was that besides targeting the government, the protesters sometimes directed their anger against regional merchants and others they perceived were getting wealthy at the farmers' expense.

The urban counterpart of farmer uprisings were known as *uchikowashi* (literally, "smashing"). These rice riots, as they are sometimes called, were held to protest the very high cost of rice. Mobs of irate—and often starving—urban poor rampaged through a city destroying rice storehouses and other merchant establishments that they deemed the source of their misery. Urban riots occurred in many cities, including Edo, Osaka, and Nagasaki. By the end of the Edo period, the severity of these riots was also connected to the waning political influence of the Tokugawa shogunate, which by this time appeared mostly helpless to either aid the poor or to suppress their protests.

4.3 Scene of an Edo-period rice riot (Illustration Grace Vibbert)

modern period, wealth increasingly resided with the merchant class, formally the lowest on the social hierarchy.

In the Heian period, control of economic resources was centered at Kyoto. By the end of the Kamakura period, however, the economy had become more and more decentralized. What this meant in practical terms was that at least some regions of Japan, now ruled by local warriors, had become independent and self-sustaining. Such regions did not have to rely on Kyoto or, for that matter, Kamakura, to maintain a functioning economy. Local markets developed around castle towns and other growing urban centers. In the early modern period, markets and commerce became more and more centered on the larger urban areas, such as Edo and Osaka.

ECONOMY

Like most other aspects of Japanese culture and society, Japan's economy was significantly impacted by the warrior class during the medieval and early modern periods. Although warriors were formally the social elite, this high standing in society did not necessarily mean that warriors held the most economic wealth. By the latter half of the early

Medieval Economy

The medieval period witnessed economic changes, including the development of markets and domestic commerce, increased agricultural production as a result of new technologies, the marketing of artisans' goods, the use of money as a means of exchange, and overseas trade. Merchants and artisans became increasingly central to these economic developments, but other classes also contributed to the medieval economy. Buddhist monks, particularly

Zen monks, who had studied in China, provided a link between Japan and China not only from a religious perspective, but also in contacts useful for those conducting trade with China. The warrior class, too, contributed to the economy as consumers of a variety of goods, both domestic and imported. The many warrior-bureaucrats dispatched by the shogunate to oversee cities and provinces also created markets for the needs of this social class. The use of coins was also associated with this phenomenon.

The development of daimyo domains in various parts of the country during the 14th and 15th centuries also impacted the economy. Regional lords wanted goods to reflect their status, and required markets and other commercial ventures to support the samurai and farmers who worked their land. Itinerant merchants traveled from domain to domain setting up markets and trading centers once or twice a month. These markets evolved into permanent market sites as the ongoing demand for goods increased. Artisans also settled in such locations to sell the goods they produced. The development of market towns was a direct result of this kind of commercial activity.

AGRICULTURE

The medieval period witnessed increased agricultural productivity. This, in part, was a result of technological advances, including the increased diffusion and use of iron tools, and the development of double cropping. One important transformation that accompanied increased agricultural production was the rise in the importance of self-ruled and self-supporting villages to medieval economic life. During the medieval period, aristocratic estates as centers of economic activity fell into decline. As a result, villages increasingly took on the role of centers of agricultural production. Such villages were ruled by the farmers who settled there. The village head served as the liaison between the farmers and the regional lord and was responsible for assessing the taxes owed by each farmer. Over time, village heads often came to be employed by the regional lord.

The village agricultural economy was in all aspects a community effort. Wet rice farming in paddy fields was a labor-intensive enterprise requiring a group effort to construct level fields and a

water system for flooding the paddies. Similarly, rice planting was an arduous process of placing seedlings one by one into the field and required everyone's cooperation. Finally, the village banded together to take care of other tasks, such as constructing houses and rice storage facilities, which were necessary for the community's economic prosperity.

MARKETS AND COMMERCE

The growth in agricultural output required new markets for these products. The development of commerce and a commercial infrastructure began to take shape in the medieval period. As aristocratic estates declined, village markets and markets promoted by warrior domains came to be the center of commercial activity. Domain authorities took several steps to promote flourishing markets: Weights and measures were standardized, currency was introduced as a medium of exchange, and tax-free trading for commercial agents was established.

Feudal lords encouraged economic development within their domains because it was one way they could raise the funds crucial to waging war. During the Warring States period, warlords utilized agents to procure the weapons and other supplies needed to field an army. Agents engaged in trade with other, nonhostile regions. This economic activity promoted trade across different regions. It also contributed to the use of gold and other money as a method of payment that was both more convenient and more efficient than barter.

Trade, however, was conducted not only between feudal domains, but also between towns and villages. Local markets, operating several days a month, were established to sell both agricultural products and artisans' crafts and daily-use items. Nonagricultural products sold at these markets might include pottery, cooking utensils, farm tools, and other household items. Although coins were sometimes used as a medium of exchange, a barter system in which farm products were traded for handicrafts made by artisans was more typical at local markets in the medieval period.

Traveling merchants were important to the growth of commerce. They brought goods to market, transporting village agricultural products to various local markets. By the Muromachi period, merchants and artisans were organized into trade guilds (*za*) to try to control the flow of goods and to gain monopoly rights over the goods they made and sold. In effect, guilds were a means to cut out the competition. Well-placed patrons—such as regional lords, temples and shrines, and the shogunate—were paid by merchants and artisans in return for these protections against others entering the marketplace selling similar goods. Membership in guilds was restricted to guarantee the ongoing monopoly benefits that guild members enjoyed. Salt, oil, silk, wood, and iron utensils were among the goods protected by guild arrangements. The influence of guilds declined in the latter half of the 16th century when regional lords began to abolish these organizations in favor of free markets.

TAXATION

Taxation in the medieval period was often a very heavy burden, especially to farmers and peasants. During the Muromachi period, for instance, taxes were constantly being increased to the point where an estimated 70 percent of everything produced by farmers and peasants was collected as tax by the Ashikaga shogunate. Under such adverse financial conditions, it did not take much else to occur for the life of a peasant to be ruined. Crop failure, for one, quickly brought about conditions of famine and starvation. Families were sometimes left with no recourse but to beg for food. Such heavy taxation also sometimes led to social protest (see "Social Protest" above).

During the medieval period, taxes were collected both on land use and production, and on households. One such tax, known as *nengu* ("annual tribute"), was an annual land tax. This represented the dues paid in rice (and sometimes barley) by farmers to estate proprietors in the first half of the medieval period and, after the decline of estates, to domain lords. This form of tax continued into the early modern period and came sometimes to be paid in currency.

Farmers and peasants were also irregularly subject to special land taxes in addition to the annual land tax. These special land taxes were collected by the social elite—including aristocrats, the shogunate, and temples and shrines—when they needed additional resources for special events, rituals, and projects. These special taxes were paid either in rice (called *tammai*) or in currency (called *tansen*). These special taxes were levied more and more frequently in the 15th and 16th centuries by regional lords.

Besides land taxes, there was a household tax (*munabetsusen*) levied on all households during the medieval period. This kind of tax, like the special land taxes, was originally and infrequently imposed by aristocrats or a religious institution to finance a special court or religious event. In the Muromachi period, it became a regular tax, used by the shogunate to collect additional funds once regional domains became free of shogunal authority—and could no longer be forced to pay taxes to the shogunate—during the long period of civil war.

Early Modern Economy

The local and fragmented nature of the medieval economy underwent a process of unification at the outset of the early modern period. This process was a by-product of the political and social unification of Japan effected by Oda Nobunaga, Toyotomi Hideyoshi, and Tokugawa Ieyasu in the late 16th century. Hideyoshi, for instance, as part of his efforts to regularize economic standards, had land surveys conducted throughout all of Japan to determine the amount of taxable income that might be realized. The consolidation of power at the beginning of the early modern period also focused economic interests on the great castles of the unifiers. Thus, Osaka Castle, for one, became the center of a vibrant market that hosted large numbers of artisans and merchants.

Once the Tokugawa shogunate established control of the country and based its ruling ideology on Chinese Neo-Confucian ideas, the market economy that had grown so rapidly as a result, in part, of military conflict was now regulated and conceptualized in such a way as to decelerate the pace of growth. Neo-Confucianism, with its emphasis on a four-class social structure that placed merchants at the lowest tier, was, in effect, an economic perspective that advocated a premarket economy. The Neo-Confucian view was that merchants were essentially parasites on the hard work of farmers and artisans, obtaining their wealth at the expense of the labor of others. As such, merchants were seen as having no positive social value.

The suppression of the market economy also had a significant impact on farmers. According to Neo-Confucian philosophy, farmers were supposed to live austere lives, laboring in the fields only to produce what they personally needed to survive. To produce more than what was personally needed was to move beyond frugality—a positive Neo-Confucian value—toward a market system where agricultural surplus could be sold. In order to induce conformity to the official ideology, the shogunate issued regulations to control the farmers and to prevent them from easy access to markets where they could sell their products. These regulations required, for instance, that farmers not abandon their land, that they pay their taxes before they could sell their rice, that they wear simple clothes, and that they always work hard. These and similar regulations were all directed toward keeping farmers living at a subsistence level.

The Neo-Confucian value system also impacted warriors in quite specific ways. For one, warriors were supposed to only live off of their military stipends, paid to them in rice by their lords. If warrior families had additional needs, they were expected to produce what they needed or obtain it for themselves, usually by exchanging rice for goods. Further, warriors were supposed to transcend money and not use it at all. Money, a need of merchants, was considered beneath the dignity of samurai.

Despite the ideal society and economy envisioned by Neo-Confucian philosophy, the reality was that a market economy was needed in the early modern period. Ironically, it was the warrior elite who demeaned the notion of monetary wealth but simultaneously drove a market in luxury and other items that they desired. At the same time that the warrior elite admonished farmers to live a frugal lifestyle, they took rice obtained through land taxes and converted it into currency to purchase the items they required at markets and at urban stores. The net result of this economic activity was the development of wholesale and retail markets, and a banking and credit system to

handle the increasing use of currency to buy and sell goods.

Another policy of the Tokugawa shogunate that inadvertently supported the expansion of a market economy was the *sankin kotai* system whereby domain lords were required to reside in Edo in service to the shogun in alternate years. As a result, Edo became an economic center dealing in the goods and services that domain lords and their retainers required. Merchants and artisans especially profited. Edo's commercial needs were fed, in turn, by other areas of Japan, which supplied the goods sold at the capital. Osaka, for instance, with its trade in regional commodities and its proximity to water transportation networks, became one of the key supply points for the Edo market.

By the end of the Edo period, despite the formal ideology, Japan had a well-developed market system covering agricultural, industrial, and other products. The infrastructure needed to support thriving markets—including a transportation system to bring goods to market and a banking system—also developed. Even in the face of these economic realities and the shogunate's complicity in advancing a market system, taxes were still primarily levied on land and not on the wealth accumulated by merchants. This was ineffective because wealth had shifted away from the countryside into the urban markets. At the end of the early modern period, this was but one problem among many that eventually led to the collapse of the Tokugawa shogunate.

AGRICULTURE

Despite the shogunate's restrictions on what farmers could produce and the emphasis on growing rice, other crops were also cultivated. In dry fields, such items as grains, hemp, and soy beans were grown. Where the local climate was favorable to cultivation, crops such as cotton and indigo were grown. Urbanization also brought with it a market for new crops not indigenous to Japan. Among these were plants that were imported from the West as a result of contact with European traders. Such crops as potatoes and tobacco became luxury items that fetched significant profits. Although the shogunate, and by extension domain authorities, officially disdained the cultivation of luxury crops, they were themselves

4.4 Example of a scale used in the conduct of business during the Edo period (Edo-Tokyo Museum exhibit; Photo William E. Deal)

among those whose desire for these items helped fuel their sale at market. Some domain lords had regulations against growing these kinds of crops, but even they capitulated and allowed these crops to be cultivated on domain lands in recognition of the financial loss of importing such items from other domains. In the end, economic realities often trumped official ideology.

MARKETS AND COMMERCE

Although merchants were looked down upon by the shogunate, they played a central role in the development of the early modern Japanese economy. It was domain merchants, for instance, who urged domain authorities to grow financially lucrative crops—despite the prevailing premarket ideology—rather than buy them from another domain and lose out on the profits to be made by producing these crops and bringing them to market.

As in the medieval period, merchants organized themselves into trade organizations. One such association was the 10 Wholesaler Group (*tokumi doiya*; the term *doiya*—"wholesale dealer"—is sometimes

pronounced *don'ya*) based in the city of Edo. This was an organization of wholesale merchants that originally consisted of 10 wholesale houses each trading in different kinds of products and commodities. At the height of its influence, the 10 Wholesaler Group grew to include nearly 100 wholesale houses. Organized in 1694, the 10 Wholesaler Group banded together to better protect their collective interests, especially when it came to disputes with other wholesalers, merchants, and shippers over goods that had been lost or damaged in transit. The Edo wholesalers group bought goods to sell in Edo from wholesalers in Osaka, known as the 24 Wholesaler Group (*nijushikumi doiya*). The Osaka association provided goods and served as shippers to the Edo group. Together, the two wholesale houses operated nearly a monopoly transportation system of cargo ships (*higaki kaisen*) that ran between the two urban centers.

The medieval merchant and artisan guilds (*za*) were slowly dismantled by regional lords starting in the middle of the 16th century on the grounds that such trade associations unnecessarily hindered economic growth. By the start of the Edo period, most of these guilds had ceased to exist. In their place, the Tokugawa government and domain lords authorized the creation of official merchant guilds (*kabunakama*;

4.5 Example of a box used as a measure in the conduct of business during the Edo period (Edo-Tokyo Museum exhibit; Photo William E. Deal)

literally, "association of shareholders"). These trade associations were first promoted by the government in the late 1600s as a way to regulate trade. These associations included merchants who were allowed to limit trade in certain commodities and to set the prices of these goods. These official merchant guilds were monopolistic by design. The shogunate and domain lords benefited from this arrangement because monopoly rights were bought by merchants by paying what amounted to a tax to the government in exchange for permitting these trade practices. At one point in the 1840s these merchant guilds were abolished only to be reinstated a few years later when high inflation was blamed on their absence from the marketplace. The 24 Wholesaler Group became an official merchant guild in the late 18th century.

Another important function played by wealthy merchants was as financiers and moneylenders. Their main clients were domain lords who were often financially overextended as a result of the requirement that they reside in Edo in alternate years. It was extremely costly for domain lords to keep two residences and to transport their households and belongings back and forth to Edo. To make matters worse, the shogunate sometimes required domain lords (daimyo) to pay for additional expenses incurred by the government for a variety of projects. As a result, financial problems were not uncommon among domain lords. Merchants charged high interest rates on these loans to protect themselves from nonpayment which sometimes occurred. Interest was typically paid in rice.

TAXATION

Taxation during the early modern period was similar to the medieval period with taxes collected on land and households. Additionally, however, taxes in the Edo period were also collected on goods and services produced by artisans, merchants, craftspeople, hunters and fishers, and others who did not pay land taxes on a regular basis.

The primary land tax during the early modern period was based on estimates of the annual yield of unpolished rice that a particular tract of land would produce. These estimates were based on land surveys conducted by Toyotomi Hideyoshi at the end of the 16th century. Farmland yield was measured in *koku*—one *koku* equaled approximately five bushels or 180 liters. Landholders were taxed on this estimate of rice yield, known as *kokudaka*. The size and importance of a particular domain can be determined in part by the amount of rice tax paid annually as measured in *kokudaka*, or the total of rice productivity. In the case of domain lands, rice productivity also determined the number of troops a domain lord was expected to maintain as a part of his responsibility to the shogunate.

Another tax, known as *kuramai* ("granary rice"), was a rice tax that peasants paid to the shogunate or to a domain lord. The rice (*mai*) collected was stored in granaries (*kura*) and was subsequently used to pay stipends to retainers of the shogunate and domain lords. Peasants and farmers were also subject to a tax that was calculated on the basis of village rice yield. This tax, known as *honto mononari*, was meant to be paid in rice but it was also sometimes paid in currency.

Besides land taxes, there were taxes levied by the government on merchants, artisans, and others who did not hold farmlands and thus were not subject to land taxes. Payment of this tax was typically made in currency, but sometimes payment was made in commercial products or in physical labor. These taxes, called *myogakin*, were assessed both on individuals and on merchant associations.

4.6 Model of a scene in front of an Edo shop (Edo-Tokyo Museum exhibit; Photo William E. Deal)

4.7 *Rice packed in straw sacks used for paying taxes. Each sack holds approximately 60 kg of unpolished rice.* (Photo William E. Deal)

Currency

The growth of markets beginning in the medieval period accelerated the use of currency as a medium of exchange. Barter was not replaced, but currency became an additional means by which goods could be bought and sold at market. Coins were first used by wealthy warriors, but as trade expanded, currency use came into vogue even at village markets. The use of coins had become widespread enough by the 15th century that counterfeiting became a lucrative activity and attracted sufficient concern from authorities to make it into the historical record.

In the medieval period, different kinds of coins were utilized for trade. Although the Japanese had minted coins during the Heian period, they used Chinese-minted coins during the medieval period. For instance, the *sosen* was a copper coin minted in Song-dynasty China (960–1279). It came into wide circulation in Japan by the 13th century due to trade between Japan and China. Another Chinese copper coin, the *kobusen*, was minted during the Ming dynasty (1368–1644) in five different denominations. These coins were used in Japan starting in the Muromachi period and continuing until the Edo period. The *eirakusen* was a copper coin minted in

early 15th-century China. In Japan, this coin was used especially in land tax transactions. In an attempt to regulate the currency system, the Tokugawa shogunate issued an edict at the beginning of the Edo period prohibiting the use of this coin. However, it remained in use until the middle of the 17th century.

These three kinds of coins—*sosen, kobusen,* and *eirakusen*—were those primarily in use in the medieval period. However, there was one Japanese-minted coin also in use, the *bitasen*. This was a copper coin that was not minted by the government but rather was privately produced. In circulation from the 16th century, the *bitasen* contained not only copper but significant amounts of lead. The value of the *bitasen* fluctuated depending on how it was valued relative to the Chinese coins. Each market region made its own determination of the *bitasen*'s value. At the beginning of the early modern period, the shogunate established a uniform valuation for *bitasen* that was used in all regions of Japan.

A new monetary development occurred at the end of the Warring States period that was largely a result of the resources needed to support an army in the field. In order to purchase weapons and other supplies, the need for more valuable coins arose as a way to more easily pay off the large amounts of money such military supplies cost. To meet this need, regional lords started mining for gold and silver. Takeda Koshu, lord of the Kai region, was the first to issue gold coins, known as *koshukin*.

Just prior to the start of the early modern period, Toyotomi Hideyoshi placed all the gold and silver mines under his control and began the process of minting gold and silver coins. Under the subsequent Tokugawa shogunate, a nationwide monetary system was instituted. This system included coins minted in gold, silver, and copper. Gold coins were used extensively in Edo, while silver coins were primarily used in Osaka and Kyoto. Copper coins were in general use throughout the country.

As part of the Tokugawa government's attempt to control the monetary system and commercial markets, the shogunate maintained direct control over the mints (*za*) that produced Edo-period coins. These mints were run by families who had the hereditary right to do so. At the beginning of the 19th century, these mints, which had originally been situated in different parts of Japan, were all moved to Edo as a way for the government to further control them.

The gold mints (*kinza*)—located until 1800 at Edo, Kyoto, and Sado—produced gold coins, such as the *koban*. The *koban* was first minted in 1601 and had a value of one *ryo* (the other standard monetary unit of value was termed *bu*). This coin was used nationally throughout the Edo period. Another gold coin was the *oban*. Although only in very limited circulation prior to the Edo period, the *oban* was used more widely in the early modern period. These gold coins, with a valuation of 10 *ryo*, were therefore many times more valuable than the *koban*. They were not, however, considered general-use coins. Rather, they were used for such special purposes as, among other things, gifts and rewards.

Silver mints (*ginza*) were located in Kyoto, Sumpu, and Edo (the famous Ginza district of modern-day Tokyo was the location of the Edo silver mint). Besides their use in the marketplace, silver coins were sometimes used by the shogunate to pay off budget deficits. Like gold coins, silver coins were often utilized in large financial transactions because of their high value.

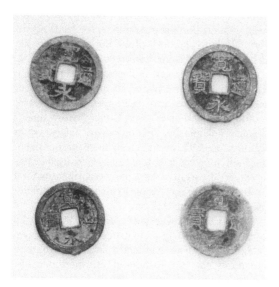

4.8 Examples of Edo-period coins (Photo William E. Deal)

Copper mints (*zeniza*) produced not only copper coins, but also coins made of iron and brass. The first government-sponsored copper mints date from 1636 and were located at Edo and Sakamoto. Copper coins were in general circulation in the early modern period and were used to purchase goods at market and to enact other daily business. There was a hole in the middle of these coins and they were often carried by stringing coins together in 100- and 1,000-coin units.

Paper currency was used only on a limited basis in the early modern period. When paper money was issued, it was done by individual domains for use only within that region, despite the fact that the value of this paper money was pegged to the shogunate's national currency system. The Fukui domain was the first to issue paper currency, doing so in 1661, and other domains followed this practice.

The use of currency, especially in the Edo period, was extremely important to the growth of commerce and to how the merchant class functioned. One of the challenges of the early modern currency system was the issue of how to value the different kinds of coins and what exchange rate to use when these coins were used at market. A shopkeeper, for instance, would need to exchange copper coins used every day for gold or silver coins that were used to pay off debts and other financial obligations. Because Edo used gold coins and Osaka used silver coins, commerce between these two regions invariably also involved currency exchange. Further complicating this matter was the fact that among specific kinds of coins, there were different levels of purity in the metals used and variation in the percentage of, for example, gold actually used in a gold coin. Government authorities tried to establish fixed rates of exchange, but fluctuating values were the norm. This matter was dealt with at the local market level by merchants known as *ryogaesho*. Often translated as "money changers," this term referred to merchants who specialized in currency exchange and other kinds of financial transactions, including the extension of credit. Some famous names in the contemporary Japanese banking world, such as Sumitomo and Mitsui, trace their origins back to the Edo-period business of currency exchange.

Foreign Trade

Throughout the medieval and early modern periods, foreign trade went through periods of great activity and periods when contact with foreign traders was forbidden or otherwise made difficult by the governing authorities. Sometimes there were official trade relations between Japan and other countries; at other times trade was conducted by enterprising private merchants or even, on occasion, Buddhist temples. This was the case, for instance, in the Muromachi period when both official and private trade was conducted with China. Foreign trade not only occurred with the Asian mainland in the medieval period, but also with Southeast Asian countries.

In the middle of the 16th century, trade began with Europe, especially Portugal and Spain, and lasted into the first half of the 17th century. At that time, Japan embarked on its more than 200-year national isolation period, in which contacts with the outside world were severely curtailed, and Japanese were forbidden from traveling overseas. Contacts with China, Korea, and Holland continued, but on a limited basis and under tight restrictions imposed by the shogunate, which closely controlled the trade activity that did exist. Any foreign trade allowed was supposed to be transacted in Nagasaki. Dutch and Chinese ships, for instance, docked at Nagasaki ports but were limited in the number of ships permitted entry into Japanese waters each year. One exception, and there were few, was trade between the Tsushima domain and Korea.

Restricted foreign-trade policy continued into the 19th century, but there were increasing numbers of encroachments, especially by European and Russian ships, seeking trade relations with Japan. These requests were always denied. It was not until the 1850s, when Commodore Matthew Perry was dispatched to Japan by the president of the United States to obtain trade relations, that this situation formally changed. In the late 1850s, trade treaties were signed between Japan and the United States. Treaties with European nations quickly followed, thus ending Japan's period of national seclusion.

TRADE WITH CHINA

During the Kamakura period, the Hojo regents strongly supported trade with the Chinese Southern Song dynasty (1127–1279). The Japanese traded gold and swords for Chinese silk and copper coins (known as *sosen*). After the Mongols took control of China, trade relations ended. In the Muromachi period, trade relations with China were once again established. Ashikaga Yoshimitsu, the third Ashikaga shogun, promoted Japanese trade with the Ming dynasty (1368–1644). Trade with China at this time, known as the "tally trade," lasted until the middle of the 16th century. The tally trade commenced in the early years of the 15th century and by the time it ended in the mid-16th century, 17 trade voyages had been conducted in fleets that numbered up to nine ships each. Among the items exported from Japan were swords, horses, copper, and lacquerware. Among the items imported from China were porcelain and silk. Much of this trade was conducted using Chinese copper and silver coins.

Formally, the Ming government did not permit Chinese ships to trade with foreign countries. This restriction, however, did not apply to ships from countries that paid tribute to the Ming dynasty. Thus, the Japanese tally trade with Ming China was conducted under the fiction that the Japanese "king"—that is, the shogun—was not trading with China, but rather offering tribute to the Ming-dynasty emperors. In return for "tribute," the Japanese received "gifts" from the Chinese emperor. Further adding to the complexity of this arrangement was the fact that it was not usually the shogunate that was conducting these trade voyages directly. Rather, trade was carried out by regional lords, such as the Hosokawa and Ouchi families, and the Sakai merchants.

The Sakai merchants were wealthy traders based in the port city of Sakai, near Osaka. They conducted foreign trade as part of the tally trade and also traded with Korea. But even after the tally trade ceased, the Sakai merchants continued their foreign trade, especially gaining prominence—and a monopoly—in the importation of raw silk. Sakai's fortunes waned after the implementation of the national seclusion policy in 1639, which decreed that Nagasaki serve as the primary foreign trade port.

The raw silk trade was operated under a system called *itowappu* that was established in 1604 by the Tokugawa government, which sought greater control over commercial activities and especially foreign trade. It allowed for Japanese merchants a monopoly to purchase raw silk from Portuguese traders who had sole right of trade in Chinese silk. As part of the *itowappu* system, a fixed price for silk was negotiated between Portuguese traders and Japanese merchants. The Sakai merchants, along with selected merchants in Nagasaki and Kyoto, were given official government approval to act as sole agents in the silk trade. As the Tokugawa shogunate moved to close down its ports and establish a national seclusion policy, it applied the monopolistic principles of the *itowappu* system to trade with China, and later to the Dutch. This system existed, with the exception of a 30-year period in the 17th century, until the middle of the 19th century and the opening of Japanese trade with the West.

There were other trading arrangements that occurred during the early modern period. Of note was a merchant organization that came to be known as the Nagasaki Kaisho. This group took advantage of its location in Nagasaki, after the implementation of the national seclusion policy designated Nagasaki as the port from which foreign trade could be conducted. Originally constituted in 1604 as one of the merchant groups allowed to trade in raw silk under the *itowappu* system, the Nagasaki Kaisho came to monopolize foreign trade in the early modern period. By the beginning of the 18th century, this merchant organization was in charge of dealing with all goods traded with Dutch and Chinese merchant ships harboring at Nagasaki. They also controlled the exchange of gold and silver that was used in trade deals with the Dutch and Chinese. As in other financial arrangements in which the Tokugawa shogunate granted monopoly rights to a merchant association, the Nagasaki Kaisho paid taxes to the shogunate.

TRADE WITH EUROPE

Japanese trade with Europe started in the 1540s when Portuguese traders and missionaries first arrived on Japanese shores. Subsequently, Spanish, English, and other Europeans commenced trade with Japan. Among the many goods introduced to

Japan at this time were firearms and European luxury items. This trade, known as the Southern Barbarian (*namban*) trade was at first conducted with few restrictions or regulations. As suspicions arose in the Japanese government about European intentions, missionary activities were curtailed or ended entirely by the shogunate, and trade was similarly restricted. Trade with Europe lasted until the commencement of the Japanese seclusion policy in the 1630s. After this time, the Dutch were the only Europeans, a small but legal presence, in Japan. It was not until the 1850s and the reopening of Japanese ports that trade with other European nations was once again permitted.

TRADE WITH KOREA

Despite Korea's proximity to Japan, the 13th-century Mongol invasions of Korea—and the later attempt by the Mongols to extend their empire to Japan in the unsuccessful 1274 and 1281 attacks on the Japanese islands—wreaked havoc on any possibility of trade between Japan and Korea. By the early 15th century, however, conditions had changed, and Japan and Korea were able to establish diplomatic relations and a trading relationship. Trade was conducted not by the shogunate, but with the lords of the So domain in Kyushu.

Warfare once again brought trade relations to a halt. This time it was a result of Toyotomi Hideyoshi's attempt to conquer both Korea and China. Invasions of Korea occurred during the 1590s. These invasions ultimately failed but in the process destroyed opportunities for trade. Tokugawa Ieyasu, who succeeded Hideyoshi, realized the potential economic benefits of a Korea trade. He revived relations with Korea and trade between the two countries was restarted. The Japanese traded items like silver and copper for Korean cotton and ginseng. This trade was conducted primarily with the So domain and continued through the rest of the Edo period.

TRADE WITH SOUTHEAST ASIA

Trade between Japan and Southeast Asia was very active in the 16th century and into the first half of the 17th century. Trade thrived because the shogunate encouraged a form of foreign trade with Southeast Asia known as the vermilion seal ship trade. The name derived from the fact that all ships had to carry a trading license that included the vermilion seal (*shuin*) of the shogun. The purpose of licensing these ships was to place foreign trade under Japanese government control.

Japanese merchants looked to Southeast Asia as a trading partner in part because, in the late 16th century, Japanese ships were forbidden from trading in China. Japanese merchants exported goods such as silver, copper, iron, and some items manufactured by Japanese artisans. They imported silk, medicine, and spices. To trade in these goods, vermilion seal ships traveled to locations that included areas of what is now the Philippines, Thailand, Vietnam, Cambodia, Taiwan, Indonesia, and Macao. The vermilion seal ship trade lasted until 1639, when the Japanese national seclusion policy effectively ended trade with these regions.

One important result of trading in such geographically distant locales was that Japanese settlements, called Nihonmachi ("Japan Town"), were founded in many of these places. In addition to housing traders, these communities also attracted Japanese who fled Japan to avoid the shogunate's persecution of Christians and the many edicts issued that severely restricted the activities associated with this religion. The largest of these settlements was reportedly an enclave in the Philippines that had a population of approximately 3,000 people. After the seclusion policies were enacted and trade with Southeast Asia was formally abolished, these communities, or what was left of them, became absorbed into the local communities.

TRADE WITH RUSSIA

Although there were sporadic interactions between Japan and Russia in the Edo period, it was not until the 1850s that any trade agreements were concluded. Prior to this time, Russian traders, often on behalf of the Russian government, requested permission to trade with Japan, but were always denied on the basis of Japan's national seclusion policy. Several attempts to establish relations were made in the late 18th and early 19th centuries. Finally, in 1855,

on the heels of the opening of Japan by Commodore Perry, Japan and Russia signed the Russo-Japanese Treaty of Amity that opened three Japanese ports to Russian traders. This treaty also established formal diplomatic relations between the two nations. Three years later, Russia and Japan signed the Treaty of Friendship and Commerce that further expanded trade and diplomatic dealings.

TRADE WITH THE UNITED STATES

The possibility for trade with the United States occurred only at the end of the early modern period. Threatening military action against Japan, Commodore Matthew Perry convinced the Tokugawa shogunate to sign the Kanagawa Treaty in 1854. This treaty set in motion the final collapse of the Tokugawa shogunate as well as the opening of Japan to trade not only with the United States, but also with Russia, England, France, and other Western nations.

The Kanagawa Treaty, despite its far-reaching ramifications for Japan's future, permitted American ships to dock at only two Japanese ports and did not formally establish trade relations. This occurred in 1858 when the United States and Japan signed the United States–Japan Treaty of Amity and Commerce, also known as the Harris Treaty, after Townsend Harris, the American consul general who negotiated the terms of the agreement. Besides establishing increased diplomatic relations, the treaty opened additional Japanese ports to American ships and guaranteed the United States the right to freely conduct trade with Japan. Other countries soon concluded similar trade and diplomatic arrangements with Japan.

READING

Society

Beasley 1999, 152–170: Edo-period society; Hall, Nagahara, and Yamamura (eds.) 1981, 65–75, 207–219, 282–286; Dunn 1969, 13–49: warriors,

50–83: farmers, 84–96: artisans, 97–121: merchants, 122–136: others, 143–145: outcastes; Ooms 1996: Edo-period village life; Jansen 2000, 96–126: early modern social class; Totman 2000, 225–230: early Edo-period society; Hane 1991, 96–98: medieval peasants, 142–155: Edo-period society and social classes; Yamamura (ed.) 1990, 301–343: medieval peasantry; Hall (ed.) 1991, 121–125: early Edo-period society

Women

Bingham and Gross 1987; Knapp 1992, 102–153; Tonomura 1997; Mulhern (ed.) 1991, 162–207; Leupp 1992, 49–65, 83–87, 137–139; Bernstein (ed.) 1991, 17–148: early modern women; Tonomura, Walthall, and Wakita (eds.) 1999; Yamakawa 1992: early modern samurai-class women

Social Protest

Jansen 2000, 232–236: social protest; Berry 1994, 37–44, 89–93, 145–170: social protest, especially Hokke ikki; Hane 1991, 197–200: late Edo peasant uprisings; Yamamura (ed.) 1990, 280–289: medieval peasant protests

Economy

Crawcour 1974, 461–486; Nagahara with Yamamura 1981, 27–63: medieval taxes; Sasaki with Hauser 1981, 125–148: medieval commerce; Wakita with McClain 1981, 224–247: medieval commerce; Yamamura 1981, 327–372: early Edo economy; Sheldon 1958: merchant class; Gay 2001: medieval moneylenders; Beasley 1999, 134–151: foreign trade; Totman 1993, 59–79, 140–159: early modern economy, including foreign trade; Totman 1981, 118–123: medieval economy; Hane 1991, 98–102: medieval economy, 189–197: late Edo economic problems, 209–214: foreign trade in the late Edo period; Yamamura (ed.) 1990, 344–395: medieval commerce; Hall (ed.) 1991, 110–121: early Edo-period economy; 121–125: Edo-period trade with China and Korea, 478–518: economic aspects of the early modern village and agriculture, 538–595: economic aspects of early modern cities; Bank of Japan Web site http://www.imes.boj.or.jp/cm/english_htmls/history.htm: history of Japanese currency

5

WARRIORS AND WARFARE

By Lisa J. Robertson

WARRIOR HISTORY

The Japanese warrior class dominated military affairs, politics, and civilian culture from the establishment of the Kamakura shogunate in 1185 until the end of the Edo period in 1868. During this nearly 700-year period, warriors controlled Japan's government, promulgated a military code of behavior, and fostered distinctive art forms that memorialized soldierly virtues and exploits. Warrior involvement in court affairs increased as government officials, aristocrats, and religious institutions relied on military bands to enforce order in the provinces. Military rule fostered advances in weapons technology and battle tactics, as well as innovations in fortifications. Martial values including a strict code of conduct and a pledge to attain honor in both life and death distinguished Japanese warriors and fueled transformations in feudal religion, philosophy, and lifestyles. Warrior patronage resulted in revitalization of visual and performing art forms. Military ideals captured in colorful tales of heroic battles and other accomplishments immortalized leaders and inspired future soldiers.

Traditionally, the medieval Japanese warrior symbolized rigor and austerity in contrast with the indulgent, courtly ideals of the Heian period. Naturally, soldiers honed their military skills, yet the warrior classes also pursued civilian arts long linked with aristocratic refinement. Recent scholarship has noted persistent court influence in the era of military government, which may have spurred warriors to cultivate elite art forms. Further, warriors required cultural and literary knowledge in order to function as successful leaders. Many authorities now question the longstanding notion that the aristocrats and the warrior class were diametrically opposed, citing instead numerous parallels between nobles who pursued military training and professional warriors who refined their abilities in the civilian arts. Ultimately, even though aristocrats cultivated military skills, they remained unable to prevail in martial training. Meanwhile, by the Edo period, members of the samurai class gradually achieved mastery of literary traditions and administrative procedures, accomplishments that had long been considered critical resources for statesmen.

The term *samurai* is used in this volume to describe professionals employed for their martial skills. However, this word does not indicate a specific rank, nor does it describe the social status of a military retainer. Readers are advised that the function and socioeconomic rank of samurai fluctuated a great deal during the medieval and early modern epochs. An armed warrior of a particular era might lack some accomplishments or aspects of samurai behavior considered below. Still, the martial training and ethical codes essential to soldiers remained relatively consistent (at least in principle) throughout the feudal era in Japan, and therefore merit close examination as a unifying component of military culture. This chapter explores the philosophy and training required of an exemplary warrior, followed by investigations of army structure, military arts, weapons, armor, battle strategies, and key battles. The following section provides a historical overview of samurai origins and related developments in medieval and early modern Japan.

Rise of the Military Class

Japanese warriors are known as samurai, *bushi*, and *buke*. These terms reflect some distinctions in the function of military figures in Japan over time, differences that are considered below in the section "Warrior Terminology." The most familiar term for a warrior, samurai, dates from the Heian period. Including military figures from various class levels over several hundred years, samurai refers to the warriors of Japan in a general sense. However, changes in military roles have been far more complex than popular understanding of the word *samurai* would suggest. The gritty existence of a medieval foot soldier bore little resemblance to the comparatively stable life of samurai residing in peacetime Edo (modern Tokyo) in the early modern period. In an age of prolonged peace, the military abilities of the warrior class eroded as their military services were no longer required.

Samurai transcended humble origins, developing from informal bands of soldiers seeking to overthrow established imperial and aristocratic rule, to emerge as members of the ruling elite. The warrior negotiated an embattled Japan in transition from a decadent, disinterested aristocratic government, in which rank was based on birthright, to a new system of military rule and a social order that validated warrior skills and values. Eventually unification, isolation from the outside world, and the disintegration of the feudal order led to the end of 700 years of samurai prowess and governance in Japan.

Early Medieval Warriors

Armies existed in Japan prior to the medieval era. For example, in the Nara period, government troops consisted of peasants recruited from provincial farm communities. In the early medieval era from about the 10th century, the government-sponsored conscription system began to falter. Despite court government efforts to establish militia units, eventually both aristocrats and the imperial family enlisted the aid of private provincial warrior bands to maintain order in remote areas where central rulers had little authority.

As the Kyoto-based aristocratic government declined during the 12th century, the warrior class emerged as the dominant political, economic, and social force, first in outlying provinces and later, throughout much of Japan. Samurai ascent to power in the middle to late Heian period was prompted in part by the widespread employment of warriors on estates held by Kyoto aristocrats (*kuge*). High-ranking courtiers residing at the cultural center of Japan were not interested in administrating their extensive provincial landholdings, private estates called *shoen*. Instead, they turned to individuals of military skill to serve as estate agents and governors. Aristocrats were effectively absent as the day-to-day management and defense of these lands became the responsibility of groups of professional soldiers.

The rise of these warrior bands, called *bushidan*, began in the late Heian period. All such militia units were regarded as professional fighters, and thus were distinct from conscripted government troops who lacked a formal military background. Some of the most formidable warrior bands were located in the eastern provinces, known as the Kanto region. In addition to court nobles, both the central government and private landholders with no aristocratic lineage employed military units for diverse purposes, such as guarding the capital and protecting villages, and they soon became indispensable.

Disregarding court authority, military bands in the provinces behaved according to lord-vassal relations, and envisioned themselves as bound to serve regional estate officials rather than the courtier-owners of the lands they defended. Often a military troop comprised warriors who shared lineage within extended families, or were local recruits serving on behalf of private interests. Some military bands included warriors who assumed or were granted family names by their employers. Historically significant clans had large percentages of armed retainers who shared no kinship ties. Many warriors serving in the provinces who would never attain court rank were simply assigned to one of the three clans—the Fujiwara, the Taira, and the Minamoto—who dominated warfare of the late Heian and early Kamakura eras. Descendants of these families (or those so assigned) struggled continually for power during the last 100 years of the Heian period.

The Gempei War (1180–85), a violent, decisive struggle for power between the Minamoto and the Taira, ended in victory for the Minamoto. The Minamoto were headquartered at Kamakura in the eastern Kanto region, where the patriarch, Yoritomo, accepted court appointment as *seii tai shogun*, "Great General Who Quells the Barbarians," and set up the first warrior government (*bakufu*, or shogunate). The abbreviated title *shogun* identified Minamoto no Yoritomo as the head of the military government and the person to whom all warriors owed ultimate allegiance. Under military rule, martial responsibilities and local power remained the purview of warrior bands unified through kinship, regional alliances, or political interests, although the shogun was the supreme leader.

Warrior units who enforced peace and defended estates were employed by provincial constables (*shugo*) and estate stewards (*jito*), offices first established by Minamoto no Yoritomo. Initially these constables and stewards were sent to outlying regions by the shogunate, although they later began to amass land and power for personal gain, thus functioning as forerunners to the military lords later known as daimyo. Samurai had long relied upon personal connections to recruit members of their band, while the central government had secured allegiance of military retainers through a system of rewards including rank, office, and land grants. Eventually, government land reserves and available positions became insufficient to ensure that samurai vassals (*gokenin*) would remain loyal to the shogunate and control of provincial estates fell to warrior alliances that consolidated power over regions in the provinces. (For more information on *shugo*, *jito*, and *gokenin* refer to chapter 1: Historical Context.)

From early medieval times, provincial *bushidan* were confederations of independent warrior bands bound by lord-vassal relations and serving different leaders. In practice, lord-vassal alliances functioned like ancestral bonds whereby descendants of a vassal served subsequent generations of the lord's family, who in turn provided ongoing support to the vassals. Despite the lack of blood ties, lords and vassals often conceived of and articulated their relationship in language suggesting kinship. For instance, vassals were described as housemen (*kenin*, or *gokenin* after the Heian period) and children of the house (*ienoko*). Vassals also sometimes characterized their lords as father figures although they were not related.

During the 13th and 14th centuries, the shogunate unwittingly hastened dissolution of central government authority by allowing *gokenin* to attain rank and wealth previously reserved for aristocrats, even as military bands also increased their might. At first, rulers valued warrior bands for their military acumen and secure regional ties or kinship bonds, which peasant forces had lacked. However, personal (or assigned) connections strengthened the commitment between the military retainer, or vassal, and the regional lord (daimyo). Capitalizing on such alliances, established daimyo and *gokenin* were able to amass significant tracts of land far from the capital, with the assurance that samurai bands could defend the domains against central government interference.

Initially such privately trained military groups were somewhat informal, although by the end of the Kamakura era, warrior bands became more organized and essentially constituted private armies. In response to threats from such forces, the Kamakura shogunate issued a new code governing *gokenin* behavior in 1232, hoping to inspire provincial order and regulate samurai activity through exhortations to honor and integrity. Yet such ideals were largely ignored among warrior classes until the samurai code was fully articulated in the Edo period. Disorder prevailed in the provinces, and samurai challenged shogunal authority in struggles for personal property, land, and financial gain—not for honor. The Kamakura shogunate finally collapsed in 1333, and the Ashikaga family assumed power, establishing the Muromachi shogunate.

Late Medieval Warriors

During the Muromachi and Azuchi-Momoyama periods (particularly after the imperial schism known as the Northern and Southern Courts period ended in 1392), warrior bands continued to increase in number and to accumulate military resources such as land, weapons, and training. While aristocrats remained isolated amid imperial court formality in the capital, Kyoto, warriors became a significant threat to central government authority, since they resided in the countryside close to regional lords and farmers who worked the land. The shogunate was unable to quell localized, small-scale disturbances and continued to simply ignore uprisings among warrior vassals. Feuding samurai wisely seized upon pervasive political instability to justify violence fomented in the provinces as they sought to annex land, casting such conflicts as warfare waged on behalf of the shogun. As provincial samurai resources and power mounted, the increasingly insolvent Ashikaga government failed to intervene as aristocrats, governors, and constables ceded land and regional authority to warrior clans.

In the end, neglectful Ashikaga shoguns helped to empower other warrior families as they competed for superiority. Kyoto was largely destroyed in the 10-year struggle known as the Onin War (1467–77). Once hostilities ended in Kyoto, another 90 years of fighting ensued among warrior vassals and lords who had constructed decentralized power bases throughout many regions of Japan. During this era, known as the Warring States period (*Sengoku jidai*, 1467–1568), these territorial lords came to be known as daimyo, meaning great (*dai*) name (*myo*). Because they exercised local and regional power without regard for central authority at a time of incessant war, these lords are often called *sengoku daimyo* (warring lords). Despite the name, Warring States, used for this period, most conflicts involved powerful but peripheral daimyo residing on provincial domains, not authorities serving as central government representatives. Amid the fracturing of government power, fierce competition developed among three successive warriors for control over Japan: Oda Nobunaga, Toyotomi Hideyoshi, and Tokugawa Ieyasu. All three worked to unify the country, although only Ieyasu was able to definitively achieve that aim under the banner of the Tokugawa shogunate. In the shadow of these three famous warriors, warrior vassals deposed shogunal representatives such as *shugo* and *jito* in the 15th and 16th centuries in a disruption of central authority and social hierarchy known in Japanese as *gekokujo* (the inferiors overthrowing the superiors).

Despite widespread destruction, the Warring States period yielded greater respect and resources for the warrior class, and enabled development of strategies and technologies that made both warfare and administration more efficient. Mounted samurai were joined by foot soldiers (*ashigaru*) recruited from the ranks of the peasantry and outfitted with weapons and armor by their wealthy domain lords. Firearms were also introduced to Japan at this time, first from China and then in the mid-16th century by Europeans. A standardized system of land valuation and taxation helped rulers maintain control of their daimyo and vassals and led to a clear articulation of samurai hierarchy through land assessments. Finally, castle construction became an important means of defending large land parcels and establishing a lord's regional status. Thus at the close of the Azuchi-Momoyama era, charismatic regional lords such as Oda Nobunaga, Toyotomi Hideyoshi, and Tokugawa Ieyasu, who once ranked as vassals or lower themselves, demonstrated that members of the samurai class merited authority by virtue of military acumen, not because of aristocratic connections or right of succession. Once unified, the country emerged from more than a century of war-

fare receptive to the mandates of a more effective, centralized form of government.

Early Modern Warriors

The Tokugawa shogunate officially assumed control of Japan in 1615, fostering more than 250 years of peace and imposing nearly complete isolation from trade as well as conflict with foreign lands. Warriors were no longer occupied with battles because the Tokugawa government instituted strict controls to maintain order in domestic affairs, especially in the provinces. Soon many samurai became government bureaucrats, serving the shogunate both in the capital and outlying regions. Other warriors became figureheads who traveled to the capital to make periodic ceremonial appearances and offer tribute to the shogun in the name of their lords. Thus, both daily experience and the social position of members of the samurai classes were transformed in the Edo period. Military ability no longer ensured that the heads of warrior clans could attain daimyo status, nor did lineage confer wealth and prestige, as lands were reallocated according to allegiances and for strategic purposes at the discretion to the Tokugawa ruler. Mounting estate taxes and tributes due to the shogun began to cause financial hardship even among elite daimyo, who could no longer rely upon a network of dutiful vassals and warriors.

The high cost of maintaining favor and position with Edo rulers increased in the third decade of shogunal rule, further depleting already dwindling samurai resources. In 1634, the Tokugawa government established a policy of obligatory alternate-year residence (*sankin kotai*) in the capital for samurai and their families. Initially, daimyo were encouraged to leave family members behind in Edo, thus making them available as hostages in the event that warrior lords collaborated in an attack on the shogun in the capital. Soon, the system also included compulsory daimyo attendance at court in Edo in alternating years, ensuring that warriors traveling to the provinces would lack time, inclination, and resources to organize factions that might overthrow the Tokugawa rulers.

Combined with other aspects of Tokugawa rule, the system of alternate attendance and hostages had significant consequences for warrior culture. The *sankin kotai* system helped to distance regional lords from their vassals and domains, and ensured that shogunal rule in the Edo period would not be disrupted by the localized power struggles that characterized the Warring States period. Although samurai could continue to bear arms in some cases, they suffered reduced stipends due the alternate residence requirement and the associated burden of frequent long-term travel, as well as expenses due to social competition among daimyo for shogunal favor. Warrior affairs were further restricted due to extensive regulations and taxes imposed on diverse circumstances—including castle construction and repair, and intermarriage of daimyo families. Compliance with shogunal edicts was assured using spies and inspectors. *Sankin kotai* did have advantages for warriors of means, since wealthy daimyo had opportunities to indulge their cultural passions. The peacetime environment of the shogunal court spawned increased warrior patronage of leisurely pleasures such as theater, literature, music, and other forms of entertainment. Finally, the significant sums spent by the large samurai population enriched the Edo economy, resulting in a bustling metropolis that ultimately benefited not only the Tokugawa shogunate, but also the merchant and artisan classes.

Thus, Tokugawa rule revolutionized both the social position and daily lives of samurai. Many former warlords were recruited as administrative figures in the shogunal bureaucracy—a position not so different from that of courtiers in attendance at the capital during the zenith of the Heian court. At first it may seem incongruous that the famous Bushido ("Way of the Warrior") code was formalized during this time of peace. Although the Tokugawa shogunate supervised warriors carefully to prevent battles and challenges to central authority, Edo-period samurai were expected to follow rigorous moral guidelines for conduct and to polish their martial skills in accord with their superior rank. Further, under Tokugawa rule, emphasis was placed on principles of warrior traditions rather than military practice, and daimyo and samurai were urged to uphold valor, honor, and duty, even as they were charged with administration of a peacetime government.

Warrior Rank and Socio-Economic Position

Throughout the medieval period, warrior hierarchies often emulated the lord-vassal networks that had long formed the basis for Japanese feudal socioeconomic structure. However, such distinctions were minimized during the era of Tokugawa peace. As Edo-period shoguns reassigned land parcels, status and wealth were dictated by proven loyalty and service to the shogun, and could subvert centuries-old feudal structures or even older aristocratic ties.

Allegiances between lords and vassals within the warrior class had been firmly established by the Warring States period (Sengoku jidai). In accord with Confucian ideals first imported from China in the seventh through ninth centuries, warrior vassals, also called military retainers, served lords in exchange for material and intangible benefits. In turn, these individual landholding vassals were bound to their superiors, such as regional rulers or, in the Edo period, the shogun. A vassal or samurai could expect tangible rewards such as land or currency (often in the form of harvested rice) from superiors in return for service. Other figures, such as farmers and peasants, worked land held by regional rulers and military figures, in return for protection and subsistence rights. Infantry members such as foot soldiers were often recruited from the peasant and farming classes, and while necessary in military encounters, these warriors had few privileges, little income, and low social status, and rarely attained rank among the ruling samurai.

Despite the growing superiority of self-made military figures over aristocrats in the early medieval era, noble ancestry could confer some status in the world of the samurai. Warriors that had (or made claims to) elite lineage were often positioned as officers in the loosely organized regional bands that flourished amid chronic warfare in the Muromachi and Azuchi-Momoyama eras. However, military lords who emerged in the late 16th century were often of humble birth, and figures such as Oda Nobunaga and Toyotomi Hideyoshi rose to power largely because of their superior strategic abilities and military resources. Notably, neither Nobunaga nor Hideyoshi ever assumed the title shogun—which had acquired negative connotations due to a long history of associations with ineffective rulers representing military aristocracy—perhaps in part due to their lower social rank.

In the early modern period, some warriors enjoyed prominence due to long-standing prestige accorded to the military class by lower-ranked social groups, such as farmers, merchants, and artisans. Yet during the more than 250-year Tokugawa peace, many samurai also confronted decreasing incomes and languished as nominal bureaucrats. Such figures were among the fortunate, for many regional daimyo were rendered ineffective or were disenfranchised under reunification, and warriors who had once served such men became masterless, since they were no longer pledged in duty to a lord. Defined by duty, these samurai without lords (*ronin*) became social outcasts and often lived destitute lives because they had no livelihood or stipend to depend upon. Others left warrior culture behind and pursued other professions despite the humiliation of being stripped of a privileged social position.

Warrior Terminology

Terminology for figures within the military power structure also varied during specific eras. While *samurai* was not the most common word used for a soldier during the early medieval period, this term has become the preferred designation for premodern military figures in Japan. First used in a Heian-period document, the term *samurai* derives from a classical Japanese verb, *saburau* (to serve), and aptly describes how duty bound warriors to their lords. At the same time, the term *bushi* (literally men, *shi*, of the martial arts, *bu*) was also used to describe warriors, although the word samurai was used to distinguish armed figures who served the aristocracy. Other less common terms such as *tsuwamono*, *musha*, and *monofu* were used to identify those possessing martial skills, mostly during the Heian to Northern and Southern Courts eras.

Under the military rule that ensued from the Kamakura period onward, soldiers holding an official rank designated by the shogun or the imperial court were considered samurai. Thus, military figures serving in ranked positions were first distinguished from general infantry through terminology early in the medieval era. After reunification was achieved in the early modern period, the term *samurai* was used to indicate warriors of a comparatively high (upper-class) social status, although by that time many samurai no longer served a lord in the original military sense.

From the Kamakura period, *bushi* were considered members of "warrior houses," or *buke*, which in principle were regulated by the shogun or overseen on his behalf by a powerful lord, later known as a daimyo. The term *buke* came to refer generally to the warrior class and was used more or less interchangeably with the term *bushi*. As noted above, warrior bands (*bushidan*), situated on provincial *shoen*, came to exert significant influence in the provinces by the 10th century. *Bushidan* became private armies associated with specific lords (daimyo) from the time of the decline of the Ashikaga shogunate in the mid-15th century. The term *daimyo* was not used extensively to refer to regional lords until the Warring States period, when these domain rulers began to direct regional politics.

The late medieval warrior negotiated a deceptive world in which rank and hierarchies were not always clear, and alliances could shift or disintegrate without warning. By contrast, in the Edo period, warriors were required to submit to a rigid system of socioeconomic classification with the shogun at the pinnacle. Rank and class hierarchies, as stipulated by the shogunate, were assiduously enforced. Under the Tokugawa shogunate, daimyo, *hatamoto* (bannermen), and other titles initially used to describe military function indicated social position, stipend (based on average annual rice consumption), and consequently, the level of respect due to a member of the samurai class. Although the various ranks were based on military terms, most warriors served the Tokugawa shogunate as administrators or bureaucrats, not as military retainers. Members of the warrior classes who were released from obligation to a lord due to death or loss of stipend were known as masterless samurai or *ronin* (literally, "one who wanders") from the Muromachi period on. Often dissatisfied with their financial situation and lack of status, masterless samurai were frequently involved in uprisings such as the Keian Incident of 1651. The Tokugawa shogunate strove to reposition these disenfranchised individuals, but many *ronin* abandoned their samurai status or eventually died out. For more information on *ronin*, see the section below entitled "Values Expressed in Life—Loyalty."

WARRIOR ETHICS

Bushido: The Way of the Warrior

The term *Bushido* literally means "the way (*do*) of the warrior (*bushi*)." In popular usage, Bushido designates a broad spectrum of traditional Japanese samurai values. However, the term originated long after the military class rose to power in the early medieval era, and carries different implications within various periods. Regardless, the "way of the warrior" was a critical philosophy and code of conduct for the martial rulers who transformed military affairs and governance in feudal Japan.

The word *Bushido* was first used in Edo-period Japan to identify the collective values and ideals of the ruling military class. Although uniformity of warrior values was promoted by the Tokugawa government, there was no official samurai code. Even during peacetime, samurai were expected to possess ardent martial spirit and military acumen as well as ultimate devotion to a lord, fervent commitment to duty, and courage to relinquish life in battle or through ritual suicide if necessary. Paradoxically, qualities sought in reliable soldiers, such as valor in battle and duty to superiors, became inextricably connected with the warrior class only during the peaceful, centralized, yet restrictive, rule of the Tokugawa shogunate. Specific examples of warrior values are discussed below in the section titled Warrior Values.

Warrior principles were first codified as a formal ethical system in the 17th and 18th centuries by the scholar Yamaga Soko (1622–85), who is credited with defining the samurai ideal. Although the term *Bushido* was not used by Yamaga, he described the military figure as a moral exemplar committed to duty and loyalty above all. The Way of the Warrior functioned effectively, Yamaga noted, as an ethos perpetuated by the warrior's lord, who rewarded samurai service with favor. The mutual dependence and bond between military retainer and lord was essential to what scholars after Yamaga called the Bushido ethic. Once Emperor Meiji was restored as ruler of Japan in 1868, the samurai class was abolished along with feudal socioeconomics. Still, the warrior archetype articulated through writings on Edo-period Bushido continued to serve as a potent ideal in Japan. In 1899, Nitobe Inazo published *Bushido: The Soul of Japan* (1899), a work that characterized warrior ethos as the embodiment of all that was most admired in traditional Japanese society and culture.

Despite the cohesive picture of samurai ideals presented by Edo-period philosophers and historians, warrior values fluctuated during the feudal era. During the middle and late Heian periods, warriors were primarily occupied with family honor, then loyalty to their lords, and third, personal benefit. From the end of the Kamakura period, samurai were less likely to consider honor, moral obligation, or duty first, focusing on professional obligations and prospects for the future in a time of widespread social, political, and economic unrest. The Muromachi shogunate prompted greater fragmentation of warrior behavior despite attempts to restore stable, centralized military rule. Ambitious warriors took advantage of the breakdown of political authority, acquiring land or consolidating power in efforts to improve their socioeconomic position. At the same time, improved weapons technology and soldiers who were better prepared for battle made warriors a more potent threat in the eyes of provincial constables (*shugo*), estate stewards (*jito*), or vassals (*gokenin*) appointed by the shogun or court nobles. Often, provincial samurai were granted or could assume positions as intermediate vassals, and thus had direct access to land and power, as well as military might to ensure their concerns were protected. Thus, throughout the Muromachi period, self-interest and opportunism thrived as warriors became increasingly aware of their access to land and power in a fractured political climate. In reality, medieval samurai behavior did not necessarily reflect Edo peacetime ideals of warrior duty and virtue. Other disjunctions between early modern samurai standards and the actual role of warriors in the medieval era are discussed below.

Aspects of the samurai code have been construed as established principles for warrior conduct dating to the Heian period, although, as noted above, this was not always the case. Recently, scholars such as Karl F. Friday have reexamined the chivalry, camaraderie, and ritualized attitudes toward warfare long seen as hallmarks of early medieval warriors. Friday and his colleagues propose that warrior lore glorified military values favored in later eras, rather than reflecting the experience of feudal military retainers. Fundamentally, samurai were professional fighters who might be reluctant to selflessly sacrifice their lives to honor their lords. In Edo Japan, the warrior tradition offered a reminder of past glories for samurai displaced from their professional role by the peaceful state engineered by the Tokugawa shogunate. In all probability, samurai virtues encompassed by the term *Bushido* were defined through such romantic retrospection rather than contemporary observation.

Today, many scholars acknowledge that the samurai heroes who conducted epic campaigns recounted in medieval tales were intended as entertainment, rather than as historically accurate descriptions of individual figures. Such warrior tales, known as *gunkimono* (sometimes also called *gunki monogatari*), first became popular during the 14th and 15th centuries, and are considered in greater detail in chapter 8: Language and Literature. Since the nostalgic allure of these dramatic accounts helped to shape the ideals embodied in the "way of the warrior," notable figures and tales from warrior literature are outlined briefly below. Later theoreticians and scholars revisited medieval visions of the romanticized Japanese samurai as they strove to forge an ethical code for the military retainer based on the ideals of the past.

Feudal Society and Bushido

Military figures influenced many aspects of politics and society in feudal Japan. Medieval authority, economy, and social hierarchies centered on the lord-samurai retainer relationship. This relationship, much like the dynamic between lord and vassals in feudal Europe, functioned through the lord's commitment to provide favor (*on*), often in the form of land grants, titles, or prestige, in exchange for service (*giri*) from the warrior retainer. *Giri* refers to notions of social obligation and indebtedness in Japanese culture in general, although contemporary understanding of this concept was largely inspired by the feudal dynamics of vassal and lord. More information on this exchange of debt and favor can be found in the section "Warrior Values," later in this chapter.

The interdependence of medieval lords and their retainers was critical to the success of the feudal system. If samurai overpowered their lords, disorder ensued, as lords did not anticipate or plan for an insurrection mounted by their own military forces. Fostering a moral and behavioral code for samurai thus served as insurance for a lord, helping to maintain a fit, well-prepared, knowledgeable army that was constantly ready for battle, outfitted with the best weapons and other resources, and devoted to duty. In return, virtuous samurai were recognized for their skill in battle and rewarded for their loyalty. As noted earlier, by the middle of the medieval era in the 14th century, armies grew increasingly privatized and professionalized, in part due to this effective system of reciprocal values.

Military success increased, too, due to the improved organization of units that trained together and operated for mutual benefit in peacetime as well as in battle. Early medieval warrior bands were often ad hoc conglomerations, even in the presence of family ties, that gathered for particular campaigns and disbanded or forged new affiliations shortly thereafter. By the late 13th century, many feudal samurai units included both foot soldiers and cavalry in mixed groups in which infantry were far more vulnerable to attack. Further, they rarely had the benefit of having trained together, either as a mixed group or with comrades using the same weaponry, whether infantry or on horseback. Achieving victory in this type of configuration was difficult, especially without significant numbers of infantry and authoritative commanders to deploy them, and samurai armies thus remained relatively inefficient. Further, a majority of battles in the early medieval era culminated in private conflicts between elite, mounted warriors engaged in ritualized maneuvers, rather than large-scale sieges using specialized units. Under the command of various locally powerful daimyo, from the late 14th century and thereafter, feudal warfare in Japan became more specialized, more decisive, and less ceremonial.

Although warrior values advocated a distinctive martial ethic centering on absolute loyalty to a daimyo, nonetheless, many feudal samurai interpreted their vassal-lord relationship as a basic economic contract endowed with potential gains for enterprising individuals. Thus in practice, warrior loyalties often fluctuated, varying with prevailing local, socioeconomic, and personal circumstances. The bonds of honor and service a samurai owed to his lord could be ruptured, as in the late medieval dynamic called *gekokujo*, "the lower [inferiors] overturning the upper [superiors]." This enterprise of warrior culture involved an inversion of Japan's normative social and economic feudal order, which kept land and power in the hands of regional daimyo.

By the middle of the Warring States era (Sengoku jidai, 1467–1568), *shugo* (provincial constables), *jito* (estate stewards) and other samurai vassals, such as *gokenin*, had overthrown daimyo and other estate owners, largely due to increased numbers of well-trained warriors that powered samurai military bands and mounted challenges to daimyo military units weakened by incessant warfare. Such disruptions of long-established medieval social and political order exemplify the conflict between individual authority, represented by various leaders at the imperial, shogunal, or daimyo level, and institutional power. Amid the upheaval of the Warring States era, this crisis of authority was manipulated by skillful vassals and samurai who were able to benefit from the power gaps inherent in the Japanese feudal system. From humble beginnings as loosely organized professional military leagues, warrior retainers ultimately gained the upper hand and came to dominate regional politics in the late medieval era, and thus the might of the samurai class led to triumph over the established supremacy of regional daimyo.

Bushido in the Edo Period

In early modern times, the Tokugawa shogunate achieved reunification and peace and maintained control of the samurai through an administration that fostered both a distinctive sense of identity and a new political role for the ruling military classes. Along with the shogunate, the enduring Edo-period peace challenged warriors to redefine their role. While Edo samurai were considered members of the ruling class, paradoxically they had little political power since they subsisted on stipends, which were distributed by domain lords who were no longer dependent upon warrior retainers for protection. With overseas travel limited and peace enforced along with isolationist policies, samurai were transformed into civil administrators and tributaries who served the shogun. Many higher-ranking samurai were charged with oversight of domains or smaller land parcels on behalf of their lords, particularly as ruling daimyo were often occupied with ceremonial responsibilities in the capital stipulated by the shogunate. The alternate-year attendance (*sankin kotai*) policy enforced by the Tokugawa rulers also meant that some samurai were required to travel frequently with the regional entourages obliged to appear before the shogunate. All of these activities helped to prevent potential uprisings within the military classes and encouraged samurai to spend any discretionary income that might otherwise enable individuals to amass resources to mount a military threat. Finally, samurai and their families helped to boost the peacetime economy as they competed among themselves in efforts to impress their leaders or the shogunate with their refinement and glamour.

Peacetime and the bourgeois culture that flourished in urban centers encouraged samurai to cultivate civil and leisurely pursuits. Several members of the warrior class turned their attention to literary arts in efforts to articulate the philosophy behind martial traditions. Many of these texts extol Bushido values, such as the will to action, purity of motivation, steadfast service, and intellectual and political leadership, that are also Confucian paradigms of human behavior. Through contact with Korea and China, Confucian traditions had long influenced Japanese notions of effective government and society. Confucian ideals became more prominent in the Edo period due to the suitability of such principles for a military government administrated by functionaries who prized loyalty, and thus notions of filial piety, above all other virtues. Assisted by the rhetoric emerging from writers of the military classes who highlighted similarities between long-standing Bushido values and Confucian ethics, the Tokugawa shoguns identified an effective means of promoting samurai civil service as representative of warrior values, even as they were able to suppress martial aspects of military culture by identifying these pursuits as civilian arts.

During the Edo period, the shogunate monitored the warrior elite to ensure that military ethics and abilities that emerged in the medieval era were transformed into peacetime values and service to the Tokugawa government. The shogunate approved of the fundamental samurai ethic of absolute loyalty, as well as the moral tone of Bushido in general. Such ideals were primary topics among the military classes, due to numerous treatises on samurai philosophy composed in the Edo period. For example, in the first decades of Tokugawa rule, Miyamoto Musashi (1584–1645) published *Gorin no sho* (ca. 1643; *The Book of Five Rings*, 1974). A master swordsman trained in Zen Buddhism, and a *ronin* whose lord had been among those defeated in the Battle of Sekigahara, Musashi detailed strategies of swordsmanship and exalted victory achieved in the name of one's lord as the supreme accomplishment and self-effacing purpose of a warrior. Upholding ideals of selfless duty provided inspiration to samurai transformed from self-reliant military adventurers to functionaries dependent upon fixed stipends awarded by shogunal or domain governments. Linking these paradigms with Confucian principles gave the warrior a higher purpose in peacetime Edo Japan.

The connections between Confucian ethics and civil responsibility promoted by Miyamoto Musashi were furthered by Yamaga Soko (1622–85), whose theories were discussed above in the section titled "Bushido: The Way of the Warrior." Unlike his predecessors, Yamaga emphasized the social debt samurai had incurred, as the protective services they had previously provided were no longer necessary in the era of Edo peace. Since the warrior's military service was his means of livelihood and was critical to Japan, samurai thus had incurred a responsibility to society in general, since the stipends earned previously became a debt that had to be repaid in peacetime. In repayment of this debt, Yamaga urged samurai to uphold Confucian values, proposing that the warrior alone could serve as a model for the virtue of duty necessary for a harmonious society. The Confucian tone in Yamaga's works coincided with the desire of the Tokugawa shogunate to recognize and reinforce the contributions of samurai-turned-bureaucrats. Yamaga also emphasized the importance of the warrior's duty to honor his lord, and above him, the shogun, as symbolic of the debt all Japanese had to serve their supreme leader, the emperor, through whom Japan's divine origins could be traced. Most Japanese viewed the emperor as a figurehead in the Edo period, although by the mid-19th century, Yamaga's writings became influential in galvanizing support for the emperor's return to power.

Some Edo-period theorists on Bushido placed more emphasis on the self-discipline required of the warrior as evocative of the self-effacing samurai tradition of ultimate devotion to one's lord. Yamamoto Tsunetomo (1659–1719) is believed to have dictated the Bushido manual *Hagakure* (full title *Hagakure kikigaki*; "Notes of What Was Heard in the Shadow of Leaves"; completed 1716) to Tashiro Tsuramoto. This collection of more than 1,300 anecdotes and brief reflections on the samurai way opens with the oft-repeated phrase "Bushido is a way of dying." This quote summarizes the pervasive theme of *Hagakure*: That only a warrior who is ready and willing to perish at any moment can be fully dedicated to his lord.

Another important Edo-period treatise on warrior conduct and philosophy entitled *Budo shoshinshu (Code of the Samurai)* was compiled by Daidoji Yuzan (also known as Daidoji Shigesuke, 1639–1730) in the early 18th century. A native of Yamashiro province (part of modern Kyoto Prefecture), Yuzan traveled to Edo to study military strategy under Hojo Ujinaga (1609–70), and produced this volume in 44 chapters that is now considered a Bushido classic. Like other Edo-period authors, he sought to preserve the values and techniques central to warrior heritage, which had become increasingly unfamiliar to peacetime samurai under Tokugawa rule. *Budo shoshinshu* stands apart from other manuals as one of the most widely circulated volumes about the warrior code. Yuzan's text may have seemed particularly accessible compared to other warrior manuals of the Edo period, since *Budo shoshinshu* was organized as a series of lessons delivered by a father to his son.

Reflections on samurai experience and moral bearing, like those described above in the work of Daidoji Yuzan, Yamamoto Tsunetomo, Yamaga Soko, and Miyamoto Musashi, offered warriors a sense of purpose and integrity, while inspiring pride in the long tradition of the samurai code. Ultimately, the warrior elite who had displaced Japan's tradition of aristocratic rule with a system of military governance dominated politics and culture for nearly 700 years. Although the Confucian leanings of Edo-period warrior treatises advocated the importance of samurai culture even in peace, economic realities helped foster discontent among warriors. By the 19th century, many samurai were trapped in a symbolic social role with dwindling resources and little actual power, resulting in dissatisfaction with shogunal rule. Warriors envisioning a better future for their country and their heirs began to support the emperor's right to serve as Japan's true ruler, leading to the dismantling of the Tokugawa shogunate and the restoration of imperial power beginning with Emperor Meiji in 1868. While the Meiji Restoration was largely supported by the samurai classes, ironically, this landmark political reform marked the end of both feudal governance and the hegemony of the warrior in Japan.

The Legacy of Bushido

Advocates of the imperial restoration prevailed and forced the last Tokugawa shogun to abdicate as the Edo period drew to a close. With Emperor Meiji restored as the supreme ruler of Japan, the Tokugawa shogunate and its feudal structure were dismantled, and the samurai class was abolished. However, Bushido remained a powerful tradition and a source of pride in Japan. Early Meiji industrialization and Western influence temporarily muted the appeal of warrior traditions, yet in the wake of the Sino-Japanese War (1894–95), the way of the warrior became a more prominent cultural force as an ex-

pression of patriotism that emphasized militarism and devotion to the emperor. A noted tribute to warrior ideals titled *Bushido: The Soul of Japan* (1899) was written by Nitobe Inazo (1862–1933), a professor, author, and diplomat, during this time of reflection on the integrity of Japanese culture. Published as Japan had begun to surge into the modern era, Nitobe's portrayal of samurai rectitude as the most admirable legacy of Japanese culture confirmed the enduring power of Bushido as both a call to arms and a call to virtue even in a time of rapid social and economic reform.

Medieval Warrior Values

The medieval warrior values similar to those described in detail below were perhaps first summarized in the *Chikubasho* (Bamboo stilt anthology), a Muromachi-period volume providing moral instruction for samurai. Completed in 1383 by an Ashikaga deputy shogun (*kanrei*) named Shiba Yoshimasa (1350–1410), the text outlined explicit rules to guide the behavior of the military class. At the same time, this work also stressed the importance of cultivating both the martial arts and the traditional four scholarly accomplishments first identified with Confucius's ideal gentleman: games of strategy, scholarship through skilled calligraphic copies of the classical texts, music, and painting. In advocating the "dual way" of both military abilities and cultural pursuits, *Chikubasho* identified the balance of cultural and martial knowledge sought by the warrior class. At the same time, this early warrior manual laid foundations for samurai of limited regional authority and humble origins to achieve social, economic, and political prominence previously available only to the cultivated aristocracy.

First and foremost, the samurai was a professional soldier, and thus was expected to perform martial duties at the request of his lord in exchange for remuneration in the form of land, subvassals who worked samurai fields and served in his military unit, and other tangible rewards, such as protection. The lord-vassal relationship was the primary factor that determined a warrior's role and socioeconomic status. Since a samurai provided service to his lord by means of achievement in combat, in both military encounters and civilian life, warriors were expected to exhibit discipline and fortitude even off the battlefield. For example, a well-known Edo-period anecdote relates the deep disgrace samurai would experience at betraying hunger through the rumbling of an empty stomach, or even by acknowledging such a basic need. Upholding such stringent ideals of honor and restraint helped to ensure that warriors were constantly prepared for battle as well as other forms of adversity, while cultivating a sense of group pride and integrity lacking in nonmilitary circles.

Warriors were expected to cultivate other exemplary traits, such as loyalty, prudence, and stability, along with military leadership. Such appropriate samurai attributes were first expounded in literary sources dating to the medieval period. Literary sources highlighted samurai devotion, such as the vow to commit seppuku (ritual suicide by disembowelment; also known as hara-kiri) if faced with disgrace, especially when confronting certain enemy triumph. Willingness to follow one's lord in death (*junshi*) was a related act of ultimate loyalty. Samurai demonstrated such values when imperial forces defeated the Hojo clan in 1333, and thousands of loyal warriors emulated the fate of their Hojo masters by performing ritual disembowelment, an event recorded in the *Taiheiki* (Chronicle of the great peace), completed by 1374.

Despite the picture of duty painted in historical accounts like the *Taiheiki*, loyalty was not an absolute for the military retainer throughout the medieval and early modern periods. In principle, a samurai might owe allegiance to a lord through his obligation to uphold loyalty and duty, but such a debt might also derive from material benefits, such as financial support and other rewards, offered to a warrior by a daimyo. Although traditionally the Japanese military class has been characterized as selfless and disinterested in personal gain, in reality warriors put their own needs ahead of those of their lords at various times. Certainly samurai were not immune to the allure of improving their socioeconomic position. Military units often fought on behalf of a distant lord, and even lofty moral principles could not prevent samurai bands from enjoying the spoils of warfare directly, rather than being satis-

fied with token parcels offered by their lords when redistribution of conquered lands occurred.

As discussed above, theoretically, Bushido principles required that samurai were chivalrous champions of the weak and the disadvantaged, and protectors of the vanquished. However, since samurai had been trained to fight until capture or casualties occurred, they were often ruthless in pursuing their objectives. From the early medieval era, both the law and widespread precedents worked to prevent warriors from pursuing private interests through violent means. In the Kamakura period, legally, samurai were granted authority only to chastise lawbreakers on behalf of a superior ruler. Many incidents occurred during the medieval era in which warriors usurped ruling authority, took advantage of disorder and military power, or simply extended their responsibilities in order to achieve personal gains. Thus, many samurai failed to consistently demonstrate honorable behavior and loyalty as extolled in Bushido principles. Eventually, the civil order established by the Tokugawa shogunate eliminated samurai incentives to pursue personal gain through military prowess.

Other warrior values attest to connections between learning, lineage, social status, and righteous administration first introduced to Japan from China, along with centralized government, during the Asuka period (552–645). Long seen as the purview of the ruling class, knowledge and education became central samurai ideals during the Muromachi era as Japan experienced renewed Chinese cultural influence. As in ancient China, learned samurai were expected to be familiar with standard Chinese texts, and to master related skills such as calligraphy, poetry, and principles of strategy. Once the Ashikaga shogunate was established in Kyoto, the residence of Japan's imperial family for nearly 1,100 years and a city distinguished by its aristocratic elegance and refinement, military rulers and other members of the warrior classes sought to establish their cultural acumen as well as the right to govern the nobility. The prominent influence of Chinese culture in the Muromachi age also contributed to the growing sense that a military figure should demonstrate characteristics typical of the superior gentleman, a moral and cultural ideal first identified by the Chinese sage Confucius (Kongfuzi), ca. 551–479 B.C.E.

Early Modern Warrior Values

During the Edo period, the enduring Tokugawa peace challenged warriors to redefine their role. By this time, samurai ranked as the ruling class, yet paradoxically had little actual power, subsisting on stipends distributed by lords of domains who served as functionaries at the behest of the Tokugawa rulers. Many higher-ranking samurai were also transformed into administrators of domains or smaller areas they controlled on behalf of daimyo. Others were occupied with the ceremonial duties associated with the alternate-year attendance (*sankin kotai*) or held positions in the Tokugawa government. Advocacy of warrior values in peacetime needed to sanction moral behavior and pride in samurai heritage without encouraging uprisings and other challenges to shogunal authority. The Tokugawa shogunate took several steps to bring about this change in the early modern era.

Warriors were located in castle towns, where they could be monitored closely, and where they were distanced from forming regional alliances and annexing land. Military adventures were thus curtailed, and direct contact with peasants and farmers who had previously served as foot soldiers was eliminated. Military commanders such as Oda Nobunaga and Toyotomi Hideyoshi realized that separating the samurai from their former subvassals (who were often infantry training under a particular military retainer's command) was not enough, and made efforts to ensure that only samurai could possess swords. With samurai isolated in areas away from their own landholdings and with no direct control of their subvassals, the warriors were more likely to remain loyal to their daimyo rather than becoming turncoats.

Foundations of Warrior Conduct

From the 14th century, and especially during the Edo period, samurai were expected to follow their code of conduct closely and adhere to warrior values. Samurai behavior was praised as a model for all Japanese to follow, and therefore, inappropriate or deviant behavior was considered particularly problematic.

Fundamental virtues such as duty and filial piety were primary among the values warriors were expected to uphold. Confucian ideals were introduced to Japan from China during the fifth or sixth centuries C.E. These principles place strong emphasis on appropriate behavior, such as social obligations in human relationships, and were also pertinent to the code of warrior conduct. A central Confucian tenet, filial piety (*ko*; also known as *koko* or *oyakoko*), stipulates that children are obligated to be obedient to their parents and to care for them as they age. Upon death and thereafter, children must continue to venerate their parents and other ancestors, since family members are seen as capable of perpetual influence in the world of the living. Further, throughout East Asia, Confucian principles have informed the perception that the family—rather than the individual as in many Western cultures—is the basic unit of society. Ideally for Japanese during the feudal era (and in many cases, today as well), proper observation of filial piety would yield a pleasant family life and, by extension, social harmony in general.

Filial piety was practically inseparable from loyalty (*chu*) and duty or indebtedness (*on/giri*) in medieval Japanese society, both of which were considered essential traits that distinguished an exemplary samurai. Duty through filial piety had first been linked with righteous governance and harmonious human relationships through Confucian hierarchies in government and bureaucratic structures imported from China and Korea especially in the fifth through eighth centuries. As military rule was instituted in the Kamakura period, these principles for government and military order continued to be foundations of shogunal authority, offering assurance of steadfast service that cemented the bonds of martial rule. As noted earlier, duty was fundamental to warrior behavior, since the samurai profession was defined by obligation to serve a lord. Other ethical concerns, including honor, obligation, perseverance, obedience, and deference, became more closely linked with samurai as they became victorious and more powerful in the medieval period. Thus respect and social position in medieval and early modern Japan were produced by, but also derived from, the institutionalization of the warrior code, Bushido.

By the 15th century, performances, written and illustrated tales, and anecdotes heralded warrior achievements, and soon samurai dedication to duty, honor, and military prowess became legendary largely through association with the heroes chronicled in these accounts. In the Edo period, Bushido principles were fundamental to maintaining peace and preserving the socioeconomic structure. Members of the ruling samurai class were exalted as model citizens and moral exemplars, while paradoxically, their earning potential declined rapidly. Although they occasionally expressed dissatisfaction with their diminished income and political might, still these warriors posed little threat to the shogunate, largely because the proud samurai tradition demanded service to their supreme lord, the shogun, and adherence to Bushido principles.

Name, class, occupation, land, and responsibilities were all matters of patrimony in medieval Japan. Thus, consciousness of heritage and filial piety suffused many aspects of warrior culture. For example, early samurai war chronicles such as the *Hogen monogatari* and the *Heike monogatari* recount the process of pedigree declarations, in which a challenger was expected to recite the achievements of all his ancestors including his own before engaging in single combat with an opponent. This procedure certainly heightened a warrior's awareness that he fought not only for the lord he served, but also in support of a reputation already established by his ancestors.

By the 14th century, pedigree proclamations were discontinued as warfare became more fast-paced and less ceremonial, although the symbolic association with ancestral duty was manifest in other aspects of a soldier's regalia. Heraldic symbols such as *sashimono* that had once consisted of a single color and often a symbol to unite and identify an entire army gradually came to be used by individuals and featured their family crest. (Further details regarding *sashimono* and other banners can be found below under "Weapons and Armor.") About 200 years later, in the 16th century, a warrior no longer needed to announce his identity in the midst of battle since his family name (or sometimes, that of his

lord) was visible on his banner and/or garments. Such expressions of duty and ancestral ties (or evidence of service to a particular daimyo) represented one form of filial piety that linked nearly all Japanese warriors, regardless of historical era or political events. For feudal samurai, filial piety represented not merely an obligation to respect ancestors, but also a sense of patrimony and military reputation that was borne into battle for all to see.

Model Warrior Values

Specific warrior ideals are discussed below in social and historical context.

VALUES EXPRESSED IN LIFE

Loyalty In the popular imagination and in various treatises on samurai behavior, warriors were portrayed as paragons of loyalty. In behavior toward both superiors and inferiors, in word and deed, and even in death, samurai were expected to demonstrate unwavering fidelity. Japanese views of loyalty were strongly informed by Confucian behavioral ideals, which were transmitted to Japan perhaps as early as the fifth century C.E.

During feudal times, loyalty was essential to the relationship between samurai and daimyo in their roles as military retainer and lord. Beyond the bonds of allegiance owed to daimyo, feudal warriors also had commitments of fealty to immediate family members, clan or *bushidan* leaders, and other samurai retainers or landowners, depending upon alliances formed by their daimyo. Further, if a lord changed allies, samurai were obligated to follow. The relative hierarchy of such loyalties varied at different points in medieval and early modern Japan, although a samurai's unconditional loyalty to his lord remained a constant. The most extreme form of loyalty expected of samurai was the act of *junshi*, described in detail below.

In some cases, standards of samurai loyalty could involve suppressing national laws in favor of the moral principles of Bushido. Since warriors were required to remain steadfast to their daimyo above all else, samurai were obligated to avenge the unjust death of their lord in order to restore his (and by extension, their own) honor. Unfortunately, the moral obligations of the warrior code sometimes conflicted with government mandates and codes of civil conduct. Tension between moral law and shogunal mandates was a critical factor in what was known as the notorious 47 Ronin Incident (Ako Jiken; literally, the Ako Incident), which occurred in the early morning hours of January 31, 1703 (although the event is now commemorated annually in Japan on December 14). Former retainers of Asano Naganori (1665–1701), the deceased daimyo of the Ako domain, descended upon the well-guarded Edo residence of Kira Yoshinaka (1641–1703), whom they assassinated in retaliation for Asano's death, which they considered unjust.

While in attendance at a reception for the shogun in Edo castle, Asano violated acceptable court behavior, reportedly due to neglect or inaccurate counsel by Kira. As chief of protocol to the Tokugawa shogunate at the time, Kira was responsible for maintaining decorum among retainers in attendance at the castle. Apparently Kira provoked Asano through his condescending and supercilious manner, and in response, Asano drew his sword in anger and attacked Kira inside the shogun's castle. This criminal act incited a swift response from the shogun, who determined that as punishment Asano would be required to perform seppuku, ritual suicide by disembowelment, and that thereafter his domain, the province of Harima (now part of Hyogo Prefecture) would become property of the shogunate, and his retainers henceforth would be considered *ronin* (masterless samurai). Of these retainers, 47 took a pledge to exact revenge for their lord's demise. After slaying Kira, these loyal *ronin* marched to Asano's grave site and presented his decapitated head.

Determining the appropriate response to this vengeful act was problematic for the shogunate in several respects. The Tokugawa rulers had helped to promote the Bushido code, which stipulated that the cardinal duty of the samurai was absolute loyalty to their daimyo. Yet the 47 *ronin* had openly violated public law, as they had committed a violent act in a group. Further, by assassinating Kira, Asano's former retainers had attempted to rectify his purported wrongful punishment as determined by the shogun,

and they had mounted their revenge in the capital, thus brazenly challenging the authority of the shogunate in both respects. The shogunate determined that the retainers would be punished as a group and ordered to commit seppuku. Perhaps because they were disciplined for upholding longstanding samurai values, and since their demise could be viewed as an act of *junshi*, the 47 *ronin* quickly became popular heroes, to the chagrin of the Tokugawa rulers. A famed play entitled *Kanadehon chushingura* appeared in 1748 on the subject and was later used as a model for future accounts of the incident.

Honor In addition to fulfilling their duty, warriors had a responsibility to conduct themselves in a manner that would reflect well upon their lord, their ancestors, and their descendants. In principle, samurai behavior was deemed a reflection of individual character, but it also affected family reputation and could enhance or mar a lord's social and political status. The notion that honor was inherent in one's name, and thus was shared with other family members, past, present, and future, became prominent in Japanese society during the 12th century. For example, in warrior tales (*gunki monogatari*) written during the Kamakura and Muromachi eras, references to shame and honor, which are frequent in such contexts, refer to both individuals and family members, as well as ancestors. Often this concept of collective prestige or disgrace is referred to as "face" in the English phrase "to lose face." Thus, in Japanese, honor (*meiyo*; literally "glory of the name") carries the additional implication for samurai that, beyond personal virtue, warriors must also uphold allegiances to family, clan, and lord, who might not have the same name but certainly shared a collective reputation. Just as honor was inherited or shared through a name, household (meaning a lord and his vassals), or clan, shame would also be borne by all who were linked by family ties or bonds of service and protection.

Favor and Debt (*On/Giri*) Since warrior existence was predicated upon duty, in everyday life, warrior values were governed by the related concepts of *on* and *giri*. These principles affected warrior behavior in relation to land, protection, and service in battle.

On can be defined as the debt incurred by the recipient of benefits (material or otherwise), and is often equated in English with the concepts of favor or indebtedness. *Giri* refers to an obligation to repay *on* incurred in receiving favors, whether material or otherwise, and is often translated as "social obligation."

Obligation could arise in a variety of relationships such as between a warrior and master, individual and family group, employee and employer, or subject and lord. For feudal samurai, this reciprocal dynamic meant that warriors incurred an enormous debt to their lords because of the benefit of receiving employment, land, and political protection, as well as associated items such as armor and weapons. Since samurai subsistence depended on the lord, the debt incurred and the associated responsibility to make repayment was immense. Warriors bore this profound obligation in an unbreakable bond of duty—a debt so significant that the samurai were bound to follow their lords even in death. If such obligations were not obeyed, the responsible party could face social disdain and even complete ostracization, thus disgracing not only individual honor, but also an extended family or even an entire domain. The interrelated dynamic of *on/giri* was central to the structure of feudal warrior society, and remains important in Japan today.

Manners and Appearance Appearance first became a central concern in Japan amid the cultural renaissance of the Heian period, when aristocrats were preoccupied with aesthetic refinement and elegance. From the rise of the warrior class in the late Heian period, certain characteristics distinguished samurai. Manuals dictated the procedure for donning armor, and by the late medieval period, volumes were compiled to instruct samurai on appropriate behavior and grooming both on and off the battlefield.

While roving mercenaries had little concern for their public image, members of the warrior elite recognized that external appearance impacted all facets of samurai experience from personal dignity to rank and even earning power. On the battlefield, helmets and armor clearly distinguished warriors by rank, division, and even region of origin. (For more information on arms and armor, see below.) Civilian samurai garments echoed the fashions that had long been favored by court nobles, and may reflect the fact that the military classes aspired to higher social status and cultural sophistication in a feudal society that prized the aristocracy despite the supremacy of its military rulers. For more information on warrior clothing, see chapter 12: Everyday Life.

Projecting a dignified and fashionable manner remained a high priority for members of the warrior classes during the Edo period, when samurai competed against each other with displays of wealth when traveling to the capital to attend upon the shogun. Samurai of the early modern era became more concerned with embellishment of warrior clothing and armor, and in peacetime, more time and resources could be devoted to such matters. Amid the growing popularity of adornment and the dramatic appearance cultivated by actors and other denizens of the pleasure districts, warriors were permitted to wear makeup. The Tokugawa government issued other regulations about appropriate samurai dress for various occasions and ranks, and (theoretically, at least) the warrior classes alone were granted the right to carry two swords, long and short, in public. As in earlier eras, manuals prescribed appropriate behavior and customs for the samurai class. Many aspects of samurai bearing and appearance were intended to ensure that the respect and honor due to members of the warrior classes were conferred in Edo culture.

Marriage Confucian ideals informed samurai marriage practices along with many other aspects of warrior life. Bushido, as a moral code, necessarily involved Confucian principles governing virtuous human relationships and social roles. The absolute subordination of a wife and children to the head of the family constitutes one powerful example of the influence of Confucian thought in feudal Japanese society. Wives who did not honor their husbands were seen as disruptive of domestic harmony and the wider social order as well.

Marital unions became a central concern of samurai from the 12th century onward, especially since political imbalances and power struggles often implicated family ties. Military alliances between families could be established or reinforced through strategic unions, and such bonds were critical during eras of civil war, such as the Warring States period (1467–1568).

Samurai marriages discontinued the matrilocal, endogamous (marriage within a limited group of households), and polygamous practices of Heian-period aristocrats. This change may have been inspired in part by practical considerations, for medieval Japanese marriages among the elite increasingly involved wives selected from distant households. Marrying within a close group had few advantages for ambitious samurai families eager to increase their landholdings or to broaden alliances across provincial territories. Further, matrilocal marriage traditions, in which, for example, couples often chose to reside with the bride's family, were impractical for warriors who had amassed land, military forces, and political connections in the region of their own family residences, and which required close supervision. The shift to more permanent marriage practices was isolated among members of the ruling military classes. Rural commoners, who often served as warriors in times of conflict, were bound to the land they worked and continued to engage in multiple liaisons and other established traditions.

Sexual Conduct Samurai often retained concubines during the medieval and early modern eras. However, in their own households, military retainers rarely practiced polygamy, which had notoriously complicated imperial succession and family structure in the Heian period. Like other social groups throughout Japanese history, warriors also engaged prostitutes of both sexes, though such practices were not widely documented until the early modern era. Under the peaceful Tokugawa shogunate, many samurai spent leisure time in the notorious pleasure districts of the capital city, Edo. Homosexuality was also a common practice among members of the warrior classes, particularly during the Edo period.

VALUES EXPRESSED THROUGH DEATH

Demonstrating honor and duty throughout life were central aspects of the samurai code, but in many respects, death was a defining moment for members of the warrior class. Death was an occasion for establishing ultimate honor, physical and moral strength, and providing a model of Bushido for one's descendants.

Ritual Suicide *Seppuku* (or hara-kiri) is the Japanese term for the practice of self-disembowelment, which originated as a way for samurai to achieve an honorable death when defeat or some other form of dishonor was imminent. Both seppuku and hara-kiri have the same meaning, although *seppuku*, which is the preferred term in Japan, has a more formal tone and involves the Chinese characters for hara-kiri arranged in a different order. While hara-kiri is often translated simply as "abdominal cutting," seppuku must be rendered more formally, as in "cutting of the abdomen." Many words in Japanese have both a Chinese-style reading and a native Japanese pronunciation, and seppuku is the Chinese pronunciation of the characters for cut and abdomen, while hara-kiri is the Japanese reading of the same characters.

In ancient Japan, the abdomen (*hara*) was regarded as the domain of the soul, and the source of tension arising from human actions. As the center of the human body, the stomach was also viewed as the point of origin for individual will, might, spirit, anger, and potential favor or generosity. Thus, a knife thrust into the abdomen was understood as an expedient means of destroying the physical core of one's humanity.

A warrior was mandated to die by seppuku if he killed another retainer without justification or drew a weapon inside a castle without need for such an action in self-defense. Even warriors sentenced to perform disembowelment as punishment (rather than to avoid dishonor in battle) were allowed to distinguish themselves in death through this exclusive samurai ritual by virtue of their social position. Although seppuku could be ordered as punishment, death by this means warranted respect, thereby maintaining the honor of the deceased warrior and his family. Further, daimyo and other lords bore an obligation to support the heirs and spouse of samurai who died honorable deaths. One of the most famous examples of seppuku as punishment involved the suicide of the 47 *ronin*, described above in "Loyalty." Thus, for members of the warrior classes, seppuku represented a solemn procedure that nonetheless upheld samurai heritage and integrity.

The process of suicide by disembowelment was prescribed in detail, and the time, location, assistance, and sequence of events were all predetermined. Ritual seppuku began as a warrior used his knife to make a shallow cut in his abdomen, considered the individual's symbolic spiritual center. After the samurai performed the initial incision, an assistant completed the event by beheading the warrior.

Junshi This tradition meant that samurai were committed to perform the ultimate sacrifice in duty to their lord, following him in death by ritual disembowelment, a method of suicide usually called *seppuku*. To distinguish the devotion exhibited by following one's lord in suicide, this particular practice is termed *oibara*, meaning "disembowelment to follow" or *tomobara*, "disembowelment to accompany" in reference to *junshi*.

Originally *junshi* was not a suicide requirement, but a practice called *junso*, described in the Chinese *Book of Rites* (*Li ji*), one of the literary works collectively known as the Chinese classics. In ancient China, rituals included the sacrifice of human beings to guard the deceased, although it is not known whether this practice was followed in ancient Japan. As the samurai class emerged, military retainers would sometimes perish in battle alongside their lord, or commit suicide upon learning of their lord's death. Gradually, *junshi* became a central component of the warrior code, Bushido, as a means of demonstrating the unconditional devotion that bound samurai to their lord, even in death.

By the early Edo period, many samurai had begun to perform *junshi* as a way of providing for their descendants, since a daimyo's heirs were obligated to provide for a samurai's family if he honored his lord through *junshi*. Subsequent or lower-ranking military retainers reasoned that they had no choice regarding suicide since superior samurai had preceded them in *junshi* to honor their lord. Criticism arose as prestige was accorded to daimyo who had the highest numbers of self-sacrificing retainers, and losses of able men increased as this practice became widespread through a need to salvage personal fortunes and family reputations rather than out of true loyalty. The prohibition of *junshi* fol-

lowed, first voiced by shogun Tokugawa Ietsuna in 1663, and added to the *Buke Shohatto*, codes of conduct issued under Tokugawa rule to increase control over daimyo, during the tenure of Tokugawa Tsunayoshi.

MARTIAL ARTS AND WEAPONRY

Martial abilities were the foundation and focus of warrior life. Today known as *bugei* or *budo*, these military disciplines originated in weapons training and tactics first employed during the medieval era. Samurai and other warriors trained both in battle techniques and in various military technologies. Until the Warring States period instruction in weapons usually included use of bow and arrow, sword, and spear and other projectile weapons, both while mounted and on foot. Specialized training for foot soldiers developed during the 16th century as infantry ranks increased significantly. Collectively, various aspects of military preparation came to be known as the martial arts—a peacetime pursuit promoting spiritual and philosophical discipline along with military training—only in the Edo period. Edo-period martial arts also involved practice with weapons that would not have been practical in many conflict situations, with mental and spiritual reflection favored over lethal potential. Popular views of samurai today largely reflect the experiences of elite warriors who cultivated martial artistry during an era of sustained peace, rather than the embattled professional soldiers who learned a patchwork of skills during the tumultuous medieval era.

The 18 martial arts (*bugei juhappan*) listed below were perpetuated by samurai during the Tokugawa shogunate at the urging of Edo-period military theorists and philosophers, who viewed these abilities as essential to the cultivation of Bushido spirit. Some of these practices had been associated with warriors in Japan since the term *samurai* came into use. Subsequently, military tactics imported from China, especially covert practices used in espionage and

5.1 Warriors preparing for battle inside Himeji Castle (Himeji Castle exhibit; Photo William E. Deal)

assassination, were incorporated with native Japanese traditions. Other techniques listed below were developed to keep warriors fit for battle (and otherwise occupied) in an era of enforced peace. Most sources define the arts and skills associated with Bushido by the middle of the Edo period as: archery (*kyudo/kyujutsu*), horsemanship (*bajutsu*), swimming (*suieijutsu*), fencing/sword fighting (*kendo/kenjutsu*), sword drawing (*iaijutsu*), short sword skills (*tantojutsu*), truncheon skills (*jittejutsu*), polearm skills (*naginata jutsu*), spearmanship (*sojutsu*), staff skills (*bojutsu*), firearms (*teppo*) skills, *yawara* (now known as judo), spying (*ninjutsu*), needle spitting (*fukumibarijutsu*), dagger throwing (*shuriken jutsu*), roping (*torite*) skills, barbed staff (*mojiri*) skills, and chained sickle (*kusarigama*) skills. Specific military techniques have been grouped together below.

Various techniques among the above 18 canonical martial arts dominated samurai drills and instruction in particular eras. For example, fencing,

sword drawing, and similar techniques using bladed weapons dominated military arts at a time when few warriors would experience armed combat. Thus the ceremonial, strategic, and moral aspects of hand-to-hand combat dominated training in the 18 martial skills that occupied warriors under Tokugawa rule. Wisely, the Tokugawa shoguns compelled idle samurai to cultivate distinctive abilities that required complex training, thus furthering collective warrior ethics and identity, while also discouraging uprisings or other intrusions in shogunal affairs. Clubs and other groups specialized in particular categories among the martial arts, and contests emphasizing protocol and form predominated. However, samurai of earlier times had concentrated on different aspects of military training.

Horsemanship and archery were the most prized military skills in the Kamakura period. As noted above, the mounted archer was considered the most effective member of an early medieval warrior band.

In the late Kamakura and early Muromachi eras, locally powerful landholders did not yet have the resources to commission and train considerable numbers of mounted warriors. At this stage, extensive forces designed for long-distance campaigns were unnecessary as well, since battles in the provinces often culminated in localized sieges to gain control of a strategically positioned castle. Thus significant numbers of well-trained foot soldiers were necessary to enter the territory of an opponent and scale his fortress. While swordsmanship began to gain prominence among samurai skills in the early medieval era, the primary warrior weapon among foot soldiers was a long pole-mounted arm called *naginata*, and this was supplemented by archery. Military drills using polearms involved learning to pull a cavalryman from his mount and engage him in close-range combat. Other practical applications of such weapons included thrusting, or throwing, a spear or other polearms in order to hit a distant target. Archers and infantry equipped with spears were also trained to send arrows over castle walls to cover the approach of foot soldiers who sought to scale the walls and thereby gain access to the castle.

By the 15th century much of the main Japanese island, Honshu, had been consolidated by the most powerful daimyo into a few large territories. Battles among these lords were necessarily fought over large distances. At this stage, regional rulers of large land parcels possessed increased resources obtained from smaller conquered daimyo, and thus had the funds required to outfit and train larger cavalry regiments. As a result the need for mounted archers combined with the resources to train them culminated in the return of the cavalry to prominence in samurai armies. However, infantry divisions remained a powerful component of a daimyo army. Foot soldiers far outnumbered those in other divisions, and the constant warfare of the mid-15th to 16th centuries drained resources and impeded proper training of archery and cavalry units, and foot soldiers were far more plentiful, inexpensive, and renewable than any other type of military force. Daimyo wisely chose to protect their core forces of officers, cavalry, and skilled archers, maintaining a stable contingent to perform supervisory and training functions. Foot soldiers were also famously

treacherous, and would shift loyalties for trifling rewards.

Early in the 16th century, firearms were introduced to Japan and quickly adapted for use in battle. By the end of the Warring States period in 1568, gunnery began to replace archery as the most prominent weapon in the military arsenal. Foot soldiers learned to use the newly acquired weapon to best advantage in various foot stances and on horseback. The introduction of guns also affected the design of fortifications, in part contributing to the dramatic surge in construction of castles, the dominant defensive architectural form in the 16th and early 17th centuries.

Most of the martial arts mentioned above were not formally codified as critical to the "way of the warrior" until the Edo period, when samurai culture elevated battle skills into a peacetime art form. During this time of warrior-administrators and leisurely study of military arts, swordsmanship and sword drawing thrived as the most prized martial skill among the warrior classes, and the sword was heralded as embodying the "soul of the samurai." Comprehensive philosophies of military preparation were developed centering on martial arts, and samurai trained and conducted contests in fencing, spear- and swordsmanship, archery, equestrian skill, jujutsu, gunnery, and military strategy, which were regarded as the seven foundations of Bushido. The Tokugawa shogunate sanctioned only military training that emphasized the form and philosophy of warrior heritage over actual warfare, and consequently samurai administrators and functionaries came to be regarded as ineffective fighters who lacked practical experience. Recognition of differences between the civilian samurai elite of the Edo period and battle-scarred medieval military retainers is captured in the dichotomy of the "field warrior" (one who possesses battlefield experience) and the "mat warrior" (a peacetime samurai who practiced only on the training mat)—a contrast often cited under Tokugawa rule.

As noted above, the stealthy ninja and inscrutable sword masters immortalized in modern samurai tales bore little resemblance to medieval archers who forged a reputation for gritty discipline in mounted battles during the formative stages of military rule. Yet both types of figures believed that they exemplified the principles of the warrior code and pursued their goals through practice of the military arts.

18 Martial Arts

archery (*kyudo/kyujutsu*)
horsemanship (*bajutsu*)
swimming (*suieiijutsu*)
fencing/sword fighting (*kendo/kenjutsu*)
sword drawing (*iaijutsu*)
short sword (*tanto*) skills
polearm or long sword manipulation (*naginata jutsu*)
staff (*bojutsu*) skills
spearmanship (*sojutsu*)
yawara (judo/*jujutsu*)
firearms (*teppo*) skills
spying (*ninjutsu*)
dagger throwing (*shurikenjutsu*)
needle spitting (*fukumibarijutsu*)
chained sickle throwing (*kusarigamajutsu*)
roping (*torite*) skills
barbed staff (*mojiri*) skills
truncheon (*jitte*) skills

ARCHERY

Archery (*kyudo*; literally "the way of the bow") was the weapon most closely associated with warriors and was in common use by the end of the prehistoric era, during the fourth or fifth centuries C.E. While the term *kyudo* is more common today, *kyujutsu* ("technique of the bow") was used to describe archery in the age of the samurai.

Warriors practiced several types of archery, according to changes in weaponry and the role of the military in different periods. Mounted archery, also known as military archery, was the most prized of warrior skills and was practiced consistently by professional soldiers from the outset in Japan. Different procedures were followed that distinguished archery intended as warrior training from contests or religious practices in which form and formality were of primary importance. Civil archery entailed shooting from a standing position, and emphasis was placed upon form rather than meeting a target accurately. By far the most common type of archery in

Japan, civil or civilian archery contests did not provide sufficient preparation for battle, and remained largely ceremonial. By contrast, military training entailed mounted maneuvers in which infantry troops with bow and arrow supported equestrian archers. Mock battles were staged, sometimes as a show of force to dissuade enemy forces from attacking. While early medieval warfare often began with a formalized archery contest between commanders, deployment of firearms and the constant warfare of the 15th and 16th centuries ultimately led to the decline of archery in battle. In the Edo period archery was considered an art, and members of the warrior classes participated in archery contests that venerated this technique as the most favored weapon of the samurai.

In the earliest Japanese literary sources, military figures relied upon horse and arrow. Yet in the popular imagination, the samurai is always linked with the sword. In fact, swords were an important symbol of samurai status, particularly during the Edo period and afterward. However, as the warrior tradition began to develop, the most important weapon was the bow. The classic image of a medieval warrior with a long bow astride a dashing stallion does not accurately describe the typical soldier of the Heian through late Kamakura periods. However, many high-ranking samurai and those employed by wealthy domain owners were known for their equestrian archery skills. By the 14th century, as armies increased in size and outfitting sizable battalions became costly, even foot soldiers (*ashigaru*) were equipped with the relatively inexpensive bow and arrow, thus shattering the legendary exclusivity of warrior arts as "the way of the bow and horse." Nonetheless, in the middle years of the feudal period, the bow gradually declined in prominence, with foot soldiers preferring to use *naginata*, a polearm with a curved blade, and then the straight spear (*yari*) after about 1450 C.E. The firearm eventually displaced archery in the arsenals of most samurai in the late 16th century. Thereafter, samurai continued to practice archery, though mostly as a spiritual and physical discipline and a popular form of entertainment, rather than as a martial skill for practical use.

Most ranking warriors carried several weapons in addition to their bows and arrows, one of which was a sword. Considered a viable defense only in hand-to-hand combat, the sword had disadvantages, such as fairly common concerns like broken blades or the prospect of complete loss if the weapon was lodged firmly in a corpse. Further, swords had symbolic associations with divinity and elite warriors, and were expensive and difficult to obtain for average samurai of low or middle rank. By contrast, arrows were plentiful, easily replaced, and more reliable. Thus, among the many military arts listed above, archery remained the traditional samurai specialty, although medieval Japanese swords were considerably more refined than those made in medieval Europe, where the sword was the weapon of choice. Foot soldiers, often excluded from the ranks of true samurai, were more likely to utilize polearms and spears.

5.2 Warrior with bow and arrows (Illustration Kikuchi Yosai from *Zenken kojitsu*, mid-19th century)

Archery was widely regarded as the best way to ascertain a warrior's abilities. In many military tales, samurai skills were assessed by the length of arrow (measured in fists or hand-widths) used to strike a target from a moving horse. Battles were occasionally settled not by entire armies but through a mounted archery duel performed by samurai leaders. Opponents would aim arrows while riding toward each other, using one arrow for each pass. Several passes might be used to determine the victor, rather than fighting until death of one party. Usually, fatal wounds were inflicted only after soldiers fired several arrows, not because their aim was poor, but rather because Japanese armor was skillfully designed to deflect such blows.

Typical samurai bows measured from about five feet long to more than eight feet, and about two-thirds of the bow was situated above the hand grip. These are generally classified as longbows, although they differ in form from similar weapons called longbows used in medieval European warfare. Japanese wooden bows had to be long to generate the power to launch arrows while remaining flexible and strong, since laminated wood and composite materials could separate if flexed strenuously. Hand-grips placed in the center of such long bows would have made equestrian archery impossible, and would not have balanced the elasticity of the upper portion of the bow. Therefore, the handgrip was placed off-center, producing bows that bent in an asymmetrical fashion, which facilitated drawing the bow, reduced stress on the bent wood, and made mounted archery possible for those who were well trained. Less-experienced archers such as foot soldiers often used bows that were shorter and easier to manipulate. However, the *Chronicle of the Wei Dynasty* (*Weizhi*) notes that Chinese envoys saw Japanese archers using bows with shorter lower portions and longer upper sections by the mid-third century, although there is no mention of equestrian practices at the time.

From the Kamakura period, bows were constructed in layers utilizing bamboo slats for added strength and flexibility. The core of the bow was made of stiff wood and was combined with laminated pieces of bamboo. After the 15th century, the sides of the bow were laminated with bamboo slats, and the wooden core of the bow was thus completely encased in bamboo. For added strength, cane was wound around the stave of the bow. While in theory the cane bow was finished with lacquer for additional protection, this was not always the case in practice.

There were numerous kinds of arrows and arrowheads, intended to perform specific functions based on the desired point of contact. The average arrows were about 12 fists in length, although both longer and shorter arrows survive. Arrow length depended upon the skill of the archer and the desired target. During the medieval era, most samurai favored arrows between 86 and 96 centimeters (about 34–38 inches) in length. Arrow shafts were made of bamboo harvested in early winter and shaved to remove the outer bark and joint nodes. The shaft was straightened and softened by placing it in hot sand.

Arrowheads were fastened to the shafts by a system of flanges similar to the tangs seen on swords. These arrows had three or four fletchings made from the wing or tail feathers of varied species of bird. The shaft of the arrow was fashioned from young bamboo. In the early medieval period, arrow shafts were carried in devices called *ebira*, which resembled a woven chair. These quivers were worn on the hip and made from pieces of woven wood. Later, quivers called *utsubo* were used, which were wood, covered in fur, and worn across the back. Like other military equipment, the various components used by archers were manufactured and distributed in various locations, but the shapes and styles of these tools of war were quite consistent throughout medieval and early modern times, and across all regions of Japan.

Some forms of archery practiced in Japan were not intended to serve as preparation for battle. Mounted archery was ritualized in Japan beginning in the early 11th century with the practice called *yabusame*. Often performed for emperors or shoguns to glorify military training and celebrate samurai achievements, this ceremonial pastime involved four distinct movements. The designated primary archer first pointed a drawn arrow at the sky, and then the ground, to symbolize harmony between heaven and earth. Mounted archers would then begin to shoot at targets two meters away composed of five concentric circles in multiple hues. These targets were about 60 meters apart with a surface area of 60 square centimeters, and the archers aimed as they rode their horses at full gallop around a track. In the third movement, soldiers who had struck all three targets were invited to aim at three clay targets that were about one-third the size of targets in the second movement. Finally, the primary archer inspected all of the targets to determine who had demonstrated the best military prowess. *Yabusame* is still practiced today and is seen as an enduring symbol of Japan's traditional military arts.

HORSEMANSHIP

Although horses existed in Japan during the Neolithic period, it was not until horses were reintroduced via China, Korea, and Central Asia in the fourth and fifth centuries that the Japanese began to recognize the advantages of mounted soldiers. Refugees from embattled kingdoms on the continent, especially the modern Korean peninsula, settled in the Kanto area (modern Tokyo and Yokohama) and continued to refine their equestrian and archery traditions during the Asuka period (mid-sixth to mid-seventh century). These families migrated to the regions north of the Kanto plain, established a reputation for their horsemanship and became a concern for regional chieftains seeking to dominate the contentious tribes for control of Japan. From the eighth century, cavalry for the imperial armies were recruited from the ranks of these northern and eastern equestrian clans. Soon, mounted archery units began to replace conscripted troops drawn from the peasant class, which had dwindled in number and skill. These professional horsemen constituted the first warrior elite and furthered the enduring association between samurai and mounted archery.

Mounted warriors came to dominate armed forces during the era of samurai rule, largely due to the fact that fewer cavalry than infantry were required to prevail in warfare. As the warrior class attained greater social and political power in the 12th century, horsemanship (*bajutsu*) and archery (*kyujutsu*) gained popularity among samurai who had no previous training in these military tactics. Mounted archery gained further attention after the Gempei War (1180–85), as the cavalry was reputed to be the leading force in the Minamoto and Taira armies. After attaining victory over the Taira clan, the Minamoto shoguns prospered during the Kamakura era, amassed significant equine reserves, and drew upon their financial resources to train superior soldiers in horsemanship.

This strong equestrian force was a critical asset for the Minamoto, as the shogun's forces often traveled long distances to quell uprisings associated with persistent civil unrest during the early years of military rule. Leaders of domains situated in the provinces had difficulty mounting a challenge against such well-organized, skillful fighters. In response, even informal groups such as provincial warrior bands cultivated mounted battle tactics that were seen as critical to military strategy during the 12th through 15th centuries. As Minamoto power began to erode by the early 14th century and provincial disorder increased, warriors and regional lords took advantage of the weakening central government by annexing nearby domains, and faced with the growing resources, equestrian skills, and organization of regional samurai, the ruling authorities were unable to regain control of the provinces.

After the Onin War (1467–77), and throughout the Warring States period (Sengoku jidai, 1467–1568), daimyo sought to consolidate power, and armies grew in size. Typically, mounts were reserved for officers and commanders, and infantry were divided into specialized groups based upon the types of weapons they used. Wealthy regional lords were able to outfit their infantry with spears, bows, and eventually, armor, but noting the fickle nature and lack of integrity among foot soldiers (*ashigaru*), they maintained a reserve corps of reliable, loyal equestrian samurai. Since preserving a faithful warrior retinue was critical to continued success in warfare, battles were waged mostly by infantry, and the mounted warrior became a symbolic figure rather than a main military force during the Warring States period. With the introduction of the firearm in the 16th century, equestrian archers were supplanted by the long range and greater effectiveness of the harquebus, which was deployed by foot soldiers. Equestrian samurai purportedly serving as guards were a familiar sight in daimyo entourages of the Edo period, and maintained a ceremonial presence that honored the mounted samurai tradition. Retaining equestrian samurai for processions required to attend court in Edo was a major expense for Tokugawa-

period daimyo, and helped to ensure that regional lords would not amass sufficient resources to challenge the shogun's right to rule.

Throughout the medieval era, equestrian schools were formed to teach different riding methods, although most training techniques emphasized a bond between horse and rider. Warriors desired well-trained horses for use in military operations, yet the most effective warrior bands, which originated in the Kanto region, used horses that were quite high-spirited and difficult to manage. Samurai horses were raised in the northeastern provinces, and were mostly short, sturdy, and somewhat wild in nature, since stallions were more imposing on the battlefield than geldings. Warriors relied upon horses to travel to the battle site and often to carry them away in case of retreat, so endurance and a powerful presence were prized. Often steeds made the initial frontline assault, or were used as a shield against the enemy in a withdrawal. Unlike those in cavalries in Europe and western Asia, Japanese horses wore no armor.

Saddlery

Japanese saddles were designed to provide the rider with a stable platform from which to stand in the stirrups and aim their longbows while moving fairly quickly. The wooden saddles (*kura*) were heavy and uncomfortable, and thus were poorly suited for riding at high speeds or over long distances. The saddletree, or *kurabane*, was fashioned from four pieces of wood, including an arching burr-plate (*maewa*) and cantle (*shizuwa*) connected with two contoured bands (*igi*), thus providing a frame for the seat of the saddle. Military saddles had especially thick cantles and burr-plates, which offered protection from bows and arrows and from shifts in the saddle when shooting from a standing position. A double-layered padded leather under-saddle (*shita-gura*) was bound by hemp cords to the wooden frame, and was sandwiched between the under-saddle and a padded leather seat (*basen*) secured by stirrup leathers (*chikaragawa* or *gekiso*). The stirrup leathers passed through slots in the contoured bands (*igi*) and saddle seat.

Saddles were fastened to the horse with three straps made of braided cord. The girth strap encircled the belly of the horse, while a chest strap secured the saddle across the horse's shoulders, and a crupper strap encircled the hindquarters. Saddles are generally classified as either Chinese-style, *karagura*, or Japanese-style, *yamatogura*, although there are also variations for ceremonial or court use, and military use.

Variations in saddle design reflect Japanese interaction with the Asian continent. During the Nara period, when trade with China proliferated, the Chinese style of saddlery known as the *karagura* was adopted. Gradually, changes to this design consistent with native Japanese preferences resulted in the *yamatogura*, or Japanese-style saddle from the Heian period onward. Further, saddles of Japanese design are distinguished as either *suikangura*, reserved for aristocratic use, and *gunjingura*, or war saddle.

Edo-period saddles became more decorative, as they were no longer used primarily as practical objects but instead served as adornments that reflected the status of the samurai who used them in ceremonial processions. The most elaborate saddles were decorated with mother-of-pearl inlay, gold leaf embedded in multiple coats of lacquer, and even classical poetry. In the Kamakura period, saddles were constructed by carpenters, although as they became more elaborate, artisans began to produce saddles, especially those reserved for wealthy domain rulers and high-ranking samurai. During the Muromachi period, the more diverse economy in the provinces supported a growing number of artisans clustered in villages and castle towns, enabling daimyo to commission saddlery to outfit an entire army.

Stirrups were employed in Japan from the beginning of equestrian culture. Early Japanese stirrups, found in fifth-century tombs, were made of wood covered with metal in the shape of a flat-bottomed ring. By the eighth century, these had been superceded by cup-shaped stirrups that enclosed the front of the rider's foot. From the late Heian period, ceremonial saddles were fitted with stirrups that no longer had sides, but encompassed the entire length of the foot. Military stirrups were similar, though thinner, longer, and fitted with a deeper pocket for the toe. Both these ceremonial and military styles were uniquely Japanese and remained in use until European ring-style stirrups were reintroduced in the late 19th century. Two practical advantages of the Japanese stirrup design attest to the preeminence of mounted warfare during most of the medieval period: The wide, stable platform was well-suited to shooting from a standing position, and the rider had little risk of being dragged by a horse if unseated.

Equestrian equipment also included bridles and accessories such as whips, and sometimes removable horseshoes. Bridles consisted of a headpiece, bit, and reins and were similar to European design in most respects. In Japan, the headpiece and reins were made of fabric, such as braided silk, as opposed to leather, which was used in Europe. Horsewhips were made of bamboo or willow, and had a hand strap to allow the rider to retain the whip when shooting. Horses were not permanently shod in Japan as in Western equestrian units. However, from the late Muromachi era, cavalrymen did outfit their horses with straw sandals called *umagutsu*, similar to those worn by human beings, to stifle the sound of their progress and provide traction in rainy weather or protection on long campaigns. Horses were not fitted with armor, and to ensure that a samurai had another mount in case a horse was wounded, a servant or foot soldier would be stationed nearby with additional steeds.

SWIMMING

The practice of swimming first developed as a martial art from the 12th to the 16th centuries. Instruction included techniques for swimming while bearing weapons, silent swimming, and underwater movement. These types of aquatic movements have long been distinguished from swimming for sport or relaxation, which is called *suie*, in Japan. Training in swimming techniques was critical during the heyday of castle building in Japan, since most castles were designed with an extensive series of moats intended to deter intruders. Ninja and similar clandestine figures often relied upon noiseless swimming techniques executed while bearing weapons to enter an enemy stronghold and obtain essential information or even commit assassinations. Twelve schools of traditional military training in swimming (*suieijutsu*) are still known in Japan today.

FENCING/SWORD FIGHTING

The sword (*nihonto*) was characterized as "the soul of the samurai" by Tokugawa Ieyasu in the 17th century. In practice medieval warriors regarded the sword as one weapon among many—useful primarily in close combat, which was to be avoided if at all possible. Although many warriors carried swords in battle, they functioned primarily as a supplement to the more effective bow and arrow. Swords were more likely to figure in conflicts apart from battles, such as assassinations or brawls, and in the Edo period, these weapons were carried as a privilege conferred by socioeconomic rank. The words of Tokugawa Ieyasu have captured the popular imagination, however, and for many in Japan and elsewhere, the sword is still the weapon most associated with Japanese warriors. While the sword may not have enjoyed a prominent role in a majority of samurai battles, sword smiths and sword polishers have garnered honor and prestige for Japanese-style swords produced for more than 1,200 years. These artisans have preserved the techniques for creating refined and powerful steel blades that are among Japan's most noted premodern technological achievements. Japanese swords are regarded as exemplary objects that demonstrate technical expertise as well as elegance of design and ornamentation.

Sword History The sword holds a high position in Japanese history and culture, in part because this weapon is one of the three imperial regalia, traditional symbols of the authority of the emperor. These three objects include the sacred mirror used to lure the sun goddess (Amaterasu no Omikami) from her cave, the curved jewels—comma-shaped precious stones—presented by heavenly deities to the goddess on her emergence from the cave, and the sacred sword removed from a serpent's tail and presented by Amaterasu's brother Susanoo no Mikoto as a sign of subservience to her authority. According to tradition, these three imperial symbols were given to the grandson of Amaterasu, Ninigi no Mikoto, when he was granted divine authority and descended from above to rule the Japanese islands. This incident constitutes the founding of the Japanese imperial line, and is venerated as representing the divine origins of the Japanese archipelago.

Shinto, the indigenous religion of Japan, holds that mountains, volcanoes, waterfalls, rocks, trees, and other phenomena are inhabited by spirits called *kami*, whose divine qualities are expressed in the beauty and power of the natural world. (For more information about Shinto, see chapter 6: Religion). Today as in the past, Japanese swords are produced from metal, water, and fire—three of the five elements believed to be the source of the universe. Swords are viewed as extensions of the powerful sacred beings that reside within such natural elements throughout the Japanese archipelago. Therefore, swords have long been revered as sacred objects deserving of respect, and for many Japanese, sword smiths merit the respect accorded to religious figures such as Shinto or Buddhist priests. This association has been furthered by sword manufacturing traditions, which include ritual purification through fasting and abstinence, special clothing worn by the smith, cold-water ablutions such as those performed at Shinto shrines, and the prohibition of women in the smithy.

Swords and other metal weapons were introduced to Japan along with metallurgy from the Asian mainland during the prehistoric period. The *Chronicle of the Wei Dynasty* (*Weizhi*) records that an envoy dispatched to China by Queen Himiko (also read Pimiko) of the country of Wa (Japan) received swords from the Wei emperor as a tribute in 239 C.E. Examples of Chinese-style swords, characterized by single cutting edges and a triangular profile, have been excavated from numerous tomb mounds that were constructed during the Old Tomb (*Kofun*) period (ca. 300–600 C.E.), named for the burial mounds that proliferated at that time. In addition, straight swords were among the many objects donated to the Shosoin circa 756 C.E. from the imperial treasury of Emperor Shomu.

The curved-profile Japanese sword originated in approximately the eighth century, coinciding with the earliest steel production in Japan and the emergence of the first professional military figures. From the first, Japanese sword blades were made from steel with a carefully monitored carbon content, rather than iron, or in the case of the first examples excavated in Japan, bronze, which had been used from around the first centuries C.E. to manufacture swords on the Asian continent.

Swords made during the medieval and early modern eras are noted for different reasons. Blades produced from the Heian period until approximately 1600, during the late Momoyama era, are classified as *koto* ("old swords") and are considered superior to Edo-period weapons. Until the Muromachi period, most swords made in Japan, known as *tachi*, emulated an earlier type originally exclusive to Heian-period nobles. These swords primarily had a ceremonial function, and were longer than later types. Further, *tachi* blades had a particularly pronounced curve. *Tachi* are distinguished from later sword forms like *katana* (see below and in Types of Swords) because they were worn suspended from a chain fastened at the waist. Nobles and other court officials of lower rank were not permitted to bear traditional *tachi*, and instead carried straight swords or *tachi* that were significantly shorter and less curved.

From the beginning of the Kamakura era to the 15th century, sword production increased markedly and great strides were made in both artistic and technical refinement. The most prized sword blades, designated national treasures (*kokuho*) by the Japanese Agency for Cultural Affairs (Bunkacho), date primarily to the Kamakura period. These swords reflect the synthesis of technical achievement and artistic embellishment that distinguishes the most refined objects made for Japanese warriors. Some swords produced prior to the Muromachi period were created in response to changing defensive technology, and demonstrate how experimental sword designs could neglect functional considerations. For example, in the late Kamakura period, novel swords sometimes exceeded three feet in length and were used exclusively by mounted warriors, most likely to little effect. Such weapons were often shortened later to make them more practical in individual combat.

The prolonged strife of the Warring States period had a powerful influence on Muromachi-era sword production. In troubled times, swords were expensive weapons and represented a poor investment for armies stretched thin and composed of untrained foot soldiers who functioned best as archers and spear-bearers. Although no longer the sole purview of elite nobles, swords produced in the Warring States period and later remained objects rightfully owned by elite samurai or warlords, and were generally associated with warriors of status and means. Still, conquerors had an opportunity to possess swords left behind in battle by the vanquished, and pirates or thieves might seize a sword (and its owner) by force. The lack of regulations and consistency in sword production and ownership mirrors the general disorder that characterized the era of civil warfare.

Sword quality gradually declined as production volume became a priority in this period of widespread unrest. Muromachi-period swords decreased in length but were heavier, wider, and less curved. These changes were probably intended to improve the effectiveness of swords against the heavier armor developed in the late medieval era. Most Muromachi blades, known as *katana*, measured about 60 centimeters (two feet) or slightly more and were often accompanied by a shorter sword, initially a form of dagger, which began to be called *wakizashi* sometime during the middle years of the medieval era. *Wakizashi* were worn thrust through the warrior's sash with the edges of both swords facing upward and blades parallel or crossing each other. This arrangement was known as *daisho* (literally, long and short).

The practice of carrying one larger and one smaller sword became popular early in the age of the warrior, although it is difficult to generalize about how widespread this custom became, and which samurai typically carried two blades. In general, sword sizes varied throughout warrior culture, with particular blade shapes and lengths dominating different periods and suiting diverse purposes. In the Edo period, regulations were imposed, and in principle only members of the warrior classes were allowed to wear two swords. Japanese and other sources have traditionally noted that samurai are easily distinguished from individuals from other classes by the two different sizes of swords they carried. However, this practice was not specifically associated with military retainers until the beginning of Tokugawa rule, and further, such displays of rank were not closely regulated. Relatively few *katana* were made after about 1500, perhaps due to the introduction of the matchlock rifle or harquebus.

Azuchi-Momoyama- and Edo-period blades made from about 1600 to 1800 are classified as *shinto*, or new swords. At this time, individual smiths set up workshops and founded schools of sword production that aimed to replicate Kamakura-era techniques that had been lost. Nearly all swords made in the *shinto* period were intended for hand-to-hand combat, and thus did not reproduce the wide variety of blades made in past eras. Characterized by brilliant surface patterns atop a well-tempered steel structure, these swords were technically refined, yet nearly all of those produced after the beginning of the Tokugawa shogunate were used solely for martial arts practice or for ornamental purposes. At the same time, sword fittings, such as sword guards, scabbards, and other equipment, became more elaborate and reflected the new role of samurai swords as a status symbol linked to social rank. Swords also came to be regarded as status symbols which identified those who belonged to the warrior classes and upheld the warrior code, and were prized as part of family heritage. After about 1800, swords are identified as *shin-shinto* (literally, "new-new swords") or as *fukkoto* (meaning "of the renewal") depending upon type. The term *fukkoto* is reserved for *katana*-type blades.

Sword Production Japanese-style swords are differentiated from other types in their consistent use of steel in different gradations of hardness attuned to the requirements of different parts of the blade. As early as the eighth century, during the Nara period, these technologically advanced blades were made of densely forged steel laboriously hammered, folded, and welded multiple times in order to create a steel fabric of superior flexibility and integrity. Due to this process, Japanese-style blades have a complex, multilayered structure similar to the grain of wood, with a more flexible, lower carbon-content steel encased in (or layered with) a harder, more brittle outer surface that is exceptionally durable. The difference in the carbon content of the steel and the positioning of the contrasting metals also results in the characteristic curve of Japanese swords.

The traits detailed above comprise the distinguishing characteristics associated with all swords produced in the traditional Japanese style. In later times, Japanese swords were forged from precisely combined blocks of steel that were prefabricated to facilitate production and then hammered into a final form that was unsurpassed by blades produced in other parts of the world in structural integrity, toughness, and sharpness.

As noted above, even in the formative years of sword production, Japanese smiths mastered steel technology. Japanese swords are noted for their controlled carbon content, which produces refined steel of superior hardness and regularity of structure. In addition, Japanese sword smiths were also skilled in shaping blades of superior strength and durability. Thus, swords made in Japan quickly gained a reputation for precision and technological refinement, and those involved in sword production attained social prominence. Beyond the respect accorded to their profession, smiths also had religious affiliations that enhanced their high social position. Some early sword smiths were members of the Shugendo sect, a religion practiced by mountain-dwelling adherents who lived in austerity and seclusion. Other sword manufacturers who worked prior to the Kamakura era were affiliated with the Tendai school of Buddhism, an eclectic religious tradition originating in China that was headquartered in Japan on Mt. Hiei, just above the aristocratic capital, Kyoto. For more information on Shugendo and Tendai Buddhism, see chapter 6: Religion.

About 200 schools of sword craft techniques existed in Japan during approximately 1,200 years of sword production, and each had particular traditions, blade marks, and other identifying characteristics that can be traced with great accuracy today. From the 10th century, smiths began to chisel signatures on the tang of the blade, thus forging an enduring bond between the reputation of a skilled artisan and the sword throughout its functional life. Inscriptions could also include the province and town where the blade was produced and even the date the sword was tempered.

Another form of signature is used by all Japanese sword smiths. A distinctive temper pattern called *hamon* on the cutting edge of the sword can indicate the specific era and place, as well as the individual smith or workshop, where the sword was produced. The *hamon* is a synergistic result of three events that contribute to the final hardening of the sword's cutting surface. First, clay is applied to the blade and allowed to dry. Then, the sword is repeatedly passed through a high-temperature charcoal fire for a specified amount of time, until it reaches the temperature desired by the smith. Finally, the blade is plunged into a tank of water, calibrated precisely to

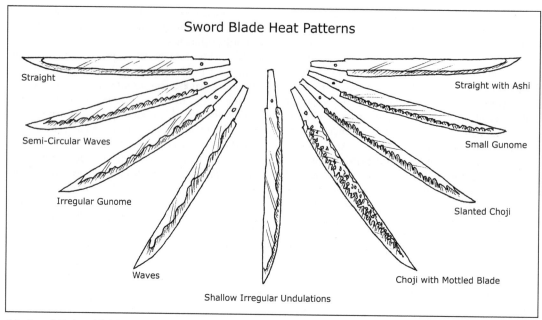

Sword Blade Heat Patterns

Straight

Semi-Circular Waves

Irregular Gunome

Waves

Shallow Irregular Undulations

Straight with Ashi

Small Gunome

Slanted Choji

Choji with Mottled Blade

5.3 Sword blades with heat-tempered patterns, like those pictured here, were a distinct feature of Japanese sword fabrication. (Illustration Grace Vibbert)

complement the amount of time spent in the fire at a certain temperature. The combination of these three factors determines the form of the *hamon*, and is a closely guarded secret in each smith's workshop. Quenching in water can also affect the curve of the blade, which is determined in part by its position in the tank and the cooling rates of the different types of steel comprising the sword.

After the blade has been carefully inspected by the smith, it is then sent to a polisher, who uses stones lubricated with water and increasingly finer in grain to shine the surface of the sword and sharpen the blade. The polisher reveals the crystalline steel structure that constitutes the unique fabric of a Japanese sword, and marks the difference in the texture and form of the two different types of steel used to craft blades of noted strength, sharpness, and flexibility.

Types of Swords: *Tachi*, *Katana*, and *Tanto* The term *tachi* is used to designate a long sword primarily used by nobles from the Heian to Muromachi

eras. *Tachi* blades were arched and longer than *katana*, and were worn in a different manner. The term *tachi* refers specifically to swords worn with the cutting surface slung down from the hip. This means of carrying a sword was standard practice in Japan except in the case of harquebusiers, who arranged their swords so that the tip would not touch the ground as they knelt to fire their weapons.

By contrast, *katana* were worn with the cutting surface facing up and thrust through the belt or sash. *Tachi* were generally produced for aristocrats as regalia indicating social position and imperial court rank. Under military rule, warlords and military retainers eschewed vestiges of the old aristocratic order, perhaps preferring swords such as *katana* for the tactical advantages they offered, as a reliable last resort for defense in hand-to-hand combat. Although they are generally described as shorter than *tachi*, *katana* were not fashioned in any standard length. Usually *katana* measured about two feet in length, while typical *tachi* were about three feet long (90 centimeters).

Tanto is a term used for blades of less than 30 centimeters (about one foot) in length, and thus this type of sword is often translated as dagger. Unlike the short sword called *wakizashi*, *tanto* usually have no sword guard. Further, *tanto* became the focus of one of the central martial arts, known as *tantojutsu*, practiced in the Edo period. In the medieval period, *tanto* were reportedly carried by figures appearing to be Buddhist monks who were actually ninja in disguise.

Since most swordsmen were right-handed, swords were carried on the left side of the body. Because sword types and shapes varied in relation to their position on the body, these blades can be differentiated from other sharp metal weapons that were mounted on long poles and manipulated differently.

SWORD DRAWING TECHNIQUES

Although many medieval samurai of low or middle rank regarded the sword as a final option in the event of hand-to-hand contests, elite warriors were commonly schooled in sword drawing (*iaijutsu*) techniques. Since battles were occasionally settled with a sword fight between commanders, sword techniques became an appropriate skill for daimyo or samurai of high rank.

Standard *iaijutsu* techniques are said to have originated in 1560 with Hayashizaki Jinsuke Shigenobu (born 1542), who founded a school in his name. Proper swordsmanship included the ability to cut an opponent, if necessary, in a single, swift movement. Yet despite the bloody descriptions of sword drawing practices, *iaijutsu* was primarily an art of defense, and samurai were taught that the sword should be manipulated to sustain one's vigor rather than with the intent to kill an opponent.

Sword drawing was the first school of warrior arts to integrate philosophical and mental preparation with martial techniques. Ideally, *iaijutsu* required mastery of fluid motions similar to dance. Development of timing and observation skills enabled practitioners to interpret clues offered by an opponent's position. Thus, tactics and preparation were emphasized over sheer athletic abilities.

Iai tactics formed the basis for *kenjutsu* (fencing), which was practiced using wooden "swords" with bamboo blades, called *shinai*, that made the practice of this art less dangerous. *Kenjutsu* was introduced during the Edo period by Sakakibara Kenkichi (1830–94) as a means of physical and mental training for youth. Banned in 1876, the pursuit was reintroduced in 1900 as *kendo*, a term that sounds less confrontational.

POLEARM AND RELATED WEAPONS

The most common type of polearm used in early medieval Japan was known as the *naginata*, and techniques for its deployment were called *naginata jutsu*. This versatile weapon is sometimes compared to the halberd, which was used by European soldiers of the 15th and 16th centuries. Unlike the halberd, however, the *naginata* had no axe, and was often longer than the six-foot European polearm. First used by the early Kamakura period, the *naginata* is closest to a European glaive in form, with an elongated shaft, and a single-edged blade curved more than that of a Kamakura-period Japanese *tachi*. Most likely, the *naginata* was based upon similar weapons introduced from China by 300 C.E. which have been unearthed in graves.

5.4 Warrior with polearm (naginata) (Illustration Kikuchi Yosai from *Zenken kojitsu*, mid-19th century)

Inspired in part by the sword, and identified by Japanese characters meaning long sword until the 15th century, the *naginata* is sometimes also called the pole-sword. Its broad blade was made of steel, was similar in shape to a sword, and was fixed to a long shaft usually made of lacquered wood. Early *naginata* had blades about 60 centimeters (two feet) long, although longer blades were used later. Blades were about 0.6 to one meter long at most (up to three and a half feet) and shafts of more than two meters (about seven feet) existed; however, these enormous dimensions meant that more than one soldier would be required to deploy the weapon, which was often impractical.

In addition, periodically there were variations, often localized, of the *naginata* produced. Ninja and members of the peasant classes sometimes utilized a *bisento*, a double-edged long sword with a thick, truncated blade. Other forms of the polearm included an intriguing rake-like object attached to a pole, called a *kumade* (bear paw), which had three or four hooks arranged like a claw and was most often used in land or sea attacks by massed soldiers. Some picture scrolls indicate that the *kumade* was used from horseback to drag opponents off their mounts. Several other types of thrusting weapons related to the *naginata* and the sword (in the early medieval era, *tachi*; later, *katana* and *wakizashi*) were used sporadically in feudal Japan. Arms with blades such as *teboko* (hand spears) and *konaginata* (small glaives) are noted in medieval sources. These appear to have been about 1 to 1.5 meters in length, with straight, short blades, although there is some disagreement on this matter since there are no extant examples that can be reliably identified. Sources that describe weapons used in the medieval era often provide extensive (and sometimes conflicting) information about arms that can be classified as swords and/or polearms, and thus this category covers a variety of objects that are described only cursorily compared with other more homogenous weapon types.

Most *naginata* had poles that reached from the ground to an average foot soldier's ears (approximately 120–150 cm, or four to almost five feet), and blades of between 30 and 60 centimeters (about one to two feet) in length. *Naginata* blades were mounted to the haft or pole by a tang inserted through an opening in the haft and secured with pegs. Poles were usually oval in profile, making them easier to grasp and maneuver.

While the length of the *naginata* kept the opponent at a distance, the leverage afforded by the long shaft enabled the foot soldiers to deliver blows with a stronger impact. From the 11th until the mid-15th century, the *naginata* was the primary weapon wielded by foot soldiers, and was especially favored by Buddhist warrior-monks (*sohei*). Although the *naginata* was most often deployed by ranks of troops, it was most effective as a personal weapon, since it could be employed in sweeping motions, or to cut, strike, or thrust. To deter multiple opponents arriving from different directions, the *naginata* could be twirled like a baton. According to battle accounts, these weapons were most often manipulated in a somewhat uncontrolled, slashing manner. From the end of the 15th century, most troops serving on foot were provided with a straight, thrusting spear (*yari*) that produced more effective results in destroying opposing forces. *Naginata* fell into disuse after the *yari* was deemed more effective for use by many soldiers in large-scale head-on confrontations. *Yari* are discussed in detail below in the section titled Spearmanship.

In the Edo period, *naginata* techniques became an established martial art and schools of instruction emerged. Daughters of samurai were expected to learn *naginata jutsu*, and the polearm was regarded as a woman's weapon from the 17th century on. Today the art of manipulating the *naginata* remains popular among women, and is presently practiced using a weapon with a blade made of bamboo.

SPEARMANSHIP

Spears (*yari*) have a long history in Japan, as the two earliest extant Japanese histories, the *Kojiki* (712 C.E.) and the *Nihon shoki* (720 C.E.) recount that the Japanese islands emerged from drops created when the gods Izanami and Izanagi used a jeweled spear to stir the cosmic brine mixture that constituted the universe.

The *yari* was one of the most important weapons in the samurai arsenal, especially in infantry units during the Warring States period (1467–1568) and thereafter when the *yari* served as a means of tactical advancement to a higher position. By the end of the Warring States period, the *yari* was much more prevalent than the *naginata*, another form of pole-

5.5 Warrior holding a spear (yari) (Illustration Kikuchi Yosai from *Zenken kojitsu*, mid-19th century)

mounted weapon (also called polearm), which is discussed above. Foot soldiers (*ashigaru*) were almost uniformly provided with spears throughout the late medieval period. The *yari* is also sometimes called a lance to underscore that in Japan spears were not thrown as in other military traditions where these arms served as projectile weapons.

Use of the spear was considered one of the seven primary abilities necessary for knowledge of the warrior arts during the formative years of the samurai tradition in the medieval era. Usually termed *sojutsu*, spear manipulation was also simply designated by the name of the type of spear commonly used in the military, called the *yari*. These weapons had a double-sided blade that could measure from 30 to 75 centimeters (12–29 inches). As with other pole-mounted weapons, *yari* were available in different lengths. Among the longest were *nagai-yari*, which were over four meters long. Warriors often had preferences for a particular length of spear, and the forms and types were often specific to a particular domain or army. The length of the shaft was determined in part by the length and shape of the blade or spearhead. Other forms were triangular in

shape. The most common were the L-shaped or cross-shaped lanceheads, which were useful in pulling victims from the saddle.

Infantry divisions bearing long spears, known as *yaribusuma* (literally, "screen of spears"), performed a decisive role in battles of the Warring States period. Ironically, though, most infantry received no instruction in spear techniques, and a majority of foot soldiers were said to deploy their weapons in a haphazard fashion.

Various methods of spear handling were developed by martial experts using diverse types of *yari*, and therefore different schools of *sojutsu* developed. In the long peace of the Edo period (1600–1868), the *yari* earned a place as an emblem of samurai status and became standard ceremonial equipment borne by retainers of high-ranking warriors.

YAWARA ("WAY OF SOFTNESS")

Yawara (literally, "the way of softness or yielding") is the term for one of the original samurai techniques now called *judo*, which was known as *jujutsu* in premodern times. Unusual among the canonical martial arts as a technique for unarmed combat, *yawara* stresses agility, precise form, and refined mental abilities as opposed to physical prowess. Standard techniques include throwing (*nagewaza*), grappling (*katamewaza*), and attacking vital points (*atemiwaza*).

During the Edo period, *jujutsu* developed as a martial art of self-defense, and was especially useful in arresting criminals, as the Tokugawa government favored strict control of arms deployment. Instruction in this technique was popular under Tokugawa rule, but once the emperor was restored to power, schools of *jujutsu/yawara* declined along with the fortunes of the samurai class.

FIREARMS

Authorities acknowledge that medieval Japanese were probably familiar with explosive weapons due to longstanding contact with China, where gunpowder had been in use for many centuries. Further, pirates (*wako*) and merchants traveling to and from the Asian continent almost certainly had observed or handled matchlock guns. However, even if firearms (*teppo*) were already known in Japan, their use was not widespread in Japanese battles until after European guns were formally introduced to Tanegashima Tokitaka, daimyo of an island domain off the southern coast of Kyushu, in 1543. From that point, firearms directed changes in battle tactics and military organization, and guns became a critical weapon in the samurai arsenal.

In 1543, two Portuguese survivors of a vessel sailing from Thailand to Ningbo, a port city in China's northeast Zhejiang province, shipwrecked on a Japanese island called Tanegashima, located at the southern tip of Kyushu. These men demonstrated use of a firearm from Portugal to the young daimyo of Tanegashima. This first Japanese encounter with a firearm for practical use so impressed the island daimyo that he ordered craftsmen of his domain to duplicate the harquebus. The Portuguese weapon they copied was a matchlock-type musket known in English as the harquebus, also spelled arquebus, and called *hinawaju* in Japan. This weapon is sometimes also called the *tanegashima*, for the island where it was first used in Japan.

The Portuguese harquebus, like its close counterpart made in Japan, was about one meter long and was equipped with a smooth bore about 15 millimeters (0.6 inch) in size. Its maximum effective range was 100 meters (328 feet) if aimed at a large target. The somewhat primitive musket took up to a half-minute to reload, and could not be fired at all in rain. Yet this weapon proved popular with the Japanese military, particularly as regional skirmishes between daimyo escalated into challenges to the authority of the shogun. Firearms similar to the Portuguese model were adopted rapidly, and soon Japan became the largest gun exporter in Asia. Centers of gun production were located in Sakai (a city near present-day Osaka), the medieval province called Omi (now Shiga Prefecture, which surrounds Lake Biwa, near Kyoto), and in Negoro (in present-day Wakayama Prefecture, near to the Kii mountains). Gunpowder was mostly imported.

As the Warring States period drew to a close, explosive weapons like the harquebus earned a figural role in large-scale conflicts. By many estimates, nearly a third of armies assembled by daimyo in the late 16th century were supplied with guns. Sometime after 1549, the great strategist general Oda Nobunaga designated a unit in his army that bore firearms, and outfitted them with 500 matchlocks purchased from the gunsmiths in Kunitomo in Omi. The daimyo of the province then known as Kai (now Yamanashi Prefecture) also established a firearms brigade in the 1550s. By the late 16th century, matchlock weapons were considered primary in importance among offensive weapons. Units bearing firearms (*teppogumi ashigaru*) were often sent ahead of other troops to mount an ambush, thereby luring enemy formations into the field of fire. This tactic proved instrumental in several victories attained during the latter half of the 16th century, such as the Battles of Anegawa in 1570, and Nagashino in 1575, under the command of Oda Nobunaga. After the Battle of Nagashino, deployment of large numbers of harquebuses became common. The successful efforts mounted by Toyotomi Hideyoshi against the Shimazu family in Kyushu in 1586, and his Odawara campaign against the later Hojo family in 1590, also depended upon the achievements of firearm units.

Beyond the advantages of the musket in military contexts, there were other benefits to the introduction of firearms in Japan. Pervasive use of muskets spurred industrial and commercial growth due to an increased demand for the manufacture and distribution of firearms, ammunition and related equipment. The effectiveness and popularity of firearms justified the establishment of armed infantry units, since operation of the harquebus required little military knowledge and almost no training. These musket-bearing infantries were recruited from the peasant classes, and the increased status of foot soldiers in a time of near-constant battles enabled individuals from the lowest classes to gain social mobility.

With the founding of the Tokugawa shogunate, firearms production was reduced and further advances in technology and design were interrupted until the inception of the Meiji Restoration in 1868 and removal of trade restrictions. Regardless, there was no requirement for firearms during the security of Edo-period peace. On a larger scale, explosive weapons were rarely used in Japan before the 19th century. Evidence indicates that samurai eschewed most forms of heavy artillery until the last major campaign of the Tokugawa shogunate, in which cannons were used against lingering Toyotomi loyalists at Osaka Castle between 1614 and 1615.

NINJUTSU (ESPIONAGE)

Reconnaissance became a primary concern during the Warring States period (Sengoku jidai, 1467–1568) and centered on the famed spies known as ninja, whose activities were called *ninjutsu* (ninja arts and training). The widespread internecine warfare of the mid- to late-Muromachi period made infiltration and information-gathering a focus of military operations. Training in ninja techniques like those described below in "Dagger Throwing" and "Needle Spitting" have relatively recent origins in Japan, despite having developed out of espionage tactics that were fairly common in the medieval era. As with legends praising brave and virtuous samurai, modern (and medieval) misconceptions about ninja traditions have enhanced the ninja mystique. Clothed in notorious secrecy and black garments, and endowed with famed accuracy, acrobatic skills, and awe-inspiring weapons, these figures have played prominent roles in film and literature concerning the martial arts. Most ninja missions supplied little such drama, although concealing the identity of successful ninja was considered paramount.

Famed ninja bands, such as the Iga school (originating in present-day Mie Prefecture) and the Koga school (part of Shiga Prefecture today), were identified with the regions in which they began. Villages in these areas were entirely devoted to instruction and mastery of ninja techniques. Ninja who trained in such regional bands served as scouts, penetrating enemy territory to gather information, conduct assassinations, or simply to distract and confuse the enemy at nighttime. Daimyo relied upon legions of these figures beginning in the 15th century as domains competed for dwindling land and other resources.

Ninja techniques, known as *shinobu* in Japanese, included strategies of artifice, camouflage, and deception, as well as an array of weapons and tools designed especially for espionage and covert use. In the Warring States period, clandestine missions were critical to military tactics, and thus ninja practices were transmitted orally to maintain secrecy. While medieval samurai enjoyed a somewhat undeserved reputation for noble intentions and valor, ninja temperament was compared to that of a trickster who eschewed the forthright bravery of military

5.6 *Ninja demonstrating stealthy jumping technique* (Illustration Kikuchi Yosai from *Zenken kojitsu*, mid-19th century)

retainers, preferring the advantages offered by ambush and sleight of hand. Opportunistic ninja offered themselves as assassins for hire and pirates during the nearly continuous unrest of the 15th to 16th centuries. They became a significant threat in the 16th century. For example, Oda Nobunaga sent 46,000 troops to Iga province in 1581, although tales recount that 4,000 were killed by the Iga ninja.

In the Edo period, threatened with extinction under the enforced Tokugawa peace, *ninjutsu* became a formal martial art which may have attracted followers simply because of the general fascination with these mysterious, elusive, seemingly magical figures. As *ninjutsu* became one of the most alluring of the standard 18 military arts (*bugeijuhappan*), samurai enthusiasts organized ninja teachers, classes, skill requirements, tools, weapons, and techniques systematically in manuals designed for instruction. One of the primary ninja manuals, the *Mansen shukai*, was compiled in 1676 by Fujibayashi Samuji. This important text detailed the traditions and techniques of the Iga and Koga schools of *ninjutsu*.

Sometimes opposition forces anticipated spy activity and sent their own ninja to trail enemy scouts back to their encampment and perform counter-spy operations. To combat this problem, many ninja forces used passwords, which were determined before the outset of an espionage mission by a leader. Upon returning from the mission, the commander would utter the password without advance notice, and every member of the ninja force would stand, as ordered before the mission when the word was determined. Anyone left seated was instantly identified as an infiltrator from enemy ranks.

DAGGER THROWING

Weapons were employed as projectiles beginning in the 11th century in Japan, but use of thrown daggers (*shuriken*) by ninja is not noted until the Edo period. Sometimes shaped like a star, with at least four sharp points radiating from the center of the steel blade, these weapons were usually deployed in groups. Most *shuriken* measured 20 centimeters or less in diameter, making them light, easy to launch, and suitable for the mobile ninja milieu. *Shuriken* is sometimes paired with a related technique using smaller metal objects called *fukumibari* which closely resembled needles. See below for more information on this approach. Schools specializing in *shuriken* were located in the Sendai, Aizu, and Mito regions.

NEEDLE SPITTING

This technique involves small metal pins (*fumibari*, or *fukumibari*) which are blown in the direction of the adversary's eyes from the ninja's mouth. The devices were intended to cause blindness or other serious injuries to an opponent. While this martial art has sometimes been included in descriptions of the standard 18 warrior techniques (*bugei juhappan*) as articulated in the Edo period, some Japanese and Western scholars, both past and present, regard this and other ninja techniques as peripheral to standard warrior training regimens. Warriors who cultivated such deadly techniques in an age of peace, the Edo period, were perhaps more drawn by the allure of the legendary secrets of the Iga and Koga ninja schools, long feared by warriors and peasants, than they were interested in physical and mental discipline. For some authorities, the lack of demand for

true espionage, or assassination attempts, in Edo peacetime justifies exclusion of ninja practices such as *fumibari* from lists of martial arts training.

SICKLE

The crescent-shaped sickle (*kusarigama*) was a weapon especially associated with ninja infiltrators. The *kusarigama* functioned as a metal weight attached to a wooden shaft that also held a long chain. The hardwood shaft measured from 20 to 60 centimeters (eight to 24 inches), while the chain was two to three meters (6.5 to 10 feet) long. By swinging the chain, the warrior generated significant velocity to disrupt use of an opponent's weapon, cause injury, or entangle the opponent with the lethal sickle-like blade. The device was also effective in securing an opponent's head before a beheading. During the Edo period this weapon was used for a martial art called *kusarigamajutsu*.

The effectiveness of the *kusarigama* depended largely on surprise and rapid deployment, and along with other ninja weapons and methods was seen as less noble than pursuits such as spear-throwing or sword-drawing. Like the other techniques described above, use of the *kusarigama* is sometimes omitted from standard lists of martial arts traditions in Japan, as this practice failed to impress critics as an appropriate technique for warriors.

WEAPONS OF RESTRAINT AND RESTRAINING TECHNIQUES

Truncheon The truncheon (*jitte*) is a weapon made of iron and later, steel, that was introduced to Japan from China. Resembling the truncheons used in feudal Europe, these arms had a shaft measuring about 45 centimeters (one and a half feet) long. Just below the hilt, an L-shaped hook that could be used to grasp an opponent's sword and wrest it from him ran parallel to the shaft. During the Warring States period, restraining and disarming techniques using the *jitte* proliferated and the weapon came to be regarded as one of the martial arts. Samurai continued to practice *jitte* techniques in the Edo period. Manuals were developed, and in Edo under Tokugawa rule, the *jitte* became a popular weapon for members of law enforcement appointed by the shogun. Elegant *jitte* plated in silver with hilts decorated with red tassels were worn by shogunal constables called *yoriki* and *doshin* as a symbol of their office.

Roping *(torite)* and the barbed staff *(mojiri)* were also employed as restraining devices.

OTHER WEAPONS USED BY WARRIORS

Beyond the weapons and restraining techniques using objects described above, samurai also employed other objects in combat, depending upon variables such as weather, availability of traditional weapons, and other circumstances. Soldiers might also use slings, iron rakes that could dislodge an opponent from a horse or boat, axes and wooden hammers to remove objects in their path.

War Fans War fans *(gunsen)* or iron fans *(tessen)* were among the items high-ranking samurai carried in times of war and peace. Although the name war fan suggests that this object was frequently used in battle situations, this equipment served warriors primarily as a weapon of last resort.

Two types of fans were used by warriors, each with a specific application based upon its design features. The folding fan *(ogi* or *sensu)* originated in Japan and served ceremonial, comfort, and occasionally, defensive functions for warriors. Folding fans had practical appeal for samurai, given that a typical warrior had a primarily itinerant lifestyle. Commanders often carried folding fans as authority symbols, just as ruling figures held short, scepter-like staffs called *shaku* as signs of their power and rank at court. Further, fans were a portable solution that offered relief from the persistent heat of Japan's tropical summers. At the same time, in a surprise attack, the folding war fan had substantial iron edges that could be deadly. Warriors also used flat fans called *uchiwa*, which originated in China. These rigid fans include a ribbed support structure overlaid with paper or silk in a rounded or occasionally trapezoidal form. Flat war fans *(gumbai uchiwa)* served warriors mostly as signaling devices and standards in battle, not as weapons of last resort. Both types of fans were often decorated with dragons or other symbols of strength, or family crests.

Controlled manipulation of the fan as a weapon, or *tessenjutsu*, originated in the feudal era, and was favored by instructors to the Tokugawa shoguns in the Edo period. According to medieval battle literature, war fans were also used by warriors performing seppuku (ritual suicide) as a place for composing poems or other final messages before death.

Oyumi While bows and arrows required repeated deployment by a regiment or even entire army, this larger weapon allowed a similar assault without such a threat to numbers of troops. The earliest record of the *oyumi* cites that a number (unspecified) of these weapons were presented to the imperial court by Korean envoys from the kingdom of Koryo in 618. Although examples have not yet been excavated, and no illustrations or precise descriptions survive, the *oyumi* appears to have been a platform-mounted catapult that operated in the style of a crossbow, although greatly enlarged. Similar devices used in ancient Greece were called *oxybeles* or *lithobolos*, and in Rome, *ballista*. These weapons were praised for their ability to release volleys of stones or arrows in a single deployment. Notorious as a complex weapon, the *oyumi* was regarded with respect and fear during the early medieval era.

ARMOR, HELMETS, AND SHIELDS

Japanese arms and armor of the early medieval period were produced by artisans clustered in the capital cities (or the city in which the shogunate was located) and were obtained by individual samurai or the leaders of regional warrior bands through distribution networks. Later, in the age of warfare, domains and castle towns relied upon a corps of local armorers and metalworkers to supply daimyo armies. By the end of the Sengoku period in the late 16th century, production of arms and armor had become a major industry. Yet typical foot soldiers in a regional lord's army often lacked a full complement of armor and up-to-date weapons. Few lords could afford to provide their troops with uniform armor, as did Ii Naomasa, famous for his "Red

Devils," troops outfitted in easily recognizable red-lacquered armor.

Despite minor variations over time, medieval and early modern Japanese armor, helmets, and shields for foot soldiers remained generally uniform in design and appearance. Certainly there were no regional differences in arms and armor. *Domaru*, a late Kamakura form of armor, manufactured in one regional center and later shipped elsewhere, closely resembled armor produced locally or in remote regions. Those of higher rank wore armor that conformed to standard styles in terms of structure, but elite samurai had suits and helmets that were ornamented with symbols and decorations befitting their superior rank. A considerable percentage of current knowledge about armor forms and production techniques originated in numerous illustrated battle tales from the late Heian period and after. Armorers were well regarded in medieval and early modern culture, for their craft was considered both an art and a science.

Armor

In Japanese, the term *bugu* (military tools) refers to all objects used for both offense and defense in battle, and armor is included in this category. Typically, armor has not always been identified as a military tool or instrument, yet armor merits consideration as a central component of the warrior regalia that offered protection first but also a sense of identity within a military force and camaraderie among samurai in general. Innovations in armor corresponded closely to changes in martial techniques and technologies, although in a few instances styles and types of armor were favored despite being somewhat impractical.

Throughout the medieval period and into the early modern era (and even the 20th century), Japanese armor was valued both as a means of defense and a source of pride. The elaborate appearance of Japanese armor from the feudal era reflects that the military elite lavished patronage on such symbols of their power. Protective gear was often passed on to future generations, and bore family crests and other historically significant symbols of lineage and status. Fortunately, examples of Japanese armor have been well

5.7 *Example of armor on display at Himeji Castle* (Photo William E. Deal)

preserved, in part because of the tradition of passing armor along within families. In addition, warriors often presented such objects to shrines as tribute for a victory or to commemorate fulfillment of a request for divine intervention. Records show that occasionally such donations were reclaimed by the owner when required in an emergency.

Types of armor, materials used, decorative details, condition, and the defensive capabilities of protective gear varied among samurai of different rank throughout the medieval and early modern eras. Foot soldiers were easily recognized on the battlefield not only because the majority of troops belonged to this class, but also because they wore relatively simple, easily adjusted armor and helmets that included minimal ornamentation. By contrast, Japanese armor produced for the elite members of the samurai class, such as daimyo or even shoguns, included sumptuous decoration, and was augmented by symbols to ensure bravery and victory as well as crests to indicate one's affiliation and service. For example, since it was believed that dragonflies could not fly backward, dragonflies were depicted on armor to represent the hope that there would be no retreat, and thus defeat, for the soldier who wore the suit.

Although most Japanese armor was created primarily with practical considerations in mind, armor also served important ceremonial functions. Armor could serve as a signature, as most important political figures wore unique suits of armor specifically designed for them. Further, armor could identify troops or unify regiments sharing a singular style, color, or emblem. One noted example is the signature red-lacquered armor reportedly worn by Ii Naomasa (1561–1602), a precedent followed by his descendants until Ii Naosuke (1815–60), whose assassination was caused in part by his negotiation of a trade agreement with the United States that was opposed by conservatives. Colors favored for decorating armor were usually bold hues, such as red, deep blue, brown, black, and gold.

Even in the case of relatively humble armor, Japanese artisans sought to make armor that was aesthetically pleasing as well as highly functional. Consequently, armor and related objects such as sword fittings are usually considered artistic objects in Japan. However, in this volume, arms and armor have been discussed as material evidence of warrior culture. Readers are advised that stylistic and decorative analysis of arms and armor have been minimized in this section. Publications that explore the artistic qualities and elements seen in warrior regalia are identified in the Reading section and in the General Bibliography.

DEVELOPMENT OF BODY ARMOR

Much of what is known of early armor in Japan has been gleaned from tomb figures dating from the Kofun period, which often depicted military figures. Early forms of armor from the Kofun period (ca. 300–710) were produced in styles known as *keiko* and *tanko*. Both types are thought to have been based on mainland prototypes.

Metal cuirasses from this era consisted of several plated sections tightly bound together and then lacquered to inhibit rust. Subsequent construction methods that were more flexible involved narrow, roughly square, strips of bronze or iron fastened using cords or leather. These metal parts are called lames in English, or *sane* in Japanese, and remained a central component of the relatively flexible armor developed in Japan throughout the medieval period.

From its inception, Japanese armor was far lighter and more flexible than the chain mail and cuirasses made of solid metal plates used at the same time in Europe. Japanese armorers did not confine themselves to metal, and instead incorporated lighter and more malleable materials such as leather and silk (or other fibers) along with iron or steel parts. Even armor made during the early feudal era in Japan typically consisted of modular steel scales called lames atop leather laced together with leather, various types of cord, and silk. The materials used, color scheme, and lacing format identified particular clans and individuals, and some materials, patterns, or designs were reserved for individuals of certain status. Further, rather than adorning the metal plates with elaborate, etched designs that were time consuming, or simply polishing the metal to a reflective shine, Japanese metalworkers chose to cover the metal components they used with lacquer.

Lacquer, a non-resinous substance similar to sap, from the lacquer tree, was added atop the metal and sometimes also covered the leather parts of early medieval body armor. Lacquer (botanical name *Rhus verniciflua*) is native to East Asia and has been used in producing objects that date back more than 3,000 years. Once dried (or, technically, hardened), lacquer functions like a natural polymer, bonding to the surface to which it is applied, and remains impervious to moisture, insects, and even mild acids for many years. Each coat of lacquer must be allowed to harden completely before another coat is applied. Once complete, the process of coating metal with lacquer enhanced the strength and durability of the metal without adding to its weight. Further, the protective lacquer reduced the shine of metal surfaces which could make approaching troops more visible both day and night.

Japanese medieval armor, which was also commonly used across Asia and the Middle East, offered portability as well as flexibility and a lighter load, since its structure allowed it to be folded or collapsed for transport and storage. Further, armor constructed with lames offered better protection than chain mail, which was the predominant choice for armor made in medieval Europe. Once pierced by a weapon, the sharp, broken metal components of chain mail could worsen or infect a wound, while the layered structure of lamellar armor absorbed shocks efficiently and covered a larger surface area than the circular links of mail. The advantages of armor composed of lames, covered with lacquer, and using a combination of materials contributed to the widespread use of this type of armor construction in Japan from the late Heian period until the middle of the 14th century.

The principal form of armor used in the medieval era was known as *oyoroi* (literally, great armor). Overall, its form was cube-like and the entire ensemble hung from the shoulders. The box-like cuirass wrapped around the torso on the front and back as well as the left side. However, the right side, necessary for entering and exiting the armor, consisted of a separate piece called a *waidate*. Unlike the other portions of the cuirass, the *waidate* was a solid metal plate enhanced by a skirt-like form in four pieces that protected the thighs. This solid element was attached to protect the more vulnerable area where the suit was fastened, on the right side of the samurai's body. Separate loosely hanging plates in slightly different shapes about 30 centimeters wide covered the gaps left where the cuirass was cut away at shoulders and armpits to allow for the archer's motion while riding, aiming, and shooting. These plates, known as *osode*, protected the collarbones and hands of the warrior.

5.8 *Warrior wearing face mask as part of his armor ensemble* (Illustration Kikuchi Yosai from *Zenken kojitsu*, mid-19th century)

Oyoroi armor was constructed of leather and iron lames bound together in horizontal layers and was ornamented and reinforced with leather, silk, and gilt metal. Elements were added to *oyoroi* body ensembles to protect specific body parts that were most exposed. These elements included the *osode* and *wakidate* described above, as well as the *nodowa*, a throat guard.

Another form of armor—essentially a simplified version of the components used in *oyoroi*—called *haramaki* appeared about the same time that *oyoroi* became the favored protection for the mounted archers that comprised early samurai bands. Made of the same materials as *oyoroi*, the *haramaki* cuirass was a single piece wrapping the warrior's chest and overlapping under the right arm. Without the solid form of the *waidate* covering the right arm, *haramaki* fit more closely about the waist and included a skirt made up of eight segments that made both running and walking much easier. *Haramaki* rapidly earned favor among elite samurai and for a quarter of the cost of *oyoroi*, *haramaki* were obtained for *ashigaru* (foot soldiers).

After the middle of the Kamakura period, new battle tactics emerged and warfare became more dynamic. Therefore, warriors required armor that would allow quick, agile movements and manipulation of a variety of types of weapons. In such circumstances, European styles of armor would have been too heavy and rigid for Japanese purposes. Japanese horses were smaller than their European counterparts, too, so armorers had to avoid further burdening mounts or foot soldiers with armor made entirely of metal, which could impede progress. Yet a typical *oyoroi* of the Heian period weighed approximately 30 kilos, or about 62.5 pounds. Weight, bulk, and cost eventually led to the decline of *oyoroi*. Although elegant and quite effective, such styles of armor offered few advantages amid dramatic changes in samurai warfare. As mounted battles dwindled and increasingly large infantry units were deployed in siegelike maneuvers, armor that was more flexible and less expensive began to supersede the bulky but effective *oyoroi* suits. *Haramaki* was particularly well suited to meet these demands. Due to the effectiveness of *haramaki*, by the end of the Warring States period, armor fit closer to the body, had parts that could be easily modified and transported, and consisted of modular forms. As the overall design of the cuirass components had not changed significantly, armorers had successfully adapted components of *oyoroi* and synthesized them into *haramaki* to meet the requirements imposed by the changing battle landscape. The ranks of foot soldiers swelled, archery on horseback and on foot were abandoned in favor of pole-arms and elongated swords (more decisive tactics requiring less training), and *haramaki* replaced *oyoroi* armor, which became obsolete by the end of the Northern and Southern Courts period (1336–92).

Notably, an ordinary warrior's arsenal did not necessarily include armor until the Azuchi-Momoyama period, when Oda Nobunaga was the first leader to issue all troops, including foot soldiers, a standard suit of armor. However, by the Muromachi period, most ranking soldiers had a cuirass, consisting of a *do*, which covered the torso, as well as a helmet of some type. As the *oyoroi* was extremely expensive to produce, it was beyond the means of all but the most wealthy samurai.

Later artisans developed armor made from solid metal plates which were hammered into shape. Cuirasses made of solid metal proved useful as weapons technology changed and the pole-arm or *naginata* preferred by foot soldiers and warrior-monks offered a formidable challenge to samurai armed only with bow and arrow.

"MODERN" ARMOR (*TOSEI GUSOKU*)

In Japanese, *tosei gusoku* literally means "modern equipment" and fittingly, the type of armor referred to by this term represents innovations made in materials and construction in response to the changing battle tactics and weaponry introduced during the last half of the 16th century. Once firearms were introduced to Japan, armor requirements and designs changed once again. In addition to matchlock harquebuses, Western armor began to be imported into Japan from the late Muromachi period. Initially, Japanese warriors adapted Western cuirasses by simply attaching protective skirts and neck guards, but soon entire sets of body armor in Western styles began to be produced in Japan. Such suits, called *nambando gusoku* in Japanese, often incorporated two single-ridged, hammered iron sheets which were hinged on one side and fastened with cord on the other.

Helmets

The basic form of helmet (*kabuto*) that dominated medieval and early modern armor was shaped generally like a skull cap with an opening at the front top and flaps at the sides intended to protect the neck and face. In addition, the neck was shielded by a series of three or five metal plates. By the end of the Muromachi period, most ordinary helmets were made from iron and/or steel. The helmet was formed from individual plates fastened with rivets or simply joined together. The top portion of the helmet, shaped like the pate of a human head, was called the *hachi*. In the early medieval period, from the 11th to 14th centuries, *hachi* were almost invariably rounded, but this shape became less common in the late 1500s. In some cases the ridges produced where plates intersected at the top of the helmet were studded with numerous raised decorative rivets that inspired the term "star helmet" for this type of *kabuto*.

As warfare proliferated in the 16th century, helmets began to be made in a wider variety of shapes, and the majority of these roughly maintained the shape of a human head if viewed from above. While many samurai wore decorated helmets, the most distinctive designs were reserved for daimyo. Helmets of the Warring States period began to reflect the grandeur of the age in their size, dimensions, and elaborate ornamentation.

Animal symbolism was a popular motif for the *maedate*, a section of the front of the helmet usually translated in English as the crest. However, crests found on helmets did not necessarily replicate the *mon* or family crests found on flags and banners. Instead, helmets belonging to high-ranking daimyo displayed a retinue of images similar to some of the animal imagery also used to adorn body armor. Often the shapes featured on helmets were derived from nature or from legends. In addition, various symbols relating to aspects of Japanese history and culture were found on the *maedate*. For example, Honda Tadatsugu wore a helmet with a design of large antlers, while Ii Naomasa, a central member of the Ii clan in Shiga Prefecture, had a helmet emblazoned with golden horns. Other noted daimyo had helmets shaped like half-moons, deer antlers, and sunbursts, and Kuroda Nagamasa owned a helmet that bore a strange curved metal plate about one foot wide and high, symbolizing the Battle of Ichinotani, a decisive event during the Gempei War (see Chapter 1: Historical Context for more information).

By contrast, most foot soldiers possessed a relatively modest helmet called a *jingasa* (war helmet). Usually, *jingasa* were made of metal or hardened leather and were conical in shape. *Jingasa* made of iron could also serve as a pot for cooking, as seen in a noted illustration from the *Zoyo monogatari* (1649) in which a foot soldier has suspended his helmet from a branch for use as a rice steamer.

Shields

Shields were commonly used in nearly all military contexts in Japan, beginning with prehistory. Chinese dynastic histories include descriptions that indicate shields were in use by the third century in Japan. Other sources such as clay figures called *haniwa*

found on or near tomb mounds and excavated objects confirm that shields made until the end of the sixth century mostly had a rectangular form, measured about 100 to 150 centimeters long, and about 50 centimeters wide. Most early shields were composed of layered leather covered with lacquer.

During the early medieval period, shields made of wood became more common, and they were designed for individual protection and to present a coordinated defense on the battlefield. From the Nara period to the early medieval period, military shields were standing wooden barriers about eye-level in height and roughly the width of human shoulders. (In English, these defensive weapons were also called mantlets because of their similarity to devices of that name which were used by European soldiers.) They were attached to poles, or feet, which were hinged so that the support could be collapsed and stored or transported flat. Approximately one and a half meters tall and less than half a meter wide, mostly such shields were made of several planks joined vertically. Although shields could withstand more force if each was made from a single board, this was the exception rather than the rule. Protective substances such as lacquer could also prolong the life of such standing shields; however, by the end of the Kamakura period, decoration usually consisted solely of a family crest. Before firearms came into widespread use in the late 16th century, shields were portable but somewhat cumbersome. Deployment and other tactical considerations involved in the use of standing shields are discussed below in the Battle Tactics section.

Another means of defense was a length of fabric draped over the back of a warrior's armor that could catch stray arrows, especially in a charge or other rapid maneuver that caused the cape to billow. Later this device, known as a *horo*, took the form of a large sack that inflated when the warrior moved, thus harnessing the force of the trapped air to repel arrows. Sometimes, this cloaklike bag positioned on the back of the armor was stiffened with a cage of reeds to ensure that few arrows would meet their target. Further, this fabric *horo* served as one means of protection for a messenger, as they possessed little other means of defense and often traveled rapidly and without accompanying troops. When a lord's seal (*mon*) was added to the cloak, the messenger could be easily identified whether approaching or retreating.

FORTIFICATIONS

Although fortifications were constructed in Japan prior to the feudal period, frequent conflicts associated with warrior ascendancy inspired new, distinctive temporary architectural forms as well as more lasting structures to protect against military attack.

Up to the beginning of the feudal era, three forms of fortifications were built, according to archaeologists. The grid-pattern city form was inspired by Chinese planning precedents, and included gates or walled enclosures. Mountain fortresses appear to be an indigenous form, and were typical of remote areas. Plateaus or plains often utilized the palisade, a semi-permanent defense. Typical defenses included a rampart, a ditch, and a palisade. Grid-pattern cities were surrounded by walls that served as a demarcation point rather than as true protection, and eventually such barriers disappeared. Remains of mountain fortresses found in northern Kyushu were a more effective means of protection, and may have belonged to ancient kingdoms that ruled parts of Japan in early times. Palisades were often constructed in the northeastern areas of the main island of Honshu. Although excavations have revealed only partial remains of such structures, they are significant since they offer prototypes for medieval fortifications.

Until the end of the Kamakura period, most fortresses built in Japan were relatively simple, and were designed for a particular siege or campaign. Terms such as *shiro* and *jokaku* (translated in later eras as "castle") appear frequently in 12th- and 13th-century accounts of warfare, but in the Kamakura era, these terms refer to temporary fortifications. Early medieval defense structures were more like barricades than buildings, and were not intended to house soldiers for extended periods. However, such fortifications could be elaborate and large in scale.

Literary and pictorial accounts confirm that extensive planning and earthworks projects were utilized throughout the medieval era for major battles. For instance, the defense works at Ichinotani erected by the Taira clan in 1184 included boulders topped by thick logs, a double row of shields, and turrets with openings for shooting. Even if descrip-

tions of such structures taken from accounts of the Gempei War dating to the late Kamakura era exaggerate these defenses, they capture the labor, time, and ingenuity involved in such efforts.

As wartime construction continued, Japanese military architects became skilled in adapting civilian structures that offered multiple options for warrior defenses. Composite barriers utilizing timber and other materials that protected crops from intruders and animals were helpful in subduing infantry offenses. Military architects familiar with agricultural irrigation principles constructed ditches and moats to deter mounted troops. In sum, military construction of the early medieval period involved tailoring familiar forms to warrior needs to provide an initial line of defense.

Some temporary construction types afforded flexibility and served well in both offensive and defensive situations. *Kaidate* (shield walls) and *sakamogi* (brush barricades; literally "stacked wood") were both in common use by the 13th century. *Kaidate*, formed of rows of standing shields, had been employed since the end of the Asuka period (eighth century), and were valuable as portable field fortifications. *Sakamogi*, which were most likely inspired by barriers for livestock, were useful in several contexts as well. These deceptively simple structures continued to be effective in the age of gunpowder as they remained difficult to cross and also resisted explosive shells. Barriers made of shields could be made more effective through deployment atop, or in front of, another defensive form. However, as the power of the Ashikaga shoguns declined in the Northern and Southern Courts era, combat conditions changed, and samurai clans confronted elevated fortresses where warriors on horseback were ineffective.

Azuchi-Momoyama- and Edo-Period Castles

After the feudal system was reorganized by the Tokugawa shogunate, castles (*shiro*) were erected in the center of a daimyo's domain, so they would be easily accessible. Without natural defenses such as hills and plateaus, these structures required additional protection compared with the elevated *shiro* built during the late Muromachi and Momoyama periods. For security, builders developed walls of enormous boulders that often had smooth surfaces that would be difficult to scale. Moats (*hori*) also provided a means to deter an attacking force.

The castle was not only a means of defense, but also served as the hub of administration and commerce in the domain. Castles housed the domain lord and chief retainers. Towns developed around the structures, called "towns beneath the castle" (*jokamachi*) since the castle was often elevated, and both literally and figuratively overshadowed all other buildings nearby. Merchants and artisans became an important aspect of life in these castle communities, as daimyo and their retainers had more time and disposable income than in the past. Further, the rise of fashion and interest in display (in the sense of decoration and adornment) that arose in the cosmopolitan Edo period made it necessary for members of the warrior class to keep up appearances, and this led to healthy economic growth even in provincial castle towns. Castle construction is surveyed in detail in chapter 10: Art and Architecture.

Warrior Ranks and Hierarchy

Military Structure

From the late Muromachi era, army organization changed significantly. One positive outcome of the long era of internecine battles was a more clearly defined military order. While the shogun still functioned as the head of the military government as well as the supreme general, military structure emerged as the basis for the socioeconomic hierarchy and also for the organization of armed forces. As in the *ritsuryo* system of conscripted military first instituted in the Nara period, the leaders of warrior bands still usually came from aristocratic backgrounds. Also as in the previous system, warriors of status were mounted, as equestrian soldiers had

higher status than infantry. Increasingly, however, figures of more humble social rank began to ascend to military positions previously reserved for aristocrats, especially as the country approached unification under the charismatic leaders Oda Nobunaga and Toyotomi Hideyoshi, both of whom initially held *ashigaru* (foot soldier) ranks. Thus, military organization began to reflect the new ethos of warrior culture, in which martial ability could confer status that had previously been inherited.

Some daimyo administered armies with a basic structure. For example, in the Muromachi period, Hojo Ujiyasu separated his bodyguards into 48 squads and placed a captain in command of each squad. These squads were then divided into seven companies. Six companies were composed of seven squads in total, and one company had six. Finally, each squad numbered 20 men. Tokugawa Ieyasu also favored dividing warriors into companies. Initially, his elite *oban* (great guard) force was separated into three companies. With the advent of the Korean invasion, the army numbered five companies, and by 1623, Ieyasu's force consisted of 12 companies. The companies were headed by a single captain, four lieutenants, and 50 guards.

There was extensive variation in the ways troops were structured for battle and the hierarchy of command that directed the troops. See the chart on page 175 for a typical configuration.

It should be noted that horse-mounted troops were also sometimes deployed, but from the late medieval period onward this practice became more and more infrequent.

Warrior Service Requirements

In medieval times, daimyo raising an army calculated warrior wealth in order to determine the amount of service, including numbers of mounted and foot soldiers, each vassal would provide. From the Momoyama period, warrior service was measured in *koku*, a unit of measure that was based upon the amount of unpolished rice normally required annually for sustenance—approximately 5.12 U.S.

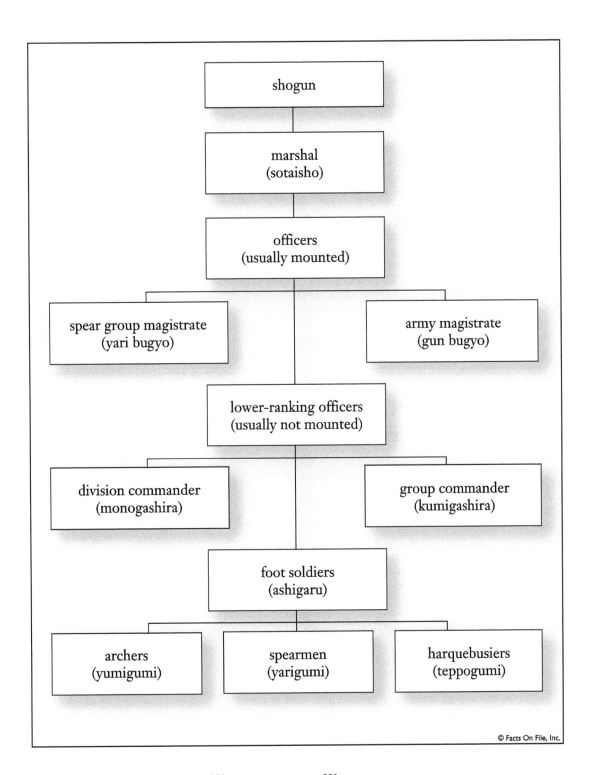

bushels or 180.39 liters. This figure was then used to assess average annual yields of a rice field within a system of four grades: 1.5, 1.3, 1.2, or 1.1 *koku* annually for each 10th of a hectare (or quarter-acre). The *koku* quantity, known as *kokudaka*, or assessed tax base measured in *koku*, replaced an earlier system used in the Kamakura and Muromachi periods that calculated annual tax in terms of monetary value.

In 1649, for instance, samurai of *hatamoto* rank with assets of 300 *koku* would be required to provide one spearman, an armor-bearer, a groom, a sandal bearer, and a *hasami-biko* bearer as well as one baggage carrier to his lord whenever called upon for service. While *hatamoto* was a relatively humble rank, providing service to the shogunate was a primary measure of loyalty among the warrior classes, and thus a critical cost of allegiance. Prior to the Edo period, there was little standardization of the service requirements incurred by a vassal, although certainly some vassals were taxed more heavily than others. The most unfortunate among the military ranks were obligated to fulfill the multiple demands of temples, shrines, and aristocratic owners of provincial estates (*shoen*).

cepts prohibiting monks from engaging in such pursuits. In addition, civil codes that limited weapons possession among priests, acolytes, and other clerics had little effect on the many *sohei* who functioned in institutions not subject to such restrictions. Another common misconception about warrior-monks also relates to terminology. Some scholars have conflated the roles of *sohei* and *yamabushi* (mountain ascetics), since both of these religious figures dwelt in mountains and are sometimes identified in medieval sources as similar figures. Despite the apparent similarity to the word *bushi*, which is also used to designate samurai, the "bushi" in *yamabushi* is written with a different character than the "bushi" for warrior. The term *yamabushi* distinguishes ascetics who engaged in mountain pilgrimages and sustained meditation as part of their spiritual practice. However, many powerful temples were located on mountains, and while *yamabushi* also occupied such territory, they were usually benign figures devoted to solitary religious practice. At the same time, the legions of warrior-monks enlisted by religious institutions were only occasionally referred to as *yamabushi* in contemporary sources,

Warrior-Monks (*Sohei*)

Armed forces known as *sohei* (warrior-monks) mounted a potent challenge to aristocrats and warriors throughout the feudal era. The term *akuso*, meaning evil monks, found in diaries of Heian-period courtiers, summarizes the general view of these soldiers that represented powerful temples. While warriors and aristocrats struggled for control of feudal Japan, from the sidelines the *sohei* fought to unseat both of these forces and instead obtain both land and wealth for the benefit of powerful religious institutions.

The origins of the bands of warrior-monks and the language used to identify these figures can be confusing. For example, the title warrior-monk (the more common English translation of the term *sohei*) carries varied connotations in different periods, and *sohei* were not always part of the monastic order at the temples they served. Further, *sohei* were well armed and skilled in the use of weapons, despite Buddhist pre-

5.9 Buddhist warrior-monk (sohei) (Illustration Kikuchi Yosai from *Zenken kojitsu*, mid-19th century)

simply because the temples they served were in mountainous locations.

Temples and other religious institutions were motivated to deploy units of warrior-monks to defend land acquired during the redistributions and lapses in administration practices on provincial estates that occurred in the 10th and 11th centuries. Young warriors employed by private estates as militiamen confused matters by shaving their heads and were often mistaken for *sohei* in practice and in historical accounts. In some cases, the warrior-monks (including those private soldiers who appeared to be monks, but often were not) became so powerful that they posed a threat to the imperial court and the shogunate. Warrior monks serving Enryakuji, Kofukuji, and Miidera, all temples located near Kyoto or the old capital, Nara, were particularly notorious.

With the burning of Enryakuji by Oda Nobunaga in 1571, the power of the *sohei* diminished significantly. Efforts mounted by Toyotomi Hideyoshi

5.10 Kamakura-period foot soldier (Illustration Kikuchi Yosai from *Zenken kojitsu*, mid-19th century)

and the weapons prohibitions instituted in the late Momoyama and early Edo periods finalized the suppression of these warriors.

Foot Soldiers (*Ashigaru*)

The term *ashigaru* (literally, "light of foot") was used for foot soldiers, or infantry, from the Muromachi through Edo periods. These soldiers first attained a reputation during the Onin War (1467–77) when, along with *nobushi* (armed peasants) and *akuto* (bandits), they laid waste to the capital city, Kyoto. Foot soldiers were inexpensive to outfit, and because these warriors had little equipment, such as armor, they could move rapidly. Subsequently, as constant warfare ensued during the Warring States period, they came to be more prominent in daimyo armies, and were outfitted more completely.

From the start, *ashigaru* weapons consisted of bow and arrow or pole-mounted arms (*naginata*, and later, *yari*). Once firearms were introduced in 1543, *ashigaru* played an increasingly prominent role in warfare and were often organized into musketeer units (*teppo ashigaru* or *teppogumi ashigaru*). By the beginning of the Edo period, *ashigaru* were granted positions as the humblest samurai, certainly an improvement upon their initial social rank.

Attendants (*Yoriki* and *Doshin*)

Even samurai of comparatively low social status were accompanied by attendants who furnished armor and supplies, tended to weaponry and horses, and provided protection. Figures who performed these assistant functions were called *yoriki* (literally, "strength that is offered") and *doshin* (literally, "like-minded" or "shared hearts"). These figures were usually considered members of the warrior class in the sense that they were also professional soldiers.

In the early medieval period, when their services were not needed in battle, attendants were likely to be engaged in farming activities. By the Muromachi period, *yoriki* was a term used for samurai who served warrior-commanders of higher rank—proof of the social mobility possible in the warrior class during feudal times. From the 16th century, *yoriki* were usually mounted samurai in command of other samurai or *ashigaru*. Under Tokugawa rule, *yoriki* managed patrol and guard units composed of *doshin*. Considered members of the *gokenin* category of vassals, both *yoriki* and *doshin* were ranked above ordinary peasants, but *yoriki* claimed higher hereditary status and accordingly merited larger family stipends. Therefore they were entrusted with more important military duties than *doshin*. In the Edo period, *doshin* (along with *meakashi*, military agents) were members of police forces in both the capital and smaller castle towns.

Masterless Samurai (*Ronin*)

The term *ronin* (literally, "floating men") is most commonly used to designate masterless samurai of the Edo period. A samurai became masterless for a variety of reasons including the death of the master—whether of natural causes or in battle—or because he abandoned his master as a samurai. However, as early as the Muromachi period, the word *ronin* was used to refer to warriors who became separated from their commanders and/or warrior stipends.

One of the most dramatic events for many *ronin* was the Battle of Sekigahara (1600) after which as many as 400,000 warriors became "floating men" due to the defeat or demise of many daimyo and other chieftains. Another effect of the events at Sekigahara was redistribution of lands held by samurai, leaving many warriors with no residence, no livelihood, and no supporting forces. Estimates indicate that some 100,000 disgruntled *ronin* joined the forces of Toyotomi Hideyoshi's heir, Hideyori, at Osaka Castle and fought during the siege of 1614–15. However, many masterless samurai also joined the ranks of Tokugawa Ieyasu, and some were rewarded with government positions and stipends when Ieyasu prevailed at Osaka. Other former samurai left behind their military vocation and sought work in provincial castle towns or adopted new professions in the rapidly growing cities of the Edo period.

Figures who remained *ronin* presented a challenge to the Tokugawa shogunate. As marginalized former military men, their dissatisfaction with their position led to uprisings, such as the Keian Incident in 1651. Some former samurai turned their attention to instruction in martial arts, or theorized about the philosophy of the warrior. In some cases, the Tokugawa shogunate attempted to stimulate employment of such figures. Eventually many samurai without masters abandoned their status or simply left no heirs. A small number of *ronin* earned their marginal role through criminal activities. In 1703, the 47 Ronin Incident caused further disorder in the Tokugawa government as a group of masterless samurai mounted an act of revenge in response to the perceived unjust death of their lord and were punished by the shogunate for this murderous act. The 47 *ronin* were then ordered to commit seppuku. See "Model Warrior Values—Values Expressed in Life—Loyalty" (pp. 145–146) for additional information.

BATTLE TACTICS

A wide range of battle tactics was used by samurai over nearly 700 years of medieval and early modern history. Warrior strategies in battle were determined in part by the weapons used and the topography of the battle site or domain where the campaign was conducted. In most geographical locations feasible for battle, such as open plains, cavalry were quite effective. However, Japanese topography includes inhospitable areas where archers on foot—and later, firearm units—were better suited to battles in these mountainous, heavily forested, or rocky terrains. Further, the size and degree of specialization of troops affected the military techniques employed by officers, and these factors also varied as the warriors of Japan encountered changing political and economic circumstances.

Training

By definition, a samurai was a professional soldier and devoted hours to preparing for warfare. Battle preparations encompassed a range of activities, including mental as well as physical exercises. Warriors were encouraged to formulate a philosophy regarding death, and most retainers incorporated aspects of contemporary Buddhist and Confucian thought into their disciplined attitude toward life, danger, and death. The legendary samurai integrity essential to the code of behavior known as Bushido (literally, "the way of the warrior"—for additional information on Bushido see above) derived in part from the powerful sense of personal responsibility assumed by self-reliant medieval warriors. In medieval times, retainers first drew upon their own resources to outfit and train military units, and later became dependent upon daimyo or other higher-ranking lords for support. Samurai training thus reflected the investment of a warrior's patron or lord as well as the individual samurai's dedication to self-improvement. Generally, during the nearly 700 years of medieval and early modern Japanese history dominated by warrior culture, samurai trained in various applied skills using the tools and principles of warfare, from basic battle maneuvers to martial strategy, and also investigated the ethical foundations of warfare.

Medieval warriors were able to train with instructor-opponents only if they had aristocratic rank or high social standing. Before the Edo peace, large numbers of peasants joined the ranks of the military in the Warring States period during the 15th and 16th centuries with little or no military background. These foot soldiers, or *ashigaru*, required schooling in traditional samurai mental discipline as well as intensive instruction in military maneuvers. In addition to individual exercises, foot soldiers participated in regiment drills, which endeavored to transform individual soldiers into a well-coordinated unit that operated in unison on the battlefield. In the latter part of the Muromachi and into the Azuchi-Momoyama period, foot soldiers were required to practice by following a mounted general through battle formations and attack-retreat sequences before they were permitted to pick up their weapons to fight. In the Edo period, wealthy and elite samurai participated in martial arts drills focusing on stances and motions both with and without weapons. Retainers from the warrior class alone were entitled to pursue the martial arts during the

Edo period. However, such activities became more a form of sport inspired by pride in military spirit rather than true combat training, as there was no arena for combat under Tokugawa rule.

Shield Deployment/ Formations

In encounters staged on open ground or slightly mountainous terrain, warriors used temporary fortifications like those discussed above. However, such building projects required significant resources, and rapid solutions were more likely to bring favorable results. In preparing for some battles, samurai armies arranged connected shields in a formation called *kaidate* designed for mobility. Linked wooden shields were an effective impediment to the progress of an oncoming opponent, much like temporary fortifications such as the stacked brush barriers called *sakamogi*, especially when conflicts took place on

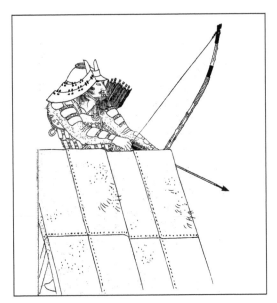

5.11 *Warrior shooting arrows from a fixed shield defensive position* (Illustration Kikuchi Yosai from *Zenken kojitsu*, mid-19th century)

fields or open plateaus. Large-scale shields were more easily deployed than brush barriers, which required significant human labor and large-scale construction, and shields could be removed to another location after use. Nonetheless, both shield walls and *sakamogi* were vulnerable if confronted with fire, a weapon favored by early medieval warriors.

Archery/Cavalry Strategy

Since *oyoroi* armor was heavy enough to slow progress and freedom of movement, and the bows used in the early medieval period were weak, Japanese archers were forced to shoot at close range. With 10 meters or less between the archer and the target, bowmen had to carefully identify and target weaknesses in the opponent's armor. Further, early medieval samurai horses had little endurance, especially at high speeds and while bearing heavy loads, so armies utilized light cavalry formations in which mounted archers were surrounded by small groups of infantry circling and regrouping in a manner that historian Karl F. Friday has compared to aviators in a dogfight.

Signals and Identification

As armies increased in size, especially during the Warring States period, opponents often had trouble identifying each other and commanders could not recognize important samurai amid the crush of bodies. Signals became an effective means of controlling troops from a distance during battles, since only coordinated efforts could be successful. Strategies included the use of items such as flags, drums, and conch shells, as well as deployment of fire signals and messengers. For instance, many samurai and *ashigaru* affixed a *sashimono*, or personal banner, on the back of their armor. The family crest (*mon*) of the army commander was usually painted on the field of the *sashimono*, which later developed into the more visible vertical banner called a *nobori* carried by standard bearers into battle. Similarly, recognizing the potential of messengers, daimyo invested in preparing elite corps of messengers. A commander relied upon his messaging system to convey orders to other generals and ensure timely compliance with directives. These messengers were specially identified by cloaks or distinctive *sashimono*. For example, Toyotomi Hideyoshi had 29 messengers, all of whom were fitted with a golden *sashimono*. Nobunaga provided his messengers with a *horo*, a fabric bag similar to a cloak attached to the back of the armor, in either red or black.

During the Warring States period, as the military became more professionalized and battles were plentiful, specialized signaling and other means of identifying entire companies as well as specific figures were instituted. To ensure quick identification of opposing forces at a distance or ready identification of a military leader in poor weather, high-ranking figures had elaborate helmets and other distinguishing characteristics that made them readily recognizable. At the dawning of this era of many feuding daimyo, the tradition of affixing a *sashimono* was abandoned, perhaps because such devices could hinder the progress of an elite warrior. Regardless, high-ranking samurai had attendants (standard-bearers) who were charged with carrying the large vertical flag known as a *nobori* identifying the entire company or unit.

Personalized armor or helmet elements functioned like a crest which might be etched into or painted on European armor to indicate one's allegiance to a particular ruler. However, overall, Japanese use of banners and flags contrasted with European styles. Apparently, free-flying banners, as commonly seen in recreations of European battles, were not favored in Japan. The most typical banner style of the 15th century and after, the *nobori*, was a long, vertical piece of fabric that hung from the arm of a pole, which could be easily seen from both sides. Essentially these were larger versions of *sashimono* made more visible as well as less personal, a change that underscores the increasing grandeur of well-orchestrated combat at the end of the Warring States period.

Other types of flags and banners served diverse purposes. Signal flags (as well as fires) could be employed in directing unit movements. Another banner used for identification was the *uma-jirushi*, or horse insignia, which was worn by the standard-bearer of a daimyo and used to determine whether a leading figure had lost his mount.

In peacetime, banners and flags served to distinguish rank and status of samurai in service to the Tokugawa shogunate. Under the reorganization of the feudal system, samurai rank was equated with banner size. For example, samurai with an income of 1,300 *koku* were entitled to bear a small flag, while those possessing more than 6,000 *koku* of annual income could display a large flag. Thus, an entourage approaching the Tokugawa castle in Edo could be identified from a distance. Such banners required three soldiers to serve as bearers, more than the single figure that had accompanied the *sashimono* of high-ranking retainers in the medieval period. However, due to the dearth of battles, such flags were displayed primarily during processions of daimyo to and from the capital, and represented no

hindrance to the typically slow and ceremonious progress of such entourages.

Battle Formations

Battle formations were predetermined, though once a battle began there was no requirement or expectation that the formation would be maintained. Some formations were specific to interaction among types of warriors. For example, Japanese cavalry units included both soldiers on foot and mounted samurai. In this configuration, the figures on foot served as attendants to the mounted warriors. This had a strong effect on the maneuverability of the cavalry

5.12 Warrior procession (Illustration Kikuchi Yosai from *Zenken kojitsu*, mid-19th century)

unit, as well as the necessary charge distance the unit required.

There were numerous battle formations utilized for different strategic moments in a battle. Among the battle situations for which a specific configuration of troops might be used were formations for the initial battle charge and for subsequent charges, formations used for surrounding enemy forces, or when the two armies were of equal strength or when one army was outnumbered, various defensive formations used to maneuver against the enemy, formations used under specific terrain conditions, formations that placed a particular part of one's army—for instance, cavalry or foot soldiers—at the front of the battle, formations for withdrawal, and formations used for a final stand against an oncoming army.

Battle Rituals

The culture of battle in the medieval and early modern periods was highly ritualized. There were, for instance, specific ceremonies enacted before going into battle and specific rituals conducted to celebrate victory. Before going into battle, it was not uncommon for prayers to be offered to the Shinto gods—such as to the war deity Hachiman—asking for divine help in securing victory. Also common was a ceremonial meal prepared prior to battle in which *sake* was drunk and foods with names suggesting victory were consumed, such as *kachi guri*, or dried chestnuts. The term *kachi* can also mean victory; hence, the association of "victory chestnuts" with this food. Finally, the commander would start his troops marching to battle by uttering a ritual phrase ("for glory") while a Shinto priest said additional prayers for victory. Victory celebrations included rituals such as bathing in a hot spring both as a means of treating wounds and for purification, the presentation of letters of commendation for bravery or other heroics, and a "head inspection" in which the severed heads of the enemy taken during the battle were presented for review and particular honors were given to the warrior who had taken the first head.

5.13 Triumphant warrior with the head of his defeated enemy (Illustration Kikuchi Yosai from *Zenken kojitsu*, mid-19th century)

WARS AND BATTLES

CHRONOLOGICAL LIST OF SIGNIFICANT WARS AND BATTLES

1180–85	Gempei War (also called Taira-Minamoto War)
	Battle of Dannoura
1189	Battle of Hiraizumi
1221	Jokyu Upheaval
1274	First Mongol Invasion (Hakata Bay)
1281	Second Mongol Invasion (Hakata Bay)
1324	Shochu Upheaval

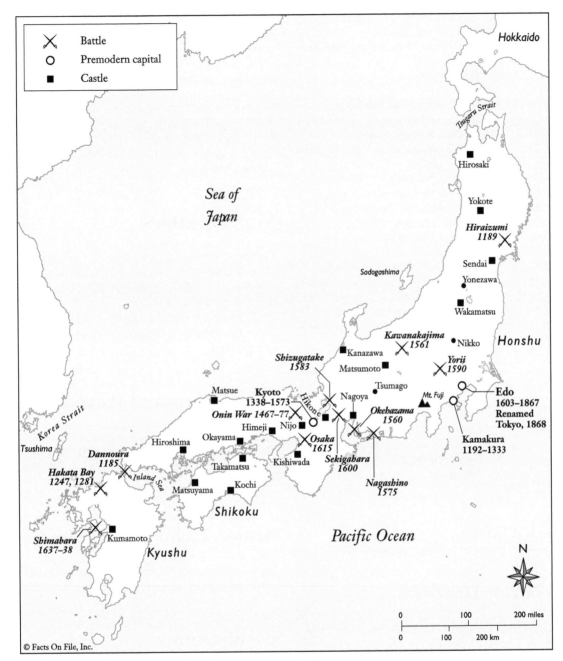

Map 4. *Major Battles in the Medieval and Early Modern Periods*

1333	Ashikaga overthrows bakufu
1336	Battle of Minatogawa
	War of the Northern and Southern Courts
1426	Ikki Uprisings
1467–77	Onin War
1488	Buddhist Ikko-Ikki Uprisings
1560	Battle of Okehazama
1561	Battle of Kawanakajima
1571	Burning of Enryakuji, temple located on Mt. Hiei
1575	Battle of Nagashino
1583	Battle of Shinzugatake
1584	Battle of Komaki-Nagakute
1592–97	Invasion of Korea
1600	Battle of Sekigahara
1615	Osaka summer and winter campaigns
1637–38	Christian rebellion in Shimabara
1825	*Bakufu* orders that foreign ships are to be fired upon
1854	Treaty of Kanagawa
1863	Chochu Han fires on British ships
1864	British, Dutch, French, and U.S. ships attack
	Bakufu launch punitive campaign against Han
1866	Second punitive expedition against Han
1868	Satsuma and Chochu army defeats Keiki's *bakufu* army at Toba-Fushimi
	New government army defeats Aizu Han rebels

READING

Warrior History

Takeuchi 1999: origins of Bushido, lord-vassal relations; Turnbull 1987: warrior history and society; Turnbull 1985: warrior history and society; Frédéric 1972: medieval warrior society; Berry 1982: biography of Toyotomi Hideyoshi; Berry 1993: history of the Onin War and the Warring States period with particular emphasis on the city of Kyoto; Varley 1974: history of the samurai; Varley 1967: Onin War; Turnbull 2003: ninja; Ikegami 1995: cultural history of the samurai from a social scientific perspective; Friday 2004: early medieval warriors; Kure 2001: historical overview; Bryant 1989: historical background; McCullough 1979: translations of medieval warrior tales; Varley 1994: the portrayal of warriors in war tales

Warrior Ethics

French 2003: warrior code; Daidoji 1999: warrior code; Butler 1969: medieval warrior values as expressed in the *Tale of the Heike*; Cleary 1999: translation of the *Bushido shoshinshu*, Hurst 1990: Bushido ideal; Leggett 2003: Zen and the samurai; Sato 1995: translations of warrior tales recounting the samurai ethos

Martial Arts and Weaponry

Tanaka 2003; arms and armor as used in Edo-period martial arts, illustrations; King 1993: Zen and swordsmanship; Kure 2001: samurai gear; Bryant 1989: weapons

Armor, Helmets, and Shields

Bryant 1989: armor; Shimizu (ed.) 1988, 228–283: armor and helmets; Murayama 1994: samurai clothing

Fortifications

Friday 2004; Coaldrake 1996

Warrior Ranks and Hierarchy

Kure 2001

Battle Tactics

Kure 2001: battle tactics in reenactment photos

Wars and Battles

Turnbull 1992: battles; Bryant 1995: battles with a focus on the Battle of Sekigahara

6

RELIGION

INTRODUCTION

Japan's Religious Traditions

Japanese religious traditions consist of both indigenous and borrowed religions. Shinto, the "way of the *kami* (gods)," is the term used to describe Japan's indigenous tradition, although Shinto as an organized tradition with common doctrines and practices probably dates back no further than the medieval period. Related, but often treated separately from Shinto, are Japan's so-called folk religions (*minkan shinko*). Rather than comprising an organized belief system, the term folk religion refers to local practices usually involving local deities and rituals that often focus on the agricultural cycle and the well-being of the local community or village.

The foreign traditions of Buddhism and Christianity impacted Japan during the medieval and early modern periods. Buddhism was introduced to Japan in the sixth century from the Asian mainland and quickly became the religion of the aristocrats and the imperial family, thus assuming political significance. It was not until Japan's medieval period that Buddhism became broadly diffused throughout Japanese society.

European missionaries and traders introduced Christianity to Japan in the middle of the 16th century. It was initially embraced by some Japanese feudal lords as much for the lure of trade as for the Christian religious message. By the middle of the 17th century, Christianity had been banned in Japan as a dangerous foreign presence. Christian missionaries were not permitted in the country again until Japan's modern period.

While Christianity was never fully embraced by the Japanese, the medieval period was a particularly active time for Shinto-Buddhist interactions, a phenomenon referred to by the term *shimbutsu shugo*, the fusion of gods and Buddhas. This fusing of religions represented reconciliation between the indigenous and foreign traditions. Sometimes, for instance, *kami* were treated as the more concrete and immediate aspect of the sacred in the natural world, while the Buddhas and bodhisattvas represented a more distant essence.

In the early 19th century, new popular religious movements were formed. Among those that attracted the largest followings were Kurozumikyo, Tenrikyo, and Konkokyo. These traditions usually arose as a result of charismatic leaders whose religious ideas and practices were based in their own religious experiences. These experiences often reflected the overlay of Shinto, Buddhist, and other aspects of existing Japanese religious traditions.

Although individual Japanese religions can be discussed, it is important to bear in mind that in many periods of Japanese history—including the medieval and early modern—distinctions between traditions were not very sharply drawn. This was true both in terms of a person's worship and in terms of Japanese culture more generally. It was typical for a person to pray to a *kami* on one occasion and to invoke the aid of a bodhisattva on another. Similarly, Japanese literature and theater often contained plots in which multiple religious ideas and practices were expressed. Thus, in medieval and early modern Japan, the Japanese tended to practice what is now referred to as multiple traditions, but which at the time would have probably been seen as multiple access points to the sacred. Interaction was as prevalent an aspect of Japanese religions as was exclusion between religious traditions.

The word *shukyo* (religion), a term referring to religion as distinguishable from other human endeavors, such as politics, only gained currency in the late 19th century. Until then, the Japanese had no single term for religion in general. Religious traditions practiced in Japan, such as Buddhism (*Bukkyo*), Shinto (also known as *kami no michi*) and Christianity (*Kurisuto-kyo*), were identified by name, but a term for the universal concept of religion (*shukyo*) was not coined until after the Meiji Restoration in 1868.

One other aspect of Japanese religions is illuminated by the term *shukyo*. If religion is thought of in the Western sense as something one professes faith in, religion is defined in terms of what people think and believe. Practice is viewed as secondary to faith. After all, it might be argued, why practice what one does not believe? But in medieval and early modern Japan, practice was far more central to religious identity than was any profession of faith. The reason, in part, is the very close connection between culture and religion at that time.

Common Characteristics

Japanese religion displays great diversity of forms and practices, but there are also aspects of Japanese religious attitudes that reflect cohesion across traditions. This introduction will briefly discuss some important themes.

CLOSE CONNECTION BETWEEN HUMAN BEINGS AND THE SACRED

An intimate relationship between human beings and the sacred exists. Sacredness is found not only in specific gods (*kami*), but also in natural phenomena and in certain human beings, both living and dead. The sacred is understood to be located within the world of humans, not in some transcendent or distant place.

RELIGION AND THE FAMILY

Japanese traditions often treat the family as a site of religious activity. Families identified a tutelary god that protected them. Deceased ancestors were propitiated to bring blessings on the living. Buddhist home altars (*butsudan*) were utilized for prayer for the happy rebirth of the deceased. Even Confucian thought, usually associated with political and moral philosophy rather than religion, placed a high premium on filial piety.

CLOSE CONNECTION BETWEEN RELIGION AND THE STATE

Unlike the contemporary United States where there is a debate about the proper relationship between church and state, in medieval and early modern Japan, a very close connection between religion and the state was deemed both proper and necessary. Though there are exceptions, religion was often treated as ancillary to politics. Used to create national identity, religion served the nation as a means of providing legitimacy for political arrangements current at any given time. Japan's national myth, that Japan was created from the sacred acts of the *kami* whose descendants form the imperial line, is one such use of religion to justify political power. The Buddhist priest Nichiren viewed Japan as a sacred country in which the truth of the Lotus Sutra would be enacted.

THIS-WORLDLINESS

There tends to be an emphasis on "this-worldly" concerns and benefits rather than an emphasis on death and the afterlife. Some Japanese Buddhist traditions express a deep concern over what happens in the next life, but this is often a subsidiary religious focus. Material benefits are sought through Shinto and Buddhist ritual practices. Religious rituals often deal with being delivered from human troubles—such as illness, debt, drought, and other causes of human misery—rather than with the final disposition of one's soul. Further, this world is not radically separated from the next, making death a transition rather than a permanent change. Unlike some Western traditions, one need not reject this world to gain spiritual benefits.

IMPORTANCE OF RITUALS AND FESTIVALS

Religious rituals, though directed to numerous different ends, were often intended for life cycle events such as birth, marriage, and death. Religion was often intimately connected to the everyday, rather than directed beyond daily life. Festivals, too, celebrated various key events in the life of a community. Festivals were held in celebration of the harvest, the New Year, and to honor the spirits of the dead. Both rituals and festivals were methods of personal purification, showing appreciation for the fertility of the land, making offerings to honor the gods, Buddhas, and ancestors, requesting help in troubled times, and seeking the welfare of the community.

SACREDNESS OF MOUNTAINS

Mountains have long held a special place in the Japanese religious imagination. Mountains, large and small, were considered to be the abode of the *kami*.

Similarly, mountains were sometimes seen as the abode of deceased ancestors. Because of the sacred nature of mountains, shrines and temples were often built in these locations. A Shinto-Buddhist fusion tradition, Shugendo, focused in part on ascetic rituals performed in desolate mountain locations.

PRAYER AND VERBAL INVOCATIONS

Both Shinto and Buddhism utilize prayer as a way to invoke the powers of gods, Buddhas, and bodhisattvas. Prayers provide a means for humans to request blessings or assistance for their material and spiritual needs. Both Shinto and Buddhism developed specific systems of prayers and invocations. *Norito* in Shinto and mantras (*shingon*) in Buddhism are two examples.

Shinto Traditions

Introduction

Shinto is Japan's indigenous religious tradition. The term Shinto means the "way of the gods (*kami*)" and is written with the Chinese characters *shin* ("god," "the sacred;" also pronounced *kami*) and *to* ("way;" also pronounced *michi*). Unlike many religions, Shinto has no founder and does not view any single text as its sole scripture. Shinto is closely associated with the Japanese sense of cultural identity. Shinto emphasizes practice over thought or formal doctrine. There is not a formal Shinto theology or rigidly codified set of moral rules. Shinto is intimately connected with the agricultural cycle and a sense of the sacredness of the natural world. The worship of *kami* and other ritual practices express these concerns.

Central to Shinto traditions is the concept of *kami*. The word *kami* refers generally to the sacred manifest in the natural world and specifically to the deities of the Shinto tradition. *Kami* can be both benevolent and destructive, but if properly worshipped, they are believed to grant blessings to

human beings. Ritual practice is central to Shinto traditions and includes such activities as purification, food offerings, dance, and festivals honoring the gods. While *kami* may be worshipped at shrines under the supervision of Shinto priests (*kannushi*), they can also be worshipped individually at a shrine or in the home. Further, Shinto associations (*ko*) provide yet another avenue for interaction with the *kami*.

Unlike the hierarchies of deities in other traditions, the pantheon of Shinto deities is only loosely structured. What structure it does have is largely the result of the imperial mythology expressed in the *Kojiki* and the *Nihon shoki*. It is said that there are 800 myriads of gods (*yaoyorozu no kami*), a huge number that represents the idea that *kami*, or the presence of the sacred, suffuses all aspects of the natural world. *Kami*, while deities, are certainly nothing like the omnipotent, transcendent God of monotheistic traditions. *Kami* are very much in the world, found both in animate and inanimate objects, such as mountains, rocks, trees, the Sun, animals, and human beings. *Kami* can be ancestors or even living people, such as the emperor, and are active in the lives of human beings, providing blessings in health and human activities, such as agriculture. In a famous description, the 18th-century Shinto scholar, Motoori Norinaga, described the term *kami* as having multiple significations. "The word *kami* refers, in the most general sense, to all divine beings of heaven and earth that appear in the classics. More particularly, the *kami* are the spirits that abide in and are worshipped at the shrines. In principle human beings, birds, animals, trees, plants, mountains, oceans—all may be *kami*. According to ancient usage, whatever seemed strikingly impressive, possessed the quality of excellence, or inspired a feeling of awe was called *kami*."

There was not a unified Shinto "tradition" until at least the medieval period, but the term is nevertheless used to describe the complex of traditions subsumed under this category. The term *Shinto* is descriptive of two different aspects of Japanese indigenous religion. On the one hand, Shinto describes an organized set of doctrines and practices related to the state. This perspective on Shinto is strongly tied to the mythology and founding stories of the imperial family, especially as expressed in the

Kojiki (Record of ancient matters, compiled in 712). Shinto was important to the legitimating narratives by which the imperial family justified its right to rule. This aspect of Shinto was conspicuous for the rituals performed expressing the intimate connection between emperor and *kami*.

The term *Shinto* also has a more generic meaning, referring generally to local practices—both in the home and in the village—focused on local deities. Worship can occur at a local shrine or at home before a family altar (*kamidana*). Rituals and festivals are directed to these local deities in hopes of receiving their blessings. Because of the association of *kami* with deceased ancestors, there is sometimes a strong sense of family connection to a *kami*. Local worship was often connected to rice deities and local festivals. These rituals were particularly concerned with the agricultural cycle and other seasonal events impacting small, agrarian communities.

Historically, one of the key concepts in Shinto thought is the idea of transgression, or *tsumi*. Although this term is sometimes translated as sin, *tsumi* was not originally associated with moral failing. Instead, this term referred to the idea of ritual impurity (*kegare*). Rather than a central concern with human agency, the traditional view of *tsumi* is concerned with the physical impurity that results from contact with such things as disease, blood, death and other elements that are, in a sense, beyond one's control. In order to counteract the deleterious effects of transgressions that result from contact with impurity, Shinto rituals are intended to restore one to purity.

In the medieval and early modern periods, Shinto thought was influenced by both Confucian and Buddhist ideas. One result of this interaction was that the original Shinto focus on *tsumi* (transgression) as one of physical impurity was transformed to include the notion of moral transgression.

Shinto Mythology

Japanese mythology, though dating back long before the medieval and early modern periods, nevertheless remained an important part of Japanese culture and identity throughout the medieval and early modern periods. In the Edo period, Shinto revivalist movements used Japanese myths compiled in texts like the *Kojiki* (Record of ancient matters, compiled in 712 at the order of the imperial family) to argue their case for Shinto as the moral and spiritual compass of the Japanese people.

The *Kojiki*, Japan's earliest extant written text, recounts the story of the creation of the Japanese islands by Izanagi and Izanani (both brother and sister and husband and wife). It tells the story of the birth of the *kami*, especially the birth of Amaterasu, the sun goddess, from whom the Japanese imperial family—and by extension the Japanese people—are descended. The narrative tells of how Ninigi no Mikoto, grandson of Amaterasu Omikami, was sent to establish sovereignty over the Japanese islands. It was Ninigi's great grandson, Jimmu, who became, according to the narrative, the first emperor of Japan. All Japanese emperors are said to descend from this sacred line beginning with Amaterasu. The three regalia—mirror, sword, and jewel—the symbols of imperial ruling authority, are said to have originated with Amaterasu who started the tradition of passing these symbols to each subsequent ruler. In the medieval and early modern periods (in fact, up until 1945), this *Kojiki* narrative was used to argue the legitimacy of the imperial family as rightful rulers. The origins of the gods are at once the origins of the Japanese islands and the Japanese people. Hence, it was argued, Japan is a sacred land.

Medieval and Early Modern Shinto

Although what is termed Shinto predates the introduction of Buddhist and Confucian traditions, medieval and early modern Shinto was often responding to Buddhist and Confucian influences, sometimes embracing them and sometimes setting itself apart. Soon after Buddhism's introduction to Japan, Shinto *kami* were often understood to be Buddhist protective deities. For this reason, Buddhist temples often included a shrine for their related *kami*. A further development, a theory known as *honji suijaku*, viewed *kami* as manifestations (*suijaku*) of Buddhas and bodhisattvas (*honji*) creating a correspondence between specific *kami* and their Buddha and bodhisattva counterparts. For example, Amaterasu Omikami and Dainichi Nyorai were sometimes connected. Such matching of *kami* with Buddhas and bodhisattvas started in the Heian period, but its importance extended well into the medieval period. Two Shinto-Buddhist fusion schools were particularly important during the Kamakura period: Ryobu ("Dual Aspect") Shinto, which blended Shingon Buddhism with Shinto ideas, and Sanno ("Mountain King") Shinto which fused Tendai Buddhism and Shinto.

Whereas Ryobu and Sanno Shinto were schools that viewed Shinto deities as manifestations of Buddhas and bodhisattvas, the medieval period also witnessed the development of Shinto schools that viewed *kami* as the essence and Buddhas and bodhisattvas as subsidiary manifestations. Yoshida Kanetomo (1435–1511) was one notable theorist who made such an assertion.

In the early modern period, Shinto, instead of encompassing Buddhism, entered into dialogue with Neo-Confucianism. By this time, Neo-Confucian ideas had become quite important as a way of thinking about ethics and political philosophy. Rather than blend or fuse Shinto with Buddhism, some Edo-period Shinto figures reconsidered Shinto in light of Neo-Confucian ideas. In the same way that Shinto and Buddhism had been blended, so Neo-Confucian ideas were combined with Shinto ones.

While some embraced a fusion of Shinto and Neo-Confucianism, others sought to purge any foreign influence from Shinto, whether Buddhist or Confucian. Especially important in this regard was the Kokugaku ("National Learning") movement, which advocated the study of Japan's ancient past through philological studies of early texts, such as the *Kojiki*, that recounted the values and attitudes that the Japanese held in the Age of the Gods (*kami no yo*). This was an attempt to return to a pristine time unsullied by the Buddhism, Confucianism, and other foreign ideas that were seen as leading Japan away from its true path. Kokugaku sought to rediscover the ancient roots of Japanese culture and religion through painstaking examination of old texts.

6.1 Buddhist protective deity (Illustration Grace Vibbert)

Shinto Schools

Ryobu Shinto Dual Aspect Shinto. Also known as Shingon Shinto. A Shinto-Buddhist fusion school developed within Shingon Buddhism. The term *ryobu* refers to the dual aspect of the universe symbolized in Shingon by the dual womb-world and diamond-world mandalas. In this view, the universe is understood as having the twofold characteristics of noumenon and phenomenon, which the mandalas symbolize. Ryobu Shinto also asserts the identity of Shingon Buddhism and Shinto. For instance, the Ise Inner Shrine corresponds to the womb-world mandala (Taizokai), and the Ise Outer Shrine corresponds to the diamond-world mandala (Kongokai). Amaterasu Omikami, enshrined in the Inner Shrine, is identified with the Buddha Mahavairocana (Dainichi Nyorai).

Sanno Shinto Mountain King Shinto. Also known as Sanno Ichijitsu ("One Reality") Shinto or Tendai

Shinto. Sanno Shinto was founded by a Tendai monk named Tenkai (1536–1643). Sanno, or "Mountain King," refers to the guardian deity of Tendai Buddhism who is enshrined at the Hie Shrine on Mt. Hiei. According to Sanno Shinto, the Mountain King deity is identified as a manifestation of Sakyamuni, the historical Buddha, and Amaterasu Omikami is a manifestation of Dainichi Nyorai. When Tokugawa Ieyasu died, his funeral was conducted according to the ritual prescriptions of Sanno Shinto.

Watarai Shinto Also known as Ise Shinto and Geku (Outer Shrine) Shinto. A form of Shinto associated with the Watarai family, a lineage of Shinto priests in charge of the Outer Shrine at Ise Shrine. The devout of the Outer Shrine worshipped the deity Toyouke no Okami, who was traditionally viewed as serving Amaterasu, worshipped at the Inner Shrine. Starting in the 13th century, Watarai family priests argued the two shrines were equal. To legitimate this perspective, Watarai priests compiled the *Shinto gobusho* (Five books of Shinto). These texts recounted the story of the imperial family's descent from the *kami* and a history of the Ise Shrine that asserted its highest position over all other Shinto shrines. Watarai theorists also claimed the priority of Shinto over Buddhism and repudiated *honji suijaku* and its view that *kami* are but manifestations of Buddhas and bodhisattvas.

Yuiitsu Shinto "Only" Shinto. Also known as Yoshida Shinto. A form of Shinto associated with the Yoshida family and especially with teachings set forth by Yoshida Kanetomo (1435–1511). Yuiitsu Shinto was particularly concerned with overturning the idea of *honji suijaku* and asserting the priority of *kami* over the Buddhas and bodhisattvas. Yuiitsu Shinto priests performed the funeral rites for Toyotomi Hideyoshi on his death in 1598.

Suika Shinto "Conferment of Benefits" Shinto. Also called Suiga Shinto. A form of Shinto that identified similarities between Shinto and Neo-Confucian ideas. Suika Shinto was developed by Yamazaki Ansai (1619–82), an ardent supporter of Shinto who had originally been a Zen monk. Ansai

asserted that the Neo-Confucian way of heaven was identical to the way of the *kami* in Shinto.

Kokugaku National Learning. A Shinto philosophical school that sought the restoration of a pure Shinto that existed prior to the Buddhist, Confucian, and other foreign influences. First developed in the 17th century, the school's most important spokesperson was Motoori Norinaga (1730–1801). Motoori, using detailed philological and philosophical study of ancient texts such as the *Kojiki*, argued that Japan must embrace the values and attitudes present during the Age of the Gods (*kami no yo*).

Shinto Rituals and Festivals

Shinto practice is characterized by an extensive ritual and festival calendar. Shinto rituals assume a variety of forms, but in general are concerned with obtaining blessings from the *kami* for a happy and prosperous family and community. These involve obtaining blessings for aspects of one's daily life and agriculture-related rituals for a bountiful harvest. Rituals can occur at both the national and local community level, or they may also be private requests to the gods. Shinto rituals often require the devotee to undergo some kind of ritual purification, such as fasting, abstinence, and/or cleansing the hands and mouth with water, to avoid offending the gods. Festivals (*matsuri*), which play an important role in Shinto tradition, are held on numerous days throughout the year and usually entail lively and colorful displays. They are designed to give thanks to the *kami* and to venerate the divinities so that they will continue to confer benevolence on their followers.

Daijosai Great Food Offering Ritual. Dates back to at least the seventh century, but was rarely practiced from the middle of the 15th century to the late 17th century, when it came to be regularly practiced again. The Daijosai is conducted by a newly enthroned emperor and is one of three rituals conducted to mark the accession of a new emperor. Rice grown especially for the ritual is offered to Amaterasu, the imperial ancestor *kami*.

Gion Matsuri Gion Festival. The most famous of the many Gion festivals held throughout the country is the one performed at the Yasaka Shrine in Kyoto in July. Yasaka enshrines the *kami* Gozu Tenno, a guardian deity with Indian origins who protects the Jetavana monastery (Gion shoja) associated with the historical Buddha. Gozu is believed to be especially efficacious in protecting one's health. The Gion Festival dates to the ninth century. During the Edo period, Kyoto merchants became patrons of the festival.

harae Purification rituals. Purification rituals are central to Shinto practice and are recounted throughout Shinto history. They are practiced, for instance, by the *kami* in the *Kojiki*. Ritual purification is required of worshippers. In order to approach the *kami* for blessings and requests, petitioners must cleanse themselves of any pollution (*kegare*) caused by transgressions (*tsumi*). Purification is accomplished by rituals involving water, prayers, offerings, and other means.

hatsumode First visit to a shrine or temple at the New Year to pray for blessings in the upcoming year.

imi Taboo. Refers to rituals used to avoid pollution or inauspicious things. Causes of impurity are called *imi*. *Imi* are related to the idea of *kegare*, ritual impurity, in the sense that impurities are to be avoided or, if encountered, purified. Death, birth, blood, and disease are some examples of *imi*. Certain words also need to be avoided and are called *imikotoba*, or taboo words. Examples include the use of the number 4 (*shi*) because it is a homonym for the word for death (*shi*).

kagura Ritual music and dances that enact the activities of the *kami* and other sacred events are conducted both at the imperial court and at local shrines.

Kannamesai New Rice Festival. Held in September during the medieval and early modern periods. Ancient annual ritual performed at the Ise Shrine by the emperor. Offerings, including rice from the year's harvest, sake, and other foods, are made to Amaterasu.

kegare Pollution in the sense of ritual impurity or defilement. Pollution originally referred to agents of defilement such as death, childbirth, and menstruation. By the early modern period, spiritual pollution came also to be included in the category of *kegare*. Regardless of the type, pollution can be removed through purification rituals. A 10th-century Shinto text refers to several categories of pollution, including contact with blood, death (both human and animal), unsanitary things, natural disasters, and sexual impropriety.

misogi A ritual of purification through the use of water after contact with a physical or spiritual pollution. The concept of water being used for personal purification originates in the *Kojiki* where the god Izanagi purified himself with water after contact with the dead. Although there are various kinds of purification rituals that involve water as the cleansing agent, perhaps the most common is the practice of *temizu*, whereby one washes both hand and mouth with water before entering the grounds of a Shinto shrine.

Niinamesai New Rice Harvest Festival. This is a festival held in the autumn after the harvest to thank the *kami* for the year's rice. Although many local autumn festivals thank the gods for an abundant harvest, the Niinamesai is a national festival that features rice offerings presented by the emperor to the gods. This ritual includes a communal meal with the gods.

norito Prayers. *Norito* are formulaic words addressed to the *kami* on ritual occasions. As sacred speech, they provide a means to connect human beings with the gods. These prayers can be considered a verbal offering to a god as well as a statement of why the *kami* is being addressed. *Norito* are used to express thanks to the *kami* for their blessings, to list offerings made, and to identify people making the prayer and their request to the gods.

okage mairi Literally, "thanksgiving pilgrimage." This term refers to the Edo-period practice of pilgrimage to the Ise Shrine. Occurring about every 60 years, these pilgrimages were usually spontaneous and involved a large number of pilgrims. The Edo

6.2 Barrels of sake given as offerings to a Shinto shrine (Photo William E. Deal)

period was witness to four major pilgrimages, the last occurring in 1830. Pilgrims especially sought the blessings of the sun goddess, Amaterasu. These pilgrimages were hardly solemn affairs—they included singing and frenzied dancing.

Shinto Ritual Objects

Shinto rituals and festivals make use of a number of different objects in the conduct of religious practices. Paper, rice, salt, wood, and branches are among the items used in the performance of ritual. These items can be intricately decorated or unadorned strips of paper. Some of the more common ritual objects and their purposes are described below.

ema Literally, "horse picture." Small wooden boards sold at Shinto shrines and Buddhist temples and used as votive offerings. The name may derive from *ema* as replacements for offerings of horses to shrines. In the medieval and early modern periods, a tradition of large *ema* (*oema*) developed whereby artists made requests to the gods for benefits or artistic ability. These large *ema* were often displayed in *emado*, halls specially built for their exhibition.

gohei A wooden staff with paper strips attached. The staff is held by a Shinto priest during a ritual to represent the presence of a *kami*.

hamaya Evil-destroying arrow. Arrows symbolizing the possibility of conquering misfortune are sold at Shinto shrines during New Year festivities.

6.3 Example of the use of ema *to request assistance from the* kami (Photo William E. Deal)

The arrows are placed in the home to ward off evil and to ensure good fortune throughout the year.

ofuda Protective amulet. *Ofuda* usually include the name of the *kami* worshipped at the shrine where the amulet was obtained. Amulets are viewed as having the power to bring health, protect the home from fire or other disasters, and ensure success in business and educational endeavors, among other things. Amulets may be carried or placed in the household shrine (*kamidana*).

omamori Protective amulet. Similar to *ofuda* (see above).

omikuji A form of divination carried out at Shinto shrines. Sticks are taken from a container and exchanged for a prediction, which is understood to be the guidance of the *kami*.

shimenawa A rope with white paper attached that is used to mark off a sacred space. It is sometimes found at the entrance of Shinto shrines or placed around trees or other objects to demarcate a place where the *kami* have appeared.

Shinto Deities

Amaterasu Omikami Sun goddess. The central deity in the *Kojiki*, born from the act of purification conducted by the god Izanagi after his escape from the world of the dead. The imperial family is descended from her lineage through her great grandson, Jimmu, the first emperor. She rules the high plain of heaven (Takamagahara), and is enshrined at the Ise Shrine's Inner Shrine (*naiku*).

Bimbogami God of poverty. This deity became important during the Edo period and is associated with urban life. There are rituals to dispel this deity and, by extension, the poverty and bad fortune he brings into the home.

Bishamonten/Tamonten One of the seven gods of good fortune (see "*shichifukujin*") and one of the four heavenly kings (see "*shitenno*").

Hachiman Shinto god of war and protector of warriors. Hachiman is usually identified with the emperor Ojin. He is also considered a Buddhist protective deity and is given the additional title of "great bodhisattva" (*daibosatsu*). Hachimangu—shrines dedicated to Hachiman—exist throughout Japan.

Inari Shinto god of rice cultivation. Often worshipped in hopes of receiving an abundant harvest, more generally Inari is worshipped for success in business. In the early modern period, Inari was worshipped in the homes of merchants and warriors who would have a small Inari shrine for this purpose. Inari is often associated with the image of a fox. In the medieval period, the fox was viewed as Inari's messenger, but later Inari became a fox himself. Inari is famously enshrined at the Fushimi Inari Shrine in Kyoto, but there are many other Inari shrines throughout Japan.

Izanagi and Izanami Izanagi no Mikoto (male) and Izanami no Mikoto (female), both brother and sister and husband and wife, are deities depicted in the *Kojiki*. They created the Japanese islands and produced many deities. Several scenes in the narrative of these two *kami* became the foundation for Japanese religious concepts and rituals. For instance, after Izanami dies giving birth to the fire god, Izanagi tries to reunite with her in the land of the dead. Izanagi suffers pollution as a result of his contact with the dead and must cleanse himself through a water purification ritual (*misogi*). It is through this act of purification that the sun goddess, Amaterasu, and the wind god, Susanoo, come into being.

Ninigi no Mikoto A deity described in the *Kojiki*. He is Amaterasu's grandson, who was sent to civilize the Japanese islands in advance of their population. What comes to be called the three imperial regalia—mirror, sword, and jewel—were given to Ninigi as symbols of his right to rule over Japan. Jimmu, Ninigi's great grandson, became the first Japanese emperor.

Okuninushi no Mikoto Shinto deity important in the *Kojiki*, where he is depicted as a benevolent god and bringer of civilization. Depending on the source, he is either the son or grandson of the god, Susanoo. Okuninushi is sometimes worshipped as an agricultural god because of his cultivation skills and farming technologies, such as irrigation. He is said to have instructed the people of Izumo in these matters. According to the many different stories about him, Okuninushi was able to subdue evil beings, cure disease, and ensure a happy marriage. He is enshrined at the Izumo Shrine, which is said to be the grounds of his palace.

shichifukujin Seven gods of good fortune who are said to travel on the Takarabune, or treasure ship. They are especially worshipped at the New Year in hopes that they will bring renewed prosperity. The seven gods are:

1. Benten/Benzaiten: goddess of music, arts, and fertility
2. Bishamonten: god of war and fortune
3. Daikoku/Daikokuten: god of wealth and of the kitchen; associated with Okuninushi no Mikoto

4. Ebisu: god of work; associated with success at various occupations, especially fishing, farming, and, during the Edo period, with commercial business
5. Fukurokuju: god of longevity
6. Hotei: god of fortune and contentment; said to be an incarnation of Miroku, the Buddha of the future
7. Jurojin: god of longevity

shitenno Four heavenly kings: Bishamonten, Jimokuten, Komokuten, and Zochoten. These four are Buddhist protective deities.

Susanoo no Mikoto A deity prominent in the *Kojiki*. He is Amaterasu's mischievous brother who is banished to the Japanese islands from the high plain of heaven (Takamagahara) because of his unruly behavior that results in pollution and defilement. He is sometimes referred to as the wind god or the storm god.

Tenjin Literally, "heavenly god." This term refers to the spirit of Sugawara no Michizane (845–903), a Heian-period courtier and scholar who was exiled from the capital as a result of political intrigue. After his death, a series of disasters befell Kyoto, and it was determined that Michizane's angry spirit was the cause. In order to end the disasters, Michizane was given a posthumous pardon and came to be considered a god. As a *kami*, Michizane is associated with learning and scholarship. He is enshrined in Tenjin shrines in many parts of Japan.

6.4 Stone sculpture of Hotei, one of the seven gods of good fortune (Photo William E. Deal)

Shinto Priesthood

The generic term for a Shinto priest is *kannushi*. However, Shinto in the medieval and early modern periods was not a centrally organized tradition. Hence, there is great variation in terminology used to denote Shinto priests. Historically, the office of shrine priest was typically passed down through a priestly family from father to son. The hereditary lines of priests associated with some larger shrines represented a particular family's significant power within a community. During the medieval period, there usually was not a formal priesthood at small local or village-level shrines. Rather, villagers—usually from the most powerful and influential families—supervised festivals and other ritual occasions. In the early modern period, priesthoods at village shrines did develop.

Shinto Shrines

Shinto shrines are places to worship the *kami*. Shrines install one or more gods. There are both local shrines and national shrines, such as the Ise Shrine. A number of different terms and suffixes are used in Japanese to designate a shrine, including:

–jinja (Yasaka Jinja = Yasaka Shrine [also used by itself to describe shrines in general])
–jingu (Ise Jingu = Ise Shrine)
–gu (Tsurugaoka Hachimangu = Tsurugaoka Hachiman Shrine)
–sha (Hie-sha = Hie Shrine)
–taisha (Izumo Taisha = Izumo Shrine)
yashiro: shrine
hokora: small wayside shrine
jinja: shrine
miya: shrine (also appears as a suffix)

In English, it is commonplace to use the word "temple" to indicate a Buddhist building, and "shrine" to indicate a Shinto building. The architectural style of shrines and some of their physical features are treated in chapter 10: Art and Architecture.

Asakusa Shrine (Asakusa Jinja) Shinto shrine built in 1649 by the third Tokugawa shogun, Tokugawa Iemitsu (1604–51). Located on the grounds of the Sensoji temple in the Asakusa section of the Taito Ward in Tokyo, this shrine pays tribute to two brothers and their lord, who found a statue of the bodhisattva Kannon in the Sumidagawa River in 628 C.E.

Dazaifu Shrine (Dazaifu Temmangu) The imperial court first erected Dazaifu Temmangu in 905 to placate the spirit of the scholar and statesman Sugawara no Michizane (posthumously known as Tenjin

of Temman). It was built again in 919 after being destroyed by a fire. Located in Dazaifu, Kyushu, at the site of Michizane's grave, the shrine has become widely associated with education. Annually, on January 7, the festival Dazaifu Usokae takes place when participants exchange bird-shaped amulets at random in hopes of attaining lucky amulets circulated by disguised shrine officials. The ceremony of *Oni-sube* also occurs on this day; it is a form of exorcism in which demons are ushered away from the main shrine.

Fushimi Inari Shrine (Fushimi Inari Taisha) The most important shrine dedicated to Inari, the *kami* of agriculture and commerce. Located in southern Kyoto and dating back to 711, the Fushimi Inari Shrine serves as the hub of more than 30,000 secondary shrines throughout Japan that venerate this

6.5 Example of a small Shinto shrine for the fox deity Inari (Photo William E. Deal)

6.6 Atagoyama Shrine (Illustration Grace Vibbert)

tain, and the West Shrine dedicated to Onamuchi no Mikoto, the guardian of the imperial court. April 14 and 15 mark the Takayama Festival held in honor of the shrine deities, when people parade through the streets with *o-mikoshi—kami* in portable shrines.

Hie Shrine (Hie Jinja; also known as Sanno Gongen until 1868) The Tokugawa shoguns built the Hie Jinja as a protector shrine of Edo (now Tokyo) and the imperial palace. Dedicated to Oya-makui no Kami, it serves as the largest of about 3,800 secondary Hie temples (Hie Taisha being the primary shrine) located throughout Japan. The Kanda and Sanno Festivals, held in alternate years in May and June respectively, celebrate the shrine deities in a similar fashion to the Takayama Festival at Hie Taisha.

Ise Shrine (Ise Jingu) Ise Jingu, located in the city of Ise in Mie Prefecture, is the most sacred shrine in all of Japan. It consists of two complexes: the inner shrine (Kotaijingu or Naiku), and the outer shrine (Toyoukedaijingu or Geku). The inner shrine houses the sacred mirror of Amaterasu, the sun goddess and ancestor to the unbroken lineage of Japanese emperors. The outer complex enshrines Toyouke, who not only serves as the *kami* of food and agriculture but also provides Amaterasu with her meals. Ever since the reign of Emperor Temmu in the late seventh century, Ise is destroyed and rebuilt every 20 years (*shikinen sengu*) (with a brief interruption during the Muromachi period due to civil wars) in the same style (*shimmei-zukuri*) and using cypress wood as in its original construction. Beginning in the 13th century, Ise became a major pilgrimage site.

kami. The Inari Matsuri takes place here every April and marks the visit by the deity to various *o-tabisho*, or sacred grounds. The Fushimi Inari Shrine also attracts hundreds of thousands of people every year for *hastumode*, the celebration of the New Year.

Hie Shrine (Hie Taisha; also known as Hiyoshi Taisha) Regarded as the main center for Sanno Ichi-jitsu Shinto—a derivation of Tendai Buddhism—the Hie Shrine served to protect the mountain deity, Sanno Gongen, the guardian of Mt. Hiei and avatar of Shakyamuni, as well as the larger Tendai Buddhist monastery Enryaku-ji. Built in 788 at the base of Mt. Hiei, it consists of two shrines: the East Shrine dedicated to Oyamakui no Kami, the *kami* of the moun-

Itsukushima Shrine (Itsukushima Jinja; also known as Aki no Miyajima) A Shinto shrine built on the small island of Itsukushima in Hiroshima Bay and dedicated to Susanoo's three daughters (Susanoo is the brother of Amaterasu), and since the Kamakura period, Benzai-ten (see *shichifukujin*). According to tradition, a local inhabitant established the shrine in 593 after receiving a visitation from the three deities, but, most likely, the shrine was built in 811. The Heian military leader, Taira no Kiyomori, lavishly restored Itsukushima in the

12th century, making it his clan's tutelary shrine. His family later donated the most elaborate of the *Lotus Sutra* scrolls—the *Heike nokyo* (Sutras dedicated by the Heike)—to the shrine. Kiyomori also constructed the predecessor of the shrine's famous *torii*: a giant, red gateway that stands 160 meters out in the bay.

Izumo Shrine (Izumo Taisha) Dedicated to Okuninushi no Mikoto; son of Susanoo and the *kami* associated with love and marriage. During the festival Kamiari Matsuri ("gods are present" festival), *kami* from all over Japan leave their permanent homes to take up residence at Izumo Shrine. Priests provide temporary lodging for the visiting *kami* by building numerous small wooden boxes around the shrine's perimeter. The festival attracts many couples requesting marriage blessings and other related matters.

Kamo Shrines (Kamo Jinja) Refers to two independent Shinto shrines located in Kyoto: the Kamo Wakeikazuchi Jinja (Kamigamo-jinja) and the Kamomioya-jinja (Shimogamo-jinja). As protector shrines of the imperial palace and capital, they enshrine Kamo Wakeikazuchi no Kami, a son of Tamayori-hime and brother of Jimmu-tenno (the legendary first emperor of Japan), and Tamayori-hime, herself, respectively. The Aoi Festival is held at both shrines every May 15 and consists of prayers for an abundant harvest.

Kasuga Shrine (Kasuga Taisha) Located in Nara and closely associated with the major Buddhist temple Kofukuji. Although Kasuga Taisha was originally founded by the Fujiwara clan and served to venerate the four deities of the family's three shrines, it typified the growing development of the shrine-temple relationship that expressed the interaction of Shinto and Buddhism in medieval and early Japan.

Kitano Shrine (Kitano Temmangu) Located in Kyoto and built on the 44th anniversary of scholar Sugawara no Michizane's death (see *Dazaifu temple* and *Tenjin*). It remains a popular destination for scholars and students who seek divine assistance with their educational endeavors.

Kotohira Shrine (Kotohiragu; Kompiragu; Kompira-san) Founded in the 11th century and located on Shikoku, Kotohira Shrine first venerated Kompira, a divinity imported from India and transmitted to Japan from China. Originally having associations with the Ganges River and its sacred waters, Kompira became recognized in Japan as the protector of sailors, fishermen, and all others who make a living from the sea. After 1868, however, the shrine was associated with Omononushi no Kami (Okuninushi no Mikoto) and was also dedicated to the spirit of Emperor Sutoku (r. 1123–42), who died exiled in the shrine's vicinity in 1164.

Kumano Sanzan Shrines (Kumano Sansha) Refers to three shrines located in Wakayama Prefecture: Kumano Hayatama Taisha dedicated to Kumano Hayatama no Kami, Kumano Hongu Taisha dedicated to Ketsumiko (Sunanoo no Mikoto), and Kumano Nachi Taisha, dedicated to Kumano Fusumi no Kami and to the worship of the Nachi waterfalls. Collectively, these shrines served as the seat of one major Shinto-Buddhist movement in which the *kami* were also considered manifestations of Amida Buddha. The Kumano shrines were also popular among the *yamabushi* (practitioners of Shugendo or mountain asceticism), for whom they additionally served as a major pilgrimage site.

Sumiyoshi Shrine (Sumiyoshi Taisha) One of the largest shrines in Osaka and dedicated to four deities. Three of them were called the "Sumiyoshi brothers," who were born from Izanagi no Mikoto after his return from the land of *yomi* and subsequent ritual purification in the sea. The fourth deity is the shrine's legendary founder—Empress Jingu Kogo, whose deified name is Okinagatarashihime no Mikoto. The shrine promises marine safety and prosperity for those whose livelihoods depend on the sea.

Toshogu Toshogu, a Shinto shrine and mausoleum honoring the first Tokugawa shogun, Ieyasu, also refers to the posthumous title given to him by the imperial court. The first Toshogu shrine, founded in 1617 in Nikko, houses his remains. More than 100 shrines throughout Japan are dedicated to Tokugawa Ieyasu.

Tsurugaoka Hachiman Shrine (Tsurugaoka Hachimangu) The Tsurugaoka Hachimangu was erected in 1063 by Minamoto no Yoriyoshi (988–1075) to honor the family's tutelary divinity Hachiman, the god of war. The shrine is dedicated to the spirits of Emperor Ojin (deified as Hachiman); his mother, Jingu Kogo; and his wife, Hime Okami. The annual festival, founded by Minamoto no Yoritomo, is held in September and includes archery demonstrations (*yabusame*) and parades of the three *o-mikoshi* (portable shrines).

Usa Hachiman Shrine (Usa Hachimangu) The Usa Hachimangu, situated in Usa, Kyushu, is regarded as the central shrine for around 25,000 Hachiman shrines throughout Japan. Like the Tsurugaoka Hachimangu, this shrine is also dedicated to the mythical emperor Ojin, his mother (Empress Jingu Kogo), and his wife (Hime Okami).

Yasaka Shrine (Yasaka Jinja) Also called Gionsha, Gion Tenjin, or Kanshinin and located in the Higashiyama district of Kyoto. The Yasaka Shrine is dedicated to Susanoo no Mikoto, the brother of Amaterasu, and the *kami* who protects against misfortunes and disasters. The Gion festival is held here and lasts the entire month of July.

JAPANESE BUDDHIST TRADITIONS

Introduction

Buddhism originated in India around the fifth century B.C.E. Buddhist thought and practice is based on the religious experience of Siddhartha Gautama, the man who became the Buddha (literally, "The Enlightened One"). Historically, two major strands of Buddhism developed, Theravada and Mahayana. Theravada, "Religion of the Elders," is most closely associated with the teachings of the historical Buddha in India and survives today in places like Thailand, Sri Lanka, and Myanmar (formerly Burma). Mahayana Buddhism, "Greater Vehicle," is the form of Buddhism that developed some 500 years after the death of the historical Buddha. It spread from India to East Asia and Tibet and is the form of Buddhism prominent in Japan during the medieval and early modern periods and today.

THERAVADA THOUGHT AND PRACTICE

Theravada Buddhism takes as its starting point the life of the historical Buddha (ca. 563–483 B.C.E.). This tradition treats the Buddha as a human being who, through spiritual practices, comprehended the nature of reality. This realization is termed *nirvana*, or enlightenment. Buddha's life stands as a model for others to follow.

After the Buddha's religious awakening, he began to expound the Dharma—the law or teaching—to others. The Dharma, as taught in Theravada, centers on religious practices that result in a transcendent understanding (enlightenment) of the human condition. This condition is expressed in the "three marks of existence"—impermanence, suffering, and absence of a permanent self or soul—that describe an unenlightened life lived in the world of samsara (the cycle of birth-death-rebirth). The morality of one's actions (karma) determines one's status in the samsaric cycle. Moral action offers the promise of a higher spiritual rebirth, while immoral action leads to rebirth in a lower spiritual state. The samsaric world, according to the Buddha, is fundamentally unsatisfactory. As a result, human beings eventually seek to escape the continual round of rebirths.

The Buddha's Four Noble Truths describe the human condition and the means to liberate oneself from the samsaric world:

1. All existence is suffering.
2. Suffering is caused by desire.
3. Cessation of desire results in the cessation of suffering.
4. The "Eightfold Path" leads to liberation (nirvana).

The Eightfold Path constitutes the Buddha's method for attaining liberation from samsara. The eight aspects of the path are divided into three components:

wisdom:
1) right views
2) right intention

morality
3) right speech
4) right conduct
5) right livelihood

concentration
6) right effort
7) right mindfulness
8) right concentration

Wisdom refers to the mental states and attitudes required to successfully practice the Buddha's Dharma. Morality concerns the way one treats others and acts in the world. Concentration encompasses the kinds of practices necessary to master the mental processes required to engage in advanced levels of meditation. Wisdom, morality, and concentration entail ardent effort that eventually leads to a transformation from ignorance to transcendent wisdom—nirvana.

MAHAYANA THOUGHT AND PRACTICE

Mahayana Buddhism arose some 500 years after the death of the historical Buddha. Mahayana includes the idea that the historical Buddha was but one of many Buddhas who have taught human beings the way to gain enlightenment. The tradition includes the important figures known as bodhisattvas (in Japanese, *bosatsu*) who have vowed to attain Buddhahood (enlightenment). Some Mahayana schools believe that bodhisattvas who have already attained enlightenment postpone their passing out of the samsaric world to help others attain salvation. Compassion is the key virtue that operates in a bodhisattva and is a concept important in medieval and early modern Japanese Buddhism.

Like Theravada, some Mahayana schools, such as Zen Buddhism, assert the possibility of enlightenment achieved through individual effort. Other schools of Mahayana stress the possibility of salvation into a Buddhist paradise on the basis of faith. Pure Land Buddhism, for instance, relates the story of Amida (in Sanskrit, Amitabha) Buddha who vows to save all sentient beings that call on him for assistance into his Pure Land, or Western Paradise.

A primary focus in Mahayana thought is on the bodhisattva. In meditation-based Mahayana, the bodhisattva is a compassionate being who vows to practice the Buddha's teaching and, once enlightened, to help others do the same. Through meditation, the bodhisattva's goal is to perceive that the universe is empty of an essential foundation, thereby overcoming the duality of our everyday, ordinary perceptions and experiences.

In faith-based Mahayana, the term bodhisattva refers to beings like Kannon (in Sanskrit, Avalokitesvara) who have already achieved enlightenment and are now endowed with great compassion and spiritual powers. Unenlightened people call upon bodhisattvas—along with Buddhas like Amida—for aid with the material and spiritual difficulties of human existence. This was an especially attractive alternative to the difficulties of meditation for laypeople. According to faith-based Mahayana, humans live in a degenerate age. At such a time, the only hope for release from the samsaric cycle is to place one's faith in the Buddhas and bodhisattvas. Out of compassion, Buddhas and bodhisattvas will relieve one of his or her pain and suffering and deliver the faithful to a Buddhist paradise in the next life.

Medieval and Early Modern Japanese Buddhism

Medieval Japanese Buddhism marks a significant departure from the forms of Buddhist thought and practice current during the aristocratic Heian period. During the Heian period, Buddhism was largely controlled by the Kyoto aristocrats and was characterized, in part, by the use of resource-intensive rituals with an emphasis on a formal Buddhist hierarchy. This style of Buddhism began to break down during the later part of the Heian period, and by the beginning of the medieval period, new Buddhist schools arose that took the Buddhist message of salvation to a much broader segment of the Japanese population. These new Buddhist schools—Pure

Land, Nichiren, and Zen—though not entirely free of political and other influences, nevertheless shifted the focus of Japanese Buddhist thought and practice, resulting in the spread of Buddhism throughout all classes of Japanese society.

Both Pure Land and Nichiren schools stressed the idea that Japan had entered a period of time known as *mappo*, the end of the Dharma. According to this view, so much time had elapsed since the historical Buddha preached the Dharma in ancient India that it had become increasingly difficult to understand the full import of what he taught. As a result, the idea of relying on one's own efforts to achieve enlightenment gave way to the notion that the only hope for salvation was to place one's faith in the powers of a compassionate Buddha or bodhisattva. To this end, Pure Land emphasized the need to practice the recitation of the name of Amida Buddha (*nembutsu*) to activate the powers of salvation that Amida offered and to achieve birth in his Pure Land (or, Western Paradise). Similarly, the Nichiren school stressed the idea of the recitation of the sacred title of the Lotus Sutra as the ritual practice that activated the possibility of salvation in a defiled and impure world. For the Nichiren school, salvation meant the conversion of the entire country of Japan to Lotus Sutra faith with the result that a Buddhist age would be inaugurated in the world. For both the Pure Land and Nichiren traditions, proof that the end of the Dharma was at hand was reflected in social and political unrest, and in human evil perceived to be rampant in the land. The solution was escape from this unhappy world. These schools, with their message of salvation, became popular during the medieval period.

Zen schools, on the other hand, repudiated the notion of *mappo*. Instead they taught the idea of enlightenment realized in the context of everyday life. This was to be achieved not through reliance on a power outside of oneself, as Pure Land and Nichiren required, but through traditional Buddhist modes of effort, particularly meditation, leading to a religious awakening. Zen, too, was well suited to monastic traditions that provided the support necessary to engage in rigorous contemplative practice. For this reason, Zen had far less popular appeal than the faith-based forms of Kamakura Buddhism.

It is important to stress, however, that the new Kamakura Buddhist schools did not replace older forms of Japanese Buddhism. The medieval period was often impacted by innovations emerging from these older schools. In the Kamakura period, for instance, priests of the Nara Buddhist schools were active in movements to revitalize monastic regulations. Myoe (1173–1232) was a Kegon priest who advocated strict adherence to the monastic precepts. Similarly, Eizon (1201–90), a Ritsu school priest, worked diligently to transmit the precepts to his generation. He lectured on the precepts, gained followers from both the aristocratic and military elite, and at the same time worked to teach the precepts to the lower classes.

By the late Kamakura and Muromachi periods, Zen Buddhism received patronage from members of the warrior class, including support from the Hojo family of shogunal regents and from the shogunate itself. One of the products of this patronage was the development of a Rinzai Zen temple system known as Gozan (Five Mountains). This was a hierarchical system of monasteries in both Kyoto and Kamakura that received the support of wealthy and powerful patrons. Zen also had a significant impact on Japanese art and literature.

The Pure Land and Nichiren schools also continued to thrive in the Muromachi period. True Pure Land Buddhism (Jodo-shinshu) was ably led by the priest Rennyo (1415–99), who embarked on activities to expand the influence of Jodo-shinshu. In the process, he created a powerful religious movement headquartered at the Honganji in Kyoto. The Nichiren school also became quite powerful in the Kyoto region in the 15th century. As a result, armies of militant monks were dispatched from the Tendai headquarters on Mt. Hiei in 1536 to destroy Nichiren-related temples in Kyoto to counter the growing success of the Nichiren schools.

The role of Buddhism in Edo-period Japan became much more complex than it had been in earlier periods. It was a period in which Buddhism's primacy as the main way of thinking about the world was challenged by new Shinto movements as well as by the influence of Neo-Confucian ideas on Japanese ways of thinking. Although Japanese Buddhism always had connections to the state and political interests, these associations became quite explicit during the Edo period. In the early 17th century, the Tokugawa shogunate prohibited the teaching of Christianity and later banned nearly all foreign contacts in Japan for fear of the power of the Christian movement. The government utilized Buddhism as a way to oversee this ban and to enforce its isolationist policies.

One way this was accomplished was by forcing Japanese Christians to renounce their Christianity. Buddhist temples were made into bureaucratic offices of the shogunate by the system of *shumon aratame*, or examination of religious affiliation. This system—called the *danka* (parishioner) system—required every Japanese family to become registered members of a local temple and to receive a certificate to the effect that they were not Christian. Temples were required to provide this information to the local lord. As the *danka* system developed, other obligatory activities were instituted, such as financial support to temples, annual visits to ancestral graves located on temple grounds, and attendance at important temple rituals. In this way, Buddhist temples became overseers of the religious lives of its patrons.

Edo-period Buddhism was not simply an organ of state control. This period also witnessed dynamic new developments in religious thinking and practice. Notably, the early modern period gave rise to a new school of Zen known as the Obaku school. It received its start as a result of the teachings of a Chinese Zen master known in Japanese as Ingen Ryuki (1592–1673), who took up residence in Nagasaki in 1654. Nagasaki's port permitted limited access by Chinese traders during the Edo isolationist period. Not only did Ingen attract many disciples, but he also attracted the interest of Tokugawa Ietsuna (1641–80), the fourth shogun. Ingen received land near Kyoto at Uji to build a temple. The Mampukuji, established in 1661, became the center of Obaku Zen. This form of Zen stressed the combined practice of both *zazen* (seated meditation) and recitation of the *nembutsu*.

Not all Edo-period Buddhist innovations involved the establishment of new schools. Already established Buddhist schools, often under the leadership of dynamic monks, also vitalized Edo Buddhism. Notable among these were such Zen figures as Suzuki Shosan (1579–1655), Hakuin Ekaku (1685–1768), and Ryokan (1758–1831). Shosan was a Soto Zen priest with a warrior background who had fought on the side of the Tokugawa at the Battle of Sekigahara and at the siege of Osaka Castle. He later became a Zen priest, advocating the need to practice Zen in the context of daily life. He stressed the importance of virtue and hard work, and viewed these as aspects of proper Zen practice. Hakuin was a Rinzai priest who sought to spread Zen teachings to all people by writing about Zen thought and practice in an easily understood manner. It was largely due to his efforts that Rinzai experienced a revival of interest during the Edo period. Ryokan was a Soto Zen priest and poet who led the life of a solitary mendicant and expressed his religious sensibilities, especially compassion for all living beings, through his poetry.

Other Edo-period Buddhist developments included the revival of the practice of monastic precepts by a Shingon priest named Jiun Onko (1718–1804) and grassroots Pure Land movements among the Jodo-shinshu (True Pure Land school) common people, who led simple religious lives and taught Pure Land practices to others. They came to be called *myokonin*, "wonderfully good ones."

Buddhist Schools

SIX NARA BUDDHIST SCHOOLS

These were six Chinese Buddhist schools introduced to Japan during the seventh and eighth centuries that became formalized in the Nara period (710–94) as the six Nara Buddhist schools, named after the capital in which they were located. These six schools are:

Sanron Sanron is a Buddhist school based on the writings of the Indian monks Nagarjuna and his disciple Aryadeva that focus on the concept of emptiness (in Sanskrit, *sunyata*), the idea that all things in the phenomenal world arise because of cause-and-effect relationships with all other phenomena. Sanron was first introduced to Japan in the early seventh century and was centered at the Gangoji and Daianji in Nara.

Jojitsu Jojitsu is a Buddhist school based on the writings of the Indian monk Harivarman. It focuses on the idea that there are two levels of truth in the world. There is the provisional truth, the reality humans experience in an unenlightened state, and the absolute truth, the enlightened realization that emptiness (in Sanskrit, *sunyata*) characterizes all of reality. Although grouped as one of the six Nara schools, Jojitsu was really a branch of the Sanron school.

Hosso This Buddhist school is based on a number of Yogacara Buddhist texts teaching the notion of "consciousness only," the idea that a careful analysis of the characteristics of worldly phenomena reveals that they do not exist outside of our minds. The Japanese monks Dosho, at the Gangoji, and Gembo, at the Kofukuji, were early proponents of this school.

Kusha This Buddhist school is based on the writings of the Indian monk Vasubandhu, teaching that dharmas, the constituent elements that make up all things, exist but that there is no enduring self or soul.

Kegon The Kegon school is based on the *Flower Garland Sutra* (*Kegon-kyo*). This text teaches that all things are interrelated and interconnected. This school was introduced to Japan by Chinese and Korean monks in the eighth century. The Todaiji at Nara is the school's center in Japan.

Ritsu The Ritsu school emphasizes the importance of closely following the rules of monastic discipline known in Sanskrit as *vinaya*. The school was founded in Japan in 753 by the Chinese monk Ganjin. He established ordination platforms (*kaidan*) for receiving the Buddhist precepts at the Todaiji and Toshodaiji in Nara.

SHINGON SCHOOL (SHINGON-SHU)

The Shingon (True Word) school was founded on Mt. Koya by the ninth-century monk Kukai (774–835), posthumously known as Kobo Daishi (Great teacher who spread the Dharma). After studying in China, Kukai established Shingon in Japan. Shingon is a form of esoteric Buddhism that places a strong emphasis on rituals and modes of practice that must be learned directly from a master. Shingon thought and practice focus on the Buddha Mahavairocana (in Japanese, Dainichi) who, it is said, expounded the ultimate truth, that is, the "True Word." According to Shingon doctrine and the Mahavairocana Sutra (Dainichi-kyo), Dainichi is the

dharmakaya (a Sanskrit term), or "Truth Body," whose essence permeates the entire universe. It is taught that the universe is composed of the body, speech, and mind of Dainichi. Kukai preached that Buddhist practitioners, under expert guidance from a Shingon teacher, could learn the esoteric rituals and forms of meditation that would enable them to realize that they are intimately connected to the essence of the universe. This realization allows one to "become a Buddha in this lifetime" (*sokushin jobutsu*).

The notion that Shingon is esoteric derives from the fact that the rituals necessary to realize the truth can only be taught directly by a teacher to a disciple. Thus, for instance, the use of hand gestures (in Sanskrit, *mudras*), chants (*dharani*), and other ritual actions can only be learned from a teacher; they can never be adequately learned from a text. Kukai also utilized artistic representations of Shingon ideas to further the practice of his followers. The Diamond World and Womb World mandalas are typical of such usage. The Diamond World mandala represents the wisdom of Dainichi while the Womb World mandala symbolizes the truth conveyed by that wisdom.

During the Kamakura period, doctrinal disputes caused Shingon to split into the Shingi (New doctrine) and Kogi (Old doctrine) schools.

TENDAI SCHOOL (TENDAI-SHU)

Tendai Buddhism was founded by the monk Saicho (767–822), posthumously known as Dengyo Daishi (Great teacher who transmits the teaching), on Mt. Hiei in the early ninth century. After studying in China, Saicho returned to Japan to establish Tendai. However, he was met with opposition from the Nara schools. Saicho wanted to create an ordination platform at Mt. Hiei, but the Nara schools opposed this because it threatened their government-recognized right to ordain monks, and thereby maintain sole control over the make-up of the monastic order. After Saicho's death, Tendai turned its focus to esoteric Buddhist practices under the direction of a series of gifted leaders.

Tendai Buddhism focuses on the *Lotus Sutra*, which teaches that although there are different and apparently contradictory Buddhist teachings, they are all expedient devices used by the Buddha to preach to human beings according to their ability to understand the profundity of the Dharma. Thus, the different sutras can be explained not as contradictory but rather as teachings accommodated to different levels of discernment. Tendai Buddhism is thus inclusive of myriad different Buddhist teachings, although it follows the *Lotus Sutra* in arguing that sutra is the pinnacle of the Buddha's Dharma. The *Lotus Sutra* and Tendai also preach the notion that bodhisattvas, such as Kannon (in Sanskrit, Avalokitesvara), are available to help others in times of spiritual and material need. Finally, the *Lotus Sutra* also teaches the concept of the end of the Dharma, a time period in which it would be exceedingly difficult for individuals to attain enlightenment through their own efforts at meditation, which was to have a significant impact on some of the new schools of Kamakura Buddhism.

The political prominence of Tendai ended when Oda Nobunaga demolished most of the Mt. Hiei temple complex Enryakuji in 1571.

PURE LAND SCHOOL (JODO-SHU)

Founded in the late 12th century by Honen, the Jodo (Pure Land) school teaches that, in a time so far removed from the era of the historical Buddha, it has become nearly impossible for human beings to attain enlightenment. The only hope for salvation in this degenerate age (known as *mappo*, the end of the Dharma) is to put faith in the vow of Amida Buddha, who resides in the Western Paradise, or Pure Land, to heed calls for help and deliver the devoted into the Pure Land upon death. The mechanism for calling on Amida for help is the recitation of the *nembutsu*—chanting the phrase *namu Amida butsu* ("hail to Amida Buddha"). Sincere and single-minded recitation of the *nembutsu* would be answered by spiritual, and even material, assistance from Amida.

Honen founded the sect in Kyoto. Not seeking to intentionally start an entirely new sect of Buddhism, he simply began to spread his interpretation of the three foundational sutras and advocate the practice of *nembutsu*. In 1198, Honen reportedly had a mystical encounter with Amida, which confirmed the truth of his teachings and his new sect. However, his teachings, which were antagonistic to worldly ideas of order, proved threatening to the government and the other established religious groups, and he was forced to flee the capital. Despite this opposition, his sect survived among the small groups of followers left in the capital and grew to gain prominence in the medieval and early modern periods.

TRUE PURE LAND SCHOOL (JODO SHINSHU)

Started by Shinran, a disciple of Jodo sect founder Honen, the so-called True Pure Land sect was originally reported to be the true essence of Honen's doctrines and was known by the name Ikkoshu until 1872. As the sect developed, however, it came to be more about the teachings of Shinran himself than his former master, and the followers of the school came to emphasize the teachings of Shinran's major work, *Kyogyoshinsho*, written in 1224. The thrust of his teaching was eschatological in its focus on a final degradation of the human race from which all would be saved by the Primal Vow of Amida Buddha.

In 1207, Shinran was exiled along with his teacher, Honen. Four years later, Shinran was allowed to return to Kyoto to lead those disciples of Honen who had avoided persecution and continued to practice *nembutsu*. As the Jodo sect developed, the disciples of Shinran split to form the Jodo Shin sect, which saw the path to the Pure Land as one illumined by the believer's embrace of the Primal Vow. In 1263, Shinran's death sent the sect into decline, only to be revived by the passionate monk, Rennyo, in the 15th century. Under Rennyo's leadership, the sect became one of the most prominent Buddhist schools in Japan.

TIME SCHOOL (JI-SHU)

Started by Ippen (1239–89) in the 13th century, the Ji school is a form of Pure Land Buddhism. Ippen had a dream in which he was told to preach the message of Pure Land salvation among the people. As a result, Ippen became an itinerant preacher, traveling throughout the countryside to instruct people in *nembutsu* practice. He attracted disciples and a large following. One of his innovations was the use of dance as part of religious practice. The *nembutsu odori*, or "dancing chant," became central to his method of teaching.

YUZU NEMBUTSU SECT (YUZU NEMBUTSU SHU)

The Yuzu Nembutsu sect embraced the ideas of the Pure Land scholar, Ryonin, who concluded that the power of *nembutsu* practice culminated in the intermingling of the individual with the whole of Pure Land devotees. Through this unification, one was reborn into the Pure Land. The sect experienced a renaissance under the direction of Ryoson in the 14th century, and a comprehensive explanation of its doctrines was finally recorded by its patriarch, Yukan, in the 17th-century work *Yuzu emmonsho*.

NICHIREN SECT (NICHIREN-SHU)

The Nichiren school, founded by the former Tendai monk Nichiren (1222–82), was a form of faith-based Buddhism that stressed the power of the *Lotus Sutra* as the sole path to salvation. Like Pure Land Buddhism, Nichiren promoted the idea of chanting as a means to tap into the saving power of Buddhism. Unlike Pure Land traditions, Nichiren advocated a practice known as the *daimoku*, chanting the sacred title of the *Lotus Sutra*: *namu myoho renge kyo* ("hail to the *Lotus Sutra*). By chanting this phrase single-mindedly and with faith, one would gain salvation.

Nichiren believed in the idea of *mappo* ("end of the Dharma"), the notion that the world has entered an age so far removed from the enlightened teaching of the historical Buddha that it is not possible for one to gain enlightenment through meditation. Instead, the only course available during this degenerate age was to chant the sacred title of the *Lotus Sutra*. Nichiren taught that if all of the Japanese people would embrace the teaching of the *Lotus Sutra*, then Japan itself would become a Buddhist paradise.

FUJU FUSE SCHOOL (FUJU FUSE HA)

A school of Nichiren Buddhism. The term *fuju fuse* ("neither giving nor receiving") refers to the idea that in order to maintain the purity of Nichiren's teachings, Nichiren Buddhists must refuse to give offerings and perform rituals for nonbelievers, and they must refuse to receive offerings and rituals from nonbelievers. This movement, started by the monk Nichio (1565–1630), was banned by the Tokugawa shogunate because of its intransigence. Throughout the Edo period, however, Fuju Fuse school adherents continued to practice in secret. It was not until after the start of the Meiji Restoration that the ban on this school was lifted.

SOTO ZEN SCHOOL (SOTO-SHU)

The Soto Zen school was founded by the monk Dogen (1200–53), who had originally trained on Mt. Hiei as a Tendai priest. Dissatisfied with Tendai teachings, Dogen traveled to China, where he engaged in intensive study and practice of Soto Zen. Tradition holds that Dogen achieved enlightenment during his stay in China. Upon returning to Japan in 1228, Dogen established Soto as a separate Buddhist school, training monks and nuns as well as writing numerous treatises regarding Zen practice. In 1243, Dogen built the monastery Eiheiji in the mountains of Echizen province (present-day Fukui Prefecture). Dogen's Zen teaching centered on *zazen*, or seated meditation, as the chief practice leading to enlightenment.

RINZAI ZEN SCHOOL (RINZAI-SHU)

The Rinzai Zen school was founded by the monk Eisai (1141–1215). Like Dogen, Eisai studied first as a Tendai priest but took up Rinzai Zen practice after two pilgrimages to China. Settling again in Japan, Eisai built Rinzai Zen temples and otherwise promoted Rinzai teachings. Eisai was also a proponent of green tea drinking as an aid to both meditation and health. To this end, he brought tea seeds with him from China to plant in Japan. Like Soto, Rinzai Zen focused on meditation as a central religious practice, but, unlike Soto, Rinzai also advocated the use of *koan*, nonlogical questions or aphorisms that were given by a Zen master to a disciple. The process of trying to find an answer or response to a *koan* was intended to move the disciple away from logical, discursive thought, to a spontaneous, non-dualistic perspective leading to enlightenment.

6.7 *Meditation hall at Engakuji, a Rinzai Zen temple in Kamakura* (Photo William E. Deal)

OBAKU ZEN SCHOOL (OBAKU-SHU)

Founded in Japan in 1654 with the permission of Tokugawa Ietsuna by the Chinese monk, Ingen, the Obaku sect of Zen combined ideas from Pure Land and esoteric Buddhist sects with traditional Zen to create a distinctive form of religious practice that included the use of *nembutsu* chant. Ingen and his students founded the Mampukuji temple near Kyoto. The Obaku monks made a large contribution to the advancement of Japanese artistic styles, especially in the disciplines of painting and calligraphy.

SHUGENDO

The Shugendo order, whose members are called *yamabushi*, combined elements of Japanese folk religion involving mountain worship with esoteric Buddhist doctrines seeking to unlock the mystical powers of the mountains that were home to their ascetic communities. The group traces its ancestry to Heian-period Buddhist hermits, known as *hijiri*, who lived in the mountains of Japan studying the secrets of Buddhist texts like the *Lotus Sutra*. Emerging as a full-fledged religious movement in the 12th century, its followers claim allegiance to the teachings of a legendary ascetic named En no Gyoja, and its practices center around seasonal holy mountain pilgrimages known as *nyubu*, which are said to transform the practitioner into a Buddha by ascending through the profane to the sacred in the course of climbing the mountain. Shugendo holy mountains include the Kumano mountains, Daisen, and Dewa Sanzan.

Buddhist Monasticism

The growth of Buddhist monasticism beginning in the early seventh century is credited largely to the patronage of the influential Soga family whose support of Buddhist monastic orders was spearheaded by Prince Shotoku who founded a number of monasteries including Shitennoji and Ikarugadera in the late sixth century. Despite this early support, by the eighth century, political involvement in the monastic life of many Buddhist sects began to feel suffocating as the government continued to tighten its control over the communities, issuing a number of administrative codes and regulations governing the activities taking place inside these monasteries. The establishment of a number of monastic offices within the government forced religious leaders to assume increasingly bureaucratic roles at the expense of their spiritual responsibilities, drawing the criticism of a number of monks who were looking for a higher standard of religious purity.

Tired of the stale and detached Buddhism of the monasteries that had become, for all intents and purposes, "state run," monks like Gyogi left to bring the Buddhist message to the common people. These monks, along with a number of other visionaries who came to Japan from China to start religious groups, soon started their own monasteries independent of government sanction. At this time, the emperor moved the capital to Kyoto to escape the influence that religious institutions were having on the government. Thus, the monastic orders seemed to free themselves from governmental interference.

During the Heian period, the monastic orders continued to grow as many new religious sects were introduced from China, including the Tendai and Shingon sects. The introduction of Zen during the 12th century also strengthened the numbers of religious people seeking a monastic lifestyle in Japan, but at this time, Pure Land Buddhism was also gaining influence, which, with its de-emphasis on meditation, led to a decline in Buddhist monasticism. The monastic orders continued to decline until the 16th century, when a renewed interest in Confucian ideals championed by the government brought new patronage of monasteries especially for Zen devotees.

Buddhist Rituals

Bon Festival Also known as Urabon or Obon, a Buddhist ritual usually observed on July 13 or 15 to honor ancestral spirits. Commonly, observers construct a *shoryodana* (spirit altar) and make other preparations for the return of their ancestors. The Bon Festival is a highlight of the yearly festival calendar on a par with the New Year celebration.

pilgrimages Pilgrimages were journeys of particular religious significance to many Japanese believers. Often such endeavors required travel to a specific religious place (a temple, mountain, or similar site) or to a series of such holy locales in a meaningful, predetermined succession.

Buddhist Ritual Objects

Buddhist ritual implements Objects or accessories that are commonly used during ritual practice and often assume larger spiritual significance. A wide assortment of implements has been used in numerous ceremonies with varied historical backgrounds. Some limited examples of ritual objects include the water jug used as a symbol of purification, a monk's robe, incense, candles, vases, and numerous instruments. One of the most prominent ritual implements is the mandala altar commonly seen in esoteric sects of Buddhism. The mandala is a symmetrical diagram that represents the Buddhist universe and is used during ritual as an object for meditation.

Buddhas, Bodhisattvas, and Buddhist Deities

Amida (Butsu) In Sanskrit, Amitabha (Buddha of Infinite Light) or Amitayus (Buddha of Infinite Life). Buddha of the Western Paradise, or Pure Land. The object of worship in Pure Land Buddhist schools. As a bodhisattva, Dharmakara—the future Amida—vowed to help all sentient beings attain

6.8 *Large bronze sculpture of Amida Buddha (Daibutsu) at Kamakura* (Photo William E. Deal)

enlightenment. Japanese Pure Land traditions stress recitation of Amida's name as a profession of faith. This is known as the practice of the *nembutsu* (Namu Amida Butsu: "I place my faith in Amida Buddha").

Birushana Another name for Dainichi Nyorai.

bosatsu In Sanskrit, bodhisattva. A being who forgoes Buddhahood to help others in their quest for enlightenment, the bodhisattva will not become a Buddha until all sentient creatures have achieved this state. The bodhisattva is an important concept in Mahayana Buddhism (Mahayana: Greater Vehicle) because it emphasizes the idea that all beings possess the power to reach nirvana.

butsu In Sanskrit, Buddha.

Dainichi Great sun Buddha. In Sanskrit, Mahavairocana; also known in Japanese as Dainichi or Dainichi Nyorai. Dainichi is especially important in Shingon (esoteric) Buddhist traditions. Dainichi is understood as the ground or essence of the universe. All phenomena are emanations of this Buddha. Dainichi's nature is expressed in the mandala of the two worlds, the *kongokai* (in Sanskrit, *vajradhatu*, diamond world) and the *taizokai* (in Sanskrit, *garbhadhatu*, womb world), which shows all aspects and manifestations of the Buddha.

Fugen In Sanskrit, Samantabhadra. Bodhisattva who represents meditation and practice. Fugen is often depicted riding an elephant.

Jizo In Sanskrit, Ksitigarbha (womb of the earth). Jizo, usually represented as a monk with a jewel in one hand and a staff in the other, protects travelers and children, and often assists followers out of the hell realms and guides them to higher levels of existence. He has been venerated since the Heian period.

Kannon In Sanskrit, Avalokitesvara; in Chinese: Guanyin. Kannon is perhaps the most popular of all bodhisattvas. Kannon represents infinite compassion and has the power to deliver all beings from danger. Kannon figures prominently in chapter 25 of the *Lotus Sutra*. Kannon is also an attendant to Amida Buddha. Other representations of Kannon include the Bato (Horse-Headed) Kannon, Juichimen (11-Headed) Kannon, and Nyoirin (Wheel of the Wish-Granting Jewel) Kannon.

Miroku In Sanskrit, Maitreya ("Benevolent One"). As the Buddha of the future, Miroku will descend to this world in its next cycle and attain Buddhahood, thereby bringing all of its inhabitants to enlighten-

6.9 Stone sculpture of the bodhisattva Jizo (Photo William E. Deal)

ment. Miroku currently resides in the Tushita heaven (in Japanese, Tosotsu), one of many Buddhist paradises.

Monju Bosatsu In Sanskrit, Mañjusri. Bodhisattva of wisdom. Monju is often depicted riding on the back of a lion.

myoo In Sanskrit, *vidyaraja* ("kings of light or wisdom"). Considered kings of magical science, *myoo* deities constitute the third class of Buddhist divinities after the buddhas (*nyorai*) and bodhisattvas (*bosatsu*). The fourth class is the *tembu* (in Sanskrit, *deva*). Originally of Hindu origin, *myoo* were adopted into the Buddhist pantheon as protectors of Buddhism. The most famous is Fudo Myoo (in Sanskrit, Achalanatha), often depicted with a fierce visage and associated with fire.

Nikko Bosatsu In Sanskrit, Suryaprabha. Attendant of Yakushi Nyori (Bhaishaijyaguru). Nikko symbolizes the light of the Sun.

Nyorai In Sanskrit, Tathagata (literally, Thus Come One). An epithet of the Buddha.

rakan Japanese term for an *arhat*, in Theravada tradition, people who have attained enlightenment.

Rushana Another name for Dainichi Nyorai.

Shaka Nyorai A term for the historical Buddha.

Shakamuni A term for the historical Buddha.

Shakuson A term for the historical Buddha.

Taho Nyorai In Sanskrit, Prabhutaratna. The Buddha "Many Jewels" who appears in the *Lotus Sutra* to witness the truth of the historical Buddha's teaching.

Seishi Bosatsu In Sanskrit, Mahasthamaprapta. The bodhisattva of wisdom. Along with Kannon, Seishi is an attendant to Amida Buddha. Seishi is mentioned in the *Sutra of Immeasurable Life*, the *Meditation Sutra*, and in the *Lotus Sutra* as one who attended Shakyamuni's teachings on Eagle Peak.

Yakushi Nyorai In Sanskrit, Bhaiṣajyaguru. Medicine Buddha.

Zao Gongen Protective deity of Shugendo mountain ascetic practice. He is especially associated with Mt. Kimpu in the Yoshino region south of Nara.

6.10 Stone sculpture of the bodhisattva Kannon (Photo William E. Deal)

Buddhist Temples

In English, the word *temple* is used to indicate a Buddhist building, and *shrine* is used to indicate a Shinto building. The suffixes *-ji, -tera (-dera), -in,* and *-do* are used to denote Buddhist temples and related structures.

Examples of this usage:

Eiheiji = Eihei Temple
Asukadera = Asuka Temple
Hokkedo = Lotus Temple (or Hall)

Chion'in Chion'in, built in 1234 by Genchi (1183–1238), honors his teacher, Honen, the founder of the Jodo sect of Pure Land Buddhism (see Pure Land Buddhism). The temple, located at the foot of the hills known as Higashiyama, marks the site where Honen settled and established his secluded residence after leaving Mt. Hiei in 1175 to proclaim his new Pure Land teachings. The temple became the head of the Jodo sect in 1523. In 1607 the temple was designated a *monzekidera*, one whose main abbot must be chosen from the imperial family or aristocracy. Its famous bell, cast in 1633, is six meters high, two meters in diameter, and weighs more than 70 tons.

Daitokuji Head temple of Rinzai Zen; located in the Murasakino section of Kyoto. Built in 1315 by Myocho, the temple became a part of the Gozan system. In 1431, however, the abbots of Daitokuji decided to make the temple private, thereby removing the temple from the Gozan ranks; it closed its doors to priests outside of Myocho's lineage. Daitokuji attracted many priests, including Kaso Sodon (1382–1412), and his disciples, Ikkyu Sojun (1394–1481) and Yoso Soi (1376–1458). The great tea master, Sen no Rikyu (1522–91), under whose auspices the tea ceremony experienced its greatest development, also studied at Daitokuji and contributed to its cultural development by building tearooms and tea gardens. Also buried here is one of the great unifiers of Japan—Oda Nobunaga.

Eiheiji Founded by Dogen in 1243, Eiheiji serves as one of two main temples of the Soto Zen sect. Dogen built Eiheiji, which he originally called Daibutsu-ji, as a place to live a life of seclusion. In 1246, Dogen changed the name to Eiheiji. The temple was damaged by fire in 1473, but not until the 16th century did Eiheiji become a prominent center of Soto Zen.

Enryakuji Founded in 785 by Saicho (767–822) (known posthumously as Dengyo Daishi) at the peak of Mt. Hiei, where he spent several years performing austerities, Enryakuji became the head temple of the Tendai school of Buddhism. Situated in the northeast of Kyoto, Enryakuji also became a protector of the city and the imperial palace because it was believed that evil spirits came from the northeast. A conflict arose in the 10th century between the "mountain faction," and the "temple faction" that led to a struggle between armies of warrior-monks lasting from 993 to the 15th century. Oda Nobunaga saw this as a great threat to the unification of the country, and therefore, destroyed much of the temple in 1571. Enryakuji is also associated with the Hie Jinja, its major tutelary Shinto shrine.

Ginkakuji (Temple of the Silver Pavilion) Built by Ashikaga Yoshimasa, Ginkakuji functioned as a pleasure villa and retreat when the shogun needed to withdraw temporarily from the pressures of administration. After Yoshimasa's death in 1490, Ginkakuji was converted into a Zen temple under the name Jishoji.

Higashi Honganji The head temple of the Otani branch of the Jodo Shinshu sect of Pure Land Buddhism, located in Kyoto. The temple was founded in 1603 by Kyonyo Koju, after an argument split the Honganji Jodo Shinshu branch into two different factions. In 1619 Tokugawa Ieyasu recognized the Otani sect as an independent branch of Jodo Shinshu, giving the temple the same status as its rival, the Nishi Honganji.

Honganji Originally a small memorial chapel and mausoleum dedicated to Shinran, the founder of the Jodo Shinshu sect of Pure Land Buddhism. Built by Kakushin-ni (1224–83), Shinran's youngest daughter, in 1272 and called Otani-byodo, it enshrined an image of her father and his remains. Not until 1321 was the building promoted to the rank of main temple by Shinran's grandson, Kakunyo (1270–1351), and renamed Honganji (Temple of the Original Vow). Honganji, however, garnered little support from other Jodo Shin subgroups even though it claimed to be the most orthodox interpreter of Shinran's teachings. The Onin War (1467–77) provided the context for the appearance of the Ikko-ikki, a military force of warrior-monks who were trained to defend the temple and their beliefs. Surpassing its rivals, Honganji was officially recognized by the emperor in 1560, whereby the abbots gained not only religious power but also secular power. Because the national power bestowed on its abbots conflicted with Oda Nobunaga's political agenda of national unification, Nobunaga attacked and destroyed the temple's political power. Honganji split into two rival branches, the Higashi Honganji and the Nishi Honganji, following a struggle between Kyonyo (1558–1614) and his younger brother Junnyo (1577–1631) for the title of 12th abbot.

Ishiyama Honganji Temple of the Jodo Shinshuu sect founded in 1496 by Rennyo (1415–99), the eighth abbot of Honganji. In the period 1533–80, it served as the center of the Honganji sect after the temple had burned, and provided a center of com-

6.11 *Example of a Buddhist temple altar* (Photo William E. Deal)

merce, culture, and most important, a headquarters of the Ikko ikki. Ishiyama Honganji reluctantly surrendered to Oda Nobunaga on September 10, 1580, due to Nobunaga's political campaigns.

Kan'eiji Located in Ueno Park, Tokyo; founded in 1625 by the monk Tenkai (ca. 1536–1643) for the Tendai sect. Situated to the northeast of Edo Castle, Tenkai beseeched the shogun Tokugawa Iemitsu that a temple should be erected to protect Edo Castle from evil spirits that emanate from the northeast. Kan'eiji also served as a cemetery for many members of the Tokugawa family.

Kenchoji Temple of Rinzai Zen; located in Kamakura and built in 1249. The fifth Kamakura shogunal regent (*shikken*) Hojo Tokiyori (1227–63), an avid supporter of Zen, served as a major patron of the temple. The temple was founded by the Chinese monk, Rankei Doryu (in Chinese, Lanqi Daolong), 1213–78, not only to make Kamakura a vital center for Rinzai Zen, but also to serve as a major Zen center and refuge for Chinese Chan (Zen) priests who fled China as it came under control of the Mongols.

Kenninji Temple and monastery of Rinzai Zen established in 1202 by the priest Eisai at the behest of the shogun Minamoto no Yoriie. Kenninji promoted Zen instruction after the warrior class and elite rulers acquired an interest in it because of its strict ideals of self-discipline and the religious idea of transcending death. Kenninji is modeled after the Chinese Baizhang monastery (built during the Tang dynasty, 618–907) and named one of the Five Mountain (*gozan*) temples of Kyoto in 1334. The name Kenninji comes from the era Kennin, in which it was built.

Kinkakuji (Temple of the Golden Pavilion) Kinkakuji, built by the third Muromachi shogun, Ashikaga Yoshimitsu (r. 1369–95), acted as a retreat after he abdicated the shogunate to his son, Ashikaga Yoshimochi. Much like the Phoenix Hall at Byodoin, the Golden Pavilion expresses Yoshimitsu's power to transcend and make permanent the temporal; the temple, covered in gold foil as its name suggests, is supported on pillars extending over a pond to give the illusion that it floats. After Yoshimitsu's death in 1408, the pavilion was converted into a Buddhist temple and given the name Rokuonji— Rokuon being Yoshimitsu's posthumous religious title. The Kinkakuji was set on fire during the Onin War (1467–77) and restored. However, it was completely destroyed by arson in 1950. The existing temple is a 1955 reproduction.

Kongobuji Main building in a complex of Buddhist temples founded in 816 by Kukai (Kobo Daishi) on Mt. Koya; belonging to the Shingon sect of esoteric Buddhism. Kongobuji (Temple of the Diamond Mountain) was the name that originally encompassed every temple and building on Mt. Koya, but in 1869, two temples, Seiganji and Kozanji, merged together to form the temple Kongobuji. Here, Kukai instituted the first teaching center for Shingon *mikkyo*, the doctrine of esoteric Buddhism that originated in India. The temple prohibited women from entering until 1872.

Nanzenji As Zen gained recognition among the Kamakura ruling elite, the cloistered emperor Kameyama (r. 1259–74) granted Mukan Gengo (1212–91) an imperial villa in Kyoto, which became Nanzenji. As a major temple in the Rinzai sect of Zen, it was ranked first among the *gozan* in Kyoto

in 1334, and, in 1386, Ashikaga Yoshimitsu gave Nanzenji a special rank above the *gozan* ranking system.

Nishi Honganji Pure Land Buddhist temple; founded in 1591 by the 11th abbot (*hossu*) of Honganji, Kennyo (1543–92). This temple replaced the Ishiyama Honganji and was founded following a dispute between Kennyo's sons, Kyonyo (1537–98) and Junnyo (1577–1631), for title of the 12th abbot of Honganji. Junnyo became the head abbot of Nishi Honganji in 1593, after which his brother built the Higashi Honganji in 1603. The Tokugawa shogunate recognized both temples as equal, independent establishments of the Jodo Shinshu sect.

Ryoanji Buddhist temple of the Rinzai Zen sect; located in Ukyo Ward, Kyoto. Built in 1450 by Hosokawa Katsumoto and patronized by Toyotomi Hideyoshi and Tokugawa Ieyasu, the temple entered into decline after being almost completely destroyed by fire in 1797. Ryoanji is famed for its dry rock garden that consists of 15 large stones in a sea of white gravel designed by Soami c. 1455.

Sensoji Also known as Asakusadera, Sensoji originally belonged to the Tendai sect of Buddhism. According to tradition, two fishermen found a statue of the bodhisattva Kannon in the Sumidagawa River in 628. Each time they tried to put the statue back in the water, it returned to them. The village head recognized the statue's divinity and renovated his home into a temple to enshrine the statue. It was completed in 645. (See also ASAKUSA SHRINE.)

Todaiji Major Buddhist temple built in Nara between 728 and 749 by the monk-architect Roben at the order of Emperor Shomu (r. 724–749). This commission signified an effort to emulate temples of the greatly admired Tang dynasty of China. Todaiji is famous for the Nara Daibutsu (The Great Buddha of Nara), the image of the Buddha Birushana (in Sanskrit, Vairocana), regarded by the Kegon sect as the cosmic, supreme Buddha. Having been severely damaged, the present Buddha was restored in 1692. Under the abbot Shunjobo Chogen (1121–1206), many of the buildings at Todaiji were reconstructed in 1180 in the style of the Southern Song dynasty in China (1127–1279). The famous Nio guardians sculpted by Unkei and Kaikei were placed at the front of the temple in 1203.

Tokeiji Rinzai Zen temple in Kamakura. Founded in 1285 by Kakusan, the widow of Hojo Tokimune, Tokeiji served as an asylum for mistreated women and for those seeking divorce.

Zojoji Edo-period Pure Land (Jodo) temple located in Edo. During the Edo period, Zojoji served as the Tokugawa family temple.

CHRISTIANITY

Christianity (in Japanese, *kirisutokyo*) was introduced to Japan in 1549 with the arrival of Francis Xavier (1506–52), a Christian missionary and one of the founders of the Jesuits (Society of Jesus). The early efforts made by Xavier and other missionaries to convert the Japanese to Christianity were modestly successful, especially given language, worldview, and other cultural impediments to understanding. Missionaries in Japan also came to include representatives of different orders, not only Jesuits, but also Franciscans and others. This resulted in a credibility problem for the missionaries when competition over who could gain the most converts emerged between these different Christian groups. Despite conversion of some powerful local lords, by the early 17th century, Christianity was deemed a threat to the ruling authority of the Tokugawa shogunate, which eventually banned all missionary activity in the 1630s, coinciding with the shogunate's national seclusion policy. The prohibition on missionary activities lasted some 200 years, until Japan was forced by the United States and other Western nations to open its ports in the 1850s to trade in material goods and, by extension, foreign ideas.

Early Christian missionaries were faced with a number of problems, including confrontation with customs and religious ideas that they neither understood nor respected. Potential Japanese converts were suspicious of the Christian idea that only those who embraced Christianity would be saved. To some Japanese, this seemed to imply that their deceased ancestors were already condemned to an eternity in hell, an idea entirely foreign to those raised at the intersection of both Buddhist ideas about universal salvation and Confucian notions of filial piety. Despite these obstacles, by 1579 the number of Christians in Japan was estimated at approximately 100,000. However, this number includes individuals who were forced to adopt Christianity by their newly converted lords.

For several decades following their arrival in Japan, Christian missionaries received powerful backing from a number of Japanese leaders, including Oda Nobunaga and Toyotomi Hideyoshi, who saw in Christianity both economic possibilities as well as a foil to powerful Buddhist monastic communities. However, Hideyoshi eventually became convinced that Christianity was a threat to his plans for unification of Japan under his control. Hideyoshi's suspicions were heightened by the actions of some Japanese Christian converts who sometimes desecrated or destroyed Buddhist and Shinto sacred sites. In 1587, infuriated by reports of these activities, Hideyoshi issued a decree banning Christianity and ordered all missionaries to leave Japan. Enforcement of this decree was sporadic at best, and missionary activity continued without significant government interference. In 1596, the Spanish ship *San Felipe* ran adrift off the shore of Japan and was captured by government authorities. Hideyoshi was convinced that this was an advance force of Westerners planning to conquer Japan just as they had other Asian nations such as the Philippines. He ordered the arrest of 26 Christians, a group comprised of both Franciscan priests and their Japanese converts, who were subsequently marched from Kyoto to Nagasaki on foot and burned at the stake.

Tokugawa Ieyasu, Hideyoshi's successor and founder of the Tokugawa shogunate, initially tolerated the Christian missionaries because it was profitable for the shogunate to maintain friendly relations with Western traders. However, once he no longer deemed Christians a strategic ally, he ordered the missionaries to leave Japan. The Tokugawa shogunate feared not only the colonization of Japan by Western powers but also the possibility that Christian missionaries would foment dissent among the Japanese populace and challenge the ruling authority of the shogunate.

After the expulsion of the missionaries, persecution of Japanese Christians became systematized under the direction of the government. Individuals were forced to renounce Christianity or face a variety of punishments, including death. It is estimated that 3,000 Japanese Christian adherents were martyred, and still others were imprisoned or exiled. In addition, the Tokugawa shogunate enacted a policy whereby all Japanese families were required to register at a local Buddhist temple in order to receive a certificate testifying to the fact that they were not Christians. In some regions of Japan, people were forced to stamp on displays of Christian images—a practice called *fumie* ("images to step on")—such as the Crucifixion, in order to prove that they were not Christians. The Tokugawa shogunate's anti-Christian policies, however, were based as much in political exigencies, such as the shogunate's fear of invasion by Western powers, as it was in any intense religious antagonism. Christianity did not return to Japan, legally, until the opening of Japan in the closing years of the Edo period.

ROLE OF WOMEN

The attitude of male-dominated Japanese Buddhism has varied in its perspectives on women and the kind of religious lives and roles women were capable of assuming. Sometimes this view was negative toward women, and other times it was significantly more positive. Both Tendai and Shingon Buddhism were headquartered on sacred mountains: Tendai on Mt. Hiei and Shingon on Mt. Koya. On both of these mountains, for much of the medieval and early modern periods, women were either forbidden to enter the mountain precincts or severely restricted in where they could go on the mountain. Women, including nuns, were believed to be spiritually inferior to men and to be subject to the "five obstruc-

tions" (*gosho*). The idea of the five obstructions asserted that women are unable to attain the five highest spiritual states, including the highest, that of a Buddha.

Some medieval Japanese Buddhist men held favorable views of women and their spiritual abilities. This was especially true among the new Buddhist schools of the Kamakura period. Pure Land traditions, for instance, with their emphasis on the possibility of universal salvation, included women in this view. Women were not only seen as capable of salvation, but were treated as full participants in the religious life. Honen, the founder of the Pure Land school (Jodo-shu), was particularly welcoming of women.

Buddhism served women in yet other ways during the Edo period. One notable example was the service a few temples provided to women who were seeking to leave a bad marriage. The Tokeiji temple in Kamakura was one such temple that included a nunnery where women could enter religious practice, and thereby be released from an abusive or otherwise problematic marriage. In this way, Buddhist temples provided women with a way to extract themselves from a marriage in a society in which there was no secular mechanism for women to end a marriage.

Some Buddhists held the view, based on a Chinese sutra, that women were impure because of the blood associated with menstruation and childbirth. It was believed by these Buddhists that not only were women impure, but that this blood inevitably polluted the nearby water and soil. The result, it was claimed, was that women were condemned to rebirth in one of the nine levels of Buddhist hells unless Buddhist rituals were performed that would obviate this transgression.

In medieval and early modern Japan, women could become Buddhist nuns. Reliable research on this aspect of Japanese Buddhism is still relatively sparse, but it was the case that women did enter the monastic life whether because of a heartfelt wish to pursue enlightenment or in order to avoid an oppressive marriage. Becoming a nun was one method by which women could take control of their own lives in a society that provided them with few lifestyle choices. One role model for a woman's Buddhist religious career was the life of Mugai Nyodai (1223–98). She was the daughter of a warrior and married into a samurai family. She took up the study of Rinzai Zen Buddhism, becoming a disciple of the Chinese monk Wu-hsueh Tsu-yuan (in Japanese, Mugaku Sogen). Later, as his spiritual heir, Mugai became the founder and abbess of the Keiaiji temple, a Rinzai Zen convent.

Shinto attitudes toward women were rather different than the attitude of Buddhists. Unlike Buddhist sutras and other Buddhist texts, Shinto had a long tradition of acknowledging and valorizing female deities, most prominently, Amaterasu, the Sun Goddess, from whose lineage the imperial family derives. The imperial shrine at Ise included among its priests a chief priestess, typically chosen from the imperial family. On the other hand, local shrines often denied women entrance into the most sacred precincts housing the altar of the enshrined deity. Similarly, women were often denied participation in shrine associations known as *miyaza*, which functioned as executive administrators over local matters.

In the late Edo period a new phenomenon arose whereby women became the founders of new religious movements. One of the most notable examples was the life and religious experience of Nakayama Miki (1798–1887). Miki, the wife of a farmer, had a series of possession experiences in which the god Tsukihi (literally, "Sun and Moon") instructed her to provide care for the poor, including faith healing and other rituals for curing disease and ensuring safe childbirth. Miki came to be seen as healer, and as a result, her popularity as a religious figure began to grow. The religion Tenrikyo (Teaching of the heavenly principle) was founded by Miki in 1838, teaching that human beings are children of God the Parent (Oyagami), a later appellation for Tsukihi.

READING

General

Ellwood and Pilgrim 1985; Yusa 2002; Earhart 2004; Kasahara (ed.) 2001; Kitagawa 1990; Kornicki and Mullen (eds.) 1996; Nishiyama 1997, 76–91: early modern Buddhist temples and Shinto shrines, especially focused on the city of Edo; Hori 1968: folk religion

Shinto

Reader 1998; Ono 1962; Muraoka 1964: Shinto thought and language; Philippi 1968: mythology in the *Kojiki*; Ellwood 1973: imperial enthronement rituals; Bocking 1997: glossary of Shinto terms, rituals, people, and places; Breen and Teeuwen (eds.) 2000: Shinto history

Buddhism

Tamura 2000; Kashiwara and Sonoda (eds.) 1994: biographies of important Japanese Buddhists; Pilgrim 1993: Buddhism and the Japanese arts; Kasahara 2001, 285–298: women in Japanese Buddhism; LaFleur 1983: Buddhism and Japanese literature

Christianity

Boxer 1951, Cooper (ed.) 1965; Elison 1973

7

PHILOSOPHY, EDUCATION, AND SCIENCE

PHILOSOPHY

Unless we make the claim that Buddhism is a philosophy, Japan did not have philosophical systems separate from explicit religious affiliations until the early modern period. The Edo period was a time of great intellectual change and development. New ways of thinking were derived from Neo-Confucian, Shinto, and Western sources. Within these three modes of thinking there was a great deal of variation between traditions and many instances of borrowing between traditions. It is Neo-Confucian thought, however, that framed much of the political, social, and moral discourse during the Edo period.

Neo-Confucian philosophy was first imported to Japan by Zen monks returning to Japan from study in China during the Muromachi period. By the Edo period, Neo-Confucian thought had become a significant influence on many aspects of Japanese culture, including political, moral, and family life. Chinese Neo-Confucianism was an elaboration on earlier Confucian thought. These earlier modes of Confucianism arrived in Japan sometime around the fifth or sixth century along with Buddhism and other aspects of Chinese culture. Although this earlier form of Confucianism impacted ideas about social relationships and education, it was not systematically studied as a particular school of thought.

Confucianism arose in China during the Warring States Period (475–221 B.C.E.), and offered a means of rectifying the harsh political realities and insecurity of a society in turmoil. Confucius looked out at his troubled world and proclaimed that one must emulate an ideal past age that once existed in China when people lived in harmony. For Confucius, cultivation of virtues such as filial piety and benevolence were the key to reinstituting this past age in the present. A central aspect of Confucian thought was the perception that there is a hierarchy of power and authority in the universe. For Confucius, heaven is above and the Earth is below.

This same hierarchy also can be seen at the social level. Confucianism posits the possibility of a harmonious society based on five human relationships: between lord and subject, father and son, husband and wife, older (brother) and younger (brother), and friend and friend (the only one characterized by mutuality). In each relationship, the former is superior and the latter subordinate, just as heaven (that is, the natural laws of the universe) is superior and Earth is subordinate. This was a rigid structure whereby one was always embedded in an ever-shifting set of unequal, hierarchical relations. Sometimes one was in the superior position, and sometimes in the subordinate position: the emperor is superior to his subjects; a child is subordinate to a parent. For Confucius, harmony exists in the world when people act in the appropriate manner given whatever hierarchical relationship they currently find themselves in. This hierarchy shifts from moment to moment as one goes in and out of different social situations. For Confucius, these relationships and their correct enactment formed the basis of morality and a harmonious society.

Although Confucianism did not include women among these five relationships, Confucianism taught that mothers must be honored in the household and may exert influence within the family. Women are expected, however, to be subordinate to their fathers until marriage, then to their husbands, and then to a son once he assumes his position as head of the household.

Confucianism shared with Daoism the idea that everything in the universe functions in accordance with the "way" (Chinese: *dao*), or in more Confucian terms, heaven (Chinese: *tian*). It is therefore a human being's responsibility to find a method to conform to and resonate with the "way," which would in turn bring peace and harmony into both one's immediate world and the world at large. Where Daoism and Confucianism differed, however, was the means by which one finds harmony with the *dao*. Daoism favored contemplation of the true nature of the *dao* as a way to understand how to live a harmonious life in accord with the natural rhythms of the universe. Confucianism, on the other hand, emphasized the "way" of social and political action with a great deal of importance placed on social hierarchy and the cultivation of personal values and virtues.

Neo-Confucianism is a general term that describes the revival of traditional Confucian thought that arose in China during the Song dynasty (960–1279). The philosophy had undergone various periods of change and development and became modernized to fit the needs of those living in Song-dynasty China. By fusing together elements of Daoism and Buddhism, Neo-Confucian thought attempted to create a philosophical and metaphysical explanation of the cosmos and of a human being's relationship to the cosmos. Neo-Confucianism taught that people can alter the state of a community and even the universe—positively or negatively—through transforming their own human nature by trying to attain the highest moral good.

In the Edo period, Neo-Confucianism was used, in part, to legitimize the workings of the state and government policies. It was patronized by the Tokugawa shogunate and the daimyo and became the prevailing ethical and philosophical doctrine adopted by the Edo government. Neo-Confucian scholars equated the moral and rational force in society and politics with the cosmos and its natural harmony. The government also officially patronized Neo-Confucian teachings because they provided the guidelines with which to maintain political order and stability. To preserve the utmost control, the shogunate promoted only one orthodox school of Neo-Confucianism, the Zhu Xi (Chu Hsi) school (see below), and banned all others as heterodox teachings.

Under the Tokugawa shogunate, the five relationships formed the basis of a strict system imposed on every aspect of society, while the educational system became saturated with Neo-Confucian moral and political ideas. By explicitly delineating every social relationship, from the elite rulers to the common people, a bureaucratic system was set in place that promised, in the ideal, a fair and just administration of government, and loyalty from the people in return. Not surprisingly this articulation of the relationship between ruler and ruled often failed to match the ideal.

Neo-Confucian Philosophical Concepts

There are a number of terms and concepts that regularly appear in the writings of Edo-period Neo-Confucians. It should be noted, though, that these terms might appear in earlier Confucian texts with different emphases. Similarly, contemporaneous Neo-Confucian schools did not always agree on the import or meaning of a particular term. Among the most important concepts are the following:

PRINCIPLE

In early Confucianism, the concept of principle (in Chinese, *li*; in Japanese, *ri*) referred primarily to propriety, that is, acting properly in accord with the way of heaven. In a limited sense, this meant acting in a moral and socially acceptable manner, and the translation of the term *ri* as ritual, propriety, or politeness reflects this meaning. But principle was not simply a social contract. Rather it was the notion that human relationships reflect the cosmic order of heaven above and Earth below. Thus, human relationships require different ways of acting depending on whether one is in the superior or inferior social position at any given moment. By acting properly, one contributes to the harmony of both the social world and of heaven.

In Neo-Confucian thought, especially as articulated by the Zhu Xi school, principle referred to the idea of a cosmic foundation to the universe. Principle is a universal regulating order that all things in the world are subject to and governed by. Principle is derived from the workings of heaven. Included in the concept of principle is the notion of both a natural law underlying all things in the world as well as a correct way for people to act that is in accord with principle.

VITAL FORCE

Vital force (Chinese: *qi*; Japanese: *ki*) was the counterpart of principle. It was the material basis of all things. While principle inhabited all things, animate and inanimate, it required vital force in order to have matter to embody. Form and matter were fully interrelated. In effect, things existed in the world as a result of the interaction of principle and vital force.

FILIAL PIETY

Filial piety (*ko*) was the idea that children owe a debt of gratitude to their parents for bringing them into the world and caring for them. Thus, children were to exhibit loyalty and obedience to their parents. In more concrete terms, this meant caring for one's parents once they became old and infirm, and, upon a parent's death, to engage in rituals of veneration that conferred the status of ancestor on the deceased. In China, the family was thought of as the basic unit of society and therefore filial piety was considered the foundation that made this social unit work properly. The Japanese also embraced this Confucian notion of filial piety but extended it to apply to the ideal of loyalty to one's lord. To be loyal was to be filial. As a result, filial piety also resonated with the warrior class and was a way to frame the lord-vassal relationship within the prevailing philosophical discourse of the Edo period.

LOYALTY

The Confucian value system places a strong emphasis on loyalty (*chu*), a concept closely related to filial piety. In medieval and early modern Japan, loyalty was especially associated with the reciprocal, but hierarchical, relationship between superior and inferior. A warrior, for instance, was obligated to serve his lord, even to the death, in exchange for the lord's patronage. In Japan, such loyalty was observed throughout both warrior culture and also in government which was organized along a series of hierarchical relationships up to the shogun, to whom loyalty was considered among the highest virtues.

BENEVOLENCE

Benevolence (*jin*) is a fundamental Confucian virtue that is concerned with the fundamentally relational and social nature of Confucian ethics and notions of government. Those who have cultivated benevolence express humanity and compassion through the way they treat other people. A person who has cultivated benevolence is able to act toward others in an altruistic way. The attainment of the virtue of benevolence is also considered transformative in the sense that one cannot be truly moral without it.

SUPERIOR PERSON

According to Confucian thought, the superior person (*kunshi*) is one who has attained the highest level of self-cultivation of Confucian values and lives in accordance with principle. Such a person has developed a heightened sense of awareness of propriety so that rules and codes of behavior are naturally enacted. The superior person thus provides a model of self-cultivation toward which others should strive.

SINCERITY

Sincerity (*makoto*; sometimes translated as "truthfulness") is a central Confucian value. The term refers to the idea of being true to one's nature. Both heaven and humanity have sincerity at their core, but human beings must cultivate sincerity to fully realize this virtue. Sincerity generally denotes the cultivation of a sincere mind and heart whereby one can endeavor to undergo self-purification and live harmoniously according to the way of heaven.

Edo-Period Philosophical Schools

Although Neo-Confucianism, especially the Zhu Xi school, represented the intellectual foundation for the Tokugawa shogunate, the Edo period was a time of vigorous philosophical speculation and debate. The following philosophical schools were among the most important.

SHUSHI SCHOOL

The Shushi school (Shushigaku), was based on the thought of the influential Chinese Confucian philosopher Zhu Xi (in Japanese, Shushi; 1130–1200). According to Zhu Xi's thought, reality consists of both principle and vital force. It is the interaction of these two that produces all things in the world, including human beings. For Zhu Xi, human beings have both an original nature, which is made up of nothing but principle and is solely good, and a nature that is the product of human interactions in the world, through which different kinds of vital force—some good, some evil—accumulates. Thus, it is possible for a person to fall away from the originally good nature. Because people interact with their environment differently, everyone possesses different kinds of vital force, which explains an individual's unique disposition. The focus of the Zhu Xi school was on the purification of vital force through self-cultivation by means of education, the study of principle, and introspection.

Although Zhu Xi's writings were transmitted to Japan in the Kamakura period, they did not have a significant impact at that time. During the Muromachi period, Zhu Xi's thought was studied by Zen monastics. However, it was not until the Tokugawa shogunate assumed power that Shushigaku became the official orthodoxy, providing specific guidance on both ethics and government. The philosophy legitimized the strict hierarchical social system advocated by the shogunate because it provided a rational order to society that the government could control. By 1790, only the Shushi school of Neo-Confucianism was formally sanctioned and all other philosophical schools were officially banned.

In the Edo period, the shogunate began to regard principle as a law with which to rule society and not just as a philosophical concept abstractly commenting on the nature of the ultimate good. If rulers enacted principle, that is, if they governed only through the ultimate good, then subjects would remain loyal and obedient. In the same way, the importance of loyalty began to take precedence over that of filial piety. Rather than the primacy of filial relations to parents and lord, there was an increasing emphasis on loyalty to institutions such as the shogunate or domain. Such a value shift provided the shogunate with the assurance of loyalty from its subjects.

YOMEI SCHOOL

The Yomei school (Yomeigaku) was a form of Neo-Confucianism based on the thought of Chinese philosopher Wang Yangming (1472–1529). Wang was born into a family of accomplished scholars and officials. After his own less-than-distinguished stint as a government bureaucrat, Wang resigned his position and took up the life of a world renunciant in order to study Daoist and Buddhist ideas. His experiences led him to formulate a new theory of Confucian learning that blended elements of Daoism and Buddhism with Neo-Confucianism.

In contrast to the Shushi school, where principle must be learned through outside sources, the main tenet of Yomeigaku was that everyone innately possesses principle, and therefore by reflecting on the mind instead of the external world, one can become a sage and live in harmony with the universe. Yomeigaku emphasizes the idea that everyone possesses the ability to become a sage and live according to the way of heaven. Knowledge of good is expressed through moral action and by extending compassion to oneself, to one's family, and one's community, continually radiating outward into the cosmos until one can show compassion for all living things.

Yomeigaku was introduced to Japan during the early Edo period by Nakae Toju (1608–48). He was the exemplar of the notion of filial piety, resigning a government position to take care of his aging mother. Nakae advocated that cultivating the mind was equally important for men and women, and that women should be given greater access to educational opportunities. Yomeigaku never received significant support from the government and was eventually banned in the late 18th century. By stressing the pursuit of personal betterment and by allowing for social equality of men and women, its doctrine threatened the ultimate supremacy of the shogunate with its stress on social hierarchy.

ANCIENT LEARNING SCHOOL

The Ancient Learning school (Kogaku) was an Edo-period movement that sought a return to the original teachings of Confucius. Confucian scholars such as Ito Jinsai (1627–1705), Yamaga Soko (1622–85), and Ogyu Sorai (1666–1728) strictly opposed Neo-Confucian thought, including both the Shushi and Yomei schools, on the basis that they had obscured the true and original teachings of Confucius. Although all three scholars developed their own systems of thought, they did share the view that there must be a return to the original teachings of Confucius, instead of reliance on Chinese commentaries and other later interpretations of Confucius, if the true import and meaning of the Confucian classic texts was to be understood.

Ito Jinsai was particularly concerned with ethics. He strongly opposed the regimented nature of Neo-Confucian thought and maintained that morality was not related to nature or the way of heaven. Although he believed that humans are inherently good, this good could only be nurtured and cultivated through actions and participation in society. He also emphasized loyalty and sincerity.

Yamaga Soko called attention to the ethical principles of Confucianism, focusing on the idle warriors of the Edo period. He was the first scholar to attempt the codification of a warrior ethic. His work, *The Way of the Warrior,* became the foundation for the development of the Bushido ideal later in the Edo period. He claimed that the warrior should serve as the paradigm of the virtue of duty to all levels of society.

Ogyu Sorai took a philological approach to the interpretation of the original Confucian texts. He claimed that the fundamental Confucian message became distorted when it was transmitted in a language other than the classical Chinese in which it was originally written. The Chinese of Confucius's day was considerably different from the Chinese in use by Edo-period Japanese Confucian scholars. He attempted to read and interpret the Confucian classics as the ancient Chinese would have done and concluded that the "way" was not innate like many scholars before him had claimed, but rather, was created and instituted by the ancient Chinese sages.

MITO SCHOOL

Scholars of the Mito school (Mitogaku), situated in the Mito domain, attempted to synthesize Confucian thought with native Japanese Shinto beliefs. The school is credited with compiling the monumental 243-volume *Dai Nihon shi* (History of great Japan), largely written by 1720 but not fully completed until the early 20th century. Some Mito school ideas were a threat to the shogunate, especially in the waning years of the Edo period, because they effectively opposed the rule of the shogun in favor of a return to rule by the emperor. According to Mito thought, the emperor stands at the top of a moral and political hierarchy, thus supplanting the shogun as head of the Japanese nation. This philosophy was used by pro-imperial advocates in making their case for a return to direct imperial rule that ultimately led to the downfall of the Tokugawa shogunate and the establishment of the Meiji Restoration in 1868.

HEART LEARNING SCHOOL

The Heart Learning school (Shingaku, or Sekimon Shingaku) is based on the teachings of Ishida Baigan (1685–1744). Baigan's thought is a moral philosophy synthesizing Zhu Xi Neo-Confucianism, as well as Zen Buddhist and Shinto ideas. Baigan was particularly interested in the problems of the merchant class, the lowest social class according to formal Edo ideology. To this end, Baigan promoted a merchant ethic called "the way of the townsman" (*chonindo*), and claimed that it was equal to the way of the samurai (Bushido). Morals, he argued, transcend the class system, and therefore the merchant could cultivate morality the same as the samurai. Among the virtues that Baigan promoted were honesty and frugality. If merchants cultivated these values, then the profit motive was in accord with the way of heaven.

SUIKA SHINTO

Suika Shinto is a synthesis of Shushi Neo-Confucianism and Shinto. Its founder, Yamazaki Ansai (1619–82), identified the "way" as being present in both Neo-Confucianism and in Shinto. He synthesized the teachings of Zhu Xi and placed a greater importance on loyalty to a ruler than on filial piety. He put the emperor at the top of the hierarchy rather than the shogun, and underscored the divinity of Japan as a nation, citing the unbroken line of emperors descended from the sun goddess, Amaterasu. Yamazaki's teachings allowed for the veneration of *kami* and other Shinto spiritual practices while Confucianism was restricted to governing and running the country. Along with Mitogaku, Suika Shinto played a role in the development of Shinto ideas in the Meiji period.

NATIONAL LEARNING SCHOOL

The National Learning school (Kokugaku) refers to a movement to rediscover a unique core of Japanese values and cultural sensibilities that, it was believed, had long been obscured by the importation of foreign religions and philosophies—including Buddhism and Confucianism—into Japan over the centuries. For Kokugaku scholars, the way back to a pristine and pure Japanese past was through the study of ancient texts such as the *Kojiki* (Record of ancient matters), Japan's earliest writing, and the *Manyoshu* (Collection of ten thousand leaves), the earliest collection of Japanese poems. By focusing on Japan's own literary tradition and classical mythology and poetry, its purpose was to rid Japanese culture of all foreign ideas and influences, whether Chinese or Western. Besides the attempt to reclaim Japan's past, one of the significant ramifications of National Learning was its use by those who wanted to return to imperial rule. The quest for a unique Japanese spirit—located in Shinto values—became, at least in the hands of some, closely aligned with a strong nationalist view of the Japanese state.

Although there are a number of philosophers associated with Kokugaku, Motoori Norinaga (1730–1801) and Hirata Atsutane (1776–1843) were particularly significant thinkers within this movement. Norinaga took a philological approach to the study of Japanese language and literature. He spent 30 years writing the *Kojikiden*, his commentary on the *Kojiki*, and systematically attempted to strip all non-Japanese notions, such as Confucianism, Buddhism, and other Chinese ideas, from this work. In his quest to locate a pure Japanese character and sensibility untainted by foreign influence, he applied these same philological methods to the examination of other ancient and classical writings such as the poetry of the *Manyoshu* and the narrative of the *Tale of Genji*. His studies of classical Japanese literature convinced him that the concept of *mono no aware*, the pathos of things, was central to a pure Japanese sensibility that valued the ability to truly feel human emotion. For Norinaga, not only was literature a way to discover the pathos of things, but reverence for the *kami* as a force of nature was central to triggering such a response. He criticized the rational and abstract views of Confucianism and Buddhism, claiming that they promote ideals impossible to attain and do not allow for the coexistence of good and evil as it is expressed in texts like the *Kojiki*.

Hirata Atsutane's National Learning movement was known as Fukko Shinto (return to ancient Shinto), which sought to reclaim a pristine Shinto purged of foreign, and especially Buddhist and Confucian, ideas. He maintained that the Age of the Gods was a paradigm for how to live in the present, and that the Ancient Way (Kodo) must be reclaimed

so the pure Japanese spirit could be actualized in the present. This meant that only by emulating the gods as described in the *Kojiki* could one understand Japan's ancient and sacred past. Atsutane claimed that Confucianism and Buddhism were false because foreign teachings corrupt the purity of the Ancient Way. With Atsutane, Kokugaku took on a decidedly nationalist flavor, especially in his notion that Shinto was superior to the ways of action and thought of all other cultures.

EDUCATION

Education in the Medieval Period

Prior to the start of the medieval period, education had been mostly confined to aristocrats and Buddhist monastics. However, with the rise of the military class at the beginning of the Kamakura period, education also spread to wealthy samurai. Samurai began to educate their children in the practical matters of warrior life, including such things as proper lord-retainer relations and rules for the inheritance of property. With the appearance and dissemination of popular Buddhism in the medieval period, education began to spread slowly to the larger nonelite population. Nevertheless, during the medieval period, the great majority of the population was illiterate. Lords who were not able to read and write would often seek assistance from literate Buddhist monks when, for instance, they needed to prepare formal documents for some bureaucratic purpose.

There was one particularly notable educational institution during the medieval period. The Ashikaga School (Ashikaga Gakko) was established in 1439 by Uesugi Norizane (1410–66), a high-ranking samurai, who donated books and named a Buddhist priest as its first administrator. Though the school, connected with the Ashikaga family, had origins dating back to prior centuries, it was not until the 15th century that it formally became a school with a curriculum centered on Confucian philosophy and military strategy. By 1550, the school enrolled 3,000 students from all over Japan. The school also attracted the attention of Catholic missionary Francis Xavier who, in 1549, expressed his admiration for the quality of the education obtained there. The school declined during the Edo period.

There were other contributions to education in the medieval period but they were neither widespread nor systematic. For instance, in the 16th century, Christian missionaries started schools to provide general education. Temple schools (*terakoya*), which became important in the early modern period, had their start around the same time. These schools, located at Buddhist temples, were attended by the children of samurai and wealthy peasants. Finally, libraries were founded by elite warrior families that collected both Chinese and Japanese texts and became centers of learning. One of the most notable was the Kanazawa Library (Kanazawa Bunko) that was founded in 1275 by Hojo Sanetoki, reflecting his interest in scholarship and learning. Besides the family, the library collection was available to scholars and priests.

Education in the Early Modern Period

In contrast to the medieval period, education became widely diffused over the course of the early modern period. Throughout the early modern period, the Tokugawa shogunate advocated the importance of learning and was particularly interested in promoting education based on the Neo-Confucian philosophy of Zhu Xi (in Japanese, Shushi) that eventually became the orthodox ideology of the shogunate.

Formal schooling was reserved for samurai and their children well into the 18th century. Edo-period education for those of the samurai class typically included learning to read and write both Japanese and Chinese, Neo-Confucian and other Chinese curricular topics, and military training—all matters deemed important to those of the samurai class, and especially males. Among the Neo-Confucian values learned were notions of loyalty to one's lord and

devotion to one's parents. One of the ways that samurai children were trained in Neo-Confucian values was through the use of readers that included excerpts from the Confucian classics. Not only did samurai children learn to read from such books, but Neo-Confucian values were inculcated in them as a result of engaging with such material.

Education for commoners during the Edo period, especially at the start of the early modern period, was not promoted by the shogunate, but neither was it forbidden. In discussing commoner education, it should be noted that education for commoners typically meant urban commoners with wealth, especially in the earlier half of the Edo period. While at least some shogunal authorities viewed commoner education, especially reading and writing, as an important tool for gaining assent for both Neo-Confucian values in general and laws in particular, literacy was not actively promoted by the shogunal authorities. Thus, the encouragement of educational opportunities for urban commoners came from this social class itself. Many from the merchant class, for instance, realized the significance to business success of being able to read and write. Besides this practical aspect to education, it also decreased at least one aspect of the class difference between warriors and commoners. By the 1750s, urban schools were attended by the children of many urban commoners.

Education in the Edo period spread through most segments of the population, resulting in a rise in literacy, a significant change from the educational situation in the medieval period. At the start of the Edo period, very few people were literate and there were very few schools. It is estimated that by 1700, most samurai were literate, even if they were not otherwise well educated. By the end of the period, it is estimated that 40 percent of the Japanese population could read and write.

As more and more schools were established, literacy spread beyond the warrior classes to include large numbers of the commoner population. Although much of the literacy among commoners was especially evident in the larger cities such as Edo and Osaka, the rise of literacy in rural areas is attested to by the increasing amount of bureaucratic and commercial documents found in town and village records of the Edo period. Overall, this dramatic rise in literacy during the Edo period impacted society in many ways, including the administration of government and the spread of trade and commerce, both of which required written records to fully function. Literacy also impacted the development of popular literary forms. Popular literature, and the demand for it, in turn spurred development of publishing that had become a significant industry by the end of the Edo period.

Edo-Period Schools

The spread in literacy was made possible in large part by the increase in the number and kind of schools that were established over the course of the Edo period. At the beginning of the Edo period, very few schools existed. By the end of the period, numerous schools of different types were thriving. The shogunate founded schools to train government bureaucrats, but other schools were also established, including domain schools, temple schools, and private schools. There were also more specialized schools that taught medicine, Dutch and Western learning, accounting, and other skills. According to estimates, at the end of the Edo period 43 percent of boys and 10 percent of girls attended school.

GOVERNMENT SCHOOLS

The Tokugawa shogunate played an important role in promoting the necessity of education during the Edo period. The government established schools to promote Neo-Confucian learning generally and to train government bureaucrats more specifically. These school became models for similar schools set up locally by domain leaders to educate the children of their warriors.

The most important of all government schools was the one known as Shoheiko (or Shoheizaka Gakumonjo). It was closely associated with Zhu Xi Neo-Confucianism and became the shogunate's official academy for training, among others, government administrators and officials, and Neo-Confucian scholars. Although the school's title, Shoheiko, was not used until 1797, its origins date to 1630. Toku-

gawa Iemitsu, the third Tokugawa shogun, became a proponent of Zhu Xi Neo-Confucianism under the influence of his Neo-Confucian adviser, Hayashi Razan (1583–1657). In 1630, at Razan's urging, Iemitsu provided him with the resources necessary to establish a school to teach Zhu Xi's philosophy to future shogunal bureaucrats and domain officials. Located in Edo, the school also included a library. It was not until 1797, seven years after the shogunate decreed Zhu Xi Neo-Confucianism the official state orthodoxy, that the Shoheiko assumed its status as the shogunate's leading educational institution. Part of the importance of the Shoheiko was that it trained students to pass exams that enabled them to assume government positions.

DOMAIN SCHOOLS

Domain schools (hanko) were institutions established by domain authorities to educate samurai children. These schools were headed by Neo-Confucian scholars and focused on teaching the Confucian classics with an emphasis on developing the samurai child into a moral human being. A domain school education also included training in military arts, reading and writing in both Chinese and Japanese, and other aspects of being a cultivated Neo-Confucian. Samurai children were expected to attend such schools to receive the orthodox training required of a samurai and a domain administrator.

Although government schools were often the model for domain schools, domains had a fair amount of autonomy in deciding the particular curriculum their schools would offer. In general, though, learning was based on memorization of Chinese texts. Instruction also differed depending on the status of a student's family. It was often the case that status was treated as more important than ability.

Later in the Edo period, domain schools expanded their enrollment and curriculum by allowing children of other social ranks to attend and by teaching the Japanese classics and aspects of Western learning such as mathematics, astronomy, military science, and ballistics. Forty domain schools existed before 1750, but by the end of the Edo period, some 225 schools had been established.

TEMPLE SCHOOLS

Despite the term, temple schools (*terakoya*) did not have any necessary connection to Buddhism or Buddhist teachings, though some schools were situated on temple grounds. In general, however, *terakoya* refers to small, local schools that were run out of a home or shop. These temple schools afforded a way for their teachers to make a living. Instruction at these schools was often provided by just one teacher, or perhaps by a married couple. It is estimated that 33 percent of the temple schoolteachers were women.

Temple schools were institutions for commoners, though samurai children might also attend. Usually samurai and commoner children were educated together. By the end of the Edo period, tens of thousands of temple schools operated throughout Japan. Although they are believed to have existed before 1700, the first literary reference to *terakoya* was not made until 1716.

These schools taught a curriculum that included reading, writing, and arithmetic, as well as practical and vocational skills. They also placed a great deal of importance on learning basic Neo-Confucian moral tenets. This curriculum was designed, in part, to give students the skills needed to take advantage of new opportunities that Edo-period urbanization offered.

PRIVATE SCHOOLS

Private schools (*shijuku*) were established throughout Japan during the early modern period. Before 1750 only 19 private schools existed in Japan. That number rose to more than 1,000 by the end of the Edo period. In the first half of the early modern period, private schools were typically found in larger cities such as Edo and Osaka. However, by the later half of the early modern period, private schools appeared even in rural locations. Regardless of location, they were often operated out of the teacher's home. As a result, private schools assumed many different teaching styles and curriculums. These schools were not under the immediate control or authority of the shogunate and they had no common administrative structure or curriculum. Many private schools were run in such a way that curriculum might change to suit the times and prevailing interests of the student body. This kind of flexibility was not available to government and domain schools with their set curriculum, largely samurai constituency, and the mandate to train government bureaucrats.

One benefit, intended or not, for private schools in not receiving funding from the shogunate was that they were given relative freedom to teach any number of subjects that would not have been included in a government-sponsored school, such as Shoheiko, or at domain schools.

Private schools were usually founded by scholars with a particular expertise or academic interest. Thus many different subjects were taught, though the study of Confucian and other Chinese texts was a typical foundation. Like other Edo-period schools, students learned to read and write both Japanese and Chinese. Other subjects were taught at the discretion and interests of a school's teacher. In addition to the subjects already mentioned, others might include Dutch and Western studies, Japanese literature, medicine, and accounting. Often, students would graduate from a private school as advocates of the particular social and political philosophy espoused by their teacher.

Because of the exclusive nature of domain schools in both curriculum and samurai clientele, private schools were established to teach commoners disenfranchised from the domain school system. Although private schools might also enroll samurai, they were particularly important to commoners. Further, while private schools might teach Neo-Confucian subjects, they also provided instruction in subjects not covered by domain schools. Some private schools, for example, offered instruction in Dutch or Western learning (discussed in more detail below).

Students might travel long distances to attend the private school that taught a curriculum they wanted to take. Students might also attend more than one private school. In the early Edo period, private schools were often attended by children—usually male—of a variety of social classes, including samurai or wealthy farmers and merchants, or aristocrats. By the end of the Edo period, private schools were attended by students from a broader socioeconomic range, and included females. The only impediment was a lack of funds to pay tuition.

Private schools were important to the development of Dutch and Western studies. The terms Dutch learning (*rangaku*) and Western learning (*yogaku*) refer to study of European science, medicine, and military technology. Although language, art, and other topics were also studied, of particular importance were the sciences. Because of the reliance on the use of Dutch for these studies, during the Edo period itself the term *Dutch learning* was often used to describe this form of study. This usage reflected the Dutch presence at Dejima during the time of national isolation when the Tokugawa shogunate banned interaction with all other European countries. As a result, the first contact with Western knowledge came through the Dutch, often as a result of Japanese translations of Dutch texts. As this knowledge spread, it became the subject of the curriculum of some private schools. It was only toward the end of the Edo period that the term *Western learning* was regularly utilized, reflecting the late Edo interactions with other Western nations, including the United States, England, and France.

Women's education was also impacted by private schools. The education of girls and young women during the medieval period was mostly confined to the aristocratic and wealthy warrior classes. They learned to read and write, and some also learned etiquette and skills that would prepare them for marriage. The expansion of education in the Edo period included even commoner girls. Further opportunities for the education of women arose with the development of private schools, where women sometimes served as teachers. While preparing girls for marriage remained a significant reason for parents to want their daughters to attend school, education was, by the end of the Edo period, a common activity for girls of all classes.

Like Edo-period boy's education, the curriculum for girls centered on reading and writing. In addition to basic literacy skills, girls—whether warrior-class or commoner—were also taught Neo-Confucian moral values. Texts expounding particular moral virtues for women, such as the famous *Great Learning for Women* (*Onna daigaku*; early 18th century), taught girls to respect their parents and husband, to avoid vices like gossip and extravagance, and to take care of their health. Interestingly, texts that on the one hand taught the subservience of women to men at the same time provided women with literacy skills that placed them on a more equal educational level with men.

SCIENCE

In medieval and early modern Japan, the natural sciences—including such disciplines as medicine, mathematics, and astronomy—were largely influenced by Chinese systems of science and classification of the natural world. From the mid-16th century, Japanese interactions with Western missionaries and traders provided exposure to European science and medical practices. Japan did not, however, simply borrow science and medicine from foreign sources. Japanese innovators transformed these borrowed systems to suit Japanese needs and interests. Among scientific fields in early modern Japan, special attention was given to medicine, astronomy, and mathematics.

In the medieval period, at least through the 15th century, science understood as empirical observation of the natural world was almost entirely lacking. The medieval world was largely caught between older assumptions based on Chinese cosmological ideas about balance and harmony and new ways of scientific thinking from renewed contacts with China and from interactions with European missionaries and traders.

In the medieval period Buddhist views were also influential in how people thought about the natural world and reasons why events occur as they do. Natural occurrences, whether earthquakes, solar eclipses, famine, or epidemic, were often interpreted from the Buddhist perspective of karmic consequence or from a more general perspective that reflected both Chinese and native Shinto sensibilities about the harmony—or its lack—operating at any moment. Lack of harmony meant the possibility of the world falling into disorder. Natural disasters were one way that one came to know of this disorder. Such medieval perspectives allowed for only the most general of predictive capabilities about the occurrence of natural phenomena. In any event, the notion of empirical measurement or experimentation that allowed knowledge and understanding of the natural world was not a part of the medieval Japanese mindset.

One way notions of harmony and karmic consequence played out in the medieval period was in terms of medical practice and ideas about the etiology of disease. Medical treatments might include exorcism of an angry spirit wreaking havoc on the body of its victim, the recitation of sutras to neutralize the deleterious action that had caused a disease, or medications intended to put the body back in harmony with its environment. In all of these instances, the functioning of the body's organs was deemed irrelevant to the underlying idea that one's vital force was driving health and sickness.

By the end of the 16th century, these traditional ideas about the natural world were beginning to undergo a significant transformation because of new contacts with China that led to a Japanese interest in Neo-Confucianism and because of encounters with Western science that accompanied European missionary and trade activity. As a result, the early modern period was a time of great intellectual and scholarly ferment, a time in which, for instance, Western taxonomic systems and other scientific ways of thinking came to impact Japan. Although the Tokugawa shogunate imposed a policy of national isolation, the introduction of Western science and medicine through interaction with the Dutch at Dejima and publication of books on Chinese science and other fields ensured that new ways of thinking about the world continued despite national policy. The seclusion policy only permitted contact with Dutch and Chinese traders, so it was largely through Dutch that the Japanese gained knowledge of Western science and medicine.

Although Chinese scientific and medical ideas were important in early modern Japan (and remain so today), it was interactions with the Dutch after Japan's formal seclusion that marked the start of investigations of the natural world within a Western scientific paradigm. Because of the contact with the Dutch, the Dutch language became the medium through which new Western scientific and medical knowledge were disseminated. Translations of Dutch scientific and medical books into Japanese led

to the advancement of Japanese scientific thinking and opened up whole new ways to think about the natural world, including anatomy, astronomy, and geography.

There were many Japanese scientists and doctors who embraced Western learning. Among them were Nishikawa Joken (1648–1724), a scholar of astronomy and Confucianism, who wrote books on astronomy and geography and who was sought out by the shogunate for his knowledge of things Western. Similarly, Arai Hakuseki (1657–1725), a Confucian scholar and shogunal adviser, studied geography and wrote a book on Western geography.

It was not just scientists, though, who found value in Western learning. The eighth Tokugawa shogun, Yoshimune (1684–1751), seeking to increase agricultural production, allowed Chinese books that treated various Western subjects to be imported to Japan. Previously, all foreign books had been banned under the national isolation policy. Yoshimune also ordered the study of Dutch. Not surprisingly, there was also deep interest in military technology, especially naval ships and weaponry.

Medicine

Japanese medicine in the medieval and early modern periods was the site of multiple and conflicting medical understandings of the human body and of its diseases and treatment. These different perspectives—especially, Buddhist, Chinese, and Western—do not reflect some inevitable movement from a less sophisticated understanding of medical science to a more sophisticated (Western) one. Rather, these different medical views often coexisted, particularly in the early modern period. Even today, for instance, traditional Chinese medicine and Western medicine coexist in Japan. While contemporary Westerners might view Chinese medicine as "alternative medicine" in a Western biomedical context, in medieval and early modern Japan there was nothing alternative about Chinese medical theory and practice. Rather, it constituted the mainstream view.

During the medieval and early modern periods, Japanese medicine was shaped by a number of influences. Native sources suggested ritual causes for disease, such as contact with impurity or punishment by irate deities. Evidence for these views derives from the earliest extant Japanese texts, such as the *Kojiki* (Record of ancient matters, 712) and the *Nihon shoki* (*Chronicle of Japan*, 720), as well as from subsequent literature, both nonfiction and fiction. Similarly, early Japanese views of disease prescribed religious rituals and herbal medicine as the cure for disease. Buddhist ideas also impacted Japanese perspectives on the etiology of disease and the possibilities for cures.

The two most important influences during the medieval and early modern periods were Chinese medicine and, eventually, Western medicine. For instance, the *Ishimpo* (Methods at the heart of medicine), composed in 982 by Tamba Yasuyori (912–995), is Japan's oldest extant medical text and displays the influence of Chinese medicine and medical treatises on Japan's understanding of medicine. Its influence lasted into the medieval and early modern periods. Contacts with the West starting in the mid-16th century gradually eroded the primacy of Chinese medical practices and introduced new, Western ways of understanding and treating disease.

Although the Japanese embraced different medical traditions, Chinese and Western medical procedures were used to treat certain common and widespread diseases. Aside from wounds resulting from accidents and warfare, Japanese physicians were confronted with a number of diseases. There are difficulties, however, in determining today exactly what these past diseases may have been. This is due in part to the ways in which Chinese and Western medicine understood, described, diagnosed, and treated these diseases. Diseases known to have afflicted the Japanese include leprosy, smallpox, syphilis, malaria, tuberculosis, influenza, and measles.

BUDDHIST MEDICINE

In the Kamakura period, as Buddhism spread throughout Japan, its perspectives on disease and treatment had a large impact on Japanese medical practice. Priests served as doctors, disseminating and applying knowledge about medicinal herbs and other remedies. In this sense, the medical arts were viewed as an important aspect of their religious activities. One way in which medieval Buddhists made sense of disease was through the concept of karmic disease (*gobyo*). According to this view, immoral acts and transgressions performed in a past life became manifest in the present life as disease. Thus, disease was the direct outcome of negative karmic acts.

Buddhist monks, besides ministering to the sick, also compiled treatises on medicine. The Zen monk Eisai (1141–1215), famous as the founder of Rinzai Zen and a promoter of green tea drinking for medicinal purposes, also wrote a medical book, the *Kissa yojoki* (Drink tea and prolong life, 1214). The Buddhist monk and physician Kajiwara Shozen (1266–1337) is noted for two volumes *Ton'isho* (Jottings on medicine, 1303) and *Man'anpo* (Prescriptions for felicity, 1327) that detailed his understanding of Chinese medicine and anatomy. The *Ton'isho* makes use of the idea that alimentary care—proper food and nutrition—had healing properties. A similar idea about the medicinal properties of certain foods is found in a medical text by the Zen monk Yurin (died 1410).

Buddhists were also known for their aid to the sick and indigent. The Buddhist priest Ninsho (1217–1303), for instance, was noted for the assistance he provided to those who were homeless and impoverished. He founded two refuge centers dedicated to ministering to the sick and poor, and worked on behalf of lepers.

CHINESE MEDICINE

Chinese medical theory and practice (in Japanese, *kampo*) was central to much of medieval and early modern medicine. It provided models for such things as the balance of vital force (Chinese: *qi*; Japanese: *ki*) in the human body, the cause of disease, and the medicinal properties of plants and other natural materials. Chinese medicine was introduced to Japan as early as the sixth century, quickly influencing Japanese medical perspectives. It was practiced with little modification until the late medieval period. In the Heian period, the aristocratic court physician Tamba Yasuyori (912–995) wrote the *Ishimpo* (Methods at the heart of medicine, 984), the oldest extant Japanese medical text that compiled Chinese medical treatises into 30 volumes. Among the topics explored in the *Ishimpo* were diseases and their origins and treatments.

From the Muromachi period, a medical perspective blending Neo-Confucianism and Chinese medicine—known as the Li-Zhu school—began to attract the interest of Japanese medical practitioners. Japanese interest was partly a result of the interest taken by Japanese Zen monks in Chinese Neo-Confucian ideas, such as vital force and principle (Chinese: *li*; Japanese: *ri*), that were a theoretical foundation to Li-Zhu medicine.

The Li-Zhu school derived its name from two Yuan-dynasty (1279–1368) Chinese physicians, Li Dongyuan and Zhu Danxi. This school viewed disease as the direct consequence of a poor lifestyle— that is, one that disregarded Neo-Confucian moral injunctions—and vital force imbalances. Treatment consisted of combinations of herbal medicine, acupuncture, and moxibustion.

Li-Zhu school medicine was founded in Japan during the Muromachi period by the physician Tashiro Sanki (1465–1537). After studying medicine in China for 12 years, he returned to Japan with Li-Zhu school medical theory and practice. He used Li-Zhu medical procedures to treat both samurai and commoners. It was under the direction of Sanki's disciple, Manase Dosan (1507–94), that Li-Zhu school medicine became established as an orthodox approach to medical theory and practice. Dosan was both a physician to the imperial family and a prominent teacher. He trained doctors in Li-Zhu medical theory and practice at his private medical school. He also wrote medical texts, including *Keitekishu* (A guide to medical practice, 1574) that viewed Chinese medicine from the perspective of Japanese values and sensibilities. The lineage of physicians that followed Dosan gained support from and served high-ranking warriors and members of the Tokugawa shogunate.

One of the great contributions made by Dosan and his followers to the Japanese practice of Chinese medicine was to establish standard procedures for diagnosing disease. According to these procedures, there were four observations that a physician needed to make to accurately assess a patient's disease: 1) visual observation, especially of such things as skin color, hair condition, feces, and urine; 2) audi-

tory observation of such things as coughs and verbal responses made to pain when the patient was touched, and olfactory observation of patient odors; 3) observation of patient responses to physician questions concerning such things as appetite and emotional state; and 4) observation of pulse and abdomen through touching the body in various ways.

The Li-Zhu school in Japan came to be called the School of Latter-Day Medicine (Goseiho) in reference to its connections with Neo-Confucianism (a latter-day Confucianism). It remained an important Chinese medical system throughout the early modern period, but there was one important competing school of Chinese medicine that developed starting at the end of the 17th century. The School of Ancient Medicine (Koiho), as this movement was called, established itself as an alternative to the School of Latter-Day Medicine. Although the Latter-Day School had transformed aspects of Chinese medicine in accord with Japanese views and sensibilities, the medical approach of the School of Ancient Medicine resulted in a more thoroughgoing Japanese transformation of Chinese medicine.

A scholarly trend in the late 17th century had a significant impact on the development of the School of Ancient Medicine. Confucian scholars increasingly rejected Neo-Confucian interpretations of the Confucian classics in favor of a direct reading of the ancient texts. This same trend occurred in medical circles where Neo-Confucian–influenced Li-Zhu interpretations of ancient Chinese medical texts were dismissed and direct readings of these texts were initiated. Thus, the School of Ancient Medicine derived its name from the idea of returning directly to the ancient sources of medical theory and practice. To this end, the School of Ancient Medicine based its medical perspective on a Chinese medical text dating back to the Han dynasty (206 B.C.E.–220 C.E.). This text, *Shang han za bing lun* (Essay on typhoid and miscellaneous diseases), was concerned with symptoms and their treatments based on the observations of physicians with long experience in treating patients.

There were several prominent physicians associated with the theoretical and practical foundations of the School of Ancient Medicine, but they did not always agree on how to interpret ancient Chinese medical texts or how to put theoretical understanding into actual medical practice. Among the most important doctors of the School of Ancient Medicine were Goto Konzan (1659–1733), Yoshimasu Todo (1702–73), and Yamawaki Toyo (1705–62).

Goto Konzan (1659–1733) viewed the cause of disease from the perspective of vital force. He believed that when vital force becomes congested or congealed in the body, disease occurs. He derived this view from the metaphysical view that just as vital force infused the universe and maintained balance and harmony, so did it infuse the body and create health. Konzan treated the congestion of vital force with moxa therapy (see below) and herbal medicine.

Yoshimasu Todo (1702–73) placed great importance on the observation of bodily symptoms in diagnosing and treating disease. He carried out empirical research that he believed proved the efficacy of medical treatments prescribed in ancient Chinese medical texts. Todo viewed all diseases as caused by a single poison that created different symptoms depending on its location in the body. He treated these poison-caused illnesses with herbal and other medicines.

Yamawaki Toyo (1705–62) represents a bridge between Chinese and Western medicine as practiced in Japan. Although he administered Chinese medicine as an imperial court physician, he doubted the traditional Chinese view of the structure of the human anatomy. According to this traditional anatomical view, the human body was conceptualized, without any empirical or visual verification, as encompassing five organs and six viscera that interacted with each other and with the meridians, paths along the body through which vital force flowed. In turn, the five organs corresponded to traditional Chinese views of the five elements: heart/fire, lungs/metal, kidneys/water, liver/wood, and spleen/earth. The organs themselves were not a site of treatment in traditional Chinese medicine, that is, disease was not caused by malfunctioning organs. Rather, this anatomical view related to the idea that disease was caused by imbalances in and disruptions to vital force and the five elements.

Toyo's doubts about the traditional view of human anatomy came about in part because of an anatomical description in one of the Chinese classics that asserted that the body contains nine organs. To determine which anatomical view was correct, Toyo

received permission to dissect a human body, which he did in 1754. In 1759, Toyo presented the results of his observations in a publication entitled *Zoshi* (Anatomical record). Although Toyo's findings contradicted the traditional view, the five organs and six viscera theory remained orthodox. The significance of Toyo's experimentation was that it set in motion the idea of performing empirical observations in a medical setting through dissection and other means, a methodology that was much more akin to Western medicine than to Chinese.

Some Forms of Treatment in Chinese Medicine

Chinese medicine is concerned with the patient as a whole person, not simply as a set of isolated, discrete organs and body parts. For this reason, practitioners of Chinese medicine did not think in terms of medical or disease specialization, but rather in terms of treating the whole patient and to restore health generally. Diseases were diagnosed through a reading of symptoms (*sho*).

Chinese medicine treated diseases and symptoms in a variety of ways. Medications, prepared from a wide variety of plants, animal parts, and other natural materials such as minerals, were one such form of treatment. They were administered on the basis of the symptoms presented by the patient and as observed by the physician. This was the same diagnosis system that Manase Dosan had systematized in the late medieval period (see above). Appropriate medicine was then administered on the basis of the results of this diagnosis.

Physicians usually grew medicinal plants and herbs themselves, and then prepared the plant material for ingestion, often by drying the medicine into powder form. Medications were prepared according to different formulae used to treat specific diseases or symptoms. Ingredients were typically mixed together to derive the desired medical result. Although there were guides to formulas for various medications, different doctors often had their own favorite formulas for treating a particular illness. When traveling, doctors often carried medicines with them in case they should be needed by those the physician chanced to meet along the way.

Another common treatment was acupuncture (*hari*). In this procedure, used both for treating specific diseases and as a preventative to health problems, thin silver needles were slowly inserted into various locations on the body of the patient. In keeping with the idea that a healthy body was a body in balance, the needles were used to restore the natural balance of the human body after disease had caused an imbalance.

A related treatment, and one sometimes used in conjunction with acupuncture, was moxibustion, or moxa (*kyu*). Moxa was a term derived from the word *mogusa*, which is the Japanese name for the artemisia plant. This procedure requires the physician to place small cones of moxa directly on the patient's skin and then to burn the cone so that the skin is heated. This treatment was used when it was diagnosed that a patient had a blockage of the vital force believed to circulate throughout the body, which, if impeded, would cause disease symptoms. Burning the moxa was thought to remove the obstruction and allow energy to once again flow properly in the body. There was a variation of this treatment in which the moxa was placed on the end of an acupuncture needle and ignited, the heat traveling down the needle and releasing the energy in that manner.

There was also a treatment that involved finger pressure (shiatsu) applied to specific locations on the body. Doing so was another way to keep the patient's energy flowing properly through the body. It was believed that energy flowed along specific paths called meridians, and finger pressure was a means to restore balance and flow to the energy in a body that had experienced the imbalancing influence of disease. Similarly, massage (*amma*) was also one of the Chinese medical practitioner's treatment set. In the Edo period, massage therapy was often administered by blind practitioners (also referred to as *amma*).

WESTERN MEDICINE

Western medicine, referred to in the late medieval period as "Southern Barbarian" (*namban*) medicine, was first introduced to Japan in the 16th century along with other aspects of Western culture that accompanied European missionaries. One item of material culture that Europeans brought with them was firearms. These soon became a part of the weaponry available to Japanese warriors. The use of firearms also resulted in wounds that were not efficiently treated by traditional Chinese medicine. Thus, European surgical methods for removing and treating bullet wounds were adopted. Beyond this, however, Western medicine was limited in its appeal to Japanese physicians. It should be noted that in this period transmission of medical knowledge worked both ways: Europeans were interested in what they could learn from traditional Chinese medicine.

After the missionaries were expelled from Japan and the shogunate instituted the national seclusion policy, it was only Dutch traders, among Europeans, who were allowed a minimal presence in Japan. Japanese first began in-depth consideration of Western medical practices through medical texts written in European languages, especially Dutch, and through the medical knowledge of physicians in service to the Dutch East India Company enclave on the island of Dejima in Nagasaki harbor. It was largely from these physicians and from Western medical books that the Japanese learned Western medical theory and practice, including surgical techniques, anatomy, the smallpox vaccination, and such medical equipment as the stethoscope.

Among the most influential of these physicians was Caspar Schambergen (1623–1706) who arrived in Japan in 1649. The following year, he accompanied the head of the Dutch East India Company to Edo for an audience with shogunate authorities. At the request of the shogun, Schambergen remained in Edo for several months to instruct shogunate physicians in Western surgical procedures and practices. In similar fashion, Engelbert Kaempfer (1651–1716), a German physician who arrived in Nagasaki in 1690 to serve as a physician to the Dutch East India Company, also traveled to Edo and consulted with the shogunate's doctors about Western medicine.

The Swedish physician Carl Peter Thunberg (1743–1828) was also a botanist who had studied with the creator of the modern plant classification system, Carolus Linnaeus (1707–78). Upon his arrival in Japan in 1775 as a doctor to the Dutch East India Company, he practiced medicine and also conducted an extensive yearlong study of Japanese flora. He collected some 800 botanical specimens and wrote a book on this subject, the *Flora Japonica* (1784).

Philipp Franz von Siebold (1796–1866) was a German physician for the Dutch East India Company, serving at Dejima from 1823 to 1829 and again from 1859 to 1861. In addition to imparting his medical expertise, he was also a student of Japanese culture providing knowledge of Japan to Europe.

For Western medicine to gain a foothold in Japan, it required acknowledgment of the possibility that traditional medicine might not be the last word in medical understanding and treatment. This did not occur in Japan until the 18th century as a result of the increasing influence of Western medical texts that were first translated into Japanese at this time.

Western medicine presented challenges to traditional Chinese medicine. For instance, Western emphasis on understanding the anatomy of the human body was largely ignored in traditional Chinese medicine. The Chinese view was that the living person was animated by a vital force known as *ki* (in Chinese, *qi*). A corpse was a body devoid of vital force. Performing dissections to understand the structures and interrelations of internal organs, musculature, and bones was considered an empty exercise. However, doubt about this traditional view grew as it became evident that traditional Chinese anatomical charts were faulty when compared to the evidence that an autopsy provided.

For some Japanese doctors, the discrepancy between the traditional view and empirical evidence became glaringly obvious in the latter half of the 18th century. In 1771, the Japanese physicians Sugita Gempaku (1733–1817), Maeno Ryotaku (1723–1803), and Nakagawa Jun'an (1739–86) observed the dissection of the corpse of an executed criminal. The three physicians were familiar with the Dutch translation of a German anatomy book and found that the anatomical features they observed at the dissection closely paralleled the anatomical charts and descriptions in the anatomy text. For these doctors, a new way of seeing and understanding the human body was revealed. As a result of this experience, Sugita and others resolved to translate the Dutch anatomy text, *Ontleedkundige Tafelen* (Illustrated anatomy), originally written in German by the physician Johann Adam Kulmus (1689–1745), in order to raise the level of Japanese medical knowledge. Their translation, *Kaitai shinsho* (New book of anatomy, 1774), marked the first translation into Japanese of a complete Western medical text.

The publication of *Kaitai shinsho* inaugurated the study of Dutch medicine (*rampo*) in Japan, as well as other Western medical and scientific disciplines. By the early 1800s, Japanese physicians increasingly studied Western medicine from the physicians assigned to the Dutch East India Company. Another result was a new interest in translating other Western medical and scientific texts into Japanese. Notable in this regard was the Udagawa family who, over the course of three generations, were strong supporters of Western scientific knowledge and who were active in the translation of Western texts.

A further consequence of this incursion of Western medical notions into Japanese medicine was that it created interest in studying affiliated areas of Western science critical to understanding European medical perspectives. Subjects such as biology and chemistry were embraced by those Japanese wishing to understand Western science and medicine. By the end of the 18th century, original Japanese texts on medical and scientific topics began to appear. In 1857, a Japanese medical school was founded by Japanese doctors trained by Dutch and other European physicians.

Astronomy

Japanese interest in astronomy was traditionally focused on issues of the calendar and timekeeping. Techniques of astronomical observation were borrowed from China. Contact with the 16th-century Catholic missionaries introduced the Japanese to the ideas of Ptolemy and Ptolemaic astronomy. Scientific ideas that emerged during the Western Enlightenment were introduced to Japan by the Dutch. The ideas of notables such as Galileo and Newton were disseminated in Japan by way of the Japanese translators working with the Dutch. The impact of these ideas on Japan, though gradual, was nonetheless significant because they forced the Japanese to consider their own assumptions about the operations of the natural world. These new astronomical ideas also had an immediate, practical benefit. The shogunate soon realized that these astronomical discoveries could be utilized to make the lunar calendar then in use more accurate. This was important in terms of maximizing agricultural production.

As the field of Western astronomy developed in Japan, the government appointed official astronomers (*temmonkata*) to serve and advise the shogunate. The first, Shibukawa Shunkai (or Harumi; 1639–1715), was a student of the theories of Copernicus. He utilized this knowledge to design a new calendar, the Jokyo calendar, based on a late 13th-century Chinese calendar that was adopted as the official Japanese calendar in 1684.

In 1782, Japan's first astronomical observatory was established in the city of Edo at Asakusa. It was used by the official government astronomers to study the movement of heavenly bodies. The observatory included an astrolabe (*kontengi*) for making precise calculations of the location of space objects.

Geography

Geography as a scientific endeavor, as opposed to descriptions of landscape and location, did not become important in Japan until the start of the early modern period. As with other new sciences in Japan, geography emerged as a science as a result of both Neo-Confucian rationalist thought and contact with Western missionaries and traders that intro-

7.1 Japan's first astronomical observatory at Asakusa. The object on the roof of the building at left is an astrolabe.
(Illustration Grace Vibbert)

duced Western scientific ideas, especially, in this case, regarding geography and navigation.

One of the immediate benefits to the Japanese of embracing geography as a science was in the areas of mapmaking, land surveying, and navigation. Greater precision in these areas gave rise to Japanese exploration of lands and seas beyond Japan's immediate shores. Among the most important Edo-period cartographers and explorers were Ino Tadataka, Mogami Tokunai, Mamiya Rinzo, and Takahashi Kageyasu.

Ino Tadataka (1745–1818) was a land surveyor and cartographer who made surveys of Japan utilizing Western geographical methods that resulted in the *Dai Nihon enkai yochi zenzu* (Atlas of coastal waterways of greater Japan, 1821), a complete geographic survey of all of Japan that took some 16 years to produce. Mogami Tokunai (1755–1836) was an explorer and surveyor who surveyed Ezochi (Hokkaido), and parts of the Sakhalin and Kuril islands. Mamiya Rinzo (1775–1844) was an explorer and cartographer who made surveys for the shogunate. In 1809, for instance, he explored the Sakhalin region and found that a strait separated Sakhalin from the Asian mainland.

While these geographers surveyed the Japanese islands and surrounding areas, others fixed their interests on regional and world geographies. Takahashi Kageyasu (1785–1829), who also made maps of Japan, produced world maps in a collection titled *Shintei bankoku zenzu* (Newly revised universal atlas) that was published in 1810. Besides maps of Japan and the world, Japanese geographers and cartographers working for lords produced maps of domain lands. These maps were ordered by the shogunate.

Mathematics

The first system of mathematical calculation in Japan was derived from seventh- and eighth-century borrowings from China. Some 800 years later, Chinese math was once again introduced to Japan in the guise of math texts imported in the late 15th or early 16th century. It was at this time that the abacus (*soroban*), borrowed from China, came to be used for arithmetic calculation. These Chinese influences fostered the development of indigenous Japanese modes of arithmetic and calculation, including the development of Japanese-style math texts and a differently configured abacus than its Chinese counterpart. Prior to the introduction of the abacus, calculations were done using the *sangi* method. This was a calculation system that used short wooden sticks aligned in various ways to represent numbers. This system was mostly discontinued by the 17th century.

Yoshida Mitsuyoshi (1578–1672) wrote a math text titled *Jingoki* (Treatise on eternal mathematical truths) in 1627 that was republished in 1641 with a new feature that was later copied by others and led to ongoing mathematical developments in Japan. This important innovation was the development of unsolved math problems known as *idai* (bequeathed questions). Yoshida included 12 math problems that had no answer. These were left as problems for others to solve. Over time, others picked up this practice and the problems often became quite sophisticated and complicated.

Japanese mathematics, or *wasan* as it came to be called by the end of the early modern period, referred to Edo-period methods of calculation and arithmetic. Seki Takakazu (or Seki Kowa, ca. 1642–1708) is usually considered the founder of Japanese mathematics and the mathematical school, Seki-ryu, that bears his name. He is noted for his systemization of algebraic notation (*tenzan jutsu*) that led to more sophisticated math problems and their solutions. Edo-period Japanese mathematics was especially concerned with its application to everyday matters as opposed to issues of proof and demonstration central to Western mathematical systems.

Japanese mathematicians of the 17th and 18th centuries typically came from the warrior class. Seki, for instance, was born into a samurai family and later became an accountant to the shogunate. By the 19th century, interest in mathematics extended beyond the samurai to include those of the merchant class.

Western mathematical theory (*yosan*) came to Japan by way of the Dutch. Among the areas studied were geometry, trigonometry, and logarithms. These areas of study gradually replaced Japanese mathematics in terms of interest by the end of the

Edo period. Western mathematics was also coupled with other Western sciences, such as astronomy, that furthered their development.

READING

Philosophy

Totman 2000, 220–221: early Edo political philosophy, 263–272: early modern thought; Varley 2000, 170–173, 205–220: early modern philosophy; Maruyama 1974: early modern philosophy and its relationship to politics; Najita 1974: Edo-period thought; Najita and Scheiner (eds.) 1978: Edo-period thought; Ooms 1985: early Edo-period thought; Nosco (ed.) 1984: Neo-Confucianism in the Edo period; Nosco 1990: Edo-period thought; Harootunian 1988: Edo-period National Learning philosophy

Education

Hall (ed.) 1991, 715–725: early modern education, including discussion of women's education; Totman 1993, 161–162, 300–303, 351–355, 429–436: education in the early modern period; Kassel 1996, 23–33: overview of Edo-period education; Dore 1965: education in the early modern period; Rubinger 1982: education in the early modern period; Lincicome 1991, 1–12: history of Japanese education; Tocco 2003, 193–218: women's education in the early modern period; Najita 1987: Kaitokudo private merchant academy

Science

Bartholomew 1989: formation of Japanese science; Morris-Suzuki 1994: early modern science and technology; Nakayama 1978, 728–758: overview of Japanese scientific thought; Sugimoto and Swain 1989: history of Japanese science

MATHEMATICS

Mikami 1974: overview of the history of Japanese mathematics; Fukagawa and Pedoe 1989: Japanese temple geometry problems; Jochi 2000, 423–454: Japanese mathematics (*wasan*); Smith and Mikami 1914: overview of the history of Japanese mathematics

MEDICINE

Cai and Zhen 2003, 49–73: background on Chinese medicine; Hsia, Veith, and Geertsma, trans. 1986: background on early Japanese medical practice; Bowers 1965: Japanese medical history; Bowers 1970: Western physicians in the early modern period; Bowers 1980: Western medicine in early modern Japan; Bowman 1987: epidemics and disease in early modern Japan; Fujikawa 1934: Japanese medicine; Otsuka 1976: Chinese traditional medicine in the early modern period; Nagayo 1991: early modern Japanese medicine; Kuriyama 1992: 18th-century Japanese anatomy; Tatsukawa 1993: disease in the medieval period; Farris 1993: disease in the early modern period; Lock 1980, 23–66: Japanese medical beliefs and practices in the medieval and early modern periods; Ohnuki-Tierney 1984, 145–166: religion and medicine in medieval and early modern Japan

8

LANGUAGE AND LITERATURE

LANGUAGE

and the current orthography of the phonetic scripts.

Historically the Japanese language developed along two major trajectories—spoken and written. The Japanese spoken language bears no linguistic relationship to Chinese, but it borrowed Chinese language for writing. The Japanese used Chinese characters for writing simply because this was the writing system they first encountered. Given the structure of the Japanese spoken language, however, it was not a very good fit.

Over time the Japanese writing system developed into a complex use of Chinese characters along with two different phonetic scripts to represent the sounds of spoken Japanese. The two phonetic scripts—hiragana and katakana—represented the same sounds but were used in different contexts reflecting, among other things, class and gender. These scripts were developed by the Japanese based on derivations made from Chinese characters. The complexity of Japanese was further increased because of the use of foreign words borrowed from Chinese, and later on, from European languages.

Historically there were also regional dialects that arose, in part, because of the natural barriers, such as mountains and islands, that separated different areas of the country. A dialect in one region was often difficult for those in another area to understand. Dialects, too, were not usually reflected in formal written Japanese.

Linguists sometimes divide the historical development of Japanese into five periods.

- Old Japanese (up to the eighth century)
- Late Old Japanese (9th–11th century)
- Middle Japanese (12th–16th century)
- Early Modern Japanese (17th–18th century)
- Modern Japanese (19th century to the present)

Our interest in this volume is with Middle and Early Modern Japanese, corresponding roughly to the historical divisions of medieval and early modern. Because of the difficulties in trying to recreate Japanese pronunciation from past times, this discussion focuses on written Japanese in the medieval and early modern periods, and utilizes the contemporary pronunciations of the Chinese characters

Genetic Affiliation

In linguistics, genetic affiliation refers to the shared relationship that certain languages have to one another. This is determined, in part, by examining common origins and historical development. Since the Japanese writing system derives from the Chinese writing system, it would appear that Chinese and Japanese must have some fundamental affiliation, similar, say, to the affiliation between German and English. In fact, this is not the case. Although they share some written aspects, the languages are not affiliated in that they do not share similar linguistic structures. Grammatical structure and syntax, for instance, are different in the two languages. Japanese follows a subject-object-verb (SOV) sentence structure, while Chinese utilizes a subject-verb-object (SVO) structure.

Japanese has no genetic affiliation with Chinese, but neither does it have any clear affiliation with any other language. There are a number of theories about the origins of Japanese. Some theories suggest a genetic affiliation with Korean, but others assert possible relationships to South Asian languages, to Altaic languages of central Asia, and to Malayo-Polynesian languages. The strongest arguments for affiliation are with Korean, on the basis of very similar syntax, and with Altaic languages, on the basis of such similarities as the number system and verb forms.

Chinese Characters

Chinese characters were first introduced to Japan in the early centuries of the common era. Contacts between Japan, China, and Korea increased significantly in the fourth and fifth centuries, and by the beginning of the eighth century when Japan's earliest extant texts were written, the Japanese had fully developed the use of Chinese characters (known in Japanese as *kanji*), though sometimes in ways that would not have been recognized in China.

Throughout the medieval and early modern periods, the Japanese employed the use of Chinese characters in several different ways depending on the linguistic and literary requirements of a particular kind of writing. Thus, for instance, there are examples of Japanese literature, history, government documents and other writings that used Chinese and Chinese characters in varied ways. Among these variations are: classical Chinese, hybrid forms of Chinese and Japanese, and classical Japanese which relies little on Chinese characters.

When the Japanese first came to use Chinese characters to write Japanese, they did so in two ways. First, they utilized the phonetic value of Chinese characters. In this usage, the meaning of individual characters was ignored and instead a Japanese sound value was given to each character regardless of the actual meaning of the Chinese character. For example, the Japanese word for *country* is *kuni*. In order to write *kuni* using the phonetic method, a Chinese character with the approximate sound value of *ku* would be combined with another Chinese character with an approximate sound value of *ni*. Chinese characters are monosyllabic so, in the case of a two-syllable word like *kuni*, two Chinese characters were needed. By writing the two Chinese characters representing *ku* and *ni* together, the word *kuni* was produced even though the original meaning in Chinese of the two characters was completely ignored. Needless to say, the Japanese use of Chinese characters in this way produced, from a Chinese perspective, complete gibberish. Not surprisingly, this mode of transcribing Japanese into written form was soon abandoned, having also been complicated by the fact that more than one Chinese character might be given the same sound value as another. For instance, in Japan's earliest extant text, the *Kojiki* (Record of ancient matters, 712), written partly in this phonetic style, there were 88 different syllables used, but they are represented by nearly 1,000 Chinese characters.

The second way Chinese characters were used was based on their semantic value. In this method, the meaning of the Chinese character was used for writing a Japanese word with the same or a similar meaning. However, the Chinese pronunciation was ignored and instead the character was pronounced using the indigenous Japanese sound value. For example, the Chinese character for the word *country* would be used but the Chinese pronunciation of that character was ignored in favor of pronouncing the character using the Japanese word for *country* (*kuni*) every time the character was encountered.

The term used for describing the phonetic use of Chinese characters is *man'yogana*, literally, "the syllabary (kana) of ten thousand leaves (*man'yo*)," a reference to the phonetic use of characters in the early poetry anthology, the *Man'yoshu* (Collection of ten thousand leaves, compiled ca. 759). Using Chinese characters was inefficient, however, not least because it took many pen strokes to convey a simple sound. Although the Japanese would continue to use Chinese characters for their meaning—using both Chinese- and Japanese-derived pronunciations (see "Kanji Pronunciation" below)—it was from the phonetic use of characters that Japan's syllabary writing system developed.

Kana Syllabaries

The term syllabary (kana) refers to the systems of writing Japanese that developed out of *man'yogana*. In Japanese, the smallest linguistic unit is the syllable. Japanese has no way of breaking syllables into smaller units of vowels and consonants. Thus, for example, the syllable *sa* in Japanese cannot be reduced to *s* and *a*. Nor, we should add, is there a need to.

There are two syllabaries that developed in Japanese: hiragana and katakana. They were in use in the medieval and early modern periods, and are used in modern Japanese. Both hiragana and katakana were created by simplifying Chinese characters into two or three brush strokes. Hiragana is rounded and was derived from a cursive style of writing Chinese characters. In contrast, katakana is angular and was derived from using only part of a Chinese character. Although both hiragana and katakana represent all the sounds of the Japanese language, the choice of which syllabary to use for what kind of writing varied in different historical periods. In the medieval and early modern periods the Japanese wrote using various combinations of kanji and kana. They also sometimes wrote in Chinese.

SYLLABIC SOUNDS IN THE JAPANESE LANGUAGE

Basic											
	a	**ka**	**sa**	**ta**	**na**	**ha**	**ma**	**ya**	**ra**	**wa**	**n**
hiragana	あ	か	さ	た	な	は	ま	や	ら	わ	ん
katakana	ア	カ	サ	タ	ナ	ハ	マ	ヤ	ラ	ワ	ン
	i	**ki**	**shi**	**chi**	**ni**	**hi**	**mi**		**ri**	**[w]i**	
hiragana	い	き	し	ち	に	ひ	み		り	ゐ	
katakana	イ	キ	シ	チ	ニ	ヒ	ミ		リ	ヰ	
	u	**ku**	**su**	**tsu**	**nu**	**fu**	**mu**	**yu**	**ru**		
hiragana	う	く	す	つ	ぬ	ふ	む	ゆ	る		
katakana	ウ	ク	ス	ツ	ヌ	フ	ム	ユ	ル		
	e	**ke**	**se**	**te**	**ne**	**he**	**me**		**re**	**[w]e**	
hiragana	え	け	せ	て	ね	へ	め		れ	ゑ	
katakana	エ	ケ	セ	テ	ネ	ヘ	メ		レ	ヱ	
	o	**ko**	**so**	**to**	**no**	**ho**	**mo**	**yo**	**ro**	**[w]o**	
hiragana	お	こ	そ	と	の	ほ	も	よ	ろ	を	
katakana	オ	コ	ソ	ト	ノ	ホ	モ	ヨ	ロ	ヲ	
Voiced											
	ga	**za**	**da**		**ba/pa**						
hiragana	が	ざ	だ		ば・ぱ						
katakana	ガ	ザ	ダ		バ・パ						
	gi	**ji**	**ji**		**bi/pi**						
hiragana	ぎ	じ	ぢ		び・ぴ						
katakana	ギ	ジ	ヂ		ビ・ピ						

		gu	zu	zu		bu/pu				
hiragana		ぐ	ず	づ		ぶ・ぷ				
katakana		グ	ズ	ヅ		ブ・プ				
		ge	ze	de		be/pe				
hiragana		げ	ぜ	で		べ・ぺ				
katakana		ゲ	ゼ	デ		ベ・ペ				
		go	zo	do		bo/po				
hiragana		ご	ぞ	ど		ぼ・ぽ				
katakana		ゴ	ゾ	ド		ボ・ポ				
Palatalized										
		kya	sha	cha		bya/pya				
hiragana		きゃ	しゃ	ちゃ		びゃ・ぴゃ				
katakana		キャ	シャ	チャ		ビャ・ピャ				
		kyu	shu	chu		byu/pyu				
hiragana		きゅ	しゅ	ちゅ		びゅ・ぴゅ				
katakana		キュ	シュ	チュ		ビュ・ピュ				
		kyo	sho	cho		byo/pyo				
hiragana		きょ	しょ	ちょ		びょ・ぴょ				
katakana		キョ	ショ	チョ		ビョ・ピョ				
		gya	ja		nya	hya	mya	rya		
hiragana		ぎゃ	じゃ		にゃ	ひゃ	みゃ	りゃ		
katakana		ギャ	ジャ		ニャ	ヒャ	ミャ	リャ		
		gyu	ju		nyu	hyu	myu	ryu		
hiragana		ぎゅ	じゅ		にゅ	ひゅ	みゅ	りゅ		
katakana		ギュ	ジュ		ニュ	ヒュ	ミュ	リュ		
		gyo	jo		nyo	hyo	myo	ryo		
hiragana		ぎょ	じょ		にょ	ひょ	みょ	りょ		
katakana		ギョ	ジョ		ニョ	ヒョ	ミョ	リョ		

Kanji Pronunciation: *on* and *kun* Readings

Because of the hybrid nature of the Japanese written language—combining aspects of both written Chinese and spoken Japanese—its historical development included two different ways of reading Chinese characters (kanji). These two different kinds of readings became known as the *on* reading (*on-yomi*) and the *kun* reading (*kun-yomi*). The *on* reading, also referred to as the Sino-Japanese reading, is the Japanese approximation of the original Chinese pronunciation. Chinese pronunciations required modification to fit with the sounds of the Japanese language. Some kanji have multiple *on* readings. This is the result of the character importation process: characters came into use in Japan that in China had different pronunciations depending on historical period and region of the country. The *kun* reading, also referred to as the Japanese reading, is a native Japanese word that has the same meaning as the character to which it is applied. Thus, for instance, the kanji for *country* has an *on* reading of *koku*. The Chinese pronounce this character *guo*—the pronunciation *koku* is the Japanese modification of the Chinese sound. The same *country* character also has a *kun* reading of *kuni*. The word *kuni* is the indigenous Japanese term for "country" that has been applied to the reading of the kanji. Like *on* readings, *kun* readings can be multiple for the same character. *Kun* readings are a result of the assignment of Japanese words with similar meanings to the same character. For characters with multiple *on* and/or *kun* readings, the choice of which pronunciation to use depends upon the linguistic context in which the kanji is being used.

EXAMPLES OF *ON* AND *KUN* READINGS FOR SOME COMMON CHINESE CHARACTERS (KANJI)

kanji	meaning	*on* reading	*kun* reading
国	country	*koku*	*kuni*
犬	dog	*ken*	*inu*

kanji	meaning	*on* reading	*kun* reading
火	fire	*ka*	*hi*
山	mountain	*san*	*yama*
人	person	*nin/jin*	*hito*
田	rice field	*den*	*ta*
水	water	*sui*	*mizu*

Japanese Vocabulary

As a result of both indigenous and foreign influences on the development of the Japanese language, there were three different kinds of vocabulary in use in the medieval and early modern periods: native Japanese words, Sino-Japanese words, and foreign words (also referred to as "loan words"). Sino-Japanese words were Japanese words of Chinese origin, usually written as character compounds, that is, two or more kanji written together to form words. Sino-Japanese words are often used to express abstract ideas. Some character compounds are entirely Japanese in origin.

In Japanese, the notion of foreign words typically refers to lexical items borrowed from languages other than Chinese. Not surprisingly, the Japanese borrowed the most words from cultures with which they had the most contact. Often loan words reflect borrowed aspects of material culture, as well as the introduction of new concepts and specialized terminology. From Portuguese traders and missionaries, for instance, the Japanese borrowed such terms as *pan* (bread, from the Portuguese *paõ*) and *tempura* (battered deep-fried vegetables and fish, from the Portuguese *tempero*). After the Portuguese were expelled from Japan in the first half of the 17th century, Dutch influence predominated. The Japanese borrowed words not only from Dutch medical and scientific discourse, but also such everyday words as *biiru* (beer, from the Dutch *bier*).

Writing Styles

The history of the varied Japanese writing styles is complex as a result of the multiple ways of reading and writing characters and kana. Texts from the medieval and early modern periods reflected this diversity of written forms. Some texts were written in classical Chinese, others used Japanese generously laced with kanji, while still others reflected a style using mostly kana. Styles were also combined in hybrid forms. The following brief list of written styles is by no means exclusive, but it does reference the most important.

CLASSICAL JAPANESE

Classical Japanese is a broad term that encompasses writing in Japanese from the Heian period through the Edo period. Classical Japanese is especially associated with the literary style of Heian-period aristocrats. There are, in fact, a number of styles that fall under this heading, including Japanese poetry that uses little Chinese vocabulary, prose that uses mostly Japanese diction, and writing that uses both Chinese vocabulary and occasional applications of Chinese syntax in otherwise Japanese sentences. From a contemporary perspective, any writing in Japanese prior to about 1900 can be considered classical Japanese.

The Heian-period style of classical Japanese that used little Chinese vocabulary was, by the start of the medieval period, undergoing significant changes as a result of interactions with Chinese. One result of Chinese influence on Japanese was the development of the Japanese-Chinese mixed style (*wakan konkobun*) in the medieval period. This writing style is treated below. In the Edo period, National Learning scholars (see chapter 7: Philosophy, Education, and Science), in their attempt to reclaim a pristine Japanese past cleansed of the taint of foreign influence, took a special interest in early Japanese poetry and hence classical Japanese prior to the medieval period.

8.1 Writing set, including brush and inkstone (Photo William E. Deal)

It is thought that the classical Japanese of Heian aristocrats was closely connected to the spoken language of the time. By the early modern period, Japanese as spoken language bore little resemblance to the spoken language of the Heian period. Hence, classical Japanese came to be more and more removed from colloquial speech. In the Edo period, however, the colloquial speech of the day did find its way into literature in which dialogue was central, such as plays and some forms of fiction. Edo-period vernacular literature, then, is also an aspect of classical Japanese, but a very different language than, say, the classical Japanese of Heian poetry and prose.

CLASSICAL CHINESE

Classical Chinese (*kambun;* literally, "Chinese writing") refers to any writings, particularly by Japanese, composed in Chinese. In the medieval and early modern periods, classical Chinese was especially associated with and sometimes used in scholarly and religious writing. It was also sometimes used as a literary language. Japanese poetry written in Chinese, known as *kanshi,* is one example. The study of classical Chinese was also central to education in the early modern period—students were expected to be able to read and recite passages from the Chinese classics both to promote literacy and to instill in children fundamental Neo-Confucian values.

Difficulties in reading classical Chinese were partly resolved through the Japanese use of a system of marks that were placed within the Chinese text and served as pointers on how to read and understand the syntax of a particular Chinese passage. While Japanese used a subject-object-verb word order, Chinese used a subject-verb-object word order. The use of these markings effectively showed the reader how to render a Chinese sentence in classical Japanese.

VARIANT CHINESE

Variant Chinese (*hentai kambun*) refers to a hybrid combination of both classical Chinese and classical Japanese. The Japanese had learned to write Chinese (*kambun*) during the centuries of contact with the Asian mainland. After ongoing contact ended in the late ninth century, Japanese writing in Chinese more and more included such anomalies as Japanese words, syntactical irregularities, and the misplacement of verbs. While this variant or hybrid form of classical Chinese might be perfectly understandable to the Japanese, it would have been peculiar at best, if not incomprehensible, to the Chinese. It was, in effect, a writing style that looked Chinese but had developed into a different language than classical Chinese.

By the end of the Heian period, variant Chinese was being used in government documents and in the conduct of everyday business. In the medieval period, variant Chinese was used to write a number of different kinds of documents, including historical narratives, shogunal records, contracts, and diaries written by men. Variant Chinese was also used into the Edo period.

JAPANESE-CHINESE MIXED STYLE

Japanese-Chinese mixed style (*wakan konkobun*) is, strictly speaking, a form of classical Japanese. It is a hybrid writing style that intermingles Japanese and Chinese character readings, grammar, and lexical items. Japanese-Chinese mixed style evolved out of the practice of adding marks to Chinese texts in order that they could be read more easily by Japanese readers. This style developed in the medieval period and was used into the Edo period. Classic examples of compositions in this style are two Kamakura-period texts, *Heike monogatari* (Tale of the Heike) and *Hojoki (An Account of My Hut).*

EPISTOLARY STYLE

Epistolary style (*sorobun*) was a formal writing style in use during the early modern period. As its name suggests, this style was used for letters—both personal and official—and also in government-related documents. The Tokugawa shogunate required that all correspondence coming into its offices—such as reports and requests—be written in this style. The term *sorobun* derives from the frequent use of the polite auxiliary verb *soro* that occurs in this writing style. The use of this verb served to humble the writer before the intended recipient—the government. Like other Japanese writing styles, *sorobun* was a hybrid form. Although it was based on classical

Japanese, it used many Chinese characters, generally left out kana used as particles and verb suffixes, and often placed words in Chinese order.

LITERATURE

Introduction

Japanese literature has a long history dating back to the early eighth century when the oldest extant texts were compiled. Literature prior to the medieval period had been almost entirely the work of aristocrats. Texts like the *Tale of Genji* (*Genji monogatari*, ca. 1000) are suffused with the sensibilities, values, and aesthetics of Heian-period aristocrats. While aristocratic literature retained its importance throughout the medieval and early modern periods, it was also supplanted in many ways by literature that reflected the sensibilities of a much broader segment of Japanese society. Warriors, Buddhists, merchants, masterless samurai, and geisha were among those who became the subjects of this literature and those whose interests this literature sometimes expressed.

Medieval and early modern literature was written in a variety of different styles, such as classical Japanese, Japanese-Chinese Mixed Style, and Variant Chinese. Literary sensibilities found expression in such textual genres as poetry, fiction, drama, literary theory, diaries, travel accounts, and journal-style writings. Within these genres, there were many different styles, such as the various kinds of poetry—for instance, haiku and linked verse—and prose writings—such as war tales and travel diaries.

The following discussion examines medieval and early modern literature in historical perspective. It should be noted that drama and other writing for theater is not treated in this chapter for two reasons. First, theater, including influential plays and playwrights, is treated in chapter 9: Performing Arts. Second, the idea that plays were literature was mostly a foreign idea in medieval and early modern Japan. Plays were first and foremost an art to be per-

formed and observed. The texts of Kabuki plays were not usually even published. Thus, to discuss drama here might be in keeping with contemporary sensibilities, but it would not reflect how theater was consumed by the Japanese in the medieval and early modern periods.

Medieval Literature

MEDIEVAL POETRY

Waka At the beginning of the medieval period, *waka* poetry, so closely associated with Heian-period aristocrats, was still a vibrant literary art. *Waka* ("Japanese poem"), also referred to as *tanka* ("short poem"), is verse that is composed of five lines with a total of 31 syllables in a 5-7-5-7-7 pattern. Despite the transformation of Japan into a country in which warrior values were newly ascendant, poetry remained a central mode of expression for aristocrats and, often, well-educated Buddhist priests. This is evidenced by the 15 imperial poetry anthologies that were compiled during the medieval period. Further, the poetry included in these anthologies followed the poetic rules set down during the Heian period.

Medieval *waka* did not express warrior values—it was still very much an aristocratic art. But the turmoil of the Gempei War and the decline of the political and social influence of the court was reflected in the darker mood and tenor of some medieval *waka*. The Buddhist notion of *mappo*, "the end of the Dharma," asserted that the world had entered an era of spiritual darkness and confusion. No doubt the period of civil war that ushered in the medieval period contributed to the belief in the veracity of this view. Buddhism also taught that life is transient and that human fortunes are ephemeral. This sense of the fundamental impermanence of human existence was expressed by some aristocrats and Buddhists through *waka*.

In the early Kamakura period, Fujiwara no Shunzei (or Toshinari, 1114–1204) and his son, Fujiwara no Teika (or Sadaie; 1162–1241), were among the most outstanding poets. Shunzei conceived of *waka* composition as a spiritual practice analogous to meditation. For him, composing *waka* was a way to attain enlightenment if practiced with "concentration and insight" (*shikan*), a Tendai school form of meditation. Both Shunzei and Teika set the aesthetic tone for Kamakura-period *waka*. They promoted the notion of "traditional language, fresh conceptions" (*kotoba furuku, kokoro atarashi*) in which the language of traditional *waka* was used in new ways. Innovative language, however, had to express the aesthetic ideal of *yugen*, "mystery and depth," that was both a literary and spiritual goal aspiring to elevate the prosaic into a profound beauty. They also prized the use of *honkadori*, a technique whereby the poet alludes to an earlier poem and then develops this imagery in new ways.

These poetic ideals found expression in the eighth imperial anthology, *Shin kokinshu* (New collection of poems from ancient and modern times) that was compiled by Teika and others around 1205. The *Shin kokinshu* was commissioned by retired Emperor Go-Toba whose poetry also appears in the

collection. Other prominent *Shin kokinshu* poets include Teika, Shunzei, Fujiwara no Yoshitsune (1169–1206), Princess Shokushi (d. 1201), Fujiwara no Ietaka (1158–1237), and the Buddhist priests Saigyo (1118–1190) and Jien (1155–1225). This collection is widely regarded as containing the finest *waka* of all medieval imperial poetry anthologies.

Renga Although *waka* continued to be written, by the time the last imperially commissioned *waka* anthology was compiled in 1439, the creativity of this poetic form was already moribund. In part, *waka* was a victim of its own poetic rules for how a poem was to be composed, including the kinds of imagery that were permissible. As a result, medieval poets eschewed the rigidity of *waka* for the new poetic possibilities of linked verse (*renga*). Between the 13th and 16th centuries, the best poets composed in the *renga* style.

The structure of *renga* is similar to *waka* but the poem created is the work of more than one poet composing a sequence of consecutive verses. In *waka*, one poet creates a 31-syllable verse of five lines in a 5-7-5-7-7 syllable structure. In *renga*, a poet composes the first three lines (5-7-5) and a second poet composes the last two lines (7-7). By continuing this process, a long chain of alternating 5-7-5 and 7-7 lines is created. There was variability in the number of lines that constituted a linked verse sequence, but over time the standard length was set at 100 stanzas.

Lines of verse are linked to each other through associative word imagery and subject matter. For instance, a poet might start with a verse about a cuckoo, a bird that symbolizes summer. The next poet might introduce the image of a pine tree which, in Japan, has poetic associations to the cuckoo. The Japanese word for pine (*matsu*) is also a homophone for the verb "to wait," a reference to waiting or anticipating some event or action. The next poet, expanding on the pine tree image, might create a verse calling to mind a shady mountain scene with a stream flowing through it. Pine trees are connected to mountains, and both mountains and the heat of summer are relieved by the mountain shade and the cool flowing stream. A fourth poet might then introduce the idea of a moonlit scene because other Japanese imagery speaks of the Moon reflected in

8.2 The late Heian–early Kamakura poet-priest Saigyo (1118–90) (Illustration Kikuchi Yosai from *Zenken kojitsu*, mid-19th century)

water. The Moon symbolizes autumn; hence, this linked sequence moves from summer to fall.

The idea of two poets composing a single *waka* dates to the Heian period when the communal composition of a 31-syllable poem was a leisurely pastime. In the Heian practice, one poet composed the first three lines and another poet the second two lines, creating what is sometimes referred to as a "short" *renga*. This practice was expanded in the medieval period and much longer links were produced, the result of several poets working together.

By the 14th century, *renga* had become a serious poetic style that eclipsed *waka* in importance. In 1356, Nijo Yoshimoto, a high-ranking Kyoto aristocrat, compiled the *Tsukuba shu* (Tsukuba Collection; the title is a reference to a *Manyo'shu* poem), a collection that secured for *renga* its status as a legitimate literary art form. Yoshimoto's successors further advanced the reputation of *renga*. Of particular note are the two *renga* masters, Shinkei (1407–75) and Sogi (1421–1502).

Shinkei, a Buddhist priest, was not only a highly regarded poet, but he also wrote theoretical treatises on the nature of poetry in general and *renga* in particular. Not unlike Fujiwara no Shunzei's view of *waka*, Shinkei found a deep connection between poetry composition and the religious quest for enlightenment. For Shinkei, pursuit of poetic ideals was deeply spiritual because it held the possibility of profound expression about the nature of the world. The aesthetic ideal of *yugen* (mystery and depth) was central to the spiritual possibilities of poetry composition. Shinkei's *Sasamegoto* (Whisperings, 1463) discusses his views of *renga* and its relationship to *yugen* and other aesthetic ideals.

Sogi, also a Buddhist priest, was an accomplished poet. He came from a commoner background, so his poetry was informed not only by the refined sensibilities of Kyoto poets but also by the lives of peasants and farmers. Sogi exemplified the communal nature of *renga* and the necessity of working closely with other poets to create a coherent series of linked verses. In 1488 Sogi traveled to Minase shrine, in a village between Kyoto and Osaka, to compose a *renga* sequence with two other *renga* masters, Shohaku (1443–1527) and Socho (1448–1532). The result of this collaboration was the 100-verse *renga* composition titled *Minase sangin hyakuin* (One hundred links by three poets at Minase), arguably the finest example of the genre. The success of this text stems from its ability to create a flow of associative word imagery and subject matter.

MEDIEVAL PROSE

Diaries The medieval period continued the tradition of diary writing begun in the Heian period. As in that period, many significant medieval diaries were composed by aristocratic and Buddhist women. The term *diary* is somewhat misleading, however, because diaries were not necessarily daily or weekly accounts written as events occurred. Rather they were often memoirs, recollections, accounts of one's travels, or a combination of these, and many also included poetry. To further complicate matters, the term *diary* has also been applied to fictional stories written in the form of diaries.

Travel diaries are sometimes treated as a separate genre, but this is problematic because travel diaries can include memories and recollections. There are also different kinds of travel diaries, such as those that recount pilgrimages to sacred places and accounts of travel from Kyoto to the shogunate at Kamakura to deal with legal matters. Diaries were also written by poets about their journeys in the countryside often to visit places associated with famous poems of the past. Poetry is typically interspersed with prose in such accounts. The famous *renga* poets Sogi and Socho both wrote poetic travel diaries in the Muromachi period.

Some representative medieval diaries include:

KAIDOKI
(JOURNEY ALONG THE SEACOAST ROAD, 1223)
Written by an unknown man, this travel diary recounts the author's walking trip from Kyoto to Kamakura visiting famous sites along the way.

KENREIMON'IN UKYO NO DAIBU NO SHU
(POETIC MEMOIRS OF LADY DAIBU, CA. 1231)
Kenreimon'in ukyo no daibu (ca. 1157–unknown), or Lady Daibu, was an aristocratic woman who served in the court of Emperor Go-Toba. Her memoir is a particularly interesting glimpse at the life of an aristocratic woman connected with the Taira family—the vanquished clan of Gempei War fame—

whose lover, Taira Sukemori, was killed at the Battle of Dannoura in the closing battle of the Gempei War in 1185.

BEN NO NAISHI NIKKI
(DIARY OF LADY BEN, CA. 1260)

Composed by the aristocratic woman Go-Fukakusa In Ben no Naishi (dates unknown), who was in service at the court of Emperor Go-Fukakusa, this diary records events that occurred at court during Go-Fukakusa's reign.

IZAYOI NIKKI
(DIARY OF THE WANING MOON, 1280)

Composed by the Buddhist nun Abutsu (d. 1283), this diary relates events connected with her journey from Kyoto to Kamakura to press her claim about a property dispute in the shogun's courts.

TOWAZUGATARI
(THE CONFESSIONS OF LADY NIJO, 1313)

This diary of Go-Fukakusa In no Nijo (1258–unknown), an aristocratic woman who served in the court of Emperor Go-Fukakusa, is commonly known as The Confessions of Lady Nijo in English translation. However, the literal meaning of the title is "A Tale Nobody Asked For." This diary recounts Lady Nijo's numerous love affairs and her eventual dismissal from service to the court. She talks about her decision to take the tonsure and become a Buddhist nun. She then embarks on a number of journeys that she describes in detail.

ISE DAIJINGU SANKEIKI (ACCOUNT OF A
PILGRIMAGE TO THE GREAT SHRINE AT ISE, 1342)

This travel diary by the Buddhist priest Saka Jubutsu records his pilgrimage to the Shinto sacred site, the Ise Shrine, in 1342. This diary is especially interesting because of the view it provides of the relationship between Buddhism and Shinto in the 14th century.

TSUKUSHI MICHI NO KI (JOURNEY ALONG
THE TSUKUSHI ROAD, 1480)

Sogi (1421–1502) was a noted *renga* poet and traveler. His diary, Journey along the Tsukushi Road, recounts his journey to Kyushu, visiting places of historic and poetic significance along the way, and interspersing poetry with his prose.

UTSUNOYAMA NO KI
(ACCOUNT OF UTSUNOYAMA, 1517)

Like his friend Sogi, Socho (1148–1532) was a noted *renga* poet and traveler. His diary, Account of Utsunoyama, is both memoir and a recollection of his travels to sites of historical and poetic interest.

Essays "Essay" refers to the genre known in Japanese as *zuihitsu* (literally, "following the writing brush"). These are miscellaneous essays or random thoughts—often personal observations about people and nature—set down with no particular structure in mind. Two classic examples of this genre are also among the most important literary works from the Kamakura period: *Hojoki* (*An Account of My Hut*, 1212) by Kamo no Chomei (1155–1216) and *Tsurezuregusa* (*Essays in Idleness*, ca. 1330) by Kenko (Yoshida Kaneyoshi, ca. 1283–ca. 1352). The authors were both Buddhist recluses, having left behind a world in a state of social and political turmoil. For Kamo no Chomei, the unsettled time period was the Gempei War (1180–85) and its aftermath; for Kenko, it was the political intrigue and warfare that occurred at the transition from the Kamakura and Muromachi periods.

Both of these works are imbued with the Buddhist idea of impermanence (*mujo*), according to which the world is a place of constant change and instability. Both Kamo no Chomei and Kenko find abundant evidence for the truth of this view in their descriptions of the world they inhabit. They also both raise questions about the nature of enlightenment and its possibility in such a tumultuous world. In the *Hojoki*, Chomei reveals his acute awareness of impermanence and the transience of human existence. He also conveys his satisfaction at living a simple, reclusive life. In the *Tsurezuregusa*, Kenko reflects on the human condition and poignantly recalls happier days now long past. Occasionally, Kenko also assumes a moral tone in his reflections on life and living.

War Tales War tales (*gunki monogatari*), composed during the Kamakura and Muromachi periods, became a very popular literary form. These tales narrated stories of great conflicts and battles, and described in detail the heroic victories and defeats of the greatest warriors. Such stories also became the source for later literary and theatrical forms, including the recitation of tales by itinerant *biwa* musicians (*biwa hoshi*) and the dramatization of warrior exploits in Kabuki and Bunraku dramas. War tales not only reflected the interests of the ruling warrior class, but they also framed a warrior ethic that, by the Edo period, became codified as part of the way of the warrior (*bushido*). Prized warrior values included bravery, loyalty, duty to one's lord, and a heroic death. A list of some of the more important war tales follows below. Special attention is given to the *Heike monogatari* (*Tale of the Heike*), widely regarded as the classic and best example of this literary genre.

Some representative medieval war tales include:

HOGEN MONOGATARI (TALE OF THE HOGEN DISTURBANCE, CA. EARLY 13TH CENTURY)

The *Hogen monogatari* recounts the events and armed conflict that occurred in 1156 when the retired emperor Sutoku made an unsuccessful attempt to gain control of imperial power against the current emperor, Go-Shirakawa.

HEIJI MONOGATARI (TALE OF THE HEIJI DISTURBANCE, CA. EARLY 13TH CENTURY)

The *Heiji monogatari* recounts the events and armed conflict that occurred in 1156–60, in Fujiwara Nobuyori's failed attempt to seize power from the Taira family.

HEIKE MONOGATARI (TALE OF THE HEIKE, FIRST HALF OF THE 13TH CENTURY)

The *Heike monogatari* recounts the political intrigue, battles, heroics, and other events that occurred before, during, and after the Gempei War (1180–85) between the Taira (or Heike) and Minamoto (or Genji) warrior families (see chapter 1: Historical Context, for details on the Gempei War). The *Heike* story focuses on the ascent of the Taira warrior clan to power in the waning years of the Heian period, their control of the imperial court, and their eventual fall and defeat at the hands of forces led by the Minamoto clan. Many classic Japanese stories of bravery, loyalty, self-sacrifice, and honor in defeat derive from the *Heike monogatari*. It is arguably the most important of all the war tales, and certainly the one that gave definitive shape to the war tale genre. This tale became widely known across all social classes by virtue of the many literary and theatrical genres used to narrate the *Heike monogatari*'s stories. Notable among these were the oral recitations of the Heike story by itinerant *biwa* players during the medieval period.

There are two important Buddhist themes that set the tone for the entire work: impermanence and karmic retribution. The famous opening lines of the *Heike* remark on the impermanence (*mujo*) of the world and the fleeting nature of human existence, a sensibility repeated throughout the text. The notion that all things necessarily perish foreshadows the inevitable downfall of the Taira family from power. The cause of their fall is not fated, but is rather a direct result of karmic retribution, that is, retribution for evil actions. The Buddhist view is that all actions, good and bad, have a positive or negative consequence. The arrogance and ruthlessness of the Taira result in a downfall that is both deserved and inescapable.

A sensibility expressed in the *Heike monogatari* that tends to run counter to Western values is the focus on the defeated rather than the victorious. There is a strong sense of tragedy and sadness that pervades the *Heike*'s account of the Tairas' downfall. Sympathy for the defeated, fueled in part by the Buddhist virtue of compassion, tempers any negative evaluations of the Taira.

One interesting theory concerning the early development of the *Heike monogatari* asserts that there may have been a ritual aspect to the early oral recitations of the events that later became the *Heike* text. There existed in Japan a tradition of chanting Buddhist texts as a way to pacify the souls of the dead that might otherwise wreak havoc on the living. The chanting of the *Heike* text may have been intended to pacify the souls of those who had died in the Gempei War.

GEMPEI SEISUIKI (AN ACCOUNT OF THE GEMPEI WAR, EARLY 14TH CENTURY)

The *Gempei seisuiki* (or *josuiki*), like the *Heike monogatari*, recounts the battles, heroics, and other events that occurred before and during the Gempei War (1180–85) between the Taira (or Heike) and Minamoto (or Genji) warrior families. Unlike the *Heike monogatari*, which developed originally out of an oral storytelling tradition, the *Gempei seisuiki* developed from the first as a written narrative.

JOKYUKI (AN ACCOUNT OF THE JOKYU DISTURBANCE, EARLY 14TH CENTURY)

The *Jokyuki* recounts the events and armed conflict that resulted from Emperor Go-Toba's failed attempt to overthrow the Hojo regents and restore full ruling power to the imperial office.

SOGA MONOGATARI (TALE OF THE SOGA BROTHERS, 14TH CENTURY)

The *Soga monogatari* details the story of the Soga brothers who, in 1193, avenged their father's murder by killing the lord whose retainers had carried out the act.

TAIHEIKI (CHRONICLE OF THE GREAT PEACE, CA. LATE 14TH CENTURY)

The *Taiheiki* recounts the years 1318–67, which included Emperor Go-Daigo's short-lived attempt to overthrow military rule and reassert imperial rule, and the resulting years of struggle between the Northern and Southern courts.

GIKEIKI (YOSHITSUNE CHRONICLE, 15TH CENTURY)

The *Gikeiki* details the life of Minamoto no Yoshitsune, a hero of the Gempei War, and later a tragic figure when he was forced to commit suicide as a result of the treachery of his brother (Minamoto no Yoritomo, the first Kamakura shogun). Some of the stories about Yoshitsune told in this war tale became the source for subsequent treatments of Yoshitsune's life in theatrical and other literary forms.

Early Modern Literature

In the transition from aristocratic rule to warrior governance that marked the beginning of the medieval period, literature came to express at least some of the interests and sensibilities of the newly emerging warrior class. In similar fashion, the transition from the medieval to the early modern was accompanied by the gradual emergence of urban centers that were home to newly important social classes, such as merchants and other commoners. The social context of urban culture—in particular, the cities of Edo, Osaka, and Kyoto—was central to the development of early modern literary sensibilities and tastes. Warrior literature was not replaced, but early modern literature is notable for its articulation of the interests and concerns of merchants, artisans, and other nonelite members of early modern society.

Just as Buddhism permeated aspects of medieval literature, in the early modern period, the Tokugawa shogunate's promotion of Neo-Confucianism influenced early modern literature. In general Neo-Confucianism was hostile to fiction, drama, the newly emerging *haikai* poetry, and other literary forms it believed played no useful role in building the Neo-Confucian state or in promulgating Neo-Confucian values. Interestingly, though, traditional *waka* and Chinese poetry (*kanshi*) were acceptable because they were literary forms that expressed true human emotion in distinction to literature that trafficked in made-up stories that often exposed human frailties or were merely frivolous. Not surprisingly, especially given the tensions already inherent in the rigid social hierarchy that the shogunate promoted, early modern literature frequently challenged the government's assertions or otherwise raised questions about values, class, and economic status.

One technological change that occurred at the start of the Edo period significantly transformed access to literature and the process of its dissemination to increasingly larger numbers of people. Prior to the early modern period, texts—whether religious or literary—were only reproduced through the hand copying of manuscripts. Besides the inevitable errors and infelicities that such a process introduced into copied texts, this low-tech mode of duplication produced relatively few texts, which were distributed on a very limited basis, usually only to aristocrats, high-ranking warriors, and clergy.

The commencement of commercial woodblock printing in 1609 began the process of shifting access to literature and texts from elitist-only circles to those that included literate commoners. The growth of so-called popular literature, that is, literature with an audience beyond the upper classes, had been a relatively minor aspect of medieval literature. This changed dramatically in the early modern period. Mass-published books accessible in bookstores at affordable prices in turn fueled the demand for more new books of fiction and poetry. Literature had become a commodity.

EARLY MODERN POETRY

***Haikai/Hokku/*Haiku** Toward the end of the medieval period, a new poetic form developed from the *renga* tradition. This form, *haikai* (or *haikai no renga*), became the central poetic style of the early modern period. *Haikai* began in the late medieval period as a comic diversion from the composition of serious *renga*. To distinguish this poetic form, it was called *haikai no renga* (often shortened to *haikai*). *Haikai* followed the usual *renga* form of repeating sets of stanzas of five, seven, and five syllables followed by two seven-syllable lines, but without the traditional restrictions on themes, word choice, and seriousness of tone. Relaxation enjoyed through transgressing the usual canons of *renga* taste, however, soon yielded to the formalization of this poetic activity. As a result, schools devoted to this literary art and promoting different *haikai* composition styles developed at the beginning of the early modern period. The two most important schools were the Teimon and Danrin.

The Teimon school was named after Matsunaga Teitoku (1571–1653), a *waka* and *renga* poet who was an advocate of traditional styles of poetry composition. Teitoku's achievement was to turn a light-hearted poetic form into serious poetry by applying formal rules to its composition and promoting an attention to aesthetics that would raise *haikai* to the level of *waka* and *renga* in its relevance as a style of poetry. For Teitoku, what distinguished *haikai* from *renga* was not so much humor as the use of a *haigon*—a colloquial Japanese word or a Chinese word. Such words were not permitted in serious *waka* and *renga*. The judicious use of such words brought structure to *haikai*, providing formal rules that serious *haikai* poets of the Teimon school were required to master.

The Danrin school, headed by Nishiyama Soin (1605–82), was, in part, a reaction against the Teimon school's formalistic approach to *haikai* composition. Soin was a *renga* and *haikai* poet who, along with Ihara Saikaku (1642–93, also a noted fiction writer—see below: "Ukiyozoshi"), advocated a move away from formal rules, applied in a painstaking manner, to an informal style in which poems were composed rapidly using colloquial Japanese. Unlike the Teimon school, the Danrin school was not concerned with the enduring quality of its poetry, but rather the immediate witty humor that it produced. The Danrin poetic style of humorous, rapid composition is exemplified by Saikaku's prodigious ability to produce large numbers of amusing, linked verses in a short time. In 1684, Saikaku reportedly managed to compose 23,500 verses in a single day. One example of Saikaku's *haikai* is the collection known as *Haikai okukazu* (A great number of haikai stanzas, 1677), a 4,000-verse linked sequence.

Originally, the goal of *haikai* was to produce a humorous link in the *renga* sequence. Over time, however, the emphasis shifted from sequential links to the first verse of the sequence (called *hokku*). The *hokku* came to be treated more and more as a verse that was independently meaningful, even without the addition of subsequent stanzas. Thus, *hokku* became a 17-syllable verse structured into three lines of five, seven, and five syllables and was regarded not as a link to another stanza, but as a separate, independent poem. *Hokku* is better known as *haiku*, but this later term was not used until the Meiji period. The neologism *haiku* was derived from the "hai" of *haikai* and the "ku" of *hokku*. The creation of the term *haiku* marked the full independence of *hokku* from its origins in *renga*.

The acknowledged master of the *hokku* form was the *haikai* poet, Matsuo Basho (1644–94), a samurai turned poet and traveler. Despite the brevity of a *hokku*—a mere 17 syllables—Basho was able to compose poems that contain very simple images of seemingly mundane scenes, but that carry with them a great deal of power to suggest larger truths or to evoke a surprisingly wide range of human emotion. For Basho, as for other Japanese poets, poetry was not simply a literary pursuit; it also had deeply spiritual implications. Basho was a student of Zen Buddhism, and Zen sensibilities inform at least some of his poetry.

Besides his *hokku*, Basho is highly regarded for his travel writing that intersperses poetry and prose. His most famous travel writing, *Oku no Hosomichi* (The narrow road to the deep north; published posthumously in 1702), recounts a journey he took in 1689 with a companion. This text exemplifies Basho's prodigious abilities at composing 17-syllable verse with accompanying prose (called *haibun*) that sets the context for his poems. Basho's *hokku* evoke his moods and feelings as he travels the countryside visiting famous historical sites and viewing scenes of nature along the way.

Following Basho, other poets continued to write fine poetry in the *hokku* style and to create their own distinctive poetic voices. Many of these poets also wrote *haikai*, but are best known for their 17-syllable compositions. Notable among Basho's successors were Yosa Buson (1716–84) and Kobayashi Issa (1763–1827). Buson was a poet and painter whose verses were particularly descriptive of worldly scenes without any overt suggestion of the spirituality found in Basho's poems. He championed the slogan, "Back to Basho," presumably referring to poetry composition that is mindful of a Basho-like quality. Issa was a poet who advanced the narrative voice that Buson had introduced into his poems. Issa's poetic narratives are chiefly concerned with commoners, expressing concern for the plight of the downtrodden and poor. His poems also sometimes express great affection for animals.

EARLY MODERN PROSE

Kanazoshi Kanazoshi, "kana books," is a term for popular literary works published in the early Edo period. Written mostly in kana (usually hiragana) and containing few Chinese characters, they had no scholarly pretensions, because all learned texts were written either in Chinese or in a mixed Chinese and Japanese style. Writings in this genre covered a wide variety of subjects, both fiction and nonfiction. Of the approximately 200 *kanazoshi* published, none are considered among the Edo period's finest literature. Nevertheless, the subjects written about illustrate popular interests and concerns in the first decades of the early modern period, such as Buddhist sermons and Neo-Confucian ethical instruction, practical guides to travel and the pleasure quarters, fictional stories about love and the lives of merchants, and critical evaluations of the skills and abilities of actors and geisha. Authors of these books included middle-ranking warriors, aristocrats, monks, Neo-Confucian scholars, and others either needing the income or wanting to get out their particular message to the population at large.

One author, Asai Ryoi (unknown–1691), a former head of a Pure Land Buddhist temple, is regarded as the best writer in this genre. He was also the most prolific and his literary output suggests the breadth of subjects taken up by *kanazoshi* authors. Among his works are travel guides, ghost stories, fiction, and sermons. He was able to earn a living as a writer and is usually described as Japan's first professional writer. His most famous work is the *Ukiyo monogatari* (Tales of the floating world; ca. 1661). Although this text is not usually categorized as a "book of the floating world," a genre developed soon after *Ukiyo monogatari* was published, it deals with the same themes: how to live life in a world that is inherently unstable and changing.

Ukiyozoshi Ukiyozoshi, "books of the floating world," is a term for popular literary works published in Osaka and Kyoto from the late 17th century to the late 18th century. The concept of the "floating world" (*ukiyo*) is central to this genre. Prior to the early modern period, "floating world" was a Buddhist metaphor referring to the impermanence of all things in the world and the transitory nature of human existence. In the Edo period, the idea of the floating world kept its Buddhist meaning, but instead of something to be escaped through meditation or ascetic practice, the floating world was to be enjoyed here and now because life was transitory and short. By extension, the pleasure quarters, the theater, and other hedonistic attractions of urban life were where the fleeting pleasures of this world could be most fully enjoyed. As a literary genre, *ukiyozoshi* explored the nature of life in the floating world, focusing on such topics as eroticism, amorous affairs, the pleasure quarters, and the lives of merchants and warriors.

A book published in 1682, *Koshoku ichidai otoko* (*Life of an Amorous Man*, 1682), by Ihara Saikaku, is usually cited as the inaugural work in this genre. Saikaku's poetic compositions have already been discussed (see above: "*Haikai/Hokku/*Haiku"), but he is best known for his fiction, and he is considered one of the finest Edo-period authors. Saikaku, himself born into an Osaka merchant family, was particularly astute in his observations of urban life. His prose explores the nature of human existence in the floating world, including erotic love (both heterosexual and homosexual), money and status, the merchant work ethic, warriors, and disparities between social classes that arise from a hierarchical society.

The following brief discussion of four of Saikaku's most important works highlights some of these themes.

Koshoku ichidai otoko (*The Life of an Amorous Man;* 1682) *The Life of an Amorous Man* was Saikaku's first novel. It details the amorous adventures of the protagonist Yonosuke, whose first sexual encounter takes place at the age of eight. At the age of 61, having finally exhausted the sexual amusements to be had in Japan, he sails away in search of an island inhabited only by women in hopes of discovering new sources of pleasure. This book is significant in part because it made erotic love (*koshoku*) the primary subject of a literary work for the first time. Prior to Saikaku, treatment of love in Japanese literature had focused mostly on the ideal of courtly love first articulated in Heian period works like *Genji monogatari* (*Tale of Genji*) that emphasized human emotion and aesthetics, not the erotic.

Koshoku gonin onna (*Five Women Who Loved Love;* 1686) *Five Women Who Loved Love* was also a groundbreaking work because it dealt with the love lives of merchant-class women. Prior to this novel, only the sexual activities of pleasure-quarter prostitutes had been addressed, never that of "respectable" women. The book tells the story of five women with an uncontrollable fondness for lovemaking. As a result, four of the five women come to shameful and tragic ends as a result of illicit affairs or adulterous relationships. Saikaku based these stories on real incidents. In addition, Saikaku explores an ethical dilemma when he takes up a theme also found in other Edo-period literature and drama—the conflict between a social sense of duty (*giri*) constantly reinforced by the government's promotion of Neo-Confucian values and the personal desires and needs that arise from one's own feelings (*ninjo*), which often are contradictory to duty.

Koshoku ichidai onna (*The Life of an Amorous Woman;* 1686) Like *Five Women Who Loved Love, The Life of an Amorous Woman* deals with uncontrollable erotic urges that lead to decadence and unhappiness. Saikaku has the protagonist tell her dark and sad story in the first person. She is descended from a family of Kyoto aristocrats, but has to rely on her own resources to survive. She works at many different jobs, including those of pleasure-quarter courtesan and common prostitute. Her downward spiral is the result, she reveals, of her love of erotic love acquired at a young age. Saikaku has once again moved his readers a long distance from the gentler side of romance expressed in the courtly ideal of love.

Nihon eitaigura (*The Eternal Storehouse of Japan;* 1688) *The Eternal Storehouse of Japan* deals with both the fortunes and misfortunes of merchant life and the struggle to make a living. This book is a collection of tales that recount the successes and failures of different merchants. Rather than deal with the success stories of wealthy merchants, Saikaku turns his attention to middle- and lower-class merchants who have to endure the vagaries of the markets and the unfair advantages to which they are subjected by the Edo-period economic system.

Gesaku *Gesaku* (playful composition) is a term used to collectively describe the different kinds of early modern prose fiction after Saikaku, that is, from the middle to the end of the Edo period. While the notion of "playful composition" refers in part to the idea that this literature was enjoyable to read, it also suggests something of the attitude of its authors, which was often irreverent toward the prevailing social mores.

As a literary form, *gesaku* not only drew inspiration from past narrative fiction, but also from some of the Edo period's allied arts. For instance, some types of *gesaku* used woodblock prints, sometimes in color, as book illustrations. In some *gesaku* forms the illustration was meant to supplement the text. In others, the illustration was primary and the textual narrative secondary. It was also common for plots and themes from popular theater, such as Kabuki and Bunraku, to find their way into *gesaku* narratives. Characters in book illustrations might even be rendered to resemble famous stage actors.

The plots and stories of some *gesaku*, and, for that matter, other popular art forms, were sometimes found to be morally offensive by the shogunate's censors. On at least two occasions, the government attempted to ban certain kinds of *gesaku* literature. During the Kansei Reforms (1787–93) and the Tempo Reforms (1841–43), some authors were effectively silenced, and the chilling effect this had on other writers lasted beyond the years of these reforms. Nevertheless, *gesaku* remained a vibrant source of literary creativity through the end of the Edo period, and the government was never fully successful in banning the books it found injurious to public morality.

A large number of books and several different categories of *gesaku* were published in the last half of the Edo period. Sometimes the names for these *gesaku* categories describe something of the subject matter of books, while at other times the category names refer to the physical appearance of books. Some categories have been used in multiple ways and some authors wrote books that fall under more than one category. Not even a specialized study of Edo-period prose literature could do full justice to the variety and complexity of *gesaku* works. However, the following discussion introduces some of the more important *gesaku* categories and briefly considers some of the genre's most influential and important authors.

Included among the important categories of *gesaku* were:

- *sharebon* (witty books)
- *kibyoshi* (yellow-covered books)
- *kokkeibon* (humorous books)
- *gokan* (bound-together volumes)
- *yomihon* (reading books)
- *ninjobon* (books about human feelings)

SHAREBON

Sharebon (witty books) were fictional stories, usually depicting the world of the pleasure quarters, written in a colloquial style considered clever or witty. This narrative form was especially popular in the 1770s and 1780s. The typical *sharebon* tells the story of a man who has a refined knowledge of the ways of the pleasure quarters, fashions, and all the latest cultural crazes.

Important *sharebon* authors:

- Ota Nampo (1749–1823)
- Santo Kyoden (1761–1816)

KIBYOSHI

Kibyoshi, or "yellow-covered books," were named for their bright yellow book jackets. They were short satirical stories written in colloquial Japanese, and

published in illustrated books starting in the 1770s and continuing through the early 19th century. Woodblock-print illustrations were central to this literary form. The text of the story was printed directly onto the blank spaces in the illustration. The book illustrators were sometimes well-known woodblock artists, such as Utagawa Toyokuni and Torii Kiyonaga. Subject matter for these stories included the licensed pleasure quarters and other aspects of contemporary society. Regardless of the subject matter, these stories were typically racy and provocative making them the object of Neo-Confucian government censors.

Important *kibyoshi* authors:

- Hoseido Kisanji (1735–1813)
- Santo Kyoden (1761–1816)

KOKKEIBON

Kokkeibon, or "humorous books," were comic compositions written starting in the middle of the 18th century and continuing until the end of the Edo period. Usually a fictional narrative, *kokkeibon* sometimes also told humorous stories about real people and events. Readers were attracted to *kokkeibon* not only because they were funny, but also because of their often penetrating, satirical view of society. *Kokkeibon* also featured dialogue spoken in colloquial Japanese.

Important *kokkeibon* authors:

- Hiraga Gennai (1728–80)
- Jippensha Ikku (1765–1831)
- Shikitei Samba (1776–1822)

GOKAN

Gokan, or "bound-together volumes," were illustrated prose fiction. *Gokan* illustrations, however, were typically more complex than the kinds of illustrations found in earlier *gesaku* forms. Originating at the beginning of the 19th century, *gokan* were volumes that took a number of smaller books and bound them together to create a larger book. One of the important effects of this change in printing and binding style was that it created a market for longer novels with more detailed plots. Romances, historical novels, and warrior adventures were among the kinds of stories that were told in this longer format. *Gokan* was one of the *gesaku* forms to be especially influenced by Kabuki plots, which frequently were reprised in book form. Of all the *gesaku* literary forms, *gokan* were published in the greatest numbers.

Important *gokan* authors:

- Santo Kyoden (1761–1816)
- Ryutei Tanehiko (1783–1842)

YOMIHON

Yomihon, or "reading books," derived its name from the desire to set these books apart from those that relied on illustrations to tell their stories. Although *yomihon* were illustrated, the text was always primary. *Yomihon* were prose fiction stories that had an overtly moral or didactic tone. Depending on the author, the moral of the story might be Buddhist or it might be Neo-Confucian. *Yomihon* plots were often placed within the context of historical events and sometimes were replete with supernatural occurrences. Influences on this literary form included Japanese *ukiyozoshi* (see above) and Chinese colloquial fiction.

Important *yomihon* authors:

- Ueda Akinari (1734–1809)
- Santo Kyoden (1761–1816)
- Kyokutei (or Takizawa) Bakin (1767–1848)

NINJOBON

Ninjobon, or "books about human feelings," were late Edo-period love stories usually set in the pleasure quarters of the city of Edo. These books first appeared at the end of the 18th century. As a genre, *ninjobon* were related to *sharebon*. Like *sharebon*, *ninjobon* utilized dialogue to portray the world of the pleasure quarters. Unlike *sharebon*, *ninjobon* were sympathetic to the travails of their characters, despite the social class or occupation of their protagonists.

Important *ninjobon* authors:

- Tamenaga Shunsui (1790–1843)
- Hana Sanjin (1790–1858)

IMPORTANT *GESAKU* AUTHORS AND THEIR MAJOR WORKS

Hiraga Gennai (1728–80)
- *Nenashigusa* (Rootless grass, in two volumes, 1763 and 1768)

- *Furyu shidoken den* (Biography of the stylish Shidoken, 1763)
- *Naemara in'itsu den* (The tale of a limp prick in seclusion, 1768)
- *Hohirin* (On flatulence, in two volumes, 1774 and 1777)

Ueda Akinari (1734–1809)
- *Ugetsu monogatari* (Tales of moonlight and rain, 1776)
- *Harusame monogatari* (Tales of the spring rain, ca. 1809)

Hoseido Kisanji (1735–1813)
- *Miru ga toku issui no yume* (Seeing is believing: dreams for sale, 1781)
- *Sato namari* (Yoshiwara dialect, 1783)
- *Nagaiki mitaiki* (A search for long life, 1783)
- *Koto shamisen* (Koto and shamisen, 1783)
- *Bumbu nido bangoku toshi* (Separating the sword from the brush, 1788)

Ota Nampo (1749–1823)
Note: Ota Nampo also wrote under the name Shokusanjin.

- *Ichiwa ichigen* (One story, one word, 1775–1822)
- *Senko banshi* (Thousand reds and ten thousand purples, 1817)
- *Hokushu sennen no kotobuki* (Northern district, one thousand years of good luck, 1818)
- *Ukiyo-e ruiko* (Lives of the ukiyo-e artists, ca. 1790)
- *Hannichi kanwa* (A half-day of leisurely talk, date unknown)
- *Zokuji kosui* (Urging secular ears, 1788)

Santo Kyoden (1761–1816)
- *Edo umare uwaki no kabayaki* (Grilled and basted Edo-born playboy, 1785)
- *Kokei no sansho* (Three madames and their dirty tale, 1787)
- *Tsugen somagaki* (Stars of the brothel, 1787)
- *Keiseikei* (Prying on courtesans, 1788)
- *Keiseikai shijuhatte* (48 techniques for success with courtesans, 1790)
- *Nishiki no ura* (The other side of the brocade, 1791)

LANGUAGE AND LITERATURE

Jippensha Ikku (1765–1831)
- *Seiro yawa irogoshaku* (Romantic lectures for Yoshiwara nights, 1801)
- *Tokaidochu hizakurige* (Travels on the eastern seaboard, 1802–22)

Kyokutei (or Takizawa) Bakin (1767–1848)
- *Sumidagawa bairyu shinsho* (The plum and the willow by the Sumida River, 1807)
- *Sanshichi zenden nanka no yume* (The complete story of Osan and Hanshichi, 1808)
- *Chinsetsu yumiharizuki* (The crescent moon, 1811)
- *Beibei kyodan* (Talk in rural dialect, 1813)
- *Kinseisetsu bishonenroku* (Golden youths in recent times, 1828)
- *Nanso satomi hakkenden* (Satomi and the eight dogs, 1814–32)

Shikitei Samba (1776–1822)
- *Ukiyoburo* (Bathhouse of the floating world, 1809–13)
- *Ukiyodoko* (Barber shop of the floating world, 1813–14)

Ryutei Tanehiko (1783–1842)
- *Shohon jitate* (Kabuki stories, 1815–31)
- *Nise murasaki inaka genji* (The false Murasaki and the rustic Genji, 1829)
- *Yama arashi* (Mountain storm, 1808)

Tamenaga Shunsui (1790–1843)
- *Shunshoku umegoyomi* (Spring colors: the plum calendar, 1832–33)
- *Shunshoku tatsumi no sono* (The Tatsumi quarter, 1833–35)
- *Harutsugedori* (Bush warbler, 1837)

Hana Sanjin (1790–1858)
Note: Hana Sanjin also wrote under the name Tori Sanjin.

- *Sato kagami* (Yoshiwara Patterns, 1822)
- *Kuruwa zodan* (Idle talk in the pleasure quarters, 1826)

READING

Language

Clarke 1999: development of Edo-period language; Habein 1984: history of the written Japanese language; Hadamitzky and Spahn 2003: kanji and kana; Miller 1967: history of the Japanese language; Quackenbush 1999: Edo dialects; Seeley 2000: history of the written Japanese language; Shibatani 1990: languages of Japan

Literature

HISTORY

Keene 1974, 375–388: general characteristics of Japanese literature, 401–405: medieval literature, 406–414: Edo literature; LaFleur 1983: Buddhism and medieval literature; Putzar 1973, 69–169: history of medieval and early modern literature; Kato 1981, 209–313: history of medieval literature; Kato 1990: history of early modern literature; Brower and Miner 1961: history of aristocratic poetry; Hibbett 1959: history of popular Edo-period literature; Hisamatsu 1976: biographical dictionary of authors; Keene 1989: travel diaries; Keene 1993, 609–1175: history of medieval literature; Keene 1976: history of early modern literature; Konishi 1986: history of early medieval literature; Konishi 1991: history of late medieval literature; Kornicki 1998: history of the book; Miner 1979: *renga*; Miner, Odagiri, and Morrell 1985, 43–63: history of medieval literature, 63–111: history of early modern literature

ANTHOLOGIES

Bownas and Thwaite (eds.) 1964: translations of selected medieval and early modern poetry; Carter (ed.) 1991: translations of selected medieval and early modern poetry; Sato and Watson (eds.) 1981:

translations of selected medieval and early modern poetry; Keene (ed.) 1955: translations of selected medieval and early modern prose; McCullough (ed.) 1990: translations of selected medieval and early modern prose; Miner (ed.) 1969: translations of selected medieval and early modern poetic diaries; Shirane (ed.) 2004: translations of selected early modern prose

9

PERFORMING ARTS

INTRODUCTION

Medieval and early modern Japanese performing arts included music, song, dance, theater, folk performing traditions, and storytelling. It is misleading, though, to assume that these different performance modes can be treated as if they are fundamentally separate arts. In fact, these different performing arts are intertwined in ways that make it difficult to create distinct boundaries. Two examples illustrate this point. First, religious performing arts included both music and dance that were often performed together. Second, Japanese theatrical forms, such as Kabuki, contain music and dance, as well as acting. While the following discussion will make certain distinctions between kinds of performing arts, they will often be interconnected.

Prior to the medieval period, Japanese performing arts were strongly influenced by continental traditions. Early Japanese music—that is, music prior to the start of the medieval period—was influenced by Chinese and Korean court music and by Buddhist ritual performance traditions. Dance and other performance arts were similarly influenced by Chinese and Korean culture. The history of traditional Japanese music and dance dates to the Nara period (710–794). These early performance arts were based in the court music of Tang-dynasty China (618–907), known as *gagaku*, and Buddhist liturgical music. *Gagaku*, the earliest extant court performance tradition of music and dance, was performed during the medieval and early modern periods, but this imperial court tradition fell out of favor with the rise of the warrior class at the beginning of the medieval period.

As in so much of medieval and early modern Japanese cultural expressions, warrior sensibilities had a significant influence on the development of performing arts. In the medieval and early modern periods, new forms of music developed alongside the older traditions, which continued throughout these periods. In the Kamakura period, the ritual performance of *gagaku* was continued on a limited basis; however, the popular music of the period was derived from new traditions of song and theatrical performance. Among these developments were chanted recitations set to *biwa* music that recounted the exploits and heroics of warriors in the Gempei War in which the Taira and Minamoto battled over control of Japan.

A later medieval development was the Noh theater. This dramatic performing art combined music and dance, and became popular with the warrior class, enjoying the patronage of Ashikaga shoguns. Noh drama consisted of highly ritualized chanted narratives wedded to Buddhist themes and aesthetics.

In the early modern period, there were two significant influences on the performing arts: the differing aesthetics of warriors and merchants. The rise of the merchant class in the large cities of Edo-period Japan became the catalyst for an urban cultural style that was significantly different from that of the warrior class. The emerging merchant culture, and the performing arts associated with it, prospered in the largest cities, Edo, Osaka, and Kyoto. The licensed pleasure quarters became the place for merchants to go for theatrical entertainment that more closely reflected their aesthetics and interests than older forms, such as Noh. Among the new types of theater were Kabuki and Bunraku, as well as new forms of music and song that were performed with koto accompaniment.

In the Edo period, three instruments that are closely associated with Japanese music today became central to different early modern musical traditions. These three instruments were the *shamisen*, the 13-string koto, and the *shakuhachi*. These instruments became important components of theatrical music as well as instruments to be played in concerts separate from the theater.

Because music was central to most medieval and early modern performing arts, musical instruments are discussed first, followed by music and dance traditions, including religious performing arts. Formal theater traditions—both medieval and early modern—are then discussed, along with brief comments on popular street performing arts in Edo.

MUSICAL INSTRUMENTS

Traditional Japanese musical instruments include a variety of wind and string instruments, as well as different kinds of drums and percussion instruments. Wind instruments include end-blown and side-blown flutes and reed instruments. Among the traditional string instruments used in traditional Japanese music are a variety of zithers, long and short lutes, and one bowed string instrument. Drums and other percussion instruments include both large and hand-held drums, and a variety of gongs, bells, and wooden clappers. Some important examples of Japanese instruments are discussed below.

WIND INSTRUMENTS

shakuhachi The *shakuhachi* is a rim-blown bamboo flute that utilizes five finger-holes to produce its dis-tinctive sound. The *shakuhachi* derives its name from its length as traditionally measured: 1 *shaku*, eight *sun* (the character for *sun* is also read *hachi*), approximately 21.5 inches. It was originally imported from China in a six–finger-hole version. Although there are references to the *shakuhachi* in medieval texts, it was not until the late medieval and early modern periods that the instrument became important through its association with Zen Buddhist monks. Later in the Edo period, the *shakuhachi* was played by warriors and others as a leisure activity. As a result, new repertoire developed to accommodate these musical interests. Ensembles known as *sankyoku* ("three parts"), consisting of *shakuhachi*, koto, and *shamisen*, also became popular in the Edo period.

hichiriki The *hichiriki* is a cylindrical double-reed instrument used in the performance of *gagaku* court music. It is made of bamboo wrapped with cherry bark and lacquered. The instrument has seven finger-holes in front and two thumb-holes in back, and it uses a reed in oboelike fashion. The *hichiriki* is

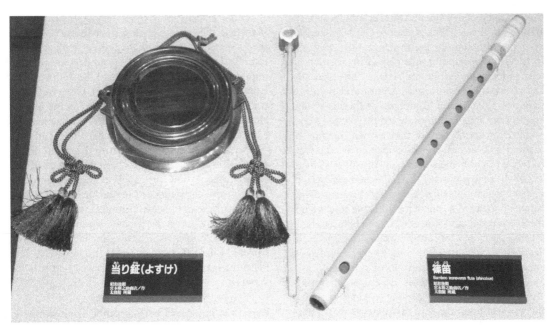

9.1 *Examples of Edo-period musical instruments* (Edo-Tokyo Museum exhibit; Photo William E. Deal)

descended from a similar instrument played in Tang-period China (618–907) court music.

sho Along with the *hichiriki*, the *sho*, a free-reed mouth organ, is integral to traditional *gagaku* court music. The *sho* is constructed of 17 bamboo pipes of different lengths set in circular fashion in a cup-shaped wind chest. The *sho* musician can produce sound by both the inhalation and exhalation of air through a mouthpiece inserted into the wind chest. By opening and closing holes in the pipes, a rather ethereal sound is produced. The full name of this instrument is *hosho*, or phoenix *sho*, a colorful reference to the idea that the instrument is like a phoenix: the *sho* is said to sound like the cry of a phoenix, its shape has the appearance of a phoenix, and the arrangement of pipes resemble a phoenix's wings. The *sho* is descended from a Tang-period Chinese instrument known as a *sheng*.

STRING INSTRUMENTS

biwa The *biwa* is a pear-shaped plucked string instrument that resembles a lute. It is descended from a Chinese instrument, the *piba*, and its appearance in Japan dates back at least to the Nara period, when it was used in the performance of court music. In the Heian period, it was played by aristocratic men and women as a leisure activity. The *biwa* also had strong associations with Shinto and Buddhist religious rituals, and Buddhist bodhisattvas and Shinto *kami* are sometimes shown playing the *biwa*.

In the medieval period, the *heikyoku* tradition of chanted war narratives—accompanied by the *biwa* and song by performers known as "lute priests" (*biwa hoshi*)—became popular. Also in the medieval period, a style of *biwa* playing, known as Satsuma *biwa*, became popular. The name for this style comes from the Satsuma domain controlled by the Shimazu family, who promoted this music as morally edifying. In the Edo period, the *biwa* was largely eclipsed in importance by the newly introduced *shamisen*.

Competing *biwa* schools developed that promoted different styles of playing, systems of tuning and musical notation, and instruments with variations in the number of strings and frets. Although four strings was the most common form, some *biwa* used three strings while others used five strings.

9.2 Musician playing a biwa (Illustration Kikuchi Yosai from *Zenken kojitsu*, mid-19th century)

shamisen The *shamisen* (or *samisen* in the dialect of the Osaka and Kyoto areas) is a three-string plucked lute. It is descended from a similar instrument imported to Japan in the middle of the 16th century from the Ryukyu Islands (Okinawa). Once in Japan, the *shamisen* quickly replaced the *biwa* as the lute of choice. It also became the central instrument in early modern Kabuki and Bunraku theater music. The instrument was associated with the geisha of the urban pleasure quarters, who played it as part of the entertainment they provided to their customers. Later in the early modern period the *shamisen* and the songs sung to its accompaniment (called *nagauta*, or "long song") were performed in concert settings, often in the homes of wealthy merchants and other patrons. Like the *biwa*, different playing styles and instrument configurations were developed for the *shamisen*.

koto The koto is a 13-string zither-like instrument with a paulownia wood soundboard. The instrument uses moveable bridges for each string to adjust the tuning, which allows for the variety of tunings used in koto music. To play the koto, the musician uses finger picks on the thumb, index, and middle fingers of the right hand to pluck the strings, and uses the left hand to press down on the strings to modulate the tone or raise the pitch that the plucked string produces. The koto is descended from the Chinese instrument known as a *zheng*.

The koto was first used in Japan in the Nara period in performances of court music. In the Heian period, the koto was used to accompany singers of popular songs, while during the medieval period, it was used as a solo instrument and as an accompaniment to Buddhist ritual chanting. As the koto grew in popularity as a solo instrument, new musical styles, sometimes including vocals, developed for the instrument. In the Edo period, the koto became a favorite instrument of urban merchants.

kokyu The *kokyu* is a bowed lute and was the only bowed musical instrument in use in Japan in the late medieval and early modern periods. The *kokyu* has a long neck and three strings, although after the late 18th century, some *kokyu* adopted a fourth string. The *kokyu* has its origins in the Ryukyu Islands (Okinawa). It is a hybrid instrument derived from both European (the Portuguese rebec) and Asian antecedents (the *shamisen*). The *kokyu* was first used in Japan in the late 16th or early 17th century, but it was not until the 18th century that the instrument became fairly widespread. It developed into an instrument used, along with the *shamisen* and koto, in a form of trio music called *sankyoku*.

PERCUSSION INSTRUMENTS

taiko The term *taiko* refers to several kinds of large drums that were used in a number of different settings, including imperial court music, Noh and Kabuki theater, and religious festivals. These large drums rest on the ground and are beaten with thick sticks to produce a deep rhythmic sound.

tsuzumi *Tsuzumi* are handheld lacquered wooden drums in an hourglass shape. Leather skins are used for the two drumheads. The use of these drums in Japan dates from before the Nara period. In the Edo period, these drums were used in both Noh and

9.3 Example of a drum (taiko) (Edo-Tokyo Museum exhibit; Photo William E. Deal)

Kabuki theater performances. There are both large (*otsuzumi*) and small (*kotsuzumi*) types of *tsuzumi*.

MUSIC AND DANCE

The association between music and dance has a long history in Japan. The earliest extant Japanese text, the *Kojiki* (Record of ancient matters), tells a story about Amaterasu, the Sun Goddess, who resides in the High Plain of Heaven. Amaterasu, in a fit of anger at her unruly brother, Susanoo, hides herself away in a cave, thereby casting the world into darkness. Amaterasu refuses repeated entreaties to emerge from the cave. Finally, one of the other gods performs a suggestive dance while stomping rhythmically on an overturned bucket, causing the other gods to laugh and applaud. The curious Amaterasu pokes her head out the cave to see what all the fuss is about. She is prevented from reentering the cave and light is restored to the world. Whether this story is read as an account of a comical music and dance performance or as a shamanic act of ritual dance and music, the later performers of the Shinto-related ritual performance of *kagura* (see below), a form of sacred song and dance, understood the cave event as the originating moment of this religious performing art. Subsequent Japanese performing art often combines music and dance to the extent that it is typically difficult to consider one without the other.

Characteristics of Traditional Japanese Music and Dance

There are many different kinds of traditional Japanese music and dance—some religious and some secular—that are performed on many different occasions. Within this variety, there are some common characteristics that are typically found in these diverse modes of performance.

Traditional Japanese music (*hogaku*) tends to be oriented toward the voice and narrative, often with simple instrumental accompaniment. Historically, though, there are also instrumental traditions; especially notable are those that developed in the Edo period. One important aesthetic in Japanese music is the significance of space (*ma*), a concept that refers, in part, to the "space" or silence between notes. Thus, this notion of space is not just about musical timing, but also concerns the idea that music is both the notes played and the silence in between. This idea of *ma* also appears in dance as pauses between movements. Such silences or pauses also add to the audience's anticipation of what will come next.

In both music and dance, aesthetics extends to the way in which the music or dance is performed. It was usual for each school of music and dance to prescribe aesthetically pleasing and ritually correct ways of performance, such as how to hold the body or intonate the words of a song. While we might view these as simply stylistic differences between competing performance schools, they were typically viewed as essential to the "correct" performance. Aesthetic considerations were never divorced from or treated as secondary to performance, and audiences were aware of these matters and responded accordingly when watching performers sing and dance.

Japanese music mostly uses a pentatonic scale that tends to focus on the horizontal aspects of music, that is, melody and rhythm, while simultaneously downplaying the use of vertical aspects of music, such as harmony or chords. Melodies can be quite complex. Japanese music is typically in duple meters (that is, 2/4 or 6/8 time). Rhythmically, however, there is sometimes no steady beat at all, or when there is, it exhibits a great deal of flexibility. Different kinds of Japanese music have different fixed rhythmic patterns. Finally, while there are Japanese forms of music notation, these were not regularly used until the Meiji period. Unlike Western music notation, it was common for each instrument to have its own separate notation system.

Traditional Japanese dance is referred to by two generic terms: *mai*, which usually refers to dance techniques through the end of the medieval period, and *odori*, which usually refers to early modern dance traditions. Japanese dance is often highly stylized with deliberate movements meant to convey the aesthetic or affective mood of the occasion as much as any specific meaning. Japanese dance also sometimes includes the use of masks, as for instance in Noh theater and some religious dances. As in music, the concept of *ma* ("space") is an important component of Japanese traditional dance aesthetics. In this instance, *ma* refers to the space between dance movements. Thus, both movement and nonmovement are equal partners in conveying meaning in Japanese dance.

Japanese dance traditions were found in the performing arts of all social classes in the medieval and early modern periods. Thus, the wide variety of dance types includes the formal dances of the aristocratic court, dances employed in Noh and Kabuki theater traditions, dances performed by geisha, and folk and religious dances performed on ritual and festival occasions.

Music and Dance Traditions

GAGAKU AND *BUGAKU*

The earliest extant forms of music and dance date back to at least the Nara period. The music tradition, known as *gagaku*, and the dance tradition, known as *bugaku*, were the music and dance of the Japanese aristocratic court. These performing arts were based on a number of influences, including court music of Tang-dynasty China (618–907), ancient Korean performing arts, Buddhist liturgical music, and indigenous Japanese music and dance traditions associated with Shinto ritual.

Given its influences, it is not surprising that the performance of *gagaku* and *bugaku* often had a ritual aspect both in its performance at court and also in its performance at Shinto shrines and Buddhist temples. Dances often included the use of masks and brightly colored costumes.

Although this performing art form continued in the medieval and early modern periods, it was eclipsed by other music and dance forms that were more in keeping with the aesthetics and values of the warrior class and, in the Edo period, the merchant class as well.

HEIKYOKU

The Kamakura period marked the beginning of the significant influence of warrior values and aesthetics on the performing arts. While different warrior tales were told, stories of the *Heike monogatari* became the most popular. This was especially the case in the development from the early Kamakura period of a tradition of chanted narratives accompanied by the *biwa* (lute) that told the story of the Gempei War between the Taira and the Minamoto that marked the beginning of warrior rule and the medieval period. The text used for these performances was the *Heike monogatari* (Tale of the Heike, ca. 1220). This performance tradition was known variously as *heikyoku* (Heike recitation), *heike katari* (Heike narrative), and *heike biwa* (Heike lute music). It included influences from both court music and Buddhist chants.

The performance of *heikyoku* was done by "lute priests" known as *biwa hoshi*. These performers were often blind. They assumed the appearance of itinerant Buddhist priests even when they were not formally ordained. The popularity of these performers is clear from the fact that in the 14th century the shogunate sponsored a guild of lute priest performers who effectively had a monopoly on the telling of Heike war stories. The *heikyoku* performance tradition continued into the Edo period.

ENKYOKU

Another form of medieval-period song was the "banquet song," or *enkyoku* (also called *soga*, or "feast songs"). These banquet or party songs were popular among warriors and court nobles at times of feasting and celebration. Songs were accompanied by rhythmic percussion and, for some songs, by *shakuhachi* accompaniment. The text of some of these songs still survives although little is known about the melodies that accompanied them. It is thought, however, that the occasions when these songs were performed were considerably less staid than traditional court performances, likely the influence of warrior sensibilities. Banquet songs were no longer performed by the beginning of the early modern period, but they were the antecedents to the Edo-period song form known as "short songs" (*kouta*).

DENGAKU AND *SARUGAKU*

In the medieval period, the two most important and popular music and dance forms were *sarugaku* and *dengaku*. They were important because they were antecedents to the development of the Noh theater. The term *sarugaku* is written with characters meaning "monkey music," but what the notion of monkey music might refer to is not known. *Sarugaku* is also a term that was sometimes used to refer to Noh theater, underscoring the historical connections between these two performing arts. The term *dengaku* means "field music," indicating its origins in rituals performed to promote an abundant rice harvest.

Historical records indicate the popularity of these two dances in both cities and provinces, and among such notables as Hojo regents and later the Ashikaga shoguns. By the Muromachi period, both *sarugaku* and *dengaku* performers were organized into guilds, called *za*, and enjoyed the patronage of important temples and shrines. Troupes traveled extensively, performing in towns, temples, and shrines in addition to such cities as Kyoto. Unfortunately, the exact nature of *sarugaku* and *dengaku* performances is unclear, though in addition to music and dance, it probably included acrobatics and plays. It is also likely that by the late 14th century, *sarugaku* and *dengaku* had developed similar repertories though they remained separate as schools of performance.

It was *sarugaku*, however, that developed into Noh theater as a result of the patronage of the third Ashikaga shogun, Yoshimitsu (1358–1408). In 1374, he attended the performance of a *sarugaku* troupe that included the actors Kan'ami (1333–84) and his son Zeami (1363–1443). Yoshimitsu was so taken with the performances that he offered Kan'ami and Zeami his financial support to further refine and develop *sarugaku* into the performing art that came to be known as Noh theater.

KOWAKAMAI

Originating in the Muromachi period, *kowakamai* was a form of dramatic song and dance that related stories of warriors and their military exploits. The narratives were taken from the *Heike monogatari* and other warrior tales. These warrior stories were chanted to music by three actors who enacted the narrated scene in a mimed dance. Musical accompaniment included drums and flute. Though *kowakamai* was a source for later theatrical works, it was largely a discarded art by the early Edo period.

JIUTA AND *KOUTA*

Both *jiuta* (regional songs) and *kouta* (short songs) were popular song forms in the early modern period that were performed to the accompaniment of the *shamisen*. *Jiuta* were particularly associated with the Osaka and Kyoto areas. These regional ballads sometimes included an accompanying dance. As this song form developed, koto and *shakuhachi* accompaniment sometimes replaced the *shamisen*. *Jiuta* was one of the important influences on the *nagauta* song form that developed in Kabuki theater. *Kouta* (also called Edo *kouta*), were popular in the city of Edo. Usually, the *shamisen* is plucked with a plectrum, but the short song tradition discarded the plectrum and instead used the fingernails. This was done in order to produce songs with a fast tempo at a high pitch. *Kouta* were often performed by geisha.

FOLK MUSIC

This is a catchall category that is the invention of modern scholars who have used the term *folk music* (*min'yo*) to describe the many local and regional song forms. It is difficult to make any but the most general of claims about folk music from the medieval and early modern periods because only scant records exist of how they were performed or what the verses might have contained. The best we can do is assume that folk music preserved today bears at least some resemblance to their earlier versions. It is also difficult to decipher the regional origin of songs that accompanied those who traversed the travel routes of medieval and early modern Japan. There is some evidence, though, that folk music traditions influenced more formal song traditions, such as the medieval banquet songs, Edo period short songs, and Kabuki songs.

RELIGIOUS PERFORMING ARTS

Medieval and early modern Japanese religious rituals utilized both music and dance. Depending on the particular tradition, music might include chanting to a rhythmic accompaniment or a dance reenacting stories of the gods. In the medieval and early modern periods, Shinto, Buddhism, and Christianity contributed to the religious performing arts.

Shinto

Shinto is especially associated with a performing art known as *kagura*. *Kagura* is the music and dance of the *kami* (deities) and is traced back to the dance performed to lure Amaterasu, the Sun Goddess, out of hiding (see "Music and Dance" above). *Kagura* was performed in medieval and early modern Japan as an aspect of rituals asking the gods for blessings and long life. There are two major categories of kagura: court *kagura* (*mikagura*) and village *kagura* (*sato kagura*).

Court *kagura* was performed at the imperial court and at important Shinto shrines connected with the imperial family. It was formally related to *gagaku* court music (see above). By contrast, village *kagura* is a term denoting the many different kinds of ritual music and dance performances that were enacted at local and regional shrines. There was great variety in village *kagura* and sometimes similar rituals went by different names in different parts of Japan. However, among the kinds of village *kagura* were performances such as *miko kagura*, a ritual dance performed by a Shinto shrine shamaness or priestess; Ise *kagura*, a ritual performance that involved an offering of boiled water to the *kami*; Izumo *kagura*, a dance utilizing sacred objects; and *shishi kagura*, a version of the so-called lion dance. The lion dance (*shishi-mai*) was a ritual performance in which the dancer or dancers wore lion masks (in some parts of Japan, the lion more closely resembled a deer). The lion dance's ritual function was to dispel evil and to bring blessings to the community.

Buddhist

Buddhist ritual practice included a number of different performance aspects. Most major ritual observances included some form of music, whether melodic or rhythmic. Sutra recitation and other forms of liturgical chant (*shomyo*) were chanted differently depending on the particular Buddhist school. Chanting and other Buddhist rituals often included accompaniment by percussion instruments and sometimes by melodic instruments. Forms of traditional court dance (*bugaku*) were sometimes also employed, especially at temples associated with the aristocratic class. Buddhist chanting styles also influenced later forms of Japanese music.

During the Kamakura and Muromachi periods, a performance known as *ennen* (long life) was conducted at Buddhist temples. Long-life ceremonies were conducted as the closing event at various kinds of religious events and included song and dance, and dramatic presentations. *Ennen* may have been a precursor to the development of the Noh theater, which was heavily influenced by Buddhist sensibilities and themes.

Playing music also sometimes had explicit religious implications. For instance, starting in the late medieval period, itinerant Zen priests known as *komuso* ("priests of emptiness") played a flute called a *shakuhachi* (see above) as an aspect of their ritual practice. Playing the *shakuhachi* was seen as a spiritual performance similar to meditation. They held to the notion that it was possible to attain enlightenment while playing the *shakuhachi* with single-minded concentration.

Dance was also an important part of the ritual practice of some Buddhist schools. Of note were the *nembutsu odori* and the Bon *odori*. The *nembutsu odori*, or "dancing *nembutsu*," was related to faith in the saving power of Amida Buddha associated with the Pure Land schools of Japanese Buddhism (see Chapter 6: Religion for details on Pure Land Buddhism). The term *nembutsu* refers to calling on the name of Amida for spiritual and material assistance with the hopes of being born in his paradise, known as the Pure Land, in the next life. The *nembutsu* dance provided a way of expressing one's faith and devotion to Amida. It was performed while chanting Amida's name or singing Buddhist hymns. This dance influenced the development of other folk performing traditions.

The Bon *odori*, or Bon dance, was performed during the annual Bon festival that occurred in either July or August, depending on the region. This was a festival in which the living welcomed the spirits of deceased relatives back to the realm of the living for a brief time. The Bon dance—derived from the dancing *nembutsu*—was one of a complex of rituals meant to honor the dead, who were believed to have the power to affect the fortunes of the living. The Bon dance originated in the Muromachi period and was performed throughout Japan during the early modern period.

Christian

In the transition from the medieval and early modern periods, during the 100 years of contact with Western European countries such as Portugal and Spain, beginning in the 1540s, Japan also had its first contact with Western music. Western musical instruments such as viols, rebecs (a 3-string bowed instrument), lutes, harps, claviers, and even a pipe organ were introduced to the Japanese by European missionaries and traders. It is reported that in 1591, a Portuguese music ensemble played a concert of Western music for Toyotomi Hideyoshi.

The exposure to Western music was largely Christian in focus. The pipe organ was used for religious music. Jesuit missionaries introduced Gregorian chant. Catholic mass was conducted in Japan using Western liturgical music. Christian influence on Japanese music was short-lived, however. Western music largely disappeared from Japan after Christianity was banned in the 1630s.

THEATER

In the medieval and early modern periods, there were four major theatrical forms: Noh, Kyogen, Kabuki, and Bunraku. Of these, Noh and Kyogen developed in the 14th century, while Kabuki and Bunraku date from the last half of the 17th century. The periods in which these theatrical forms originated suggest the initial patrons for these performing arts. Noh and Kyogen, dating from the medieval period, were first patronized by the warrior class, and especially the shoguns and regents who controlled the military government. Kabuki and Bunraku developed in the early modern period and were

an urban art form. The style and stories of these two theatrical forms were especially appealing to the newly rising merchant class who patronized both Kabuki and Bunraku.

One aspect is worth highlighting about the nature of medieval and early modern Japanese theater that on first glance may seem self-evident: it was quintessentially a performing art. The notion that one might read a play was a relatively foreign idea. Regardless of the playwright's creative process, the end product for the audience was the performed play, not a read one. Thus, although plays are often treated as Japanese literature, this would have been a peculiar thought to most medieval and early modern Japanese literati.

Noh

The Noh theater originated in the late 14th and early 15th centuries through the artistic creativity of the actor and playwright Kan'ami (or Kanze Kiyotsugu, 1333–84) and his son, Zeami (or Kanze Motokiyo, 1363–1443), an actor, playwright, and Noh theorist. They were both *sarugaku* performers (see above), and it was out of their elaborations on and refinements of *sarugaku* that Noh evolved into its own performing arts tradition, with an emphasis on mime and stylized dance accompanied by music and song. Noh theater might not have developed had it not been for the patronage and financial backing of the third Ashikaga shogun, Yoshimitsu, who had become an enthusiastic supporter of Kan'ami and Zeami's *sarugaku* troupe. It was this patronage that afforded Kan'ami—and later, Zeami—the resources needed to expand their theatrical ideas.

As the head of his own *sarugaku* troupe, Kan'ami was both the director and main actor, as was the custom of the day. He thus had the opportunity to introduce innovations into the usual repertoire of *sarugaku*. One such innovation was to interpose a song and dance form called *kusemai* into the short plays that by Kan'ami's time had become part of the standard repertoire of *sarugaku*. Explicitly Zen Buddhist themes also informed the new plays authored by Kan'ami and Zeami. This new theatrical form came to be referred to as Noh ("ability" or "talent").

After his father's death, Zeami continued to refine this new performing art, writing theoretical treatises on such topics as Noh aesthetics, the structure of plays, and the relationship between actor and audience. Like the plays he wrote, Zeami's theoretical perspectives were also imbued with Zen Buddhist ideas.

As a theatrical form, Noh revolves around human emotion expressed in movement and dance that is highly stylized with a strong suggestion of religious ritual. The development of plot is always secondary, in part because the audience usually already knows the story being performed. Rather, it is the slow and plodding expressive movements, relating tales of high emotional potency, that drives a Noh play.

The symbolic nature of a Noh performance is evident from the lack of concern shown for realism. There is nothing about the stylized movements and vocalizations that suggest the everyday world. Nor is there any concern for trying to match the actual appearance of an actor with the part the actor performs in the play. As in Kabuki, all performers are male, and thus men play women's roles. Similarly, an older actor might perform the role of a boy or a young man. It is not the physical appearance that is important, but the ability to properly perform the movements and convey the emotions expected for a particular role.

Noh utilizes stylized gestures and movements meant to suggest actions that do not actually take place on stage. Thus, for instance, a secondary character might express the wish to travel to some location. A simple turn of the head in a new direction symbolizes the travel and arrival at the new location. These fixed gestures and movements are called *kata* ("pattern" or "form"). Besides actions, they can also indicate emotions. Some 30 fixed gestures were commonly used, though many more existed. These gestures were fixed not only within the same school of Noh performance, but also between schools. Thus, a gesture indicating sadness would be more or less the same regardless of which school was performing.

The quality of acting and the emotional impact of the performance were critical in Noh because the plot of a play was usually already known to the audience. Thus, a plot's climax and conclusion rested not on anticipation or suspense at what the outcome might be, but on the ability of the actors to express emotion and provide the audience with a sense of connection to the plight of the protagonist.

A Noh actor was required to undergo extensive training. An important part of this training was directed toward the cultivation of proper skills and qualities, similar to cultivating spiritual awareness and abilities. Two of the most important of these qualities, as articulated by Zeami, were related to aesthetic aspects of Noh: *monomane*, the "imitation of things," and *yugen*, "refined elegance" or "profound beauty." The concept of *monomane* is closer to mime than to imitation, in the sense of imitating reality. Rather, in Noh, it is the ability to properly represent—or mime—the classic fixed gestures and actions that is prized.

The concept of *yugen* refers to "mystery and depth," but in Zeami's conceptualization, the meaning and significance of this aesthetic term expanded. For Zeami, it was paramount that actors be able to express *yugen*, which for him meant the skill to convey to the audience a sense of the profundity and beauty of the situation being enacted. *Yugen*, in effect, stresses the connection between actor and audience at an aesthetically rich emotional level.

Noh plays were enacted on a mostly bare stage and utilized only minimal props. Both masks and costumes were central to conveying the symbolic meanings of a play and the emotions of a character. Masks, for instance, were only worn by the main character and the main character's companions. Masks were used to represent character types such as old men, young women, demons, gods, and others. The mask worn by the character in the first part of a play was sometimes exchanged for a different mask in the play's denouement where the main character's true form is revealed. In keeping with the aesthetic requirements of Noh plays, specific costumes were designed to accompany the particular mask worn.

The few props that were used in a Noh performance by either the main or secondary character were typically hand props, such as a folding fan, Buddhist prayer beads, a letter, or an umbrella. Like other aspects of Noh, these objects were often used in a symbolic way so that the prop's shape suggested some other kind of object than the actual one carried. The folding fan, for instance, was used especially in this way. The fan might be closed to represent a knife or opened to represent the moon.

The other essential aspect of a Noh performance was the musicians. They sat on the stage, providing accompaniment to the verse sections of the play. A usual grouping of Noh instruments included flute and drums. There was also a chorus—usually eight people—that sat in view of the audience. They sang in unison between the songs performed by the main and secondary characters.

Among Zeami's many accomplishments were his theoretical treatises. He theorized, for example, about the correct elements required for a Noh play. In brief, he laid down rules about a play's subject matter, its literary style, and its formal structure. Subject matter varied, but often it derived from stories already known to the audience concerning figures, both historical and literary, for whom unresolved conflict made for an unsettled life and, at death, prevented a transition to the next life. This subject matter required a literary style that was, among other things, aesthetically appropriate, poetic, affective, and elegant.

Subject matter and style were molded by a prescribed structure that traced a pattern of 1) introduction (*jo*), 2) development (*ha*), and 3) climax (*kyu*). Not all Noh plays had the same structure, but this was a common arrangement. Translating this structure into the actual plot and performance of a play typically yielded the following sequence of events:

Introduction: entrance of secondary character (*waki*); the secondary character is typically a traveler who explains the place and time of the play's dramatic locale.

Development: (in three sections)

Section 1: entrance of the main character (*shite*) and, in some plays, the main character's companions or attendants (*tsure*)

Section 2: dialogue between the secondary and main characters. The secondary character is a stranger, a traveler, who does not know about the history and other details concerning the location he has come to. He therefore asks the main character about the locale and to explain what important events have transpired there.

Section 3: explanation. The main character explains what important events have transpired in the locale that the stranger has come to. This narrative of historical details usually occurs as a dance (*kusemai*). The detail provided by the main character leaves the secondary character wondering how anyone can have such intimate knowledge of events that transpired so long ago.

Climax: Reappearance of the main character in changed form, revealing her or his true identity. The revelation usually includes a dance performance. Once all is revealed, the protagonist receives some form of assistance from the secondary character and is now freed from the karmic ties binding her or him to this world.

By the end of the Edo period there were around 250 plays in the standard Noh repertoire. These plays were organized into five groups according to subject matter. One play from each group constituted a traditional Noh performance program. Thus, a medieval or early modern theatergoer would have seen a play from each category in an afternoon of Noh theater. The five groups are:

God Plays: a religious play in which a deity figures prominently

Warrior Plays: plays about warriors or male protagonists; the plots are often taken from tales told about the warriors who fought in the Gempei War (1180–85) found in the *Heike monogatari* (*Tale of the Heike*).

Women Plays: plays about elegant, courtly women; these plays are often referred to as "wig" plays.

Miscellaneous Plays: these plays often have a living person or "madwoman" as the protagonist; these plays deal with human character traits and emotions, such as bravery, jealousy, and love.

Demon Plays: plays that deal with beings such as demons and ghosts.

Noh play texts are composed of both poetry (*utai*) and prose (*kotoba*). Prose sections of plays are chanted rather than spoken in a conversational tone, and there are prescribed rules for the speed and cadence of the chanting. Poetry sections are sung to the accompaniment of music. They include verse from classical Japanese poetry collections and sometimes passages from Buddhist texts.

Buddhist aspects of Noh plays are significant. In fact, Noh plays cannot be understood without an understanding of the Buddhist assumptions that drive the plot and the resolution of a play's tensions. These ideas would have been immediately recognizable to medieval and early modern audiences. For instance, a play's protagonist (the *shite* role) often appears in one guise at the beginning of a play only to transform into another form by play's end. Because the protagonist is often the unsettled spirit of a warrior or some other famous figure seeking resolution to some longstanding conflict, the themes of Japanese Buddhist thought, stressing notions of karmic consequence and the fundamental instability and impermanence of the world, are critical. Reality is not fixed and stable, but fluid and changing. Thus, the otherworldly sensibility conveyed in many Noh plays and the movement of spirits in and out of the perceptions of the living would have seemed natural to most medieval and early modern theatergoers. The notion of the priest as intermediary between the world of the living and the world of the dead was symbolically enacted by the actors of the Noh play.

SOME REPRESENTATIVE NOH PLAYS LISTED ACCORDING TO THE FIVE TYPES

God Plays

- *Chikubujima*
- *Kamo*
- *Oimatsu*
- *Takasago*
- *Yoro*
- *Yumi yawata*

Warrior Plays

- *Atsumori*
- *Kiyotsune*
- *Sanemori*
- *Tadanori*
- *Tomoe*
- *Yashima*
- *Yorimasa*

Women Plays

- *Hagoromo*
- *Izutsu*

- *Matsukaze*
- *Nonomiya*
- *Obasute*
- *Saigyo zakura*
- *Yuya*

Miscellaneous Plays

- *Aoi no ue*
- *Ataka*
- *Aya no tsuzumi*
- *Dojoji*
- *Kantan*
- *Kinuta*
- *Sumidagawa*
- *Uto*

Demon Plays

- *Funa benkei*
- *Momijigari*
- *Nue*
- *Shakkyo*
- *Tsuchigumo*
- *Yamamba*

Kyogen

Kyogen ("mad words") was a comic theatrical form with close associations to Noh. Kyogen performances were either independent plays or comic interludes interspersed within the scenes of a serious play. Kyogen is also sometimes referred to as *ai-kyogen* ("*kyogen* in the spaces") in reference to its performance between Noh scenes. Like Noh, Kyogen traces its development back to medieval *sarugaku* traditions. It represents the extension of comic aspects of *sarugaku* into early modern Kyogen. In modern scholarship, Kyogen's connection with Noh has often overshadowed the study of Kyogen as a separate and distinct tradition. But Kyogen had distinct schools of performance and its own repertoire of plays even though it shared the same stage with Noh performers.

Kyogen was integrated into Noh performances in different ways. Sometimes Kyogen actors performed between acts in a Noh play, offering comic relief from the seriousness. The Kyogen actor, in the simple garb of a commoner, would explain to the audience in colloquial language aspects of the Noh play being performed, including plot and background information. This provided the audience with potentially greater clarity than the difficult literary language used in the play might otherwise provide. Kyogen actors sometimes performed within the play itself, dancing or playing a role, such as a beggar, that had the purpose of conveying some additional meaning or significance to the plot. Besides their functions within Noh, Kyogen comedies were sometimes performed as independent plays.

Originally, Kyogen was an improvised performance in which the actors worked only from a synopsis of the plot. It was not until the 17th century that Kyogen plays were written down, thereby largely fixing the play's performance according to the written text. The Kyogen repertoire included more than 200 plays.

Kyogen humor makes light of most social classes and a variety of human foibles, including clever retainers and dimwitted lords, husbands and wives, social snobbery, sons-in-law, and Buddhist clergy. Its comedic effects are accomplished through a number of different theatrical strategies including physical humor, stylized vocalization, verbal puns, mime, and mimicry. There is also the use of some dance, but masks are used sparingly, and there is usually no musical accompaniment.

There are numerous contrasts that can be drawn between Noh and Kyogen to underscore the fundamentally different natures of these two performing arts. For instance, unlike the characters found in Noh theater, Kyogen characters are commoners. Interestingly, the social status of Noh and Kyogen actors reflected this same distinction between upper class and commoner, and Kyogen actors were treated as inferior to Noh actors. Noh plays are imbued with Buddhist sensibilities that make many plays seem quite ethereal, focusing the real concern on the next world or an afterlife. By contrast, Kyogen is firmly grounded in the concrete, here and now, material world.

Kabuki

Together with Bunraku, Kabuki developed in the early modern period and was a theatrical form espe-
cially associated with the urban merchant class in such cities as Edo, Osaka, and Kyoto. Kabuki became a popular theater form that, like Bunraku, included music and dance to tell stories about the exploits of historical figures and about the lives of merchants and other townspeople.

Kabuki has its origins in women's traveling performance troupes dating from the late 16th and early 17th centuries. The leader of one such troupe, a woman named Okuni, is commonly given credit for creating Kabuki. Her troupe performed music and dance, and acted both comedic and dramatic stories. So-called women's Kabuki became quite popular, at least in part because the women performers were also prostitutes. In 1629, the Tokugawa shogunate banned Kabuki performances that featured women performers. In their place, young men and adolescent boys became the star Kabuki performers. But these young male performers also worked as prostitutes and, in 1652, the government banned young men and adolescent boys from acting in Kabuki performances.

In order to control the moral lapses associated with Kabuki, the shogunate decided to allow only performances by adult males who could legitimately claim to be serious actors. This stipulation was to have a profound effect on the future development of Kabuki. By the latter half of the 17th century, Kabuki had become a performing art in which men played all the roles, including women's roles (*onnagata*). It was around this same time that Kabuki theaters were constructed in such large cities as Edo, Osaka, and Kyoto.

As Kabuki became an important theatrical form in the Edo period, it incorporated aspects of other theatrical forms, including Noh, Kyogen, and Bunraku. Both Noh and Bunraku plays, for instance, were adapted into the Kabuki play repertoire. By the late 17th century, Kabuki revolved around three different kinds of performances: 1) historical plays (*jidaimono*) that dealt with historical figures, particularly warriors; 2) contemporary plays (*sewamono*) that dealt with the lives and loves of merchants and other townspeople; and 3) dance dramas (*shosagoto*) that included music and pantomime.

Music was an essential element of Kabuki, and its primary function was to accompany a dance segment. Like Bunraku, the newly popular *shamisen* became the favored instrument driving the melody of Kabuki music. Kabuki music consisted of both onstage and offstage music. Onstage music was divided into two kinds: lyrical (called *utamono*) and narrative (called *joruri* or *katarimono*). The most important lyrical form was *nagauta* (long song), in which verses were sung to accompany a dance. This musical style was particularly important in Edo Kabuki. The most important narrative forms were *kiyomoto bushi* (Kiyomoto style) and *tokiwazu bushi* (Tokiwazu style), both named after their creators. Kiyomoto *bushi* was happy and bright, while Tokiwazu *bushi* was heavily influenced by a Bunraku musical style known as *gidayu bushi* (Gidayu style).

These musical forms were performed by onstage musicians. But there was also music performed off-stage. Offstage music (*geza*) served several functions such as creating special sound effects, suggesting moods, establishing the locale in which a scene occurs, identifying characters, and signaling the beginning and end of a play.

There were different styles of Kabuki dance, but they generally shared a penchant for the spectacular and flashy. The most famous Kabuki dances were those choreographed for *onnagata* (women's roles). Another important aspect of dance was the effecting of a dramatic pose called a *mie*. The dancer would stop, turn his head, sometimes cross his eyes, and strike a pose that indicated a climatic moment in the play. The striking of wooden clappers (*tsuke*) served to heighten the drama and tension as the actor moved into the pose.

9.4 Replica of the Nakamuraza, a Kabuki theater (Edo-Tokyo Museum exhibit; Photo William E. Deal)

PERFORMING ARTS

9.5 Recreation of a scene from an Edo-period Kabuki play (Edo-Tokyo Museum exhibit; Photo William E. Deal)

EXAMPLES OF ROLES PERFORMED IN KABUKI PLAYS

Roles in Kabuki plays were quite varied, but they were usually assigned to specific categories.

Male Roles (*Otokogata*)
good male characters (*tachiyaku*)
- handsome men and amorous men (*wagoto*)
- straightforward men (*jitsugoto*)
- heroes and brave men (*aragoto*)
- warriors (*budogata*)

Evil Male Characters (*Katakiyaku*)
- evil men, often warriors (*jitsuaku*)
- amorous evil men (*iroaku*)
- old evil men (*oyajigata*)
- evil men who work for merchants (*tedaigataki*)
- fools (*dokegata*)
- comic evil men (*handogataki*)

Female Roles (*Onnagata*)
- twenty-something young women (*wakaonnagata*)
- high-ranking courtesans of the pleasure quarters (*tayu*)
- young commoner women (*musumegata*)
- evil women (*akuba* or *dokufugata*)
- old women (*kashagata*)

Other Roles
- boys or young men (*wakashugata*)
- old men (*oyajigata*)
- children (*kokata*)

SOME IMPORTANT FIGURES IN EDO-PERIOD KABUKI

Sakata Tojuro I (1647–1709): a Kyoto-Osaka–area actor who developed a realistic acting style known as *wagoto* ("soft business") that focused especially on a play's plot, dialogue, and character development.

Chikamatsu Monzaemon (1653–1724): a playwright especially associated with Bunraku plays, but who also wrote plays specifically for the Kabuki stage. Some of his puppet plays were adapted for Kabuki performance.

Ichikawa Danjuro I (1660–1704): an Edo-area actor who developed a flamboyant and particularly masculine acting style known as *aragoto* ("rough business") that focused on the exploits of brave heroes who overcame great odds.

Yoshizawa Ayame I (1673–1729): a Kyoto-Osaka–area actor who established the conventions for the performance of women's roles (*onnagata*).

Namiki Shozo I (1730–73): a playwright and creator of the revolving stage (*mawaributai*).

Tsuruya Nanboku IV (1755–1829): a playwright known for the use of dramatic theatrical effects and for plays about the lowest classes of Edo society.

Kawatake Mokuami (1816–1893): a playwright who wrote plays about the lowest classes of Edo society and whose dramatic sensibilities mark the transition between late Edo and modern Kabuki.

SOME IMPORTANT EDO-PERIOD KABUKI PLAYS

The repertoire of Kabuki plays was quite large. Aside from plays written explicitly for the Kabuki stage, there were many scripts that were adapted from plays written originally for Bunraku. To further complicate matters, many plays written for Kabuki and Bunraku have the same title and subject matter but were written by different playwrights. Despite these complications, some of the most famous Kabuki plays include the following:

Japanese Title	Common English Title
Aoto-zoshi hana no nishiki-e	Benten the Thief
Ichinotani futaba gunki	Chronicle of the Battle of Ichinotani
Kagamijishi	The Lion Dance
Kanadehon Chushingura	Treasury of Loyal Retainers
Kanjincho	The Subscription List
Kenuki	Hair Tweezers
Kokusen'ya kassen	Battle of Coxinga
Kuruwa bunsho	Love Letter from the Licensed Quarter
Kyo-ganoko musume Dojoji	Young Woman at Dojoji Temple
Meiboku sendai hagi	The Disputed Succession
Narukami Fudo Kitayama zakura	Narukami and the Deity Fudo
Sakura hime azuma bunsho	The Scarlet Princess of Edo
Sanja matsuri	Sanja Festival
Shibaraku	Wait a Minute
Soga no taimen	The Soga Confrontation
Sonezaki shinju	Love Suicide at Sonezaki
Sugawara denju tenarai kagami	Secret of Sugawara's Calligraphy
Sukeroku yukari no Edo zakura	Sukeroku: Flower of Edo
Tokaido Yotsuya kaidan	The Ghost of Yotsuya
Tsumoru koi yuki no seki no to	Love Story at the Snow-Covered Barrier
Ya no ne	Arrowhead
Yoshitsune sembon zakura	1,000 Cherry Trees

Bunraku

Bunraku, the puppet theater that developed in the late 16th and 17th centuries, was originally referred to as *ningyo joruri* (puppetry with chanted accompaniment). The name "Bunraku" dates from the early 1800s. Although the idea of puppet theater might conjure up notions of plays and storytelling for children, Bunraku was serious theater with stories, both serious and comedic, intended for adults.

Puppet theater originated from the combination of other performing arts—including chanted narrative (*joruri*), puppets to illustrate the story, musical accompaniment on the newly popular *shamisen*, and dance—into a new theatrical form. *Joruri* is a general term referring to chanted narratives accompanied by *shamisen* music. Another important influence on Bunraku was Kabuki. Especially important in the development of Bunraku was its borrowing of some of the technical aspects of Kabuki production.

The origins of puppet theater can be traced to the 11th century, although its history up to the Edo period is not well known. In the mid-17th century, puppet theater, combining the manipulation of puppets with chanted narrative, was already popular in cities such as Osaka and Kyoto. It was not until the late 17th century, however, that Bunraku became a fully developed performing art. This occurred because of the collaboration between a *joruri* chanter, Takemoto Gidayu (1651–1714), and a playwright, Chikamatsu Monzaemon (1653–1724). Together they gave a new and dramatic form to the theatrical style that would become Bunraku.

Gidayu made a name for himself as a master of narrative chant. His *joruri* chanting style bears his name: Gidayu-bushi (Gidayu-style recitation). He employed this style of narrative chanting, with solo *shamisen* accompaniment, in a puppet theater he founded in Osaka in 1684. This style would later have a significant influence not only on other styles of *joruri* chanting, but also on the styles of music that developed within Kabuki. Gidayu engaged Chikamatsu, who was already well known for his Kabuki plays, to write plays for his theater. In the years of collaboration with Gidayu, Chikamatsu wrote plays that dealt with historical themes and plays that took up contemporary issues. Plays composed after Chikamatsu's time sometimes merged the historical and contemporary play categories.

Chikamatsu's fame stems primarily from his Bunraku plays rather than those he wrote for the Kabuki stage. His puppet plays can be categorized into two major groups based on the narrative story line of the play. The first group is called *jidaimono*, or period plays, that narrated historical stories, most often about warrior exploits. Tales about famous battles or battlefield heroics were not new, and his audiences would have known the stories. Yet Chikamatsu and Gidayu were able to create a theatrical experience that included not only Gidayu's masterful chanting and Chikamatsu's engaging scripts, but puppets made to perform acrobatics and other seemingly impossible movements much to the delight of the audiences. One of the most famous examples of a Chikamatsu *jidaimono* play is *Kokusen'ya kassen* (Battle of Coxinga), a story of Chinese patriotism in the face of the Manchu invasions of China in the 17th century.

The second group of plays is termed *sewamono*, or contemporary plays. These plays were often based on real events and considered issues of immediate interest to his audience. Through his use of current events, Chikamatsu explored the morality of the times and the dilemmas confronted by those whose lives led them to deviate from the Neo-Confucian values set down by ruling-class warriors. One famous example—and the first *sewamono* that Chikamatsu wrote—is *Sonezaki shinju* (Love Suicide at Sonezaki, 1703), which dealt with the illicit love affair between a merchant and a prostitute. Tragedy, often resulting in suicide, was the usual denouement of such plays dealing with the conflict between emotional attachment and social mores. This play became very popular, reflecting the strong audience interest in the exploration of such themes.

The popularity of Bunraku continued to grow even after the deaths of Gidayu and Chikamatsu in the first quarter of the 18th century. In the 1740s, for instance, three plays were written that became among the most famous in the Bunraku repertoire. Among these three was *Kanadehon Chushingura* (1748), based on a true incident, which tells the story of a group of masterless samurai who avenge the forced ritual suicide of their lord. Bunraku's success as a theatrical form presented a challenge to Kabuki, with which it competed. In order to counter some of Bunraku's popularity, Kabuki productions incorporated aspects of Bunraku style. Kabuki actors, for instance, sometimes used a style of movement that mimicked the way puppeteers moved the puppets. Sometimes, too, Kabuki used Bunraku stage techniques to try to heighten interest in its plays. After the middle of the 18th century, however, Kabuki was able to eclipse Bunraku in popularity.

The style of Bunraku created by Chikamatsu and Gidayu—that elevated puppet theater into one of early modern Japan's important performing art forms—was the consequence of successfully and creatively combining three elements: recitation, music, and puppetry. Recitation is performed by the *joruri* chanter (known as a *tayu*). The chanter's role is to serve as the voice for all the puppet characters. Since there can be many different roles in a particular play, the chanter must be capable of projecting a wide range of voices that include males and females of differing ages, social classes, and other characteristics that require speaking in a particular way.

The music performed in Bunraku usually consists of a solo *shamisen* (see above for details on this instrument), but *shamisen* ensembles sometimes provide rhythmic accompaniment in plays adapted from Kabuki. Both the musical performance and the chanted word are tied intimately to the movement of the puppets. It is the puppet, however, that must follow the lead of the *shamisen*, which sets the narrative pace and timing through the way the *shamisen* is strummed. These aural cues are necessary because there is little if any eye contact between the puppeteers, the chanter, and the *shamisen* player.

Bunraku theater would not exist without puppets, but the way that puppets have appeared on stage and how they have been manipulated by puppeteers (*ningyo zukai*) has changed over time. In its earliest stages, Bunraku puppets were the only figures seen on stage. Puppeteers, chanters, and musicians were hidden behind a curtain. By the beginning of the 18th century, however, the tradition developed to make them visible to the audience and thus a part of the on-stage entertainment. Puppets also evolved. They came to have movable mouths, eyes, eyebrows, eyelids, and hands. With these elaborations in the form of puppets, it now required three puppeteers, dressed in black, to operate the puppets on stage. Puppets ranged in size from one-half to two-thirds of life size and weighed as much as 50 pounds. There were also smaller puppets used for a play's minor characters that were operated by only one puppeteer. As puppets became more intricate, so did other aspects of a Bunraku production, such as set designs and costumes.

In order for the three elements of Bunraku—recitation, music, and puppetry—to be compelling and entertaining, they needed the structure of a well-told tale. Chikamatsu provided such plays, as did subsequent Bunraku playwrights.

SOME IMPORTANT EDO-PERIOD BUNRAKU PLAYS

Japanese Title	Common English Title
Kanadehon Chushingura	Treasury of Loyal Retainers
Kokusen'ya kassen	Battle of Coxinga
Shusse Kagekiyo	Kagekiyo Victorious
Sonezaki shinju	Love Suicide at Sonezaki
Sugawara denju tenarai kagami	Secret of Sugawara's Calligraphy
Tokaido Yotsuya kaidan	The Ghost of Yotsuya
Yoshitsune sembon zakura	1,000 Cherry Trees

STREET ENTERTAINERS AND STORYTELLERS

There were other forms of performance that operated outside of the formal music, dance, and theater traditions. Street entertainment, for instance, became a significant phenomenon during the Edo period and contributed to the rise of cities as important cultural centers. Such performance modes took on a variety of forms, and it has been estimated that there were as many as 300 different kinds of street entertainers. One might enjoy plays, trained animals, magic, song and dance, comedic dialogues, and puppetry on the streets, and vendors sold food, drink, and even medicine to spectators. While street entertainment came to have wide popular appeal, the performers themselves were usually itinerants and therefore of a very low social class.

In addition to street entertainers, other forms of performance emerged in the early modern period. *Yose* was a kind of Edo-period theater that is often likened to vaudeville because of the different types of performances that one might enjoy there, which included song and dance, comedy, storytelling, parody, mime, and acrobatics. The popularity of *yose* is evident from the 390-odd *yose* theaters that existed in Edo at the close of the early modern period. Of particular importance to the development of *yose* were storytelling traditions, some dating back to the medieval period, that evolved into performance traditions during the Edo period. These include *rakugo* and *koshaku*, which were performed at *yose*.

Rakugo, a comic monologue often with a strong dose of satire, was performed by professional storytellers known as *rakugoka*. The *rakugo* performer was essentially presenting a play in which he played all the parts, including narration, and used changes in facial expressions and vocal intonation to present the different characters in the story. The performer typically sat on a cushion in the center of a bare stage, using only a fan for a prop. One important feature of a *rakugo* performance was the rapport that developed between *rakugoka* and the audience, especially since the stories told were often already well known. The performer created a sense of connection to the audience by the unique way in which he told the story.

Koshaku, called *kodan* since the Meiji period, was a popular Edo-period performance tradition in which storytellers recited tales based on historical narratives and legends. This storytelling tradition had its origins in the reading and explanation of Buddhist and other religious texts. By the Edo period, *koshaku* had lost its connections to religion, and the repertoire of stories expanded to include tales recounting dramatic events concerning warriors, lords, merchants and other urban commoners, and the unsavory side of those living in the cities. Tales of heroism were also popular. The storyteller would sit at a desk and narrate a story, clapping wooden blocks or beating a fan against the desk in order to build dramatic interest at important junctures in the story.

READING

Musical Instruments

de Ferranti 2000; Malm 2000; Kishibe 1982

Music and Dance

Ortolani 1995; Malm 2000; Kishibe 1982

Religious Performing Arts

Ortolani 1995; Malm 2000; Kishibe 1982

Theater

Ortolani 1995; Inoura and Kawatake 1981; Miner, Odagiri, Morrell (eds.) 1985, 307–316: Noh, 316–320: Kyogen, 322–325: Joruri/Bunraku, 326–332: Kabuki, 333: *kagura* and *dengaku* stage layouts, 334–335: Noh theater stage layout, 350–357: list of Noh plays, 357–360: list of Kyogen plays; Dunn 1969, 137–145: Edo-period actors and entertainers; Kato 1981, 303–313: Noh and Kyogen; Keene 1966: Noh and Kyogen; Keene (ed.) 1970: Noh plays; Komparu 1983: Noh; Takeda and Bethe 2002: Noh and Kyogen costumes, robes, masks, and musical instruments; Brandon (ed.) 1982: Kabuki and Bunraku; Brandon 1975: Kabuki plays; Hare 1986: Zeami; Rimer and Yamazaki 1984: Zeami; Gerstle 1984: Chikamatsu; Gerstle 2001: Chikamatsu plays; Brazell (ed.) 1998: anthology of traditional plays; Brazell (ed.) 1988: Noh and Kyogen plays; Yasuda 1989: Noh plays; Morley 1993: Kyogen plays; Gerstle 1999: Kabuki; Torigoe 1999: Joruri and Bunraku

Street Entertainers and Storytellers

Nishiyama 1997, 228–241

10

ART AND ARCHITECTURE

With Lisa J. Robertson

INTRODUCTION

Developments in visual art and architecture paralleled transformations in medieval and early modern Japanese religion, government, and society. Once the military class attained power in the Kamakura era and instituted a new form of government, they sought to assert their values, political aims, and social status. One way they accomplished this was through patronage of art and architecture, a practice that continued throughout the medieval and early modern periods despite variations in warrior sensibilities expressed at different times during this nearly 700-year period.

Members of the warrior classes favored certain themes, techniques, and styles in art and architecture that distinguished their patronage from that of established aristocrats and, in the Edo period, from nouveau-riche merchants and artisans. Further, the military classes grasped the power of visual art and considered its effects as they chose their commissions. For example, art created for Buddhist institutions at the request of elite samurai leaders could help restore the reputation of a particular temple, further the career of an important priest, or simply inspire other forms of patronage at the local level. At the same time, regional lords could enhance the prestige and authority of both patron and domain by commissioning Buddhist images.

Medieval Art and Architecture

High-ranking warrior leaders recognized the arts as a powerful arena in which to define the central military government, the shogunate, as a rival to the imperial court in Kyoto in artistic and cultural discernment. Through sponsorship of the arts, the medieval warrior elite promoted samurai tastes as distinct from the sensibilities of aristocrats who had directed artistic production to the end of the Heian period. Warriors were drawn to images and art forms that highlighted their martial lifestyle and code of honor. Examples of such masculine art

forms—as they came to be known, in contrast with the "womanly" elegance of Heian court romance tales and paintings—included war epics illustrated with battle scenes glorifying samurai conquests, portraits of noted shoguns and military lords, and suits of armor distinguished by both aesthetic and technological achievement. Regionally powerful warriors also found that commissions such as arms and armor, battle chronicles, and portraiture expressed military sensibilities in keeping with their status. Although shogunal rule rendered the emperor a figurehead and afforded aristocrats little input into military government, elegant Heian cultural preoccupations lingered in the medieval period alongside military tastes. Contrasting, yet coexisting, styles included established aristocratic tastes such as Tosa school painting.

During the Muromachi period, the Ashikaga shoguns enjoyed prominence even among the cultural elite during their tenure in the capital, Kyoto, in part due to their enthusiastic support for performing arts such as Noh drama, linked verse (*renga*), tea gatherings, and flower arranging, as well as garden arts and architecture in the Chinese style. Beyond the political role of the Ashikaga shoguns, their patronage helped to create a legacy that extended beyond the medieval era. For example, academic styles in painting such as the Kano school and the Japanese literati school were rooted in the monochrome ink traditions introduced by monk-painters in the Muromachi era.

The Kamakura-period shoguns and other high-ranking warriors were patrons of religious art and architecture. For example, Minamoto no Yoritomo made generous donations for rebuilding key Nara temples such as Todaiji and Kofukuji destroyed during the Gempei War. While Yoritomo's generosity could be considered a simple act of Buddhist piety, his financial assistance also offered potential political rewards, as popular support furthered government authority and even economic conditions.

Other influential currents in medieval art originated outside Japan. The rate of cultural exchange between Japan and China during the Kamakura period declined in comparison to the deluge that characterized earlier eras, such as the Nara period. Still, the newly established Kamakura shogunate encouraged introduction of ideas and imagery from abroad, especially from China. Opportunities for cultural exchange with Song-dynasty China (960–1279) increased due to China's active merchant navy and, at least during the Kamakura era, a desire to disentangle the shogunate and its affairs from the preoccupations of the Heian court with its aristocratic sensibilities. The final element that emerged from a renewed relationship between China and Japan during this period was the introduction of the meditative Zen (Chinese: Chan) Buddhist tradition.

Zen Buddhism first arrived in Japan from China beginning in the late 12th century. Soon after the Japanese monks Eisai and Dogen returned from travels in China with Chan teachings and seeds for growing green tea plants, the samurai elite embraced this austere tradition. Warrior involvement in Zen Buddhism quickly became visible, as temples modeled on Chinese Zen architecture, such as Kenchoji and Engakuji, were constructed in the city of Kamakura. In addition, emphasizing direct, intuitive perception of reality, Zen espoused succinct, incisive literary forms, a straightforward ethical code, and discipline, rather than scripture, dogma, or ritual—all of which were well received by the military and cultural elite. Compared with the complex subtleties of Heian society, the spare Song literary forms, serene landscape paintings, and subtle monochrome ceramics probably seemed immediately accessible to the military and intelligentsia. Zen and its cultural permutations could inspire without daunting those who had little exposure to Chinese poetry, Confucian classics, and other pillars of Japanese aristocratic education. As Zen and related cultural traditions eschewed the worldly orthodoxy and iconic imagery of other Buddhist schools, the boundaries between sacred and secular were blurred. Further, medieval monastics were active in secular circles, attending civil ceremonies, advising about political affairs, and practicing distinctively Zen arts such as poetry and calligraphy. These monks began to introduce their military patrons to the reserved character of Song literary and visual arts. Thus, through formal restraint and directness in accord with Zen traditions, Song culture provided warriors with a foundation for further arts patronage, as well as a cause to which they became dedicated.

Many scholars have asserted that samurai were attracted to Zen largely due to its insistence on self-discipline. Compared with other schools of Buddhism practiced in Japan, Zen especially emphasized poverty and seclusion for monastics, although interaction between clerics and the laity was acceptable and encouraged. Zen practices originating in China included long hours of intense meditation, ritualized tea gatherings to promote health and concentration, composition of poetry, calligraphy, and paintings with a distinctive Zen flavor, and even gardens designed to inspire insight. Monk-painters in Japanese monasteries began emulating the minimalist monochrome landscape paintings first brought to Japan by Chinese monastics as part of their training. Such images were thought to cultivate intuition and insight. However, many practices associated with Zen also served as leisure and cultural activities for privileged members of Japanese society. Daimyo and shoguns amassed notable collections of painting and calligraphy in the Zen idiom, especially in the Muromachi era. Elite warriors sought to learn painting and calligraphy techniques through study with Zen monastics. Chinese architectural styles used in Japan for Zen temples were admired by Japanese military figures, who borrowed the Zen aesthetic in designing cultural retreats surrounded by Chinese-inspired gardens, where they could indulge in aesthetic pursuits. Zen promoted study of Chinese literature and history, which offered models for successful administration and righteous rule that assisted members of the military classes, while also affirming the virtues of education and contemplation. Thus, Zen represented not only a religious tradition, but also the possibility of a broader cultural horizon deemed necessary for warrior-class rulers who sought to place themselves on an aesthetic and intellectual par with the nobility.

As Japan emerged from the Warring States period, three warlords attempted in sequence to seize political control of the country during the brief Azuchi-Momoyama era. Some aspects of the patronage of this era reflect the grandiose excesses of which daimyo were capable. Numerous castles were erected, only to be conquered and destroyed by competing lords, and are evidence of the frequent shifts in authority that marked this tumultuous age. Fortifications constructed during the rule of the

Ashikaga shoguns had been designed primarily for military purposes. In contrast, although the palatial castles of the Azuchi-Momoyama period were erected with defense against gunfire in mind, they were primarily a setting for daimyo displays of military and political power. Warlords also favored extravagant paintings for their castle interiors, and were particularly fond of gold pigments and gold leaf. Considerable resources were devoted to commissions that would promote the political and cultural superiority of elite lords.

Early Modern Art and Architecture

The unification of Japan under the leadership of the Tokugawa family in 1615, and the establishment of a stable government in the city of Edo, marked the end of decades of war and political upheaval, and the start of a 250-year period of peace. The combination of increased leisure time, the redefinition of the military classes in peacetime, and the rise of an increasingly wealthy class of merchants and artisans, with their interest in urban amusements, contributed to the artistic variety that marked the early modern period.

The focus of the visual arts changed, in part, because the prosperity and the security of peace allowed time for leisure pursuits. Amusing pastimes, local scenery, and images of everyday life replaced battle chronicles, religious themes, and flashy compositions that had been favored by warrior patrons since the 16th century. The prohibition on overseas travel for Japanese, and strict trade limitations with foreigners, meant that Japanese artists produced their works with the indigenous population in mind, with the exception of ceramics exported to China during the 17th century. An increase in disposable income and the growth of the leisure industry also spurred demand for a greater variety of functional art objects, such as ceramics, lacquer, and textiles.

Although they controlled the government and most of the wealth, Tokugawa patronage produced probably the least innovative development in Edo art. The Kano school, a studio of extended family members who exemplified the regime's conservative approach, dominated works completed for the shoguns from the 1620s onward. Kano painters utilized a decorative manner first favored by Tokugawa forbears in the Momoyama era in conjunction with Chinese subjects that highlight Confucian themes and characters. Models of good government drawn from Confucian sources adorned painted sliding doors and screens in reception rooms where official business was conducted, thus reinforcing shogunal policies. While Tokugawa commissions lacked drama, they certainly fulfilled the shogunate's central ambition by keeping tradition intact.

As in past eras, religion and philosophy continued to inform Edo-period artistic and cultural developments. The ethical implications of Neo-Confucianism—principles for maintaining an ordered government and social structure originating in China—became especially vital as Tokugawa shoguns aimed to shepherd the self-reliant lords and retainers of about 250 domains into a genial, cohesive bureaucracy. Brush and ink compositions, including various forms of calligraphy and painting styles inspired by Chinese Ming-dynasty works, promoted the Confucian scholar-official ideal to which samurai were expected to aspire.

Beyond the shogun's residence at Edo Castle, a vast array of visual art forms flourished, in a testament to the cultural diversity of the early modern period. A healthy economy, changing aesthetics, and social competition helped the arts to become more accessible during the Edo period. Artists enjoyed a better standard of living, were able to specialize and attract clients seeking their particular abilities, and experienced more freedom than in earlier periods. Censorship occurred, although sumptuary laws and restrictions on content often spurred artists to creative circumvention.

The maintenance of clearly demarcated social classes was an important component of Tokugawa policy that affected art, consumption, and currents in visual culture. All citizens were required to observe various statutes regarding proper appearance as determined by the social hierarchy. Individuals and family groups were closely identified with visual and contextual symbols that indicated one's position in life at a glance. High sensitivity to status fueled competition among those of means.

One Edo cultural institution largely eluded the shoguns' far-reaching regulations: the sometimes bawdy diversions found in the pleasure quarters. Despite several edicts by Tokugawa rulers that attempted to quiet the boisterous world of theaters, street performers, vendors, public baths, teahouses, and brothels, the pleasure districts maintained a prosperous urban leisure culture. One of the first licensed districts, the Yoshiwara, was located in the Tokugawa capital, and became a main attraction of Edo urban life. These quarters, known as the floating world, or *ukiyo* (see below in ukiyo-e), spawned colorful new trends in the visual arts.

Like the changing of the political guard, the shifting economic circumstances also affected Edo-period arts as a new class of patrons emerged who favored the glamour and unique flavor of urban centers. Many artists formulated their aesthetics to appeal to the fashion-conscious merchants, money-lenders, and other discerning urban residents who made up the wealthiest portions of the population. Edo-period artists often looked to past artistic trends, yet reworked earlier styles and techniques into a new idiom that accorded with the tastes and sensibilities of such patrons as warriors, merchants, artists, and aristocrats.

ART

Sculpture

Prior to the medieval period, Japanese sculpture was fabricated in a variety of mediums including wood, bronze, clay, and dry lacquer modeled over wood. By the beginning of the Kamakura period, wood had become the primary medium for sculpture. Medieval wood sculpture, which was mostly Buddhist in subject matter, was either carved from a single solid block of wood (*ichiboku zukuri*) or made from parts carved separately and then joined together (*yosegi zukuri*).

MEDIEVAL PERIOD

Heian- and Kamakura-period Buddhist sculptors were typically organized into workshops (*bussho*), independent or associated with a particular temple, which consisted of a group of Buddhist sculptors (*busshi*) working in a similar style, passed down from a teacher to students and studio assistants.

Although Kamakura-period sculpture still sometimes used styles derived from Chinese and Heian-period precedents, there were significant stylistic innovations in the construction and decoration of Buddhist sculpture in the medieval period. The Heian-period style of gilded statues continued, but from the late 12th century, a dramatic sculptural style grounded in realism dominated, especially in images by sculptors of the Kei school. These works were executed using the joined-wood technique (*yosegi zukuri*). Realism was enhanced by the use of crystal insets for eyes (*gyokugan*, "jewel eyes").

The most important workshop in the Kamakura period, the Kei school (*Keiha*) was so called because the important figures all shared the character *kei* in their names. These sculptors worked within sculpture studios that were commissioned to work on images for temples. The Kei-school style ranges from stark to dramatic to beatific realism, and as these artists worked in the former capital at Nara, they were also affected by the classicism of the eighth-century works that remained in Nara temples. However, works by Kei-school artists often venture beyond realism to exaggeration, especially in depictions of unenlightened beings. Thus the Kei-school of Kamakura sculpture can be understood as a response to and dramatization of earlier realistic modes in Japanese sculpture. For further clarification, some have characterized the Kei style as "exaggerated realism." Perhaps the sensational appearance of dramatic Kei figures, like the pair of guardians located beneath the Great South Gate (*nandaimon*) at Todaiji, can be connected with the brutal nature of military experience, as seen in illustrated battle tales and other examples of medieval warrior patronage.

There were a number of Kei masters. Unkei (d. 1223) and Kaikei (active ca. 1185–1223) worked on both collaborative and individual projects. Their most famous collaboration is the pair of Buddhist guardian figures (*ni-o*) crafted for the newly reconstructed Great South Gate (*nandaimon*) at Todaiji. This project received support from the Kamakura shogunate.

Separately, Unkei was noted for a number of works including a pair of wooden sculptures located at the Kofukuji in Nara. These are images of two Indian Buddhist monks named Muchaku (in Sanskrit, Asanga) and Seshin (in Sanskrit, Vasubandhu) that utilize such Kamakura-period sculptural innovations as a high level of realism realized, in part, through the use of crystal for the eyes. In contrast to Unkei, Kaikei's images are sometimes less expressive of realism and tend more toward idealism. Kaikei also uses gold and paint on the surface of some of his images. Particularly well-known are his images of Hachiman, a Shinto god portrayed wearing a Buddhist monk's garb, and the bodhisattva Jizo.

Unkei's six sons were also sculptors. Of special note were the eldest son, Tankei (1173–1256), and the fourth son, Kosho (active late 12th to early 13th century). Tankei and his workshop sculpted some of the many Buddhist images at Rengeoin (popularly known as Sanjusangendo (Hall of 33 bays) in Kyoto. Images of the gods of thunder and wind are particularly famous. Kosho's most famous work is an image of the Heian-period Japanese Buddhist priest Kuya (903–972). Kuya was an advocate of the practice of reciting the *nembutsu: namu Amida butsu*, meaning "Praise to Amida Buddha," as a means to gain birth in the Pure Land, or Western Paradise, of Amida. Kosho's realistic sculptural portrait of Kuya shows the monk chanting the *nembutsu*. Emerging from Kuya's mouth are six tiny images of Amida, each figure representing one of the six characters that comprise the *nembutsu* (*na-mu-a-mi-da-butsu*).

While Buddhist sculptures were the most commonly produced, there were other trends in Kamakura-period sculpture that included secular subject matter. Portrait sculptures, though they might be of important monks, were also made of famous warriors such as the late 13th-century image of Minamoto no Yoritomo, the founder of the Kamakura shogunate. Like other Kamakura-period sculpture, this seated portrait employs realism and inlaid crystal eyes. In a similar style is the seated sculpture of Uesugi Shigefusa, a 13th-century adviser to the shogunate.

By the Muromachi period, the earlier emphasis on Buddhist sculpture rendered in a realistic manner was largely discontinued. Religious sculpture was no longer produced by sculpture workshops like the Kei, but instead by artisans without the kind of formal ties to Buddhist temples that Kamakura-period sculptural schools had. This was less because a new form of sculpture had taken its place and more due to changing warrior sensibilities, especially as the result of the importation of Zen Buddhism and the arts this religious tradition engendered. Interest shifted from Buddhist sculpture to new art forms such as ink painting. While ink painting could be a powerful medium for expressing Buddhist ideas, it accomplished this in a much different way than the realism of Kamakura-period sensibilities.

EARLY MODERN PERIOD

Edo-period sculpture is sometimes described as insignificant compared with its medieval antecedents. While it was the case that impressive workshops of gifted sculptors were no longer the norm, there were nevertheless important works produced in the early modern period. One avenue for sculptural creativity resulted from the rebuilding of Buddhist temples destroyed during the Warring States period. These temples commissioned sculptors to reproduce the images that had been lost when buildings were burned or razed. Often these images were made in imitation of the earlier styles of the destroyed images.

The most original early modern sculptor was the artist Enku (1632–95). Enku was a Buddhist priest who wandered the countryside preaching and creating religious images. His sculptural style is usually classified as *natabori*, in which the wood is only roughly carved and the finished surface shows the wood grain and the marks made by the chisel or ax. His many works suggest a spontaneity of both concept and execution.

Painting

Artists produced paintings of both secular and religious subjects throughout the medieval and early modern eras. The breadth and richness of Japanese painting traditions are evident in the numerous formats, styles, and diverse subjects represented in the many surviving works from feudal times. Yet the variety of approaches to painting produced during military rule complicates a brief survey of this form of artistic expression during a period of nearly 700 years. For instance, Buddhist figures and themes were painted in several different formats and styles—resulting in images that defy association with discrete categories. Images rendered in monochrome ink, a widely used technique in the medieval era, encompass both secular and religious subject matter, and were executed in diverse formats such as screens, doors, and hanging scrolls. Thus, a single chapter examining painting in medieval and early modern Japan cannot summarize the many important artists and significant trends in detail. Instead this section provides an overview of painting formats and techniques employed in the age of warrior rule, along with a general survey of major movements in painting.

At the outset of this brief introduction to medieval and early modern painting in Japan, one aspect of art historical terminology must be clarified. The stylistic terms *kara-e* (Chinese-style pictures) and *yamato-e* (Japanese-style pictures), first employed in the Heian period, persist in descriptions of Japanese painting throughout the medieval era. Although these terms may initially seem straightforward, in fact they are used to designate varied styles, techniques, and content in painted images. *Kara-e* can refer to works made by Chinese painters or images by Japanese artists utilizing Chinese painting styles. Images executed by Japanese artists that feature Chinese subject matter, such as a landscape depicting a locale in China (whether mythic or real) are also described as *kara-e*. Chinese landscapes are visually distinct from Japanese outdoor scenes, for *kara-e* paintings feature the precipitous mountains typical of many areas of China, while *yamato-e* images focus on the gently rolling landscapes that characterize the Japanese archipelago. Although the term can also refer to landscape scenes, the word *yamato-e* was first used to identify images rendered in a distinctive Japanese manner, involving application of thick layered pigments in rich jewel tones by Japanese artists. (*Yamato* is an old Japanese word

for "Japan.") Poignant subjects drawn from aristocratic literature dominate *yamato-e* or Japanese-style painting from the Heian period onward. However, Edo-period approaches, such as the Rimpa style, incorporate typical *yamato-e* content presented in painting techniques that depart from established *yamato-e* traditions—thus reworking familiar themes in a new manner. Quintessentially Japanese painting formats, such as hand scrolls (*emakimono*) and six-panel folding screens (*byobu*) that incorporate literary tales, seasonal imagery, or scenes of everyday life, are also identified as representative examples of Japanese-style painting that proliferated throughout the medieval and early modern eras.

MAJOR PAINTING FORMATS

Formats such as hand scrolls (*emakimono*) and hanging scrolls (*kakemono* or *kakejiku*) were introduced to Japan from China before the Heian period. These types of paintings could be easily transported, and would be displayed for brief periods of time. Often hand scrolls and hanging scrolls have survived in fairly good condition since they were protected when stored and could be removed quickly in case of fire or other disasters. Other formats for painting were more interrelated with architectural settings, such as wall painting (*hekiga*), screens (*byobu*), and sliding doors (*fusuma*).

Hand Scrolls Pieces of silk or paper attached horizontally comprise Japanese hand scrolls (*emakimono*, "rolled object with images"), which are fastened on the left side to a dowel-like rod (called a *jiku*). Handscrolls are unrolled and read from right to left. In the medieval and early modern eras, handscrolls measured approximately 20–50 centimeters in height (eight to 20 inches) and could be many meters long. These painted scrolls were designed to be held by one or two people and viewed in sections approximately 30 centimeters (one foot) wide as they were unrolled from right to left, in the same direction that Chinese and Japanese characters are traditionally written. As viewing proceeded, the portion of the scroll that had already been seen would be rolled up on the right-hand side, while the unseen content was unrolled on the left. When viewing was complete, the entire scroll would be rolled up on the left-hand side, fitted with a dowel for that purpose, and fastened with a cord made of silk. Works in horizontal scrolled format soon departed somewhat in style and technique from Chinese antecedents, and by the early Kamakura period, these types of paintings were well established as formats favored for native Japanese-style (or *yamato-e*) painting. The hand scroll format allows the artist to depict an illustrated narrative in an extended manner. Images on a hand scroll sometimes include text. Hand scrolls were especially prized during the Kamakura period, though the format was used through the Edo period. They are often associated with the *yamato-e* picture style.

Hanging Scrolls The center panel of a hanging scroll (*kakemono* or *kakejiku*) consists of a piece of silk or paper on which the image, which may be painting, calligraphy, or a combination of both, is rendered. This panel is attached to a backing made of paper, which is fixed to a dowel-like rod at the bottom of the image. This rod allows the image to be rolled up for storage, and when unrolled for display, its weight helps to keep the scroll evenly extended. Atop the original panel, hanging scrolls are fitted for display with a mounting, or frame, made of silk or brocade. Hanging scrolls are meant to be hung on a wall and are typically changed with the seasons so that the subject matter of the scroll is congruent with the time of year.

Screen, Door, and Wall Paintings Paintings were executed on paper-covered sliding doors (*fusuma*), freestanding folding screens (*byobu*), freestanding single-panel screens (*tsuitate*), and sometimes directly onto walls. These painting formats were especially important in the latter half of the medieval period and in the early modern period. *Shoin*-style architecture made particular use of screen and door paintings executed in a variety of styles. (For a description of the architectural features of screens and doors, see "Architecture" below.)

PAINTING IN THE MEDIEVAL PERIOD

Religious and Secular Painting Religious images were an important subject for medieval painters.

Paintings included illustrated biographies of famous Buddhist priests, such as the *Ippen hijiri-e* (Pictures of the Buddhist ascetic Ippen, 1299), a set of 12 hand scrolls depicting the life of the monk Ippen Shonin (1239–89) by En'i (active late 13th century).

Depictions of Buddhist and Shinto mandala (*mandara*) were also a common subject for medieval painting. Mandalas are typically abstracted representations of the Buddhist universe and often depict the Buddhas and bodhisattvas. Borrowing from Buddhism, Shinto mandalas were also painted in the medieval period. Unlike their more abstract Buddhist counterparts, Shinto mandalas depicted a bird's eye view of a shrine in its natural setting.

Another subject for Buddhist paintings were images called *rokudo-e*, or pictures of the six kinds of rebirth in the samsaric world (see chapter 6: Religion). These six realms were understood as the six possible states of existence for those bound to the cycle of rebirth, a cycle which could be transcended through the intervention of Buddhas and bodhisattvas who could sever one's samsaric connections and facilitate birth in a Pure Land. Religiously *rokudo-e* were visual reminders of how nasty existence could be for those who did not strive toward Buddhist enlightenment. Particularly vivid were paintings of the different levels of hell and the horrible experiences awaiting one reborn there. A well-known example is the *Jigoku zoshi* (Hell scrolls; late 12th-century hand scroll).

In contrast to *rokudo-e* were images called *raigozu* ("welcoming pictures"). *Raigozu* depict the descent of Amida Buddha to the bedside of a dying adherent to the Buddhist Pure Land school. According to a Pure Land school sutra, Amida comes to welcome the faithful to the Pure Land upon their death. The *raigozu* genre was pictorial representations of this idea and were meant to bolster the faith and resolve of Pure Land Buddhists that they would be born into the Pure Land at death.

Many religious paintings utilized the illustrated hand scroll (*emakimono*) format, but hand scrolls were also used in paintings with secular themes, such as war tales, aristocratic literature, and historical biographies. The *Heiji monogatari emaki* (Tale of Heiji scrolls; later half of the 14th century), recounting clashes between the Taira and the Minamoto prior to the start of the Gempei War in 1180, is a famous example of a secular hand scroll. Kamakura-period hand scrolls used realist modes of representation, much in the way that Kamakura-period sculpture did. Realist detail is also seen in both secular and religious hanging scrolls that depict landscapes.

Ink Painting In the 13th and 14th centuries, Chinese Zen ink painting was imported into Japan. The Japanese interest in ink painting was largely the product of the emerging importance of Zen Buddhism in Japan. Ink painting, or *suibokuga* ("water-ink painting"), blossomed especially during the Muromachi and Momoyama periods. This form of painting is also called *sumi-e*, or "ink pictures." Solid black ink, made of soot or charcoal, is ground on an inkstone. Once water is added to the ground ink, it is ready to use for painting or calligraphy.

Ink painting styles, subjects, and techniques were first introduced through hanging scrolls and hand scrolls executed by Chinese artists of the Song dynasty (960–1279). Once Zen Buddhism became established in Japan during the Kamakura period, Chinese ink paintings were also brought to Japan, since they constituted a key element of Zen tradition passed to Japanese monastics by their Chinese counterparts. In the 14th century, Japanese painters began to adopt the techniques and subjects they observed in Chinese works in temple collections. Unlike *raigo* images, *emakimono*, and other genres of Buddhist and secular painting, the power of *suibokuga* lay in evocative, minimalist techniques.

A brief explanation of the origins of the two similar terms *suibokuga* and *sumi-e* indicates something of the history of the technique in Japan and its cultural role. The character for *ink* in Japanese can be read, or pronounced, in two different ways: *boku*, an approximation of the Chinese pronunciation (*on-yomi*) for the same character, or *sumi*, the native Japanese term (*kunyomi*) for the concept *ink*. These two terms used for ink painting, *suibokuga* and *sumi-e*, carry different connotations in Japanese that help illuminate the origins of the painting method. The former suggests the Chinese origins of this painting practice, while the latter term has a more native sound. While some Japanese artists executed ink paintings in a Chinese style, other painters created a distinctive Japanese ink-painting style. Although ink paintings made during the medieval period usually use a single color of ink, and are thus called monochrome works, variations of tone, texture, and style in brushstrokes create visual interest.

Muromachi-period ink paintings were commonly executed by Zen priest-painters. Among the important Japanese ink painters were Mokuan Reien (active ca. 1330–45), Kao Ninga (active early 14th century), Josetsu (active early 15th century), Tensho Shubun (active 1425–50), Sesshu Toyo (1420–1506), and Sesson Shukei (ca. 1504–89). Not all ink painters, however, were Zen priests, including a notable group of artists—Noami (1397–1471), Geiami (1431–85), and Soami (1455–1525)—who were Pure Land Buddhists.

Typical subjects of medieval ink paintings included portraits of important priests (*chinso*); Zen aphorisms; landscapes; bamboo, flowers, birds, and animals; images meant to aid the viewer to awaken to enlightenment (*doshakuga*); and depictions of Kannon, the bodhisattva of compassion, and Bodhidharma (in Japanese, Daruma), the legendary founder of Zen Buddhism in China. By the middle of the 15th century, a Zen ink-painting format known as *shigajiku* was also becoming popular. *Shigajiku* were hanging scrolls that coupled an imaginary landscape ink painting with a poetic inscription usually written by one or more Zen priests.

The priest-painter Sesshu arguably represents the pinnacle of Muromachi-period Zen ink painting. Although he traveled for two years in China, Sesshu's landscapes are imbued with a Japanese sensibility. Besides landscapes, Sesshu painted birds, flowers, and other natural images. Sesshu did utilize painting techniques learned during his sojourn in China. Of particular note was his use of splashed ink (*hatsuboku*) landscapes, in which ink is spattered onto the paper or silk. Sesshu also employed a similar technique called "broken ink" (*haboku*), creating a raised wash effect that gave texture and volume to shapes within the landscape painting. Sesshu's work was a model for subsequent artists.

Kano School The Kano school of painters, a single family, dominated the art of opulent decorative painting for the interiors of both castles and temples. The Kano school became an academy with a genealogy of known masters bound by stylistic affinities as well as by family ties. Part of the success of the Kano school was the result of patronage by the Ashikaga and subsequent shoguns through the end of the Edo period.

Kano school painters were versatile, working in a number of different styles and formats. Kano painters were especially famous as the foremost Japanese school painting in Chinese style (*kanga*). Subject matter for these paintings included landscapes and images of birds and flowers. Kano painters were also capable ink-painting artists and executed compositions on all the major formats of the day such as handscrolls, hanging scrolls, screens, and doors.

Kano Masanobu (1434–1530) is considered the founder of the Kano school. He was appointed the official painter to the Ashikaga shogunate. He specialized in the Chinese style of monochrome ink painting, and later passed his skills on to his son, Motonobu. It is Kano Motonobu (1476–1559) who is usually credited with bringing real fame to the family. Like his father, Motonobu worked in the Chinese style, but he was also known for his paintings in the Japanese style (*Yamato-e*), a manner of painting that had fallen out of favor with the rise of Zen ink painting and its associations with the warrior class. Motonobu was able to blend the Japanese and Chinese styles to create a dynamic new mode of painting. Motonobu's paintings executed on sliding doors (*fusuma*) are particularly famous.

Motonobu's grandson, Kano Eitoku (1543–90), was the most important and famous of the medieval Kano-school artists. During the Azuchi-Momoyama period, he was chosen to paint for the warriors Oda Nobunaga and Toyotomi Hideyoshi. In 1576, Eitoku provided paintings for Nobunaga's Azuchi Castle. Though both the castle and Eitoku's art were destroyed, historical accounts record that Eitoku executed monochrome ink paintings as well as color paintings with a great variety of subjects including natural scenes, Buddhist imagery, and depictions of Chinese sages.

One of Eitoku's contributions to Japanese painting was his use of ink painting with the addition of bright colors and gold washes to his compositions. Eitoku had a well-developed sense of decorative style that he employed in his ink painting, thus innovating while maintaining the Kano school's reputation as the premiere monochrome-ink specialists. Eitoku's decorative style, however, eventually led to the development of a new school of painting known as Rimpa (see below) that focused on decoration in painting.

Hasegawa Tohaku Hasegawa Tohaku (1539–1610) worked as an independent artist during the Momoyama period. He established himself as a virtuoso painter of landscape subjects who was accomplished in employing two rather distinct manners simultaneously. Like Kano school painters, Tohaku showed mastery of the screen (*byobu*) and sliding door (*fusuma*) formats, executing splendid works in vivid colors accented with gold leaf. A set of screens depicting an autumn maple and other fall foliage in brilliant hues that are today housed in the Chishakuin temple in Kyoto constitutes one of the best examples of his work in this manner.

Genre Painting In the 16th century genre painting became a popular artistic style. Genre painting refers to works that depict the everyday life and activities of the different social classes. A famous work, and the oldest extant example of a genre painting, is a pair of six-paneled screens titled *Rakuchu rakugai zu* (Scenes Inside and Outside of Kyoto; 1525). The screens portray Kyoto and the surrounding area from a bird's-eye view. Scenes of daily life are visible with images of people working and relaxing, a snapshot of a day in early 16th-century Kyoto. Visible, also, are celebrated temples, palaces, and other buildings, as well as famous areas in the city and its environs. This subject matter, life in the city, was often depicted in subsequent genre paintings.

Another popular theme of genre paintings was leisure activities. Paintings portrayed shrine festivals, cherry blossom and maple viewing, horse racing, theater performances, odd-looking Westerners, and the pleasure quarters. Such paintings continued to be made through the 17th century when they were largely eclipsed by the new techniques that gave rise to woodblock prints, which portrayed similar kinds of subject matter.

Namban Paintings Another form of genre painting is called *namban* (southern barbarian) painting.

The word *namban* refers to images connected with European merchants and missionaries who were in Japan for approximately a 100-year period starting in the mid 16th century. Europeans, except for a small Dutch enclave on Deshima island in Nagasaki harbor, were expelled from Japan in the 1630s. In a broad sense, *namban* art encompasses works incorporating European figures as well as those created by Europeans and brought to Japan. More specifically, *namban* refers to pairs of screens painted during a period of less than 50 years, beginning in the last quarter of the 16th century. The term *namban* comes from the route many of these travelers used to reach Japan, since the Portuguese and Spanish arrived from the south. Japan, following China's precedent, generally used the word *namban* to describe inhabitants of all countries to the south of China who, as foreigners, were considered barbarians.

Some *namban* works are essentially copies of religious paintings and related objects brought by Jesuits to aid in spreading their cause throughout Japan. Few of these works survive, due to the persecution of Christianity. However, the vast majority of *namban* works were secular and were likely inspired by books, prints, and atlases displaying artistic styles and content popular in 16th-century Europe. As imported styles and forms became popular, Japanese artists were commissioned to render images with the flavor of distant lands and cultures. Scenes include Portuguese and Dutch traders as well as Jesuit prelates who settled in Japan during this era. Some Japanese artists adopted Western conventions such as the bird's eye perspective used for maps. Yet even when experimenting with foreign formats and subjects, painters of *namban* works otherwise worked in traditional Japanese modes.

PAINTING IN THE EARLY MODERN PERIOD

The early modern period witnessed both the continuation of some late medieval painting styles, but it also gave rise to new schools that innovated from older painting trends or created new modes of artistic expression. The Kano school, for instance, continued to be a significant artistic force during the Edo period, but new movements such as Rimpa and Maruyama-Shijo took painting in new directions. Ink painting, for instance, continued to be an important style but it was taken in new stylistic directions by literati- and Rimpa-school painters.

Kano School The Kano school continued to be the official painters to the shogunate. Of special note is Kano Tan'yu (1602–74) who was appointed at age 15 to be the first official painter of the Tokugawa shogunate. Tan'yu, Eitoku's grandson, was an especially fine and prolific artist. He, along with his brothers, painted interior doors and screens of the newly built Nijo Castle in Kyoto. Like Kano painters before him, Tan'yu was an ink painter, but he pioneered a new style of ink painting that made creative use of empty space while at the same time displaying a knack for refined brushwork. Although the Kano school maintained its reputation and served the shogunate subsequent to Tan'yu, other painting schools also attained important stylistic and aesthetic achievements.

Tosa School The Tosa school, another dominant lineage of master painters, was established in the 15th century and continued to prosper into the Edo period, although through intermarriage with the Kano-school artists, the two styles became less distinct over time. Just as the Kano painters were employed by the shogunate, so did Tosa artists serve as official painters to the imperial court. The Tosa school, which dates from the early 15th century, specialized in traditional *yamato-e* style painting. Tosa paintings often used subjects taken from classical literature such as the celebrated Heian-period work, *Genji monogatari* (Tale of Genji). The use of gold and bright colors was one characteristic of Tosa paintings. Although one of the Tosa school's most famous painters, Tosa Mitsunobu (ca. 1434–ca. 1525), worked in the medieval period, the school continued through the 19th century.

Rimpa School One important decorative school of painting was called Rimpa. A painter named Tawaraya Sotatsu, who began his career as proprietor of a fan-painting shop (active 1600–40), is most closely associated with the strongly expressive decorative styles popular in the early Edo period. He is best known for his dappled brush effects. Sotatsu used a painting technique known as *tarashikomi*, in which pigment is applied to a wet area of another pigment, causing a decorative puddling effect.

Sotatsu also lent his painting to collaborations with calligrapher and connoisseur Hon'ami Koetsu (1558–1637). Koetsu was fascinated with Japan's early poetry, brushing his elegant, bold calligraphy of classical poems and Noh plays over Sotatsu's paintings in gold or silver ink washes on decorated paper. Koetsu and Sotatsu chose images to complement seasonal themes, often reworking the same theme many times in different compositions.

Koetsu and Sotatsu are the first artists associated with the Rimpa school of painting, a group linked by styles rather than a formal school (like the Kano). Rimpa artists were inspired by the literary and pictorial themes of classical hand scrolls. Rimpa artists reworked *yamato-e* subjects and techniques into a personal and more dynamic manner, often rendered on a monumental scale.

The term Rimpa refers specifically to a later artist influenced by content drawn from classical Japanese painting: Ogata Korin (1658–1716). *Rimpa* means "the school of Korin." Korin was also influenced by content drawn from classical literature. He specialized in bold, decorative paintings using techniques inspired by Sotatsu. Korin copied many designs authored by Sotatsu, but he was quite successful in his own right. He worked less freely than Sotatsu, utilizing a more precise outline and relatively regular color application, thus refining Sotatsu's technique. Korin also excelled in other media, such as ceramics, often utilizing compositions and motifs drawn from his painted works. Like Sotatsu, Korin also worked in collaboration with other artists. Korin's lyrical designs influenced subsequent Edo-period artists.

Literati (or Southern School) Painting The interchangeable terms literati painting (*bunjinga*) and southern-school painting (*nanga*) refer to an artistic movement that began in the 18th century. It was a style of painting (*ga*) that borrowed the manner of Chinese literati artists (*bunjin*) from southern (*nan*) China. Despite its Chinese origins, the Japanese literati school also incorporated some Western painting techniques. In China, literati artists might be Confucian scholars who were amateur painters.

In Japan, however, most of the literati artists were professionals who painted for a living. Two literati artists, Yosa Buson (1716–83) and Ike no Taiga (1723–76), were particularly important.

In general, literati artists painted traditional Chinese subjects such as landscapes, birds, flowers, and bamboo. The literati style of Ike no Taiga, however, was rather eclectic with influences including Chinese landscapes, medieval Japanese monochrome ink paintings, and Western artistic techniques. Yosa Buson was not only a painter but also a haiku poet. He often created images to accompany poems, a style known as *haiga*, or "haiku paintings." Although Buson painted in a Chinese style, his landscapes were imbued with a distinctively Japanese sensibility.

Zenga *Zenga*, or "Zen painting," is a modern term usually used in reference to Edo-period Zen Buddhist painting and calligraphy, as distinguished from medieval-period Zen ink painting. Note, however, that the term is sometimes used to refer to medieval Zen ink painting as well.

The term *zenga* as it is used here refers to the revival of Zen painting by Zen priest-painters. After the initial flowering of Zen painting by Zen priests in the medieval period, the Zen ink-painting style was taken up more and more by professional artists without any necessary connection to Zen as a religious tradition. Zen priests in the 18th century sought to revive the Zen painting tradition. Zen priest-painters such as Hakuin Ekaku (1685–1768) and Sengai Gibon (1750–1837) actively promoted a style of Zen painting that was often playful, humorous, and spontaneous.

It is sometimes argued that Edo-period Zen paintings reflect the enlightened minds of their artists. This is likely an idealized interpretation, especially since it is known that *zenga* were sometimes painted as gifts for temple patrons. Nevertheless for priests like Hakuin, painting seems to have been a form of religious practice directed toward the goal of enlightenment, much as one might seek the same goal through other forms of practice, such as meditation.

Western-Style Painting While the Edo period has largely been identified as an age of isolation, there were exceptions, such as the persistent presence of

Dutch traders on the island of Deshima in Nagasaki harbor, and widespread private trade, a convenient euphemism for smuggling, which was hidden from the shogunate. One result was that foreign visitors to Japan, particularly the Dutch, also influenced the subjects, artistic styles, and techniques in Edo arts during the 18th century.

Western-style painting (*yofuga*), an Edo-period artistic movement, refers to Japanese use of Western painting techniques including perspective, realism, and tonal variation. Western-style paintings might employ oil paints or use traditional Japanese pigments. Hiraga Gennai (1728–79), a Western learning scholar, is credited with starting this movement. He spent time in Nagasaki studying Dutch and Western science, and at the same time learned Western painting techniques. After moving to Edo, he introduced Western painting to his circle of like-minded intellectuals. Of particular note among those introduced to Western-style painting was Shiba Kokan (1738–1818) who expanded the study of Western painting styles and techniques. His paintings were oils on silk and included use of single-point perspective and some European themes.

Maruyama-Shijo School While Gennai and Kokan painted in a Western style, Maruyama-Shijo school painters borrowed selected aspects of Western painting, such as realism, for use in otherwise Japanese-themed works. The 18th- and 19th-century Maruyama-Shijo school, mostly operating in Kyoto, is the collective name given to the work of two founding artists and their students: Maruyama Okyo (1733–95), who founded the Maruyama school, and his student Matsumura Goshun (1752–1811), who founded the Shijo school.

The Maruyama-Shijo school is notable for its synthesis of Western artistic elements and for incorporating them into paintings of traditional Japanese subjects and themes. Inspired by imported Western botanical studies, Okyo did many sketches and drawings from nature, which are both detailed and realistic. His finished paintings are a blend of traditional and Western artistic styles. For instance, he sometimes combines a decorative style suggestive of the Kano school (he trained in the Kano school earlier in his career) with Western realism and shading. Goshun, on the other hand, employed heightened realism but combined this with a Chinese-inspired literati style that he learned from his earlier study with Yosa Buson, a *nanga* painter.

Eccentrics Three Edo period artists are referred to as the "three eccentrics" because of their idiosyncratic styles that did not fit any of the styles of the traditional painting schools, such as the Kano school. The three were Nagasawa Rosetsu (1754–99), Ito Jakuchu (1716–1800), and Soga Shohaku (1730–81).

Ukiyo-e

Ukiyo-e ("pictures of the floating world") are woodblock prints, and sometimes paintings, produced during the Edo period that depict scenes of the pleasure quarters, Kabuki actors, and other urban amusements. Prior to the early modern period, the term *ukiyo-e* referred to the Buddhist idea of the impermanent and fleeting nature of the world and human existence. This was a world that needed to be escaped or transcended through Buddhist religious practices. In the Edo period, the ephemeral "floating world," was thought about in a new way—instead of avoiding this world the idea was to embrace its sensual pleasures made all the more enticing because they were illusory and temporary, requiring enjoyment now before they were gone. This discussion focuses on woodblock prints which is the most important medium used to depict scenes of the floating world.

As an art form, ukiyo-e woodblock prints held particular appeal for urban commoners. Prints in this genre were usually inexpensive (about the same price as a bowl of noodles in the mid-19th century) and could be purchased from street vendors, common in the pleasure districts, or directly from publishers' shops. Prints were often pasted on walls or sliding screens, souvenirs of a visit to the pleasure district, or later, with the development of landscape prints, as souvenirs of journeys to scenic spots along Japan's growing road system.

Ukiyo-e prints originally featured images of the floating world, including depictions of courtesans and beautiful women, Kabuki actors, sumo wrestlers, and other pleasures and pastimes. Prints later came to include nature scenes, scenes of country life, and, by the 19th century, scenes of famous Japanese places and landscapes.

The first ukiyo-e prints appeared around 1660, the work of urban artisans. They were printed in black and white. It was another century before woodblocks were printed in full color. These early ukiyo-e depicted scenes of the pleasure quarters, or floating world, and were first used as illustrations to accompany simple novels and short stories called *ukiyo zoshi* (see chapter 8: Language and Literature) that told stories about the lives of courtesans and urban commoners.

Early woodblock artists, such as Hishikawa Moronobu (1618–94), created black-and-white prints that were hand-tinted in color. These prints had a simple calligraphic beauty, in contrast to the later use of pattern and color as prints become more complex. It was not, however, until the middle of the 18th century and the work of Suzuki Harunobu (1725–70) that the technology was developed to print in colors from multiple woodblocks to create one often brightly colored image. This multiblock color process was known as *nishiki-e* ("brocade pictures"). The first color print using this technology appeared in 1764. Within just a couple of years, most woodblock artists were using this color process.

Although images of denizens of the pleasure quarters, popular actors, and sumo wrestlers remained popular subjects for ukiyo-e through the end of the 18th century, by the 19th century landscape prints emerged as an important new genre of woodblock prints. Whereas earlier Japanese landscape paintings had often depicted Chinese locales, ukiyo-e landscapes were of actual scenes in Japan. Two woodblock artists were especially prominent in landscape prints: Katsushika Hokusai (1760–1849) and Ando Hiroshige (1797–1858). They both published a number of different print series depicting famous places and landscape vistas. Both artists also used realistic perspective, a borrowing from Western painting technique.

Woodblock prints involve transferring a raised image, which has been carved into a wooden block, to a sheet of paper. Printing presses were not used in traditional Japanese woodblock printing. Printmaking is a process requiring a team of people who have different responsibilities at various stages of production. Once an image has been designed by an artist, it must be transferred to a wooden block or blocks, which look like thin boards. Carvers apply the design by cutting or chiseling areas of the wood block to leave a raised surface that will be printed. Then, paper must be prepared for printing and the blocks inked, tasks performed by the printmaker. Publishers, who often had input regarding the subject of the print and selection of the artist, were responsible for overseeing the production process and distribution and sale of the completed print. Since prints could be produced in large numbers with a minimum of effort, they were less expensive than more traditional artistic formats like calligraphy and painting, and woodblock prints became a very popular artistic form.

IMPORTANT WOODBLOCK ARTISTS

Some of the most famous Edo-period woodblock artists included:

Hishikawa Moronobu (1618–1694) Moronobu is usually cited as the first artist to create popular prints that established ukiyo-e as a valid art form. His subjects included courtesans and Kabuki actors, as well as a genre of sexually explicit prints known as *shunga* ("spring pictures"). *Shunga* became a popular, and officially banned, genre for subsequent woodblock artists. Moronobu designed the first single-sheet illustrations for floating world novels (*ukiyo zoshi*). He also pioneered prints that featured no accompanying text, which established the print as an independent art form. Whereas prints made to accompany novels did not indicate the name of the artist, Moronobu insisted on adding his name to his individual woodblock prints, thus elevating the importance and status of the individual artist.

Okumura Masanobu (1686–1764) Masanobu was both a woodblock artist and a painter. He was also an innovator who played a role in creating several of the new ukiyo-e printing and design techniques that began to appear in the early 18th century. For instance, he pioneered the application of Western perspective to his prints to create a genre known as *uki-e* or "floating picture." He used this technique in his depictions of the interiors of Kabuki theaters, merchant shops, and the pleasure quarters.

Suzuki Harunobu (1725–1770) Harunobu is important for his efforts to develop multicolored prints known as *nishiki-e* ("brocade pictures"). Subsequent woodblock artists utilized Harunobu's color printing techniques in their works. Harunobu's own color prints were widely popular. His subject matter included images of graceful women.

Torii Kiyonaga (1752–1815) Kiyonaga was a woodblock artist associated with the Torii school. He was known for his color prints of actors and beautiful women. He also did work for illustrated books. His images of women, depicted with elegance and dignity, were instrumental in creating a late 18th-century ideal of beauty that influenced subsequent woodblock artists.

Kitagawa Utamaro (1753–1806) Utamaro was famous for his prints depicting the pleasure quarters. His prints of women are also highly regarded for their portrayal of an ideal of feminine beauty. Utamaro represents a generalized type of female beauty rather than specific courtesans. These prints are quite sensual, often showing women with bare breasts or hair and clothing askew, and intimate, framing his subjects so that only the head and shoulders are viewed. It is the closed nature of these compositions that induces a feeling of being witness to a private moment. Utamaro was thus important for his enhanced depiction of the female body, something new in a culture whose previously privileged aristocratic ideals of beauty had not included portrayal of the human body.

Toshusai Sharaku (dates unknown; active 1794–1795) Sharaku produced relatively few prints made during less than a one-year period from 1794 to 1795. Less than 160 of his prints remain. Of those that do, the majority are of Kabuki actors. Though the subject matter was nothing new, Sharaku's artistic style was unusual, and not entirely popular in his own day. His prints are the opposite of those that depict idealized versions of actors or of beautiful women. Instead, Sharaku's depictions exaggerate, in caricature fashion, the physical attributes of the actors he portrayed.

Katsushika Hokusai (1760–1849) Hokusai was a prolific artist famous for his landscape prints of Japanese scenes rendered using techniques derived from Japanese, Chinese, and Western artistic traditions. Works, such as *Fugaku sanjurokkei* (*Thirty-six Views of Mt. Fuji*, 1823) created a market for landscape prints that rivaled the popularity of images of the pleasure quarters. His landscapes often adapted Western painting perspective to a print medium. Hokusai's print, "Mt. Fuji Seen Below a Wave at Kanagawa" (but popularly known in English as the "Great Wave"), is arguably the best-known view of Japan by a Japanese artist and a well-known image outside of Japan as well. After Hokusai, landscape became a popular subject for woodblock artists.

Utagawa Toyokuni (1769–1825) Toyokuni was a woodblock artist, painter, and book illustrator. He is especially well known for his portraits of Kabuki actors. His style in depicting theatrical scenes included the use of dramatically exaggerated poses and expressions, and sometimes the portrayal of two actors interacting on stage. Toyokuni's theatrical print style became a standard for subsequent prints in this genre.

Ando Hiroshige (1797–1858) Like Hokusai, Hiroshige was an innovator in the creation of landscape prints using techniques of Western perspective to depict Japanese scenes. Hiroshige's most famous work is a series of prints titled *Tokaido gojusantsugi* (*Fifty-three Stations of the Tokaido Road*; 1833–34) in which he depicts the various locales and vistas one would encounter in a trek along the Tokaido Road running between Edo and Kyoto. Hiroshige's landscape prints are noteworthy for their portrayal of weather and the changing seasons, and the challenges that nature presents to human beings traveling along the road.

Utagawa Kuniyoshi (1798–1861) Kuniyoshi was a woodblock artist and book illustrator. Among Kuniyoshi's many subjects were theater-related scenes and landscape prints. The latter were usually executed in a manner quite different from that used by landscape print masters such as Hokusai and

Hiroshige. Kuniyoshi's included influences from European prints then circulating in Japan. One of Kuniyoshi's most famous works was a series of 108 prints depicting Chinese warriors based on characters from a Chinese novel. His later prints often focused on historical figures. He also produced popular prints of women and cats.

Ceramics

Japanese ceramics are called *yakimono* ("fired object"), or sometimes *setomono* ("Seto object," named after a famous site for pottery production). Ceramics made in a certain region and sometimes a particular kiln complex are known as "ware" or "wares" (*yaki*) of that location. Thus, for example, *bizen-yaki* refers to Bizen ware, or ceramics produced at the Bizen kilns in west-central Japan. Pottery traditions are sometimes dated by referring to their oldest or antecedent wares by using the prefix *ko* ("old"). *Ko Bizen*, therefore, refers to the earliest forms of Bizen ware.

Ceramics are treated here as an artistic medium, but they were also utilitarian objects with specific practical uses. Among the ceramic objects traditionally produced at Japan's many kiln sites were tea bowls, tea storage jars, sake cups and bottles, various sizes of bowls, flower vases, and incense burners. Any discussion of ceramics must also take into account the many regional and technical variations that impacted ceramic production. Thus, for instance, different regions had different kinds of soil for clay, developed glazes producing a variety of colors and surface finishes, and used kilns designed to fire clay at particular temperatures in order to obtain a desired effect.

The history of Japanese ceramics dates back long before the medieval and early modern periods. Contact with the Asian mainland prior to the medieval period introduced Japan to the use of high-firing kilns and applied glazes, techniques that came into common use by the beginning of the medieval period. Ko Seto ware, made at a location near modern-day Nagoya, is a well-known, early medieval example of a ceramic type using high-fired, intentionally glazed ceramics. Medieval ceramics also used incised decorations. Medieval ceramics then began to develop a distinctive Japanese aesthetic style. This became especially pronounced with the later rise of pottery tea wares.

Three factors in the Muromachi period helped to elevate ceramics from utilitarian wares to art objects: trade, technology, and chemistry. Renewed trade with China and Korea gave the Japanese access to celadon wares and other types of ceramics. New kiln technologies developed, particularly the oxidation kiln that allowed air to enter during the firing process. This produced hotter flames and stronger wares resulted. Finally, the chemistry of glazes was further developed to allow for greater and more exact manipulation of natural ash glazes. Mino ware potters were especially noted for their glaze technology.

The development of tea ritual and related arts had a significant impact on ceramic production. Tea masters had specific aesthetic needs and tastes, especially favoring simple, unglazed ceramic tea bowls. While Chinese ceramics were first used for this purpose, Japanese ceramicists soon began to produce the desired wares. Important ceramics types used in tea ceremony included Raku, Shino, Oribe, Shigaraki, Bizen, and Iga. Shigaraki, Bizen, and Iga were particularly important examples of unglazed ceramics whose distinctive surfaces were created through the firing process in which intermittent areas of ash (sometimes referred to as "ash glaze") and fire marks created designs and patterns. Patronage of the tea ritual by powerful warriors, such as Toyotomi Hideyoshi, further stimulated the growth of ceramics as an art form. Contextually, ceramics made for preparing, serving, and enjoying tea could be discussed here. However, because they are also part of a larger aesthetic tradition sometimes referred to as "tea ceremony" they are covered in the section below titled "Tea and Related Arts."

Besides the development of tea ritual and its impact on ceramics, the most important occurrence impacting pottery production at the time of the transition from the medieval to the early modern period was the Korean invasions orchestrated by Toyotomi Hideyoshi in the last decade of the 16th century. Although Hideyoshi's incursions into Korea were a military failure, they did result in the forcible relocation of Korean potters to the Kyushu region of Japan. Korean potters were prized for their artistic and technical knowledge of ceramic production, including kiln design and glazes. Kilns, such as the one at Karatsu, produced wares highly sought after by tea connoisseurs.

One other very important outcome of the presence of Korean potters in Japan was the development of Japanese porcelain production. In the early 17th century, the Korean potter Ri Sampei (in Korean, Yi Sam-p'yong; 1579–1655) discovered kaolin clay, the kind used for porcelain, in the Arita region of Hizen province in Kyushu. Arita ware became the first true porcelain produced in Japan, and porcelain manufacture soon spread to other areas of Hizen province and included Ko Kutani, Imari, Kakiemon, and Nabeshima wares. Besides the Japanese market, a growing European export market for Japanese porcelains developed in the later half of the 17th century. As important as the Kyushu porcelain market became, there were other areas of Japan producing quality ceramics in the Edo period. Kyo ware, produced in Kyoto, is one notable example.

IMPORTANT CERAMIC AND PORCELAIN TYPES

Among the many important types of ceramics and porcelains are:

Arita Ware Arita-yaki. Arita ware refers to porcelains produced in the Arita area of Hizen province (present-day Saga Prefecture) in Kyushu. Porcelains such as Imari, Kakiemon, and Nabeshima were all produced in the Arita region from the middle of the 17th century.

Bizen Ware Bizen-yaki. Located in Imbe in Bizen province (present-day Okayama Prefecture) in west-central Honshu near the city of Okayama. One of the so-called Six Ancient Kilns. Bizen ware is unglazed but uses a firing process that creates a distinctive orange-red surface color. Bizen ware dates to the late Heian period. During most of the medieval period, Bizen produced utilitarian jars and other daily-use items. However, these products were distributed to other parts of central Honshu as a result of Bizen's proximity to ports on the Seto Inland Sea. From the 16th century Bizen gained new markets for its pottery, prized for its use in the tea ceremony.

Echizen Ware Echizen-yaki. Located near the city of Kanazawa on the west coast of central Honshu. One of the so-called Six Ancient Kilns. Ceramic production started in the late Heian period.

Iga Ware Iga-yaki. Located in Iga village (now called Maruhashira village) in Iga province (present-day Mie Prefecture). In the medieval period, Iga produced utilitarian items, but it became popular for use in the tea ceremony because its unglazed surfaces reflected the *wabi* tea aesthetic (see "Tea and Related Arts" below).

Imari Ware Imari-yaki. The name comes from Imari port, where porcelain was shipped to both domestic and foreign markets. Imari ware is a general term used to describe porcelain produced in the Arita region of Hizen province (present-day Saga Prefecture) in Kyushu. Nabeshima and Kakiemon wares, also Hizen province porcelains, are not included under Imari ware. See also ARITA WARE.

Kakiemon Ware Kakiemon-yaki. Located in the Arita region of Hizen province (present-day Saga Prefecture) in Kyushu. From the middle of the 17th century, the potter Sakaida Kakiemon (1596–1666) created new decoration techniques for porcelain, including the use of overglazes that made possible porcelains with colors in addition to the traditional blue. Kakiemon ware was made using such colors as green, blue, yellow, and black.

Karatsu Ware Karatsu-yaki. Located in Karatsu in Hizen province (present-day Saga Prefecture) in Kyushu. Karatsu ware, a Korean-style ceramic, was produced beginning in the late 16th century and expanded with the relocation of Korean potters there after Toyotomi Hideyoshi's failed attempt to conquer Korea. Karatsu produced utilitarian items, but also found favor with tea masters such as Furuta Oribe.

Kutani Ware Kutani-yaki. Located in Kutani in present-day Ishikawa Prefecture in central Honshu. The term Ko Kutani refers to Kutani ware fabricated in the Kutani kiln (as opposed to other kilns where Kutani ware was later made) during the Edo period. Kutani ware is a porcelain that uses a five-color glaze of red, green, yellow, blue, and purple.

Kyo Ware Kyo-yaki. Located in Kyoto. Kyo ware was a ceramic produced with traditional Japanese decorative designs in brightly colored overglaze enamels. It is a style particularly associated with the potters Nonomura Ninsei (active last half of the 17th century) and Ogata Kenzan (1666–1743), brother of the famous Rimpa-style painter Ogata Korin. Kyo ware competed with the Kyushu porcelain market.

Mino Ware Mino-yaki. Mino ware is a general term used to refer to ceramics produced in Mino province (present-day Gifu Prefecture). Pottery was made in this area from at least the seventh century. In the medieval period, Mino-style ceramics were shaped on a potter's wheel and used different kinds of glazes. With the rise of tea practice in the Momoyama period, Mino became a center for tea bowls and other related items. Ceramics labeled Mino-style include Shino Ware, Seto Ware, and Oribe Ware.

Nabeshima Ware Nabeshima-yaki. Located in the Arita region of Hizen province (present-day Saga Prefecture) in Kyushu. Production of Nabeshima porcelain began in the early 17th century. Nabeshima ware, including blue and white, celadon, and multicolored glazes, became widely distributed in Japan from about the beginning of the 18th century. It was used especially for gifts for the shogunate, domain lords, and aristocracy.

Oribe Ware Oribe-yaki. Located in Mino province (present-day Gifu Prefecture). Oribe ware is one of the Mino-style ceramics (see MINO WARE). It is associated with the tea master Furuta Oribe (1544–1615) whose aesthetic tastes included the use of green glaze and painted design applied to asymmetrical forms. Oribe ware was produced mostly in the early 17th century.

Raku Ware Raku-yaki. Located in Kyoto. Raku ware was produced from the Momoyana period. Its tea bowls—with black, red, or white glazes and

shaped without use of a potter's wheel—became highly prized for use in the tea ceremony. The Raku ware style was started by Raku Chojiro (1516–92) and continued by later generations.

Seto Ware Seto-yaki. Located in the city of Seto northeast of Nagoya. One of the so-called Six Ancient Kilns. Seto is the most important of the Kamakura-period pottery sites because of its pioneering use in Japan of high-fired, intentionally glazed ceramics. This early type of Seto ware is called Ko Seto and it used simple decorations with incised or applied designs, usually floral motifs. Ko Seto ware enjoyed the patronage of both Zen temples and the Kamakura shogunate. Later Seto ceramics included glazes of yellow and green.

Shigaraki Ware Shigaraki-yaki. Located in Shigaraki (in present-day Shiga Prefecture) near Kyoto. One of the so-called Six Ancient Kilns. Shigaraki ware, which uses a sandy, coarse clay with bits of feldspar, dates to the end of the Heian period. Shigaraki pottery was produced during the Kamakura and Muromachi periods. With the beginning of tea ritual in the late 15th century, Shigaraki ware became popular among tea practitioners, such as the famous tea master Sen no Rikyu, because it was seen as exemplifying the *wabi* tea aesthetic (see "Tea and Related Arts" below). From the early 17th century, Shigaraki tea jars were used for packaging the highly prized Uji (a site near Kyoto) tea leaves that were presented to the Tokugawa shoguns on an annual basis.

Shino Ware Shino-yaki. Located in Mino province (present-day Gifu Prefecture). Shino ware is one of the Mino-style ceramics (see MINO WARE). It started production during the Momoyama period. Shino ware was highly prized for tea ritual use.

Tamba Ware Tamba-yaki. One of the so-called Six Ancient Kilns. Located in Tamba between Kyoto and Osaka. Ceramic production started in the Kamakura period and included jars and sake bottles. Tamba ware uses either no glaze or a natural glaze that is reddish black. Ko Tamba refers to pottery made prior to the early modern period.

Tokoname Ware Tokoname-yaki. One of the so-called Six Ancient Kilns. Located in the town of Tokoname near Nagoya, Tokoname ware produced a reddish brown ceramic starting in the 11th century.

Lacquerware

Strictly speaking, "lacquer" (*urushi*) refers to the toxic non-resinous sap of the lacquer tree, *Rhus verniciflua*, a member of the same genus as poison ivy. Lacquerware refers to the objects made using lacquer, a substance which hardens like a natural polymer. In practice, the terms "lacquer" and "lacquerware" tend to be used interchangeably in English discussions of lacquerware. In Japanese, there are different terms for lacquerware, such as *shikki* (lacquer vessel) and *nurimono* ([lacquer-]coated object).

In the fabrication of lacquerware, a three-step process is used. First, a base is created from a material such as wood, paper, or leather. Then, lacquer is applied to the base, which, when hardened, effectively seals the base inside. Finally, the hardened lacquer surface is decorated. There are numerous techniques and materials used for decorating lacquerware. In the Heian period, *maki-e* ("sprinkled picture") was a decorative technique in which powdered metal, such as gold or silver, was sprinkled onto the lacquer before it had completely hardened. This practice, with refinements, was used in the medieval and early modern periods as well.

Lacquer was used in the manufacture of many different kinds of objects in the medieval and early modern periods. Lacquer was employed to make items for daily use, such as toiletry boxes and inkstone cases carried by writers. Various eating utensils, plates, bowls, and containers were also made. Some furniture items were also made using lacquer. The popularity and long history of lacquerware manufacture in Japan was the result of both its decorative value and beauty, as well as its qualities as a protective finish.

Historically, lacquerware was made and used in Japan for a long time prior to the medieval period. Nara- and Heian-period lacquer styles and techniques, however, were important antecedents to the lacquerware produced in the medieval period. Kamakura- and Muromachi-period lacquerware continued the use of *maki-e* lacquer techniques first developed in the Heian period. Lacquer was used in the production of such objects as bowls, trays, furniture, toiletry boxes, and saddles and stirrups.

In the Kamakura period, a new decorative style called *ikakeji* ("gold ground") made refinements in the use of gold powder first employed in Heian period *maki-e*. A finely ground gold powder was sprinkled in sufficient quantities on the lacquered surface of an object to mimic the appearance of solid gold. In addition to this kind of decoration, Kamakura-period lacquerware artisans continued the Heian practice of using polished shell inlaid into lacquerware. Among the popular design motifs used for lacquerware surface decorations during the medieval period were images of water, rocks, trees, and flowers. New types of lacquerware were introduced in the medieval period, such as Negoro-nuri, prized for ritual objects by Buddhist temples, Kamakura-bori, a style of carved wood lacquerware, and *chinkin*, which used decorative inlaid gold on lacquer.

By the end of the medieval period and into the early modern period, lacquerware aesthetics had moved from the more ornate *maki-e* decorations to simpler designs. Among these new styles were Kodaiji *maki-e* that utilized floral motifs and Koetsu lacquerware that used decorative themes derived from classical Japanese literature.

In the early modern period, demand for lacquerware proliferated, and it came to be used for both decorative objects as well as a variety of everyday items such as combs, tables, bottles, headrests, small boxes (*inro*), writing cases, and smoking kits. These kinds of objects were used by merchants, artisans, and others of the growing urban commoner class, a shift from earlier periods in which only the aristocrats and Buddhist temples could afford such items. Warriors also prized lacquerware, and the wealthiest among them employed their own lacquerware artisans.

EXAMPLES OF LACQUERWARE STYLES AND TECHNIQUES

Some important lacquer styles and techniques used in the medieval and early modern periods included:

Kamakura-bori Kamakura-bori, or Kamakura carving, refers to a decorative lacquerware style originally created and produced in the city of Kamakura. Kamakura-bori uses a carved wooden base on which red or black lacquer is applied.

Chinkin Also referred to as *chinkin-bori. Chinkin* is a type of lacquerware that uses inlaid gold to emphasize decorative images. It is made by incising designs into the surface of the lacquer. Additional thin layers of lacquer are then applied to the incisions. Gold powder or gold foil is then placed on the newly applied lacquer to create contrast.

Negoro Ware Negoro ware (*negoro-nuri*) refers to a regionally produced lacquerware originally fabricated at the Negoro Buddhist temple (Negoroji) near Nara starting in the 12th century. Negoro ware is made by applying red lacquer over a base of black lacquer. As Negoro ware is used, the thin layer of red lacquer begins to wear away revealing patches of the black lacquer underneath. The result is an aesthetically attractive contrast between red and black. This lacquerware style enjoyed sufficient popularity that it was often imitated in other places.

Kodaiji *Maki-e* Kokaiji *maki-e* refers to a style of *maki-e* created at the Kodaiji temple in Kyoto during the Momoyana period. This lacquerware style, used for such things as writing boxes, furniture, and Buddhist hand-scroll texts, used gold powder heavily sprinkled on black lacquer that was then incised to create embossed decorative details.

Namban Style Lacquerware The term *namban*, or "southern barbarian," referred to Westerners who visited Japan for trade and missionary purposes starting in the middle of the 16th century. Attracted to the aesthetic qualities of Japanese lacquerware, Western missionaries commissioned Japanese artisans to create decorative furnishings and ritual implements for the churches then being built in Japan. Western traders commissioned artisans to create lacquerware items that could be used for export back to Europe. This kind of lacquerware was called Namban-style lacquerware.

Koetsu Lacquerware Koetsu lacquerware refers to an early Edo period lacquerware style. The name derives from the use of lacquerware designs utilizing images made by the famous artist, Hon'ami Koetsu. Koetsu, sometimes in collaboration with another artist, Tawaraya Sotatsu, created designs taken from Heian-period literary themes. These were then used as decorations on lacquerware. This style also used mother-of-pearl inlays.

TEA AND RELATED ARTS

Tea Ceremony Practice

Formal tea gatherings in Japan blend social, religious, and spiritual functions with a profound appreciation for subtle beauty expressed in nature. Initially, Japanese tea rituals may appear straightforward and effortless, although tea and related arts are truly complex. Mastery of tea preparations requires discipline and hours of practice, yet accomplished tea participants are unpretentious and spontaneous. On a basic level, tea gatherings involve simply preparing and enjoying tea in a congenial setting. However, tea preparations could require years, for a host in 15th-century Kyoto could not quickly procure a complete set of tea implements; rather, such objects had to be obtained gradually, and collections reflected both a host's efforts and acquired tastes. Further, in order to fully appreciate the setting provided by their host, guests needed specialized knowledge of myriad art forms including ceramics, bamboo carving, lacquer, metalwork, calligraphy, painting, flower arranging, architecture, poetry, and garden design. Finally, while tea practice incorporates numerous established traditions, each tea gathering also constitutes a shared, transient moment through which, it is hoped, participants may derive renewal. Perhaps the spirituality, subtlety, and years of experience necessary in preparing and enjoying tea traditions are best summarized in the phrases used in Japan for these art forms. *Chanoyu*, meaning hot water for tea, evokes the basic components necessary to prepare tea—fire, wood, water, the metal tea kettle, and the clay tea bowl (representing earth). *Chado*, another Japanese phrase for the tea ritual, means the way of tea. Both of these terms capture the discipline and aesthetic awareness necessary to transform fundamental elements of the natural world into an opportunity to refresh both body and spirit while savoring the moment.

Guests are presented with tea in understated yet elegant surroundings that merit careful consideration, for the discernment of the host is implicit in every detail. For those who participate in *chado*, the simple forms, serene communal setting, prized objects, and prescribed actions of tea traditions offer refuge from the solipsism and mundane affairs of everyday life. Thus, for many, tea is a spiritual practice that can yield greater physical well-being, concentration, insight, and a restored connection to both humanity and nature—much as meditation may benefit body, mind, and spirit. Such metaphysical ideals and rituals seem to parallel religious goals and beliefs. Notably, though, tea practitioners prefer not to describe their gatherings as "ceremonies," for this word implies a stiffness that tea participants aim to eliminate through the uncomplicated harmonies and rhythms of the natural world.

Tea Ceremony History

From the early seventh century, Japanese monks traveled to China to study Buddhism. The Chan school, which became known as Zen in Japan, emphasized lengthy meditation sessions. Japanese monks practicing this tradition also learned to drink tea, which was considered a medicinal beverage, in order to remain alert while meditating.

Tea made from the leaves of the *Camellia sinensis*, a flowering plant native to China, was introduced to Japan during the eighth century in a bricklike form favored in Tang-dynasty China (618–907). Until the early Kamakura period, tea was prepared by steeping fermented leaves in hot water. Powdered, unfermented green tea whisked in individual bowls as in Chinese monasteries did not become popular until Zen Buddhist teachings, along with tea seedlings and etiquette for preparing tea, came to Japan in about 1191. *Matcha*, the type of tea still used today in formal Japanese tea gatherings, is produced from the choicest leaves of the tea plant. After steaming to preserve color and halt fermentation, *matcha* leaves are dried and ground into a fine powder that is whisked with warm water until slightly frothy in texture.

As Zen Buddhism proliferated during the medieval period, both monks and amateurs from the Japanese military elite began to enjoy this hot beverage. Eventually, tea preparation became a formal affair that mirrored the hierarchy of feudal society, and wealthy patrons began to engage individuals who could advise them about appropriate tea practice and aesthetics. The Ashikaga shogun Yoshimasa frequently hosted large-scale tea gatherings, and employed cultural advisers to guide him in selecting items such as celadon-glazed wares and *temmoku* bowls from China to complement paintings and calligraphic scrolls in the impressive Ashikaga collection. As in the Kamakura era, Chinese art and architecture had a powerful effect on the tastes of patrons from the warrior classes under the rule of the Ashikaga shoguns.

The Zen priest Murata Shuko (or Juko, 1422–1502) served as an adviser to Ashikaga Yoshimasa, and became an important arbiter of taste during the Muromachi era. A student of the influential priest Ikkyu, who had been an energetic proponent of tea ritual for its benefits in Zen practice, Shuko advocated an approach to tea rooted in Zen austerity. He chided tea adherents who indulged in pride, envy, and self-aggrandizement, and championed Zen views claiming that spiritual fulfillment was possible only through poverty and restraint. Shuko also felt that the atmosphere of intimate hospitality appropriate to a tea gathering was enhanced if the host prepared tea personally, rather than assigning servants to perform the task.

In articulating his convictions, Shuko anticipated two sensibilities: *wabi*, the spiritual wealth gained in poverty and humility; and *sabi*, the faded beauty of prized objects tarnished by age and repeated use—

both concepts integral to later tea aesthetics. So figural were these terms that the understated aesthetics of Murata Shuko, and his heirs Takeno Joo and Sen no Rikyu, became known as *wabi* tea to distinguish them from more ostentatious tea preparations favored by the feudal lords.

In addition to contributing to a philosophy of tea, Shuko also influenced tea architecture through his service to Ashikaga Yoshimasa. At the eastern Kyoto villa today known as Ginkakuji, Shuko hosted tea gatherings on behalf of Yoshimasa that took place in a room designed with only four and a half *tatami* mats. These mats consisted of woven grass covering a thick filling of rice straw. The configuration and number of *tatami* used by Shuko in this intimate tea setting later became a standard format for tearooms.

Sen no Rikyu (1522–91) formalized tea ideals first articulated by Murata Shuko. However, Rikyu was more influential than Shuko both in terms of access to prominent tea patrons and adherence to tea sensibilities that typified Zen austerity and understatement. During his merchant upbringing in the prosperous port city of Sakai on the eastern Inland Sea, Rikyu was exposed to continental imports such as tea ceramics that appealed to wealthy Sakai merchants, whose patronage and cultural aspirations fueled new currents in tea aesthetics from the late Muromachi era to the 17th century. Further, Rikyu studied with Takeno Joo (1502–55), a Sakai-based Zen priest, poet, and tea aficionado who first followed the teachings of his teacher, Shuko, and then strove to improve upon them later in his career. Joo eventually exercised considerable influence, for he possessed a sizable and enviable collection of tea utensils, and his innovations were carried as far as Kyoto.

Rikyu, a student of Joo, grew to prominence in this environment, where he was particularly noteworthy for his pursuit of the *wabi* aesthetic. Rikyu followed both of his predecessors in the way of tea, as he too harbored a profound appreciation of *wabi*—purity and harmony expressed in the humble appearance of the rustic tearoom and related tea objects, as well as the uncomplicated allure of austerity and restraint. As noted earlier, *wabi* has been an especially figural sensibility in tea culture, although it is somewhat incomplete unless paired

with its aesthetic complement, *sabi*, which evokes the loneliness and quietude of age, as well as the natural tarnish and worn surfaces that can be acquired only through time and frequent use.

As Oda Nobunaga (1534–82) ascended to power in the late 1560s, he summoned Rikyu to serve as his tea officer and cultural adviser. After Nobunaga's assassination in 1582, Toyotomi Hideyoshi followed his former general both in unifying Japan and engaging Rikyu. Both Nobunaga and Hideyoshi recognized the importance of tea and related arts in military culture and enjoyed the heightened political and cultural supremacy Rikyu conferred through his status as highest authority of the *wabi* tea tradition. Although officially a cultural adviser, Rikyu could serve as social agent, go-between, or even diplomat, thus intervening in various delicate political contexts even while reflecting favorably upon the cultural acumen of his overlord. Further, Nobunaga and Hideyoshi had acquired coveted tea implements originating in the Ashikaga collections. Armed with the bounty of their conquests, these military lords demonstrated to conquered daimyo tea enthusiasts that they had supplanted the old regime, yet appreciated its cultural heritage.

Soon after achieving his goal of unifying Japan, Hideyoshi ordered Rikyu to commit seppuku, or ritual suicide, in 1591 for reasons that remain unclear. Despite his demise, aspects of Rikyu's taste and ideals persisted in tea practice amid the sweeping cultural changes of the Edo period.

Tea rituals became less exclusive and tea masters grew more accessible as Rikyu's grandson, Sen Sotan (1578–1658) and his three heirs, Soshitsu (1622–97), Sosa (1619–72), and Soshu (1593–1675), founded schools and established publications to disseminate tea traditions. Initially, daimyo patronage dominated, but later adherents grew to include samurai, artisans, merchants, and other commoners. Some of Rikyu's innovations helped to further the broad access to tea that characterized the Edo period. For example, in a break with prior protocol, Rikyu had stipulated that tea should be made in front of guests, rather than prepared in one room and later served in another. Practices such as this fostered the egalitarian image of tea projected by Rikyu descendants who formed the Urasenke school, a tradition aimed at attracting more humble members of society to tea practice. The ascetic spirituality of medieval Buddhism that suffused the *wabi* style of tea most closely connected with Rikyu began to fade as tea patronage shifted from wealthy merchants and ambitious military lords to peacetime samurai who favored a style sometimes described as "daimyo tea."

Despite his significant political and spiritual contributions, Rikyu most affected tea and related arts through his exacting connoisseurship—enabling him to identify tea utensils that embodied his ideals of restraint, simplicity, and directness. Although Rikyu's greatest legacy may be his exquisite sense of design and discernment, subsequent generations have credited him with numerous other achievements. Principles of tea ascribed to Rikyu codified by his great-grandsons in the Edo period propose that he established the four ideals of tea captured in the Japanese characters *wa* (harmony), *kei* (respect), *sei* (purity), and *jaku* (tranquility or natural elegance). Below, these concepts are presented in terms of the role and relevance of each term in the world of tea ritual.

harmony (*wa*): a desire for reciprocity, both at the tea gathering and in the outside world
respect (*kei*): awareness of one's individual role and responsibilities, and appropriate decorum
purity (*sei*): a commitment to preserve social and spiritual integrity
tranquillity or natural elegance (*jaku*): savoring the transient moment to gain renewal

Tea Preparations

The host's procedure for preparing tea (*temae*) demonstrates both economy of motion and grace. Each action flows into the next in a measured, seamless choreography interrupted only by periodic taps and flourishes that punctuate stages of preparation. Typically, the *temae* involves six basic steps:

1. All tea implements, except the iron water kettle, which is usually placed on the hearth or brazier before the guests enter, are carried into the tearoom and arranged.

2. The host purifies the tea container (*natsume* or *chaire*) and bamboo tea scoop (*chashaku*) by wiping them with a silken cloth (*fukusa*).

3. Hot water poured into the tea bowl (*chawan*) warms both the bowl and bamboo tea whisk (*chasen*).

4. Using the bamboo tea scoop, the host places powdered green tea in the bowl. Hot water is added to the tea and whisked until the texture is frothy.

5. After guests have enjoyed their tea, the bowl and whisk are cleaned along with the tea scoop.

6. The host withdraws from the tearoom, returning all implements except the kettle to the preparation room.

Typical tea gatherings conclude as the host passes tea utensils for guests to appreciate and inspect. Fulfilled by the tea and atmosphere of camaraderie, guests leave the gathering refreshed by their shared experience.

Tea Utensils (*chadogu*)

Hanging Scroll (*jiku*) When entering the tearoom, guests should approach and honor the scroll first, by bowing. Unlike many of the implements, the scroll is not part of the process of preparing tea. Still, the *jiku* is essential to the tea gathering, and may be the most revered object in the tearoom. Scrolls may feature painted images, although calligraphic works are also favored. Mounted on backings made of textiles attached to a dowel to facilitate storage, *jiku* are placed in the *tokonoma*, an alcove reserved for displaying scrolls, flower arrangements, and sometimes an incense container. Scrolls are also known as *kakejiku* or *kakemono*.

Flower Container (*hanaire*) Flowers for tea are arranged to appear as if still growing in the fields. The flower container, or *hanaire*, is selected to suit the buds, blossoms, and/or grasses, to harmonize with seasonal themes, and to complement the tearoom itself. *Hanaire* may be bronze, copper, ceramic, or bamboo.

Tea Kettle (*kama*) The *kama* comes in many sizes and shapes. Larger kettles are placed on the *ro* (fireplace or hearth) and smaller versions are placed on the *furo* (brazier). In *chanoyu*, the kettle is used to boil water, not to steep tea, as in many other countries. There are many shapes of kettles, and although they are usually made of iron, *kama* are also crafted from gold or silver.

Portable Brazier (*furo*) The *furo* is a portable brazier that is used for ceremonies from May to October. *Furo* are made of earthenware, bronze, iron, wood, and other ceramic materials. During the winter, the tea kettle is heated on the fireplace or hearth (*ro*) itself. An iron *furo* is always placed on the *shiki-gawara* (fire tile).

Fresh Water Jar (*mizusashi*) This covered jar holds cool water used to regulate the temperature of the water in the *kama* or to rinse certain utensils. While *mizusashi* are ceramic, wooden or metal jars are also used.

Tea Caddy (*chaire* and *natsume*) The *chaire* is a type of tea caddy used for thick tea and the *natsume* is used for thin tea. *Chaire* are kept in *shifuku* (small silk bags). A *chaire* is usually ceramic and has an ivory lid. *Natsume* may also be called *usuki* or *chaki*.

Tea Scoop (*chashaku*) Crafted from various materials ranging from ivory to bamboo, the *chashaku* is used for scooping powdered tea from the caddy into a tea bowl.

Teabowl (*chawan*) The teabowl plays a central role in the art of *chanoyu* as the link between host and guest. Made in a wide variety of sizes, shapes, and types, *chawan* are selected by the host to express the degree of formality of the occasion, seasonal preferences, and contemporary sensibilities.

Lid Rest (*futaoki*) for the Tea Kettle and Water Ladle There are seven kinds of famous *futaoki* selected by noted tea master Sen no Rikyu (1521–91). Each has its own specific rule for use. In general, however, the most common *futaoki* is a small bamboo mat.

Bowl for Waste Water (*kensui*) Water used to rinse utensils is discarded in this bowl. *Kensui* are sometimes called *koboshi*.

Water Ladle (*hishaku*) There are many types of *hishaku*, defined by the cut of their handles. Those that have handles cut from the outside diagonally may only be used with a *ro* (winter tea). Those with a handle cut from the inside diagonally may be used with the *furo* (summer *chanoyu*).

Bamboo Whisk (*chasen*) *Chasen* are made of different types of bamboo. Some examples of materials used to make tea whisks include smoked and dried bamboo. Participants from different schools of tea prefer certain types of tea whisks.

Tea Cloth (*chakin*) This piece of linen—used to wipe tea bowls—measures about a foot long and five inches wide.

Role of Nature in the World of Tea

Chanoyu involves both social and religious principles. However, appreciation of nature is also a central component of preparing and enjoying tea in Japan. Shinto and Buddhism have long coexisted in Japan, and both religions also incorporate profound regard and respect for the natural world. The Shinto tradition proposes that sacred beings (*kami*) are manifest in nature. According to Shinto, *kami* may reside in rivers, rocks, mountains, or even trees. Tea utensils, architecture, and related art forms favor undecorated surfaces and rough or weathered textures that highlight nature's beauty, just as these elements are prized in Shinto rituals and sanctified Shinto sites. As in Shinto practice, purification also has a vital role in tea gatherings. Buddhists have established perspectives on the import of the natural world, which is a reminder of the transience of human existence. Buddhism celebrates this belief through heightened awareness and acceptance of seasonal changes and other temporal rhythms. Monks are trained to meditate through concentration on the present moment, without regret for the past or desire for the future, and thereby attain release. Similarly, *chanoyu* urges participants to cherish the fleeting beauty of nature's cycles while sharing a bowl of tea and quiet conversation in natural surroundings. In addition, most tea wares reflect Buddhist preferences for economy of design and subtle decoration.

Tea Ceramics

Ceramics for use in tea gatherings have been carefully selected to echo the rustic setting and understated pleasures central to the way of tea. Initially, ceramics used for preparing and enjoying tea were Chinese and Korean objects imported by monks and art enthusiasts, especially during the late Kamakura and Muromachi eras. Soon, Japanese potters began to craft wares emulating these imported ceramics, and some ceramicists emigrated from China and Korea, thus transmitting ceramic production techniques and types directly to artisans working in the Japanese archipelago.

While various tea traditions espouse particular aesthetic sensibilities regarding ceramic types for tea preparations, many schools agree on the most desirable varieties of ceramic wares for the tea bowl. Raku ware, Karatsu ware, and Hagi ware are all ceramic types favored for tea bowls. However, other varieties, such as Shino, Seto, and Oribe wares, are also frequently used. Regardless of its origin, the tea bowl has a special role in tea preparation as the tea implement that is handled the most, and the object that best embodies the desired connection between the host and guest.

ARCHITECTURE

There are at least two ways in which the study of medieval and early modern architecture might be organized: temporally—in sequential order from style to style—and functionally—buildings typed as

religious or secular. Both these approaches seem commonsensical, but both also introduce particular difficulties with regard to architecture in medieval and early modern Japan.

In the temporal approach, for instance talking about "medieval" or "early modern" architecture, there is a need to account for the fact that temples and shrines might be constructed in one period but have additions or other stylistic changes made to them over the centuries. Initially, a structure might be constructed in one style but come to reflect the accretion of multiple styles belonging to different time periods. Similarly, shrine and temple buildings, despite the vagaries of weather, fire, and other natural predators of wood construction, sometimes endured over the centuries and were important in multiple time periods, their architectural styles a part of periods far removed from their original time of construction. In at least one famous instance—the Ise Shrine—the architectural style is very old but the shrine buildings are rebuilt every 20 years as a means of ritual purification. Hence, the buildings are always new but exhibit an old architectural style.

The distinction between religious and secular architecture is also fraught with problems and ambiguities. Some architectural forms, such as the Shoin style (see below), were derived from both Buddhist and aristocratic sources. Secular retirement villas might be turned into Buddhist temples, as in the case of Kinkakuji and Ginkakuji (see below). The blending of the religious and secular was not unique to Japanese architecture, but was rather indicative of a worldview that did not make sharp distinctions between the sacred and the profane. While temporal and functional categories are suggested below, they should not be treated as definitive categories for organizing medieval and early modern Japanese architecture.

Buddhist Architecture

Buddhist architecture refers to building styles associated with temples and temple complexes. Buddhist temple complexes consisted of multiple structures functioning in concert to create a contained community that met both the spiritual and material needs of those residing there. Fundamentally, temples were places dedicated to a variety of Buddhist practices and functions. Different buildings were constructed for these different functions. Temple compounds had buildings for worship of the Buddhas and bodhisattvas, dwellings for monks or nuns, halls for religious training and practice, and also places to house texts and other important religious objects. In most cases, temples also served as gathering places for members of the laity.

Prior to the medieval period, there had been ideas about the proper number and configuration of buildings for a Buddhist temple complex. However, by the Kamakura period, temples were typically designed according to one of three different styles, or in a style combining the three. Thus, not all temples were designed in the same way or with the same layout of buildings and grounds, and different Buddhist schools utilized different configurations.

STYLES OF BUDDHIST ARCHITECTURE

Styles of Buddhist architecture changed over the centuries. In general, they were a combination of both Chinese and indigenous Japanese styles. In the medieval period, the preexisting Japanese style (*wayo*) of Buddhist architecture was used, along with two new important Buddhist architectural styles first developed in the early medieval period: the Great Buddha style (*daibutsuyo*) and the Zen or Chinese style (*karayo*). By the end of the Kamakura period, temple construction started to borrow from the different Buddhist architectural styles to create a hybrid or eclectic style (*setchuyo*) that utilized elements from the Japanese, Great Buddha, and Zen styles. While use of the three main architectural styles continued in the early modern period, a fourth style—Obaku style—was imported from China and was primarily associated with the Obaku Zen school.

One of the distinguishing characteristics of Buddhist architecture generally is the style of bracketing used to support the roof and eave of a temple on the outside of a building and the ceiling on the inside. Bracketing served both structural and aesthetic functions. Different Buddhist architectural styles used different bracketing systems and thus bracket-

ing became one of the architectural features that set different styles apart from each other.

Japanese Style (*wayo*) In its use as an architectural term, *wayo* or Japanese style refers to the style of Buddhist architecture current in Japan beginning in the Nara period. Despite the term, Japanese style is in fact the overlay of Japanese architectural styles—such as the use of unpainted and untreated wood, simple ornamentation, and curved lines—over styles imported from Tang-dynasty (618–906) China. Once Tang-style architecture was introduced to Japan, it evolved into a Japanese style throughout the course of the Heian period. The term *wayo* was created in the early medieval period to contrast the older architectural style with new styles then becoming prevalent, imported from the Asian mainland.

Although Japanese-style Buddhist architecture was largely supplanted in the Kamakura period by new styles, it was nevertheless employed in some important temple rebuilding projects. Of particular note was the use of Japanese style to rebuild structures at two Nara temples, the Kofukuji and the Todaiji, that were destroyed during the Gempei War.

Great Buddha Style (*daibutsuyo*) or Indian Style (*tenjikuyo*) The Great Buddha style (*daibutsuyo*) of Japanese Buddhist architecture is also referred to as Indian style (*tenjikuyo*). The term *tenjikuyo* was used in the medieval period; *daibutsuyo* is a modern term coined to more accurately describe this aspect of Japan's architectural history. Although *tenjikuyo* means "Indian style," this architectural style actually makes no visual reference to Indian design modes. Rather, it refers to south China architectural style blended with traditional Japanese design features.

The term *daibutsuyo* was named after the style of the Todaiji Great Buddha Hall (*daibutsuden*) when it was rebuilt through the efforts of the priest, Chogen (1121–1206), who had introduced Indian style to Japan after returning from his travels in southern China during the Song dynasty. The Great South Gate (*nandaimon*) at Todaiji, designed by Chogen and built at the same time as the Great Buddha Hall, is an important example of the Great Buddha style still extant. Chogen's Great Buddha Hall construction burned in 1567 and was later rebuilt in a similar style. Use of the Great Buddha style was largely abandoned soon after Chogen's death, though some of its details and elements were incorporated into other architectural styles.

Zen Style (*zenshuyo*) or Chinese Style (*karayo*)
The Zen style (*zenshuyo*) of Buddhist architecture was imported from China during the Kamakura period. An important extant example of this style is the Relic Hall (*shariden*) at the Engakuji constructed in the medieval period in the city of Kamakura. The Zen style, as an architectural term, is a modern coinage. The term used during the medieval period was Chinese style or *karayo*, reflecting the importation of this style from Song-dynasty (960–1279) China. As the name implies, the Zen style was particularly associated with design elements used for building Zen temple complexes in the medieval period.

The Zen style introduced new design elements into the construction of temples. Among these innovations were novel styles of ornamentation, upwardly curved fan rafters, and bell-shaped windows. Although Zen style was based on Chinese models, Japanese designers innovated on the borrowed design to create an architectural style different from its Chinese counterpart. The roof structure, for instance, was modified to meet Japanese practical and aesthetic needs.

Obaku Style The Obaku style of Buddhist architecture was introduced to Japan in the late 17th century and is associated with Zen temples belonging to the Obaku school. The Obaku school of Zen Buddhism was imported from China to Japan in the middle of the 17th century. The Mampukuji in Uji (south of Kyoto), constructed in the 1660s, exemplifies the Obaku style. The Obaku architectural style uses traditional Zen features, but also incorporates design elements from Chinese Buddhist architectural forms of the late Ming (1368–1644) and early Qing (1644–1912) dynasties, including the physical layout of the temple grounds. Among the Chinese architectural innovations apparent at Mampukuji and other Obaku temples are such features as open corridors running between temple buildings, a four-tiered bracketing system, intricately carved pillar base stones, and decorative railings.

BUDDHIST COMPLEXES AND BUILDINGS

Typical kinds of buildings and structures found at a temple complex—besides those for everyday functions such as kitchen, dining hall, dormitory, bathhouse, and latrine—included those in the following list. Note that not all temple complexes necessarily had all of these kinds of buildings and structures, and some may have had variants of these buildings, depending on the particular Buddhist school.

main hall (*kondo* or *hondo* or *butsudo* or *butsuden* or *Amidado*) The location of a temple's most important images of Buddhas and bodhisattvas. The term *kondo* (golden hall) was used particularly in the Nara and Heian periods. Although the term was also used during the medieval and early modern periods, the term *hondo* (main hall) became much more widely used to refer to a temple's main hall. The term *butsudo* (Buddha hall) is a generic term for a main hall housing a Buddha image. The term *butsuden* (Buddha hall) refers to the main hall at a Zen temple. The term *Amidado* refers to the main hall at a Pure Land temple.

lecture hall (*kodo* or *hatto*) The term *kodo* refers to a lecture hall used by Buddhist schools other than Zen. Buddhist statues are usually placed inside the *kodo*, and the lecturing priest stands in front of them. The term *hatto* (literally, "Dharma Hall") refers to the lecture hall at a Zen temple. Typically, Buddhist imagery is not used in a Zen lecture hall.

meditation hall (*zendo*) A Zen temple meditation hall used especially for the practice of *zazen*, or seated meditation.

pagoda (*to*) The Buddhist structure known as a pagoda (*to*; literally, "tower") was, in Japan, usually a wooden, multitiered structure that housed relics of the historical Buddha's bodily remains. The pagoda form and function originated in Indian Buddhist architecture where the stupa, as it was called in Sanskrit, was a hemispherical dome made of earth and stone. The stupa became formalized into the East Asian pagoda, a much taller and narrower structure made of wood. Both stupas and pagodas are crowned with a spire. According to early documents, the pagoda as a central feature of important Buddhist complexes was introduced to Japan by the end of the sixth century.

sutra repository (*kyozo*) A text repository housing Buddhist scriptures and commentaries as well as temple documents

bell tower (*shoro*) Housing for the temple bell that was rung to mark specific ritual occasions or other events

gates (*mon*) Buddhist temple gates functioned to set apart the temple grounds from the outside world. Gates within a temple complex created spaces within the larger temple grounds that were set apart as especially sacred or ritually important. Temples were sometimes divided according to an inner and outer precinct demarcated by a gate. Some gates could be quite large and imposing, signifying the importance and power of a particular temple complex.

ARCHITECTURE UNDER THE ASHIKAGA SHOGUNS

Two Muromachi-period pavilions that attest to the pervasive influence of Zen Buddhism also reflect the seamlessness of secular and religious culture under the patronage of the Ashikaga shogunate (1333–1573). Originally constructed as villas for retirement, these two structures are known today as Kinkakuji (Temple of the Golden Pavilion; originally Rokuonji) and Ginkakuji (Temple of the Silver Pavilion; originally Jishoji), although the buildings were not converted into temples and given their present names until after the deaths of their owners.

The third shogun, Ashikaga Yoshimitsu, demonstrated his passion for Chinese visual and literary arts when he ordered his three-story, double-roofed pavilion constructed in the Kitayama (Northern Hills) district of Kyoto. The pavilion is modeled on a type of scholarly retreat seen in Chinese painting. Situated within an extensive array of gardens for strolling modeled on Chinese precedents, Kinkakuji is resplendent with gold foil covering the exterior. Inside, the structure includes space

on the first floor dedicated to informal leisure activities such as contemplating the gardens and lake, and an L-shaped veranda on the second level for Moon-viewing. During Yoshimitsu's lifetime, the pavilion served as an appropriate spot for the poetry gatherings he liked to host, and upon his death, its conversion to a temple memorialized his enthusiasm for cultural pursuits connected with Chinese aesthetics. Thus, Kinkakuji was among the most visible manifestations of Chinese influence in Japanese art and architecture of the 14th century.

In the later half of the 15th century, Yoshimasa (1436–90), eighth Ashikaga shogun (ruled 1449–74) and Yoshimitsu's grandson, continued the tradition of Ashikaga patronage established by his grandfather as he erected a pavilion dedicated to cultural pursuits in the eastern hills of Kyoto (Higashiyama district). Today, Yoshimasa's villa is popularly known as Ginkakuji (Temple of the Silver Pavilion) due to the spurious legend that the entire exterior was to have been covered with silver leaf, just as the exterior of Kinkakuji is covered with gold foil. Yoshimasa may have intended to cover the interior second floor of the two-story pavilion, a Kannon hall, with silver leaf, although this project was not accomplished. The first floor of the double-roofed structure was used for meditation and had sliding doors (*fusuma*) that could open to reveal the gardens and lake also designed for the complex.

Another building on the site, a single-story structure known as the Togudo, housed a room created for preparing and enjoying tea in the style favored by the tea connoisseur and Zen monk Murato Shuko (1422–1502). Under the influence of Shuko (also known as Juko), who encouraged adhering to Buddhist precepts while making and sharing tea, tea consumption and related arts became a formalized ritual known today as *chanoyu*. Today, Yoshimasa's pavilion is officially known as Jishoji, a temple affiliated with the Rinzai school of Zen Buddhism. Although not formally dedicated as a temple until the death of Yoshimasa, this structure had a prominent place in the Zen-infused environment of 15th-century Kyoto.

Yoshimasa's ineffectual rule aggravated political and civil unrest in the capital that eventually culminated in the Onin War of 1467–77 and subsequent internecine conflicts. However, his artistic preoccu-

10.1 Bell tower and temple bell at the Engakuji in Kamakura. This bell, designated a National Treasure by the Japanese government, was cast by members of the Mononobe family, the best-known bronze artisans of the Kamakura period. Donated in 1301 by Hojo Sadatoki to the Engakuji in Kamakura, unlike Western bells, this bell has no clapper and is traditionally struck by a log to create a deep resonance. (Photo William E. Deal)

had. However, many of these figures left the unstable climate of the capital for provincial temples and domains, and Yoshimasa turned to a family of nominal clerics known as the San'ami, who advised him on connoisseurship and display and served as curators of the Ashikaga collection. These men had a family affiliation with the Pure Land school of Buddhism, a clerical connection in name alone that was reflected in their use of the suffix *ami* (from Amida). Under the influence of these figures, Noami (1397–1471), Geiami (1431–85), and Soami (1455–1525), both townspeople and regional lords participated in tea gatherings, garden design, connoisseurship of ceramics and lacquerwares, and flower arranging at Ginkakuji. The cultural milieu of this pavilion and its adherents was thus flavored with the aristocratic heritage of Kyoto, the old capital, as well as the sensibilities of the newly powerful warrior classes.

Shinto Architecture

Shrine (*jinja*) architecture refers to building styles associated with Shinto shrines. Shrines are located within a space demarcated as sacred because a *kami* (deity) is enshrined there. Shinto shrine precincts include not only a building or buildings for worshipping the *kami* but also buildings for ritual performances. Shinto architecture incorporates both indigenous design elements and borrowings from Chinese and Buddhist architecture. Thus, for instance, some shrines utilize the indigenous aesthetic of plain wood while others are painted a bright vermilion color.

STYLES OF SHINTO ARCHITECTURE

There were many thousands of Shinto shrines in Japan during the medieval and early modern periods (as there are today) of varying importance and size. The majority were small and shared a similar architectural style, typically *nagare-zukuri* or *kasuga-zukuri* (see below). Larger shrines, however, often had their own distinctive design style. A particular style of Shinto architecture was usually named after the style of the main sanctuary (*honden*) of the shrine

pations yielded significant developments in various cultural spheres during his tenure as shogun. Ginkakuji, where he settled in 1483, became a haven for cultivating leisure pursuits. At first, Yoshimasa relied upon *tonseisha* (nominal Buddhist clerics) for discernment in cultural matters as his grandfather

10.2 Ginkakuji, in Kyoto (Photo William E. Deal)

precincts. Among the most important Shinto architectural styles are:

Shimmei Style (*shimmei-zukuri*) The Shimmei ("sacred brightness") style is associated with the earliest Shinto shrines. These ancient shrines evolved from the design of granary storehouses. This style is exemplified by the Inner Shrine (*naiku*) at the Ise Shrine. It is here that Amaterasu, the sun goddess, is enshrined. According to Japanese mythology, the imperial family is descended from her lineage. The Ise Shrine, an important Edo-period pilgrimage destination, is rebuilt every 20 years as an act of purification.

Nagare Style (*nagare-zukuri*) Nagare ("flowing") style is the most common form of main sanctuary (*honden*) Shinto architecture. It is a style that is found throughout Japan, especially in smaller regional shrines. Nagare-style shrines have an asymmetrical gable roof with a long, extended sloping front. The two Kamo Shrines in Kyoto typify this style.

Kasuga Style (*kasuga-zukuri*) The Kasuga style refers to the architectural style found at the Kasuga Shrine in Nara and widely used at smaller shrines in the Nara and Kyoto areas. The Kasuga style is second only to the Nagare style in its prevalence in shrine construction.

Hachiman Style (*hachiman-zukuri*) The Hachiman style is used in the main sanctuary (*honden*) and worship hall (*haiden*) at shrines dedicated to the *kami* Hachiman. This style is distinguished by its use of two Nagare-style shrines, one in front and one in back, with the two buildings touching at the roof eaves. This linked building style was borrowed from Buddhist architecture. The building in front is the worship hall and the back building houses the main sanctuary. The Iwashimizu Hachiman Shrine in Kyoto and the Tsurugaoka Hachiman Shrine in Kamakura are extant examples of shrines using the Hachiman style for their main sanctuaries and worship halls.

Hiyoshi Style (*hiyoshi-zukuri*) The Hiyoshi style, also commonly referred to as the Hie style (*hie-zukuri*), is particularly associated with the extant Hiyoshi (or Hie) Shrine. This shrine is located at the foot of Mt. Hiei and is the guardian shrine of the Enryakuji, the Tendai-school headquarters atop the mountain. The Hiyoshi style is a variation of the Nagare style.

Taisha Style (*taisha-zukuri*) The Taisha ("grand shrine") style is associated with the extant Izumo Shrine (*taisha*) in present-day Shimane Prefecture. Like the Shimmei style, the main sanctuary has a raised floor suggestive of ancient granaries that required an elevated floor for air circulation. Other shrines in this region of Japan also use a similar construction technique. Other distinctive features of this architectural style include a roofed staircase leading into the main sanctuary.

Sumiyoshi Style (*sumiyoshi-zukuri*) The Sumiyoshi style is associated with the style of the main sanctuary (*honden*) at such Shinto sites as the Sumiyoshi Shrine in the Osaka area. This style is characterized, in part, by the division of its interior space into two parts, and by the use of a gable roof covered with cypress bark and extended eaves.

Gongen Style (*gongen-zukuri*) Gongen style refers to Tosho Daigongen (Eastern Light Great Incarnation), the posthumous name of Tokugawa Ieyasu (1542–1616). The term *gongen* (or *daigongen*, great *gongen*) means "incarnation." The posthumous name for Ieyasu, "the great incarnation Tosho," implies his manifestation as a deity at his death. As a *kami*, Ieyasu is enshrined in the Toshogu at the famous Nikko Shrine, an important early modern edifice. The Toshogu architectural style, conspicuous for its ornate decorative elements, is known as

the Gongen style. This style has a complicated roof design that joins together the main sanctuary and the worship hall.

SHRINE COMPLEXES AND BUILDINGS

The number, kinds, and arrangement of buildings at a shrine complex varied depending on the size and importance of the shrine. Minimally, a typical shrine included a main sanctuary and a worship hall. A large shrine might also include a meeting hall for shrine members, a storehouse, a hall for ritual meals, a shrine office, a hall for ritual purification, and priest quarters. Although shrine buildings might be placed in a number of different physical configurations, the precincts, regardless of size, typically had a gate to mark the entrance to the shrine grounds. Water basins (called *temizuya* or *chozuya*) were accessibly placed so that worshippers could purify themselves by rinsing their hands and mouth with the water before entering the central area of the shrine grounds. Pathways lead to the main sanctuary and worship hall.

In the medieval and early modern periods, it was not unusual to find Shinto shrines and Buddhist temples occupying adjoining spaces. This was the result of the medieval tendency to view gods, Buddhas, and bodhisattvas as different aspects of the same sacred power (see chapter 6: Religion). Thus, a shrine-temple (*jinguji*) might be located at a Shinto shrine complex. Or a temple-shrine (*jisha*) might be located at a Buddhist temple.

Typical kinds of buildings and structures found at a shrine complex included those in the following list. Note that not all shrine complexes necessarily had all of these different kinds of buildings and structures, and some had variants of these buildings depending on size, location, and relative importance of the shrine.

gate (*torii*) The gate structure at the entrance to a Shinto shrine is known as a *torii* (literally, "bird perch"). In the medieval and early modern periods, they were usually made of wood or stone. The *torii* marks the gateway into the sacred precincts of the Shinto shrine. Some are quite large and others small, and a shrine may have one or many within the shrine grounds. As an architectural form, the *torii* is a simple structure with two vertical posts surmounted by a single or double lintel that extend beyond the space framed by the posts.

There is debate over the origin of the *torii*, with some theories favoring the view that this design element was imported from non-Japanese architectural forms found, depending on the particular theory, in China or Korea, or even as far away as India. Other theories argue that the *torii* is a Japanese invention. Regardless of its origins, historical records suggest that the *torii* was in use in Japan by the 10th century and possibly before. There are many different styles of *torii*, but the basic shape is similar from style to style.

main sanctuary (*honden*) The main sanctuary (sometimes called *shoden*), located behind other shrine buildings, was where a *kami* was enshrined. It was the most sacred area of a shrine precinct. Only a Shinto priest was allowed into this part of the shrine. Unlike Buddhist temples where it was usual to find a sculptural representation of a Buddha or bodhisattva, Shinto shrines only rarely utilized such images. Rather, the *kami* was symbolically represented by a sacred mirror, an

10.3 Example of a Shinto shrine gate (torii) (Photo William E. Deal)

idea derived from Japan's early mythology. The style of the main sanctuary was usually considered the defining architectural feature of a shrine complex.

worship hall (*haiden*) A worship hall was central to the plan of a Shinto shrine. Some shrine precincts, such as those located in the mountains, only had a worship hall because the entire mountainous site was considered the abode of the *kami* and therefore a special sanctuary (*honden*) in which to enshrine the deity was not needed.

ritual dance hall (*maidono*) Ritual music and dance has always been associated with Shinto religious ceremonies (see chapter 9: Performing Arts). As a result, some shrine complexes included a separate hall set aside for such ritual performances. Prior to the medieval period, temporary stages were used for ritual music and dance, but by the Kamakura period, permanent structures were built for this purpose.

offering hall (*heiden*) A shrine offering hall was used to make offerings to the *kami* and to recite prayers. These offerings (known as *gohei* or *heihaku*) were typically made of white paper, silk, or cloth.

ceremonial kitchen (*shinsenden*) Usually only found at larger shrines, the ceremonial kitchen was the place where food offerings were prepared for ritual use.

Domestic Architecture

In the 16th and early 17th centuries, two new building styles arose that were closely connected to the interests and concerns of the warrior class: the castle and the *shoin*-style residence.

CASTLES

The Japanese castle, an indigenous architectural form, was the product of only about 100 years of construction, roughly 1530–1630. This corresponds to a time in which struggles to unify Japan were begun by powerful military lords and finally accomplished by the Tokugawa shogunate. Oda Nobunaga, Toyotomi Hideyoshi, and Tokugawa Ieyasu were among those powerful lords who built large-scale and elaborate castles. Although there were precedents for Japanese castles in the Kamakura and Muromachi periods, these were designed and used almost solely as military fortifications. The castle form discussed here came to serve a number of different purposes that went well beyond strategic defense.

Castles served military, political, domestic, symbolic, cultural, and other functions. The castle served as a military garrison for troops and arms, and a fortress from which to defend oneself from attack. Besides this overt military purpose, the castle was also home to the castle's lord, his family, and his closest retainers. As such, it was the place where the lord received his retainers and conducted much of his business. Within the direct vicinity of the castle, castle towns (*jokamachi*; see chapter 2: Land, Environment, and Population) developed as both economic and administrative centers of the region. Thus, a castle and its town was the political center of domain power and influence.

Castles were imposing structures that required significant wealth to build, run, and maintain. The bigger the castle and castle grounds, and the higher the main tower, the more prestige was conveyed. Castles served, therefore, as powerful reminders of the military and political might of the resident lord. They also served as the location for cultural and other leisure pursuits that projected the image of the refined lord conversant with aesthetic pursuits. To this end, warriors patronized the arts and commissioned artists to create works for their castles. For instance, Oda Nobunaga brought the famous painter Kano Eitoku (see above) to Azuchi Castle to produce wall and screen paintings with landscape and other motifs.

Castle construction peaked between 1600, when Tokugawa Ieyasu defeated the Toyotomi at the Battle of Sekigahara, and 1615, when the remaining Toyotomi forces were routed at the siege of Osaka Castle. After 1615, the Tokugawa shogunate limited to one the number of castles that could be built in each domain. This attempt to secure political and military control over Japan led, in 1620, to a complete ban on castle construction. Thus, the architec-

Castle	Principal Lord(s)	Location	Principal Construction Date
Inuyama Castle	Oda Nobuyasu	Inuyama (Aichi Prefecture)	1537
Azuchi Castle	Oda Nobunaga	Mt. Azuchi (on Lake Biwa)	1576–1579
Himeji Castle	Toyotomi Hideyoshi Ikeda Terumasa	Himeji (Hyogo Prefecture)	1581 1601–1609
Osaka Castle	Toyotomi Hideyoshi	Osaka	1583
Matsumoto Castle	Ishikawa Kazumasa	Matsumoto (Nagano Prefecture)	1590
Fushimi Castle	Toyotomi Hideyoshi	Momoyama district, Kyoto	1594
Okayama Castle	Ukita Hideie Ikeda Tadatsugu	Okayama	1597 1603
Edo Castle	Tokugawa Ieyasu	Edo	1603 (begun)
Hikone Castle	Ii Naomasa	Hikone (Shiga Prefecture)	1603
Nijo Castle	Tokugawa Ieyasu	Kyoto	1603
Nagoya Castle	Tokugawa Ieyasu	Nagoya	1612

tural style and design of castles spanned barely 100 years before it was ended by this edict.

Over time, castles were built, destroyed, and rebuilt. They changed ownership, sometimes frequently, and with each change of lord usually came additions or other changes to the castle that, among other things, asserted the power of the current inhabitant. The following is a very partial list of castles, and the lord or lords most closely or famously associated with them, along with locations and the year in which their principal construction occurred or was completed.

Castle Design

There are few extant castles existing in their original form. One exception is Himeji Castle, also known as the White Egret Castle (*shirasagijo*) because of its white-walled design. Castles like Himeji were built with many levels to present an imposing image and to afford a view of the lord's domain. In 1581, after defeating a rival lord in battle, Toyotomi Hideyoshi constructed a three-storied castle tower (*tenshu*) on the defeated lord's land. This was the beginning of Himeji Castle. The site was not fully developed as a castle until 1601 when Tokugawa

Ieyasu gave the site to Ikeda Terumasa (1564–1613), his son-in-law. Terumasa constructed Himeji Castle, completing work in 1609. The structure and design of Himeji Castle is indicative of late medieval and early Edo-period castle architecture. The following description of some of the more important architectural features of castles is generic but makes special reference to Himeji Castle where illustrative.

CASTLE SITE

Historically, there were three main castle types according to geographic location: 1) castles built in mountains (*yamajiro*), 2) castles built on plains (*hirajiro*), and 3) castles built on a hill or low mountain surrounded by a plain (*hirayamajiro*). Himeji Castle is an example of this last type of castle. These varied castle sites had different strategic strengths and weaknesses. In general, the lower the elevation of a castle, the more fortifications it required.

MAIN TOWER (*TENSHU*)

A castle's main—and usually multistoried—tower (*tenshu* or *tenshukaku*) was sited at the center of the castle complex (*hommaru*) at the highest location in the castle grounds. This placement provided both a strategic view of the adjoining area and an imposing symbol of the castle lord's power. The term *tenshu*, or main tower, is often translated into English as "donjon," a word used to describe a medieval European castle's inner tower.

There were four major types of main towers:

- **single tower**
- **compound tower:** a main tower that included attached secondary buildings or towers
- **linked tower:** a main tower connected by a passageway to a secondary tower or other structure
- **connected tower:** a main tower connected by passageways to multiple secondary towers

There were also castles constructed that employed variations on these four major tower types by combining features of more than one tower style. Himeji Castle is an example of a connected tower construction style. In addition to the main tower, there were additional small towers (*yagura*) with a design similar to the main tower. These small towers were used for different purposes, including as guard towers and as weapons storage.

INNER CITADEL (*HOMMARU*)

The focal point of castle design was the inner citadel called the *hommaru*. It was within this central enclosure that the main tower was sited. Additional compounds, arranged in different configurations

10.4 Main tower (tenshu) *of Himeji Castle* (Photo William E. Deal)

ART AND ARCHITECTURE

10.5 Steep wall of the main tower (tenshu) *at Himeji Castle* (Photo William E. Deal)

within compounds and charge along paths that had no obvious logic to them. They would also have had to deal with multiple gates and towers from which they would surely have been fired upon.

MOATS (*HORI*)

Castle designers utilized water-filled moats to deter invaders from successfully breaching the castle grounds. Himeji Castle used such a defensive system.

STONE FOUNDATION WALLS (*ISHIGAKI*)

Even if an attacking army were able to cross the moats, they would be met with steep stone foundation walls that were designed not only for their structural use as retaining walls but also to be difficult to climb. To this end, foundation walls were typically constructed so that they rose steeply from the base and were curved somewhat outward at the top.

CASTLE GATES

For an invader the easiest way into the castle was through one of the castle gates. There usually existed both a main gate in front (*otemon*) and also a rear entrance gate (*karametemon*). Secondary gates also were used. Gates, however, did not lead directly into the main part of the castle grounds. Rather, they were designed so that the path to the castle's interior included zigzags, additional gates, dead ends, and other mazelike methods for confusing anyone not already familiar with the castle plan. Interior gates sometimes included a two-story gatehouse that could be used to further defend against entry into the heart of the castle.

WEAPON PORTALS (*SAMA*)

Weapon portals, often called "loopholes" in English, were openings in walls and floors through which an arrow could be shot or a musket fired at the enemy. These openings could be round, square, or triangular in shape. This was another of a castle's defenses. Portals for archers were call *yazama* (arrow portals) and those for muskets were termed *teppozama* (musket portals). Besides accommodating these weapons, portals had a narrower openings onto the outside surface and wider openings on the inside surface. This design allowed castle warriors room to maneuver their weapons while providing only a very limited access target for enemy arrows and bullets.

depending on the castle and the physical space it occupied, enclosed this central space, spiraling out in many instances in a circular fashion from the center. These compounds bore names such as *ni-no-maru* ("second circle") and *san-no-maru* ("third circle"). The lord's business was conducted in the inner citadel, but the family residence was located in one of the secondary compounds.

There was a strategic function to these multiple compounds. The fact that castles had different arrangements meant that the enemy could not be sure how to quickly and effectively reach the inner citadel. At Himeji Castle, for instance, the compounds were laid out in interlocking sections. In order to successfully breach the castle, enemy attackers would have had to traverse open areas

10.6 Wall and gate at Himeji Castle (Photo William E. Deal)

SHOIN-STYLE WARRIOR RESIDENCES

In addition to castle construction, the development of the Shoin (writing hall) style (*shoin-zukuri*) residence was the second major architectural innovation that occurred in the late medieval and the beginning of the early modern period. The Shoin style traces its origins in part to the aristocratic Shinden residential style (*shinden-zukuri*) prevalent in the Heian period and adapted to warrior tastes in the medieval period. Though elements of Shoin-style design were used in commoners' dwellings later in the Edo period, it was this form of architecture that was particularly associated with the warrior class by the beginning of the early modern period.

In addition to the functionality of the Shoin style, there was an important political aspect to this architectural design element that expressed the social hierarchy explicit between lord and retainer. The reception room in a Shoin-style structure was where, for instance, a lord would receive his retainers. The placement of people within this space—lord seated on the upper of two floor levels and retainers on the lower—expressed a clear power differential between the two.

Beginning in the 14th century, Shoin-style architectural details began appearing in the private quarters of Zen monasteries, especially the temple residences of abbots and other high-ranking monastics. Buddhist abbots, for instance, utilized rooms that included a writing desk, a feature that became central to the Shoin style. An important prototypical example of the architectural style that developed into the Shoin style is the extant Dojinsai, a tea ceremony room at the Togudo, a hall that is part of the Ginkakuji temple complex in Kyoto.

By the Azuchi-Momoyama period, the design elements characteristic of the Shoin style were formalized. These new and newly elaborated features included an alcove for the display of important hanging scrolls (or for wall paintings), a set of staggered shelves for treasured objects in the military lord's collection, and a floor of grass mats with a place of honor reserved for the highest-ranking individual. Shoin-style architecture also included a built-in desk in the alcove. This feature of the room was utilitarian, but it also provided a way of showing that the lord was a person of culture. These are the same features used today in the formal rooms of contemporary Japanese homes.

Shoin-Style Design Elements

Buildings incorporating the Shoin style contain rooms, such as a formal reception room (*zashiki*), that utilize at least some of the following distinctive design elements:

DECORATIVE ALCOVE (*TOKONOMA*)

The decorative alcove, known as a *tokonoma*, was a raised floor that created a niche built into a back wall. It was used for displaying such things as a prized object, a flower arrangement, or a hanging scroll (*kakejiku*).

STAGGERED SHELVES (*CHIGAIDANA*)

Staggered shelves were usually two shelves set at different levels. Unlike the formality of the *tokonoma*,

10.7 The Ho Gate of Himeji Castle leads to the entrance of the First Water Gate, which is the most direct route to the main tower (tenshu). One of many gates that soldiers would encounter en route to the castle, these fortifications were designed to confuse as well as to protect. The iron plating on the gate door provided additional means of defense. (Photo William E. Deal)

10.8 Warriors firing from castle weapon portals (Himeji Castle exhibit; Photo William E. Deal)

the *chigaidana* were sometimes used for keeping personal items. In the dwelling of a wealthier person, the staggered shelves might also have a decorative purpose.

BUILT-IN DESK (*TSUKESHOIN*)

The Shoin style derives its name from the built-in desk (*tsukeshoin*) that was situated next to the *tokonoma*. The built-in desk faced toward the outside of the building and used four small sliding paper screens (*shoji*; see below) for the window between interior and exterior.

DECORATIVE DOOR (*CHODAIGAMAE*)

The decorative door of a Shoin-style room, located to the viewer's right of the *tokonoma*, originally led to a bedroom or other space. As this style developed, however, it sometimes became a purely ornamental design feature. The door consisted of four painted sliding panels.

TATAMI MAT

Tatami mats are a floor covering made of a straw base and a surface of tightly woven grass. Class distinctions were evident from the thickness and pattern of mats. Individual mats were rectangular and of varying sizes depending on region. The number of mats that fit into a room came to be the standard measure of a room's size.

SLIDING DOOR (*FUSUMA*)

Sliding doors known as *fusuma* were used to create partitions between interior spaces. The *fusuma* is made by pasting paper or silk on a thin wood-latticed frame. Sliding doors were often adorned with monochrome ink paintings, decorative compositions, and other designs.

SCREEN PARTITIONS (*SHOJI*)

Similar to *fusuma*, screens (*shoji*) were used to create partitions between inside and outside, or between

10.9 Model of the Edo residence of the domain lord (daimyo) Matsudaira Tadamasa (1597–1645), who headed the Fukui domain (han). This residence, in the Shoin style, burned to the ground in the Meireki Fire (1657). Thereafter, such luxurious compounds were no longer constructed. (Edo-Tokyo Museum exhibit; Photo William E. Deal)

interior spaces. Both fixed and sliding partitions were used as either windows or doors. *Shoji* also used a lattice-work frame, but the paper pasted on to cover the frame was a translucent white. This created a more diffused lighting effect where it was used.

TRANSOM (*RAMMA*)

A *ramma*, or transom, was a fitted into a rectangular space located between a sliding door (*fusuma*) and the ceiling of a room. Made of wood, *ramma* were carved or painted with various designs and themes. Functionally, *ramma* provided a room with light and air circulation.

EXTERIOR SLIDING DOOR (*AMADO*)

Amado are exterior wooden sliding door panels used to separate the interior and exterior spaces of a building. These heavy panels were used at night or as protection during bad weather.

10.10 Example of an Edo-period woodcutter's house (Photo William E. Deal)

10.11 Example of an Edo-period farmhouse (Photo William E. Deal)

COMMONER RESIDENCES

The term *minka*, or "folk dwellings," is a generic term used to describe the residences of commoners that existed prior to the Meiji Restoration in 1868. By the early modern period, there were many different types of housing depending on region, weather, and other factors such as the social class and wealth of the resident. Despite this variety, commoner residences can be divided into two major categories: rural dwellings and urban dwellings. Rural dwellings included farmhouses (*noka*), fishermen's houses (*gyoka*), and mountain houses (*sanka*). Urban dwellings included townhouses (*machiya*).

In the early modern period, blending of residential styles also occurred. For instance, by the middle of the Edo period, Shoin-style architectural details, originally a feature of warrior dwellings, started being utilized in the design and construction of commoner homes. Thus, sitting rooms (*zashiki*), used in warrior residences as a place to receive vassals, became a detail in the homes of wealthy commoners. The Tokugawa shogunate, however, tried to control such architectural style–blending in order to maintain distinct boundaries between social classes.

Rural dwellings used regional design styles and architectural elements, as well as regional building materials. Generally, though, rural dwellings were constructed of wood. A house would have a packed-earth floor (*doma*) space used for cooking and other such tasks, and a raised-timber floor space used as living quarters. Urban dwellings followed a similar design, but tended to be smaller than their rural counterparts as a result of the differences in available space between city and countryside. *Machiya* often consisted of two stories. These dwellings might also

10.12 Model of commoner residences (machiya) *in Edo* (Edo-Tokyo Museum exhibit; Photo William E. Deal)

have an adjoining space used for the family's business, whether a shop or a small factory.

READING

Art

Addiss 1996: introduction to visual aspects of medieval and early modern art; Mason 2005: historical survey including medieval and early modern art; Munsterberg 1974, 344–369: historical survey of medieval and early modern art; Murase 1986: medieval and early modern scrolls and prints; Noma 1966: historical survey including medieval and early modern art; Sadao and Wada 2003: historical survey including medieval and early modern art; Stanley-Baker 1984: historical survey including medieval and early modern art; Wilson 1995: ceramic materials and techniques; Yamasaki (ed.) 1981: chronology of art history; Yoshiaki and Rosenfield 1984: medieval and early modern calligraphy; Lane 1978: ukiyo-e; Guth 1996: Edo-period art; Akiyama 1961: medieval and early modern painting; Shimizu (ed.) 1988: medieval and early modern art; Grilli 1970: screen

paintings; ten Grotenhuis 1998: mandala paintings; Cort 1992: Seto and Mino ceramics; Impey 1996: early modern porcelain

Tea and Related Arts

Pitelka (ed.) 2003: tea art, culture, and practice; Anderson 1991: tea ritual; Hayashiya 1979: tea ceremony; Tanaka and Tanaka 1998: tea ceremony; Varley and Kumakura 1989: tea history; Fujioka 1973: tea ceremony utensils; Hayashiya, Nakamura, and Hayashiya 1974: tea ceremony and the arts

Architecture

Coaldrake 1996: selected religious and secular architecture with emphasis on the early modern period; Kuitert 2002: history of medieval and early modern gardens; Nishi and Hozumi 1985: medieval and early modern religious and secular architecture; Inaba and Nakayama 2000: medieval and early modern domestic architecture; Hashimoto 1981: Shoin-style architecture; Hinago 1986: castles; Hirai 1973: medieval architecture.

11

TRAVEL AND
COMMUNICATION

INTRODUCTION

Unlike the contemporary world in which one can communicate with others by telephone, the internet, e-mail, and other means requiring no physical movement from one place to another, in medieval and early modern Japan, communication across distances required travel. The topography of the land had a significant impact on the difficulty of long-distance travel and communication. Oceans separated Japan from other countries, and mountains and plains separated different regions within the Japanese islands. Thus, travel and communication were closely connected matters in Japan during this time period. Further, the development of commercial markets required dependable transportation networks so that travel and communication always had economic implications. Specific economic issues are discussed in chapter 4: Society and Economy.

There were a number of different social, economic, religious, and political developments that strongly influenced the development of possibilities for travel and communication in the medieval and early modern periods. Not surprisingly, shogunal officials were concerned with controlling and regulating travel. The government sought control over the distribution of commercial products, the movement of people, and the spread of ideas that might challenge government authority.

Another aspect of travel in the medieval and early modern periods was related to religious pilgrimage. Particularly popular was travel to Japanese sacred sites, such as the Ise and Izumo Shrines, the Shikoku 88-temple pilgrimage connected to the Shingon Buddhist school founder, Kukai, and the 33 pilgrimage temples dedicated to the worship of the bodhisattva Kannon. While pilgrimage was a feature of medieval Japanese religious life, it was not until the relative stability of the Edo period that religious travel became widespread among all social and economic classes. Besides a system of roads to carry pilgrims on their journeys, other infrastructure developed to service the needs of pilgrims, including inns for food and lodging, and shops where both religious and other goods could be purchased. The lines between pilgrimage and tourism began to blur in the Edo period. Religious aspects of pilgrimage are treated in chapter 6: Religion, but pilgrimage is discussed in this chapter because of its impact on travel and communication, especially in the early modern period.

Significant to the development of transportation and communication systems in the Edo period was the practice of alternate-year attendance (*sankin kotai*) established in the 1630s. This system required daimyo to set up residences at Edo and to appear before the shogun every other year. Though this served ostensibly ceremonial purposes, there was also a strategic feature: daimyo families, that is daimyo wives and children, were forced to live permanently in Edo as—effectively—hostages. The daimyo traveled to Edo every other year but their families were made to remain in Edo. This was one way for the shogunate to induce obeisance from the daimyo, especially those that might have ideas of asserting their power and influence against shogunal

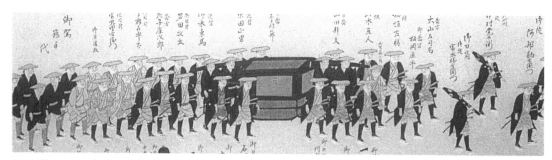

11.1 Procession of a domain lord (Edo-Tokyo Museum exhibit; Photo William E. Deal)

interests. This system held rival daimyo in check because of the great expense of maintaining two separate administrative locations (both in their own domain and a residence at the capital) and because of the great expense required to travel to Edo every other year.

It is estimated that a daimyo spent as much as 80 percent of his income traveling to Edo and maintaining two residences. Part of the traveling expense was the result of the large retinue of vassals, servants, and others who traveled with the daimyo back and forth from Edo. Daimyo and their supporting legions were required to use the main roads because these roads were under direct control of the shogunate. Daimyo processions to and from the capital could sometimes exceed 300 persons, though the size was a reflection of daimyo wealth and power.

The *sankin kotai* system produced a number of direct effects on modes of early modern travel and communication. It resulted in the systematization of highways needed to convey people to and from the capital. In turn, this improved communication between different regions of Japan. It also helped to establish an infrastructure needed to ease the movement of people across the road network. Thus, facilities for travelers were established, including inns, shops, and other services supplying the needs of travelers.

Commercial traffic was always a catalyst for the development of roads throughout Japan's medieval and early modern periods. As early as the late seventh century, roads were constructed so that rice could be delivered to the capital. It was not until the Edo period that the movement of large amounts of commercial goods became commonplace in Japan. Thus, the increased commerce of this time required more and better roads, and, at the same time, the improved road system helped the economy to grow. The road system aided in the growth of Edo and Osaka as urban centers because markets and commerce became much more widespread with improved travel and communication. Of further importance for the increase of trade was the use of coastal water routes to ship goods around Japan. Although international trade was severely limited in the Edo period by the Tokugawa shogunate's national seclusion policy, some trade was carried on with the Chinese and the Dutch.

LAND TRAVEL AND COMMUNICATION

Modes of Land Travel and Communication

Travel throughout the medieval and early modern periods was conducted almost entirely on foot. The wealthy might be carried in palanquins, and goods and communications were sometimes conveyed by horse, but the chief mode of transport—and hence communication—was on foot.

PALANQUIN

For those who were wealthy—such as aristocrats, lords, and important clergy—the palanquin (*kago*) was the preferred mode of travel. The palanquin is an enclosed portable seat, constructed of wood or bamboo, mounted on two long poles that extend beyond the front and back of the seat. The wood of fancy palanquins might be lacquered. It was carried on the shoulders of two men. Generally, a palanquin was used to convey one person. First used in the medieval period, the use of palanquins became widespread in the early modern period with the increased road traffic. As it did with so many symbols of power, the Tokugawa shogunate strictly controlled the use of palanquins based on social class.

PACKHORSEMEN

As commerce increased in the early modern period, the need for more efficient ways to transport people and goods along the roads became more important. The occupation known as packhorseman (*bashaku*) developed. Packhorsemen used packhorses to transport people and commodities along the road system. In the Kamakura period, packhorsemen were used by village communities to transport their goods to town markets. In the latter part of the medieval period, packhorsemen held a great deal of control over land transportation, and they sometimes protested over conditions they viewed as unfavor-

11.2 Palanquin (Photo William E. Deal)

able for their business, such as toll barriers established by the government to regulate the movement of people and goods. By the early modern period, their services were in great demand. Like other tradespeople, they organized themselves into guilds. Some packhorsemen became wholesale merchants, obtaining significant wealth in the process.

COURIERS

One way in which communications were expedited in the medieval and early modern periods was by the use of running couriers known as *hikyaku* ("flying feet"). Although the use of couriers dates back to the early medieval period, their utilization did not

11.3 Travel by oxcart (Illustration Grace Vibbert)

become prevalent until the early modern period. In the Edo period, couriers were used in a number of ways by different social classes. They were utilized by the shogunate in the conduct of government business. Domain lords used couriers to maintain communications between their domain and Edo residences. Merchants—especially those in Edo, Osaka, and Kyoto—relied on couriers for the conduct of business between cities. A postal system developed using couriers to deliver correspondence between cities. It took six days for a courier to deliver a letter from Edo to Osaka.

Early Modern Road System

Road systems date back to the Nara period when the government established a road network connecting the capital at Nara—and later Kyoto—to the provinces. During the Warring States period, the road network fell into disrepair and became very fragmented. In some areas, travel was treacherous, if not impossible, due to both the bandits who often found easy prey along the roads, and the barrier stations meant to restrict access and communication into and out of domains. It was only in the late 16th century that military leaders such as Oda Nobunaga and Toyotomi Hideyoshi recognized the importance of a functioning road system to their quest for the unification of Japan. To this end, they inaugurated efforts to improve the roads and make them safe for travel, and to abolish the barrier system, which hindered both mobility and trade.

The subsequent Tokugawa shogunate carried forward this agenda by establishing a five-road system (*gokaido*) directly maintained by the government. These roads were intended to serve the bureaucratic and military interests of the shogunate by linking the government's base at Edo with the provinces. The Edo-period road system included not only the five main roads, but many secondary roads that lead into the five main roads at various locations. Thus, the Edo period witnessed a dramatic increase in travel along roads developed to handle the traffic created by commerce, pilgrimage, mandatory domain lord attendance at Edo, and other travel needs.

FIVE MAIN ROADS

The five main roads developed, controlled, and maintained by the government were the Tokaido, Nakasendo, Koshu Kaido, Nikko Kaido, and the Oshu Kaido (*do* and *kaido* mean "road"). The government regulated travel along this road system by checking the identification of travelers at various points along the roads. This gave the government a mechanism for monitoring both travel and communications between regions. The shogunate required domain lords to use the five roads in their travels back and forth from the capital under the alternate-year attendance edict. All five roads led to and from a terminal point in Edo, at a bridge known as the Nihombashi. The Nihombashi area was a center of commerce during the Edo period.

Tokaido The Tokaido ("Eastern Sea Road"), the 303-mile main road that ran mostly along the coastline between Edo and Kyoto, was the most important and most traveled of the five roads in the system. According to period records, the roadbed consisted of either gravel or stone depending on the terrain over which the road passed. The average width of the road was about 18 feet. Travelers mostly went on foot, though palanquins were used by the upper classes. Horses were used to carry light goods and sometimes passengers.

The Tokaido route was serviced by 53 post stations that attended to the needs of travelers. These post stations were important because they were busy with the traffic that moved along this road, and they later became famous as the subject of a series of woodblock prints by the noted artist Hiroshige, called the *Fifty-three Stations of the Tokaido Road* (*Tokaido gojusantsugi*). The post stations from Edo to Kyoto were:

Start	Nihonbashi (Edo)
1	Shinagawa
2	Kawasaki
3	Kanagawa
4	Hodogaya
5	Totsuka
6	Fujisawa
7	Hiratsuka
8	Oiso
9	Odawara
10	Hakone
11	Mishima
12	Numazu
13	Hara
14	Yoshiwara
15	Kanbara
16	Yui
17	Okitsu
18	Ejiri
19	Fuchu
20	Mariko
21	Okabe
22	Fujieda
23	Shimada
24	Kanaya
25	Nissaka
26	Kakegawa
27	Fukuroi
28	Mitsuke
29	Hamamatsu
30	Maisaka
31	Arai
32	Shirasuka
33	Futagawa
34	Yoshida
35	Goyu
36	Akasaka
37	Fujikawa
38	Okazaki
39	Chiryu

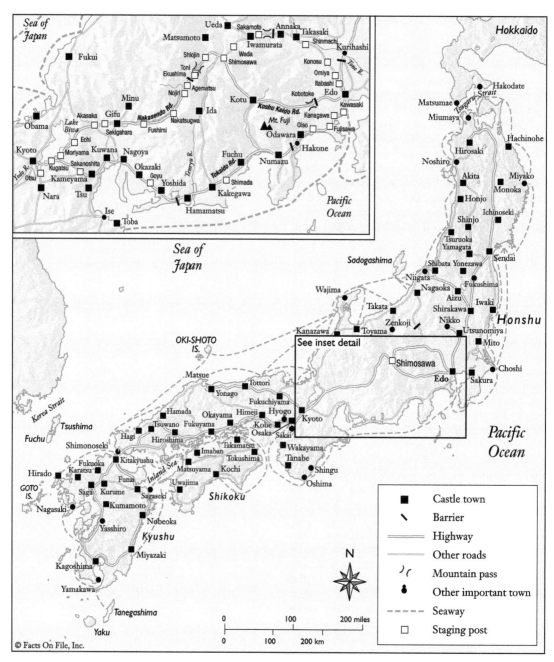

Map 5. *Major Roads in the Early Modern Period*

40	Narumi
41	Atsuta (Miya)
42	Kuwana
43	Yokkaichi
44	Ishiyakushi
45	Shono
46	Kameyama
47	Seki
48	Sakanoshita
49	Tsuchiyama
50	Minakuchi
51	Ishibe
52	Kusatsu
53	Otsu
End	Kyo (Kyoto)

Nakasendo The Nakasendo, also referred to as the Kiso Kaido or Kisoji, ran some 310 miles between Edo and Kyoto. Unlike the Tokaido, however, the Nakasendo traversed an inland course through the mountains. It was a much more arduous journey, taking a longer time to complete, and was, as a result, much less traveled than the Tokaido. The Nakasendo road went through 67 post stations.

Koshu Kaido The Koshu Kaido, also referred to as Koshu Dochu, ran for 86 miles from Edo to Shimosuwa in Shinano province (present-day Nagano Prefecture) by way of Kofu, with a view of Mt. Fuji. The road intersected the Tokaido and Nakasendo, linking with the Nakasendo at Shimosuwa. This road was reportedly the one that Tokugawa Ieyasu conceived of as the shogun's escape route in the event that Edo Castle was besieged.

Nikko Kaido The Nikko Kaido, also referred to as Nikko Dochu, ran 91 miles from Edo north to Nikko, the site of Tokugawa Ieyasu's mausoleum, the Toshogu. The road passed through 21 post stations.

Oshu Kaido The Oshu Kaido, also referred to as Oshu Dochu, ran 488 miles from Edo north to the Mutsu and Dewa provinces, terminating at Minmaya (present-day Aomori Prefecture). The road started at Edo going north along the same route as the Nikko Kaido. At the Utsunomiya post station, the Oshu Kaido branched off, heading farther

north. Past the Shirakawa post station, the shogunate gave control of this road to the various domains through which it passed, indicating the extent to which northern Japan was still relatively underdeveloped and only lightly populated in the early modern period compared with areas south and west of Edo.

SECONDARY ROADS

In addition to the five main roads, a system of secondary roads connected the provinces to the five main roads. Among the most important of these secondary roads were the following:

Chugoku Kaido (also referred to by other names, such as Chugokuji, San'yodo, and Saigoku Kaido): ran along the Seto Inland Sea from Osaka to Kokura in Kyushu.

Mito Kaido (also referred to as Mitoji): ran from Edo northeast to Mito in Hitachi province (present-day Ibaraki Prefecture).

Sayaji (also referred to as Saya Kaido): ran from Atsuta (or Miya) in Owari province (present-day Aichi Prefecture) through the Saya post station and on to Kuwana in Ise province (present-day Mie Prefecture).

Minoji (also referred to as Mino Kaido): ran from Nagoya to Ogaki in Mino province (present-day Gifu Prefecture), connecting the Tokaido at Atsuta (Miya) to the Nakasendo at Tarui.

Nikko Onari Kaido (or Nikko Onarido) and the **Reiheishi Kaido** (or Reiheishido): these two roads both traversed the space between Edo and Nikko. Unlike the Nikko Kaido, however, these roads were only used by government officials in their pilgrimages to Nikko for ritual services for Tokugawa Ieyasu at the Toshogu shrine and mausoleum.

Iseji (also referred to as Ise Kaido and Sangu Kaido): ran along the east coast of the Kii peninsula from Yokkaichi in Ise province (present-day Mie Prefecture), passing through seven post stations before arriving at the Ise Shrine.

ROAD BUILDING AND MAINTENANCE

The five main roads were maintained by the Tokugawa shogunate. The government issued strict regulations concerning the upkeep of road conditions. Generally, the shogunate required post stations and local villages to maintain the roads in their vicinity. This maintenance included keeping the roads in good travel condition by removing any debris that littered the roadbed, patching any potholes, planting trees along the route, and building and repairing necessary bridges across rivers. The government dispatched inspectors along the five main roads to ensure that maintenance work was properly performed in a timely fashion.

One other important responsibility given to post stations and local villages was the maintenance of the milestone marker (*ichirizuka*; literally, "milestone mounds") system that provided travelers with information about their location along the road. Milestone markers, 10-foot-high square earthen mounds, measured the distance from Edo in *ri*, equivalent to 2.4 miles.

BARRIERS

Although Tokugawa Ieyasu's predecessors, Oda Nobunaga and Toyotomi Hideyoshi, had abolished the kind of road barriers controlled by local lords that hindered travel and trade prior to the Edo period, the Tokugawa shogunate nevertheless instituted its own system of national barrier stations (*sekisho*)—more than 50 on the five main roads—in order to ascertain the identity of travelers and ensure they had the proper travel permits. The government was especially concerned with the illegal movement of warriors and weaponry that might be used against it. It also sought to maintain the requirement that the wives and children of domain lords remain in Edo, and hence was especially suspicious of women and children traveling away from Edo. The Hakone Barrier, located at the Hakone Pass south of Edo on the Tokaido, was strictly controlled because the shogunate viewed this particular area as the most significant point of entry into the Edo region, and thus in need of special protection and control.

POST STATIONS

Government-controlled post stations (*shukueki*) were situated along roads and offered travelers food, shelter, and other services. Post stations that were not directly controlled by the Tokugawa shogunate were usually run by regional domain lords. The number of post stations grew over time, and by the latter part of the Edo period, there were an estimated 250 post stations along the different road systems. Post stations were spaced at different intervals depending on the road and terrain. Along the Tokaido and the Nakasendo, for instance, post stations were generally located every three to 10 miles.

The size of post stations varied greatly. Some were very small stations situated in remote mountain areas that provided only food and lodging. Others were agricultural villages or market towns. The largest post stations were located in castle towns. Even the smaller post stations in rural areas possessed a more urban feel because of the service-centered nature of their economies that belied their location in otherwise agricultural areas.

Services varied at post stations depending on size and location. In general, post stations included inns for overnight lodging, restaurants, public baths, pubs, and shops selling a variety of goods including medicine, clothing, and footwear. Post stations were also required by government regulation to provide both packhorses and porters for hire, to facilitate the movement of people and commodities. The movement of people and goods along roads and through the post stations was overseen locally by a post station manager known as a *ton'ya*. This manager supervised the overall functioning and efficiency of the post station.

In keeping with social class distinctions that marked Edo-period society, post stations also institutionalized class hierarchy through the kinds of inns available to travelers. Inns called *honjin* ("principal headquarters") were available to such elites as domain lords and their retainers traveling to and from Edo under the required attendance regulation, as well as government officials and aristocrats. These upper-class inns included especially well-appointed rooms and gardens for the enjoyment of their privileged guests. Other inns serviced other social classes. There were inns for lesser government officials and middle-ranking warriors, as well as inns for commoners.

MARITIME TRAVEL AND COMMUNICATION

Domestic waterways, both the seas surrounding the Japanese islands and the inland freshwater rivers and lakes, were utilized for warfare, trade, fishing, passenger transport, and leisure activities. Similarly, the seas beyond Japan's immediate shores were used for trade, transporting government officials on missions, and warfare. The seas were also a source of anxiety because they brought potential enemies—as they did with the late 13th-century Mongol invasions—and if not enemies, then contacts with societies that presented challenges to Japan's status quo—as occurred when the Jesuits appeared in the mid 16th century and when Admiral Perry arrived in 1853.

Maritime travel was also intimately linked to issues of communication. Trends and fashions in one Japanese city were communicated to another by virtue of the maritime trade that moved both material goods and various aspects of culture, including music, theater, and literature. Similarly, in addition to commodities, Chinese cultural values were communicated to Japan as a result of trade and diplomatic relations conveyed by ship. These cultural commodities included ideas about government, religion, morality, and the arts. Finally, it was the image of the "black ships" of Admiral Perry that signaled the final years of the Tokugawa shogunate and the end of the early modern period. These ships, and those that followed from other Western countries, communicated the foreign interest in—and insistence on—having Japan as a trading partner.

This section examines the historical importance of domestic and international maritime travel and the ships that undertook these voyages. Specific waterways are covered in chapter 2: Land, Environment, and Population, and specific economic developments that spurred the use of waterways to conduct trade are treated in chapter 4: Society and Economy.

Medieval Maritime Travel and Communication

In medieval Japan, ships plied both local and international waters to conduct trade. In many ways, the more remarkable achievement was in international

11.4 Model of an Edo-period riverboat (Edo-Tokyo Museum exhibit; Photo William E. Deal)

maritime activity. Japanese ships sailed to Korea, China, and as far away as Southeast Asia for trade and also to transport embassies on their foreign missions. In the Kamakura period, for instance, ships traded with Southern Song–dynasty (1185–1333) China, although this was not an extensive trade arrangement. Both trade and the exchange of envoys expanded in the Muromachi period. Ashikaga shoguns promoted the so-called tally trade (see chapter 4 for details) with Ming-dynasty (1368–1644) China. These activities required the ability to build boats both large and strong enough to make the hazardous ocean crossing. In the medieval period, sailing ships were constructed expressly for trade and for dispatching envoys to China and Korea.

Ocean travel was possible, in part, because of advances in technology. Among significant advancements in the medieval period was the use of navigational charts that included latitude and longitude markings. Charts became available for areas including China, Korea, and Southeast Asia. By the end of the medieval period, the magnetic compass and such astronomical instruments as the quadrant and the astrolabe were being utilized for more accurate navigation, especially on long voyages.

Another aspect of medieval maritime travel and communication that impacted both the movement of ships generally and trading vessels in particular was the activity of Japanese pirates (*wako*). Although *wako* were referred to as Japanese pirates, in fact, Koreans, Chinese, and others sometimes participated in these illegal bands. Active mostly in the medieval period, pirates attacked and pillaged the coasts of both Korea and China. In the 13th century, pirates raided the coast of Korea, and such attacks continued intermittently for two centuries. Although the Korean government appealed to the shogunate to control the pirates, they were mostly ineffective in dealing with the problem. In the late 14th century, Korea successfully fought back against the pirates, though pirate activities continued in diminished form through the 16th century.

By the middle of the 14th century, Japanese pirates were venturing further from Japan. They attacked the Chinese coast in 1358, and for the next 200 years they continued to harass Chinese communities up and down the mainland coast. In an effort to combat these raids, the Chinese set up coastal defenses and limited coastal trade. One result of the Japanese pirate activity was that the Chinese government placed increasing pressure on Japan to control or destroy the pirates. Trade agreements between China and Japan began to hinge on the ability of the shogunate to suppress pirate activity. The medieval tally trade, for instance, was predicated on Japanese control of pirate bands. During the Warring States period, pirate activity increased because there was no central power available to keep them in check. It was only after Toyotomi Hideyoshi took control of Kyushu—one of the staging grounds for pirates—in his late 16th-century quest to unify Japan that pirate activity diminished.

Early Modern Maritime Travel and Communication

Medieval period accomplishments in foreign trade and travel were abandoned in the early modern period. International trade and long-distance travel were forbidden by the Tokugawa shogunate once the national seclusion policy was decreed in the first half of the 17th century. In order to assure adherence to this ban on international travel, the shogunate further restricted the size of ships that could legally be constructed. Thus, the order was issued forbidding the building of ships with capacities of more than 500 *koku* (49 gross tons).

In the Edo period, the development of a regulated road system was vital to the expansion of travel and communication, which were closely connected to the development of the early modern economy. Also vital to this process was the development and improvement in maritime travel and transport capabilities. To this end, maritime infrastructure—including docks, warehouses, and canals—was built or improved, and new coastal shipping routes were established to better link the provinces with major cities like Osaka and Edo.

Because of the ban on the construction of large ships, domestic maritime travel was mostly restricted to the use of small wooden sailing ships appropriate for use on Japan's coastal and inland waterways. During this time, such ships played a vital role in the expansion of the economy and the growth of urban centers, such as Edo. Over time, the shogunate continued to forbid foreign trade and travel, but it did relent on the maximum size of trading ships because of their importance to the burgeoning domestic economy that relied on coastal shipping to transport rice and other staple goods from area to area. The route between Osaka and Edo was particularly important, as were routes from other areas of Japan into these two large urban areas.

As the populations of urban centers grew over the course of the early modern period, and consequently the demand for essential commodities, the need for more efficient transportation and distribution networks to deliver these goods to market also increased. Osaka developed as a central collection and distribution center for goods produced in various parts of Japan. It was necessary to create an efficient method to transfer goods to Osaka, and then from there to Edo. The transportation routes then in use combined sea transport to a particular collection point where goods were offloaded from ships and taken by land to Edo, Osaka, or some other destination. The solution was to use ocean routes that linked provincial ports directly with Osaka, and Osaka with Edo.

The Tokugawa shogunate embarked on such a project in the latter half of the 17th century when it engaged the wealthy merchant Kawamura Zuiken (1617–99) to establish new coastal shipping routes. Kawamura set up a complete circuit around Japan using two primary routes, the eastern sea circuit (*higashi mawari*) and the western sea circuit (*nishi mawari*). Prior to Kawamura's endeavor, ships had avoided certain ocean areas because of the fear of shipwrecks in particularly treacherous waters. Kawamura charted the coastal waters and established lighthouses to guide ships through dangerous stretches of ocean. The eastern sea circuit ran from the Sea of Japan to western Honshu and then through the Inland Sea (Seto-naikai) to Osaka and Edo. The western sea circuit took ships from the Sea of Japan north through the Tsugaru Strait and then down the Pacific Ocean border of Japan into Edo Bay.

Japan's isolation from most of the rest of the world lasted more than 200 years, until it was interrupted when Admiral Perry arrived in 1853 and demanded that Japan open its ports to foreign trade. Aside from the political fallout from this event, it became evident to Japanese shipbuilders that Japan had fallen behind technologically in its ship designs. The subsequent Meiji period witnessed not only the revival of foreign trade, but the design and construction of new ships using Western technologies. Alternate modes of propulsion, such as steam engines, were introduced at this time.

Examples of Boat and Ship Types

Boats and ships were an important mode of domestic and international travel in the medieval and early modern periods. Because of their diverse uses, ships came in many different sizes and shapes but were always made of wood or other natural materials, until the end of the early modern period when Western shipbuilding techniques were formally introduced to Japan. Ships used for trade were built in ways different from ships used in warfare. A fishing boat was appointed differently than a boat used to take leisurely cruises down a river. The boats that carried lords to their duties in Edo were different from the boats that carried sake to market. The following list details some of the different kinds of ships and boats in use during the medieval and early modern periods.

ATAKE-BUNE

The *atake-bune* was a type of naval warship that was used in battles during the Warring States period and into the early Edo period. These vessels were anywhere from about 20 to 65 feet in length. *Atake-bune* included a wooden tower from which arrows or matchlock guns could be fired at the enemy. Twenty to 25 oarsmen were needed to propel these large ships.

BEZAISEN

Bezaisen, also known as *sengoku-bune* (1,000-*koku* ships), were large ships widely used from the end of the medieval period to transport goods to market. These ships had a flat keel and were propelled by a single square sail on one mast. The earliest *bezaisen* had a relatively small capacity, but as the need to carry more commodities per voyage increased, so did the capacity of the newer versions of this ship design. By the beginning of the 18th century, the usual capacity of a *bezaisen* was 1,000 *koku* (98 gross tons), thus earning the vessel the name *sengoku-bune*. These larger *bezaisen* carried a crew of 15 or so.

They operated originally in the Inland Sea, but later traveled a much longer distance, including voyages in the southern part of the Sea of Japan and up to Edo. These ships also sometimes took another route to Edo, sailing through the strait between Honshu and Hokkaido, and then traveling south to Edo. From the beginning of the early modern period, *bezaisen* played an active role in the growth of domestic maritime trade. *Bezaisen* were related to such other transport ships as *higaki kaisen* and *taru kaisen* (see below under *kaisen*) as well as *kitamae-bune* (see below).

CHOKI-BUNE

The *choki-bune* was a riverboat used especially in cities as a water taxi to ferry passengers from shore to shore.

GOZA-BUNE

Generally, *goza-bune* were large boats used by aristocrats or high-ranking warriors. They were also brightly decorated for use in a festival and on other occasions. *Goza-bune* were built both for use in the ocean and on rivers. Oceangoing *goza-bune* (*umi-goza-bune*) were essentially warships used to demonstrate a warrior's power during peaceful times of the Edo period. One famous example of an oceangoing *goza-bune* was the ship known as Tenchi Maru, a vermilion-lacquered vessel built by the third Tokugawa shogun, Iemitsu, in the 1630s.

In contrast, rivergoing *goza-bune* (*kawa-goza-bune*) were elegant vessels designed for use by high-ranking warriors for travel by river. Rivergoing *goza-bune* used oars and poles instead of sails.

HIGAKI KAISEN

Higaki kaisen were cargo ships that transported essential commodities—such as oil, vinegar, soy sauce, wood, and cotton—from Osaka to Edo. A kind of circuit ship (see *kaisen*), *higaki kaisen* were related to the cargo ship known as a *bezaisen* (see above). *Higaki kaisen* were used especially by the Sakai merchants.

HIRATA-BUNE

The *hirata-bune* was a large riverboat from 50 to 80 feet long, similar to a *takase-bune* (see below). This long and narrow boat with a flat bottom was used to transport freight. The largest of the *hirata-bune* had a capacity of 300 *koku* (53 gross tons).

KAISEN

The term *kaisen*, or "circuit ship," is a generic term for cargo ships used to ship goods on consignment or to deliver goods to market. Such boats were first used with some regularity in the middle of the 13th century in the Inland Sea. By the late Kamakura period, however, circuit ships were transporting goods back and forth from distant ports both north and south. The government issued maritime rules known as *kaisen shikimoku* (literally, "circuit ship regulations") to regulate the use of circuit ships in trade.

From contemporary records, it is apparent that circuit ships were important to economic growth in the medieval period. Various kinds of circuit ships were also central to the development of trade in the early modern period, and are notably associated with the transport of goods between Osaka and Edo. Circuit ships made good use of the new sea-circuit trade routes established in the last half of the 17th century. It was not until the late 19th-century importation of Western technology, such as the steamship, that the use of circuit ships diminished. See also *higaki kaisen* and *taru kaisen*.

KEMMINSEN

In the last half of the 14th century, Ashikaga shoguns inaugurated the so-called tally trade with Ming-dynasty China (1368–1644). From 1404 to 1547, 17 missions involving 84 ships made the journey to China. The ships that made this crossing were known as *kemminsen* (ships dispatched to the Ming dynasty). They combined two purposes: foreign trade and foreign relations. Thus, these ships carried both goods to trade and official envoys, known as *kemminshi* (envoys to the Ming dynasty). Merchants also accompanied these voyages. In total, a single ship might carry as many as 200 people, including the crew.

Kemminsen were newly built to meet the needs of these voyages. They were large: records report that they had a capacity between 1,000 and 2,500 *koku* (between 98 and 245 gross tons). These ships sailed using two masts with matted square sails. There was a cabin on deck that was specially appointed to accommodate the needs and tastes of the envoys on board.

KITAMAE-BUNE

Kitamae-bune, also known as *hokkoku-bune*, were a regional variation of a *bezaisen* (see above). These were very large ships—some with a capacity as great as 1,000 *koku* (98 gross tons)—used to transport cargo during the Edo period. The term *kitamae* means "northern area," and *kitamae-bune* operated from northern areas of the Sea of Japan transporting commodities to markets in central Japan. *Kitamae-bune* were designed so they could carry the greatest capacity for their size. Although a square sail was the primary means of propulsion, these ships could also be rowed. Northern Japan was only sparsely populated, and few of its customs were known in the central parts of Japan. One of the consequences of the *kitamae-bune* trade was that northern styles of clothing, song traditions, and differences in dialect became known to a wider Japanese audience.

SEKI-BUNE

Seki-bune was a type of Japanese warship used in the Warring States period and at the beginning of the early modern period. Unlike its contemporary, the *atake-bune*, the *seki-bune* was much smaller and faster.

SHUINSEN

At the end of the Azuchi-Momoyama period and the beginning of the early modern period, the government tried to control overseas commerce and travel by issuing trading permits known as "vermilion seal licenses" (*shuinjo*) to those who desired to engage in foreign trade. Merchants from Kyoto, Sakai, and Nagasaki were particularly involved in international trade under this arrangement.

The ships used by merchants with permits were known as "vermilion seal ships" (*shuinsen*). Vermilion seal ships were oceangoing sailing ships that were built within Japan and also imported from China and Siam (Thailand). These were large ships that could be as much as 130 feet in length with a capacity of up to 4,225 *koku* (750 gross tons). Their design features were a hybrid of Chinese, Portuguese, and Spanish ships. *Shuinsen* had three masts and double keels. They reportedly used a crew of 80 and could accommodate as many as 320 passengers. Before foreign trade was forbidden by the shogunate in the 1630s, some 350 *shuinsen* voyages were made to locations as far away as Southeast Asia.

TAKASE-BUNE

Like the *hirata-bune*, the *takase-bune* was a type of long and narrow riverboat with a flat bottom. It was used to transport freight (typically on the Takase River) and also for work in rice paddies.

TARU KAISEN

Taru kaisen were cargo ships that were used specifically to transport sake in barrels (*taru*), though these boats sometimes carried other products, from Osaka to Edo. A kind of circuit ship (see *kaisen*), *taru kaisen*, like the *higaki kaisen*, were related to the cargo ship known as a *bezaisen* (see above). *Taru kaisen* were propelled by a single sail and had reinforced hulls in order to hold the heavy barrels they transported.

11.5 Model of a takase-*style boat used during the Edo period* (Edo-Tokyo Museum exhibit; Photo William E. Deal)

YAKATA-BUNE

Yakata-bune was a type of luxury riverboat used for leisure activities by the wealthy.

YU-BUNE

An unusual boat, a *yu-bune* was a floating public bath. At the center of the boat was an enclosed central space for the bathtub. Water for the bath was heated using firewood. Customers, who were typically crews from cargo ships and dock workers, paid a fee to use the bathing facilities on board the *yu-bune*.

EUROPEAN SHIPS IN JAPAN

Japanese exposure to the West in the transition period from the medieval to the early modern period, and again in the middle of the 19th century, introduced the Japanese to new shipbuilding styles and methods. In the early 17th century, for instance, the Japanese built two English-style ships with the guidance of Will Adams, an English sailor living in Japan. With the help of the Spanish, a larger Western-style ship was built a decade or so later. This particular engagement with Western shipbuilding was cut short, however, by the national seclusion policy enacted by the Tokugawa government in the 1630s.

Interest in Western ships and shipbuilding was revived when, in 1853, Admiral Perry sailed into Uraga Bay in his "black ships" (*kurofune*), named for their color. Of the four ships that Perry commanded, two used sails and two were steamships. The Japanese were at once intrigued by the possibilities of a steam-powered ship, but they were also aware of the necessity of updating their own warships to match the power of their Western rivals. The government received a steam warship from Holland and purchased another one. It was not until the Meiji period, however, that Japan developed the technology to build its own modern warships.

READING

Travel and Communication

Frédéric 1972, 88–89: travel in the medieval period; Nishiyama 1997, 104–109: transportation and travel in the early modern period, 132–135: Ise pilgrimage, 135–137: Kompira pilgrimage, 131–132: Kumano pilgrimage, 139: Shikoku pilgrimage, 139–140: Shinran pilgrimage, 137–139: 33 sites pilgrimage; Dunn 1972, 23–28: samurai travel and roads in the early modern period; Cullen 2003, 53: roads, 82–83: commercial transportation, 89: Nakasendo, 88–90: road traffic, 70, 89: Tokaido; Totman 1993, 153–157: roads, travel, maritime transportation, and communication in the early modern period, 443–445: early modern pilgrimage, 325–327: road construction and maintenance in the early modern period, 71–72: promotion of commercial travel in the early modern period; Cortazzi 1990, 145–146: road and maritime transportation in the early modern period; Totman 2000, 233–235: early modern roads and transportation; Totman 1974, 101–102, 116: early modern communications; Jansen 2000, 134–141: early modern communication and travel; Yamamura (ed.) 1990, 364–366, 381–383: transportation in the medieval period; Hall (ed.) 1991, 114–115, 117, 530–531, 551–553, 567–568: early modern transportation; Jansen (ed.) 1989, 64–65: travel in the 19th century; Traganou 2004: travel and communication along the Tokaido in the Edo period

12

EVERYDAY LIFE

THE FAMILY

Family Structure

Medieval and early modern Japanese society was hierarchical. By the end of the 17th century, this hierarchy was divided, at least in the ideal, into four distinct classes: samurai, peasant, artisan, and merchant. In turn, this overarching hierarchical framework shaped the composition of the family unit. Interclass marriage was not legally permitted, thus forcing individuals to marry along socioeconomic lines. This structure perpetuated the dominant hierarchical paradigm, preventing individuals from attempting to change their social and occupational status.

In both medieval and early modern Japan, the basic family unit was the *ie* (house). While the *ie* traditionally consisted of a nuclear family, it typically expanded to incorporate an assortment of other members, including blood relatives, such as grandparents, and nonrelatives, such as servants and their kin. In addition to being the foundational component of social organization, the term *ie* also referred to notions of family property, reputation, and the principle of continued familial succession. Typically, the eldest son became the inheritor of the family. However, when there were no legitimate blood kin to assume control, external heirs unrelated to the family were often adopted into the household as successors to carry on the family lineage. This ethos of generational continuity and heritage reflects the Confucian influence on early modern Japanese culture. Particularly during the Edo period, the upper classes adopted the familial tenets of Confucianism, leading to the priority of filial obligation, obedience, and loyalty. Overall, individuals were expected to sacrifice their own well-being or personal desires for the greater good of the family structure. *Ie* as a unit or principle can be seen throughout Japanese culture well before the medieval era. However, *ie* was particularly prominent during the Edo period when strong economic developments allowed even commoners to establish their own line of succession for the first time.

The traditional size of the *ie* was around five people. If a person within the family was lost, extra responsibility was either assumed by the other family members (within poor classes) or delegated to servant workers (within wealthier families). The head of the household (*koshu*) was traditionally male and held the greatest responsibilities for running the *ie*. However, women could also assume a position at the helm of the household when a suitable male was unavailable. Likewise, the female partner to the *koshu* was usually the most powerful and respected woman in the household; she retained the responsibilities of overseeing the traditional household duties.

As this suggests, men alone were not the only individuals who could wield power in early modern Japanese society. Elaborating on this idea is the fact that the *koshu*'s authority was often tempered and undermined by the traditional moral principles of obedience to all elders. This ethical standard was valued highly, as it granted respect to all individuals of elderly rank, regardless of their sex or position. In this way, women and servants could also attain esteem by exercising their duty to the *ie*.

Housework

During the normal day of a peasant woman, her duties included daily chores, household work, and often physically demanding agricultural labor. Such activity kept lower-class women very busy, often occupying their entire day. In contrast, wealthy upper-class women, such as the spouses of warriors, frequently enlisted the help of maids, servants, and other helpers to assume the majority of daily household responsibilities. Even so, these women still remained occupied in some manner or another—complete idleness, regardless of gender or socioeconomic position, was looked down upon in early modern Japanese society. For instance, wealthier women were still responsible for entertaining guests, waiting on their husbands, and managing the household servants. Younger girls were also obligated to assist in the process of completing household labor as they were typically assigned the more tedious responsibilities and less desired everyday chores.

Despite common assumptions to the contrary, Japanese men also made significant contributions to the work of the home by assisting in the child-rearing process. In particular, lower-class men were important figures in educating their children. Often they were instrumental in teaching their progeny vital vocational skills needed on the farm or in the merchant trades.

Children

Children were often trained to be competent in housework early on in life due to the general demand of many families for household workers. It was not uncommon for children to work collaboratively with older individuals to learn a specific trade or skill. Even though formal schooling became increasingly available during the later stages of the

12.2 Model of a scene of daily life in Edo: hanging laundry (Edo-Tokyo Museum exhibit; Photo William E. Deal)

12.1 Scene of daily life in Edo: women drawing water from a well (Edo-Tokyo Museum exhibit; Photo William E. Deal)

Edo period, children still frequently received education from their own parents within the home.

While some young Japanese received training at home, the Edo period also developed the custom of *satogo* offspring, children who were sent away from the home to be raised by foster parents. Many parents made arrangements to entrust their children to rural peasants for several years. This was done in an effort to give the *satogo* a stronger upbringing. Along with the *satogo* children, the practice of infant abandonment known as *sutego* was also practiced in Japan at this time. Ill or otherwise unwanted infants were left at a predetermined location where a chosen "finder parent" (*hiroioya*) would take in and raise the child. The *hiroioya* were selected based on their character, reputation, and child-rearing ability.

Another common practice involving children was adoption. Differing from the contemporary conception of the process, Japanese adoption was often employed as a means to ensure the legacy and longevity of the family line. This was done particularly when there was no appropriate natural male successor to be the head of the household. Developing in the Kamakura period, adoption was also used to create strategic associations and familial alliances. The process of adoption became more detailed and complex during the Edo period.

Household Property

Because the *ie* was conceived of as an indissoluble entity, its property and assets were never divided among human constituents; instead, they always belonged to the household as a larger collective. This meant that no one individual, not even the head of the household, could freely utilize the material goods solely for personal gain. This stipulation preserved the continuity of the household for future generations. Changes in inheritance law during the Edo period were detrimental to women: property was controlled by the head of the household—typically male—and inheritances descended through the male line of the family. Consequently, women rarely had property in their own name.

The *ie* was usually represented by only one individual, the household head, who was respected for his rank, not individual personal merits. Because of this emphasis on one representative per household, in addition to the traditional customs that discouraged females from registering their names in the administrative records, women were frequently prevented from being recognized or involved in the social sphere. All of these factors regarding the structure and rights of household property systematically subordinated women, making them very dependent upon the men within the family.

THE HOME

(For specific information on the architecture and building materials of the home see chapter 10: Art and Architecture)

Due to the volatile conditions of climate and natural disasters, Japanese houses were often built as temporary, adaptable structures rather than permanent, fixed dwellings. Thus, despite an overall population expansion during the 16th and 17th centuries, there are few houses that have endured from that time to today.

Furnishings

Traditional forms and styles of Japanese furniture have been used consistently throughout the history of the country with the only significant changes being caused by an influx of Western ideas and influences. A variety of furnishings were common to the Japanese home during the early modern period, many of which were primarily constructed with wood in combination with other materials such as ceramics and lacquer.

Japanese houses commonly included relatively few furnishings compared with other cultures whose populations concentrated in urban centers or farming communities. Like other resources, residential possessions differed in number and quality at various levels of Japanese society. Interiors were sparsely furnished, often with rudimentary items, in all but the most prosperous households during the medieval period. From the 16th century through the Edo period, newly prosperous merchants, samurai, and other members of the middle and upper classes

12.3 Model of the exterior of an Edo commoner's house (Edo-Tokyo Museum exhibit; Photo William E. Deal)

were able to outfit their homes with basic items such as furniture and some luxuries. Still Japanese households possessed few furnishings compared with dwellings in Europe or North America during the 16th through 19th centuries. The design of Japanese interiors and the articles used inside were determined largely by the small size of most residences, especially in cities. Some items found in family residences are categorized by type and summarized below. Items such as screens and sliding doors, which functioned both as part of an interior environment and as artistic objects, are considered in chapter 10: Art and Architecture.

Furniture and Other Interior Objects

From medieval times, interiors in Japan consisted of a floor—made of earth in farmhouses and other humble dwellings, and wood planks in upper-class residences or temples—which was covered with tatami mats in structures inhabited by the middle classes and above. From the late medieval period, such floors were raised above the foundation level of the structure. Room appointments included floor cushions known as *zabuton* as well as tables and desks (*chabudai* and *tsukue*) for serving or writing. These were lower and often smaller in scale than similar items used in the West. Medium-size storage cabinets (*kodansu*, *kodana*, or *todana*, for shelves with doors, or *chigaidana*, for open staggered shelves) were sometimes made with unusual types of wood appreciated for their decorative effect. Placement of these cabinets was designed to harmonize with the layout of a room, and the storage areas, complete with drawers or open shelves, were sometimes permanent aspects of interior design. Cupboards, called *zushi*, traditionally had the form of tiered shelves (*tanazushi*) and could be disguised behind sliding screen panels (*shoji* or *fusuma*). Usually cabinets and cupboards were found only in upper-class dwellings. Smaller freestanding boxes made from lacquer, or bamboo, or other types of wood, were used for storing writing materials, cosmetics, food, and weapons. Larger items were stored in chests (*tansu*) that

ranged from basic box forms to chests with drawers adorned with precious materials and elaborate designs. Other functional furnishings such as *hibachi* (charcoal braziers), used for warming the interior of a house, and *iko*, clothing stands or towel racks, were found in many residences.

Japanese decor differed widely from Western standards of furnishing. Rather than utilizing numerous pieces of furniture to satisfy domestic needs, the Japanese home often integrated features into the structure of the building itself, making it more streamlined than its Western counterpart. Unlike the larger, unwieldy fixtures common in Western culture, Japan used lighter, less bulky items that were readily portable. For instance, cushions and pillows served as substitutes for traditional chairs and couches with legs; floor mats were used instead of larger mattresses and bed frames; and trays or smaller stands replaced larger tables. These flexible furnishings allowed for efficient and easily adaptable living arrangements that could meet different needs and changing conditions. This flexibility was especially important given the limited natural and spatial resources at the disposal of most Japanese families.

Bedding

FUTON

Typical Japanese bedding ensembles included a futon, which is a mattress padded with cotton, wool, or traditionally, straw. A futon is pliable and compact enough to store out of sight in a cabinet or simply set aside in a corner during the day, and later spread on a floor (usually made of tatami) for sleeping at night. Thus, due to the portable nature of Japanese futon, a room could have many functions. A traditional futon set consists of a *shikibuton* (tufted or padded mattress) and a *kakebuton* (thick quilted bedcover), which is placed on top of the mattress and used as a covering for sleeping. Futon similar to those used in Japan today probably originated in the mid-16th century, replacing rush or straw mats, or in modest settings, loose straw, materials that were commonly used as bedding in the medieval period.

QUILTS AND COVERLETS

Use of cotton or wool quilting for bedding first began around the mid-16th century. Previously, members of the ruling classes and samurai slept on thick woven rush matting similar to tatami, and commoners used mats of straw or loose straw. Coverlets with sleeves and neckbands similar to such daytime garments as kimono provided coverage. By the mid-1500s, quilted covers—in a heavier weight for winter and a lighter weight for summer—were standard in many ruling-class residences.

MOSQUITO NETS

Evidence indicates that mosquito nets (*kaya*) have been used in Japan since ancient times. By the early Edo period, the nets were a standard summer item found in houses at all social levels. Several sleepers could be accommodated by the nets, which were suspended overhead.

Standard Interior Structure and Seating

By the early Edo period, items such as sliding doors, tatami mats for flooring, and cushions for sitting on the floor were standard furnishings in almost all Japanese domestic settings. Such items were considered portable, although architectural in function, and tenants were expected to install such items when outfitting a new home.

Shoji and Other Types of Sliding Doors

Sliding screens were in use in Japan from the Heian period to separate one room from another, or to distinguish a passageway from a room. Sliding screens with decoration on one or both surfaces were known as *fusuma shoji*. These screens incorporated a removable wooden door frame with cloth or paper applied on both sides. Because they allowed diffused light to enter, these sliding screens were also used as windows and for interior ornamentation. Traditionally, Japanese residences had *shoji* for room dividers and terrace doors, as well as *shoji*-style fixed windows, to allow air circulation when desired. Decorated sliding doors (*fusuma*), and folding screens, which are similar in construction to decorated *fusuma*, are examined in chapter 10: Art and Architecture.

Tatami

This natural, woven mat has been used as a flooring material in traditional Japanese-style rooms since at least the Heian period. Tatami is a noun derived from the Japanese verb *tatamu*, meaning "to fold or pile." The etymology of this word may correspond to the original function of the mats, since evidence suggests that thin woven tatami were piled in layers to create a more cushioned surface, and could be folded for storage when not in use. From the Muromachi period, tatami mats have been made with a thick, straw base (*toko*) beneath a softer surface covering (*omote*) woven from rush (*igusa*). A fabric border was usually added to protect the edges from fraying, and tatami were closely fitted, covering the room from wall to wall. In some dwellings, rooms with tatami were reserved for the most formal occasions. Tatami dimensions differed from one geographic region to another.

Zabuton

These small, often slightly rectangular cushions were designed for sitting on tatami mats or wooden floors. Small rectangular portions of tatami fitted with woven fabric borders were used for seating on interior floors during the Heian period, and were replaced by the Edo period with padded or cushioned pillows stuffed with cotton batting. Traditionally visitors were supplied with *zabuton* only during the winter months, although ruling nobles or ranking samurai would be more likely to use them throughout the year.

Heating and Lighting

The Japanese home was typically heated by a centrally located fireplace. While medieval heating systems were somewhat inefficient and posed numerous problems, heating techniques improved with the development of the *irori*, an open, centralized fireplace around which several individuals could simultaneously receive heat, socialize, or cook meals. Despite this advancement, early modern heating still created a substantial amount of smoke and soot that accumulated within the home.

These factors contributed to an overall domestic environment that was often dark and murky. Compounding this problem was an overall lack of daylight received into the home, as well as crowded living conditions within townhouses. Wealthier classes were able to use oil lamps to provide some lighting, although these fixtures did not supply great illumination. Lamps were not used with any frequency by the lower classes, which instead employed long wooden torches if light was needed. However, the poor typically relied solely upon natural daylight for their needs, basing their waking hours on the cycle of the Sun.

MARRIAGE AND DIVORCE

Marriage

Within the warrior class, marriage assumed great political significance from the late 12th century and extending into the Warring States period. During that time, marriage functioned to create familial associations and strategic political alliances for the samurai. Eventually, upper-class warriors began to select wives from a greater distance than ever before in order to strengthen such family connections. Within the marriage itself, the samurai wife was expected to be able to defend the home in the absence of her spouse and was even given a dagger at her wedding for this purpose.

As a philosophy advocated by the government, Neo-Confucianism exerted much influence on warrior marital practices, something that can be seen in the patrilocal traditions (*yomeirikon*) of the time. *Yomeirikon* was the custom in which a woman entered her husband's abode and the couple lived in close proximity to the man's parents. This living arrangement reflected the Confucian virtue of a woman's duty to her spouse. During the Edo period, *yomeirikon* became more prominent, and while it was traditionally practiced in the samurai classes, the custom was eventually adopted by people of other classes.

Generally, rural marriages were far less formal than the maneuvering practices of the elite. Instead they were marked by more unruly activity such as *yobai*, "night visit," a nocturnal sexual rendezvous. The *yobai* occurred between both marital and premarital couples and was commonly seen within the *mukoirikon* living arrangement, when a wife would reside with her parents. This practice was often embellished, especially in folk traditions, and developed into an immoral activity subject to moral disdain. But commoners began to adopt the marital practices of the samurai during the Edo period, diminishing these differences.

At this same time, other new marital developments occurred. Some of these included the *yuino*, an engagement gift exchange, and the *miai*, a formal, organized gathering of eligible marital partners and their families. Marriages were highly regulated during the Edo period as all unions were required to be registered with and approved by governmental officials.

Divorce

Marriage during the Edo period did not provide for an egalitarian relationship between husband and wife. While women were not afforded marital rights with regard to divorce, men enjoyed substantial freedom in separating from their wives. Further, women could be executed for adulterous activity, while men were free to have affairs with concubine women.

For the divorce process, husbands had the sole authority in deciding if the proper grounds for separation had been met. Their decision was not subject to regulation or administrative review. While the samurai classes had a more complex divorce process, a non-samurai male only had to give his wife a three-and-a-half-line letter notifying her of the separation, something which was not subject to appeal.

Because the wife had no legal ability to divorce her husband, one of her few options was to escape to a Buddhist convent if she was unhappy or abused. The refuge temples that provided such safety for women were known as *kakekomidera* ("temples to run into for refuge"). Under proper conditions, the leaders of these asylums could issue women a legal divorce if needed. The *kakekomidera* were common from the 13th to the 19th centuries. The two most famous—and the only formally sanctioned "divorce temples" (*enkiridera*) during the Edo period—were the Mantokuji (in Kozuke province, northern Honshu) and the Tokeiji (in Kamakura). Finally, although men retained the primary rights to a divorce, marital separation was generally more of an organized, collaborative effort between both families within the marriage, something which added a degree of equity to the process.

Marriage Alternatives

There were some alternatives to the marital life for Japanese women. Some exceptional, more talented women could make a living through their trade or vocation. However, the most common alternative option was to enter the religious life or convent in order to avoid marriage. Even though the religious denial of marriage is seemingly contrary to the traditional Edo-period Confucian ideal of a woman's duty to labor in support of the domestic life, such marriage alternatives were at least sometimes valued by the authorities at the time. Often marital renun-

ciants would contribute to the household by supporting their parents.

SEXUALITY

To a great degree, Japanese religious traditions were quite liberal in their attitudes toward sex. Religious narratives such as those found within the *Kojiki* are filled with sexual imagery and symbolism. Japanese culture was not ashamed of promiscuity; instead, many practices suggest that society appeared to revel in sexual activity. Some of these include the *yobai* night visits and the *kogai* festival, which featured songs, poetry, and premarital sexual activity among young adults.

The unabashed, open attitudes toward sex were especially found within the lower classes and folk traditions. Festivals, songs, and tales often included sexual references, and sexual activity abounded among commoners during days of celebration and revelry. Promiscuity was a common theme in much of the popular literature of the day.

Homosexual relationships were also common at the time, particularly between masters and disciples at Buddhist temples and between samurai and elder statesmen with political influence. Again, there was no idea of shame or loss of status due to premarital sexual activity. Thus, it was acceptable for men to be engaged with multiple sexual partners. Concurrently, there was little reference to the concept of virginity or sexual purity within medieval Japanese culture.

As Japan developed an increasingly militaristic and paternalistic society during the Edo period, however, Confucian thought began to impact societal attitudes toward women and sexuality, much in the same way it influenced marital arrangements at that time. Consequently, these ideas and conventions propagated more conservative views of sexuality and fostered attempts to restrict the activities of women so that their behaviors were in keeping with Confucian values.

PREGNANCY AND CHILDBIRTH

Pregnancy

In the early modern period, the first decision to be made by a family once it was discovered that a woman was pregnant was whether or not the fetus should be carried to term. Many families, especially those who were feeding and clothing a number of children already, felt that they could not afford to bring another child into the world. Abortion, despite being illegal and also dangerous to the life of the mother given the lack of understanding about infection, was not uncommon in the cities. The countryside witnessed a different method of birth control, namely smothering the baby after birth, perhaps due to the family's desire to discover if they had conceived a son or a daughter before making such a decision.

If the decision was made to carry the pregnancy to term, special rituals were performed that were believed to protect the health of both the mother and her unborn fetus. One such ritual, *obi iwai*, called for a sash (*obi*) to be tied round the mother's waist at the fifth month of pregnancy to help guarantee a safe and painless delivery. Depending on the local customs, this sash could be fashioned out of a loincloth belonging to the husband, or sent to the mother-to-be by her parents, or even borrowed from a shrine whose deity specialized in matters of childbirth. As the weeks passed, the family made religious prayers and offerings, and the mother was cautious to avoid certain foods deemed detrimental to the natal process.

Childbirth

According to Shinto tradition, birth was defiling because blood caused ritual impurity. In order to minimize this impurity, a family with sufficient economic resources typically erected a special building

12.4 Scene of Edo-period urban domestic life: giving birth (Edo-Tokyo Museum exhibit; Photo William E. Deal)

outside the home, inside which the labor and delivery, overseen by a midwife, took place. The mother delivered the child either in a squatting position or in a specially designed bed, and the umbilical cord was cut with a bamboo or steel knife. Seven days later, relatives and friends were invited to pay a visit to the new family. It was on this day that the newborn received his or her name. (See *"Shichiya"* in the section on Festivals and Yearly Rituals below.)

The upper classes often availed themselves of foster mothers or wet nurses, particularly if the mother was too busy to nurse or had died in childbirth. A typical lower-class woman, however, rarely spent a minute of her time apart from her infant. A baby spent most of its daytime hours strapped to its mother's back by a broad cloth wrapped across its back and underneath its buttocks. It was intermittently taken out for feedings which, it should be noted, were carried on for far longer than Western standards of that time. Even when the child grew old enough to spend the night in its own bed, it continued to sleep in the company of its parents.

FOOD AND DRINK

Japanese eating customs varied widely depending on socioeconomic status. Typically, religious figures and those in the upper classes ate about two meals per day, one before noon and the other in the late afternoon or early evening. Later, following the lead of the warrior classes during the mid-Edo period, nobles and monks developed the habit of eating three meals per day, with the largest meal being consumed in the evening. Meanwhile, the poor involved in physical labor might consume up to four meals a day.

Buddhist dietary guidelines banned the consumption of meat because it was deemed impure and spiritually defiling. Correspondingly, nobles typically did not eat meat products, although some of the upper class did enjoy it in secret. In contrast, it was fairly common for those of the warrior and lower classes to consume meat on a regular basis.

Cooking

Japanese cooking was filled with the staples of seafood, marine vegetation, and rice. Because of religious stipulations, animal products were not typically used in food preparation. Instead, common ingredients included soybean products such as *miso*, a nutritious grain and soybean paste made with rice or barley, and *mirin*, a sweetened version of sake used in combination with vinegar and soy sauce. Common spices used included ginger, *wasabi* (Japanese horseradish) and *sansho* (a dried green powder made from grinding the seedpods of the prickly ash tree). Usually, these products could be found at local town markets, which often had a great supply of fruits, vegetables, seafood, and other food products for the general populace.

In the 13th century, a form of cooking known as *shojin ryori* ("diligence cuisine") was introduced to Japan by Chinese Zen monks. This is a form of vegetarian cooking that utilizes fresh, seasonal vegetables, seaweed, tofu, and other fresh ingredients prepared in a simple manner. This form of Buddhist cooking reflects the Buddhist admonition against killing any form of life. During the Edo period, Japanese cuisine acquired an assortment of new influences from China, Korea, and Western countries such as Portugal and Spain.

Sake

One of the most popular drinks within Japan was sake, or rice wine. This alcoholic beverage began as a drink commonly consumed within group or social settings, such as celebrations, festivals, or parties. During the Edo period, however, sake developed into an everyday drink that could easily be purchased at local markets and was consumed with regularity.

Dining Etiquette

The manner in which meals were consumed depended on several factors, including a family's

12.5 Kitchen stove in a traditional country home (Photo William E. Deal)

socioeconomic status and the rank of individual members within a family, and could differ widely from household to household. The male head of the household, who typically dined with guests and, on occasion, his eldest son, was served his meals by his wife and/or daughter-in-law. The women dined separately from the men, catching quick bites of their meal in the time between trips to serve the head of household. The head's wife was generally served by her daughter-in-law and, in more affluent households, both of these women were assisted by maid-servants.

The traditional style of serving meals was fairly systematic. The person serving the meal would place an individual lacquer tray, approximately 18 inches square and on legs roughly nine inches high, in front of the diner. The entire meal, except for the rice, was presented on this tray. The rice, served next, constituted the bulk of the meal and was therefore eaten in generous amounts. Proper etiquette advised that one leave a few grains of rice in the bowl when passing it back for more, and it was not unusual for each person to consume three full bowls of rice at a single meal. Either disposable chopsticks (*hashi*) made of untreated wood or reusable chopsticks made of lacquer, ivory, or expensive metal were utilized during the meal. The meal was officially concluded after green tea made from the unfermented leaf (unlike the powdered tea of the tea ceremony) had been served, toothpicks had been utilized, and thanks had been given.

The assortment of food items, like many other things in life, was often an accurate indicator of a family's position in society. Those at the lower rungs of Japanese society often ate markedly simple meals consisting of a *miso*-based soup, vegetables, rice or a mixture of rice and wheat, pickles, and tea.

12.6 Sake shop in Edo-period style (Photo William E. Deal)

DRESS AND PERSONAL APPEARANCE

Hair

Hair was a powerful symbol in Japan as it reflected status, age, class, and sexuality. Samurai hairstyles were pragmatic. Men wore their hair in a topknot, and this style influenced commoner fashion in the 13th century. Women's hair was usually long, worn down, and kept straight. During the 16th century, women began to put their hair up and utilize styles that were more elaborate and decorative. Sometimes, women were punished by being forced to cut their hair, a symbolic gesture representing humiliation and debasement.

Most decorative hair ornaments were made of bamboo, wood, tortoise shell, or ivory. One such common item was the comb. Combs were crafted out of gold and pearl in the medieval period. Elaborate forms, styles, and designs developed during the Edo period. Other decorative items found in the early modern period included the stylized *kanzashi* hair ornament and the *kogai* hairpin, used by both men and women to manage their hair. Also developing in the Edo period were the *kamiyui*, hairstylists who made house calls or opened up their own salons, most notably within big cities.

Cosmetics and Accessories

Facial cosmetics were worn by both male and female aristocrats on a regular basis during the medieval and early modern periods. A pale complexion was considered to be most desirable and was sought after by many women. The traditional white face powder, *oshiroi*, was often employed to achieve such an effect. Other popular fashions for women included applying a red dot on their lower lip using a flower-based paste, and the practice of *okimayu*, in which aristocratic women shaved and re-drew their eyebrows using a paint called *mayuzumi*. *Okimayu* was practiced starting in adolescence within the wealthy classes and was practiced by everyday women during special life events such as marriage and childbearing. *Beni* was a rouge applied to the lips, and during the 18th century, *sasabeni*, a fashionable form of rouge with a green hue, also became popular. Other skin care items included *nukabukuro*, a face and body wash made of rice bran, and various facial lotions made from cucumber and gourd juice.

A common trend in dental fashion was *ohaguro*, the practice of using an oxidized liquid to blacken one's teeth. This custom was thought to increase attractiveness in addition to preserving the teeth. While *ohaguro* was originally practiced only by women, it became common among noblemen and warriors during the 12th century before later reverting to a practice only for women in the 18th century.

Tattoos as cosmetic items have a varied history in medieval and early modern Japan. Until 1720, tattoos were used as punishments. Designs were placed on the arm and face to mark offenses. In the Genroku period (1688–1704), tattoos became fashionable

Clothing

During the Kamakura period, the typical warrior uniform consisted of a hunting jacket, *kariginu*, and a cloak (*suikan*). Women's formal attire included the *uchiki* robe and *hakama* skirt-trousers with the *kosode*, a silk garment with short sleeves added to the ensemble at a later time. The *uchikake* or *kaidori*, a long jacket, developed in the Muromachi period, while the *kamishimo*, a matching sleeveless top and bottom ensemble worn by the samurai, arose during the Azuchi-Momoyama period, an era in which Japanese fashion began to show Chinese and Portuguese influence. During the late 14th and early 15th centuries, the use of cotton became widespread for people of all socioeconomic classes. Individuals enjoyed the texture and washability of the fabric, especially commoners, whose attire was often uncomfortable. Led by the Kabuki theater fashions, Edo-period clothing saw the expansion of elaborate, lavish fashion designs, decorated with newly developed dyes. Toward the end of the period, the government placed restrictions on such overly flashy attire, causing citizens to modify their standards of

12.7 *Kamakura-period aristocratic woman* (Illustration Kikuchi Yosai from *Zenken kojitsu*, mid-19th century)

among prostitutes who often received *kisho-bori* tattoos or "pledge marks" to indicate their favorite clients. However, tattoos reached their artistic and popular peak during the mid-19th century. Especially trendy among the townspeople, tattoos of the time exhibited elaborate, colorful designs that often covered an extensive portion of the body. To make these intricate, designs, great skill was needed, creating a market for specialized tattoo artists called *horishi*.

A final type of fashion accessory was the fan or *uchiwa*, used in a wide range of contexts, including within battle, during ceremonies, and as personal accessories. Folding fans, or *ogi*, were status symbols that were also used in a variety of settings, including dance performances, theatrical productions, and tea ceremonies.

12.8 *Everyday medieval warrior attire* (Illustration Kikuchi Yosai from *Zenken kojitsu*, mid-19th century)

12.9 Edo-period spinning wheel (itoguruma) *used for making cloth* (Photo William E. Deal)

fashion and beauty. Typical apparel of this time included the *kosode*, a sash, and the *haori*, a short jacket. Military uniforms also incorporated the *kosode*, *hakama*, and *haori*.

Commoners often wore simple outfits consisting of a smock, trousers, and an overcoat. Women traditionally wore kimonos with girdles called *yumaki*, often layered if the weather demanded. Sometimes commoners went barefoot or wore straw sandals called *ashinaka*. Due to especially hot summers, nudity was acceptable and not subject to embarrassment or scorn within the working classes. Thus, it was not uncommon or inappropriate for men to wear only a loincloth or for women to work the fields topless.

While the shogunate stipulated that courtesans should wear only simple clothing, it was clear that they did not always follow such guidelines. Courtesans were, however, not permitted to wear any socks, leaving them barefoot even during the winter. Going barefoot became a valued symbol of discipline for these women. Furthermore, naked feet were considered sexually alluring, especially since the courtesans often used nail polish.

Japanese clothing varied greatly among social classes. Both the style and color of attire were markers of socioeconomic status and gender distinctions. Despite this diversity, however, one article of clothing that was commonly used by people of all classes was the *kosode*, or kimono, as it came to be known

during its widespread use in the 18th century. The kimono was an efficient form of clothing—it was easy to create, wasted no fabric in the manufacturing process, and was readily adaptable to fit different individuals and body types. Two special types of kimono were the *yukata*, commonly worn in the summer and made of white cotton occasionally with blue dye, and the *furisode*, worn by young women of nobility in the Edo period and marked by longer, extended sleeves.

Traditional Japanese headgear included the *kasa*, a hat made of straw, sedge, and other materials, and often formed into different shapes symbolic of an individual's class status. Headcoverings included the cotton cloth *tenugui* and *zukin*, and headbands called *hachimaki*. Hachimaki were typically worn by individuals under great duress, such as warriors in battle, women giving birth, and men involved in strenuous physical labor.

Sandals were the most common form of footwear, as they were cheap, convenient, and easy to make. The most notable forms of such footwear were the straw *waraji* used for long trips by foot, *geta*, which were wooden clogs often worn by urban dwellers, and *zori*, a sandal commonly worn with kimono. Typical raingear included the *kasa* hat, the Portuguese-influenced rain cape known as a *kappa*, and a type of *geta* used as rain footwear, the *ashida*.

12.10 Straw boots (zunbe) *worn in the countryside during winter* (Photo William E. Deal)

Everyday Etiquette

Guidelines for personal decorum differed depending on such factors as an individual's social class, gender, and rank within his or her family. For example, a wife was expected to walk a pace behind her husband when they appeared together in a public setting, a relatively infrequent occurrence. In the household, individuals were expected to situate themselves in a very particular sitting position that had been taught to them since childhood. Sitting back on the heels, with the ankles nearly sideways on the floor, allowed the feet to form a cup which comfortably accommodated the buttocks. When a woman was receiving guests, bidding farewell, or taking orders, she placed her hands on the floor and bowed quite low to the ground, lowering her forehead between her hands. Men bowed in a similar fashion, but not quite so low, and were permitted to sit in a cross-legged position in less formal situations. Outside of the home, people simply bowed to each other from the waist, only demonstrating respect by bowing to the ground when a personage of high authority, such as a daimyo, passed by.

When greeting others, it was expected that people would remove items worn for work, such as protective clothing or spectacles. Since it was considered rather rude to breathe on other people, the custom was to position the hand in front of the mouth while speaking to superiors. For the same reason, when handling sacred or otherwise important objects, a piece of paper was placed in the mouth to protect the items from desecration.

SPORTS AND DIVERSIONS

Sports and Games

In addition to the martial arts outlined in chapter 5: Warriors and Warfare, Japan also enjoyed a handful of other sporting activities. One of the most renowned and distinctive of these sports was the form of wrestling called *sumo*. In sumo two wrestlers, wearing only a special loincloth belt called a *mawashi*, compete in a *dohyo*—a central clay ring surrounded by bags of straw—where they must force their opponent to step out of the circle or touch the ground with any part of their body except the feet. The match lasts for only a brief amount of time and is arbitrated by the *gyoji* (referee). Sumo dates back to before the medieval period, but it first became a professional sport during the Edo period. Other sports included cockfighting, fishing, and falconry.

Outside of the traditional sports of the day, the athletic kickball game *kemari* was popular among the nobility during the Kamakura period. *Kemari* consisted of people trying to kick a ball around a circle while not letting it touch the ground. This game, along with the associated handball *temari*, eventually was picked up and enjoyed by the lower classes as well. *Hanetsuki*—a badminton-like game played by girls with wooden paddles and a shuttlecock—and the *otedama* beanbag game were two other athletic diversions found in early modern Japan.

Two of the most prominent board games played in Japan were go and *shogi*. Go is a classic game of strategy played by two individuals moving black and white stones across a wooden board. During the 17th century, annual go matches were held for the shogun at Edo castle. Go competition was exceptionally competitive and specialized schools were established to train individuals in the art of playing this game. *Shogi* was a related game that resembles the Western game of chess. An official governmental agency to oversee go and *shogi* was established by the Tokugawa shogunate in 1607. Finally, a board game played with dice called *sugoroku*, comparable to backgammon, became especially popular from the 17th century. The goal of the game was to move all of one's pieces into the opponent's territory. One version of *sugoroku* was played on a board inscribed with scenes of both the Buddhist Pure Land and the Buddhist hells. The goal of Pure Land *sugoroku*, as it was called, was to attain entry into the Pure Land associated with Amida Buddha. (see chapter 6: Religion, for details on the Pure Land school of Buddhism.)

Besides board games, card playing was also a common pastime. Two popular forms were the *uta karuta* (poem cards), a game played with cards on which a famous poem is written, and *hanafuda* (flower cards), a game played with cards depicting flora and fauna. Card playing was often associated with gambling, both of which were banned by the Tokugawa shogunate after a dramatic increase in such activity.

Children's play during the medieval and early modern periods included the following games:

MENKO

Dating back to the Kamakura period, *menko* was a game in which a player placed a game piece on the ground. An opponent would try to flip the piece over by flinging another game piece at the one on the ground. These game pieces, made of clay or some other material, were usually decorated. In the Edo period, images of sumo wrestlers became a popular subject for the pieces.

KAGOME KAGOME

"Bird in a cage" game. This was a guessing game in which children formed a circle around a child and sang a song called "Kagome kagome." While the song was being sung, the children moved in a circle around the child in the middle. When the song ended, the children stopped circling and the one in the middle tried to guess who stood immediately behind him or her. A correct guess released the child from the circle (or the bird from the cage), replaced by the child whose identity had been guessed.

NEKKI

In this game, a one-foot-high wooden stake is placed upright into the ground. The object of the game is to knock down the stake by throwing a stick against it.

JANKEN

This is a game of "rock, paper, scissors." Pairs of children would say "*jan, ken, pon*" in unison and then

12.11 *Princess Sen, eldest daughter of the second Tokugawa shogun Hidetada, engaged in an aristocratic pastime called* kaiawase. *From the Heian period, this traditional game involved players competing to identify shells with matching scenes or poems taken from classical literature.* (Himeji Castle exhibit; Photo William E. Deal)

12.12 *Example of an Edo-period toy doll* (Photo William E. Deal)

hold out their hands. A closed fist was a stone, a hand held out flat was paper, and a hand with two fingers extended was scissors. Paper covered stone, stone broke scissors, and scissors cut paper.

Other forms of leisure and entertainment found throughout the medieval and early modern periods included *nazo nazo*, the recitation of funny riddles that became very popular during the Edo period, and *origami*, the art of paper-folding to create intricate shapes and figures. Flying elaborately decorated kites, playing with children's tops, and collecting dolls that were often used in ceremonial celebrations were additional leisure activities.

Household Pets

Children in medieval and early modern Japan rarely possessed household pets. If an animal was cared for by a human, it was usually because the animal served some useful purpose. Insects such as crickets, valued for the soothing effects of their chirping, and fireflies were often caught and kept in cages in Japanese homes. Wild Japanese monkeys were sometimes caught and trained to perform acts of entertainment, such as dancing, for the public. With the exception of some Pekinese dogs imported by the Dutch, dogs in Japan were rarely kept as pets. Domestic cats, imported into Japan in ancient times from China and Korea, were rare and prized possessions until the 10th century. However, by the Kamakura period, they were fairly common in households as vermin-catchers but not as treasured family pets. The traditional Japanese breed of cat has been described as short-haired, mostly white with black and brown markings, and round-faced. Felines were a common theme in traditional Japanese literature, and folk beliefs revolved around the notion that cats avenge themselves when killed.

Animals enjoyed significant protection under Buddhism, which forbade the taking of any life. The release of caged animals back into the wild was highly regarded, and many people believed that such an act would bring rewards in the next life. Merchants on the street often sold live fish and caged animals, such as birds and tortoises, specifically bred or caught for this purpose.

CALENDAR

In the medieval and early modern periods, the Japanese utilized the traditional lunar calendar. Dates on this calendar represented the day, month, and year, the last of which could be determined by several methods. Two such methods included the 60-year time cycle and the use of the era name, or *nengo*. *Nengo* was a unit of time comparable to an era, commonly employed to date events or chronological periods. The use of this measure of time began in the seventh century. The change of emperor included a change in era name. However, in the early modern period, the *nengo* did not simply represent the duration of a governmental regime. New era names might be declared when auspicious events occurred or at certain points in the traditional 60-year (sexagenary) calendar cycle.

Both telling time and naming months utilized two separate methods. The time of day was typically divided into 12 sections. Under the sexagenary system, however, one set of six sections was not the same time span as the other set. Likewise, months had both formal or traditional names as well as alternative titles with symbolic folk meanings.

Despite the official use of the lunar calendar, the solar calendar was also employed and was very important for farmers. This calendar accurately pinpointed the seasons, and thus farmers depended upon it to know the proper time for planting and harvesting. In addition, the solar calendar was important for the influence it had on the structure of the traditional lunar calendar.

FESTIVALS AND YEARLY RITUALS

As in other periods of Japanese history, festivals and yearly rituals were important to the conduct of everyday life in the medieval and early modern periods. Festivals (*matsuri*) have their origins in Shinto rituals often associated with the agricultural cycle and obtaining blessings from the *kami* for a plentiful harvest and other benefits. Annual rituals (*nenchu gyoji* or *nenju gyoji*) were related originally to the imperial court calendar and date back to before the medieval period. These annual rites often had a Buddhist or astrological significance and were intended to ensure the blessings of the Buddhas and bodhisattvas, as well as the proper functioning of the court. In the medieval and early modern periods, especially with the reduced significance of the imperial court, there came to be shared elements between festivals and yearly events.

Festivals

Often tracing their origins to folk traditions, Japanese festivals were numerous in the medieval and early modern periods. Festivals existed in a multitude of forms, and were present in all seasons and regional locations. Despite the diversity of form, the purpose of *matsuri* typically was to cultivate harmony within the local community and to effect human-divine contact—often as a means to express gratitude to the *kami* or to petition them for assistance in agricultural matters. Because festivals were often held to assure an abundant harvest, the occurrence of *matsuri* was tied to the seasonal cycle. Thus, the most important celebrations occurred during the spring and autumn to coincide with the planting and harvesting periods. However, winter and summer festivals were also held, the latter of which were often rituals conducted to prevent the occurrence of anything that might destroy the crops in midseason. In the early modern period, city festivals arose as a means to protect the population from epidemics and natural disasters. Although there was obvious religious significance to *matsuri*, they also came to have a more general celebratory tone and included events such as dancing and contests.

Festivals included ritual elements that made it possible to establish a connection between humans and the *kami*. Among these rituals were rites of purification and offerings to the gods of rice, sake,

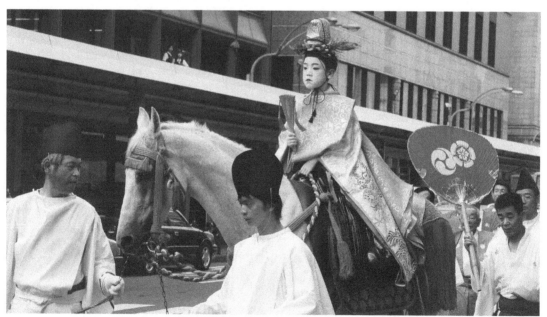

12.13 Scene of a Gion Festival parade in the streets of present-day Kyoto (Photo William E. Deal)

vegetables, and other nonmeat products emblematic of an agricultural community. Purification, central to Shinto conceptions of the sacred, was required of both Shinto priests and festival participants before they could engage in these rituals of thanksgiving and supplication. One other common aspect of festivals was a communal feast between people and the gods.

Yearly Rituals

Yearly rituals had their origins in Buddhist and other rites performed on a regular schedule by the imperial court. Starting in the Kamakura period, however, these rituals were diffused into the larger population, and at least some of the rituals once performed only at court came to be practiced more generally. Yearly rituals were integrated into the cultural calendar, so communities throughout different regions of Japan came to observe them at similar times of year. Over the course of the medieval and early modern periods, the yearly ritual calendar was revised and adapted to meet changing cultural and social needs, reflecting the interests of warriors and other social classes. This was especially the case in the Edo period when merchant and artisan values informed the kinds of rituals that were performed annually.

The following are examples of just a few of the yearly rituals celebrated in the medieval and early modern periods:

SETSUBUN (EVE OF THE FIRST DAY OF SPRING)

The performance date varied from year to year because the first day of spring was traditionally calculated using the lunar calendar. Also referred to as *oni harai* ("sweeping away the demons"), Setsubun was a ceremony in which beans were thrown both inside and outside the house to ward off evil demons.

SHICHIGOSAN (SEVEN-FIVE-THREE)

Observed on November 15, Shichigosan was a ritual for children at the ages of seven, five, and three. Boys and girls of these ages were thought to be particularly susceptible to malevolent forces, so they were taken to a Shinto shrine to gain the blessings of the gods. This ritual was believed to provide divine assurance of a safe and prosperous future for children.

OBON (OR URABON-E, BON FESTIVAL)

Observed from July 13 to 15 (or from August 13 to 15 in some parts of Japan). The Bon Festival, dating back to the seventh century in Japan but performed prior to that in China, was a Buddhist practice in which families honored their ancestors. Families would welcome the souls of their ancestors back for a three-day visit, at which time various rituals were performed.

SHICHIYA (SEVENTH NIGHT)

This was a ritual performed on the seventh day after a child's birth and was associated with the gradual fading of the 21 days of impurity that Shinto tradition associated with childbirth. It was believed that on this seventh day it was safe to take a baby outdoors. This ritual also included a gathering of the extended family for the formal naming of the newborn.

ENNICHI (DAY OF SACRED CONNECTION)

Ennichi was a ritual where people went to a Buddhist temple or Shinto shrine on a day associated with a particular god, Buddha, or bodhisattva. For instance, the 18th day of each month was associated with the bodhisattva Kannon. Going to a temple on this day ensured the practitioner of gaining a connection with Kannon and receiving the bodhisattva's spiritual assistance. Because large numbers of people visited temples and shrines on connection days, the temple and shrine precincts became places where food and other items were sold to the visiting pilgrims. In the Edo period, this ritual often became as much an occasion for merry-making as it was for religious behavior.

SHOGATSU (NEW YEAR)

Observed from January 1 to 3. New Year's celebrations constituted the largest and most prominent of all annual rituals. The Oshogatsu, or "Big New Year," celebration included family gatherings, worship at temples, and visits to the emperor's palace grounds. The Koshogatsu, or "Small New Year," took place around January 15 and was observed by the rural populace. This ritual included a series of events surrounding the harvest.

GA NO IWAI (OR TOSHIIWAI, BIRTHDAY CELEBRATION)

This rite of passage marked the attainment of certain ages in the life cycle. Although this ritual had its origins in China, the Japanese version became established sometime in the late medieval period and became popular in the Edo period. Of particular importance were the ages of 60, 70, 80, 88, 90, and 99. Of these, *kanreki*, or "the 60th birthday," marked the beginning of a new life cycle according to the 60-year Chinese lunar calendar. Usually the person wore red to symbolize this new cycle, and the day was celebrated by a feast with friends and relatives.

DEATH AND DYING

Life Expectancy

In the early modern period, the Japanese had remarkably high life expectancy rates compared with contemporary western European populations. Although life expectancy rates differed significantly depending on factors such as geographical region and the period of time during which samples were collected, rates for 18th- and 19th-century Japan ranged roughly between 35 and 45 years of age, sometimes hovering higher than 50 for men and women in some localities. Although these rates may appear low when measured by current standards, they are surprisingly high for a preindustrialized society that endured three major famines between the years 1732 and 1836. By way of contrast, it is instructive to note that at the beginning of the 19th century, European life expectancy at birth was around 35 to 40 years of age at the very highest end of the scale.

Disease

Due to its relative geographical isolation and prohibitions on travel into and out of the country, Japan escaped comparatively unscathed from many of the major epidemics that decimated the populations of Europe. However, diseases such as influenza, smallpox, measles, and leprosy continued to afflict the inhabitants of Japan, particularly the poorer segments of society. In addition to periodic countrywide famines, epidemics of cholera occasionally swept through Japanese cities, and many people suffered from the disease beriberi, also known as the "Edo disease" due to its prevalence in the city of Edo. Beriberi was characterized by a nutritional deficiency stemming from a diet heavily dependent on polished white rice. Methods of dealing with sewage, although more sanitary than those used in Europe at the time, were nevertheless unhygienic and encouraged numerous stomach and intestinal disorders, earning the country a reputation as a haven for parasites. Treatments for disease traditionally relied on Chinese medicine, though in the second half of the Edo period, Western medicines and medical practices began to be used in treatments as well.

Suicide

In contrast to the opprobrium placed on suicide in Western culture, the taking of one's life was not a disgraceful act in Japan. Suicide was considered an honorable means of ending one's life and a legitimate way of dealing with inexorable conflicts or intense social pressure. While suicide was not accepted by all individuals within society, it represented an important aspect of a Japanese view of life and death.

The Afterlife

The Japanese believed that when people died their spirits entered *shigo no sekai*, "the world after death," or Yomi no Kuni, "the Land of Darkness." During the afterlife these spirits interact with the world at times of celebrations such as the Bon Festival and New Year's festivities. In addition to this view, Buddhism influenced beliefs in reincarnation and the existence of realms such as hells and the Pure Land. These Buddhist views of death were central to life in the medieval and early modern periods.

Cremation

Cremation (*kaso*) was the most common way of treating the corpse in Japan. This process was espoused by Buddhists, who believed that the deceased person's body must be disposed of quickly in order for his or her soul to transmigrate and be reborn. Cremation spread to Japan from China and Korea and was practiced by the general populace in the Kamakura and Muromachi periods. Confucianism, however, advised against cremation and advocated coffin burial (*taiso*) instead. As Confucianism gained popularity during the Edo period, increasing numbers of shogun and daimyo chose burial as their preferred method of postmortem treatment, ultimately leading to a ban on cremation for the common people. However, following the Meiji Restoration, cremation was reinstated in an effort to curb the spread of certain diseases.

Mourning

In addition to being a process of emotional catharsis or grieving, mourning (*mo*) was a way to deal with the impurity one encountered in close proximity to death. During mourning, one was secluded within the home, not allowed to eat meat, contact Shinto deities, or perform his or her traditional duties. The length of this process varied depending on one's intimacy with the deceased.

READING

General

Frédéric 1972: everyday life in the medieval period; Dunn 1969: everyday life in the early modern period; Hanley 1997: everyday life in the early modern period; Edo-Tokyo Museum (ed.) 1995: everyday life in the early modern period in the city of Edo

The Family

Frédéric 1972, 34–45: medieval children and childhood, 53–56, 60–65: the medieval family; Hanley 1997, 137–150: early modern family structure; Dunn 1969, 165–174: early modern children and childhood

12.14 Grave markers at the Hasedera Temple in Kamakura (Photo William E. Deal)

The Home

Frédéric 1972, 104–112: medieval homes and furnishings; Hanley 1997, 25–50, 54–63: early modern homes and furnishings, 94–97: early modern bedding; Dunn 1969, 158–160: lighting and heating

Marriage and Divorce

Frédéric 1972, 45–51: medieval marriage, 56–60; Hanley 1997, 141–143: early modern marriage; Dunn 1969, 173–174: marriage and divorce

Sexuality

Edo-Tokyo Museum (ed.) 1995

Pregnancy and Childbirth

Frédéric 1972, 30–34: medieval birth; Hanley 1997, 141–150: early modern family size and abortion; Dunn 1969, 164–165: early modern childbirth

Food and Drink

Frédéric 1972, 69–77: medieval food; Hanley 1997, 63–68, 77–94: early modern food; Dunn 1969, 150–158: early modern food and cooking; Nishiyama 1997: 144–178: early modern food and restaurants

Dress and Personal Appearance

Miner, Odagiri, and Morrell 1985: 493–501: historical clothing styles; Frédéric 1972, 77–83: medieval dress, 83–86: medieval cosmetics, 86–88: medieval personal hygiene; Hanley 1997, 68–73, 94–97: early modern clothing, 97–103: early modern bathing; 104–128: early modern sanitation and personal hygiene; Dunn 1969, 160–161: summer clothing, 161–162: personal hygiene

Sports and Diversions

May 1989

Calendar

Dunn 1969, 146–148: calendar
Miner, Odagiri, and Morrell 1985: 399–407: calendar and time

Festivals and Yearly Rituals

Miner, Odagiri, and Morrell 1985: 407–414: list of annual rituals (*nenju gyoji*); Brandon and Stephan 1994: New Year rituals and customs; Ashkenazi 1993: festivals (*matsuri*)

Death and Dying

Frédéric 2002: see specific topics; Hanley 1997, 129–137: early modern life expectancy; Frédéric 1972, 51–53: medieval death; Edo-Tokyo Museum (ed.) 1995

MUSEUMS OUTSIDE JAPAN WITH NOTED JAPANESE ART COLLECTIONS

UNITED STATES

Ann Arbor, Michigan: University of Michigan Museum of Art

Boston, Massachusetts: Museum of Fine Arts, Boston

Brooklyn, New York: Brooklyn Museum of Art

Cambridge, Massachusetts: Harvard University Art Museums

Chicago, Illinois: Art Institute of Chicago

Cleveland, Ohio: Cleveland Museum of Art

Dallas, Texas: Trammell and Margaret Crow Collection of Asian Art

Denver, Colorado: Denver Art Museum

Detroit, Michigan: Detroit Institute of Arts

Hanford, California: Ruth and Sherman Lee Institute for Japanese Art at the Clark Center

Honolulu, Hawaii: Honolulu Academy of Arts

Kansas City, Missouri: Nelson-Atkins Museum of Art

Los Angeles, California: Los Angeles County Museum of Art

Minneapolis, Minnesota: Minneapolis Institute of Arts

New Haven, Connecticut: Yale University Art Gallery

New York, New York: Metropolitan Museum of Art

Oberlin, Ohio: Allen Memorial Art Museum

Philadelphia, Pennsylvania: Philadelphia Museum of Art

Portland, Oregon: Portland Art Museum

Princeton, New Jersey: Princeton University Art Museum

Richmond, Virginia: Virginia Museum of Fine Arts

Salem, Massachusetts: Peabody Essex Museum

San Francisco, California: Asian Art Museum of San Francisco

Seattle, Washington: Seattle Asian Art Museum

St. Louis, Missouri: Saint Louis Art Museum

Washington, District of Columbia: Freer Gallery of Art and Arthur M. Sackler Gallery (Smithsonian Institution)

Worcester, Massachusetts: Worcester Art Museum

CANADA

Montreal: Montreal Museum of Fine Arts

Toronto: Royal Ontario Museum of Archaeology

BELGIUM

Brussels: Musées Royaux d'Art et d'Histoire

FRANCE

Paris: Musée National des Arts Asiatiques-Guimet

GERMANY

Berlin: Museum für Ostasiatische Kunst

Cologne: Museum für Ostasiatische Kunst, Köln

ITALY

Genoa: Museo d'Arte Orientate "Edoardo Chiossone"

NETHERLANDS
Amsterdam: Rijksmuseum Amsterdam

SWITZERLAND
Geneva: Bair Collection

UNITED KINGDOM
London: British Museum
London: Victoria and Albert Museum
Norwich: Sainsbury Institute for the Study of Japanese Arts and Cultures
Oxford: Ashmolean Museum

Addiss, Stephen. *The Art of Zen.* New York: Abrams, 1989.

———. *How to Look at Japanese Art.* New York: Abrams, 1996.

Adolphson, Mikael S. *The Gates of Power: Monks, Courtiers, and Warriors in Premodern Japan.* Honolulu: University of Hawaii Press, 2000.

Akiyama, Terukazu. *Japanese Painting.* Geneva: Skira, 1961.

Anderson, Jennifer L. *An Introduction to Japanese Tea Ritual.* Albany: State University of New York Press, 1991.

Anesaki, Masaharu. *Nichiren, the Buddhist Prophet.* Cambridge, Mass.: Harvard University Press, 1916.

Arai, Hakuseki. *Told Round a Brushwood Fire: The Autobiography of Arai Hakuseki.* Translated by Joyce Ackroyd. Princeton, N.J.: Princeton University Press, 1980.

Araki, James T. *The Ballad-Drama of Medieval Japan.* Berkeley: University of California Press, 1964.

Arnesen, Peter Judd. *The Medieval Japanese Daimyo: The Ouchi Family's Rule of Suo and Nagato.* New Haven, Conn.: Yale University Press, 1979.

Arnott, Peter. *The Theatres of Japan.* London: Macmillan, 1969.

Ascher, Marcia. *Mathematics Elsewhere: An Exploration of Ideas Across Cultures.* Princeton, N.J.: Princeton University Press, 2002.

Ashkenazi, Michael. *Matsuri: Festivals of a Japanese Town.* Honolulu: University of Hawaii Press, 1993.

Association of Japanese Geographers, eds. *Geography of Japan.* Tokyo: Teikoku Shoin, 1980.

Avitabile, Gunhild. *Early Masters: Ukiyo-e Prints and Paintings from 1680 to 1750.* New York: Japan Society, 1991.

Baird, Merrily. *Symbols of Japan: Thematic Motifs in Art and Design.* New York: Rizzoli, 2001.

Barnet, Sylvan, and William Burto. *Zen Ink Paintings.* New York: Kodansha International, 1982.

Bartholomew, James R. *The Formation of Science in Japan: Building a Research Tradition.* New Haven, Conn.: Yale University Press, 1989.

Beard, Mary Ritter. *The Force of Women in Japanese History.* Washington, D.C.: Public Affairs Press, 1953.

Beasley, W. G. *The Japanese Experience: A Short History of Japan.* Berkeley: University of California Press, 1999.

Bellah, Robert N. *Tokugawa Religion: The Values of Pre-Industrial Japan.* Glencoe, Ill.: Free Press, 1957.

Bernstein, Gail Lee, ed. *Recreating Japanese Women, 1600–1945.* Berkeley: University of California Press, 1991.

Berry, Mary Elizabeth. *The Culture of Civil War in Kyoto.* Berkeley: University of California Press, 1994.

———. *Hideyoshi.* Cambridge, Mass.: Harvard University Press, 1982.

Bielefeldt, Carl. *Dogen's Manuals of Zen Meditation.* Berkeley: University of California Press, 1988.

Bingham, Marjorie Wall, and Susan Hill Gross. *Women in Japan: From Ancient Times to the Present.* Edited by Janet Donaldson. St. Louis Park, Minn.: Glenhurst Publications, 1987.

Bix, Herbert P. *Peasant Protest in Japan, 1590–1884.* New Haven, Conn.: Yale University Press, 1986.

Blacker, Carmen. *The Catalpa Bow: A Study of Shamanistic Practices in Japan.* Boston: Allen and Unwin, 1986.

Blomberg, Catharina. *The Heart of the Warrior: Origins and Religious Background of the Samurai System in Feudal Japan.* Sandgate, U.K.: Japan Library, 1994.

Blood, Katherine L., James Douglas Farquhar, Sandy Kita, and Lawrence E. Marceau. *The Floating World of Ukiyo-e: Shadows, Dreams, and Substance.* New York: Abrams, 2001.

Bloom, Alfred, *Shinran's Gospel of Pure Grace.* Tucson: University of Arizona Press, 1965.

Blum, Mark L. *The Origins and Development of Pure Land Buddhism: A Study and Translation of Gyonen's Jodo Homon Genrusho.* Oxford and New York: Oxford University Press, 2002.

Bocking, Brian. *A Popular Dictionary of Shinto.* Chicago, Ill.: NTC Publishing Group, 1997.

Bodart-Bailey, Beatrice M., ed. and trans. *Kaempfer's Japan: Tokugawa Culture Observed.* Honolulu: University of Hawaii Press, 1999.

Bodiford, William. *Soto Zen in Medieval Japan.* Honolulu: University of Hawaii Press, 1993.

Bogel, Cynthea J. *Hiroshige: Birds and Flowers.* New York: George Brazillier, 1988.

Bolitho, Harold. *Treasures Among Men: The Fudai Daimyo in Tokugawa Japan.* New Haven, Conn.: Yale University Press, 1974.

Bottomley, Ian, and Anthony Hopson. *Arms and Armour of the Samurai: The History of Weaponry in Ancient Japan.* New York: Crescent Books, 1996.

Bowers, John Z. *Medical Education in Japan: From Chinese Medicine to Western Medicine.* New York: Harper and Row, 1965.

Bowers, John Z. *Western Medical Pioneers in Feudal Japan.* Baltimore: Johns Hopkins University Press, 1970.

———. *When the Twain Meet: The Rise of Western Medicine in Japan.* Baltimore: Johns Hopkins University Press, 1980.

Bowman, Jannetta Ann. *Epidemics and Mortality in Early Modern Japan.* Princeton, N.J.: Princeton University Press, 1987.

Bownas, Geoffrey, and Anthony Thwaite, eds. *The Penguin Book of Japanese Verse.* Baltimore: Penguin Books, 1964.

Bowring, Richard, and Peter Kornicki, eds. *The Cambridge Encyclopedia of Japan.* Cambridge: Cambridge University Press, 1993.

Boxer, Charles R. *The Christian Century in Japan, 1549–1650.* Berkeley: University of California Press, 1951.

Brandon, James R., ed. *The Cambridge Guide to Asian Theatre.* Cambridge: Cambridge University Press, 1993.

———, ed. *Chushingura: Studies in Kabuki and the Puppet Theater.* Honolulu: University of Hawaii Press, 1982.

———, trans. *Kabuki: Five Classic Plays.* Cambridge, Mass.: Harvard University Press, 1975.

Brandon, James R., William P. Malm, and Donald H. Shively. *Studies in Kabuki: Its Acting, Music, and Historical Context.* Honolulu: University of Hawaii Press, 1978.

Brandon, Reiko Mochinaga, and Barbara B. Stephan. *Spirit and Symbol: The Japanese New Year.* Honolulu: Honolulu Academy of Arts, 1994.

Brazell, Karen, ed. *Traditional Japanese Theater: An Anthology of Plays.* New York: Columbia University Press, 1998.

———, ed. *Twelve Plays of the Noh and Kyogen Theaters.* Ithaca, N.Y.: Cornell University East Asia Program, Cornell University, 1988.

———, trans. *The Confessions of Lady Nijo.* Stanford, Calif.: Stanford University Press, 1973.

Breen, John, and Mark Williams. *Japan and Christianity: Impacts and Responses.* New York: St. Martin's Press, 1996.

Brower, Robert H., and Earl Miner. *Fujiwara Teika's Superior Poems of Our Time: A Thirteenth Century Poetic Treatise and Sequence.* Stanford, Calif.: Stanford University Press, 1967.

———. *Japanese Court Poetry.* Stanford, Calif.: Stanford University Press, 1961.

Brown, Delmer M. *Money Economy in Medieval Japan: A Study in the Use of Coins.* New Haven, Conn.: Yale University Press, 1951.

Brown, Delmer M., and Ichiro Ishida, trans. *The Future and the Past, A Translation and Study of the Gukansho, An Interpretative History of Japan Written in 1219.* Berkeley: University of California Press, 1979.

Brown, Kendall H. *The Politics of Reclusion: Painting and Power in Momoyama Japan.* Honolulu: University of Hawaii Press, 1997.

Brownlee, John S. *Political Thought in Japanese Historical Writing: From Kojiki (712) to Tokushi Yoron (1712).* Waterloo, Ontario: Wilfrid Laurier University Press, 1991.

Bryant, Anthony J. *Samurai 1550–1600.* London: Osprey Publishing, 1994.

———. *The Samurai.* London: Osprey Publishing, 1989.

———. *Sekigahara 1600.* London: Osprey Publishing, 1995.

Butler, Lee. *Emperor and Aristocracy in Japan, 1467–1680: Resilience and Renewal.* Cambridge, Mass.: Harvard University East Asian Monographs, 2002.

Cahill, James. *Scholar Painters of Japan.* New York: Asia Society, 1972.

Cai, Jingfeng, and Zhen Yan. "Medicine in Ancient China." In *Medicine Across Cultures: History and Practice of Medicine in Non-Western Cultures.* Edited by Helaine Selin. Dordecht and Boston: Kluwer Academic Publishers, 2003, 49–73.

Carter, Steven D. *Waiting for the Wind: Thirty-six Poets of Japan's Late Medieval Age.* New York: Columbia University Press, 1989.

———, ed. *Traditional Japanese Poetry: An Anthology.* Stanford, Calif.: Stanford University Press, 1991.

Castile, Rand. *The Way of Tea.* Tokyo and New York: Weatherhill, 1971.

Chan, Alan K. L., Gregory K. Clancey, and Hui-chieh Loy, eds. *Historical Perspectives on East Asian Science, Technology, and Medicine.* Singapore and River Edge, N.J.: Singapore University Press and World Scientific, 2001.

Childs, Margaret H. *Rethinking Sorrow: Revelatory Tales of Late Medieval Japan.* Ann Arbor: Center for Japanese Studies, University of Michigan, 1991.

Clark, Timothy. *100 Views of Mount Fuji.* New York: Weatherhill, 2001.

Clark, Timothy. *The Dawn of the Floating World 1650–1765: Early Ukiyo-e Treasures from the Museum of Fine Arts, Boston.* London: Harry N. Abrams, 2001.

———. *Ukiyo-e Paintings in the British Museum.* London: British Museum Press, 1992.

Clarke, H. B. D. "The Development of Edo Language." In *18th Century Japan: Culture and Society*, edited by C. Andrew Gerstle. Richmond, U.K.: Curzon Press. 1999, 63–72.

Cleary, Thomas, trans. *Code of the Samurai: A Modern Translation of the Bushido shoshinsu.* Boston: Tuttle Publishing, 1999.

Coaldrake, William H. *Architecture and Authority in Japan.* London and New York: Routledge, 1996.

———. *The Way of the Japanese Carpenter: Tools and Japanese Architecture.* New York: Weatherhill, 1990.

Cole, John. *Geography of the World's Major Regions.* London and New York: Routledge, 1996.

Collcutt, Martin. *Five Mountains: The Rinzai Zen Monastic Institution in Medieval Japan.* Cambridge, Mass.: Harvard University Press, 1981.

Collcutt, Martin, Marius B. Jansen, and Isao Kumakura. *Cultural Atlas of Japan.* New York: Facts On File, 1988.

Conlan, Thomas. *The Culture of Force and Farce: Fourteenth-Century Japanese Warfare.* Cambridge, Mass.: Reischauer Institute of Japanese Studies, Harvard University, 2000.

———. *State of War: The Violent Order of Fourteenth-Century Japan.* Ann Arbor: Center for Japanese Studies, University of Michigan, 2003.

Cook, Harry. *Samurai: Story of a Warrior Tradition.* New York: Sterling, 1993.

Cooper, Michael. *Rodrigues the Interpreter: An Early Jesuit in Japan and China.* New York and Tokyo: Weatherhill, 1974.

———, ed. *João Rodrigues's Account of Sixteenth-Century Japan.* London: Hakluyt Society, 2001.

———, ed. *The Southern Barbarians: The First Europeans in Japan.* Tokyo: Kodansha International, 1971.

———, ed. *They Came to Japan: An Anthology of European Reports on Japan, 1543–1640.* Berkeley: University of California Press, 1965.

Cornell, Laurel L. "Peasant Women and Divorce in Preindustrial Japan." *Signs* 15 (1990): 710–32.

Cort, Louise Allison. *Seto and Mino Ceramics.* Washington, D.C.: Freer Gallery, 1992.

———. *Shigaraki: Potter's Valley.* New York: Kodansha International, 1979.

Cortazzi, Hugh. *The Japanese Achievement.* London: Sidgwick and Jackson, 1990.

Court and Samurai in an Age of Transition: Medieval Paintings and Blades from the Gotoh Museum, Tokyo. New York: Japan Society, 1989.

Courtly Splendor: Twelve Centuries of Treasures from Japan. Boston: Museum of Fine Arts, 1990.

Craig, Albert M. *The Heritage of Japanese Civilization.* Upper Saddle River, N.J.: Prentice Hall, 2003.

Craig, Albert M., and Donald Shively, eds, *Personality in Japanese History.* Berkeley: University of California Press, 1970.

Crawcour, E. S. "The Premodern Economy." In *An Introduction to Japanese Civilization,* edited by Arthur E. Tiedemann. New York: Columbia University Press, 1974, 461–486.

Cullen, L. M. *A History of Japan, 1582–1941: Internal and External Worlds.* Cambridge: Cambridge University Press, 2003.

Cunningham, Don. *Taiho-jutsu: Law and Order in the Age of the Samurai.* Boston: Tuttle, 2004.

Cunningham, Michael, ed. *Buddhist Treasures from Nara.* Cleveland: Cleveland Museum of Art, 1998.

———, ed. *The Triumph of Japanese Style: 16th Century Art in Japan.* Cleveland: Cleveland Museum of Art, 1991.

———, ed. *Unfolding Beauty: Japanese Screens from the Cleveland Museum of Art.* Cleveland: Cleveland Museum of Art, 2001.

Cunningham, Michael, et al., ed. *Ink Paintings and Ash-Glazed Ceramics: Medieval Calligraphy, Painting and Ceramic Art from Japan and Korea.* Cleveland: Cleveland Museum of Art, 2000.

Dalby, Liza Crihfield. *Geisha.* Berkeley: University of California Press, 1983.

———. *Kimono: Fashioning Culture.* New Haven, Conn.: Yale University Press, 1993.

de Ferranti, Hugh. *Japanese Musical Instruments.* Oxford and New York: Oxford University Press, 2000.

Denoon, Donald, Mark Hudson, Gavan McCormack, and Tessa Morris-Suzuki, eds. *Multicultural Japan: Palaeolithic to Postmodern.* Cambridge: Cambridge University Press, 2001.

Deutsch, Sanna Saks, and Howard A. Link, eds. *The Feminine Image: Women of Japan.* Honolulu: Honolulu Academy of Arts, 1985.

Dictionary of Japanese Art Terms. Tokyo: Tokyo Bijutsu, 1990.

Dobbins, James C. *Jodo Shinshu: Shin Buddhism in Medieval Japan.* Bloomington: Indiana University Press, 1989.

Doi, Tsugiyoshi. *Momoyama Decorative Painting.* New York: Weatherhill, 1977.

Dore, Ronald P. *Education in Tokugawa Japan.* Berkeley: University of California Press, 1965.

Draeger, Donn F. *Classical Bujutsu.* New York: Weatherhill, 1996.

Dumoulin, Heinrich. *Zen Buddhism: A History.* Vol. 2, *Japan.* New York: Macmillan, 1990.

Dunn, Charles J. *Everyday Life in Traditional Japan.* Rutland, Vt.: Tuttle Publishing, 1972.

Duus, Peter. *Feudalism in Japan.* 2nd ed. New York: Knopf, 1976.

Earhart, H. Byron. *Japanese Religion: Unity and Diversity.* 4th ed. Belmont, Calif.: Wadsworth, 2004.

Elison, George. *Deus Destroyed: The Image of Christianity in Early Modern Japan.* Cambridge, Mass.: Harvard University Press, 1973.

Elison, George, and Bardwell L. Smith, eds. *Warlords, Artists, and Commoners: Japan in the Sixteenth Century.* Honolulu: University of Hawaii Press, 1981.

Elisseeff, Danielle, and Vadime Elisseeff. *Art of Japan.* New York: Harry N. Abrams, 1985.

Ellwood, Robert S., and Richard B. Pilgrim. *Japanese Religion: A Cultural Perspective.* Englewood Cliffs, N.J.: Prentice-Hall, 1985.

Eng, Robert Y., and Thomas C. Smith. "Peasant Families and Population Control in Eighteenth-Century Japan." *Journal of Interdisciplinary History* 6, no. 3 (1976): 417–445.

Ernst, Earle. *The Kabuki Theatre.* Oxford: Oxford University Press, 1956.

Farris, W. Wayne. "Diseases of the Premodern Period in Japan." In *The Cambridge World History of Human Disease.* Edited by Kenneth Kiple. Cambridge: Cambridge University Press, 1993, 376–84.

Farris, William Wayne. *Heavenly Warriors: The Evolution of Japan's Military, 500–1300.* Cambridge, Mass.: Council on East Asian Studies, Harvard University, 1992.

Faure, Bernard. *The Red Thread: Buddhist Approaches to Sexuality.* Princeton, N.J.: Princeton University Press, 1998.

Fiévé, Nicholas, and Paul Waley, eds. *Japanese Capitals in Historical Perspective: Place, Power and Memory in Kyoto, Edo and Tokyo.* London and New York: RoutledgeCurzon, 2003.

Fischer, Felice, et al. *The Arts of Hon'ami Koetsu, Japanese Renaissance Master.* Philadelphia: Philadelphia Museum or Art, 2000.

Fister, Pat. *Japanese Women Artists, 1600–1900.* Lawrence, Kans.: Spencer Art Museum, 1988.

Fontein, Jan, and Money L. Hickman. *Zen Painting and Calligraphy.* Boston: Museum of Fine Arts, 1970.

Frédéric, Louis. *Daily Life in Japan at the Time of the Samurai, 1185–1603.* New York: Praeger Publishers, 1972.

———, ed. *Japan Encyclopedia.* Cambridge, Mass.: Harvard University Press, 2002.

French, Calvin L. *The Poet-Painters: Buson and His Followers.* Ann Arbor: University of Michigan Press, 1974.

———. *Shiba Kokan: Artist, Innovator, and Pioneer in the Westernization of Japan.* Tokyo: Weatherhill, 1974.

Friday, Karl F., with Seki Humitake. *Legacies of the Sword: The Kashima-Shinryu and Samurai Martial Culture.* Honolulu: University of Hawaii Press, 1997.

Friday, Karl L. *Hired Swords: The Rise of Private Warrior Power in Early Japan.* Stanford, Calif.: Stanford University Press, 1992.

———. *Samurai, Warfare, and the State in Early Medieval Japan.* New York and London: Routledge, 2004.

Fruin, W. Mark. *Kikkoman: Company, Clan, and Community.* Cambridge, Mass.: Harvard University Press, 1983.

Fu, Shen, Glenn D. Lowry, and Ann Yonemura. *From Concept to Context: Approaches to Asian and Islamic Calligraphy.* Washington, D.C.: Freer Gallery, 1986.

Fujikawa, Yu. *Japanese Medicine.* New York: P.B. Hoeber, 1934.

Fujioka, Ryoichi. *Shino and Oribe Ceramics.* Tokyo: Kodansha International, 1977.

———. *Tea Ceremony Utensils.* New York: Weatherhill, 1973.

Fukagawa, H., and D. Pedoe. *Japanese Temple Geometry Problems = Sangaku.* Winnipeg: Charles Babbage Research Centre, 1989.

Gay, Suzanne Marie. *The Moneylenders of Late Medieval Kyoto.* Honolulu: University of Hawaii Press, 2001.

Gerhart, Karen M. *The Eyes of Power: Art and Early Tokugawa Authority.* Honolulu: University of Hawaii Press, 1999.

Gerstle, C. Andrew. *Circles of Fantasy: Convention in the Plays of Chikamatsu.* Cambridge, Mass.: Council on East Asian Studies, Harvard University, 1986.

———. "Flowers of Edo: Kabuki and Its Patrons." In *18th Century Japan: Culture and Society*, edited by C. Andrew Gerstle. Richmond, England: Curzon Press. 1999, 33–50.

———, ed. *18th Century Japan: Culture and Society.* Richmond, U.K.: Curzon, 2000.

———, trans. *Chikamatsu: 5 Late Plays.* New York: Columbia University Press, 2001.

Gerstle, C. Andrew, Kiyoshi Inobe, and William P. Malm. *Theater as Music: The Bunraku Play "Mt. Imo and Mt. Se": An Exemplary Tale of Womanly Virtue.* Ann Arbor: Center for Japanese Studies, University of Michigan, 1990.

Gluckman, Dale, and Sharon Takeda. *When Art Became Fashion: Kosode in Edo Period Japan.* New York and Tokyo: Weatherhill, 1992.

Goble, Andrew Edmund. *Kenmu: Go-Daigo's Revolution.* Cambridge, Mass.: Council on East Asian Studies, Harvard University, 1996.

Goble, Andrew E. "Medicine and New Knowledge in Medieval Japan: Kajiwara Shozen (1266–1337) and the *Man'anpo* (1)." *Journal of the Japan Society of Medical History (Nihon Ishigaku Zasshi)* 47, no. 1 (2001): 193–226.

———. "Medicine and New Knowledge in Medieval Japan: Kajiwara Shozen (1266–1337) and the *Man'anpo* (2)." *Journal of the Japan Society of Medical History (Nihon Ishigaku Zasshi)* 47, no. 2 (2001): 432–452.

Goff, Janet. *Noh Drama and the Tale of Genji: The Art of Allusion in Fifteen Classical Plays.* Princeton, N.J.: Princeton University Press, 1991.

Goodman, Grant K. *Japan: The Dutch Experience*. London: Athlone Press, 1986.

Goodwin, Janet. *Alms and Vagabonds: Buddhist Temples and Popular Patronage in Medieval Japan*. Honolulu: University of Hawaii Press, 1994.

Grilli, Elise. *The Art of the Japanese Screen*. New York: Weatherhill, 1970.

Grossberg, Kenneth A. *Japan's Renaissance: The Politics of the Muromachi Bakufu*. Cambridge, Mass.: Council on East Asian Studies, Harvard University, 1981.

Grossberg, Kenneth A., and Nobuhisa Kanamoto, trans. *The Laws of the Muromachi Bakufu: Kemmu Shikimoku (1336) and the Muromachi Tsuikaho*. Tokyo: Sophia University, 1981.

Gunji, Masakatsu. *Buyo: The Classical Dance*. New York: Walker/Weatherhill, 1970.

———. *Kabuki*. Tokyo: Kodansha International, 1969.

———. *The Kabuki Guide*. Tokyo: Kodansha International, 1987.

Guth, Christine. *Art of Edo Japan: The Artist and the City, 1615–1868*. New York: Harry N. Abrams, 1996.

Habein, Yaeko Sato. *The History of the Japanese Written Language*. Tokyo: University of Tokyo Press, 1984.

Hadamitzky, Wolfgang, and Mark Spahn. *Kanji and Kana: A Handbook of the Japanese Writing System*. Rev. ed. Boston: Tuttle Publishing, 2003.

Hall, John Whitney. *Government and Local Power in Japan, 500–1700: A Study Based on Bizen Province*. Princeton, N.J.: Princeton University Press, 1966.

———. *Japan: From Prehistory to Modern Times*. New York: Dell Publishing, 1970.

———, ed. *The Cambridge History of Japan*. Vol. 4, *Early Modern Japan*. Cambridge: Cambridge University Press, 1991.

Hall, John Whitney, and Toyoda Takeshi, eds, *Japan in the Muromachi Age*. Berkeley: University of California Press, 1977.

Hall, John Whitney, and Jeffrey P. Mass, eds. *Medieval Japan: Essays in Institutional History*. New Haven, Conn.: Yale University Press, 1974.

Hall, John Whitney, and Marius B. Jansen, eds. *Studies in the Institutional History of Early Modern Japan*. Princeton, N.J.: Princeton University Press, 1968.

Hall, John Whitney, Nagahara Keiji, and Kozo Yamamura, eds. *Japan Before Tokugawa: Political Consolidation and Economic Growth, 1500 to 1650*. Princeton, N.J.: Princeton University Press, 1981.

Hane, Mikiso. *Premodern Japan: A Historical Survey*. Boulder, Colo.: Westview Press, 1991.

Hanley, Susan B. *Everyday Things in Premodern Japan: The Hidden Legacy of Material Culture*. Berkeley: University of California Press, 1997.

———. "Fertility, Mortality, and Life Expectancy in Pre-Modern Japan." *Population Studies* 28 (1974): 127–142.

Hanley, Susan B., and Kozo Yamamura. *Economic and Demographic Change in Preindustrial Japan, 1600–1868*. Princeton, N.J.: Princeton University Press, 1977.

Hanley, Susan B., and Arthur P. Wolf, eds. *Family and Population in East Asian History*. Stanford, Calif.: Stanford University Press, 1985.

Hare, Thomas Blenman. *Zeami's Style: The Noh Plays of Zeami Motokiyo*. Stanford, Calif.: Stanford University Press, 1986.

Harich-Schneider, Eta. *A History of Japanese Music*. Oxford: Oxford University Press, 1973.

Harootunian, Harry D. *Things Seen and Unseen: Discourse and Ideology in Tokugawa Nativism*. Chicago: University of Chicago Press, 1988.

———. *Toward Restoration: the Growth of Political Consciousness in Tokugawa Japan*. Berkeley: University of California Press, 1970.

Harries, Phillip T., trans. *The Poetic Memoirs of Lady Daibu*. Stanford, Calif.: Stanford University Press, 1981.

Harris, Victor, and Ken Matsushima. *Kamakura: The Renaissance of Japanese Sculpture, 1185–1333*. London: British Museum, 1991.

Hashimoto, Fumio. *Architecture in the Shoin Style: Japanese Feudal Residences*. New York: Kodansha International, 1981.

Hauser, William B. *Economic Institutional Change in Tokugawa Japan: Osaka and the Kinai Cotton Trade*. Cambridge: Cambridge University Press, 1974.

———. "Why So Few? Women Household Heads in Osaka Choin Families." *Journal of Family History* 11 (1986): 343–351.

Hayakawa, Masao. *The Garden Art of Japan*. New York: Weatherhill, 1973.

Hayashiya, Seizo. *Chanoyu: The Japanese Tea Ceremony*. Tokyo: Weatherhill and Japan Society, 1979.

Hayashiya, Tatsusaburo, Masao Nakamura, and Seizo Hayashiya. *Japanese Arts and the Tea Ceremony*. Tokyo and New York: Weatherhill, 1974.

Henderson, Dan F., and James L. Anderson. "Japanese Law: A Profile." *An Introduction to Japanese Civilization*, edited by Arthur E. Tiedemann. New York: Columbia University Press, 1974, 569–91.

Herrigel, Eugen. *Zen in the Art of Archery*. New York: Pantheon Books, 1953.

Hesselink, Reiner H. *Prisoners from Nambu: Reality and Make-Believe in Seventeenth-Century Japanese Diplomacy*. University of Hawaii Press, 2001.

Hibbett, Howard S. *The Floating World in Japanese Fiction*. New York: Oxford University Press, 1959.

Hickman, Money L. *Painters of Edo Japan, 1615–1868*. Indianapolis: Indianapolis Museum of Art, 2000.

———, ed. *Japan's Golden Age: Momoyama*. New Haven, Conn.: Yale University Press, 1996.

Hillier, Jack. *The Art of the Japanese Book*. 2 vols. London: Sotheby's Publications, 1987.

Hinago, Moto. *Japanese Castles*. New York: Kodansha International, 1986.

Hirai, Kiyoshi. *Feudal Architecture of Japan*. New York: Weatherhill, 1973.

Hirota, Dennis. *Wind in the Pines: Classic Writings of the Way of Tea as a Buddhist Path*. Fremont, Calif.: Asian Humanities Press, 1995.

———, trans. *No Abode: The Record of Ippen*. Honolulu: University of Hawaii Press, 1997.

Hisamatsu, Sen'ichi. *The Vocabulary of Japanese Literary Aesthetics*. Tokyo: The Centre for East Asian Cultural Studies, 1963.

———, ed. *Biographical Dictionary of Japanese Literature*. Tokyo: Kodansha International, 1976.

Hisamatsu, Shin'ichi. *Zen and the Fine Arts*. Tokyo: Kodansha International, 1971.

Hoff, Frank. *Song, Dance, Storytelling: Aspects of the Performing Arts in Japan*. Ithaca, N.Y.: China-Japan Program, Cornell University, 1978.

Holtom, Daniel Clarence. *The Japanese Enthronement Ceremonies*. Tokyo: Sophia University, 1972.

Honjo, Eijiro. *The Social and Economic History of Japan*. New York: Russell & Russell, 1965 [1935].

Hori, Ichiro. *Folk Religion in Japan: Continuity and Change*. Chicago: University of Chicago Press, 1968.

Hsia, Emil C. H., Ilza Veith, and Robert H. Geertsma, trans. *The Essentials of Medicine in Ancient China and Japan: Yasuyori Tamba's Ishimpo*. 2 vols. Leiden the Netherlands: E.J. Brill, 1986.

Huber, Kristina R. *Women in Japanese Society: An Annotated Bibliography of Selected English Language Materials*. Westport, Conn.: Greenwood Press, 1992.

Hume, Nancy G., ed. *Japanese Aesthetics and Culture: A Reader*. Albany, N.Y.: State University of New York Press, 1995.

Hurst, G. Cameron, III. *Armed Martial Arts of Japan: Swordsmanship and Archery*. New Haven, Conn.: Yale University Press, 1998.

———. "Death, Honor, and Loyalty: The Bushido Ideal." *Philosophy East & West* 40, no. 4 (1990): 511–527.

Hyoe, Murakami, and Thomas J. Harper, eds. *Great Historical Figures of Japan*. Tokyo: Japan Culture Institute, 1978.

Ihara, Saikaku. *Five Women Who Loved Love*. Translated by Wm. Theodore deBary. Rutland and Tokyo: Tuttle, 1956.

———. *The Great Mirror of Male Love*. Translated by Paul Schalow. Stanford, Calif.: Stanford University Press, 1990.

Ikegami, Eiko. *The Taming of the Samurai: Honorific Individualism and the Making of Modern Japan*. Cambridge, Mass.: Harvard University Press, 1995.

Impey, Oliver. *The Art of the Japanese Folding Screen*. New York: Weatherhill, 1997.

———. *The Early Porcelain Kilns of Japan: Arita in the First Half of the Seventeenth Century*. Oxford: Clarendon Press, 1996.

Inaba, Kazuya, and Shigenobu Nakayama. *Japanese Homes and Lifestyles: An Illustrated Journey through History*. Tokyo and New York: Kodansha International, 2000.

Inoura, Yoshinobu, and Toshio Kawatake. *The Traditional Theater of Japan*. New York: Weatherhill, 1981.

Irvine, Gregory. *The Japanese Sword: The Soul of the Samurai*. Trumbull, Conn.: Weatherhill, 2000.

Ito, Teiji. *The Gardens of Japan*. New York: Kodansha International, 1984.

———. *The Japanese Garden: An Approach to Nature*. New Haven, Conn.: Yale University Press, 1972.

Iwamiya, Takeji. *Imperial Gardens of Japan*. New York: Walker Weatherhill, 1970.

Iwao, Seiichi, ed. *Biographical Dictionary of Japanese History*. New York: Kodansha International, 1978.

Jannetta, Ann Bowman. "Diseases of the Early Modern Period in Japan." In *The Cambridge World History of Human Disease*. Edited by Kenneth Kiple. Cambridge: Cambridge University Press, 1993, 385–388.

———. *Epidemics and Mortality in Early Modern Japan*. Princeton, N.J.: Princeton University Press, 1987.

Jansen, Marius B. *China in the Tokugawa World*. Cambridge, Mass.: Harvard University Press, 1992.

———. *The Making of Modern Japan*. Cambridge, Mass.: Harvard University Press, 2000.

———, ed. *The Cambridge History of Japan*. Vol. 5, *The Nineteenth Century*. Cambridge: Cambridge University Press, 1989.

———, ed. *Warrior Rule in Japan*. New York: Cambridge University Press, 1995.

Jansen, Marius B., and Gilbert Rozman, eds. *Japan in Transition: From Tokugawa to Meiji*. Princeton, N.J.: Princeton University Press, 1986.

Japan House Gallery. *Spectacular Helmets of Japan, 16th–19th Century*. New York: Japan Society, 1985.

Japan: An Illustrated Encyclopedia. 2 vols. Tokyo: Kodansha, 1993.

Jenkins, Donald. *The Floating World Revisited*. Portland, Oreg.: Portland Art Museum, 1993.

Jochi, Shigeru. "The Dawn of *Wasan* (Japanese Mathematics)." In *Mathematics Across Cultures: The History of Non-Western Mathematics*. Edited by Helaine Selin. Dordrecht and Boston: Kluwer Academic Publishers, 2000, 423–54.

Johnston, William D. *The Modern Epidemic: A History of Tuberculosis in Japan*. Cambridge, Mass.: Council on East Asian Studies, Harvard University, 1995.

Kageyama, Haruki. *The Arts of Shinto*. New York: Weatherhill, 1973.

———. *Shinto Arts: Nature, Gods, and Man in Japan*. New York: Japan Society, 1976.

Kakudo, Yoshiko. *The Art of Japan*. San Francisco: Asian Art Museum, 1991.

Kanazawa, Hiroshi. *Japanese Ink Painting: Early Zen Masterpieces*. New York: Kodansha International, 1979.

Kanda, Christine Guth. *Shinzo: Hachiman Imagery and Its Development*. Cambridge, Mass.: Council on East Asian Studies, Harvard University, 1985.

Kapp, Leon, Hiroko Kapp, and Yoshindo Yoshihara. *The Craft of the Japanese Sword*. Tokyo: Kodansha, 1987.

Kashiwara, Yusen, and Sonoda Koyu, eds. *Shapers of Japanese Buddhism*. Tokyo: Kosei Publishing, 1994.

Kassel, Marleen. *Tokugawa Confucian Education: The Kangien Academy of Hirose Tanso (1782–1856)*. Albany: State University of New York Press, 1996.

Kasulis, Thomas P. *Zen Action, Zen Person*. Honolulu: The University of Hawaii Press, 1981.

Kato, Shuichi. *A History of Japanese Literature*. Vol. 1, *The First Thousand Years*. Tokyo: Kodansha International, 1981.

———. *A History of Japanese Literature*. Vol. 2, *The Years of Isolation*. Tokyo: Kodansha International, 1990.

———. *A History of Japanese Literature*. Vol. 3, *The Modern Years*. Tokyo: Kodansha International, 1990.

Katsu, Kokichi. *Musui's Story: The Autobiography of a Tokugawa Samurai*. Tucson: University of Arizona Press, 1988.

Keene, Donald. *Bunraku: The Art of the Japanese Puppet Theatre*. Tokyo: Kodansha International, 1965.

———. *The Japanese Discovery of Europe, 1720–1830*. Rev. ed. Stanford, Calif.: Stanford University Press, 1969.

———. "Literature." *An Introduction to Japanese Civilization*. Edited by Arthur E. Tiedemann.

New York: Columbia University Press, 1974, 375–421.

———. *No and Bunraku: Two Forms of Japanese Theatre*. New York: Columbia University Press, 1990.

———. *No: The Classical Theatre of Japan*. Tokyo and Palo Alto, Calif.: Kodansha International, 1966.

———. *Seeds in the Heart: Japanese Literature from Earliest Times to the Late Sixteenth Century*. New York: Henry Holt, 1993.

———. *Travelers of a Hundred Ages: The Japanese as Revealed Through 1,000 Years of Diaries*. New York: Henry Holt, 1989.

———. *World within Walls: Japanese Literature of the Pre-Modern Era, 1600–1867*. New York: Holt, Rinehart and Winston, 1976.

———. *Yoshimasa and the Silver Pavilion: The Creation of the Soul of Japan*. New York: Columbia University Press, 2003.

———, ed. *Anthology of Japanese Literature from the Earliest Era to the Mid-Nineteenth Century*. New York: Grove Press, 1955.

———, ed. *Twenty Plays of the No Theatre*. New York: Columbia University Press, 1970.

———, trans. *Essays in Idleness: The Tzurezuregusa of Kenko*. New York: Columbia University Press, 1967.

———, trans. *Major Plays of Chikamatsu*. New York: Columbia University Press, 1961.

Keirstead, Thomas. *The Geography of Power in Medieval Japan*. Princeton, N.J.: Princeton University Press, 1992.

Kennedy, Alan. *Japanese Costume*. Paris: Adam Biro, 1990.

Kenny, Don. *A Guide to Kyogen*. 4th ed. Tokyo: Hinoki Shoten, 1990.

———, comp. *The Kyogen Book: An Anthology of Japanese Classical Comedies*. Tokyo: Japan Times, 1989.

Kim, Hee-jin. *Dogen Kigen—Mystical Realist*. Tuscon: University of Arizona Press, 1975.

King, Winston L. *Zen and the Way of the Sword: Arming the Samurai Psyche*. Oxford: Oxford University Press, 1993.

Kishibe, Shigeo. *The Traditional Music of Japan*. 2nd ed. Tokyo: Japan Foundation, 1984.

Kitagawa, Hiroshi, and Bruce T. Tsuchida, trans. *The Tale of the Heike*. Tokyo: University of Tokyo Press, 1975.

Kitagawa, Joseph M. *Religion in Japanese History*. New York: Columbia University Press, 1966.

Kiyota, Minoru. *Shingon Buddhism: Theory and Practice*. Los Angeles: Buddhist Books International, 1978.

Knapp, Bettina L. *Images of Japanese Women: A Westerner's View*. Troy, N.Y.: Whitston Publishing Co., 1992.

Kodansha Encyclopedia of Japan. 9 vols. Tokyo and New York: Kodansha International, 1983.

Komparu, Kunio. *The Noh Theatre: Principles and Perspectives*. New York and Tokyo: Weatherhill/Tankosha, 1983.

Kondo, Ichitaro. *Japanese Genre Painting: The Lively Art of Renaissance Japan*. Tokyo and Rutland, Vt.: C. E. Tuttle Co., 1961.

Konishi, Jin'ichi. *A History of Japanese Literature*. Vol. 2, *The Early Middle Ages*. Princeton, N.J.: Princeton University Press, 1986.

———. *A History of Japanese Literature*. Vol. 3, *The High Middle Ages*. Princeton, N.J.: Princeton University Press, 1991.

Kornicki, Peter F. *The Book in Japan: A Cultural History from the Beginnings to the Nineteenth Century*. Leiden, The Netherlands: Brill, 1998.

Kornicki, Peter F., and I. J. McMullen, eds. *Religion in Japan: Arrows to Heaven and Earth*. Cambridge: Cambridge University Press, 1996.

Koschmann, J. Victor. *The Mito Ideology: Discourse, Reform, and Insurrection in Late Tokugawa Japan, 1790–1864*. Berkeley: University of California Press, 1987.

Kuck, Loraine. *The World of the Japanese Garden*. Corrected ed. New York: Weatherhill, 1970.

Kuitert, Wybe. *Themes in the History of Japanese Garden Art*. Rev. ed. Honolulu: University of Hawaii Press, 2002.

Kunio, Minami, and Yoshiro Tamura. *Art of the Lotus Sutra*. Tokyo: Kosei Publishing, 1987.

Kure, Mitsuo. *Samurai: An Illustrated History*. Boston: Tuttle Publishing, 2001.

Kuriyama, Shigehisa. "Between Mind and Eye: Japanese Anatomy in the Eighteenth Century." In *Paths to Asian Medical Knowledge*. Edited by

Charles Leslie and Allan Young. Berkeley: University of California Press, 1992, 21–43.

———. "Concepts of Disease in East Asia." In *The Cambridge World History of Human Disease*, edited by Kenneth Kiple, 52–8. Cambridge: Cambridge University Press, 1993.

Kuroda, Taizo, Melinda Takeuchi, and Uzu Yamane. *Worlds Seen and Imagined: Japanese Screens from the Idemitsu Museum of Arts*. New York: Asia Society, 1995.

Kuroda, Toshio. "Shinto in the History of Japanese Religion." *Journal of Japanese Studies* 7, no. 1 (1981): 1–21.

Kuwayama, George. *Shippo: The Art of Enameling in Japan*. Los Angeles: Far Eastern Art Council, 1987.

LaFleur, William R. "Hungry Ghosts and Hungry People: Somaticity and Rationality in Medieval Japan." In *Fragments for a History of the Human Body, Part 1*. Edited by Michael Feher. New York: Zone Publications, 1989, 270–303.

———. *The Karma of Words: Buddhism and the Literary Arts in Medieval Japan*. Berkeley: University of California Press, 1983.

———. *Liquid Life: Abortion and Buddhism in Japan*. Princeton, N.J.: Princeton University Press, 1992.

Lamers, Jeroen P. *Japonius Tyrannus: The Japanese Warlord, Oda Nobunaga Reconsidered*. Leiden, The Netherlands: Hotei Publishing, 2000.

Lane, Richard. *Images from the Floating World: The Japanese Print*. New York: Putnam, 1978.

Lee, Sherman E. *A History of Far Eastern Art*. Englewood Cliffs, N.J.: Prentice Hall and Abrams, 1994.

———. *The Sketchbooks of Hiroshige*. George Braziller, 2001.

Lee, Sherman E., Michael R. Cunningham, and Ursula Korneitchouck. *One Thousand Years of Japanese Art, 650–1650: From the Cleveland Museum of Art*. New York: Japan Society, 1981.

Lee, Sherman E., Michael R. Cunningham, and James T. Ulak. *Reflections of Reality in Japanese Art*. Cleveland: Cleveland Museum of Art, 1983.

Leggett, Trevor. *Samurai Zen: The Warrior Koans*. London and New York: Routledge, 2003.

Leiter, Samuel L., ed. *A Kabuki Reader: History and Performance*. Armonk, N.Y.: M. E. Sharpe, 2002.

Leslie, Charles, and Allan Young, eds. *Paths to Asian Medical Knowledge*. Berkeley: University of California Press, 1992.

Leslie, Charles, ed. *Asian Medical Systems: A Comparative Study*. Berkeley: University of California Press, 1976.

Leupp, Gary P. *Interracial Intimacy in Japan: Western Men and Japanese Women, 1543–1900*. New York: Continuum, 2003.

———. *Male Colors: The Construction of Homosexuality in Tokugawa Japan*. Berkeley: University of California Press, 1995.

———. *Servants, Shophands, and Laborers in the Cities of Tokugawa Japan*. Princeton, N.J.: Princeton University Press, 1992.

Leutner, Robert W. *Shikitei Samba and the Comic Tradition in Edo Fiction*. Cambridge, Mass.: Council on East Asian Studies, Harvard University, 1985.

Lidin, Olof G. *Tanegashima: The Arrival of Europe in Japan*. Copenhagen: Nordic Institute of Asian Studies, 2002.

Lillehoj, Elizabeth. *Women in the Eyes of Man: Images of Women in Japanese Art*. Chicago: Field Museum and DePaul University, 1995.

Link, Howard A., et al. *Exquisite Visions: Rimpa Paintings from Japan*. Honolulu: Honolulu Academy of Arts, 1980.

Little, Stephen. *Visions of the Dharma*. Honolulu: Honolulu Academy of Arts, 1991.

Lock, Margaret M. *East Asian Medicine in Urban Japan: Varieties of Medical Experience*. Berkeley: University of California Press, 1980.

Lu, David J. *Japan: A Documentary History*. Armonk, N.Y.: M. E. Sharpe, 1997.

Malm, William P. *Six Hidden Views of Japanese Music*. Berkeley: University of California Press, 1986.

———. "Some of Japan's Music and Musical Principles," in *Music of Many Cultures: An Introduction*. Edited by Elizabeth May. Berkeley: University of California Press, 1980, 48–62.

———. *Traditional Japanese Music and Musical Instruments*. New ed. Tokyo and New York: Kodansha International, 2000.

Marks, Alfred H., and Barry D. Bort. *Guide to Japanese Prose*. 2nd ed. Boston: G. K. Hall, 1984.

Marra, Michele. *The Aesthetics of Discontent: Politics and Reclusion in Medieval Japanese Literature.* Honolulu: University of Hawaii Press, 1991.

Maruyama, Masao. *Studies in the Intellectual History of Tokugawa Japan.* Tokyo: University of Tokyo Press, 1974.

Maruyama, Nobuhiko. *Bushi no yosoi* (Clothes of Samurai Warriors). Kyoto: Kyoto Shoin, 1994.

Mason, Penelope. *History of Japanese Art.* 2nd ed. Revised by Donald Dinwiddie. Upper Saddle River, N.J.: Pearson Prentice Hall, 2005.

Mason, R. H. P., and J. G. Caiger. *A History of Japan.* Rev. ed. Rutland, Vt.: Tuttle Publishing, 1997.

Mass, Jeffrey P. *Antiquity and Anachronism in Japanese History.* Stanford, Calif.: Stanford University Press, 1992.

———. *The Development of Kamakura Rule, 1180–1250: A History with Documents.* Stanford, Calif.: Stanford University Press, 1979.

———. *Lordship and Inheritance in Early Medieval Japan: A Study of the Kamakura Soryo System.* Stanford, Calif.: Stanford University Press, 1989.

———. *Warrior Government in Early Medieval Japan: A Study of the Kamakura Bakufu, Shugo, and Jito.* New Haven: Yale University Press, 1974.

———, ed. *Court and Bakufu in Japan: Essays in Kamakura History.* New Haven, Conn.: Yale University Press, 1982.

———, ed. *The Origins of Japan's Medieval World: Courtiers, Clerics, Warriors, and Peasants in the Fourteenth Century.* Stanford, Calif.: Stanford University Press, 1997.

Mass, Jeffrey P., and William B. Hauser, eds. *The Bakufu in Japanese History.* Stanford, Calif.: Stanford University Press, 1985.

Matisoff, Susan. *The Legend of Semimaru: Blind Musician of Japan.* New York: Columbia University Press, 1978.

Matsunaga, Daigan, and Alicia Matsunaga. *The Foundation of Japanese Buddhism.* 2 vols. Los Angeles: Buddhist Books International, 1974–1976.

Matsuo, Basho. *The Narrow Road to the Deep North and Other Travel Sketches.* Translated by Yuasa Nobuyuki. Harmondsworth, U.K.: Penguin Books, 1966.

Matsushita, Takaaki. *Ink Painting.* New York: Weatherhill, 1974.

Mayo, Marlene J. "Late Tokugawa and Early Meiji Japan," in *An Introduction to Japanese Civilization.* Edited by Arthur E. Tiedemann. New York: Columbia University Press, 1974, 131–180.

McCallum, Donald F. *Zenkoji and Its Icon: A Study in Medieval Japanese Religious Art.* Princeton, N.J.: Princeton University Press, 1994.

McClain James, L. *Kanazawa: A Seventeenth-Century Japanese Castle Town.* New Haven, Conn.: Yale University Press, 1982.

McClain, James L., John M. Merriman, and Ugawa Kaoru, eds. *Edo and Paris: Urban Life and the State in the Early Modern Era.* Ithaca, N.Y.: Cornell University Press, 1994.

McClain, James L., and Wakita Osamu, eds. *Osaka: The Merchants' Capital of Early Modern Japan.* Ithaca, N.Y.: Cornell University Press, 1999.

McCullough, Helen Craig, ed. *Classical Japanese Prose: An Anthology.* Stanford, Calif.: Stanford University Press, 1990.

———, trans. *The Taiheiki: A Chronicle of Medieval Japan.* New York: Columbia University Press, 1959.

———, trans. *The Tale of the Heike.* Stanford, Calif.: Stanford University Press, 1988.

———, trans. *Yoshitsune: A Fifteenth-Century Japanese Chronicle.* Stanford, Calif.: Stanford University Press, 1966.

McMullin, Neil. *Buddhism and the State in Sixteenth-Century Japan.* Princeton, N.J.: Princeton University Press, 1984.

Mikami, Tsugio. *The Art of Japanese Ceramics.* Tokyo and New York: Heibonsha/Weatherhill, 1972.

Mikami, Yoshio. *The Development of Mathematics in China and Japan.* 2nd ed. New York: Chelsea Publishing, 1974.

Miller, David. *Samurai Warriors.* New York: St. Martin's Press, 1999.

Miller, Roy Andrew. *The Japanese Language.* Chicago: University of Chicago Press, 1967.

Milton, Giles. *Samurai William: The Englishman Who Opened Japan.* New York: Farrar, Straus and Giroux, 2003.

Miner, Earl, and Hiroko Odagiri. *The Monkey's Straw Rain-Coat and Other Poetry of the Basho School.* Princeton, N.J.: Princeton University Press, 1981.

Miner, Earl, Hiroko Odagiri, and Robert E. Morrell. *The Princeton Companion to Classical Japanese Literature*. Princeton, N.J.: Princeton University Press, 1985.

Miner, Earl. *Japanese Linked Poetry: An Account with Translations of Renga and Haikai Sequences*. Princeton, N.J.: Princeton University Press, 1979.

———. *Japanese Poetic Diaries*. Berkeley: University of California Press, 1969.

Mitchelhill, Jennifer, and David Green. *Castles of the Samurai: Power and Beauty*. London: Kodansha Europe, 2003.

Miyajima, Shin'ichi, Yasuhiro Sato, and George Kuwayama. *Japanese Ink Painting*. Los Angeles: Los Angeles County Museum of Art, 1985.

Miyamoto, Musashi. *The Book of Five Rings*. Translated by William Scott Wilson. Tokyo: Kodansha, 2002.

Mizuo, Hiroshi. *Edo Painting: Sotatsu and Korin*. New York: Weatherhill, 1972.

Momoyama: Japanese Art in the Age of Grandeur. New York: Metropolitan Museum of Art, 1975.

Mori, Hisashi. *Japanese Portrait Sculpture*. New York: Kodansha International, 1977.

———. *Sculpture of the Kamakura Period*. New York: Weatherhill, 1974.

Morley, Carolyn A. *Transformation, Miracles, and Mischief: The Mountain Priest Plays of Kyogen*. Ithaca, N.Y.: Cornell University East Asia Papers, 1993.

Morrell, Robert E. *Early Kamakura Buddhism: A Minority Report*. Berkeley, Calif.: Asian Humanities Press, 1987.

Morris, Ivan. *The Nobility of Failure: Tragic Heroes in the History of Japan*. New York: Holt, Rinehart and Winston, 1975.

———. *The Tale of Genji Scroll*. Tokyo: Kodansha International, 1971.

Morris, Mark. "Group Portrait with Artist: Yosa Buson and His Patrons," in *18th Century Japan: Culture and Society*. Edited by C. Andrew Gerstle. Richmond, U.K.: Curzon Press, 1999, 87–105.

Morris-Suzuki, Tessa. *The Technological Transformation of Japan: From the Seventeenth to the Twenty-First Century*. Cambridge: Cambridge University Press, 1994.

Morse, Anne Nishimura, and Samuel Crowell Morse. *Object as Insight: Japanese Buddhist Art and Ritual*. Katonah, N.Y.: Katonah Museum of Art, 1995.

Morton, W. Scott. *Japan: Its History and Culture*. 3rd ed. New York: McGraw-Hill, 1994.

Mostow, Joshua S., Norman Bryson, and Maribeth Graybill. *Gender and Power: In the Japanese Visual Field*. Honolulu: University of Hawaii Press, 2003.

Mulhern, Chieko I., ed. *Heroic with Grace: Legendary Women of Japan*. Armonk, N.Y.: M.E. Sharpe, 1991.

———, ed. *Japanese Women Writers: A Bio-Critical Sourcebook*. Westport, Conn.: Greenwood Press, 1994.

Munsterberg, Hugo. "The Art of Japan," in *An Introduction to Japanese Civilization*. Edited by Arthur E. Tiedemann. New York: Columbia University Press, 1974, 329–74.

———. *The Arts of Japan: An Illustrated History*. Tokyo: Tuttle, 1957.

Murase, Miyeko. *Bridge of Dreams: The Mary Griggs Burke Collection of Japanese Art*. New Haven, Conn.: Yale University Press, 2000.

———. *Byobu: Japanese Screens from New York Collections*. New York: Asia Society, 1971.

———. *Emaki: Narrative Scrolls from Japan*. New York: Asia Society, 1983.

———. *Tales of Japan: Scrolls and Prints from the New York Public Library*. New York: Oxford University Press, 1986.

———. *Turning Point: Oribe and the Arts of Sixteenth-Century Japan*. New Haven, Conn.: Yale University Press, 2003.

Nagayo, Takeo. *History of Japanese Medicine in the Edo Era: Its Social and Cultural Backgrounds*. Nagoya, Japan: University of Nagoya Press, 1991.

Naito, Akira. *Edo, the City That Became Tokyo: An Illustrated History*. Illustrated by Kazuo Hozumi. Tokyo: Kodansha International, 2003.

Najita, Tetsuo. *Visions of Virtue in Tokugawa Japan: The Kaitokudo Merchant Academy of Osaka*. Chicago: University of Chicago Press, 1987.

———, ed. *Tokugawa Political Writings*. Cambridge: Cambridge University Press, 1998.

Najita, Tetsuo, and Irwin Scheiner, eds. *Japanese Thought in the Tokugawa Period, 1600–1868:*

Methods and Metaphors. Chicago: University of Chicago Press, 1978.

Nakai, Kate Wildman. *Shogunal Politics: Arai Hakuseki and the Premises of Tokugawa Rule*. Cambridge, Mass.: Council on East Asian Studies, Harvard University, 1988.

Nakane, Chie, and Shinzaburo Oishi, eds. *Tokugawa Japan: The Social and Economic Antecedents of Modern Japan*. Tokyo: University of Tokyo Press, 1990.

Nakata, Yujiro. *The Art of Japanese Calligraphy*. New York: Weatherhill, 1973.

Nakayama, Shigeru. "Japanese Scientific Thought," in *Dictionary of Scientific Biography*. Vol. 15, supplement 1. Edited by Charles C. Gillispie. New York: Charles Scribner's Sons, 1978, 728–758.

Nishi, Kazuo, and Kazuo Hozumi, *What Is Japanese Architecture?* New York: Kodansha International, 1996.

Nishikawa, Kyotaro, and Emily J. Sano. *The Great Age of Japanese Buddhist Sculpture A.D. 600–1300*. Fort Worth, Tex.: Kimball Art Museum, 1982.

Nishiyama, Matsunosuke. *Edo Culture: Daily Life and Diversions in Urban Japan, 1600–1868*. Honolulu: University of Hawaii Press, 1997.

Nitschke, Günter. *Japanese Gardens: Right Angle and Natural Form*. Cologne, Germany: Taschen Verlag, 1999.

Noma, Seiroku. *The Arts of Japan*. 2 vols. Tokyo: Kodansha International, 1967.

———. *Japanese Costumes and Textile Arts*. New York: Weatherhill, 1974.

Nosco, Peter. *Remembering Paradise: Nativism and Nostalgia in Eighteenth-Century Japan*. Cambridge, Mass.: Council on East Asian Studies, Harvard University, 1990.

———, ed. *Confucianism and Tokugawa Culture*. Honolulu: University of Hawaii Press, 1984.

Numata, Jiro. *Western Learning: A Short History of the Study of Western Science in Early Modern Japan*. Tokyo: Japan-Netherlands Institute, 1992.

Ohnuki-Tierney, Emiko. *Illness and Culture in Contemporary Japan: An Anthropological View*. Cambridge: Cambridge University Press, 1984.

Okamoto Yoshitomo. *The Namban Art of Japan*. New York and Tokyo, Weatherhill/Heibonsha, 1972.

Okawa, Naomi. *Edo Architecture: Katsura and Nikko*. New York: Weatherhill, 1975.

Okazaki, Joji. *Pure Land Buddhist Painting*. New York: Kodansha International, 1977.

Okudaira, Hideo. *Narrative Picture Scrolls*. New York: Weatherhill, 1973.

Okyo and the Maruyama-Shijo School of Japanese Painting. St. Louis: St. Louis Art Museum, 1980.

Ono, Sokyo. *Shinto: The Kami Way*. Tokyo and Rutland, Vt.: Bridgeway Press, 1962.

Ooms, Herman. *Tokugawa Ideology: Early Constructs, 1570–1680*. Princeton, N.J.: Princeton University Press, 1985.

———. *Tokugawa Village Practice: Class, Status, Power, Law*. Berkeley: University of California Press, 1996.

Ortolani, Benito. *The Japanese Theatre: From Shamanistic Ritual to Contemporary Pluralism*. Rev. ed. Princeton, N.J.: Princeton University Press, 1995.

Otsuka, Yasuo. "Chinese Traditional Medicine in Japan," in *Asian Medical Systems: A Comparative Study*. Edited by Charles Leslie. Berkeley: University of California Press, 1976, 322–40.

Packard, Jerrold M. *Sons of Heaven: A Portrait of the Japanese Monarchy*. New York: Scribner's, 1987.

Paine, Robert Treat, and Alexander Soper. *The Art and Architecture of Japan*. 3rd ed. Baltimore: Penguin, 1981.

Pandey, Rajyashree. *Writing and Renunciation in Medieval Japan: The Works of the Poet-Priest Kamo no Chomei*. Ann Arbor: Center for Japanese Studies, University of Michigan, 1998.

Papinot, Edmond. *Historical and Geographical Dictionary of Japan*. Rutland, Vt.: C.E. Tuttle, 1972.

Parker, Joseph D. *Zen Buddhist Landscape Arts of Early Muromachi Japan (1336–1573)*. Albany: State University of New York Press, 1999.

Passin, Herbert. *Society and Education in Japan*. New York: Teachers College, Columbia University, 1965.

Payne, Richard K., ed. *Re-visioning "Kamakura" Buddhism*. Honolulu: University of Hawaii Press, 1998.

Pekarik, Andrew J. *Japanese Lacquer, 1600–1900*. New York: Metropolitan Museum of Art, 1980.

Perkins, George W. *The Clear Mirror: A Chronicle of the Japanese Court during the Kamakura Period*

(1185–1333). Stanford, Calif.: Stanford University Press, 1998.

Perrin, Noel. *Giving Up the Gun: Japan's Reversion to the Sword, 1543–1879.* Boston: David R. Godine Publisher, 1979.

Pflugfelder, Gregory M. *Cartographies of Desire: Male-Male Sexuality in Japanese Discourse 1600–1950.* Berkeley: University of California Press, 1999.

Phillips, Quitman E. *The Practices of Painting in Japan, 1475–1500.* Stanford, Calif.: Stanford University Press, 2000.

Picken, Stuart D. B. *Essentials of Shinto: An Analytical Guide to Principal Teachings.* Westport, Conn.: Greenwood Press, 1994.

Pilgrim, Richard B. *Buddhism and the Arts of Japan.* 2nd rev. ed. Chambersburg, Pa.: Anima Publications, 1993.

Pineau, Roger, ed. *The Japan Expedition, 1852–1854: The Personal Journal of Commodore Matthew C. Perry.* Washington, D.C.: Smithsonian Institution Press, 1968.

Pitelka, Morgan. *Japanese Tea Culture: Art, History, and Practice.* New York: RoutledgeCurzon, 2003.

Plutschow, Herbert, and Hideichi Fukuda. *Four Japanese Travel Diaries of the Middle Ages.* Ithaca, N.Y.: China-Japan Program, Cornell University, 1981.

Pollack, David. *The Fracture of Meaning: Japan's Synthesis of China from the Eighth through the Eighteenth Centuries.* Princeton, N.J.: Princeton University Press, 1986.

———. *Zen Poems of the Five Mountains.* New York: Crossroad Publishers, 1985.

Pronko, Leonard C. *Guide to Japanese Drama.* 2nd ed. Boston: G. K. Hall, 1984.

Putzar, Edward. *Japanese Literature: A Historical Outline.* Tucson: The University of Arizona Press, 1973.

Quackenbush, Hiroko C. "Edo and Tokyo Dialects," in *18th Century Japan: Culture and Society,* edited by C. Andrew Gerstle. Richmond, U.K.: Curzon Press. 1999, 73–84.

Ramirez-Christensen, Esperanza. *Heart's Flower: The Life and Poetry of Shinkei.* Stanford, Calif.: Stanford University Press, 1994.

Raz, Jacob. *Audience and Actors: A Study of Their Interaction in the Japanese Traditional Theatre.* Leiden, The Netherlands: Brill, 1983.

Reader, Ian. *A Simple Guide to Shinto.* Folkestone, U.K.: Global Books, 1998.

Reid, David. *New Wine: The Cultural Shaping of Japanese Christianity.* Berkeley, Calif.: Asian Humanities Press, 1991.

Reischauer, Edwin O., and Albert M. Craig. *Japan: Tradition & Transformation.* Boston: Houghton Mifflin Company, 1989.

Rimer, J. Thomas. *A Reader's Guide to Japanese Literature.* Tokyo: Kodansha International, 1988.

Rimer, J. Thomas, and Robert E. Morrell. *Guide to Japanese Poetry.* 2nd ed. Boston: G. K. Hall, 1984.

Rimer, J. Thomas, and Yamazaki Masakasu, trans. *On the Art of the No Drama: The Major Treatises of Zeami.* Princeton, N.J.: Princeton University Press, 1984.

Roberts, Laurance P. *Dictionary of Japanese Artists.* Trumbull, Conn.: Weatherhill, 2000.

Roberts, Luke S. *Mercantilism in a Japanese Domain: The Merchant Origins of Economic Nationalism in 18th Century Tosa.* Cambridge: Cambridge University Press, 1998.

Rodd, Laurel Rasplica, trans. *Nichiren: Selected Writings.* Honolulu: University of Hawaii Press, 1980.

Rogers, Minor, and Ann Rogers. *Rennyo: the Second Founder of Shin Buddhism.* Berkeley, Calif.: Asian Humanities Press, 1991.

Rosenfield, John M. *Song of the Brush.* Seattle: Seattle Art Museum, 1979.

Rosenfield, John M., and Elizabeth ten Grotenhuis. *Journey of the Three Jewels.* New York: Asia Society, 1979.

Rosenfield, John M., and Shujiro Shimada. *Traditions of Japanese Art: Selections from the Kimiko and John Powers Collection.* Cambridge, Mass.: Fogg Art Museum, 1970.

Rothman, Tony. "Japanese Temple Geometry." *Scientific American* 278 (May 1998): 85–91.

Rousmaniere, Nicole Coolidge, ed. *Kazari: Decoration and Display in Japan, 15th–19th Centuries.* New York: Harry N. Abrams, 2002.

Rozman, Gilbert. *Urban Networks in Ch'ing China and Tokugawa Japan.* Princeton, N.J.: Princeton University Press, 1973.

Rubinger, Richard. *Private Academies of Tokugawa Japan.* Princeton, N.J.: Princeton University Press, 1982.

Ruppert, Brian D. *Jewel in the Ashes: Buddha Relics and Power in Early Medieval Japan.* Cambridge, Mass.: Harvard University Asia Center, 2000.

Sadao, Tsuneko S., and Stephanie Wada. *Discovering the Arts of Japan: A Historical Overview.* Tokyo and New York: Kodansha International, 2003.

Sanford, James H. *Zen-Man Ikkyu.* Chico, Calif.: Scholars Press, 1981.

Sanford, James H., William R. LaFleur, and Masatoshi Nagatomi, eds. *Flowing Traces: Buddhism in the Literary and Visual Arts of Japan.* Princeton, N.J.: Princeton University Press, 1992.

Sansom, George B. *A History of Japan to 1334.* Stanford, Calif.: Stanford University Press, 1958.

———. *A History of Japan, 1334–1615.* Stanford, Calif.: Stanford University Press, 1961.

———. *A History of Japan, 1615–1867.* Stanford, Calif.: Stanford University Press, 1963.

———. *Japan: A Short Cultural History.* New York: Appleton Century Crofts, 1962.

Sato, Hiroaki. *Legends of the Samurai.* Woodstock, N.Y.: Overlook Press, 1995.

Sato, Hiroaki, and Burton Watson, ed. *From the Country of Eight Islands: An Anthology of Japanese Poetry.* Garden City, N.Y.: Anchor Books, 1981.

Saunders, E. Dale. *Mudra: A Study of Symbolic Gestures in Japanese Buddhist Sculpture.* New York: Pantheon Books, 1960.

Sawa, Takaaki. *Art in Japanese Esoteric Buddhism.* New York and Tokyo: Weatherhill/Heibonsha, 1976.

Schaap, Robert. *Heroes and Ghosts: Japanese Prints by Kuniyoshi 1797–1861.* Leiden, The Netherlands: Hotei Publishing, 1998.

Screech, Timon. *The Lens Within the Heart: The Western Scientific Gaze and Popular Imagery in Later Edo Japan.* 2nd ed. Honolulu: University of Hawaii Press, 2002.

———. *Sex and the Floating World: Erotic Images in Japan, 1700–1820.* Honolulu: University of Hawaii Press, 1999.

———. *The Shogun's Painted Culture: Fear and Creativity in the Japanese States, 1760–1829.* London: Reaktion, 2000.

Seattle Art Museum. *A Thousand Cranes.* Seattle: Seattle Art Museum, 1987.

Seckel, Dietrich. *Emakimono: The Art of the Japanese Painted Hand-scroll.* New York: Pantheon, 1972.

Seeley, Christopher. *A History of Writing in Japan.* Honolulu: University of Hawaii Press, 2000.

Seigle, Cecilia Segawa. *Yoshiwara: The Glittering World of the Japanese Courtesan.* Honolulu: University of Hawaii Press, 1993.

Selin, Helaine. *Science Across Cultures: An Annotated Bibliography of Books on Non-Western Science, Technology, and Medicine.* New York: Garland, 1992.

———, ed. *Astronomy Across Cultures: The History of Non-Western Astronomy.* Dordrecht, the Netherlands, and Boston: Kluwer Academic Publishers, 2000.

———, ed. *Encyclopaedia of the History of Science, Technology, and Medicine in Non-Western Cultures.* Dordrecht, the Netherlands, and Boston: Kluwer Academic Publishers, 1997.

———, ed. *Medicine Across Cultures: History and Practice of Medicine in Non-Western Cultures.* Dordrecht, the Netherlands, Boston, and London: Kluwer Academic Publishers, 2003.

———, ed. *Nature Across Cultures: Views of Nature and the Environment in Non-Western Cultures.* Dordrecht, the Netherlands, and Boston: Kluwer Academic Publishers, 2003.

Sen, Soshitsu. *Chado: The Japanese Way of Tea.* New York: Weatherhill, 1979.

Sen, Soshitsu. *The Japanese Way of Tea: From Its Origins in China to Sen Rikyu.* Honolulu: University of Hawaii Press, 1998.

Sheldon, Charles David. *The Rise of the Merchant Class in Tokugawa Japan, 1600–1868: An Introductory Survey.* Locust Valley, N.Y.: Association for Asian Studies, 1958.

Shibatani, Masayoshi. *The Languages of Japan.* Cambridge: Cambridge University Press, 1990.

Shimizu, Yoshiaki, and John Rosenfield. *Masters of Japanese Calligraphy: 8th–19th Centuries.* New York: Asia Society Galleries and Japan House Gallery, 1984.

Shimizu, Yoshiaki, ed. *Japan: The Shaping of Daimyo Culture, 1185–1868.* Washington, D.C.: National Gallery of Art, 1988.

Shimizu, Yoshiaki, and Carolyn Wheelwright, eds., *Japanese Ink Paintings from American Collections:*

The Muromachi Period. Princeton, N.J.: Art Museum, Princeton University, 1976.

Shinoda, Minoru. *The Founding of the Kamakura Shogunate, 1180–1185: With Selected Translations from the Azuma Kagami.* New York: Columbia University Press, 1960.

Shirane, Haruo. *Traces of Dreams: Landscape, Cultural Memory, and the Poetry of Basho.* Stanford, Calif.: Stanford University Press, 1998.

Shirane, Haruo, ed. *Early Modern Japanese Literature: An Anthology, 1600–1900.* New York: Columbia University Press, 2004.

Shively, Donald H., ed. and trans. *The Love Suicide at Amijima: A Study of a Japanese Domestic Tragedy by Chikamatsu Monzaemon.* Cambridge, Mass.: Harvard University Press, 1953.

Singer, Robert T., ed. *Edo: Art in Japan, 1615–1868.* Washington, D.C.: National Gallery of Art, 1998.

Skord, Virginia. *Tales of Tears and Laughter: Short Fiction of Medieval Japan.* Honolulu: University of Hawaii Press, 1991.

Smethurst, Mae J. *The Artistry of Aeschylus and Zeami: A Comparative Study of Greek Tragedy and No.* Princeton, N.J.: Princeton University Press, 1989.

Smith, Thomas C., Robert Y. Eng, and Robert T. Lundy. *Nakahara: Family Farming and Population in a Japanese Village, 1717–1830.* Stanford, Calif.: Stanford University Press, 1977.

Smith, David Eugene, and Yoshio Mikami. *A History of Japanese Mathematics.* Chicago: Open Court Publishing Company, 1914.

Smith, Henry D., II, and Amy Poster. *Hiroshige: One Hundred Famous Views of Edo.* New York: Brooklyn Museum of Art, 2000.

Smith, Robert J. *Ancestor Worship in Contemporary Japan.* Stanford, Calif.: Stanford University Press, 1974.

———. "The Domestic Cycle in Selected Commoner Families in Urban Japan: 1757–1858." *Journal of Family History* 3 (1978): 219–235.

Smitka, Michael, ed. *The Japanese Economy in the Tokugawa Era, 1600–1868.* New York: Garland Publishing, 1998.

Smits, Gregory. *Visions of Ryukyu: Identity and Ideology in Early-Modern Thought and Politics.* Honolulu: University of Hawaii Press, 1999.

Souyri, Pierre François. *The World Turned Upside Down: Medieval Japanese Society.* New York: Columbia University Press, 2001.

Stanley-Baker, Joan. *Japanese Art.* Rev. ed. London: Thames and Hudson, 2000.

Statler, Oliver. *Japanese Inn.* New York: Random House, 1961.

Steenstrup, Carl. *A History of Law in Japan until 1868.* 2nd ed. New York: E.J. Brill, 1996.

———. *Hojo Shigetoki, 1198–1261, and His Role in the History of Political and Ethical Ideas in Japan.* London: Curzon Press, 1979.

Stevens, John. *Sacred Calligraphy of the East.* 3rd ed. Boston: Shambhala Publications, 1995.

———. *Zenga: Brushstrokes of Enlightenment.* New Orleans: New Orleans Museum of Art, 1990.

Stinchecum, Amanda Mayer, et al. *Kosode: 16th–19th Century Textiles from the Nishimura Collection.* New York: Japan Society and Kodansha International, 1984.

Sugimoto, Masayoshi, and David L. Swain. *Science and Culture in Traditional Japan.* Rutland, Vt.: C. E. Tuttle, 1989.

Sugiyama, Jiro. *Classic Buddhist Sculpture.* New York: Kodansha International, 1982.

Suzuki, Daisetz T. *Zen and Japanese Culture.* Princeton, N.J.: Princeton University Press, 1959.

Swann, Peter C. *Concise History of Japanese Art.* New York: Kodansha International, 1979.

Swinton, Elizabeth de Sabato, ed. *The Women of the Pleasure Quarter: Japanese Paintings and Prints of the Floating World.* New York: Hudson Hills Press, 1995.

Takashige, Susuma. "The System of Space in the Medieval Period," in *Geography of Japan.* Edited by Association of Japanese Geographers. Tokyo: Teikoku Shoin, 1980, 121–45.

Takeda, Tsuneo. *Kano Eitoku.* Tokyo and New York: Kodansha International, 1977.

Takeda, Sharon Sadako, with Monica Bethe. *Miracles and Mischief: Noh and Kyogen Theater in Japan.* Los Angeles: Los Angeles County Museum of Art and the Agency for Cultural Affairs, Government of Japan, 2002.

Takei, Jiro, and Marc P. Keane. *Sakuteiki: Visions of the Japanese Garden.* Boston: Tuttle Publishing, 2001.

Takekoshi, Yosaburo. *The Economic Aspects of the History of the Civilization of Japan*. 3 vols. New York: The Macmillan Company, 1930.

Takeuchi, Melinda. *Taiga's True Views: The Language of Landscape Painting in Eighteenth-Century Japan*. Stanford, Calif.: Stanford University Press, 1992.

Tamura, Yoshiro. *Japanese Buddhism: A Cultural History*. Tokyo: Kosei Publishing Co., 2000.

Tanabe, George J., Jr., ed. *Religions of Japan in Practice*. Princeton, N.J.: Princeton University Press, 1999.

Tanabe, George J., Jr., and Willa Jane Tanabe, eds., *The Lotus Sutra in Japanese Culture*. Honolulu: University of Hawaii Press, 1989.

Tanabe, Willa J. *Paintings of the Lotus Sutra*. Tokyo: Weatherhill, 1988.

Tanaka, Fumon. *Samurai Fighting Arts: The Spirit and the Practice*. Tokyo: Kodansha International, 2003.

Tanaka, Ichimatsu. *Japanese Ink Painting: Shubun to Sesshu*. Tokyo and New York: Weatherhill, 1972.

Tanaka, Sen'o, and Sendo Tanaka. *The Tea Ceremony*. Rev. ed. Tokyo and New York: Kodansha International, 1998.

Tatsukawa, Shoji. "Diseases of Antiquity in Japan," in *The Cambridge World History of Human Disease*. Edited by Kenneth F. Kiple. Cambridge and New York: Cambridge University Press, 1993, 373–375.

Tazawa, Yutaka, ed. *Biographical Dictionary of Japanese Art*. Tokyo: International Society for Educational Information, 1981.

ten Grotenhuis, Elizabeth. *Japanese Mandalas: Representations of Sacred Geography*. Honolulu: University of Hawaii Press, 1999.

Thompson, Sarah E., and Harry D. Harootunian. *Undercurrents in the Floating World: Censorship and Japanese Prints*. Seattle: University of Washington Press, 1992.

Thornhill, Arthur. *Six Circles One Dewdrop: The Religio-Aesthetic World of Komparu Zenchiku*. Princeton, N.J.: Princeton University Press, 1993.

Tiedemann, Arthur E., ed. *An Introduction to Japanese Civilization*. New York: Columbia University Press, 1974.

Toby, Ronald P. *State and Diplomacy in Early Modern Japan: Asia in the Development of the Tokugawa Bakufu*. Princeton, N.J.: Princeton University Press, 1984.

Tocco, Martha C. "Norms and Texts for Women's Education in Tokugawa Japan." In *Women and Confucian Cultures in Premodern China, Korea, and Japan*. Edited by Dorothy Ko, JaHyun Kim Haboush, and Joan R. Piggott. Berkeley: University of California Press, 2003, 193–218.

Togi, Masataro. *Gagaku: Court Music and Dance*. New York: Walker/Weatherhill, 1971.

Tonomura, Hitomi. *Community and Commerce in Late Medieval Japan: The Corporate Villages of Tokuchin-ho*. Stanford, Calif.: Stanford University Press, 1992.

———. "Re-envisioning Women in the Post-Kamakura Age." In *The Origins of Japan's Medieval World: Courtiers, Clerics, Warriors, and Peasants in the Fourteenth Century*, edited by Jeffrey P. Mass, 138–69. Stanford, Calif.: Stanford University Press, 1997.

———. "Women and Inheritance in Japan's Early Warrior Society." *Comparative Studies in Society and History* 32 (1990): 592–623.

Tonomura, Hitomi, Anne Walthall, and Wakita Haruko, eds. *Women and Class in Japanese History*. Ann Arbor: Center for Japanese Studies, University of Michigan, 1999.

Torigoe Bunzo. "Edo Joruri." In *18th Century Japan: Culture and Society*, edited by C. Andrew Gerstle, 51–9. Richmond, U.K.: Curzon Press, 1999.

Totman, Conrad. *Collapse of the Tokugawa Bakufu, 1862–1868*. Honolulu: University of Hawaii Press, 1980.

———. *Early Modern Japan*. Berkeley: University of California Press, 1993.

———. *The Green Archipelago: Forestry in Pre-Industrial Japan*. Berkeley: University of California Press, 1989.

———. *A History of Japan*. Malden, Mass.: Blackwell, 2000.

———. *The Lumber Industry in Early Modern Japan*. Honolulu: University of Hawaii Press, 1995.

———. *Japan Before Perry: A Short History*. Berkeley: University of California Press, 1981.

———. *Politics in the Tokugawa Bakufu, 1600–1843*. Cambridge, Mass.: Harvard University Press, 1967.

———. *Tokugawa Ieyasu, Shogun: A Biography.* South San Francisco: Heian International Inc., 1983.

———. "Tokugawa Japan." In *An Introduction to Japanese Civilization,* edited by Arthur E. Tiedemann, 97–130. New York: Columbia University Press, 1974.

Traganou, Jilly. *The Tokaido Road: Traveling and Representation in Edo and Meiji Japan.* New York and London: RoutledgeCurzon, 2004.

Trewartha, Glenn T. *Japan: A Geography.* Madison: University of Wisconsin Press, 1965.

Tsukahira, Toshio G. *Feudal Control in Tokugawa Japan: The Sankin Kotai System.* Cambridge, Mass.: East Asian Research Center, Harvard University, 1966.

Tsunemoto, Yamamoto. *Hagakure: The Book of the Samurai.* Tokyo: Kodansha International, 1983.

Tsunoda, Rusaku, Wm. Theodore de Bary, and Donald Keene, eds. *Sources of Japanese Tradition.* New York: Columbia University Press, 1958.

Turnbull, Stephen R. *Ashigaru 1467–1649.* Oxford: Osprey, 2001.

———. *Battles of the Samurai.* London: Arms and Armor Press, 1987.

———. *The Lone Samurai and the Martial Arts.* London: Arms and Armor Press, 1990.

———. *Nagashino 1575* (Campaign Vol. 60). Oxford, U.K.: Osprey, 2000.

———. *Ninja A.D. 1460–1650.* Oxford, U.K.: Osprey, 2003.

———. *Ninja: The True Story of Japan's Secret Warrior Cult.* Dorset, U.K.: Firebird, 1991.

———. *Samurai Armies 1550–1615.* London: Osprey Publishing, 1979.

———. *The Samurai: A Military History.* Richmond, Surrey, U.K.: Japan Library, 1996.

———. *The Samurai Sourcebook.* London: Cassell, 2002.

———. *Samurai Warfare.* London: Arms and Armor Press, 1996.

———. *Samurai Warlords: The Book of the Daimyo.* New York: Sterling, 1989.

———. *Samurai Warriors.* London: Blandford Press, 1987.

———. *Samurai: The Warrior Tradition.* London: Cassell, 1996.

———. *Samurai: The World of the Warrior.* Oxford, U.K.: Osprey, 2003.

———., ed. *The Samurai Tradition.* 2 vols. Tokyo: Edition Synapse and Richmond, Surrey, U.K.: Japan Library, 2000.

Tyler, Royall. *Japanese No Dramas.* London: Penguin, 1992.

Ueda Akinari. *Ugetsu Monogatari: Tales of Moonlight and Rain.* Trans. Leon Zolbrod. Vancouver: University of British Columbia Press, 1974.

Ueda, Makoto. *Basho and His Interpreters: Selected Hokku with Commentary.* Stanford, Calif.: Stanford University Press, 1992.

———. *Literary and Art Theories in Japan.* Cleveland: Press of Western Reserve University, 1967.

———. *The Path of Flowering Thorn: The Life and Poetry of Yosa Buson.* Stanford, Calif.: Stanford University Press, 1998.

Ury, Marion, trans. *Tales of Times Now Past: Sixty-Two Stories from a Medieval Japanese Collection.* Berkeley: University of California Press, 1979.

Vaporis, Constantine N. *Breaking Barriers: Travel and the State in Early Modern Japan.* Cambridge, Mass.: Council on East Asian Studies, Harvard University, 1994.

Varley, H. Paul. "The Age of the Military Houses." *An Introduction to Japanese Civilization,* edited by Arthur E. Tiedemann. New York: Columbia University Press, 1974, 61–95.

———. *Imperial Restoration in Medieval Japan.* New York: Columbia University Press, 1971.

———. *Japanese Culture.* 4th ed. Honolulu: University of Hawaii Press, 2000.

———. *The Onin War: History of Its Origins and Background with a Selective Translation of the Chronicle of Onin.* New York: Columbia University Press, 1967.

———. *A Syllabus of Japanese Civilization.* 2nd ed. New York: Columbia University Press, 1972.

———. *Warriors of Japan as Portrayed in the War Tales.* Honolulu: University of Hawaii Press, 1994.

———, trans. *A Chronicle of Gods and Sovereigns: Jinno Shotoki of Kitabatake Chikafusa.* New York: Columbia University Press, 1980.

Varley, H. Paul, with Ivan and Nobuko Morris. *The Samurai.* London: Weidenfeld & Nicolson, 1970.

Varley, H. Paul, and Isao Kumakura, eds. *Tea in Japan: Essays on the History of Chanoyu.* Honolulu: University of Hawaii Press, 1989.

Vlastos, Stephen. *Peasant Protests and Uprisings in Tokugawa Japan.* Berkeley: University of California Press, 1986.

von Ragué, Beatrix. *A History of Japanese Lacquerwork.* Toronto: University of Toronto Press, 1976.

Wakabayashi, Bob Tadashi. *Anti-Foreignism and Western Learning in Early-Modern Japan: The "New Theses" of 1825.* Cambridge, Mass.: Council on East Asian Studies, Harvard University, 1986.

Wakita, Haruko, Anne Bouchy, and Ueno Chizuko, eds. *Gender and Japanese History.* 2 vols. Osaka: Osaka University Press, 1999.

Walker, Brett L. *The Conquest of Ainu Lands: Ecology and Culture in Japanese Expansion, 1590–1800.* Berkeley: University of California Press, 2001.

Walthall, Anne. *Social Protest and Popular Culture in Eighteenth-Century Japan.* Tucson, Ariz.: Association for Asian Studies, 1986.

———, ed. *Peasant Uprisings in Japan: A Critical Anthology of Peasant Histories.* Chicago: University of Chicago Press, 1991.

Warner, Langdon. *The Enduring Art of Japan.* Cambridge, Mass.: Harvard University Press, 1952.

Watanabe, Akiyoshi. *Of Water and Ink.* Detroit: Detroit Institute of Arts, 1986.

———, ed. *Of Water and Ink: Muromachi-Period Paintings from Japan, 1392–1568.* Detroit and Seattle: Detroit Institute of Arts and University of Washington Press, 1986.

Watsky, Andrew M. *Chikubushima: Deploying the Sacred Arts in Momoyama Japan.* Seattle: University of Washington Press, 2004.

Webb, Herschel. *The Japanese Imperial Institution in the Tokugawa Period.* New York: Columbia University Press, 1968.

Weidner, Marsha, ed. *Flowering in the Shadows: Women in the History of Chinese and Japanese Painting.* Honolulu: University of Hawaii Press, 1990.

Wheelwright, Carolyn, ed. *Word in Flower: The Visualization of Classical Literature in Seventeenth-Century Japan.* New Haven, Conn.: Yale University Press, 1989.

White, James W. *The Demography of Sociopolitical Conflict in Japan, 1721–1846.* Berkeley: Institute of East Asian Studies, University of California, 1992.

Wigen, Karen. *The Making of a Japanese Periphery, 1750–1920.* Berkeley: University of California Press, 1995.

Wilson, Richard L. *The Art of Ogata Kenzan: Persona and Production in Japanese Ceramics.* New York: Weatherhill, 1991.

———. *Inside Japanese Ceramics: A Primer of Materials, Techniques, and Traditions.* New York: Weatherhill, 1995.

Witteveen, Guven Peter. *The Renaissance of Takefu: How People and the Local Past Changed the Civic Life of a Regional Japanese Town.* New York and London: Routledge, 2004.

Yamakawa, Kikue. *Women of the Mito Domain: Recollections of Samurai Family Life.* Edited and translated by Kate Wildman Nakai. Tokyo: University of Tokyo Press, 1992.

Yamamura, Kozo. *A Study of Samurai Income and Entrepreneurship: Quantitative Analyses of Economic and Social Aspects of the Samurai in Tokugawa and Meiji Japan.* Cambridge, Mass.: Harvard University Press, 1974.

———, ed. *The Cambridge History of Japan.* Vol. 3, *Medieval Japan.* New York: Cambridge University Press, 1990.

Yamane, Yuzo. *Momoyama Genre Painting,* New York and Tokyo, 1973.

Yamasaki, Shigehisa, ed. *Chronological Table of Japanese Art.* Tokyo: Geishinsha, 1981.

Yampolsky, Philip, ed., *Selected Writings of Nichiren.* New York: Columbia University Press, 1990.

Yampolsky, Philip, trans. *The Zen Master Hakuin: Selected Writings.* New York: Columbia University Press, 1971.

Yasuda, Kenneth. *Masterworks of the No Theatre.* Bloomington: Indiana University Press, 1989.

Yonemoto, Marcia. *Mapping Early Modern Japan: Space, Place, and Culture in the Tokugawa Period, 1603–1868.* Berkeley: University of California Press, 2003.

Yonemura, Ann. *Japanese Lacquer.* Washington, D.C.: Freer Gallery, 1979.

Yonezawa, Yoshiho, and Chu Yoshizawa. *Japanese Painting in the Literati Style.* New York: Weatherhill, 1974.

Yuasa, Nobuyuki, trans. *The Narrow Road to the Deep North, and Other Travel Sketches.* Baltimore: Penguin Books, 1966.

Yumoto, John M. *The Samurai Sword: A Handbook.* Rutland, Vt.: Charles E. Tuttle, 1996.

Yusa, Michiko. *Japanese Religious Traditions.* Upper Saddle River, N.J.: Prentice Hall Inc., 2002.

INDEX

Page numbers in **boldface** indicate major treatment of the subject; those in *italics* refer to illustrations. Page numbers with the suffix *m* refer to maps.

A

abacus *(soroban)* 239
Abe Masahiro **21–22**
Abe Shoo **22**
abortion 347
Abutsu-ni **22**, *252*
Account of My Hut, An (Kamo) 248, *252*
acupuncture *(hari)* 235–236
Adams, William **22**, 338
Administration Board (Mandokoro) **92**, *93, 95*
adoption 341
aesthetics 268, 304. *See also* art; dress and personal appearance; performing arts
afterlife **359**
agriculture. *See also* rice production
    in early modern economy **122–123**
    in medieval economy **120**
Aida Yasuaki **22**

ai-kyogen (*kyogen* in the spaces) 275
Aizu domain **81**
Aizu Wakamatsu **65–66**
Ajima Naonobu **22**
Akakusadera temple 216
Akamatsu Mitsusuke **22**
Akasaka (section of Edo) 68
Akashi **66**
Akechi Mitsuhide 11, **22**
Aki no Miyajima (shrine) 200
Akita **66**
Ako **66**
Ako Incident 146
Alcock, Rutherford **22**
alliances by marriage. *See* marriage
altars, Buddhist *215. See also* shrines, Shinto; temples, Buddhist
alternate attendance system. *See sankin kotai*
amado (exterior sliding door) 322
Amagasaki **66**

Amakusa **66**
Amakusa Shiro **22**
Amanohashidate **66**
Amaterasu Omikami (deity) **197**
    in creation myth 191, 267–268
    imperial regalia and 157
    Ise Shrine and 200, 312
Amida Buddha **210–211**, *211*
    salvation and 204, 207
    statue of 73
Amidado (main hall) **309**
amma (massage) 236
Amoenitatum exoticum (Kaempfer) 33
amulets 196–197
anatomy, human 235, 237
Ancient Learning (Kogaku) (school of philosophy) **225–226**
Ando Hiroshige **22**, 296, **297**, 329
animal life 59
animals as pets 355

demon plays 274, 275
dengaku (field music) **269–270**
Dengyo Daishi (Saicho) 206, 214
deputy land stewards *(jitodai)* *95*, **96**
deputy military governors *(shugodai)* *95*, **96**
deputy shogun *(kanrei)* 8, **94–96**, *95*
desks, built-in *(tsukeshoin)* 321
Deus Destroyed (Fabian) 26
Dharma 202, 204, 207. *See also* *mappo* (the end of Dharma)
Dharma Hall **309**
Dharmakara (bodhisattva) 210–211
dialects, regional 242
diaries **251–252**
diet **348–349**
diligence cuisine *(shojin ryori)* 348
dining etiquette **348–349**. *See also* food and drink
discrimination against outcastes 114
disease 235, **358**. *See also* medicine
disembowelment. *See* suicide, ritual *(seppuku* or hara-kiri)
divination 197
divorce **345–346**
doboshu (curator) 26, 39, 44
Dogen **25**, 208, 214
dogs 355
do ikki (land protest leagues) 117
dolls *354*
domainal codes *(bunkokubo)* 103
domains *(han)* **62**, 120. *See also* daimyo (domain lords)
gazeteer of place-names **81–83**
domain schools *(hanko)* **229**
domaru armor 168

door paintings **290**, *292*
doshin (attendants) **177–178**
dragonflies *61*
drama. *See* theater
dress and personal appearance **350–353**. *See also* armor
clothing *351*, **351–352**, *352*
cosmetics and accessories **350–351**
hair **350**
of warriors 112–113, **147**
Dutch 64, 236–237. *See also* European contacts; trade, foreign
Dutch East India Company 236–237
Dutch learning *(rangaku)* 44, 231
Dutch medicine *(rampo)* 237

E

early modern period, historical overview of **11–15**
earthquakes **57**
Eastern Light Great Incarnation (Tosho Daigongen) 313. *See also* Tokugawa Ieyasu
eastern sea circuit *(higashi mawari)* 335
East Indian Company 22
ebira (quivers) 154
Ebisu (deity) 198
"eccentric" painting styles 295
Echizen ware (Echizen-yaki) **299**
economy **119–129**
agriculture **120**, **122–123**
and collapse of *bakufu* 14
currency **125–126**
early modern **121–124**
foreign trade. *See* trade, foreign

and Kamakura shogunate, decline of 6
legal reforms in Edo period 104
markets and commerce **120–121, 123–124**
medieval **119–121**
rice production on domains 62
taxation **121**, 124
in Warring States period 9
edicts, supplemental *(tsuika)* 102
Edo **67–69**, *68*, *69*
amusement area model *63*
city commissioners *97*, **98**
commoner residences in *324*
population growth 63, 67–68
renamed as Tokyo 12, 67
shopfront model *124*
Sumida River 56, *56*
Yoshiwara district, brothels in 117
Edo Castle 67, 98
Edo *machi bugyo* (Edo city commissioners) *97*, **98**
Edo period **11–15**. *See also* Tokugawa *bakufu* (shogunate)
bakufu, collapse of 14–15
bakuhan system of government 13
chronology of events 18–21
education in 228–231
law, crime, and punishment in **104–105**
national seclusion policy 13–14, 104
philosophical schools in 224–227
Edo River 54, *56*

fencing/swordfighting
(*kendo/kenjutsu*) 37, 50,
157–161
festivals. *See* rituals and festivals
feudal system. *See also* class system, hierarchical
   Bushido and **139–140**
   decline of 2
   European vs. Japanese
      2–3
   lord-retainer relationships
      109, 134, 136, 139–140
*Fifty-three Stations of the Tokaido
   Road* (Ando Hiroshige) 22,
   297, 329
filial piety (*ko*) 144, **223–224**
Fillmore, Millard 41
firearms (*teppo*) 151, **163–164**
   muskets 11, 65, 164
   wounds from 236
fireplaces 345
fishermen's houses (*gyoka*) 323
Five Mountain Convents Association 38
five obstructions (*gosho*) 218
five-road system (*gokaido*) 329
Five Women Who Loved Love
   (Saikaku) 257
flags 180–181
flat fans (*uchiwa*) 167, 351
flat war fans (*gumbai uchiwa*) 167
floating world (*ukiyo*) 256, 287,
   295
flora and fauna **59**
Flora Japonica (Thunberg) 32
Flower Garland Sutra 206
folding fans (*ogi*) 167, 351
folk dwellings (*minka*) 322, 323,
   323–324, *324*, *342. See also*
   homes
folk music (*min'yo*) **270**
folk religion 188
food and drink **348–349**
   cooking **348**
   dining etiquette **348–349**

medicine and 233
   sake *195*, **348**
foot soldiers 151
   ashigaru 177, **177**, 179
   zusa 110
footwear 352, *352*
forests 58
fortifications **173–174**. *See also*
   castles
fortune, gods of 197, 198
47 Ronin Incident 146, 178
fostered children (*satogo*) 341
foundation walls, stone (*ishigaki*)
   318
Four Noble Truths 202
Friday, Karl F. 139, 180
Frois, Luis **26**
Fugaku sanjurokkei (Katsushika
   Hokusai) 34, 297
Fugaku hyakkei (Katsushika
   Hokusai) 34
Fuga wakashu (Collection of elegance) (Eifuku Mon'in) 25
Fugen (bodhisattva) **212**
Fuji, Mt. 57–58
Fujiwara family, strategic marriage in 116
Fujiwara no Kanezane **26**
Fujiwara no Shunzei (Toshinari)
   249–250
Fujiwara no Takanobu **26**
Fujiwara no Teika (Sadaie)
   249–250
Fujiwara no Toshinari no
   Musume (Shunzei no
   Musume) **26**
Fuju Fuse school of Buddhism
   208
Fukko Shinto 28, 227
Fuku (Kasuga no Tsubone) **34**
Fukui **69**
fukumibarijutsu (needle spitting)
   166
Fukuoka **70**
Fukurokuju (deity) 198

furnishings **342–343**
furniture and other interior
   objects **343**
furo (portable brazier) 306
Furuta Oribe **26**
Furyu Shidoken den (Brave story
   of Shidoken) (Hiraga) 28
fusama shoji 344
Fushimi **70**
Fushimi Inari Shrine **199–200**
fusuma (sliding doors) 292, 321,
   344
fusuma shoji 344
futaoki (lid rest) 306
futons **343**

G

gagaku (court music) 264, 265,
   266, **269**
games **353–355**, *354*
ga no iwa (birthday celebration)
   358
gates
   castle gates 318, *320*
   Great South Gate at
      Todaiji 308
   mon **310**
   torii **313–314**, *314*
Geiami **26**, 311
geisha 117
gekokujo (those below overthrowing those above) 11,
   140
Geku (Outer Shrine) Shinto
   193
Gempei seisuiki (An account of
   the Gempei War) 253
Gempei War 67, 133, 154–155,
   253
genetic affiliation in language
   242
genin class 111
Genko Incident 27

Inari (deity) 197, *199*
Indian-style *(tenjikuyo)* architecture **308–309**
infantry. *See* foot soldiers
Ingen **31**, 209
Ingen Ryuki 205
inheritance 6, 340, 342
ink painting *(suibokuga)* 26, **291**
inner citadel *(hommaru)* 317–318
inns *(honjin)* 332
Ino Jakusui **31**
Inokuchi 70
Ino Tadataka **32**, 239
inspectors *(metsuke)* 97, **100**
inspectors general *(ometsuke)* 97, **98**
intendants *(daikan)* 97, **98**
Inuyama **72**
invocations, verbal **190**
Ippen **32**, 207
Ippen hijiri-e (Pictures of Ippen) 290
iron fans *(tessen)* 167
irori (open fireplaces) 345
Ise Daijingu Sankeiki (Account of a pilgrimage to the great shrine at Ise) 252
Iseji (road) 331
Isesaki **72**
Ise Shinto 193
Ise Shrine **200**
    Inner Shrine at 312
    pilgrimage to 194–195, 252
    Ryobu Shinto and 192
Ise/Uji-Yamada **72**
ishigaki (stone foundation walls) 318
Ishimpo (Tamba) 233–234
Ishiyama Honganji (temple) 78, **214–215**
islands 54, 55*m*, 63–65
Itami **72**
Ito Gemboku **32**

itoguruma (spinning wheel) *352*
Ito Jakuchu **32**, 295
Ito Jinsai **32**, 225–226
Ito Keisuke **32**
itowappu system 128
Itsukushima **64**
Itsukushima Shrine 64, **200–201**
Iwakuni **72**
Iwashimizu Hachiman Shrine 313
Izanagi no Mikoto (deity) 194, 197
Izanami no Mikoto (deity) 197
Izayoi Nikki (Diary of the waning Moon) 22, 252
Izumi Otsu **73**
Izumo **73**
Izumo Shrine **201**

J

jaku (tranquillity or natural elegance) 305
jangasa (war helmet) 172
janken (game) **354–355**
Japan, Sea of 54
Japanese-Chinese mixed style writing *(wakan konkobun)* **248**
Japanese-style *(wayo)* architecture **308**
Japan towns (Nihonmachi) 129
jidaimono (historical plays) 276, 280
Jien **32**
"Jikaishu" (Ikkyu) 31
jiku (hanging scrolls) 305
Jimyoin lineage 27, 89
jin (benevolence) **224**
Jingoki (Treatise on eternal mathematical truths) (Yoshida) 239
jingu. See shrines, Shinto
jinja. See shrines, Shinto

Jinno shotoki (Record of the legitimate succession of the divine emperors) (Kitabatake) 35
Jippensha Ikku 258, 260
jisha bugyo (commissioners of temples and shrines) 97, **99**
Jishoji. *See* Ginkakuji (Temple of the Silver Pavilion)
Ji-Shu (Time school of Buddhism) **207–208**
jito (land stewards) **94**
    Board of Retainers and 92
    shogunate and 4
    in shogunate structure 93, 95
    warrior bands and 133–134
jitodai (deputy land stewards) *95*, **96**
jitte (truncheon) skills **166–167**
Jiun Onko **32**, 205
jiuta (regional songs) **270**
Jizo (bodhisattva) *212*, **212**
Jodo Shinshu. *See* True Pure Land school of Buddhism
Jodo-Shu. *See* Pure Land school of Buddhism
Joei Code 5, 101–102
Joetsu 80
Jojitsu school of Buddhism 205–206
Jokei **32**
Jokyo calendar 238
Jokyu Disturbance 5, 27, 30, 88
Jokyuki (An account of the Jokyu Disturbance) 254
joruri (chanted narrative) 279–280
Josetsu **32–33**
judiciary. *See* courts, judicial
judo **163**
jujutsu **163**
Juko (Murata Shuko) 303–304, 310

junior councillors (*wakadoshi-yori*) 97, **100**

junshi (following one's lord in death) 143, 146, **149**. *See also* suicide, ritual (*seppuku* or hara-kiri)

junso (human sacrifice) 149

Jurojin (deity) 198

K

Kabuki theater **276–279**, *277, 278*

kabunakama (merchant guilds) 123–124

kabuto (helmets) **171–172**, 180

Kaempfer, Engelbert **33**, 236

Kaga/Daishoji **73**

Kaga domain **82**

kagome kagome (game) **354**

Kagoshima **73**

kagura (Shinto music and dance) 194, 271

kaiawase (game) **354**

kaidate (shield walls) 173, 179–180

Kaidoki (Journey along the seacoast road) 251

Kaiho Yusho **33**

Kaikei **33**, 287–288

Kai oi (Covering shells) (Basho) 24

Kaitai shinsho (New book of anatomy) 45, 237

Kajiwara Shozen 233

kakekomidra (refuge temples) 346

kakemono or *kakejiku* (hanging scrolls) **290**

Kakiemon ware (Kakiemon-yaki) 42, **299**

Kakitsu Incident 22

kama (tea kettle) 306

Kamakura **73**

Kamakura-bori lacquerware **302**

Kamakura *kubo* (Kamakura governor-general) *95*, **96**

Kamakura period and shogunate **3–7**
  chronology of events 15–16
  city of Kamakura and 73
  decline of Kamakura shogunate 6–7
  Hojo regency 4–5, 6
  law, crime, and punishment in **101–102**
  list of shoguns 100
  Mongol invasions 5–6
  shogunate, establishment of 3–4
  structure of shogunate **92–94**

kambun (classical Chinese writing) 248

Kameyama 89

kami (Shinto gods) **197–198**. *See also* Shinto religion
  Buddhism and 191–192
  concept of 190
  emperors and 28
  festivals and 356–357
  mountains and 189
  shrines and 311
  swords and 157
  tea ceremony and 306
  typhoons sent against Mongols by 5

Kamiari Matsuri (festival) 201

Kamo Mabuchi **33**

Kamo no Chomei **33**, 252

Kamo River 56

Kamo Shrines **201**, 312

Kanadehon Chushingura (Bunraku play) 280

Kanagawa Treaty (1854) 41, 70, 79, 129

Kan'ami (Kanze Kyotsugu) 270, 272

kana syllabaries **243**

Kanazawa **73**

Kanazawa Library 228

kanazoshi (kana books) 256

Kanda (section of Edo) 69

Kan'eiji (temple) **215**

Kan'ei no sampitsu (Three brushes of the Kan'ei era) 30

kanji (Chinese characters) **242–243**. *See also* language
  on and *kun* pronunciation of **246**
  writing, Classical **248**

kanjo bugyo (commissioners of finance) 97, **98**

kanjo gimmiyaku (comptrollers) 97, **98**

Kannamesai (New Rice Festival) 194

Kannon (bodhisattva) **212**, 357

Kano Eitoku 33, 292, 315

Kano Masanobu **33–34**, 292

Kano Mitsunobu **34**

Kano Motonobu **34**, 292

Kano school of painters
  in early modern period **293**
  Hasegawa Tohaku and 28
  Kano Tan'yu and 34
  in medieval period **291–292**
  Tokugawa patronage and 286

Kano Tan'yu **34**, 293

kanrei (deputy shogun) 8, **94–96**, *95*

Kansei calendar 45

Kansei reforms 36, 104, 257–258

Kanto *kanrei* (Kanto deputy) *95*, **96**

flora and fauna **59**

islands **55***m*, **63–65**

mountains, volcanoes, and earthquakes **57–58**

natural resources **58**

oceans, bays, lakes, and rivers **54–57**

land stewards. *See jito*

land taxes 121, 124

land tenure 4, 6, 103

language **242–249**

    overview 242

    Chinese characters **242–243**

    genetic affiliation **242**

    kana syllabaries **243**

    kanji pronunciation *246,* **246**

    missionaries and Western languages 24, 50

    syllabic sounds *244–245*

    vocabulary **246**

    writing equipment 247

    writing styles 247–249

        classical Chinese **248**

        classical Japanese **247–248**

        epistolary **248–249**

        Japanese-Chinese mixed style **248**

        variant Chinese **248**

laws and legal system. *See also* courts, judicial

    bukebo 101

    Buke shohatto 47, 104, 149

    crime and punishment **101–105**

        in Azuchi-Momoyama period **103**

        in Edo period **104–105**

        in Kamakura shogunate **101–102**

        in Muromachi shogunate **102–103**

        in pre-Kamakura shogunate **101**

    domainal codes 103

    group responsibility principles 102–103

    Joei Code (1232) 5, 101–102

    sakoku **13–14,** 104, 232

    samurai loyalty and 145–146

    Taiho Code 89

    Tokugawa restrictions on imperial family 13

    under Tokugawa Shogunate (1615) 12

League of the Single-Minded (Ikko ikki) 118

lecture hall *(kodo* or *hatto)* **309**

libraries 228

life, warrior ideals expressed in **145–148**

life expectancy **358**

Life of an Amorous Man, The (Saikaku) 256, 257

Life of an Amorous Woman, The (Saikaku) 257

lighting in homes **345**

Li ji 149

Linnaeus, Carolus 31, 46, 236

literacy 116–117, 227, 228–229

literati painting *(bunjinga)* **294**

literature **249–260**

    among samurai 140

    early modern **254–260**

        poetry **255–256**

        prose **256–260**

    medieval **249–254**

        poetry **249–251**

        prose **251–254**

    overview 249

    plays. *See* theater

Li-Zhu school of medicine 234

loan words 246

long-life ceremonies 271

Lotus Sutra 39, 206–207, 208, 212

loyalty *(chu)*

    as Neo-Confucian concept **224**

    as warrior value 140, 141, 143, **145–146**

lunar calendar 355

lute priests *(biwa hoshi)* 269

M

ma (space) 268

machiya (townhouses) 323–324, *324*

Maebashi **76**

Maeda family 73

Maeno Ryotaku 237

Mahayana Buddhism **203**

mai dance 268

maidono (ritual dance hall) **315**

main hall **309**

main sanctuary *(honden)* **314–315**

main tower *(tenshu)* 316–317, *317, 318*

make-e decorations 301

makoto (sincerity) 32, **224**

Mamiya Rinzo **36,** 239

Mampukuji temple 205, 309

Man'anpo (Prescriptions for felicity) (Kajiwara) 233

Manase Dosan 234

mandalas 290

Mandokoro (Administration Board) **92,** *93, 95*

maneki neko (welcoming cat) *113*

manners as warrior value **147**

Mansen shukai (Fujibayashi) 165

man'yogana (phonetic use of Chinese characters) 243

murder of 22

and structure of shogunate
99

tea and 304

title accumulation by 89

unification of Japan and 11

Odate **77–78**

Odawara **78**

odori dance 268

offering hall *(heiden)* **315**

offerings of sake *195*

ofuda (protective amulets) 196

Ogata Kenzan **40**

Ogata Korin **40,** 294

ogi (folding fans) 167, 351

Ogyu Sorai **40–41,** 225, 226

ohaguro (teeth blackening) 350

oil lamps 345

Oi River 56

okage mairi (thanksgiving pilgrimage) 194–195

Okayama **78**

Okayama domain **82**

Okazaki **78**

Oki Islands **65**

Okumura Masanobu **296–297**

Okuni **41,** 276

Okuni Kabuki 41

Okuninushi no Mikoto (deity)
197, 201

Oku no hosomichi (Narrow road
to the deep north) (Basho)
24, 255–256

omamori (protective amulets) 197

ometsuke (inspectors general)
97, **98**

Omi, Eight Views of 54

Omi Hachiman **78**

omikuji divination 197

Omna daigaku (Kaibara)
116–117

on and *giri* (favor and debt) 139,
146–147

One Hundred Views of Mt. Fuji
(Katsushika Hokusai) 34

ongoku bugyo (commissioners
of distant provinces) *97*,
98

oni harai (sweeping away the
demons) 357

Onin War **8–9**

foot soldiers and 177

Hino Tomiko and 23

Hosokawa Katsumoto and
30–31

Kyoto and 75

legal system and 103

Yamaguchi and 81

Oni-sube ceremony 199

Onna daigaku 231

onnagata (female roles in
Kabuki) 276, 277, 278

Ono Ozu **41**

Ono Ranzan **41**

on pronunciation 246, *246*

on reading (*on-yami*) 246, *246*

Ontleedkundige Tafelen (Illustrated anatomy) 237

Oribe ware (Oribe-yaki) **300**

Osaka 63, **78**

Osaka *jodai* (keepers of Oksaka
Castle) *97*, **99**

Oshu Fujiwara 71, 94

Oshu Kaido 331

Oshu *sobugyo* (Oshu general
commissioner) *93*, **94**

Oshu *tandai* 95

Otagaki Rengetsu **41**

Ota Nampo 258, 259

otogata (male roles in Kabuki)
278

Otomo Sorin 80

Otsu **78**

outcastes *(eta* and *hinin)* **111,
114–115**

Owari domain **82**

Owari family 77

oxcart travel *328*

oyori (great armor) 170, 171

oyumi (weapon) **167**

San'yodo (Southern Mountain Region) 83, 84*m*
Saron school of Buddhism 205
sarugaku (monkey music) **269–270**, 272
Sasaki Shogen **43**
sash (obi) 347
satogo (fostered) children 341
sato kagura (village *kagura*) 271
Satsuma *biwa* 266
Satsuma domain 14–15, 41–42, **82**
Sayaji 331
scales for business *123*
Schambergen, Caspar 236
School of Ancient Medicine (Koiho) 234–235
School of Latter-Day Medicine (Goseiho) 234
schools. See education
schools of Buddhism **205–209**
    Fuju Fuse **208**
    Nara schools **205–206**
    Nichiren Sect of Buddhism 76, 118, 204, **208**
    Obaku Zen 205, **209**
    Pure Land 203, 204, **207**, 218, 290. *See also* Amida Buddha
    Rinzai Zen 204, **208**, *209*, 310–311
    Shingon 192, **206**
    Shugendo 190, **209**
    Soto Zen **208**
    Tendai **206–207**
    Time **207–208**
    True Pure Land 73, 78, 204, **207**
    Yuzu Nembutsu Sect **208**
schools of philosophy 224–227
science **231–240**
    archaeology 35
    astronomy 23, 43, 45, **237–238**

geography 32, 36, 45, **238–239**
mathematics 22, 45, 51, **239–240**
medicine **232–237**
overview 231–232
screen of spears *(yaribusuma)* 163
screen paintings **290**, 292
screen partitions *(shoji)* 321–322, **344**
scrolls
    hand **289–290**
    hanging **290**, 305
sculpture **287–288**
seas 54
sei (purity) 305
seii taishogun (barbarian-subduing great general) 4. *See also* shogunate *(bakufu)*
Seishi bosatsu (bodhisattva) **213**
seki-bune (warships) **337**
Sekigahara **79**
Sekigahara, Battle of 12, 79, 178
Seki Kowa **43**
Sekimon Shingaku (Heart Learning school) **226**
Seki-ryu mathematical school 22, 43, 239
sekisho (barrier stations) 332
Seki Takakazu (Seki Kowa) 239
Sen, Princess *354*
Sendai **79**
Sendai domain **82**
Sengai Gibon **43**
sengoku-bune (ships) 335–336
sengoku daimyo (warring lords) 9, 135
senior councillors *(roju)* *97*, **98**
Sen no Rikyu **43**
Sensoji temple 199, **216**
seppuku. See suicide, ritual *(seppuku* or hara-kiri)

servants, household 115
Sesshu Toyo **43**, 46, 291
Sesson Shukei **43**
Seto **79**
Seto Inland Sea 54
Seto ware (Seto-yaki) 79, **300**
Setsubun (Eve of the First Day of Spring) **357**
Setsumon teishi (Fundamental advice for students) (Sesson) 43
Seventh Night (Shichiya) **357**
Seven-Five-Three festival (Shichigosan) **357**
sewamono (contemporary plays) 276, 280
sexuality **148**, 345, **346**
Shakamuni (Buddha) 213
Shaka Nyorai (Buddha) 213
shaku (staffs) 167
shakuhachi (flute) **265**, 271
Shakuson (Buddha) 213
shamisen (lute) **266**
    in Bunraku 279, 280–281
    in Kabuki 276–277
Shang han za bing lun (Essay on typhoid and miscellaneous diseases) 234
sharebon (witty books) 258
shiatsu (finger pressure) 236
Shiba Kokan **43**, 295
Shibata Katsuie 51, 69
Shibukawa Shunkai (Harumi) **43**, 238
shichifukujin (deities) 198
Shichigosan (Seven-Five-Three festival) **357**
Shichiya (Seventh Night) **357**
shield deployment and formations **179–180**
shields **172**
shield walls *(kaidate)* 173, 179–180
Shigaraki ware (Shigaraki-yaki) **300**

Yamana Sozen (Mochitoyo) 8, 30–31, **50**
yamato-e (Japanese-style) painting 26, 289
Yamawaki Toyo 235
Yamazaki Ansai **50–51**, 193, 226
yari (spears) 162–163, *163*
Yari, Mt. 58
yaribusuma (screen of spears) 163
Yasaka Shrine 194, **202**
yashiro. See shrines, Shinto
yawara (way of softness) **163**
yobai (night visit) 345
Yodogimi **51**
Yodo River 57
yofuga (Western-style painting) **294–295**
yogaku (Western learning) 42, 231
Yokohama **81**
yomeirikon (patrilocal traditions) 345
Yomei school of philosophy **225**
yomihon (reading books) 259
Yomi no Kuni (Land of Darkness) 359
Yonezawa **81**
yoriki (attendants) **177–178**

Yorokan school 80
Yosa Buson (Buson) **24**, 256, 294
yosan (Western mathematical theory) 239–240
yose performance 281
Yoshida Kanetomo **51**, 192, 193
Yoshida Kaneyoshi (Kenko) 252
Yoshida Kenko **51**
Yoshida Mitsuyoshi **51**, 239
Yoshida Shoin **51**
Yoshida/Toyohashi **81**
Yoshikawa Koretari **51**
Yoshimasu Todo 235
Yoshiwara (section of Edo) 69
Yoshizawa Ayame I **279**
yu-bune (public-bath boats) 338
yugen (mystery and depth) 250, 251, 273
Yuiitsu ("Only") Shinto 193
Yukan 208
Yurin 233
Yuzu emmonsho (Yukan) 208
Yuzu Nembutsu Sect of Buddhism **208**

Z

za (mints) 125–126
za (trade guilds) 121, 123

zabuton (cushions) **344**
Zao Gongen (deity) **213**
Zeami (Kanze Motokiyo) 270, 272–274
Zen Buddhism
  art and architecture, influence on 34, 285
  enlightenment in 204
  monastery architecture 319
  Obaku school of 31, **205**
  patronage of 204
  Rinzai school of 25, 31, **208**
  Soto school of 25, **208**
  tea ceremony and 303
  temple architecture 309, 310–311
zendo (meditation hall) **309**
zenga (Zen painting) **294**
Zen-style *(zenshuyo)* architecture **309**
zenzia (copper mints) 126
Zhu Xi 224–225, 229. *See also* Shushi school of philosophy
Zojoji (temple) **217**
Zoshi (Anatomical record) 235
Zuiganji 65
zuihitsu (essays) 252
zunbe (straw boots) *352*
zusa (foot soldiers) 110